Arctic AMBITIONS

Arctic AMBITIONS

Captain Cook and the Northwest Passage

EDITED BY *James K. Barnett* AND *David L. Nicandri*

PREFACE BY ROBIN INGLIS

ANCHORAGE MUSEUM
Anchorage, Alaska

COOK INLET HISTORICAL SOCIETY
Anchorage, Alaska

WASHINGTON STATE HISTORY MUSEUM
Tacoma, Washington

in association with

HERITAGE

Victoria • Vancouver • Calgary

Heritage House Publishing Company Ltd.
heritagehouse.ca

Published in the U.S. by University of Washington Press
washington.edu/uwpress

Cataloguing information available from
Library and Archives Canada

ISBN 978-1-77203-061-7 (hardcover)

DESIGN BY Thomas Eykemans

FRONTISPIECE: John Webber, *Portrait of Captain James Cook* (detail), circa 1780. Oil on canvas. Museum of New Zealand TePapa Tongarewa. Gift of the New Zealand Government, 1960, 1960-0013-1.

DEDICATION PAGE: *Map of the Arctic Regions* (detail), A. Fullarton & Company, London, 1856. University of British Columbia Library, Rare Books and Special Collections, G3271.S12.F84.1856.

The interior of this book was produced on acid-free paper.

Heritage House acknowledges the financial support for its publishing program from the Government of Canada through the Canada Book Fund (CBF), Canada Council for the Arts, and the Province of British Columbia through the British Columbia Arts Council and the Book Publishing Tax Credit.

19 18 17 16 15 1 2 3 4 5

Printed in China

To the generations of scholars
who have laid the foundation for
this study in exploration history

Contents

Foreword

AS DIRECTOR OF THE ANCHORAGE MUSEUM AT Rasmuson Center, I am delighted to present this anthology of illustrated essays, published to accompany an exhibition of the same name presented in Anchorage and Tacoma during 2015. *Arctic Ambitions: Captain Cook and the Northwest Passage* was developed in cooperation with our partners, the Cook Inlet Historical Society and the Washington State Historical Society, with the goal that both exhibition and anthology would bring fresh perspectives to a new generation of visitors and readers alike as to the importance of Cook's third Pacific voyage, especially the key stories regarding the earliest recorded history of coastal Alaska and the Pacific Northwest, as well as his search for a navigable Northwest Passage, which today is becoming a reality.

Bringing to the north Pacific and Arctic his unsurpassed skills as a navigator and surveyor, developed during two extensive voyages in the South Seas, Cook was the first to define the coastline of continental Alaska, from Cross Sound in Southeast Alaska to Icy Cape in the Arctic Ocean. With its charts, written descriptions, artifact collections, and artistic record of the Native Americans encountered and their homelands, the Cook expedition's contribution—Eurocentric as it undoubtedly was—is of inestimable value. And today, in a period of unprecedented climate change Cook's experience with Arctic sea ice and the challenges it brings to navigation, long considered a footnote in Arctic exploration, is increasingly relevant rather than increasingly distant.

Writing in his journal in June 1778, after visiting Cook Inlet and the site of the present-day city of Anchorage, Cook foresaw great commercial potential for this "vast coast." *Arctic Ambitions,* therefore, provides us with a timely and valuable historical context for the centennial of Anchorage, which the city and museum will celebrate in 2015. We recognize Cook for what he and his expedition did and meant for Alaska and the wider north Pacific coast of America, and we ourselves chart from his first, pioneering foray into the Arctic waters off northwestern Alaska the stories of those who came later, also from the west, and pushed farther into the seas of the Northwest Passage—Native Americans, whalers, and explorers. Today we arrive at the prospect of an open, navigable body of water for longer and longer each year, and the realization of that link between Europe and Asia, across the top of North America, for which Cook searched so diligently over two hundred and thirty years ago.

I would like to acknowledge my friends and colleagues in the Cook Inlet Historical Society and those at the Washington State History Museum in Tacoma—Jennifer Kilmer, director, and Redmond Barnett, head of exhibits—who have been essential partners in this overall project. This publication would not have been possible without the dedicated work of our two editors, Jim Barnett and David Nicandri, who have worked to bring the efforts of the twenty contributing scholars to publication. The support of Robin Inglis and Hannah Moderow has also been vital to the completion of this volume. Finally, my predecessor, Jim Pepper Henry, was an early and enthusiastic supporter of *Arctic Ambitions,* and we also thank Aron Crowell, Nils Andreassen, and Evguenia Anichtchenko in Anchorage, as well as Bill Smith, Tim Halloran and Howard Litwak of Storyline Studio in Seattle, for their contributions.

Julie Decker, PhD
Director/Chief Executive Officer
Anchorage Museum

Preface

ROBIN INGLIS

DESPITE THE OPENING SENTENCE OF J. C. Beaglehole's preface to his magisterial edition of James Cook's manuscript journal of his voyage to the north Pacific and Arctic—"No-one can study attentively the records of Cook's third, and last, voyage without being convinced that it was of the same order of greatness as its two predecessors"[1]—it is perhaps inevitable that the third voyage has suffered in comparison to that first pioneering expedition, which shattered forever the still-vague concept of the Pacific, and the second, which added so much more to the picture and epitomized "enlightened voyaging" at its very best. At the same time, in the history of exploration and discovery, proving a negative—disproving the existence of a navigable Northwest Passage, for example—never rates as highly as a dramatic discovery, such as Cook's meticulous survey of New Zealand or first contact with the east coast of Australia. Yet it remains perplexing that the negative of the Great Southern Continent was—and perhaps still is—somehow less disappointing than the failure to find a navigable Northwest Passage. The latter, maybe, was closer to the European consciousness, and thus the dashing of so keenly held an expectation was felt more profoundly. In addition, the shocking, almost unbelievable death of Cook cast a pall over the whole enterprise. These two things have seemingly conspired to cast a long shadow over the achievements of the third voyage: the discovery of Hawai'i; the complete success of the long and difficult survey of the high north Pacific and Arctic coasts of America and their relationship to Asia; the meticulous charts produced, as good as any ever created under Cook's supervision; the descriptions of the peoples encountered; the collections made and the images drawn and painted; the cordial relations established with the Russians, which fostered a better understanding of the role of Russia on its eastern periphery; and, last but not least, the contacts that established the maritime fur trade. These clearly served as good enough reasons at the time for the British government—in addition to honoring a fallen hero—to publish a lavish three-volume account of the voyage, with an accompanying atlas of charts and engravings of people and places.

The essays in this anthology have been published to complement the exhibition *Arctic Ambitions: Captain Cook and the Northwest Passage,* presented between March 2015 and January 2016 in Anchorage, Alaska, and Tacoma, Washington. The goal of the exhibition was to revisit, through the art, artifacts, charts, and records of the encounters between Native peoples and the explorers, the story of a remarkable voyage—at four years, two months, and twenty-two days, the longest expedition of its kind until that of George Vancouver some fifteen years later—and particularly its achievements and experiences in the north Pacific and Arctic Oceans. We were also very keen to use the events of 1778 and 1779 as a opportunity to look at today's rapidly changing Arctic in light of Cook's achievements and legacy, and to explore such issues as resource exploitation, indigenous cultural change, navigation, mapping, and sovereignty, which resonated along the coasts of the Pacific Northwest and Alaska in the decades after Cook's visit—as they do now, in our own time, in the ice and waters of the Northwest Passage. Thus the contributions that follow here speak not only of James Cook and his companions and contemporaries but also of the years that followed, the ultimate conquest of the Northwest Passage, and the changes being wrought on that elusive prize by global warming. In this context, Harry Stern's discussion of the sea ice that so unexpectedly and surprisingly halted Cook's progress in August 1778 also ponders the question: if he had arrived off Icy Cape some 237 years later, how far east would he have been able to sail? Could he have returned in triumph to Britain, or would he still have had to retrace his steps and escape through Bering Strait? Or might he have been drawn, even today, into a dead end, forced to winter over, either successfully like William Parry or Roald Amundsen or disastrously like John Franklin?

In their compendium of papers *Captain James Cook and His Times,* presented at the seminal conference of the same name at Simon Fraser University in 1978, the editors, Robin Fisher and Hugh Johnston, noted that "it has been from the south Pacific that much of the best Cook scholarship has come," and "because, in the past, much emphasis has been laid on the south Pacific, our intention has been to assert the importance of the north."[2] While Cook's exploration of the south, perhaps inevitably, continues to dominate Cook historiography, the study of the man and his voyages has increasingly involved scholars from a wider world. We hope that this anthology will shine more light on the north and provide some useful and interesting insights for those who find it difficult to imagine Cook voyaging beyond Polynesia, its adjacent islands, and Australia.

The first five essays in this collection both sketch the background to the third voyage and take the story into the voyage itself. John Gascoigne provides an overview of the world of the Enlightenment that underpinned the achievements of Cook's previous two voyages; the experiences gained by those who sailed with Cook or read the accounts of previously unfamiliar navigation, places, and people; the growing confidence of the commander as he warmed to the task of exploring and charting the South Pacific; and the development of his sensitivity to and interest in the native peoples he encountered. Glyn Williams, Iris Engstrand, and Evguenia Anichtchenko then focus our attention firmly on the north: on the new impetus for renewing the search for the Northwest Passage seemingly offered by Russian activity in the north Pacific in the 1760s and 1770s; on the nature of that activity as Russian fur traders and naval expeditions purposefully followed the route of Vitus Bering toward America, trying to sift fact from fiction in defining the region's geography; and on the Spanish response, in the context of Madrid's long-held view of the Pacific as a "Spanish Lake," to perceived threats to the viceroyalty with voyages north from New Spain in the mid-1770s, and the order to impede Cook's progress. Finally, Richard Dunn demonstrates the extent to which Cook's achievements epitomized the revolution in navigational and surveying techniques and instrumentation, and above all precise location finding, that made possible the grand surveys of his successive, and successful, crossings of the great ocean, west, east, south, and north.

The next group of contributions is framed by David Nicandri's overview of Cook's third voyage and Robert Miller's discussion of the doctrine of discovery with reference to explorations of the Pacific coast of America in the last quarter of the eighteenth century. Taking his cue from Nicholas Thomas, Nicandri's survey challenges the still-dominant view that Cook's last voyage was largely a failure, one whose lasting image is that of a weary Cook who should not have undertaken the assignment and who was therefore prone to making critical errors of judgment. Richard Inglis and Aron Crowell explore and interpret the nature of the Native encounters at Nootka Sound and around the Gulf of Alaska, from Prince William Sound and Cook Inlet to Unalaska. And, complementing these two essays, Adrienne Kaeppler discusses the nature, scope, and often-circuitous routes into museums and private collections of the materials traded or gifted to the explorers by the Native peoples they met as they made their way from Oregon toward the Arctic Ocean.

Thereafter, the focus of the essays shifts away from Cook's achievements to his legacy as contained in the charts and journals we have inherited. John Robson discusses the collaborative nature of the significant cartographic achievement of the third voyage. Ian MacLaren reminds us, in his analysis of Cook's manuscript journal, that for nearly two hundred years, what the world knew of Cook and his voyages came principally through the editorial efforts of John Hawkesworth and Canon John Douglas. Whereas the former took huge liberties with the narrative of the first voyage, Douglas was constrained by Cook's determination to author his own record, particularly on the third voyage. The nuances, however, are intriguing, and we can still find much of the true

Cook in the 1784 published account despite Douglas's attempt, in polishing his "stile,"[3] to develop a persona for the captain that fit the contemporary desire for a commanding and heroic figure, fulfilling the imperial requirements of his nation, as he charts his new discoveries and meets new people on the other side of the world. Moving beyond Cook's charts and journal, Jim Barnett's essay shows how George Vancouver carried forward the mission of discovery with his comprehensive three-season survey of the Northwest Coast of North America, an enterprise fully worthy of his former commander and mentor's highest accomplishments. Filling in the gaps of the coast from California to the Gulf of Alaska, including the waters behind Vancouver Island and throughout the Alexander archipelago, Vancouver proved once and for all that no passage to the far north was to be found in the numerous inlets surveyed by his expedition. Vancouver came to the Northwest Coast assuming the roles of both explorer and diplomat at a time when frenetic fur-trading activity was signaling the beginning of international maneuvering for commercial advantage. Barry Gough narrates this story from discovery to sovereignty, a clash of commercial and political empires that ultimately found expression, by the middle of the nineteenth century, in the division of the region among Russia, Britain, and the United States.

The final set of contributions leads us from the Cook expedition's fleeting visits to the Arctic Ocean into a discussion of the promises, potential, and challenges of the region today. James Delgado's essay bridges the gap between Cook's explorations and the voyage of the *Manhattan* in 1969, years that saw a continuing search for the Northwest Passage from both the Atlantic and the Pacific sides until it was finally found in the 1850s and traversed in the twentieth century. Despite its difficulties, the voyage of the *Manhattan* appeared to promise the establishment of a commercially navigable passage. As Harry Stern and Lawson Brigham note, however, the hostile and dangerous conditions that still prevail for much of each year, despite the unprecedented annual sea-ice melting of today, suggest that this prospect is still many years away. Meanwhile, however, global warming is rapidly changing the face of the Arctic, threatening the well-being of indigenous communities and raising issues of environmental protection and sovereignty. In their essay, Gudrun Bucher and Robin Inglis place the American Arctic in focus, finding national interests tempered by a significant spirit of international cooperation and a willingness to share science and resources to chart the way toward sustainable development in the Northwest Passage region in the future.

NOTES

1 Beaglehole, J. C. ed., *The Journals of Captain James Cook on His Voyages of Discovery,* vol. 3, *The Voyage of the* Resolution *and* Discovery, *1776–1780* (Cambridge: Cambridge University Press for the Hakluyt Society, 1967), v.

2 Fisher, Robin, and Hugh Johnston, eds., *Captain James Cook and His Times* (Vancouver, BC: Douglas & McIntyre, 1979), 3.

3 Cook, *Voyage of the* Resolution *and* Discovery, ccxcix.

Prologue

Three Comments on Cook's Third Voyage

NICHOLAS THOMAS

SINCE HIS DEATH, CAPTAIN JAMES COOK HAS been a legendary figure, an iconic explorer in the historical imagination, and the subject of a vast array of scholarly and popular biographies. In recent decades, new perspectives in maritime history, colonial history, anthropology, art history, the history of science, indigenous studies, and English literary studies have generated new academic interest in voyages, cross-cultural encounters, and Cook in particular.

Yet Cook remains a difficult character to know. This is in part because our richest sources are his voyage journals. Although illuminating in multiple ways, these are in the end official rather than private or personal papers, and they relate only to the voyages themselves. The voyages, needless to say, are the focus of most readers' interest, but the journals give us little sense of Cook's personal formation or inner life. And this is only part of the difficulty. Cook comes across as a contradictory personality, a man who would not be easy to describe, assess, or understand even if we knew a good deal more about him. This matters, and not necessarily because we are especially interested in him as a character. What sense he made of people, places, and circumstances, and how he acted and reacted, are vital to a larger story of formative encounters between Europeans and various peoples of the Pacific and the Pacific Rim.

Amid a proliferation of biographies and commentaries, some of them conflicting, a dominant narrative has emerged with respect to Cook's third voyage. This narrative largely reflects the views of J. C. Beaglehole, the editor of Cook's journals and author of the most exhaustive though now dated biography, *The Life of Captain James Cook* (1974). Beaglehole held that after his second voyage, Cook was a tired man who should not have embarked on a third expedition. Beaglehole sees Cook's inner fatigue as being exacerbated by a voyage that was as demanding as, or more demanding than, its predecessors. The commander is seen to become more impatient with his men and with indigenous people. His death on the rocky shores of Kealakekua Bay is ultimately due to his poor judgment and diminished capacities. This theme, shorn of Beaglehole's own propensity to question and weigh up the evidence, has been rehashed in many popular and even ostensibly scholarly biographies, and it was enlarged on and given a more negative cast by Gananath Obeyesekere in *The Apotheosis of Captain Cook* (1992). In what at the time appeared a bold postcolonial retelling, though clearly a flawed one, Obeyesekere drew on most of the same evidence cited by Beaglehole, evoking a Cook sliding into irrationality and violence, a figure explicitly compared with the character Kurtz from Joseph Conrad's *Heart of Darkness.*

The first point I wish to make is: not so fast. Beaglehole's argument was at best speculative. It was driven by the essentially heroic quality of his narrative: Beaglehole's protagonist needed to rise but also to suffer a fall. The evidence for Cook's decline is in fact uneven, and reported changes in his concerns and responses are not necessarily symptoms of fatigue. For example, Beaglehole considers it highly anomalous that Cook chose not to explore the Fijian archipelago, having heard of it during his Tongan visit. This assertion is largely spurious. On previous voyages, too, Cook was well aware that other islands in relative proximity could be investigated, but he did not do so. In general, this was because he was concerned about adhering to a plan. He pursued his core project relentlessly (on the second voyage, this was the confirmation or disconfirmation of the existence of the southern land), but he would not necessarily make detours to visit places like Bora-Bora, the Tuamotus, or Fiji, for the sake of completing a chart.

Cook was concerned about posterity. He took seriously the notion that the voyages might be benevolent, and he was therefore concerned to distribute breeding pairs of useful animals among islanders and also to limit the spread of sexually transmitted disease. There is no doubt that he became progressively more estranged from his men because he was dismayed by their conduct, particularly when they introduced new diseases among populations they encountered. This concern is evident, for example, from the self-justifying effort by David Samwell, the expedition surgeon, to argue that diseases were prevalent among Hawaiians before the arrival of the British. This mounting estrangement should not be equated with an "inner tiredness."

The second point is obvious yet nevertheless important. Cook's main objective on the third voyage was fundamentally different from that of the second. Despite the grueling nature of the Antarctic voyages, it was in a sense easier to establish definitively whether land existed or not than it was to seek out a Northwest Passage. Cook's deep intuitive oceanography allowed him to sense, when he was in the middle of the Southern Ocean in long, rolling seas, that no land mass was near. Sailing through hundreds of miles of open ocean established the point definitively. As Glyn Williams has shown, the search for the Northwest Passage was compromised from the start by the crucially misleading nature of Jacob von Staehlin's chart. But it was an entirely different endeavor to seek a passage into or through a landmass to find a strait than it was to find land or not find it.

The third point is that over the course of the voyages, Cook and certain of his companions became much more sophisticated in their observation of indigenous life. With their inclination toward natural history—an inquisitive, comparative, environmentally sensitive, observation-centered mode of knowledge—observers were prompted to consider the affinities and differences between Tahitians and Maori, and Tahitians and Tongans, for example. Their grasp of one language made it easier to make at least basic sense of another. The similarities among Polynesians threw into relief the distinct cultures of western Oceania, in Vanuatu and New Caledonia. During the third voyage, Cook was preoccupied above all by his expeditionary objectives, but his own proto-anthropological curiosity was intensified. Nothing in the eighteenth-century voyage archive quite compares with his absorbed account of the Tongan *'inasi* ritual. He reached America with a more refined capacity to observe and comment on indigenous life than he had shown at any point previously. Of course, the peoples of the Northwest Coast, Alaska, and Siberia were unrelated to those he had encountered so extensively before. Yet, as is discussed elsewhere in this book, the encounters were epoch making, if only in the sense that the great Native American art forms were described, delineated, and published, to become known to the West for the first time.

There has been much myth making about Cook the man and Cook the navigator. In the twenty-first century, Cook's voyages remain foundationally important, and fascinating, for the history of cross-cultural encounter—for better or worse.

Arctic AMBITIONS

James Cook, Navigator and Explorer

The Pacific Experience, 1768–1776

JOHN GASCOIGNE

1

WHEN JAMES COOK SET OFF IN 1767 ON HIS *ENDEAVOUR* VOYAGE, THE first of his three great Pacific voyages, he was drawing on both his own and his nation's growing experience and understanding of a world beyond the shores of Great Britain. Born the son of an agricultural laborer, he had succeeded in becoming an officer in the Royal Navy through proven ability and a single-minded determination that was to be his hallmark. Trained as a seaman in the challenging school of North Sea navigation as an apprentice in the coal trade from Newcastle-on-Tyne to London, he had turned from the merchant navy to the Royal Navy in 1755 on the eve of the Seven Years' War (1756–63).[1] This was a major chapter in the "second Hundred Years' War" for world mastery between Britain and France, which culminated in British victory after the battle of Waterloo in 1815. This can be considered the first world war following the European powers' struggles for dominance in India and North America.

As a member of the navy, Cook was thrust into the battles for British supremacy in North America. There he learned the surveying and cartographical skills that were to underpin the enduring significance of his three Pacific voyages. Following the British capture in 1758 of the great French fort of Louisbourg

Thomas Luny, *The Bark,* Earl of Pembroke, *later* Endeavour, *leaving Whitby Harbour in 1768* (detail of fig. 1.5).

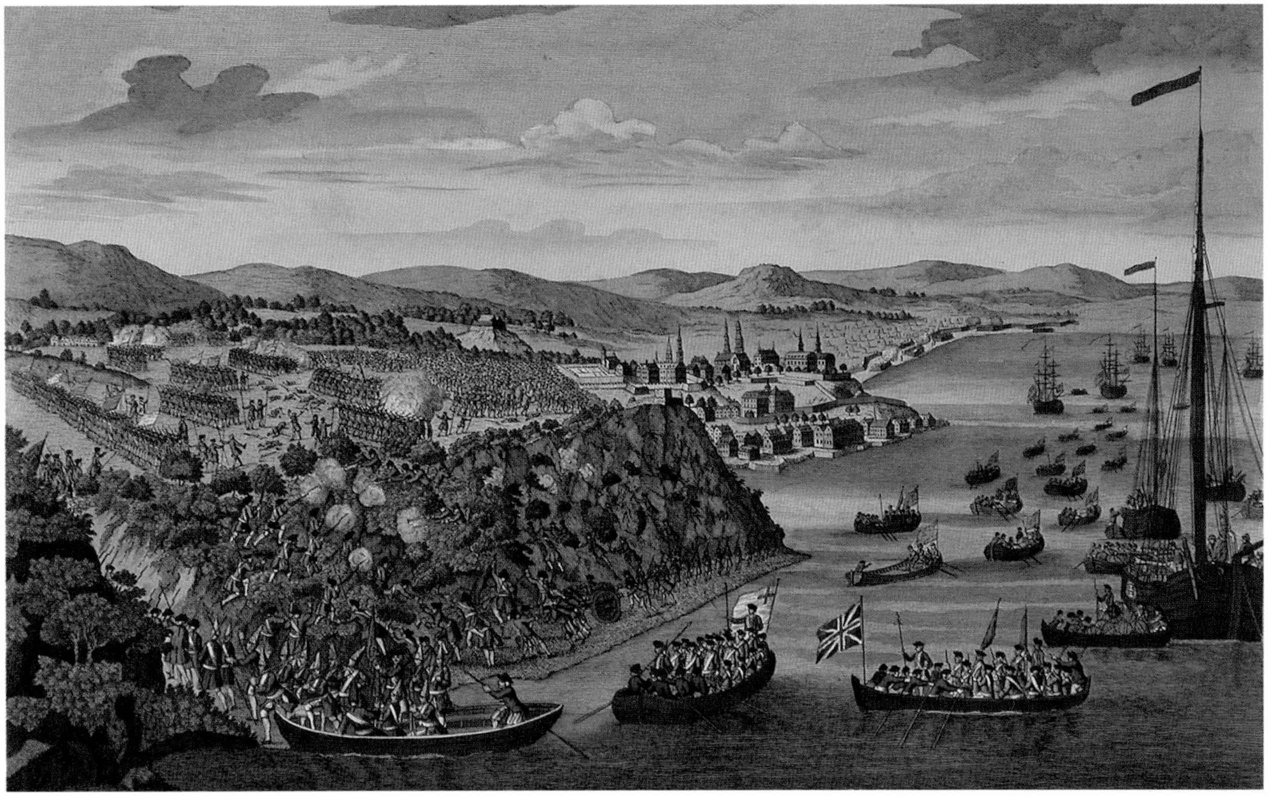

1.1 *A View of the Taking of Quebec,* September 13, 1759. This engraving after Captain Sir Hervey Smythe depicts the capture of Quebec by General James Wolfe. The event marked Cook for future advancement. Thanks to his meeting with the army engineer Samuel Holland at Louisbourg in 1758, Cook learned to apply the increasingly sophisticated techniques of land surveying to nautical mapping. Their partnership led to a joint compilation of the "New Chart of the River St Lawrence," which was a key to Wolfe's strategy. Cook later wrote that he "conducted the embarkation to the Heights of Abraham; examined the passage and laid buoys for the security of the large ships in proceeding up the river." McCord Museum, Montreal, M3971.

at the mouth of the St. Lawrence River, Cook made the acquaintance of the army engineer Samuel Holland, from whom he learned the increasingly sophisticated techniques being used by land surveyors. In particular, he learned the importance of establishing a reliable baseline and the use of triangulation and trigonometric readings from a series of landmarks to obtain accurate coordinates. Cook's determination to use such techniques at sea as well as on land was later strengthened by another Canadian encounter, with the accomplished land surveyor Joseph DesBarres, at Newfoundland in 1762.[2]

Cook's meticulous charting of the St. Lawrence River, in conjunction with Holland, played a part in the success of General James Wolfe's landing on the shores of that river and his capture of Quebec, which secured British dominance in North America (fig. 1.1). Once the French conceded British victory after the Peace of Paris in 1763, Cook was enlisted in the task of extending British control over its newly acquired possessions in North America. From 1763 to 1767 he made an annual transatlantic crossing to conduct his painstaking surveys of Newfoundland, in the course of which he honed his surveying and cartographic skills. He also displayed his abilities as an astronomer, which were naturally linked with his surveying skills. His paper in the *Philosophical Transactions of the Royal Society* on the eclipse of the sun observed from Newfoundland in 1766 drew further attention to this up-and-coming member of the Royal Navy. With the end of the Seven Years' War, interest was renewed in the exploration of the Southern Hemisphere. Cook was identified as a figure naturally equipped for the career of explorer and mapmaker, one who could expand the sphere of British geographic knowledge and power.

For Britain and the European powers, strategic and imperial goals were still important, but to varying degrees these nations were also keen to expand the realm of science. Voyages of exploration were intended not only to map the entire globe but also to observe and describe its scientific characteristics. The motives were various. Among the Spanish and Portuguese, the quests for gold and in the service of the Christian God were often intertwined. The Protestant culture of England, however, was not yet persuaded of the value of missionary activity outside Europe, so the English lust for wealth was naked of pious justifications. Imperial ambition was another constant, with the warring states of Europe seeking strategic as well as commercial advantages over their rivals.

At the same time, the developing Scientific Revolution was stimulating interest in the unknown and the curious and fostering the intellectual daring to venture beyond the boundaries set by the ancients.[3] Ingrained attitudes of European superiority, especially in religious matters, were to some extent offset by curiosity about new peoples and new lands. The force of such scientific curiosity had gathered pace by the eighteenth century, fortified by the confidence of Enlightenment thinkers that the methods of science could unravel the secrets of the globe for the betterment of humankind. Belief in the possibilities of human reason was fueled by the successes of the Scientific Revolution, and a greater willingness to understand other societies was strengthened by a decline in religious chauvinism. The search for knowledge became ever more a cultural value, though, inevitably, it was combined and often shaped by the more familiar goals of national strategic and commercial advantage. Such was the cultural matrix out of which Cook's voyages emerged.

The first voyage was prompted initially and overtly by the goal of demonstrating Britain's status as a scientific power through active participation in the observation of the 1769 transit of Venus. As part of this endeavor, Cook was ordered to Tahiti by the Admiralty at the behest of Britain's premier scientific body, the Royal Society. Observing the passage of the black dot of Venus across the disk of the sun offered a means of calculating the trigonometric determination of the exact distance

1.2 *Fort Venus in Tahiti.* Engraving based on a sketch by the botanical draftsman Sydney Parkinson. From Sydney Parkinson, *A Journal of a Voyage to the South Seas* (London: Richardson and Urquhart, 1773), plate 4. As its name suggests, the primary purpose of the fort was to provide security for Charles Green (the astronomer appointed by the Royal Society) and those involved in the observation of the transit of Venus while the *Endeavour* was anchored at Matavai Bay from April to August 1769. Protection was afforded by mounting the ships' guns along with earthworks and palisades on three sides, and digging deep channels on the fourth, though these measures did not prevent the (temporary) theft of a quadrant. The ambiguity of the reference to the planet and to the classical goddess of love was not lost on contemporaries. University of British Columbia Library, Rare Books and Special Collections, FC 3821.241P37 A3 1773.

1.3 Benjamin West, *Portrait of Joseph Banks,* 1771. This portrait was painted some months after the return of the *Endeavour* in July 1771. West, who specialized in history paintings, was at the peak of his fame after the display of his celebrated *Death of General Wolfe* (1770). Banks's portrait emphasizes his contact with Pacific cultures: he is wrapped in a Maori flax coat fringed with dog hair. Near his left foot is a Tahitian adze, and other Polynesian artifacts form part of the background. The book is left open to show an illustration of New Zealand flax (phormium), a potentially valuable commodity for naval stores. Lincolnshire County Council, Usher Gallery, Lincoln, UK / Bridgeman Art Library. LCNUG: 1989/9.

from the Earth to the sun—the basic astronomical yardstick. Since such transits come in pairs, eight years apart, the 1769 observations could draw on the experience gained from the transit of 1761. During the earlier observation, the European powers had been hampered by the lack of observation points in the Southern Hemisphere. In 1769, they cooperated across the globe to advance the cause of astronomy. Since the end of the Seven Years' War, the British had been extending their survey of the southern seas, with the voyages of John Byron from 1764 to 1766 and Samuel Wallis from 1766 to 1768—both captaining the same ship, the *Dolphin,* and many of the same men. Wallis's voyaging had led, in 1767, to the first European encounter with Tahiti, which thereafter became an icon of the Pacific.

Tahiti offered a convenient point from which to observe the transit of Venus. Moreover, Wallis's voyage had provided valuable information about navigating across the Pacific and for keeping the ship's crew in good health (fig. 1.2).[4] Further scientific significance was attached to the voyage by the fortuitous decision of the wealthy and well-connected naturalist Joseph Banks to come aboard with a wide-ranging scientific party and top-of-the-line equipment (fig. 1.3). Such an accommodation of Banks's party was an innovation that provided the precedent for a combination of British naval might and inquiry into the natural world, which reached its acme in Darwin's involvement in the great *Beagle* voyage, probably the most successful scientific research project of all time.

Cook's ship became a floating platform for the promotion of astronomy and natural history, but the Admiralty's willingness to fund such an expensive enterprise was inevitably linked to other strategic goals. After the transit of Venus, Cook opened his secret instructions, which emphasized both the importance of "Attaining a Knowledge of distant Parts . . . but imperfectly explored" and the way in which such activity might "tend greatly to the advancement of the Trade and Navigation" of the British nation.[5] Accordingly, Cook turned southward to explore the coastline of New Zealand, only sketchily known from Abel Tasman's 1642 expedition, and the east coast of Australia, hitherto a blank on European maps of the globe. It was a voyage that very nearly ended in disaster when the ship ran aground on the Great Barrier Reef in 1770 (fig. 1.4).

1.4 *The* Endeavour *Beached for Repairs after Hitting the Great Barrier Reef.* From J. Hawkesworth, *An Account of the Voyages . . .* (London: W. Strahan and T. Cadell, 1773), plate 19. Engraving probably based on a lost drawing by Sydney Parkinson. The scene is at the mouth of the Endeavour River near what is today Cooktown, in northern Queensland. It shows the *Endeavour* under repair after its near-fatal collision with the Endeavour Reef, a part of the larger reef, on June 11, 1770. Cook's state of mind is evident in the name he gave the coast nearby: Cape Tribulation. The vessel remained beached until August 4, when it was sufficiently patched up to sail again, though major repairs were required at Batavia. University of British Columbia Library, Rare Books and Special Collections, 1773. FC 3821.241.H3 1773.

1.5 Thomas Luny, *The Bark,* Earl of Pembroke, *later* Endeavour, *leaving Whitby Harbour in 1768.* Oil painting. In 1768, the Admiralty purchased this collier, which had been constructed three and a half years previously at Whitby in the Fishburn yard owned by Thomas Milner. It was the sort of ship on which Cook had been trained, and, though slow, it could carry ample stores. Thanks to its shallow draft, the ship could come in close to shore for mapping and, as figure 1.4 shows, could be dragged ashore for repairs. National Library of Australia, an2280897.

One lesson that this experience drove home for Cook was the importance of traveling with two ships—a goal he realized with much more success on the third voyage than on the second, when his two vessels frequently lost contact in high seas, and Cook's consort abandoned the voyage after an unusually hostile encounter with Maori warriors in New Zealand. More positively, the experience of repairing the *Endeavour* after its encounter with the Great Barrier Reef confirmed the merits of the vessels on which Cook had trained: the low draft of the Whitby colliers meant that they could be readily beached for repairs.[6] They could also carry a great deal of cargo and come in close to shore to facilitate the mapping of the coast, which was Cook's central mission. Thus Cook chose Whitby colliers for his subsequent voyages also (fig. 1.5). The *Endeavour* was followed on the second voyage by the *Resolution* and the *Adventure;* on the third, the *Resolution* was again pressed into service, along with the *Discovery.*

Effective navigation of new areas of the globe also allowed an evaluation of their natural resources. This was the enterprise to which Banks and his party particularly devoted themselves, though all on board played a role. This entailed an orderly and comprehensible cataloguing of the animal, vegetable, and mineral kingdoms, using systems of classification such as that of Carl Linnaeus, which had become widely disseminated by the time of Cook's voyages. This remit, too, was spelled out in the secret instructions for Cook's *Endeavour* voyage: "You are also carefully to observe the Nature of the Soil, and the Products thereof; the Beasts and Fowls that inhabit or frequent it, the fishes that are to be found in the Rivers . . . ; and in case you find any Mines, Minerals or valuable stones you are to bring home Specimens of each, as also such Specimens of the Seeds of the Trees, Fruits and Grains" so that "We may cause proper Examination and Experiments to be made of them." These orders were followed by the injunction "to observe the Genius, Temper, Disposition and Number of the Natives."[7]

Astronomy, too, played its part in this imperial project, since it provided the basis for accurate mapping. This was particularly true on the first voyage because determinations of longitude and latitude were based on astronomical readings. On the second voyage, the newly devised chronometer provided another means of determining longitude. Because the performance of the device was untested, it was used in conjunction with the traditional astronomical methods. By the third voyage, the superiority of the chronometer was well established, though astronomical methods still had a place as a form of checking accurate time (figs. 5.4 and 5.6). The astronomers on board were also expected to record other data to enable others to navigate the route as safely as possible. The *Endeavour*'s instructions required them to record "Latitude and Longitude" along with "Variation of the Needle," that is, declination of the compass needle according to the changing position of magnetic north with respect to true north. They were also to assist the commanding officers in collecting the raw material for accurate mapping, including "bearings of Head Lands, Height, direction and Course of the Tides and currents, Depths and Soundings of the Sea, Shoals, Rocks, & c."[8]

Science, then, was enlisted to effectively encompass the globe and illuminate its dark corners. Such a quest drew on the cultural capital of the eighteenth-century Enlightenment and its belief that knowledge offered a means of challenging ancient certainties and illustrating the capabilities of human reason. But, as Francis Bacon, one of the Enlightenment's heroes, well knew, knowledge and power were closely intertwined. Mapping brought with it great power, enabling more and more of the globe to be studied in metropolitan centers and facilitating return voyages to advance imperial and commercial goals.[9]

The practices established on Cook's first voyage continued to shape scientific observations on the second and third voyages. Astronomy was considered a natural extension of the haven-finding arts of the navigator. Furthermore, the possibility of observing the heavens from new vantage points helped to untie the tight purse strings of the British government and allowed for the employment of professional astronomers linked to the Board of Longitude or the Royal Observatory at Greenwich. On the second voyage, astronomers were attached to both vessels: William Wales to the *Resolution* and William Bayly to the *Adventure.* On the third voyage, the task of keeping astronomical and related records on the *Resolution* was allocated to Cook and Lieutenant James King. Bayly returned to serve as astronomer on the *Discovery.* King and Bayly produced the official astronomical volume from the third voyage, which appeared in 1782.

Natural history was a less obvious extension of a naval ship's activities, though Banks's activities on the *Endeavour* established a tradition that was continued on the second and third voyages. On the second voyage, Banks attempted to include an even larger scientific party but withdrew in high dudgeon when it could not be accommodated. Instead, the formidably learned German naturalist Johann Reinhold Forster was employed; as a bonus, his precocious son, Georg, accompanied him. Cook and others on the second voyage may have rued the prickly Forsters' presence on board, but posterity has reason to be grateful that this intellectually omnivorous duo was taken along. In ethnology particularly, their knowledge of a vast array of languages and societies provided a range of intellectual reference and resonance that has rarely been surpassed.[10] But after the prima-donna antics of Banks and the obstinacy of the Forsters, by the third voyage Cook had enough of civilian naturalists. Plausibly, he is reported by Lieutenant James King as saying, "Curse the scientists, and all science into the bargain."[11]

Part of the issue was control. Civilians were foreign bodies on ships organized according to naval hierarchy. Their intractability became a major bone of contention on French voyages into the Pacific, which often included much larger complements of scientists. Disputes were frequent, as the naval personnel were sometimes treated rather like water-taxi drivers. Cook liked to be in charge, without backchat from people he could not order about. But perhaps there were advantages in having people on board who shared the Great Cabin with Cook and the other officers and who could put forward dissenting views. When commenting on the absence of civilian scientists on Cook's third voyage, Johann Reinhold Forster suggested that Cook might not have been killed in Hawai'i if he or Banks had been on board.[12] That observation draws a long bow, but some element of independent comment and even criticism on Cook's treatment of indigenous peoples might have had some bearing on that outcome.

Despite Cook's refusal to have civilian naturalists on board for the third voyage, he was not hostile to natural history as such. He allocated the task of naturalist to William Anderson, a surgeon subject to naval discipline. It was a good choice, even though the haul of natural specimens brought back from the third voyage was smaller than those of the other two voyages—not simply because of Anderson's divided responsibilities but also because he died on August 3, 1778, two years before the voyage's end. Anderson was an astute student of indigenous societies, and his contributions to the study of Pacific languages were particularly important. The judicious Lieutenant King commended him for the wide view he held of natural history, which "took in all natural objects," and the way in which "he apply'd & studied the different Species of Natural history & of the human Species."[13] Along with Anderson was another naturalist of a much more lowly kind: David Nelson, the gardener-botanist who was listed as a servant to the astronomer, William Bayly, on the *Discovery*. As a mere gardener sent by Banks to collect specimens for Kew Gardens, he was not, however, likely to talk back to Cook.

The fruits of Cook's voyages provided the materials with which to reconstruct the world of the Pacific back in London—and the basis for the rational analysis of the globe that was central to Enlightenment thinking. Cities such as London, Paris, and Madrid provided repositories for what voyagers brought back with them, and these imperial capitals became, in the words of the French sociologist of science Bruno Latour, "centers of calculation," as the data thus assembled were subjected to patient scrutiny.[14] First and foremost, Cook was a cartographer. (One of the most notable consequences of his mapmaking achievements was the arrival of the First Fleet at Botany Bay in 1788 and the foundation of the British penal colony of New South Wales.) Cook and his men also brought back a vast quantity of indigenous artifacts, which provided insights into the ways of life of the Pacific peoples they had encountered. Many of these objects were incorporated into the great museums of Britain, Europe, and the Eurocentric cultures of Australasia and America. Such collections provided fuel for developing what the Enlightenment called "the science of man"—what today we would call

1.6 *The Natche, a Ceremony in Honour of the King's Son, in Tongataboo.* Engraving after John Webber. From James Cook and James King, *A Voyage to the Pacific Ocean in the years 1776, 1777, 1778, 1779 and 1780* (London: G. Nicol and T. Cadell, 1784), vol. 1, plate 22. This ceremony to honor the god Hikulea marked the coming of age of the Tongan king's son. It showed the extent to which religious and political beliefs were integrated within Polynesian society. Cook was so keen to observe it that, to the dismay of some of his men, he complied with the local custom of literally letting his hair down and going naked to the waist. University of British Columbia Library, Rare Books and Special Collections, FC 3821.241.243.A1 1784.

the social sciences—applying the techniques of the natural sciences to the world of human society.

Though such indigenous artifacts provoked great interest and curiosity, they also created a problem. One of the great quests of the Enlightenment was to provide ways of classifying the products of the natural and the human world. But such artifacts, referred to as "artificial curiosities" because they were manmade, resisted ready classification. The great quantities of "natural curiosities" that Cook and other Pacific explorers brought back lent themselves more readily to taxonomic classification. Joseph Banks was inspired particularly by the great Swedish naturalist Carl Linnaeus, whose system of classification and particularly his enduring device of binomial nomenclature seemed to provide a means of reducing the bewildering array of Nature into a manageable form. Banks wrote a letter of tribute to Linnaeus before setting off, though the two never met, and Linnaeus's pupil, Daniel Solander, accompanied Banks on the *Endeavour* voyage.

The study of human societies with the tools of natural history was, then, an inseparable part of exploration. The guiding ideas that shaped the voyagers' reactions to the Pacific were largely passed from voyage to voyage. The first Pacific voyage in the *Endeavour* was critical in shaping the ways in which the indigenous peoples were understood and the ways in which the voyagers dealt with the people they encountered on the shore. Moreover, the instructions that Cook was given for the first *Endeavour* voyage were largely repeated for his third voyage. Again he was instructed "to observe the Genius, Temper, Disposition and Number of the Natives and Inhabitants." Good relations were to be cultivated by presents of "Trinkets" and "Traffick"; trade was also encouraged, though Cook was warned "to be always on your guard."[15] The instructions underline the importance of relations with the indigenous people. The long Pacific voyages were impossible without regular stops to obtain fresh water, firewood, and, if at all possible, fresh food. They sometimes required spending a good deal of time on shore, such as the three months that had to be spent on Tahiti on the first voyage, much to the sailors' delight, in order to observe the transit of Venus.

The intellectual baggage that was loaded on board the ships was shaped by long theorizing about the nature of human variety. Race became a particularly important issue with the increasing scale of the slave trade, in which, by Cook's time, Britain played the largest part as the world's leading maritime power. This role, in turn, had begun to prompt a reaction that eventually led to the abolition of the slave trade in 1807. This eventual victory stemmed in large measure from the fact that the dominant view was the monogenist one that all human beings had a common origin. This had behind it the weight of scripture, which spoke of all human beings as being of "one blood," as well as the force of Enlightenment theorizing. The dominant strand of Enlightenment thinking about human difference was that it stemmed chiefly from environmental factors, particularly climate.[16] When, for example, James King encountered the Hawaiians on the third voyage, he attributed their similarity to the peoples of Tahiti and Tonga to their "living on Islands in the same climate, upon the same food, & with the same objects before them."[17] Georg Forster used some of the material he had collected on the second voyage to question this dominant view, and he even edged toward polygenism, that is, a belief in multiple origins of the human race, but this was a radical and minority position.

On the first voyage, Cook largely deferred to Joseph Banks when it came to describing indigenous peoples and accounting for their differences, even on occasions closely following Banks's own account in his voyage journal. As the *Endeavour* sailed on, however, Cook gained greater confidence and interest in the subject and wrote more and more with his own voice. On the second and third voyages, Cook's interest in indigenous cultures grew ever more pronounced. On the third voyage, in particular, Cook demonstrated a thirst for observing their rituals, an inclination that broke with the conventions of naval life and may have contributed to his own demise. On Tonga he shocked some of his officers by literally letting his hair hang down and stripping to the waist to observe the *'inasi* ceremony, which inaugurated the planting of a new crop of yams and also served to mark the coming of age of the king's son (fig. 1.6). Shortly afterward, on

1.7 John Webber, *A Human Sacrifice, in a Morai, in Otaheite.* Watercolor, circa 1780–84. This is another illustration of the extent to which Cook, on the third voyage particularly, was keen to observe indigenous Polynesian rituals at firsthand. Those sacrificed were generally Tahitian commoners who had offended the *ari'i* or aristocracy. Only males could be offered as sacrifices. They were killed by surprise, and sometimes their bodies were stored for days before being offered to the gods at a ritual site or *marae* constructed of stones. Such an offering often took the form of removing the victim's eyes. Dixson Library, State Library of New South Wales, PXX 2:10.

Tahiti, Cook took a voyeuristic interest in attending a human sacrifice (fig. 1.7).

In his descriptions of the Pacific societies he encountered, Cook, like Banks, does not seem to have been influenced by the increasingly strong belief in evolutionary, hierarchical models that placed human societies in a pecking order according to their degree of conformity with the model of a commercial society.[18] Quite obviously, this model of human development placed European society at its acme. It owed much to French Enlightenment theorists but was developed most fully in the Scottish Enlightenment.[19] (Hence Walter Bagehot's jibe that it sought to describe the ascent from savage to Scotsman through such stages as hunter-gatherer, pastoral, agricultural and, finally, commercial societies.)[20] On the first voyage, Cook had followed Banks in taking the contrary view that hunter-gatherer societies such as the Australian Aboriginals might be "far more happier than we Europeans."[21] In saying so, he rejected the unflattering view of the Aboriginals of the west coast put forward by William Dampier in his widely read *New Voyage round the World* of 1697.

There is no indication that Cook adopted the increasingly fashionable evolutionary view on subsequent voyages, even though the Forsters' accounts of the second voyage are strongly influenced by it. On the third voyage, the Scottish-educated William Anderson also appears to have thought in such evolutionary terms, seeking to place Pacific societies in a gradation from "a very barbarous state" to more enlightened ones according to their treatment of women, an issue that attracted the attention of some of the theorists of the Scottish Enlightenment.[22]

Cook was skeptical about classifying societies according to their customs and placed much more faith in the evidence of language. In Unalaska on the third voyage, Cook described the way in which the Aleut people made fire, commenting that such methods were common to many different societies. This, he noted critically, had been used by "some learned and inginious men" to argue "that this and that Nation are of the same extraction," but, he continued, "accidental agreement in a few particular manners or customs is no proof that two different Nations are of the same extraction." He placed much more faith in the linguistic evidence. This was a point that Banks had stressed on the first voyage and had been the subject of considerable investigation by the Forsters on the second. "The language of the Greenlanders, and Esquimaux," Cook observed, provided "great reason to believe that all these nations are of the same extraction." If so, the inference was promising: "There can be little doubt but there is a northern communication of some sort by sea between this Ocean and Baffins bay." Such communication was probably over land, he concluded ruefully. His doubts about the existence of the Northwest Passage increased as the ships sailed west, then southwest along the impenetrable Alaska coast, and, he eventually noted, "it may be effectually shut up against Shipping."[23]

Knowledge of indigenous societies was largely the outcome of trading relations (fig. 1.8). These interactions colored the descriptions in voyage journals of different peoples of the Pacific. The accounts of the language and customs of those, such as the Australian Aboriginals, who had no interest in trade, were relatively sketchy, even though both Banks and Cook had a certain respect for people who did not want more than they already had. Over the course of the three voyages, the significance of trade between ship and shore became increasingly evident. When Cook first arrived in Polynesia and introduced metal to the islands, it commanded hefty prices, in terms of food, sex, or curiosities, that were not sustained on the later voyages. By the third voyage Cook and his men had a better understanding of the goods that indigenous peoples valued. On the second voyage, for example, Cook drew up a list of tradable goods for the next voyage that extended to "Axes and Hatchets, Spike Nails, Files, Knives, Looking Glasses, Beads & c. Sheets and Shirts."[24] Voyagers came to understand that metal goods were most appreciated if they corresponded in shape to traditional tools. On the second voyage, Cook brought red feathers back from Tonga to Tahiti and fortuitously discovered that because of the sacred overtones of the color red, these could command remarkably high prices. The result was that on the third voyage, the expedition carried large quantities of red feathers to Tahiti, though, inevitably, some measure of inflation set in.

Relations between ship and shore were largely determined by the two sides' understanding of trade. On the whole, relations at Nootka Sound on the third voyage were harmonious because the local people were willing to engage in trade, as Europeans understood it, reflecting well-established traditions of long-distance trading across the American continent (fig. 7.2).[25] Societies along the Northwest Coast were also familiar with metal, one of the staples of trade for Cook's men. There was some cultural dissonance over the trading value of things like grass to feed the livestock, which Cook's men considered as common property but which the people of Nootka Sound regarded as requiring payment. Within Polynesian societies, the main source of conflict was breaches of trading relations, which the Europeans considered theft. Indeed, this was the most immediate cause of the conflict at Hawai'i that led to Cook's death.[26] Conflict over such matters was much greater on the third voyage than on the previous two, perhaps simply because of the increasing determination of the Polynesian peoples to obtain more valuable European goods.

Over the course of the three voyages, Cook's basic assumptions about human equality did not change; nor did his way of understanding human differences. His ever-keener interest in the cultures he encountered was reflected in his journals, as he moved from his dependence on Banks's ethnological accounts in the first voyage to a more confident and original voice in the journals of the second and third voyage. Ironically, however, as his fascination with the Pacific increased, so too did his appreci-

1.8 Tupaia, *Englishman Bartering with a Maori,* 1769, probably at Tolaga Bay, New Zealand. Watercolor. Tupaia was a priest from the Leeward island of Ra'iatea, who was driven out by invaders from the neighboring island of Bora-Bora in 1760. He came aboard the *Endeavour* in Tahiti in 1769, providing valuable service as both navigator and Polynesian interpreter. As this illustration shows, he mastered the use of Banks's coloring box to depict scenes he saw as being particularly important on his voyage on the *Endeavour* (which lasted until his death in Batavia in December 1770). Here he reduces cross-cultural trade to its emblematic essentials, with a Maori exchanging a crayfish with an Englishman (possibly Banks) in return for a piece of cloth (possibly bark cloth from Tahiti). © British Library Board, MS 15508, f.11a, #12.

ation of the hierarchical character of Polynesian societies. This made him increasingly aware of the extent to which thefts of European goods were, to a large extent, controlled by the chiefs; hence he came to regard such thefts as a form of defiance of his own authority. He thus became increasingly determined not to be outdone by the chiefs, and his desire to stamp his own presence and authority on the Pacific probably contributed to his eventual undoing.[27]

The cumulative effect of Cook's voyages, then, was to provide both the man and the country he served with a wider education in the conduct and possibilities of exploration. During his training in the merchant and Royal navies, Cook learned the basics of his craft as a seaman. His time in North America developed his skills as a cartographer—the key to his success. The accuracy of such cartography rested on precise determination of latitude and longitude. Latitude could be determined with increasing accuracy thanks to the invention by John Hadley in 1731 of an octant (the forerunner of the sextant), which could provide double reflections of a heavenly body (fig. 5.1). Determining longitude, a much more taxing problem, became possible using astronomical methods after the publication of Nevil Maskelyne's *Nautical Almanac* in 1767 (fig. 5.3).[28] But it was the alternative method, based on John Harrison's chronometer, that triumphed. This outcome owed something to Cook's advocacy after he took with him on both the second and third voyages a replica of Harrison's famed H4, made by Larcum Kendall in 1769 (fig. 5.4). Since this device was available for the second voyage from 1772 to 1775, along with the *Nautical Almanac,* this provided an opportunity for testing both methods of arriving at an accurate calculation of longitude. Cook's great second voyage not only served to demystify the globe by disproving the existence of the conjectured Great South Land but also provided an object lesson in navigating with accuracy to the farthest reaches of the planet.

The Enlightenment quest to apply the methods of science to studying the globe promoted the scientific classification of as much of the Earth's surface as possible. Natural history provided wide and flexible methods of both collecting and classifying the products of the three kingdoms of nature—animal, vegetable, and mineral. Following the inclusion by Linnaeus of the human species in the animal kingdom, the study of nature extended to the study of human society, and Cook's voyages were to provide rich materials for the development of the Enlightenment's "science of man." Knowledge was pursued out of curiosity and a love of learning that transcended national rivalries, as with the *Endeavour*'s involvement in the observation of the transit of Venus.

But knowledge also brought with it greater imperial power. Cook's observations of the Pacific peoples were prompted in part by the need to assess their likely compliance with British imperial designs. The possibility of settlements under the British flag shaped Cook's reflections on the places he encountered. On the first voyage he reflected about his time in New Zealand that "should it ever become an object of settleing this Country the best place for the first fixing of a Colony would be either in the River Thames [now Waihou River] or the Bay of Islands," on account of their harbors. His observations of Maori society led him to conclude that "they seem to be too much divided among themselves to unite in opposing, by which means and kind and gentle usuage the Colonists would be able to form strong parties among them."[29]

Cook was ever conscious of the imperative to lay claim to territories before other European powers did so. Though his instructions ordered him to take possession of Australia only with the consent of the natives, he dispensed with such negotiations. Hence on August 22, 1779, he raised the Union Jack on Possession Island in the Torres Strait to lay claim to the east coast of Australia before France, the Dutch Republic, or Spain did so. The second voyage was undertaken in order to prove a negative, that there was no Great South Land, but it was prompted by the Admiralty's conclusion that if such a land did exist, Britain would be the first to benefit from the discovery of another New World.

The level of seamanship and navigational exactitude that Cook displayed on the second voyage awed his contemporaries. When the Royal Society, the promoter of Cook's first voyage, set in train proposals for a voyage to shed light on the scantily understood geography of the north Pacific, they naturally turned to Cook. Again, the objective was to prove a negative: that there was no Northwest Passage between the Atlantic and the Pacific.

By the time of the third voyage, Cook and the British nation as a whole had accumulated the expertise to make possible lengthy voyages to unknown shores. Thanks to his dietary measures, Cook had learned how to keep his men at sea for long periods without contracting scurvy. Cook had also embraced increasingly accurate techniques of navigation and become a master of cartography. Increasing contact with the peoples of the Pacific had likewise given Cook a reputation for being able to deal with indigenous societies effectively. Ironically, this proved to be his undoing, as these previous experiences led to overconfidence and confrontation with the Hawaiians at Kealakekua Bay (fig. 12.5). There his fleshly parts were consigned to a watery grave while his bones became sacred relics and sources of *mana* or spiritual power for the Hawaiian chiefs. Cook became a part of the Pacific that he had opened up to European scrutiny and imperial expansion.

NOTES

1 On Cook's early years in the merchant navy, see Rosalin Barker, "Cook's Nursery: Whitby's Eighteenth-Century Merchant Fleet," in *Captain Cook: Explorations and Reassessments,* ed. Glyndwr Williams (Woodbridge, UK: Boydell, 2004), 7–20, and John Gascoigne, *Captain Cook: Voyager between Worlds* (London: Continuum, 2007), 17–20, 49–55. On his career in the Royal Navy, see John Robson, *Captain Cook's War and Peace: The Royal Navy Years, 1755–1768* (Sydney: University of New South Wales Press, 2009).

2 On Cook's Canadian years, see V. Suthren, *To Go upon Discovery: James Cook and Canada, 1758–1767* (Toronto: Dundurn, 1999).

3 John Gascoigne, "Crossing the Pillars of Hercules: Francis Bacon, the Scientific Revolution and the New World," in *Baroque Science,* ed. Ofer Gal and Raz Chen-Morris (Dordrecht: Springer, 2013), 217–38.

4 Randolph Cock, "Precursors of Cook: The Voyages of the *Dolphin* (1764–8) as Precursors of Cook's Voyages of Exploration," *Mariner's Mirror* 85, no. 1 (1999): 30–52.

5 *The Journals of Captain James Cook on His Voyages of Discovery,* vol. 1, *The Voyage of the* Endeavour, *1768–1771,* ed. J. C. Beaglehole (Cambridge: Cambridge University Press for the Hakluyt Society, 1955), cclxxxii.

6 On the structure and dimensions of these ships, see the definitive study by Ray Parkin, *H.M. Bark* Endeavour: *Her Place in Australian History* (Melbourne: Melbourne University Press, 1997).

7 Cook, *Voyage of the* Endeavour, cclxxxiii.

8 "Additional Instructions for Lt. James Cook," in *The Journals of Captain James Cook on His Voyages of Discovery,* vol. 3, *The Voyage of the* Resolution *and* Discovery, *1776–1780,* ed. J. C. Beaglehole (Cambridge: Cambridge University Press for the Hakluyt Society, 1967), part 1, cclxxxii. On Cook as a navigator, see J. C. Beaglehole, "Cook, the Navigator," *Explorers' Journal* 48 (1970): 264–73, and G. Ritchie, "Captain Cook's Influence on Hydrographic Surveying," *Pacific Studies* 1 (1978): 78–95.

9 Matthew Edney, "Reconsidering Enlightenment Geography and Mapping," in *Geography and Enlightenment,* ed. David Livingstone and Charles Withers (Chicago: University of Chicago Press, 1999), 165–98; John Gascoigne, "Joseph Banks, Mapping and the Geographies of Natural Knowledge," in *Georgian Geographies: Essays on Space, Place and Landscape in the Eighteenth Century,* ed. Miles Ogden and Charles Withers (Manchester, UK: Manchester University Press, 2004), 151–73.

10 Michael E. Hoare, *The Tactless Philosopher: Johann Reinhold Forster* (Melbourne: Hawthorn, 1976).

11 James Cook and James King, *A Voyage to the Pacific Ocean in the years 1776, 1777, 1778, 1779 and 1780. In three volumes: vol. 1 and 2 written by Captain J. Cook, vol. 3 by Captain J. King* (London: G. Nicol and T. Cadell, 1784), 3:49.

12 H. Zimmerman, *Account of the Third Voyage of Captain Cook, 1776–1780*, trans. from the German by U. Tewsley (Wellington: W. A. G. Skinner, Government Printer, 1926), 48–49.

13 Cook, *Voyage of the* Resolution *and* Discovery, part 2, 1430.

14 Bruno Latour, *Science in Action: How to Follow Scientists and Engineers through Society* (Cambridge. MA: Harvard University Press, 1987), 215–57; David Miller, "Joseph Banks, Empire and 'Centers of Calculation' in late Hanoverian London," in *Visions of Empire: Voyages, Botany, and Representations of Nature,* ed. David Miller and Peter Reill (Cambridge: Cambridge University Press, 1996), 21–37.

15 Cook, *Voyage of the* Resolution *and* Discovery, part 1, ccxxiii.

16 Bronwen Douglas, "Climate to Crania: Science and the Racialization of Human Difference," and "*Novus Orbis Australia:* Oceania in the Science of Race, 1750–1850," in *Foreign Bodies: Oceania and the Science of Race, 1750–1940,* ed. Bronwen Douglas and Chris Ballard (Canberra: Australian National University E Press, 2008), 33–96, 99–156.

17 Cook, *Voyage of the* Resolution *and* Discovery, 613.

18 John Gascoigne, *Joseph Banks and the English Enlightenment: Useful Knowledge and Polite Culture* (Cambridge: Cambridge University Press, 1994), 171.

19 Ronal Meek, *Social Science and the Ignoble Savage* (Cambridge: Cambridge University Press, 1976).

20 H. M. Höpfl, "From Savage to Scotsman: Conjectural History in the Scottish Enlightenment," *Journal of British Studies* 17, no. 2 (1978): 19.

21 Cook, *Voyage of the* Endeavour, 399.

22 Cook, *Voyage of the* Resolution *and* Discovery, part 2, 933.

23 Ibid., part 1, 462, 468.

24 *The Journals of Captain James Cook on His Voyages of Discovery,* vol. 2, *The Voyage of the* Resolution *and* Adventure, *1772–1775,* ed. J. C. Beaglehole (Cambridge: Cambridge University Press for the Hakluyt Society, 1961), 411.

25 R. Fisher, "Cook and the Nootka," in *Captain Cook and His Times,* ed. R. Fisher and H. Johnston (Vancouver, BC: Douglas & McIntyre, 1979), 81–98.

26 R. Borofsky and A. Howard, "The Early Contact Period," in *Developments in Polynesian Ethnology,* ed. A. Howard and R. Borofsky (Honolulu: University of Hawai'i Press, 1989), 241–75.

27 Anne Salmond, "Tute: The Impact of Polynesia on Captain Cook," in Williams, *Captain Cook,* 77–93.

28 Eric Forbes, *The Birth of Navigational Science: The Solving in the Eighteenth Century of the Problem of Finding Longitude at Sea* (Greenwich, UK: National Maritime Museum, 1973), 3, 9.

29 Cook, *Voyage of the* Endeavour, 278.

James Cook and the Northwest Passage

Approaching the Third Voyage

GLYN WILLIAMS

2

COOK'S THIRD AND FINAL VOYAGE PRESENTS A SERIES OF PUZZLES AND conundrums, among them the state of his health, his attitude toward the Pacific islanders, and above all the circumstances surrounding his death in Hawai'i. Scholars have argued incessantly and often passionately about these issues, and in the heat of their debates other crucial questions can be lost to sight: Why did Cook embark on his third voyage? What was his state of mind *before* he sailed? And what information did he have about the geography of the north Pacific?

Cook had arrived home on the *Resolution* in July 1775 after one of the greatest of all seaborne voyages of discovery. He had disposed of the imagined southern continent, Terra Australis Incognita, reached closer to the South Pole than any man before him, and touched on a multitude of lands, revisiting New Zealand and Tahiti and seeing Easter Island, the Marquesas, Tonga, New Caledonia, the New Hebrides (Vanuatu), and South Georgia for the first time. There was, Cook judged, little more to do in the South Pacific, where "the Southern Hemisphere [is] sufficiently explored and a final end put to the searching after a Southern Continent."[1] It had been an exhausting, grueling voyage in high latitudes, crossing and recrossing the Ant-

2.1 John Cleveley, *Hauling Boats over the Ice off Spitsbergen,* August 7, 1773. Watercolor. By the end of July 1773, Captain Constantine John Phipps's ships, the *Racehorse* and the *Carcass,* were trapped in the ice just north of latitude 80°N, among the Seven Islands northeast of Spitsbergen, and Phipps decided to attempt an escape to open water in the ships' boats. This painting, based on a drawing by Philippe d'Auvergne, a midshipman on the voyage, shows the launch from the *Racehorse* being hauled across the ice. After three days of laborious work, a strong breeze enabled the ships to win clear of the ice and reach the Dutch whaling base at Smeerenberg. © The Trustees of the British Museum, #1888-1211.3.

arctic Circle in a series of long, methodical sweeps, and Cook's health suffered. Acute stomach pains and violent vomiting weakened him to the point where there were fears for his life. Seafaring was a young man's occupation, as Rosalin Barker explains in her analysis of the age profile of the crews on the Whitby colliers where Cook learned his trade. Even the ships' masters "felt themselves hard done by when their aching limbs were still at sea at the age of 40."[2] On his second voyage Cook was in his mid-forties; on his third he passed fifty.

None of this seemed to matter after Cook's return in the summer of 1775. He was presented to the king and promoted to post captain (for a naval officer a key promotion, leading, if he lived long enough, to the rank of admiral). In the months that followed, Cook was elected a fellow of the Royal Society and was painted by the well-known portrait artist Nathaniel Dance (fig. 6.1). His conversation was even recorded by James Boswell. In his own professional circles Cook was on easy terms with the Earl of Sandwich, first lord of the Admiralty, and other members of the Board of Admiralty. His most immediate commitment was preparing his account of his recent voyage for publication, a daunting task for "a man, who has not the advantage of Education, acquired, nor Natural abilities for writing," but one he would undertake in the security of a comfortable retirement post at Greenwich Hospital, a well-deserved reward for the achievements of two great voyages that had seen him at sea for all but one of the previous seven years.[3] It was not complete retirement, for the *Resolution* was being refitted for another "voyage to remote parts," and in December 1775 Cook, sensibly, was involved in inspections to find a suitable consort vessel for the forthcoming expedition. By this time he presumably had been informed of the purpose of the new voyage, simply expressed in the first sentence of the instructions of the following July, that "an attempt should be made to find out a Northern passage by Sea from the Pacific to the Atlantic Ocean."[4]

While Cook had been away on his second voyage and out of contact with events at home, there had been a revival of interest in exploration to the north. The search for a Northwest Passage had been a constant theme in English maritime enterprise since the late Tudor and early Stuart period, when small vessels struggled through the eastern fringes of the Arctic archipelago in search of an open strait. The main features of this vast region were named after the commanders of the discovery vessels: Davis Strait, Baffin Island and Baffin Bay, Frobisher Bay, Hudson Strait and Hudson Bay, Foxe Basin, James Bay. Those names stood like hopeful signposts on the maps, pointing the way to the Pacific and the lands of the East; but for all the determination of the navigators, there was no way through. In Hudson Bay they reached their westernmost point, only to be blocked by icebound shores. In Cook's own lifetime there had been further attempts to force a passage west of Hudson Bay by Christopher Middleton in 1741–42, William Moor in 1746–47, and

William Christopher of the Hudson's Bay Company in the 1760s, but all had failed.

Since the end of 1772 a new generation of enthusiasts had approached ministers with proposals for northern voyages that avoided the frozen cul-de-sac of Hudson Bay. The files of the Earl of Dartmouth contain several proposals for such voyages, but since he was secretary of state for the American colonies at this time of crisis, it is unlikely that he paid them much attention.[5] Yet even if requests and petitions from individuals could be set aside, an approach from the Royal Society was another and weightier matter altogether. The society had a long tradition of interest in voyages and travels, and its influence both with the king and with the Admiralty had been demonstrated by Cook's first voyage. Central to the events of the next few years was a vice president of the society, Daines Barrington, who was a jurist, antiquarian, and naturalist and a recent convert to the cause of northern exploration. One of his correspondents was the Swiss geographer Samuel Engel, whose *Mémoires et observations géographiques et critiques* of 1765 advocated an attempt to find an Atlantic-Pacific link across the North Pole. Engel claimed that most of the ice encountered in high northern latitudes came from continental rivers when they broke up in early summer, and so he maintained that the ice was thick only near land. Barrington supported this theory in a series of tracts read to the Royal Society, with reports of experiments that seemed to show that salt water could not freeze, and examples of whalers who were alleged to have found an ice-free sea near the pole.[6] Barrington's undiscriminating enthusiasm was a subject of amusement to his contemporaries, but in these years as a council member of the Royal Society and a friend of the Earl of Sandwich, he was the link between the society and the Admiralty in negotiations that resulted in Cook's third voyage.

First, though, there was the pole and the ice-free sea to consider. At a council meeting in early 1773, Barrington stated that he had already discussed the possibility of a polar voyage with Sandwich, and encouraged by this, the society's secretary, Dr. Matthew Maty, wrote to the first lord proposing such an expedition.[7] After some hesitation the Admiralty agreed, and in June 1773 Captain Constantine John Phipps took two bomb vessels, the *Racehorse* and the *Carcass,* north to Spitsbergen (the largest island in the Svalbard Archipelago). Already strong enough to take the shattering recoil of heavy mortars, the ships were further strengthened with double bottoms and fortified bows. Greenland whaling masters were appointed as pilots. Even so, Phipps could not penetrate the ice barrier he encountered north of Spitsbergen and only with difficulty extricated his battered ships from the ice (fig. 2.1). As Phipps wrote in his published account of the voyage, he had run against a "wall of ice, extending for more than twenty degrees between the latitudes of eighty and eighty-one, without the smallest appearance of any opening."[8] For Barrington there was an obvious explanation for Phipps's difficulties: he had been sent in a "bad year."[9]

Undeterred by this failure, Barrington turned his attention to the Northwest Passage, proposing to the Royal Society in February 1774 that an expedition should be sent to find the Pacific entrance of the passage.[10] This was by no means a novel suggestion. Francis Drake on his circumnavigation of 1577–80 may have been attempting to return home by the supposed Strait of Anián when he sailed along the Pacific coast of North America after seizing huge amounts of Spanish silver in the South Sea. In 1603, on a voyage back to England from the Moluccas with East India Company ships, James Lancaster wrote a letter home in which he added a cryptic postscript: "The Passage to the East India lieth in 62½ . . . degrees by the North-west on the America side."[11] Reports of openings, real and imagined, entered by Spanish navigators along that coast—by Juan de Fuca in 1592, Martín de Aguilar in 1603, and the fictitious Bartholomew de Fonte in 1640—increased speculation about the possibility of some dramatic discovery north of Drake's "New Albion." In his *New Voyage round the World* in 1697, William Dampier made a more reasoned case for a Pacific approach to the long-standing enigma of the Northwest Passage:

> If I was to go upon this Discovery, I would go first into the *South-Seas,* bend my course from thence along to *California,* and that way seek a passage back [into the Atlantic]. For as others have spent the Summer, in first searching on this more known side nearer home, and so before they got through, the time of the Year obliged them to give over their Search, and provide for a long course back again, for fear of being left in the Winter; on the contrary, I would search first on the less known coast of the South-Sea-side, and then as the year past away, I should need no retreat, for I should come farther into my Knowledge.[12]

The first Pacific voyage of George III's reign directed Commodore John Byron to the Northwest Coast of America in 1763, where he was told that Drake, Dampier, and other navigators "have thought it probable that a passage might be found between the Latitude of 38° and 54° from that Coast into Hudson's Bay."[13] The stretch of coast mentioned was significant, for 38°N was the supposed location of Drake's Californian landing place, while 54°N lay just to the north of the openings reported by the Spanish expeditions of Fuca, Aguilar, and Fonte. The possibilities raised by the exploration of this region were illustrated in the maps of the French geographers Joseph Nicolas Delisle and Philippe Buache, which showed northwest America sliced by the straits and rivers supposedly entered by the Spanish navigators (fig. 2.2). Fanciful though they were, the maps were taken seriously by the prestigious Paris Academy of Sciences, and they were reprinted and copied many times. Buache was the leading French geographer of the day; Delisle had returned to France in 1747 after more than twenty years at the St. Petersburg Academy of Sciences,

2.2 Joseph Nicolas Delisle, *Carte générale des découvertes de l'amiral de Fonte,* 1752. Delisle's speculative map portrays the supposed discoveries made by Admiral Bartholomew de Fonte along the Northwest Coast of America in 1640, as well as a huge Mer de l'Ouest, entered by Juan de Fuca in 1592 and Martin de Aguilar in 1603. Delisle claimed that Fonte's inland waterway explorations took him within a short distance of the west coast of Hudson Bay, and his map stands as a prototype of later maps of North America that were influenced by the fictitious Fonte account. Rasmuson Library, University of Alaska Fairbanks, G3205.1752.D44—Rare Maps.

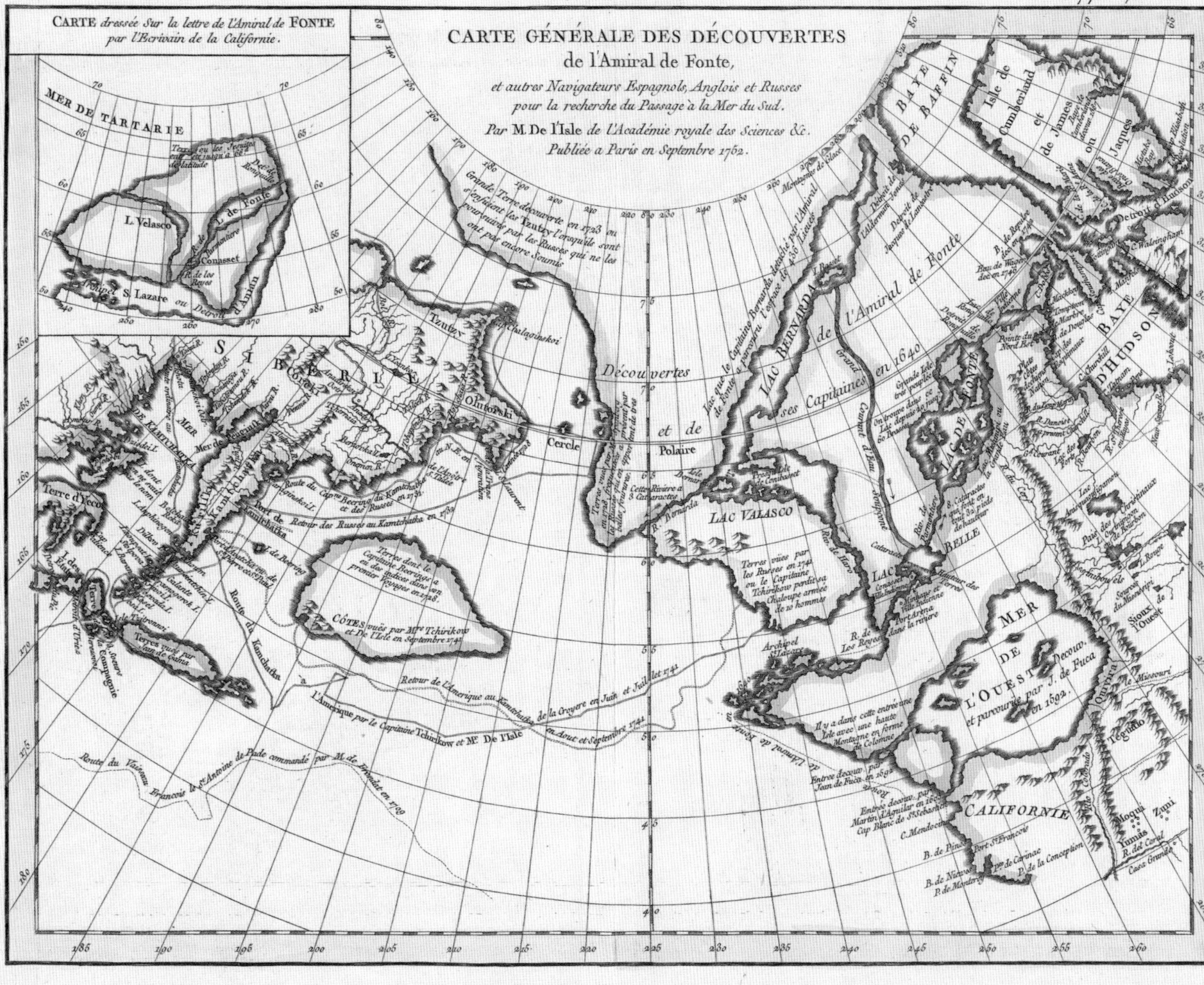
CARTE GÉNÉRALE DES DÉCOUVERTES
de l'Amiral de Fonte,
et autres Navigateurs Espagnols, Anglois et Russes
pour la recherche du Passage à la Mer du Sud.
Par M. De l'Isle de l'Académie royale des Sciences &c.
Publiée a Paris en Septembre 1762.
CARTE dressée Sur la lettre de l'Amiral de FONTE
par l'Ecrivain de la Californie.
MER DE TARTARIE
L. Velasco
L. de Fonte
Conasset
S. Lazare
BAYE DE BAFFIN
Isle de Cumberland
BAYE D'HUDSON
Detroit d'Hudson
LAC BERNARDA
Découvertes de l'Amiral de Fonte et de ses Capitaines en 1640
Cercle Polaire
LAC VALASCO
LAC DE FONTE
LAC BELLE
MER DE L'OUEST
Decouv. et parcourue par J. de Fuca en 1592.
Entrée decouv. par Jean de Fuca en 1592
CALIFORNIE
C. Mendocino
Moqui
Zuni
Missouri
Sioux de l'Ouest
SIBERIE
Tzutzy
Oluttorski
Kamtschatka
Terre d'Yeço
Terres vües par les Russes en 1741 ou le Capitaine Tchirikow perdit sa Chaloupe armée de 10 hommes
Retour de l'Amerique au Kamtschatka de la Croyere en Juin et Juillet 1741
Route du Capne Beering du Kamtschatka et des Russes en 1731
Route du Vaisseau François le St Antoine de Pade commandé par M. de Frondat en 1709
Côtes vües par Mrs Tchirikow et De l'Isle en Septembre 1741

bringing with him maps and manuscripts relating to the recent Russian discoveries.[14]

Europe's obsession with exotic South Sea islands makes it easy to overlook the fact that the first major increase in European knowledge of the Pacific in the eighteenth century had come from Russia, where Vitus Bering and other navigators sailing east from Kamchatka had cast a flickering light on the geography of the north Pacific. In his first voyage, in 1728, Bering sailed as far as the strait that now bears his name. Haze hid the American shore, and when Mikhail Gvozdev sighted it four years later, he simply gave it the name of Bolshaya Zemlya, or "great land." Bering's next voyage, the second Kamchatka expedition or great northern expedition, added both to knowledge and to confusion as he and the commander of the consort vessel, Alexei Chirikov, made isolated sightings of land along the coast of Alaska. It was uncertain whether these sightings were part of the coastline reached by Gvozdev across the Bering Strait or whether they had found mainland or islands near North America, but the failure of the Russian government to publish the charts of its explorers allowed the speculative geographers to fill the spaces with their own bizarre creations. The first semiofficial account of the Russian voyages was compiled by Gerhard Müller of the St. Petersburg Academy of Sciences, whose book on Bering's voyages was translated into English in 1761 and 1764 (as *Voyages from Asia to America*) and into French in 1766. It became the standard account of the "Bering phase" of exploration in the north Pacific. Müller thought that the landfalls of Bering's second voyage were probably sightings of the coast of the American mainland, and this assumption resulted in his map's showing a huge, inflated Alaskan peninsula (fig. 2.3). He emphatically rejected the Delisle-Buache system of inland seas and straits, commenting that "it is always better to omit whatever is uncertain, and leave a void space, till future discoveries shall ascertain the affair in dispute."[15] He concluded by pointing out that since the American coast beyond New Albion seemed to curve away to the northwest, this made the existence of a Northwest Passage less likely.

Any hopes that Byron might throw light on the situation vanished when, after struggling through the Strait of Magellan, he decided that "our Ships are too much disabled for the California Voyage" and headed home across the Pacific.[16] Barrington's proposal for a new voyage to the north Pacific raised hopes of a more successful search for a passage. Once again ministers were approached with letters supporting such a scheme, among them a proposal from a junior naval officer, Lieutenant John Blankett, for a voyage to the north Pacific. Blankett had been encouraged by Sandwich to visit St. Petersburg to obtain more detail about the Russian discoveries, and he later claimed to be the true progenitor of the expedition that left England in 1776.[17] Barrington and Engel were among others who might have claimed that distinction, but in the political world of budgets and priorities it is clear that the decisive role was played by Sandwich. Now

2.3 Thomas Jefferys, *A Map of the Discoveries Made by the Russians on the North West Coast of America*, 1761. Based on a map by Gerhard Müller. Müller's map, first issued under the auspices of the St. Petersburg Academy of Sciences in 1754, represented the official Russian view of the discoveries made by Vitus Bering's two expeditions. It marked Bering's track to the eastern tip of Siberia in 1728, together with Mikhail Gvozdev's American landfall four years later. To the east, Müller showed the tracks of Bering and Alexei Chirikov in 1741 and the scattered landfalls along the Alaskan coast made on their desperate return voyages. Most navigators, including Cook, preferred Müller's tentative outlines to the beguiling maps of the Delisle/Philippe Buache school. Rasmuson Library, University of Alaska Fairbanks, G9236.S12.1761.J431—Rare Maps.

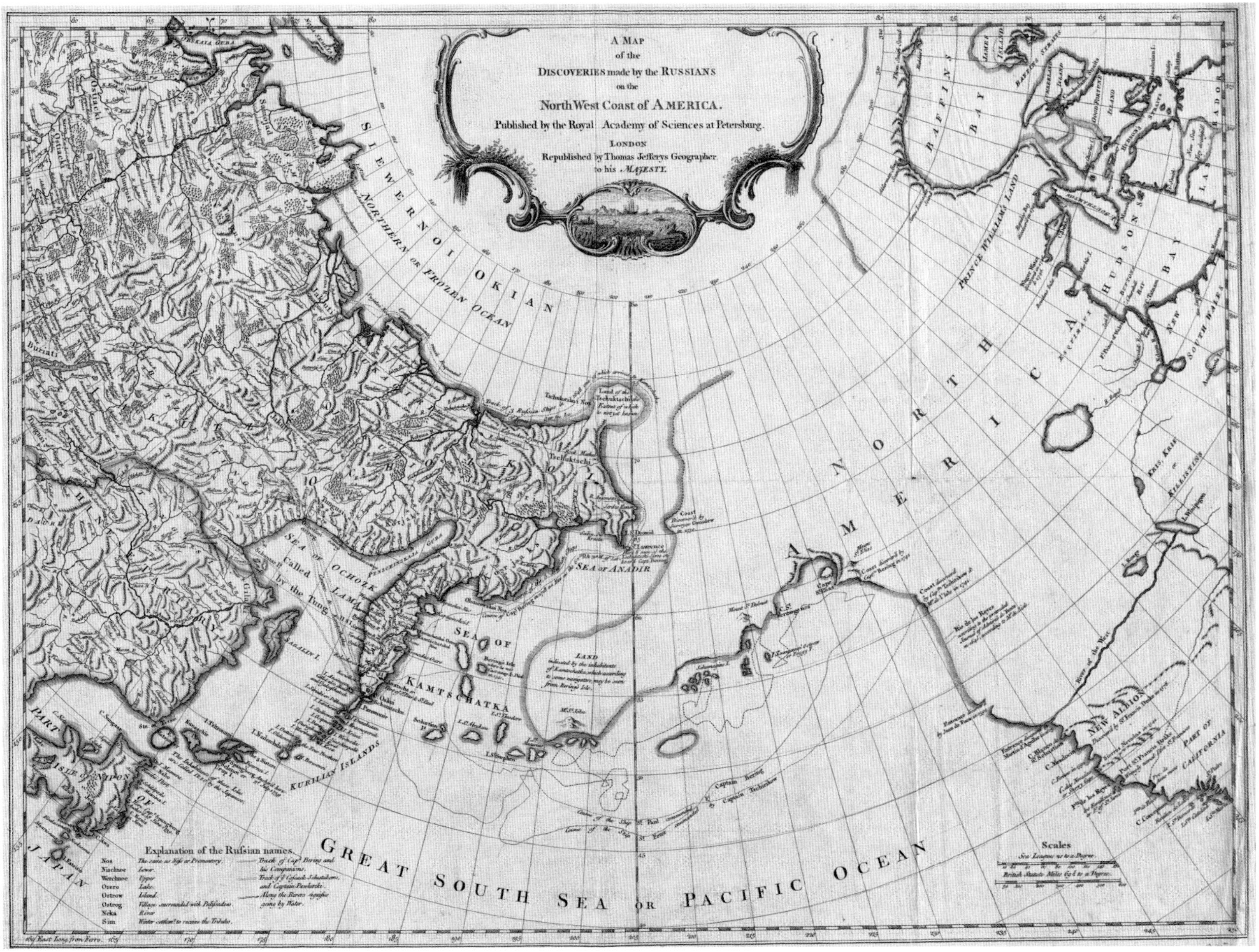

A MAP
of the
DISCOVERIES made by the RUSSIANS
on the
North West Coast of AMERICA.

Published by the Royal Academy of Sciences at Petersburg.

LONDON
Republished by Thomas Jefferys Geographer
to his MAJESTY.

SIEWERNOI OKIAN

NORTHERN OR FROZEN OCEAN

BAFFIN'S BAY

HUDSONS BAY

NORTH AMERICA

SEA of ANADIR

SEA OF OCHOTA

KAMTSCHATKA

KURILIAN ISLANDS

JAPAN

ISLE of NIPON

LAND

NEW ALBION

PART OF CALIFORNIA

GREAT SOUTH SEA OR PACIFIC OCEAN

Explanation of the Russian names.

Nos	The same as Ness or Promontory.
Nischne	Lower
Werchnoe	Upper
Osero	Lake
Ostrow	Island.
Ostrog	Village surrounded with Pallisadoes
Reka	River
Sim	Winter cabbin't to receive the Tribute.

Track of Capt Bering and
his Companions.
Track of Lt Colonels Schestakow.
and Captain Pawluzki.
Along the Rivers signifies
going by Water.

Scales
Sea Leagues 20 to a Degree
British Statute Miles 69 1/2 to a Degree

in his third and longest spell as first lord of the Admiralty, Sandwich had shown consistent support for discovery ventures. When Spanish concern had threatened to cancel Cook's second voyage, the expedition was saved by what Cook called the "perseverance" of Sandwich as first lord and Hugh Palliser as comptroller of the navy. Maty's proposal of February 1774 on behalf of the Royal Society, advocating an expedition to the north Pacific, was put on hold by the Admiralty on the grounds that the year's estimates would not cover it, but Sandwich had a "very full conversation" with Barrington in which he reassured him that when Cook returned from the Pacific, an expedition would be fitted out to make the discoveries suggested in Maty's letter.[18] Evidence of the Admiralty's interest came in intervention in a parliamentary bill offering a reward of twenty thousand pounds for the discovery of a Northwest Passage. It was a revised version of a bill passed in 1745 at the time of the Hudson Bay expeditions, with significant differences.[19] The earlier act had specified that the passage must run into Hudson Bay, and it limited the reward to privately owned ships. The new act, passed in December 1775, offered the reward to naval as well as trading vessels and stipulated that the passage should lie north of latitude 52°N. The first provision opened the way to what became Cook's third voyage; the second shaped the course that voyage would follow.

By the end of the year, preparations for the new voyage were well under way. The *Resolution* was being refitted at Deptford, and on Cook's recommendation, a consort vessel, to be named the *Discovery,* had been purchased. It was becoming a matter of urgency to appoint a commander for the voyage. Charles Clerke, who had been the *Resolution*'s second lieutenant on the previous voyage, was favored, but the new year arrived without any appointment being made. For what happened next we have to rely on the testimony of Andrew Kippis, a contemporary of Cook's and his first biographer. In early February 1776, Sandwich, Palliser, and Philip Stephens (the indispensable secretary to the Admiralty) arranged a dinner party to discuss with Cook the details of the forthcoming voyage. To consult the officer described by Sandwich in a speech to the House of Lords as the "first navigator in Europe" made sense, but it would have made even more sense to include the officer who was to command the voyage, and the failure to make the appointment raises some suspicions about the motives behind the meeting. Kippis admitted that Cook "was of all men the best qualified" for the task, but insisted (and his information seems to have come from Sandwich) that "the labours and dangers he had gone through, were so many and great, that it was not deemed reasonable to ask him to engage in fresh perils." The choice of a commanding officer was among the subjects discussed at the dinner along with "the grandeur and dignity" of the venture, on which Kippis wrote, "Captain Cook was so fired with the contemplation and representation of the object, that he started up, and declared that he himself would undertake the direction of the enterprise."[20] Biographers must be allowed their moments of drama, but apparently Cook needed little persuasion. When appointed to Greenwich Hospital on his return from the second voyage, he had made it clear that he would gladly return to active service. To John Walker, his old master at Whitby, he had written wondering whether "I can bring my self to like ease and retirement" and suspecting that the limits of Greenwich Hospital "are far too small for an active mind like mine."[21]

Had the proposed voyage been of a more routine nature, taking home Mai, the Polynesian islander brought to England, or refining the charts of the South Pacific, Cook probably would not have been tempted. But the challenge of the Northwest Passage was different. It was as long-standing an objective of European ambition as the imagined southern continent that had dominated his first two voyages. For all the important discoveries of those voyages there was, perhaps, a feeling of anticlimax when Cook returned in 1775. As he wrote, "If I have failed in discovering a continent it is because it does not exist . . . and not for want of looking."[22] In contrast, he was now presented with the possibility of taking the first ships through the Northwest Passage, and with the fame and honor would come a major share of the financial reward. This may have been an important motive for one who did not possess any inherited wealth but who was moving in circles of society well beyond the means of an ordinary naval officer. Four days after his appointment, Cook wrote again to John Walker, telling him about the new voyage and adding, "If I am fortunate to get safe home, there is no doubt that it will be greatly to my advantage."[23] These words suggest some quiet pledges and commitments by those in authority.

Cook's commission was dated February 10, 1776, and that day he went on board the *Resolution* "and began to enter men." Charles Clerke was to sail on the voyage, but in a subordinate role, as captain of the *Discovery*. The first day's entry in Cook's journal concluded: "These two Ships were at this time both in the Dock at Deptford under the hands of the Shipwrights." There are only two other entries in his journal before June 8, the day on which Cook hosted a farewell dinner on the ship for the Board of Admiralty. Although such negative evidence is not conclusive, it suggests that Cook was not totally preoccupied with shipboard matters. Before leaving England, he needed to hand over his narrative of the second voyage to Dr. John Douglas, canon of Windsor, who had agreed to edit it for publication.

Bruised by the offhand treatment of his *Endeavour* journal by Hawkesworth, Cook had been determined to give his own account of the second voyage. For most of the voyage he kept three different versions of his journal, in addition to a number of manuscript fragments. The various revisions, additions, and deletions show that from the beginning, he was writing not only for his superiors at the Admiralty but for the public at large. Although not an author as such, he had written that he was "a man Zealously employed in the Service of his Country and obliged to give the best account he is able of his proceedings."[24] The completion of the second voyage journal was no light task, nor a straightforward one, for as late as the spring of 1776 there was uncertainty as to who was writing the official account of the voyage: Cook or the senior naturalist, Johann Reinhold Forster. In April, when Cook originally hoped to be setting sail on the third voyage, Sandwich was still trying to sort this out. A compromise was reached by which Cook would write one volume and Forster a second. This arrangement was never likely to succeed. When Sandwich found a specimen chapter written by Forster unacceptable, the insulted naturalist withdrew from the enterprise.

Cook meanwhile was continuing to labor at his own account. In March he had asked Douglas whether he should be writing in the present or past tense, a sign that there was still work to do, and although in late April he had drafted a contents list for fifty-four of the book's final sixty-one chapters, the introduction was not ready until mid-June. It must have been a close-run thing for Cook to finish his narrative before sailing, and his journal has some hint of this. On June 16 both the *Resolution* and the *Discovery* were at the Nore, and that day the *Discovery* sailed for Plymouth, but as Cook wrote, "the Resolution was ordered to remain at the Nore till I joined her, being at this time in London," and there he remained until June 24.[25] The two-volume *Voyage towards the South Pole, and round the World* was finally published in May 1777.

The evidence therefore suggests that Cook, in the months before sailing, had other matters on his mind than the forthcoming voyage. These preoccupations probably explain much that is puzzling about the expedition's preparations. Crucial among them were Cook's instructions, signed by the lords of the Admiralty, dated July 6, 1776. There is a consensus that by this time Cook wrote his own instructions, at least with respect to navigational directions and geographical discovery, but a question mark hangs over this assumption. On this voyage he was expected to reach Drake's New Albion in the early summer of 1777 and then to sail more than 1,500 miles along the coast of northwest America to latitude 65°N, "taking care not to lose any time in exploring Rivers or Inlets" on the way.[26]

On the face of it, this was a surprising prohibition, for it was along the stretch of unknown coastline that the openings associated with Aguilar, Fuca, and Fonte were reported to lie. This was the stretch that the Admiralty had ordered Byron to search only twelve years earlier. But Cook's instructions specified that only when he reached latitude 65°N was he "very carefully to search for, and to explore, such Rivers or Inlets as may appear to be of a considerable extent, and pointing towards Hudsons or Baffins Bay." Hudson Bay had been explored so many times that its mention here seems out of place. On the other hand, although whalers visited the southeast coast of Baffin Bay each year, its northern stretches had not been explored since 1616, when William Baffin had sailed as far north as

2.4 Hudson Bay and Baffin Bay. Detail of *The British Empire in North America,* from Thomas Jefferys, *The American Atlas,* 1776. Jefferys' chart is representative of those supplied to the commanders of the *Lyon* on their voyages to Baffin Bay in 1776 and 1777. Its northern section is sparse in geographical detail. Apart from some detail obtained from whaling voyages along the west coast of Greenland, it shows that little information had been gained since the voyages of William Baffin in the early seventeenth century. He alone had explored the northern stretches of the bay that bore his name, and his chart had disappeared, leaving some geographers to doubt the very existence of Baffin Bay. University of British Columbia Library, Rare Books and Special Collections, G1100.J4.1974.

THE BRITISH EMPIRE IN NORTH AMERICA Contains
1 The Hudsons Bay Company's Territories
New South Wales, New North Wales, Prince Williams Land with the Artic Lands down to the London Coast in Greenland: & New Britain or Labrador.
2 Canada or the Province of Quebec.
3 Newfoundland containing the Coast of Labrador & Anticosti I.
4 Nova Scotia and Isle St. John
5 New England Subdivided into Four Colonies
6 Rode Island
7 New York Comprehending Long Island
8 New Jersey
9 Pennsilvania and Delaware Counties
10 Maryland
11 Virginia
12 North Carolina
13 South Carolina
14 Georgia
15 East Florida
16 West Florida
17 The Reserved Lands which contain all the countries comprehended between the Apalachee, Ohio & Missisipi
ARTIC LANDS
PRINCE WILLIAMS LAND
BAFFINS or BYLOTS BAY
Discover'd in 1622 & 1624.
CHRISTIAN SEA
JAMES'S ISLAND
BAFFINS STRAITS
DAVIS'S STRAITS
CUMBERLAND ISLAND
Cumberland Straits
NEW GREENLAND
SEKAMUNGA
called by the Natives
Arctic Circle
If there is a North West Passage it appears to be through one of these North West Inlets.
NEW NORTH WALES
ESKIMAUX
ISLE OF GOOD FORTUNE
HUDSONS STRAITS
St. Thomas Roe's WELCOME
New Denmark
HUDSONS BAY
New Sea
LABRADOR or NEW BRITAIN
ESKIMAUX COUNTRY
NEW SOUTH WALES
The Climate of this land is a great deal more temperate than Hudsons Bay
The Lands Height
ASSINIBOELS of the North
KRISTINAUX
ASSINIBOELS of the South
Nation of the Bear
Monsonis a Tribe of the Chipewas
NEW FOUNDLAND
GULF OF St. LAURENCE
C. Farewell
C. Desolation
False Frobishers Strait

2.5 Samuel Hearne, *A Map of Part of the Inland Country to the NW of Prince of Wales Fort,* 1772. This manuscript map shows the great extent of country covered by Hearne and his Chipewyan companions on their overland trek in 1771–72 from Prince of Wales Fort, Churchill (bottom right-hand corner of map), to the Coppermine River (top). A dotted line traces Hearne's outward route; a solid one traces his return track farther to the west by way of Great Slave Lake ("Arathapes Cow Lake"). Although Hearne's account and map were not published until 1795, the Hudson's Bay Company made them available to the Admiralty and cartographers. Hudson's Bay Company Archives, Archives of Manitoba, HBCA G. 2/10.

Smith Sound in latitude 78°N (fig. 2.4). It was there that the Admiralty decided to send the unstrengthened brig *Lyon* in 1776 and again in 1777 to search for the Atlantic entrance to the passage. In the fantasy world of Barrington and other enthusiasts, the *Lyon* might meet Cook's ships coming eastward through the passage and guide them home. In the real world of Arctic navigation, both voyages were failures, and in 1777 the *Lyon* was lucky to escape disaster, for that year saw the greatest ever losses in the Greenland whale fishery: twenty-six vessels and more than three hundred men.[27]

In the years since Byron's voyage, much had happened to explain the dramatic change of emphasis in the search for the Northwest Passage: the overland explorations of Samuel Hearne for the Hudson's Bay Company, the publication in England of a map thought to be based on the latest Russian explorations, and the theories of Engel and others on the formation of sea ice. It seems evident that this gathering of information influenced the key stipulation in the parliamentary act of 1775 that the passage should lie north of latitude 52°N. The negotiations leading up to the act began while Cook was still away on his second voyage, and they received royal approval some weeks before he was appointed to command the third voyage. His instructions pushed the search even farther north, but the change in its direction had been signaled long before he was involved.

In 1771, Hearne and Chipewyan guides had journeyed across some of the most inhospitable terrain in North America, from the company fort at Churchill on the west coast of Hudson Bay to the rock-strewn shallows of the distant Coppermine River, and down it to the shores of the Arctic Ocean at Coronation Gulf (the name given by John Franklin fifty years later). It is doubtful whether Hearne reached the actual shoreline, but "with the assistance of a good pocket telescope," he reported that he sighted the sea, which was full of islands and shoals, and that the ice was broken up three-quarters of a mile from the shore. Frustratingly to all who read his journal, Hearne noted at this point that "I did not think it worth while to wait for fair weather to determine the latitude exactly by observation."[28] Instead he relied on dead reckoning to estimate his latitude as 71°54'N. This was about four degrees or two hundred miles too far north of his actual location (fig. 2.5). His journey was hugely significant, for it eliminated the possibility that a passage for shipping could be found *through* North America. He had crossed the continent's northeast shoulder to the Arctic Ocean without finding a saltwater strait or even a sizeable river. He and his Chipewyan companions had walked right across the elaborate network of waterways shown on the maps of Delisle, Buache, and the speculative geographers. If a passage existed, it must lie much farther north, along the edge of the continent, through that partly frozen sea that Hearne had glimpsed from the mouth of the Coppermine River.

In earlier years, the explorations of the Hudson's Bay Company had been shrouded in secrecy, but the

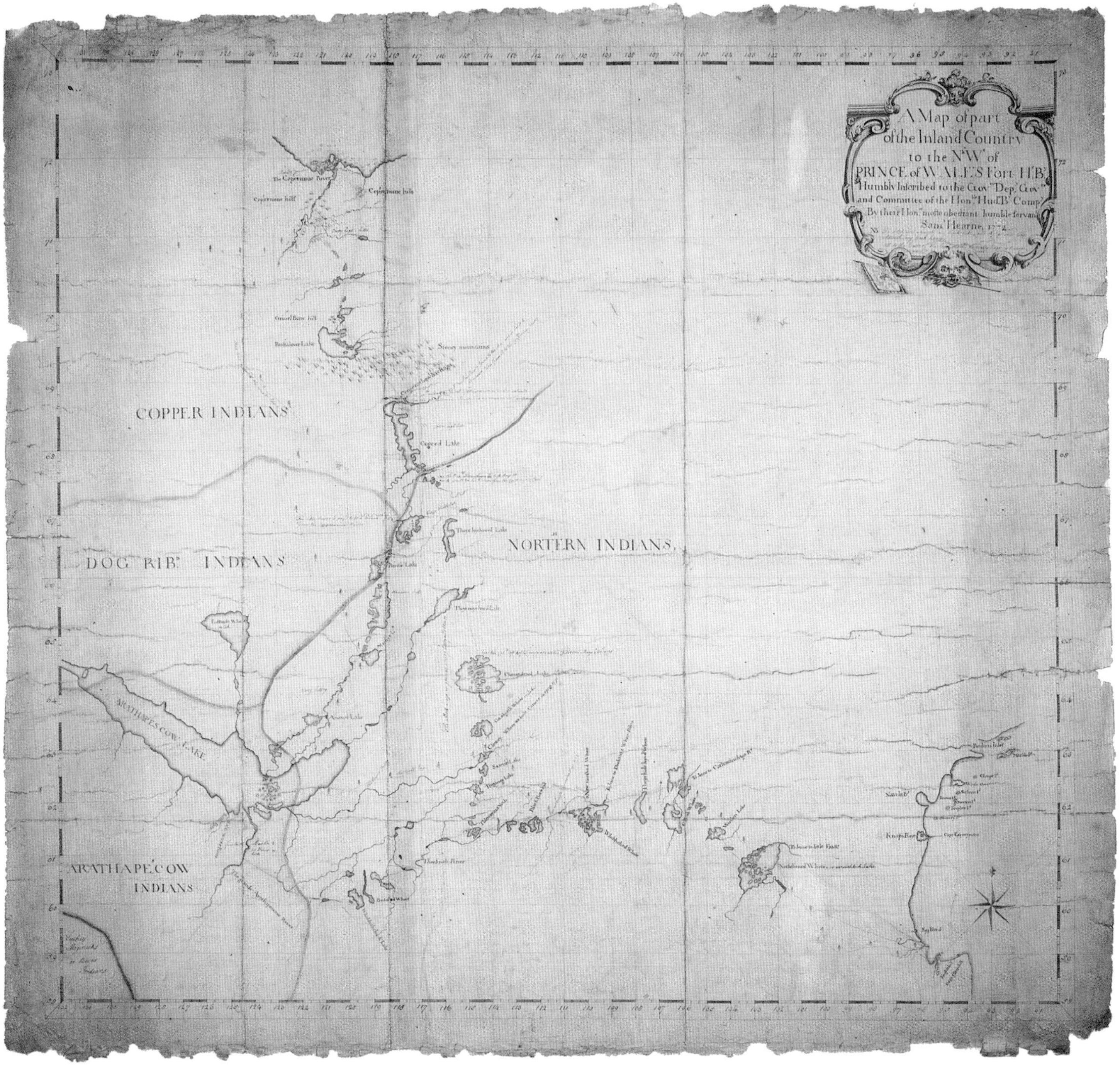
A Map of part
of the Inland Country
to the NᵒWᵗ of
PRINCE of WALES Fort H.B.
Humbly Inscribed to the Govʳ Depᵗ Govʳ
and Committee of the Honᵇˡᵉ Hudˢ Bʸ Compʸ
By their Honˢ moste obediant humble servant
Saml Hearne, 1772.
COPPER INDIANS
DOG RIBᴰ INDIANS
NORTERN INDIANS
ARATHAPESCOW LAKE
ARATHAPESCOW INDIANS
The Copermine River
Copermine hills
Conged Lake
Knaps Bay
Cape Esquimaux

2.6 Jacob von Staehlin, *A Map of the New Northern Archipelago,* 1773. The influence of Staehlin's map, first issued in an English version under the auspices of Matthew Maty in 1774, was short-lived but crucial. It determined the route planned for Cook once he reached the Northwest Coast of America and sailed north to find the map's wide strait leading into the Arctic Ocean between Alaska and the American continent. The latter is shown here cut short at 140°W. Cook's belief in the map is difficult to understand, for although it marks the tracks of the main Russian expeditions commanded by Semyon Dezhnev (1648), Vitus Bering (1728), and Ivan Sindt (1764–68), none is shown approaching the wide strait between "Alaschka I." and North America. Rasmuson Library, University of Alaska Fairbanks, A0631—Rare.

attitude of the company's deputy governor, Samuel Wegg, differed in many ways from that of his predecessors. He was a council member of the Royal Society and friendly with Barrington and others interested in northern exploration. As a demonstration of this, at some point before Cook sailed, Wegg sent Sandwich the vital evidence of Hearne's journey and of the company's seaborne explorations of the 1760s.[29]

The possibility raised by Hearne's journey that there might be a passage along the northern edge of the continent was strengthened by the publication in London in 1774 of an account of recent Russian discoveries, published in German the year before by Jacob von Staehlin, the secretary of the St. Petersburg Academy of Sciences. It was produced under the auspices of Matthew Maty, not only secretary of the Royal Society but also chief librarian of the British Museum. Staehlin's book, *An Account of the New Northern Archipelago, Lately Discovered by the Russians,* seemed to provide a welcome survey of Russian explorations since Bering. In the 1760s, the Russian government sent naval vessels to Alaskan waters to regulate and protect the activities of the *promyshlenniki,* fur traders who were moving from island to island in search of sea-otter pelts. Among the voyages was that of Lieutenant Ivan Sindt, and Staehlin's book contained an account and map of Sindt's voyages (fig. 2.6). The account was uninteresting, but the map was sensational, for on it the inflated Alaskan peninsula of Müller's map had disappeared. On the new map, "Alaschka" was not a peninsula at all but a large island, and between it and the truncated North American continent lay a wide strait in latitude 65°N leading into the Arctic Ocean. What Maty and those who relied on this edition of Staehlin's book did not realize was that there had been no collaboration between the Russian Admiralty, which held many post-Bering charts and surveys, and the St. Petersburg Academy of Sciences. The book was not, to use the standard English term, "published by authority."

Cook's search for a passage was to begin in latitude 65°N, and the chances of success would be greater if Engel and Barrington were correct that the ice of the northern seas was limited in extent and duration. Even if the ice field that had blocked Phipps's progress in latitude 80°N stretched right across the polar regions, its southern edge would be several hundred miles north of the point where Hearne had reached the American coastline. Just when Hearne's overland journey had proved there could be no passage in temperate latitudes, it appeared possible that the dreaded polar sea was ice free for most of the year. On this unproven assumption, Cook's ships were not strengthened against ice. This decision was especially surprising given Cook's experience of ice in the Baltic, off Newfoundland, and in the Antarctic Ocean. As he sailed far south on his second voyage, he had shown his awareness of current speculation on the matter. "Some curious and intresting experiments are wanting to know what effect cold has on Sea Water in some of the following instances: does it freeze or does it not? if

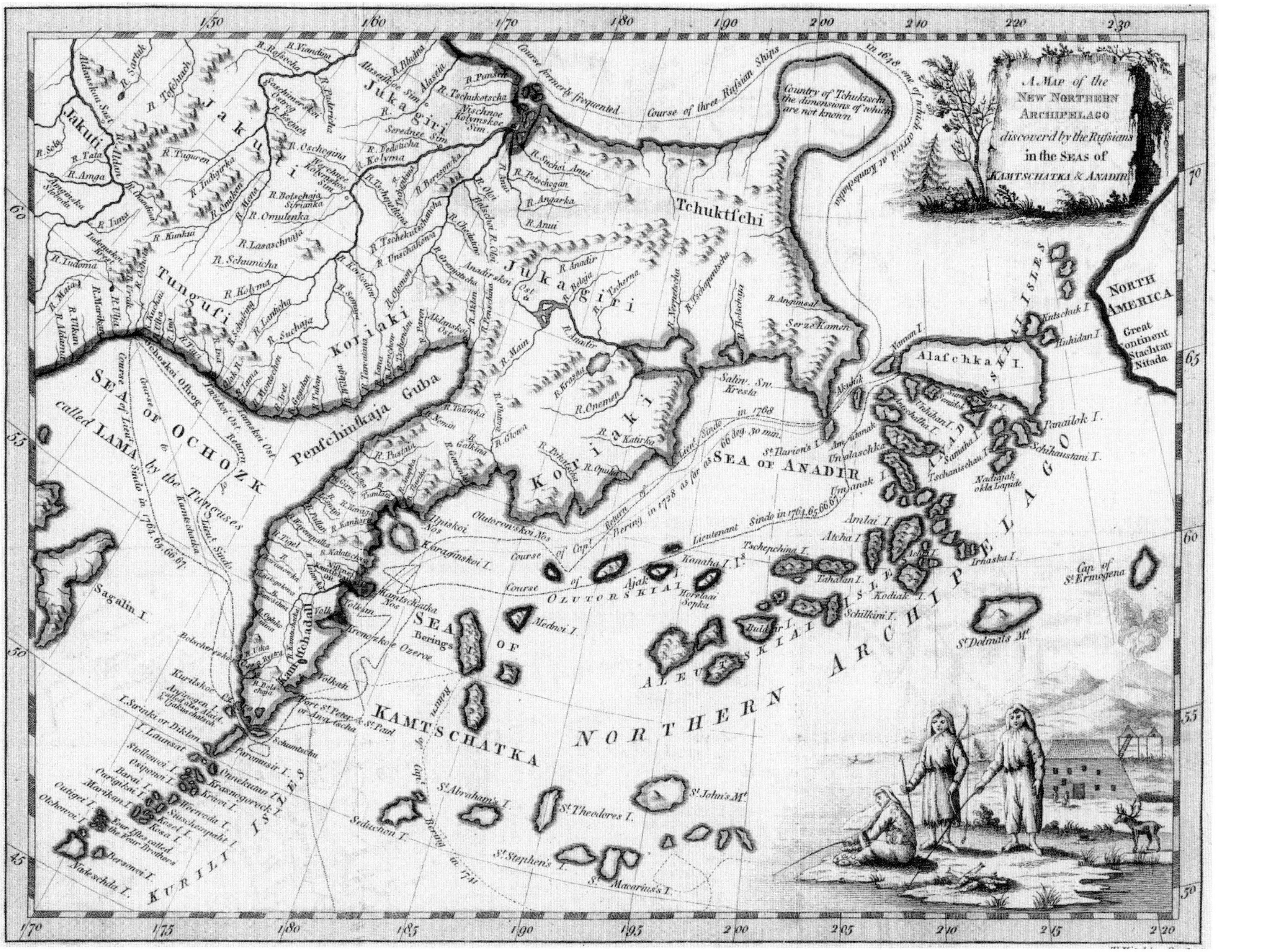

A Map of the
New Northern
Archipelago
discoverd by the Rufsians
in the Seas of
Kamtschatka & Anadir
Course formerly frequented
Course of three Rufsian Ships in 1648, one of which arrivd at Kamtschatka
Country of Tchuktschi the dimensions of which are not known
Tchuktfchi
Jukagiri
Jakuti
Tungufi
Koriaki
North America
Great Continent Stachtan Nitada
Alafchka I.
Sea of Ochozk called Lama by the Tunguses
Penfchinfkaja Guba
Sea of Anadir
Lieut. Sindo in 1768
Lieut. Sindo as far as 66 deg. 30 min.
Course of Capt. Bering in 1728 as far as 66 deg. 30 min.
Lieutenant Sindo in 1764,65,66,67
Olutorskia Isles
Aleutskia Isles
Anadirskia Isles
Northern Archipelago
Sea of Kamtschatka
Kamtschatka
Sagalin I.
Kurili Isles
Sea of Bering
Cap of St. Ermogena
St. Dolmats Mt.
St. Abraham's I.
St. Theodores I.
St. John's Mt.
St. Stephen's I.
St. Macarius's I.
Seduction I.
Capt. Bering in 1741
Karaginskoi I.
Mednoi I.
Kodiak I.
Schilkin I.
Buldir I.
Tahalan I.
Tschepchina I.
Amlai I.
Atcha I.
Irnaska I.
Unalaschka
Umnak I.
Kutschuk I.
Inhidan I.
Panailok I.
Schihaustani I.
Naman I.
Port St. Peter & St. Paul
Kamtschatka Nos
Olutorovskoi Nos
Ukinskoi Nos
Kurilskoe Ozero
Kronozkoe Ozero
Ochozkoi Ostrog
Anadirskoi Ost.
Serze Kamen
Saliv. Sv. Kresta
R. Anadir
R. Kolyma
R. Indigirka
R. Omolon
R. Aldan
R. Amga
R. Penschina
Paramusir I.
Sirinki or Diklin
Four Isles called the Four Brothers
Bersonoi I.
Nadeschda I.
150
160
170
180
190
200
210
220
230
175
185
195
205
215
70
65
60
55
50
45

it does"—and here, in one draft of his journal, Cook added "of which I make no doubt"—"what degree of cold is necessary . . . ?"[30]

Cook's ship for the third voyage was a familiar and trusted one. The *Resolution,* a 462-ton former Whitby collier, had served him magnificently on the second voyage, coping with the incessant battering in the ice on those long sweeps through the southern ocean. Clearly, it needed a thorough inspection and refitting before making another voyage likely to last three or four years. However, during its months at the Deptford shipyard, even routine maintenance tasks seem to have been botched. Cook's biographer, J. C. Beaglehole, writes of "dishonest work and slovenly supervision," and as we have seen, Cook was not at hand during the crucial months of the refitting.[31] Problems began in the very first weeks of the voyage. At the Cape Verde Islands, Cook wrote that he found "the Ship exceeding leaky in all her upper works, the hot and dry weather we had just passed through had opened her Seams, which had been badly Caulked at first, so wide that they admitted the Rain water through as it fell and there was hardly a Man who could lie dry in his bed; the officers in the gunroom were all driven out of their cabins by the Water that came thro' the sides. The sails in the Sail rooms got wet before we had weather to dry them, many of them were quite ruined."[32]

Throughout the voyage, Cook criticized the quality of the rigging, and, while approaching Hawai'i in December 1778, the *Resolution* narrowly escaped shipwreck when the ropes holding the main topsail parted. An infuriated Cook entered a complaint in his journal in language so strong that when Palliser read it on the expedition's return to England, he insisted that such "improper" comments be deleted from the published account.[33] Some months earlier, at Nootka Sound, there had been problems with both the foremast and the mizzen mast. The carpenters found that the cheeks supporting the foremast were so rotten that the mast had to be taken out and new cheeks put in. "It was evedent," Cook wrote, "that one of the Cheeks had been defective at the first, and the defective part had been cut out and a piece put [in], what had not only weakened the mast head, but had in great measure been the occasion of roting all the other part."[34] The mizzen mast was in even worse condition, and as the men were taking it out, the head fell off while the mast was still in its sling. The problem with the foremast was to persist, and four days after leaving Hawai'i in February 1779, both the strengthening pieces put in at Nootka, made from old driftwood, were found to have sprung. After some hesitation Cook decided to return to Kealakekua Bay. This decision was the turning point of the voyage and had fatal consequences.

We know less about the consort vessel, the three-hundred-ton *Discovery.* Originally named the *Diligence,* she was yet another Whitby-built collier. Only eighteen months old at the time of purchase, she would have been in better condition than the *Resolution* when she was sent for refitting at Deptford. Even so, there were problems on the voyage. In December 1778, her master, Thomas Edgar wrote, "Our Sails & Rigging being very much Worn & Decay'd Something or other is Constantly Giving way which keeps our Ships Compy in Continual Employment in Knotting & Splicing unbending & bending Sails."[35] Both ships were sheathed for protection against teredo worms, but the lack of extra protection against ice was in contrast to the strengthening given Phipps's two ships in 1773. There are two explanations for what seems, in hindsight, to be a curious decision. The first was the misplaced faith in Staehlin's strait and the expectation that the ships would not encounter ice. The second was the knowledge that the addition of heavy beams and other forms of strengthening would slow the ships' progress on a voyage that would last many thousands of miles before they reached the north Pacific.

The crews were a mixed bunch: among both officers and men, some had sailed with Cook before, others not. Charles Clerke, captain of the *Discovery,* had been on both Cook's previous voyages, as well as on the earlier circumnavigation under the command of Samuel Wallis. John Gore, the first lieutenant on the *Resolution,* was another vastly experienced officer who had been on three circumnavigations and in the end was to bring the ships home. James Burney, Clerke's first lieutenant, had been on the second voyage, albeit with the consort vessel that did not often sail in company with Cook. Among the more junior ranks, master's mates Henry Roberts and William Lanyon, mate William Harvey, and midshipman George Vancouver had sailed before either with Cook or on his consort vessel. Among those new to the Pacific was James King, the scholarly second lieutenant on the *Resolution,* whose journal was used to complete the official account of the voyage; William Bligh, the ship's surprisingly young master (twenty-two at the time of sailing); and the murky figure of John Williamson, forever suspect for his inglorious part in the events that led to Cook's death.

One surprising omission was that there were no Russian speakers on the expedition, although Cook was heading for a region where he could expect to meet Russian traders and seamen. By contrast, when Jean-François de La Pérouse sailed for the north Pacific in 1785, he took the precaution of including a crew member fluent in Russian, the young Jean-Baptiste Barthélemy de Lesseps, whose father had been consul general in St. Petersburg.

Even more noticeable was the paucity of civilian supernumeraries. The astronomer William Bayly and David Nelson, one of Joseph Banks's gardener-collectors, sailed on the *Discovery* and the artist John Webber on the *Resolution,* but in general the expanding realm of natural history was left to the part-time attention of the able young surgeon of the *Resolution,* William Anderson, in Lieutenant King's estimation "the freest from that narrow confind spirit which is fond of hiding its light under a bush of any man I ever knew." Again the expedition of La Pérouse affords a sharp contrast, for

fifteen savants sailed with him, although not all were civilians. To explain this discrepancy between the British and French discovery expeditions, we are reliant, perhaps unduly so, on a remarkable outburst attributed to Cook before the voyage. When James King reported on board, he apparently expressed his regret at the lack of scientists on the expedition, only to be told by Cook: "Curse the scientists, and all science into the bargain." The evidence for this outburst is not quite straightforward. It comes five years after the fact from Johann Reinhold Forster, hardly a dispassionate witness on the subject of scientists and Cook. In his preface to the German edition of an anonymous account of Cook's third voyage, Forster recalled being told by King of "this discourteous reply" only a day after the event.[36] By his own account, Forster played, unusually for him, a conciliatory role, although it was hardly as reassuring as he imagined. Forster later wrote: "I took the opportunity of setting things right by describing Cook's character and pointing out that it was in reality not as bad as it appeared, but that he was a cross-grained fellow who sometimes showed a mean disposition and was carried away by a hasty temper."[37]

One could wish for a supporting witness to the conversation between Cook and King; in its absence the plain facts of the situation can be set out. On the third voyage there would be no team of civilian scientists, no equivalent of Banks and Daniel Solander on the first voyage, or of the Forsters, Johann and his son Georg, and Anders Sparrman on the second. It may be that the arrogant behavior of Banks after his return from the first voyage, and the rancorous presence of Johann Forster on the second, had turned Cook against taking on board any more "philosophical gentlemen," but of this we have no further proof. As it was, Anderson's appointment as surgeon on the *Resolution* had several advantages. Cook knew his abilities from his service as surgeon's mate on the second voyage, when in addition to his medical duties he had made, in Solander's words, "a good Botanical Collection."[38] And, unlike his naturalist predecessors on Cook's ships, he would be subject to naval discipline. Unfortunately for Cook and posterity, Anderson died of consumption during the voyage.

Cook sailed from Plymouth on July 11, 1776. Shortly before sailing he had read accounts in English newspapers of a Spanish expedition to the Northwest Coast by Juan Pérez in 1774, which reached latitude 55°N, and another by Juan Francisco de la Bodega y Quadra the following year, which sailed as far as latitude 57°N.[39] There was little further information about the voyages, and neither had approached the latitude where Cook was to begin his search (see fig. 3.8). Cook reached Alaskan waters in May 1778, and although he was a year behind schedule, there was a palpable sense of excitement on board the ships as the deck officers compared the accounts of Müller and Staehlin with the actual coastline in sight. Their journals sound a continual refrain after they reached Alaskan waters. On May 12 there were three hopeful entries: "We have Dr

2.7 John Webber, *The* Resolution *Beating through the Ice,* August 1778, engraving printed in London by J. Webber, 1792. One of several depictions by Webber of the *Resolution* and *Discovery* attempting to find a way through the ice north of Bering Strait. The *Resolution,* in the foreground, is in clear water, but the *Discovery,* in the distance, is apparently trapped in the ice and "in the most eminent danger." This engraving may represent the moment near Icy Cape described by Cook on August 18: "Our situation was now more and more critical, we were in shoald water upon a lee shore and the main body of the ice in sight to windward driving down upon us." © The Trustees of the British Museum, #1917-1208.16.

Matys map of the N°ern Archipelago constantly in our hands" (King);[40] "Opened a large strait . . . probably the same called on our map the Straits of Anian" (Rickman);[41] "No land was seen to the North, which gave us some hope that here would be found the western termination of America" (Burney).[42] On May 17, Cook noted, "If the land on the west should prove to be islands agreeable to the late Russian discoveries, we could not fail of getting far enough to the north."[43] On May 24, Cook was still optimistic: "There is here a space where Behring is supposed to have seen no land; it also favoured the account published by Mr Staehlin . . . so that everything inspired us with hopes of finding here a passage."[44]

Unfortunately the coast, instead of trending north, steadily turned west, then southwest. Prince William Sound and then Cook Inlet were explored without success, and the ships slowly edged their way along the tongue of the Alaska Peninsula until, on August 9, they reached the strait discovered by Bering fifty years earlier. It was hundreds of miles west of the great opening shown on Staehlin's map, but at least it was roughly in latitude 65°N and pointed north. King wrote in his journal, "We are in high spirits," for they could glimpse open sea ahead, "free of land, and we hope ice."[45] On August 17 came the most disillusioning moment of the voyage, as a great mass of ice, rising ten or twelve feet above the water, filled the northern horizon (fig. 2.7). The ships were in latitude 70°41'N, ten degrees farther south than Phipps had been when he encountered the Spitsbergen ice barrier. As Cook pointed out, the sheer bulk of the slow-moving mass bearing down on the ships made nonsense of the assumption that it was the product of one season's breakup of the shallow rivers of the northern lands. Only "Closet studdying Philosiphers" would maintain this, he wrote, in a tilt at Barrington, Engel, and their circle.[46]

Once back through Bering Strait, the crews spent three weeks at Samgoonoodha, Unalaska. There they met Russian traders led by Gerasim Izmailov, who had sailed with Sindt in the 1760s. "I felt no small Mortification," Cook wrote, "in not being able to converse with him any way then by signs," but Izmailov's charts confirmed his belief that Alaska was a peninsula, not an island. Staehlin's map had been a false guide, and Cook expressed his feelings in a few furious sentences. "What could induce him to publish so erroneous a Map? In which many of these islands are jumbled in regular confusion, without the least regard to truth and yet he is pleased to call it a very accurate little Map? A Map that the most illiterate of his illiterate Sea-faring men would have been ashamed to put his name to."[47] Cook's outburst was provoked by his realization of how seriously he had been misled. His normally shrewd judgment of the works of theoretical geography had deserted him, with the result that the efforts of his crew had been guided in the wrong direction.

Over the years Cook had developed a keen sense of the spurious and the fanciful, and it did not need very close scrutiny to raise doubts about the Russian maps he carried. Müller had described his effort in self-deprecating terms as "no more than to connect together according to probability, by points, the coast that had been seen in various places."[48] That Cook should have placed any credence in Staehlin's map almost defies belief. The accompanying text was vague and jumbled, and even Daines Barrington, not the most critical of men, in a paper read to the Royal Society before Cook sailed, thought that the map "bears so little of the look of truth . . . that no credit can be given to it."[49] A glance at it adds to the puzzle of why its representation of Alaska as an island was ever taken seriously. It marks Sindt's track only as far as the *west* coast of "Alaschka," and no voyager, Russian or otherwise, is shown reaching that strait on the east side of the island that promised a short route into the polar sea.

At the time of Cook's voyage, scholars such as William Robertson and William Coxe were busy collecting information about the Russian voyages. Robertson had in his possession, probably before Cook sailed, a journal of the important expedition of Petr Krenitsyn and Mikhail Levashov in 1768 to the Aleutian Islands. In Germany, geographers were receiving accounts from their colleagues in Russia and were preparing books and articles for publication.[50] None of this information seems to have been known to Cook and his superiors at the Admiralty. As we have seen, the weeks between his appointment to command the expedition in February 1776 and his sailing in July were crowded ones. All the signs are that he had little time and perhaps little inclination to conduct any thorough inquiry into the latest information about the Russian discoveries. In October 1778 Cook admitted that errors had been made. "We were upon a Coast where every step was to be considered, where no information could be had from Maps, either modern or ancient: confiding too much in the former we were frequently misled to our no small hinderance."[51]

NOTES

1 *The Journals of Captain James Cook on His Voyages of Discovery,* vol. 2, *The Voyage of the* Resolution *and* Adventure, *1772–1775,* ed. J. C. Beaglehole (Cambridge: Cambridge University Press for the Hakluyt Society, 1961), 643.

2 Rosalin Barker, "Cook's Nursery: Whitby's Eighteenth-Century Merchant Fleet," in *Captain Cook: Explorations and Reassessments,* ed. Glyndwr Williams (Woodbridge, UK: Boydell, 2004), 20.

3 Cook, *Voyage of the* Resolution *and* Adventure, 2.

4 *The Journals of Captain James Cook on His Voyages of Discovery* , vol. 3, *The Voyage of the* Resolution *and* Discovery, *1776–1780,* ed. J. C. Beaglehole (Cambridge: Cambridge University Press for the Hakluyt Society, 1967), ccxx.

5 See Dartmouth MSS., William Salt Library, Stafford: D 1778, V 284–88.

6 See Daines Barrington, *The Probability of Reaching the North Pole Discussed* (London: C. Heydinger, 1775).

7 Royal Society Council minutes, January 19, 1773. Royal Society Archives, VI, 160.

8 Constantine John Phipps, *A Voyage towards the North Pole* (London: J. Nourse, 1774), 74.

9 Barrington, *Probability of Reaching the North Pole,* 13.

10 Royal Society Council minutes, February 10 and 17, 1774, Royal Society Archives, VI, 214, 216.

11 Samuel Purchas, *Hakluytus Posthumus, or Purchas His Pilgrimes* (Glasgow: J. MacLehose, 1905–6), 14:435.

12 John Masefield, ed., *The Voyages of Captain William Dampier* (London: E. Grant Richard, 1906), 1:287–88.

13 John Byron, *Byron's Journal of his Circumnavigation, 1764–1766,* ed. Robert E. Gallagher (Cambridge: Cambridge University Press, 1964), 3.

14 For the apocryphal voyages and their representation on maps, see Glyn Williams, *Voyages of Delusion: The Northwest Passage in the Age of Reason* (London: HarperCollins, 2002), especially chapter 8, "Maps, Hoaxes and Projects"; and Lucie Lagarde, "Le passage du Nord-Ouest et la Mer de L'ouest dans la cartographie française au XVIIIe-siècle," *Imago Mundi* 41 (1989): 19–43.

15 Gerhard Müller, *Voyages from Asia to America,* 2nd ed. (London: S. Jefferys, 1764), 116.

16 *Byron's Journal,* 159.

17 See Sandwich Papers, Royal Museums Greenwich (formerly National Maritime Museum), F 6/29.

18 See Royal Society Council minutes, February 10 and 17, March 7 and 30, in Cook, *Voyage of the* Resolution *and* Discovery, 1483–84.

19 For the wording of the two acts, see *The Statutes at Large,* 18:327–29, 31:155–57.

20 Andrew Kippis, *The Life of Captain James Cook* (London: G. Nicol, 1788), 324–25.

21 Cook, *Voyage of the* Resolution *and* Adventure, 960.

22 Ibid., 693.

23 Cook, *Voyage of the* Resolution *and* Discovery, 1488.

24 Cook, *Voyage of the* Resolution *and* Adventure, 2.

25 Cook, *Voyage of the* Resolution *and* Discovery, 4.

26 Ibid., ccxxi.

27 For the Baffin Bay naval voyages of 1776 and 1777, see Williams, *Voyages of Delusion,* 302–6.

28 Samuel Hearne, *A Journey from Prince of Wales's Fort in Hudson's Bay to the Northern Ocean,* ed. Richard Glover (Toronto: Macmillan Company of Canada, 1958), 106.

29 See James Cook and James King, *A Voyage to the Pacific Ocean . . . for making Discoveries in the Northern Hemisphere* (London: G. Nicol and T. Cadell, 1784), 1:lv.

30 Cook, *Voyage of the* Resolution *and* Adventure, 77.

31 Cook, *Voyage of the* Resolution *and* Discovery, lxix.

32 Ibid., 14.

33 Ibid., 482 n.

34 Ibid., 300.

35 Ibid., 481 n.

36 Ibid., 1430.

37 Ibid., xlvi–xlvi n.

38 Cook, *Voyage of the* Resolution *and* Adventure, 950.

39 See *London Evening Post,* May 29, 1776.

40 Log of Lieutenant James King, National Archives, UK, ADM 55/122, fol. 31d.

41 John Rickman, *Journal of Captain Cook's Last Voyage* (London: E. Newberry, 1781), 247.

42 James Burney, *A Chronological History of North-eastern Voyages of Discovery* (London: Payne and Foss, 1819), 221.

43 Cook, *Voyage of the* Resolution *and* Discovery, 353.

44 Ibid., 358–59.

45 Log of Lt. James King, fol. 72.

46 Cook, *Voyage of the* Resolution *and* Discovery, 425.

47 Ibid., 450, 456.

48 Müller, *Voyages,* 115.

49 Barrington, *Probability of Reaching the North Pole,* 14.

50 For more on this topic, see my comments in "Alaska Revealed: Cook's Explorations in 1778," in *Exploration in Alaska: Captain Cook Commemorative Lectures*, ed. Antoinette Shalkop (Anchorage: Cook Inlet Historical Society, 1980), 81–84.

51 Cook, *Voyage of the* Resolution *and* Discovery, 1531.

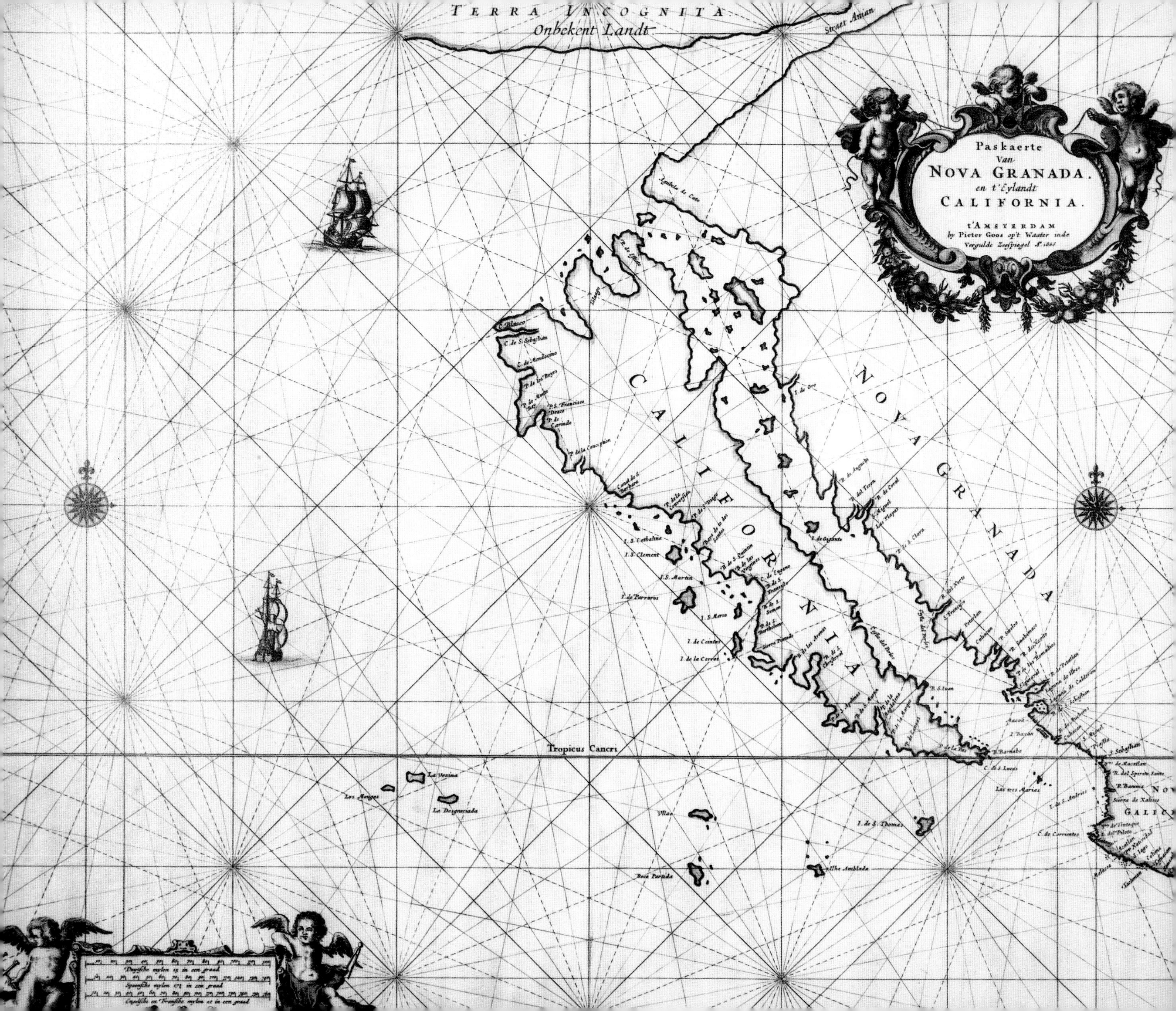

TERRA INCOGNITA
Onbekent Landt
Straet Anian
Paskaerte Van NOVA GRANADA. en t'Eylandt CALIFORNIA.
t'AMSTERDAM by Pieter Goos op't Waater inde Vergulde Zeespiegel
CALIFORNIA
NOVA GRANADA
C. de S. Sebastian
C. de Mendocino
Canal de S. Barbara
I. S. Cathalina
I. S. Clement
I. S. Martin
I. S. Marco
I. de Cedros
I. de Gigante
Tropicus Cancri
C. de S. Lucas
La Vezina
Los Monges
La Desgraciada
Villao
I. de S. Thomas
Las tres Marias
C. de Corrientes
Roca Partida
Ilha Amblada
Sierra de Xalisco

Setting the Stage

Spain in the Pacific and the Northern Voyages of the 1770s

IRIS ENGSTRAND

3

When it became apparent that Christopher Columbus's Atlantic voyages in the 1490s had not reached India, speculation began about the location of the land he actually did reach.[1] The answer did not become certain until September 1513, when Vasco Núñez de Balboa crossed the Isthmus of Panama on foot and reached the Mar del Sur (South Sea), opening up an equally significant period of Pacific exploration (fig. 10.2).[2] The ten-thousand-mile expanse of the Pacific Ocean limited its access by Europeans, and Pacific voyages were neither as numerous nor as successful as those crossing the Atlantic until well into the late eighteenth century.[3] Even by this time, the southern extent of the Pacific Ocean was still unknown, and the existence of a southern continent was still a matter of conjecture.[4]

The first recorded crossing is the well-known and often-reported circumnavigation of the globe from 1519 to 1522 begun by Ferdinand Magellan (Fernão de Magalhães), a Portuguese navigator sailing for Spain. It is a classic tale of disaster mitigated only by the success of having one ship—*La Victoria*—complete the voyage under the command of Juan Sebastián de Elcano, a Basque from northern Spain. Magellan began his journey in charge of five ships and some 235 men from several nations. Only

3.1 Pieter Goos, *The Island of California* (Paskaete van Nova Granada en t' Eylandt California), Amsterdam, 1666. Although Francisco de Ulloa had explored the Gulf of California and the outer coast of Baja California in 1539–40, proving the notion of the "island of California at the right hand of the Indies" of romantic legend to be a cartographic fiction, the idea was revived in the influential writings of Antonio de la Ascensión after Sebastián Vizcaíno's expedition of 1602–3. It appeared on maps well into the eighteenth century. This depiction of the coast is one of the few to focus primarily on the "island" as its central feature. San Diego History Center Research Archives.

3.2 Antonio Mendoza, 1495–1552. Portrait from *Iconografía de gobernantes de la Nueva España* (1921) by Eusebio Gómez de la Puente. Mendoza was the first viceroy of New Spain (1535–50). A member of a respected Castilian family, trained as a diplomat with experience in missions requiring great loyalty and ability, he proved worthy of the enormous responsibilities of developing and implementing policies to establish royal authority over the new territories. Expanding the horizons of New Spain, he sent the expedition led by Francisco Vásquez de Coronado to explore lands to the north, Juan Rodríguez Cabrillo along the coast toward what is today California, and Ruy López de Villalobos to the Philippines. Art & Architecture Collection, Miriam and Ira D. Wallach Division of Art, Prints and Photographs, The New York Public Library, Astor, Lenox and Tilden Foundations.

eighteen men survived. They included Antonio Pigafetta, who kept a daily account of the voyage that ended in Spain in September 1522.[5] Because of the tragic outcome of this around-the-world journey, it was not reattempted for several years. In 1525, however, Garcia Jofre de Loaísa left Spain with Elcano to follow Magellan's route and claim the Moluccas (now a part of Indonesia). Both died at sea, and most of their crews met a similar fate.

Following Magellan's disastrous voyage, which nevertheless proved that India could be reached by sailing west, a number of unsuccessful forays into the Pacific from Mexico (New Spain) were carried out. After the Spanish conquest of the Aztecs, contemporary with Magellan's voyage between 1519 and 1522, Hernán Cortés reached the Pacific at the port city of Zacatula and ordered the construction of four ships for northward exploration along the coast. Three instead were sent to the Moluccas in 1527 to strengthen Spanish claims in the East Indies, while the remaining one, and two additional ships, sailed across the Gulf of California.[6] A significant discovery was made in 1539 under the command of Francisco de Ulloa, who proved that the land mass referred to as the Island of California was actually an inhospitable peninsula. This discovery aroused little attention, and the "island" of California persisted on maps as late as the mid-1750s (fig 3.1).[7]

By 1535, the Spanish government had appointed Antonio de Mendoza as viceroy of New Spain, the highest-ranking official in Spain's New World province (fig 3.2). Mendoza believed that the prospect of great wealth certainly existed to the west—across the Pacific Ocean—as well as to the north, somewhere along the Pacific coast. Toward the end of the 1530s, Juan Rodríguez Cabrillo, a crossbowman and shipbuilder who had served under Cortés in the conquest of Mexico, took charge of a shipbuilding enterprise on the Central American coast near today's boundary between Guatemala and El Salvador. Out of thirteen ships that were completed by the early 1540s, three were ordered to sail northward along the coast in search of a Northwest Passage, called by the Spaniards the Strait of Anián.[8] The remaining vessels were dispatched to the Moluccas under the command of Ruy López de Villalobos in 1541. After a number of significant discoveries, and the naming of the islands of Samar and Leyte, they christened the archipelago Las Islas Filipinas in honor of Philip II. López de Villalobos, however, was imprisoned by the Portuguese for trespassing and died in prison in 1544.

During the voyage of Cabrillo, recognized for its discovery of San Diego Bay (which Cabrillo named San Miguel on September 28, 1542), the Spaniards established a limited but successful trade with the Kumeyaay natives and continued northward perhaps as far as Cape Mendocino, named after Mendoza (fig. 3.3).[9] Cabrillo died on January 3, 1543, as a result of a fall and was buried on an island the Spaniards had named La Posesión a few months before; it was renamed Isla de Juan Rodríguez in his honor.[10] Cabrillo's final words encouraged the crew to continue their reconnaissance of California's coastal waters before returning to New Spain.[11] They reached the port of Navidad on April 14, 1543, with the sad news of Cabrillo's death and a pessimistic report of their limited discoveries. Cabrillo's own journal, perhaps kept a secret, has yet to be found.[12]

The establishment of the Manila galleon trade stands next in the line of Spanish enterprises in the Pacific. With the weakening of Portuguese defenses in the East Indies, plans were made by Philip II to establish trade between New Spain and the Philippines. Viceroy Luis de Velasco (1551–64) initiated a campaign for Pacific conquest. Miguel López de Legazpi, with a military force of some four hundred men, sailed from Acapulco and conquered the island of Luzon in 1565.[13] Andres de Urdaneta, an Augustinian priest, led the way to find a return route to New Spain by following the Japanese Current. A regular trade between Asia and New Spain began in the late seventeenth century and lasted until the early 1800s.[14]

For 150 years, Spain enjoyed almost uncontested occupation of the Pacific Ocean—so much so that its waters have been referred to as "the Spanish Lake" by European historians. Nevertheless, the galleon trade was seriously interrupted twice by English pirates: first by Francis Drake on his voyage around the world from 1577 to 1579, and second by Thomas Cavendish's capture of the galleon *Santa Ana* in 1587.[15] Spain's major contribution to the exploration of the Pacific coast of North America resulted from its attempt to find a suitable landing place for the Manila galleons to take on supplies prior to reaching Acapulco.[16] This plan failed, and one galleon—the *San Agustín,* commanded by the Portuguese Sebastián Rodríguez Cermeño—was wrecked on the California coast in 1595.[17]

A more positive outcome of the Manila galleon trade involved Sebastián Vizcaíno, a passenger on the *Santa Ana* who had survived its capture by Cavendish and returned to New Spain with plans to settle California. Vizcaíno led a second voyage after Cabrillo in 1602–3 to explore the coast of California with explicit instructions to find a usable port for the galleons. He chose the bay he named Monterey on the central California coast, discounting Cabrillo's San Miguel (which Vizcaíno named San Diego). Vizcaíno's voyage marked the end of Pacific exploration to the north of Mexico until the era of Captain Cook some 166 years later. Despite the friendly relations that both Spanish voyages had established with the native inhabitants, no forms of trade or settlement were accomplished.

As the political environment in Spain declined during the seventeenth century, no major attempts were made to sponsor voyages of exploration into the Pacific.[18] The Spanish Crown's difficulties primarily concerned the Hapsburgs' inability to control their European possessions, especially the Spanish Netherlands. Dutch explorers set out from their East Indian colonies to chart portions of Australia and New Zealand.[19] The problem of finding a port for the Manila galleons was obviated by improvements in ship design and construction that added

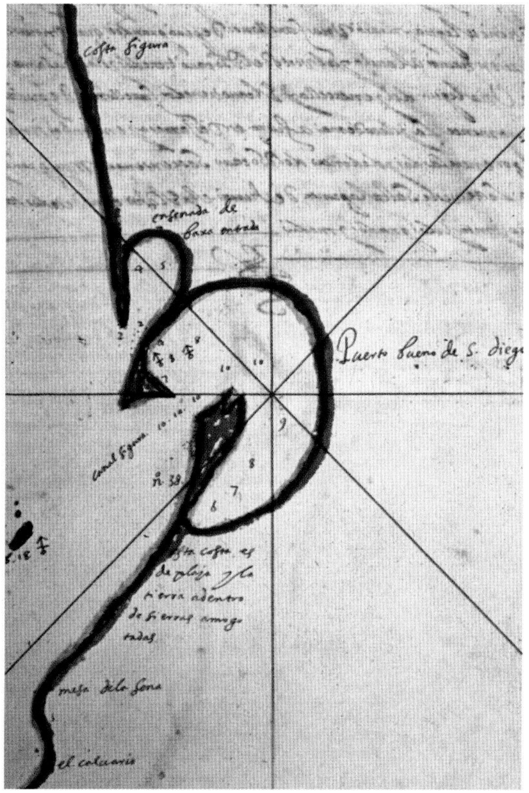

3.3 *Port of San Diego,* 1602. This, the first map of San Diego, appeared in the account of the Sebastián Vizcaíno expedition written by Antonio de la Ascensión, a Carmelite priest who had studied at the pilot academy in Seville. Rodríguez Cabrillo had named the bay San Miguel in 1542, but the name bestowed by Vizcaíno, San Diego de Alcalá, on that saint's day in 1602, survived. San Diego became the site of California's first mission and presidio as a result of the Portolá-Serra expedition of 1769, through which José de Gálvez launched the settlement of Alta California as a defensive measure against possible Russian maritime incursions from the north. San Diego History Center Research Archives.

3.4 *José de Gálvez.* Artist and date unknown. *Visitador general* (royal inspector) to New Spain from 1765 to 1771, Gálvez was later Minister of the Indies under Carlos III. A towering figure in the history of the viceroyalty, Gálvez initiated economic reforms to maximize tax revenue, supervised the expulsion of the Jesuits, undertook substantial reorganization of the political infrastructure, and supervised military operations on the northern frontier. He was responsible for initiating the colonization of Alta California and, as minister, never lost interest in promoting northern voyages to press Spanish claims to the Pacific Northwest coast. Gálvez Family Collection, Buenos Aires, Argentina.

space for carrying provisions. It was thus possible for the galleons to proceed directly to Acapulco.

By the latter half of the eighteenth century, the quest for gold and silver from Mexico had long been abandoned in favor of more enlightened pursuits such as the classification of natural resources according to the Linnaean system and the plotting of the transit of Venus to calculate the distance of the sun from the Earth.[20]

The plans for observing the transit of Venus in 1761 as an international event had a most significant impact on Pacific exploration, since many nations were, by that time, involved in the peaceful pursuit of science.[21] The German astronomer Johannes Kepler (1571–1630) had used his calculations of planetary motion to predict both the transit of Venus on December 6, 1631, and a second passing of Venus across the sun eight years later. He further predicted that the next one would occur after some 125 years. As it turned out, the eighteenth-century transits occurred in 1761 and 1769. Because observations of the 1761 transit yielded incomplete results, it was imperative that more accurate measurements be undertaken in 1769.

The stage was thus set for international travel in pursuit of this goal. Captain James Cook's first engagement with the "Spanish Lake" came when he was chosen by the Admiralty to observe the transit in the Pacific on behalf of the Royal Society. The location chosen was Tahiti, an island already visited by the English navigator Samuel Wallis in 1767 and the Frenchman Louis Antoine de Bougainville in 1768.[22] If the earlier Spanish discovery and exploration of the Pacific had brought the ocean into the consciousness of Europe, the second half of the eighteenth century confirmed that its destiny was to reflect the shifting balance of power in the struggle for European hegemony—essentially one between France and Britain.[23] At the same time that Cook set out for Tahiti, a combined French and Spanish expedition traveled to New Spain to observe the transit from San José del Cabo and Real de Santa Ana in Baja California.

Because the Russians, working hand in hand with the French, had observed the 1761 transit from both the Siberian steppe and St. Petersburg, they were determined to observe the 1769 transit from the Pacific.[24] The international observations of the transit of Venus coincided with the decision of José de Gálvez, appointed *visitador general* (royal inspector) to New Spain by the reform-minded King Carlos III in 1765, to initiate plans to secure more effectively the northern perimeter (approximately 60°N) of the viceroyalty (fig. 3.4).[25] This goal had already involved a campaign to subdue the Seri Indians of Sonora, which had enabled the establishment of the port of San Blas in 1768. This obviated the need to transport soldiers and supplies over difficult and dangerous land routes from centers in the south. It was from this new port that the second phase of Gálvez's plan was undertaken: the settling of Alta California in 1769.[26]

All of these expeditions resulted in a renewed interest in exploration. More significantly, however, they magnified for the governments in Madrid and Mexico City the perceived threat of Russian expansion in the north Pacific. This paved the way both for the establishment of missions in Alta California under Father Junípero Serra and for attempts to reach the sixtieth parallel north just a few years later.[27]

After the initial settlement of Alta California in 1769, the defensive policies of Viceroy Antonio de Bucareli were governed by California's strategic value as a buffer against foreign aggression from the north—especially, but not only, by the Russians, who by that time were well established on the Kamchatka Peninsula, and whose *promyshlenniki* were hunting furs across the Aleutian Islands toward North America. There were rumors of an English voyage to the North Pole—in actuality, the expedition of Constantine John Phipps in 1773, prompted by the continuing belief of many cartographers and armchair geographers in Europe that the fictional Admiral Bartholomew de Fonte had indeed sailed across North America through a strait from the Pacific to Hudson Bay in 1640. New reports from the Spanish ambassador in Moscow about the Russian threat led Bucareli to write: "I deem it well that any establishment of the Russians on this continent or any other foreign power ought to be guarded against, not because the king needs to enlarge his realms . . . but in order to avoid consequences brought about by having any other neighbors than the Indians."[28]

For over two decades, the government in Madrid had tended to discount the diplomatic reports from its ambassadors about Russian activities, but Ambassador Conde de Lacy's dispatches in late 1772 and early 1773 seemed to signal a new urgency. These reports, probably based on old information (but new to him), chronicled not only the rapid advances of the fur traders but also the naval expedition of Petr Krenitsyn and Mikhail Levashov to the eastern Aleutian Islands in 1768–69. Although Bucareli personally doubted that the Russians had reached America and questioned the reports of a vibrant transpacific trade, he understood that the coast was unknown, that anything was possible, and that a voyage of exploration and reconnaissance was necessary to ascertain whether the Russians could be located. The viceroy also wanted to find suitable sites for future Spanish settlements and fortifications in defense of its sovereignty in the north Pacific.[29]

Ensign Juan Pérez, who had commanded the *San Antonio* on its initial voyage from San Blas to found San Diego in the spring of 1769, and had returned in April 1770 with provisions to save the original missionaries and soldiers, was chosen to lead the expedition. The lengthy instructions he was given on December 24, 1773, would regulate all subsequent voyages of exploration from San Blas to the Pacific Northwest. The thirty-two articles covered a multitude of details about keeping logs, approaching the coasts, taking possession, handling foreign contacts, maintaining friendly contact with the Natives, taking care of medicines and supplies, and ensuring proper discipline.[30]

3.5 Gordon Miller, Santiago *off Langara Island (Haida Gwaii), 1774.* Oil, 1997. A veteran pilot on the Manila galleons, Juan Pérez became attached to the Naval Department of San Blas in 1768. He subsequently established himself as a dependable sailing master on the supply ships to California before being given command of the first Spanish voyage to the far north in 1774. He reached latitude 54°40'N, the current boundary between Alaska and British Columbia, and, although criticized for not landing and performing acts of possession, gained knowledge about sailing conditions on the coast that assisted preparations for the subsequent 1775 voyage of Bruno de Hezeta and Juan Francisco de la Bodega y Quadra. Courtesy of the artist.

Pérez, sailing the 225-ton frigate *Santiago* from San Blas on January 25, 1774, headed first to Monterey with Junípero Serra, who was returning from a visit to Mexico City. Pérez, with Fathers Juan Crespí and Tomás de la Peña as chaplains and diarists, continued his voyage into unknown waters north of the Queen Charlotte Islands at approximately 55°N. It was later established that Pérez had reached 54°40'N.[31] Here, on July 20, he encountered Haida Indians, who paddled out to meet him and to engage in a brisk trade that included furs (fig. 3.5) and, especially, basketry hats and woolen blankets. These caused a sensation when they were examined by Carlos III and his court in Madrid because they suggested "more culture than is common among the Indians."[32] Dense fog, contrary winds, and currents prevented the crew from making a landfall, however, and Pérez, plagued by constant sickness and concerned about a shortage of fresh water, turned back well short of his official goal of 60°N. He sailed the *Santiago* along the coast of Vancouver Island, and on August 9, 1775, anchored off the southern edge of a large bay outside the entrance to a harbor that he named Surgidero de San Lorenzo, later known as Nootka Sound. Twenty-one canoes containing nearly 150 amazed Indians approached the *Santiago*. A Spanish diarist later reported: "The view of this ship at first filled the natives with terror . . . and they were seized with fright from the moment they saw the giant 'machine' on the horizon, which little by little approached their coasts. They believed that Qua-utz [the Creator] was coming to make a second visit, and were fearful that it was to punish their misdeeds."[33]

Pérez did not land at Nootka, but Cook in 1778 found evidence of the Spanish voyage there. A launch from the *Santiago* was "put in the water, fitted out with sails and masts, with the purpose of locating a good anchorage," but at the last minute, an unexpected west wind nearly drove the *Santiago* onto the rocks, and a crucial opportunity to take possession of the coast was lost. Nevertheless, Pérez exchanged some gifts with the Indians. He then set his course for Monterey, arriving on August 27 with a crew ridden with scurvy. Serra was keenly disappointed that the expedition had failed to achieve its objective of 60°N, and he criticized Pérez, who was still in poor health, for refusing to stay in California and help establish a settlement in San Francisco. The veteran mariner returned to San Blas early in November and almost immediately began to prepare for further exploration.[34]

Bucareli advised his superiors in Madrid that no contact with Russian traders had been made and that a second expedition, scheduled to depart in the spring, would further investigate and take possession of northern lands.[35] The viceroy might have been disappointed that Pérez had not been able to land and perform any acts of possession, but he was less critical than later historians who have studied the period and deemed the voyage largely a failure. Bucareli wrote to Madrid, for example: "I always hold experience very useful, not that so much is accomplished in the first attempt as that it facilitates the outcome of those that follow, and it affirms that in the 19 degrees [of latitude] to which we have advanced there is no fear of foreign settlement."[36] Nevertheless, Pérez was legitimately criticized for his apparent failure to produce any chart from the expedition. Even though it was constructed after the event, and by someone who was not on the voyage, a chart by José Cañizares "prepared in accordance with the observations and surveys . . . of Don Juan Pérez" was found in the National Archives in Washington, DC, in 1988. The historian Herbert Beals stated that although this cartographic image was "far from flawless, it represents the first attempt to map the northwest coast up to the 54th parallel."[37]

As a follow-up expedition, three vessels left San Blas in March 1775 and headed into the Pacific. The *Santiago* was commanded by Bruno de Hezeta, a native of Bilbao, and the thirty-six-foot schooner *Sonora,* under Juan Manuel de Ayala, sailed as consort. The expedition was under instructions similar to those given to Pérez. Again they were to attempt a landfall at 60°N. The San Blas supply ship *San Carlos,* under Manuel Manrique, was to make a thorough reconnaissance of San Francisco Bay for its proposed occupation.[38] Unfortunately, shortly after the ships set sail, Manrique suffered a mental breakdown. Hezeta ordered his return to San Blas and transferred command of the *San Carlos* to Ayala. Propitiously, this change elevated the Peruvian-born ensign Juan Francisco de la Bodega y Quadra, recently arrived with five companions to bolster the capacity of the naval department of San Blas, to the position of captain of the tiny *Sonora* (fig. 3.6).[39]

The *Santiago,* with Juan Pérez as chief pilot, and the *Sonora* sailed directly to the north Pacific without stopping at Monterey. On June 9, 1775, the two Spanish vessels anchored in Trinidad Bay, in northern California, and took possession of the harbor in the name of Carlos III. After a few days of sailing north, Hezeta viewed the mouth of a river and recorded his discovery as the Entrada de

3.6 Julio García Condoy, *Juan Francisco de la Bodega y Quadra,* after José María Vásquez, ca. 1962. Arguably the most experienced and knowledgeable European mariner on the Northwest Coast of America in the late eighteenth century, Bodega made an epic voyage from Mexico to southern Alaska in 1775. He sailed again to the far north in 1779. In 1792 he was seconded from the naval department of San Blas to act as Spanish commissioner, responsible for enforcing in Nootka Sound the terms of the 1790 Nootka Convention, which had prevented war between Britain and Spain over the arrest of British fur traders there in 1789. Bodega's negotiations with his counterpart, George Vancouver, however, proved inconclusive. Maritime Museum of British Columbia, Victoria.

3.7 *Francisco Mourelle de la Rua.* Artist unknown. Eighteenth century. Oil. Mourelle rose from beginnings as a humble pilot to the highest ranks of the Spanish navy. Early in his career, still in his twenties, he joined Bodega y Quadra on the *Sonora* in 1775 and the *Favorita* in 1779 on two important voyages from Mexico to Alaska. In the years 1780–81, on one of a number of voyages between Manila and New Spain, he discovered and explored several islands in the South Pacific. In 1792, instead of commanding the voyage into the Strait of Juan de Fuca for which he had been chosen, he authored a lengthy report on all the Spanish voyages to the Northwest Coast since 1774. Museo Naval, Madrid, A 143.

Hezeta.[40] Continuing northward, the crewmen of the *Sonora* landed at Port Grenville on the coast of present-day Washington State and, in an eerie replay of the apparent fate of Alexei Chirikov's men off Yakobi Island in the Alexander Archipelago of southeastern Alaska in 1741, were ambushed by some three hundred Indians who sprang from the nearby bushes.[41] Seven men—half the *Sonora*'s crew—were killed, and Bodega was powerless to avenge the loss. Hezeta, the senior commander of the enterprise, transferred some men from the *Santiago* to replenish the *Sonora* and suggested they return home.

Bodega and his second officer, Francisco Antonio Mourelle de la Rua from Galicia in northern Spain (fig. 3.7), daringly planned to continue the voyage, despite Hezeta's reluctance.[42] During a dark, foggy night in the latitude of the yet-to-be-discovered Strait of Juan de Fuca, they allowed their vessel to drift away from the *Santiago* until it was out of sight and they could set sail for the north. Bodega and his men struggled against prevailing winds in an effort to reach the sixtieth parallel. The *Sonora* hove to in the latitude of Kruzof Island, where they noted the distinctive volcanic cone immediately west of modern-day Sitka, naming it San Jacinto. Three years later, Cook would call it Mount Edgecumbe. Bodega strengthened Spain's claim to the territory by taking possession at Puerto de los Remedios (today Sea Lion Cove, at the top end of Kruzof Island at 57°20'N), where they encountered a group of Tlingit Indians. Well armed with long, flint-tipped lances, they were less than friendly when the Spaniards came ashore to fill their water casks, making it clear that mere trifles were not an acceptable payment for the water being taken. Nevertheless, as Bodega's men were also heavily armed, a clash was avoided.

Sailing west to achieve a northing, Bodega approached 58°N—just two degrees short of the aspired goal of 60°—before reluctantly deciding, with a majority of his men already suffering from scurvy, to turn back: "I resolved to return on a course east-southeast, reconnoitering the coast at a distance of one mile. I contented myself with having gone up almost to 58°, in a vessel from which one had no right to expect such success. For having been in situations countless times from which I might have retreated, I never failed in my primary intentions, even under pressure."[43] Hugging the coast, Bodega and Mourelle searched in vain for anything like "the entrance that was supposedly discovered by Admiral Fonte, but I have not encountered that extensive archipelago of San Lázaro into which he says he entered" (fig. 2.2).[44] Toward the end of August, however, the *Sonora* sailed into a large bay surrounded by islands on the ocean side of Prince of Wales Island. A second act of possession was performed here in Puerto de Bucareli (55°18'N), today's Bucareli Bay. The safe anchorage and the chance to rest in warm weather, to replenish their supplies of wood and water, to enjoy excellent fishing, and to eat berries gathered on shore all revived the group's health and morale. Sailing south past

Dall Island, the *Sonora* was off toward what is today Dixon Entrance, which Pérez had seen the previous year. As the winds changed, making their southeasterly course difficult to pursue, Bodega persuaded Mourelle that they should turn north again in an attempt to reach 60°N. The weather soon turned stormy, however, and cold and signs of scurvy reappeared. The second try at 60° was abandoned just short of latitude 57°.

On the basis of their discoveries, as delineated on the charts completed by Bodega and Mourelle, Spain had established a solid foundation for its claim of sovereignty over the Pacific coast from Monterey to the Gulf of Alaska (fig. 3.8). On the return trip, despite his crew's suffering mightily from scurvy, Bodega managed to survey one final port, the one he would leave as a namesake: Puerto de Capitan de la Bodega, present-day Bodega Bay, on the northern coast of California. The *Sonora* anchored alongside its flagship *Santiago* in Monterey harbor on October 7, 1775. Everyone, including Bodega, was so ill and weak that they had to be carried ashore. Bodega's epic exploration in a thirty-six-foot schooner gives ample testimony to the courage of these early navigators, and on their safe return they were able to dispel Bucareli's fears about the presence of Russian traders in the north.

The San Blas supply ship *San Carlos,* also lying at anchor in Monterey, had just returned from its forty-four-day survey of San Francisco Bay. Captain Ayala had sailed to the entrance of the bay on August 4, 1775, but strong currents and tides pre-

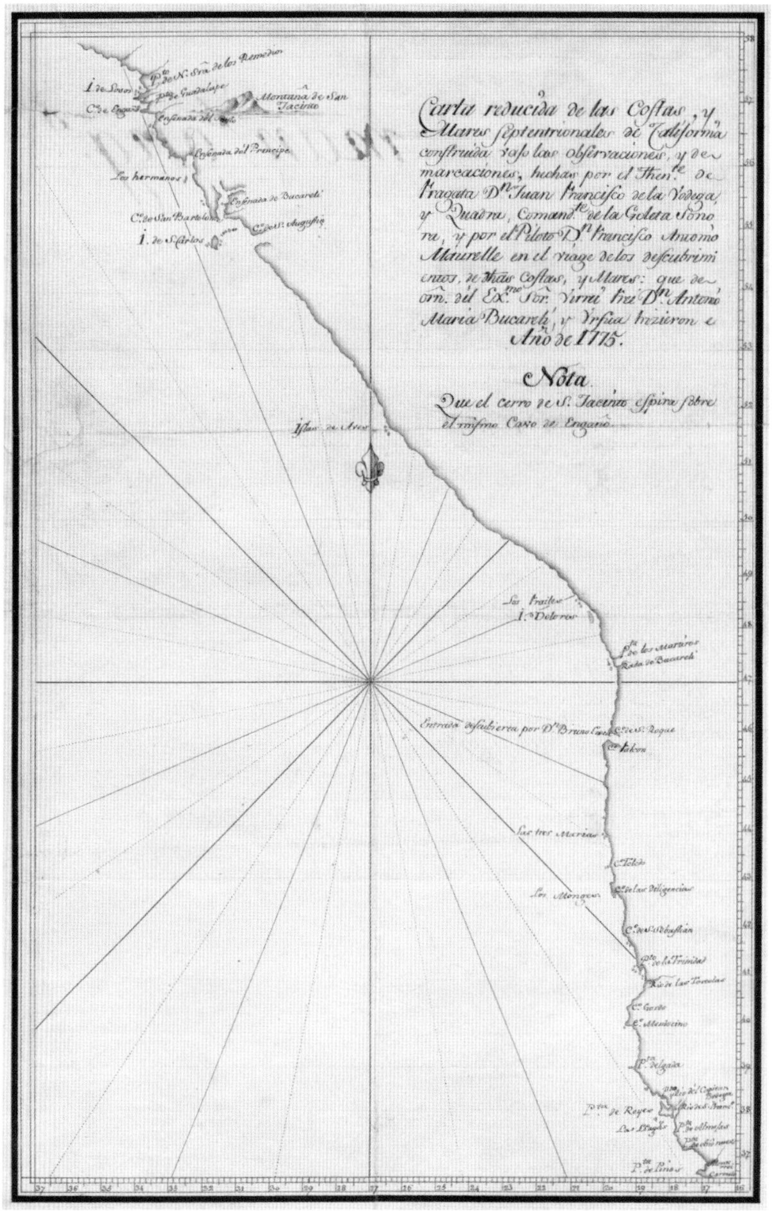

3.8 Juan Francisco de la Bodega y Quadra and Francisco Mourelle, *Chart of the Northern Coasts and Seas of California.* This was the first chart to accurately establish the trend of the coast north and west of Alta California. When a British version was published in 1781 and studied alongside Cook's chart from 1778, a clear picture of the coast emerged—minus the delineation of Vancouver Island and details of the Alexander Archipelago—from New Spain to the Arctic Ocean. A final, definitive, image based on subsequent work by British and Spanish naval vessels was reflected in George Vancouver's summary chart of 1798. Museo Naval, Madrid, Carpeta III, B4.

vented him from passing through the narrow entry (today's Golden Gate) until the next day, when the *San Carlos* became the first European ship to enter California's largest natural port. Ayala anchored off present-day North Beach and, with a small launch, explored every part of the bay, a reconnaissance that set the stage for the occupation of San Francisco and the foundation of its presidio and mission in the early fall of 1776.[45]

The American War of Independence had little effect upon Spanish California, save for the request by Carlos III that the missionaries and their Indian charges contribute to the cause of the Americans who were attempting to free themselves from British rule.[46] As fighting between Britain and the American colonists intensified on the east coast of America in July 1776, James Cook embarked on his third voyage—this time aimed at the north Pacific coast on the other side of the continent and a search for the Northwest Passage. Spanish espionage in London had picked up news of the proposed expedition in March, shortly after Cook had been appointed as its leader. His reputation as an explorer and mapmaker was of immediate concern to the Spaniards because any subsequent publication of observations and charts exposing the Pacific coast—let alone any successful discovery of a navigable passage between the Atlantic and Pacific—could only threaten Spain's assumption of sovereignty over the Costa Septentrional de California.[47] It would also inevitably promote increased foreign maritime activity, which in turn would lead to more smuggling along the Pacific coasts of the Americas, something about which the Spanish government was always intensely concerned. Cook's imminent arrival was a challenge that demanded a response.

Spain's minister of the Indies, José de Gálvez, immediately issued orders to Viceroy Bucareli to ensure that everything possible be done to impede Cook's progress. In line with the established Laws of the Indies, there was no question of offering assistance or supplies; on the contrary, if his ships were encountered (or for some reason came into port in the Americas), they were to be stopped, the ships' papers examined, and Cook himself fully interrogated as to his intentions so that a formal protest might be lodged with London concerning his egregious trespass in Spanish waters. When informed about the explorations and discoveries of Hezeta and Bodega in 1775, Gálvez also immediately ordered a third northern voyage to further improve Spain's understanding of the coast and to uphold its sovereignty. Nevertheless, Bucareli suggested that the situation in New Spain made further exploration difficult. The American war was shifting Spain's Pacific focus toward the Caribbean, and supplying Alta California was still a priority for the small inventory of ships operating out of San Blas. He rejected the idea of another expedition, but Gálvez reiterated his demand with a strongly worded order.[48] Reluctantly, however, Gálvez realized that Bucareli's concern about available ships was valid, and the viceroy of Peru was charged with providing a vessel for the new northern expedition. Bodega sailed to Lima's port of Callao early in 1777 but did not return to San Blas with a refitted vessel, the *Favorita,* until the following February—too late for the proper preparations necessary to mount a northern expedition.

As events turned out, Cook had made his run up the Northwest Coast in 1778, and the expedition designed to challenge his presence did not sail until February 11, 1779. Cook scrupulously complied with his instructions "not to touch upon any part of the Spanish Dominions on the Western Continent of America," meaning any known settlements.[49] As a result of these orders, Cook was long gone from American waters (and facing imminent death in Hawai'i) by the time the two vessels, the *Princesa* (also known as *Nuestra Señora del Rosario),* commanded by Ignacio de Arteaga, and the *Favorita* (also known as *Nuestra Señora de los Remedios*), with Bodega y Quadra once more in charge, sailed for the north. Francisco Mourelle, second in command on the *Favorita,* again served as pilot for Bodega.[50]

Following up Bodega's previous visit and positive impression from 1775, the expedition headed for Bucareli Bay, where initially friendly relations with the Indians soon turned sour. Although the ethnographic descriptions and collections that resulted from the two-month visit (May–June) were extensive, the Natives stole anything they could get their hands on, and a good deal of tension resulted from incidents of hostage taking. Added to these difficulties, many of the crew members came down with a strange, severe illness.[51] Although Bucareli Bay and its environs were extensively explored, the months spent greatly reduced the time available for further discoveries at 60°N. The Spanish expedition followed Cook into Prince William Sound and along the Kenai Peninsula, but it did not explore Cook Inlet, and the ships returned home after encountering stormy weather and experiencing scurvy among the men off Afognak Island between the Alaska Peninsula and Kodiak Island.

Despite the expedition's high ambitions—to challenge Cook's presence, to discover the elusive Northwest Passage, and to find useful information about the perceived Russian threat—the ships were forced to return with little more than transiently useful geographic knowledge and some items received in trade with the Indians they had met. Initially firmly involved in the American war, and then slow to react to the implications of a blueprint for the development of a lucrative fur trade (as recorded by Lieutenant James King in Cook's published account in 1784), Spain never again gained the initiative in its attempt to control the coast and the lands north of Vancouver Island. That region would be left to British, Russian, and American fur traders who arrived after the northern exploratory voyages of the 1770s. A settlement at the presidio of Santa Cruz de Nutka, however, was maintained between 1789 and 1795 to further the practical and diplomatic struggle with Great Britain for control of the lands and commerce between San Francisco Bay and Vancouver Island (figs. 3.9 and 13.7).

3.9 *View of the Interior of Friendly Cove at the Entrance to Nootka Sound,* 1802. Engraving after a drawing by José Cardero of the Malaspina expedition (1791). The scene shows the fort, buildings, and gardens of the Spanish establishment, first occupied in 1789. That year, Esteban José Martínez arrested British fur traders who had come to establish their own outpost on Vancouver Island, thus precipitating the Nootka crisis. Between 1790 and 1795 there was a permanent Spanish presence on the site of the native village of Yuquot, visited by James Cook in 1778 and reflected in the drawings of his expedition artist, John Webber. Instituto de Historia del Pacífico Español, Vancouver.

Meanwhile, in 1782, two vessels once again embarked upon a voyage of exploration to Alta California and beyond. The flagship *Princesa* and the *Favorita,* the veterans of the 1779 expedition, were chosen for the task, and Juan Pantoja y Arriaga, who had studied at the Seminario de San Telmo in Seville and served as a pilot for Bodega y Quadra in 1779, was second in command. Pantoja was the key figure in a reconnaissance of the coast of Southern California that contributed a number of important logs, charts, and descriptions of the ports of San Diego and Santa Barbara.[52]

In addition to controlling territory, spreading Christianity, and settling new lands, Spain also sought to expand the frontiers of knowledge. While the Enlightenment might have come to Spain late and finished early, Carlos III, who ascended the throne in 1757, followed the lead of his Bourbon predecessors and supported a renaissance in art, architecture, medicine and science, as well as the development of a more effective colonial administration and new avenues of trade. To encourage scientific studies, and to compete with scholars sent out by Great Britain, France, Germany, Austria, Russia, and other nations, he promoted half a dozen major expeditions during the last quarter of the eighteenth century, including the Malaspina expedition, which was active on the Northwest Coast in 1791 and 1792. Carlos III urged the explorer-naturalists to continue "with effectiveness the paths of Cook and La Pérouse."[53] Capable viceroys and other colonial officials carried out detailed, fully illustrated scientific projects, and a number of studies were completed.[54]

Unfortunately, with the king's untimely death and the subsequent lack of any support or encouragement from Carlos IV (1788–1808) to assemble and edit the results of these investigations, they brought the Spaniards little or no recognition. Despite numerous publications—books and articles, many of them in English—over the past four decades, Spain's naval commanders, scientific investigators, and botanical artists have never been accorded the renown given to Cook and La Pérouse.[55] This essay endeavors to help correct the balance, as it is obvious that the British, French,

Americans, Russians, and others who traveled, explored, and traded in the "Spanish Lake" were not operating in a Spanish vacuum.

In 1781, Daines Barrington, the noted eighteenth-century English jurist, antiquarian, amateur naturalist, member of the council of the Royal Society, and pursuer of the dream of a navigable Northwest Passage, published an eclectic collection of articles titled *Miscellanies,* whose principal interest lay in the presentation of Francisco Mourelle's journal from 1775 and an accompanying map of his and Bodega y Quadra's discoveries on the Northwest Coast.[56] Cook, of course, could not have seen this book, as he had been killed in 1779, but he notes when discussing Indian tools seen at Nootka that "some account of the Spaniards having visited this Coast was published before I left England." He probably read a newspaper account of the voyage translated from a substantial report in the *Gaceta de Madrid* (Madrid Gazette).[57] He may or may not have seen the map, as it is unclear when the pirated copy of Mourelle's journal actually reached England. Nevertheless, on the Northwest Coast in the spring of 1778, Cook was clearly aware that he was not the first explorer to run the coast so far north of New Albion. The northernmost discoveries of the earliest Spanish voyages, beginning with the Manila galleon trade in the late sixteenth century, had indeed set the stage for continued exploration by other European nations well into the eighteenth century.

NOTES

1 Both the papal bull of Alexander VI in 1493 and the Treaty of Tordesillas of 1494, which divided the newly discovered non-European lands of the world between Spain and Portugal, did specify exact lines of demarcation. Spain's claim to exclusive sovereignty over the entire Pacific Ocean, as well as over various islands lying therein, was rarely challenged over the following two hundred years. Beginning in the late seventeenth century, however, Dutch, British, French, and other privateers (pirates) began challenging ownership of those territories occupied or claimed by Spain and Portugal.

2 See Carla Rahn Phillips, "Spain and the Pacific: Voyaging into Vastness," in *Spain's Legacy in the Pacific,* special issue of *Mains'l Haul: A Journal of Pacific Maritime History* 41–42 (Fall 2005–Winter 2006): 4–11. See also Carlos Martínez Shaw, *Spanish Pacific: From Magellan to Malaspina* (Madrid: Ministerio de Asuntos Exteriores and Lunweg Editores, 1988). The ocean had of course been crisscrossed by Pacific Islanders for hundreds of years, using navigational techniques that predated the Columbian era, but this essay does not deal with the details of these Native voyages.

3 The consequences of Christopher Columbus's arrival in America have been studied in great detail. Less emphasis, however, has been placed upon the subsequent role of the Pacific Ocean and the early efforts made by Europeans to determine its limits and explore the islands lying within its boundaries. For an excellent survey, see Tony Ballantyne, ed., *The Pacific World: Lands, Peoples and History of the Pacific, 1500–1900* (Aldershot, UK: Ashgate, 2004).

4 The possibility of a southern continent, Terra Australis, balancing the land masses of North America, Greenland, and Eurasia was still being promoted by such armchair geographers as Alexander Dalrymple until Cook's several forays approaching or crossing the Antarctic Circle during his second voyage proved otherwise. See Grenfell Price, "Captain James Cook's Discovery of the Antarctic Continent," *Geographical Review* 51 (October 1961): 575.

5 The dismal survival rate of one in thirteen (vastly surpassed by Cook on all of his voyages) shows how poorly

provisioned these sixteenth-century ships were. By March 1521, having passed through the Strait of Magellan, the fleet reached the Mariana Islands and Guam with three ships and a crew of 150. Just a month later, in April, Magellan was killed in the Battle of Mactan (Philippines) by Natives, and the rest of the crew attempted to return to Spain. For a complete account of Magellan's voyage, see Antonio Pigafetta, *Magellan's Voyage around the World* (original title *Primer viaje entorno del globo*), ed. and trans. James Alexander Robertson (Cleveland: Arthur H. Clark, 1906), and Laurence Bergreen, *Over the Edge of the World: Magellan's Terrifying Circumnavigation of the Globe* (New York: Harper Collins, 2003).

6 Cortés sent three ships under Alvaro de Saavedra. Two of these parted company with Saavedra's ship one thousand leagues from port and were never seen again. Saavedra reached the Moluccas but could not rescue anyone, so he attempted to return to Mexico. Driven back by contrary winds, he coasted along the shores of New Guinea but eventually died at sea.

7 This knowledge was lost at various times, and maps prepared by Dutch, French, and even Spanish cartographers during the mid- to late 1600s show California as an island. In the early eighteenth century, the Jesuit father Eusebio Kino temporarily laid to rest the island theory by traveling overland across the headwaters of the Gulf of California (Mar del Cortés) in 1710. Nevertheless, the myth persisted until Fernando VI of Spain proclaimed in a royal decree of 1747 that "California is not an island." See Doris Beale Polk, *The Island of California* (Spokane, WA: Arthur H. Clark, 1991), 155.

8 This semi-mythical strait at the eastern end of Asia first appeared on a map drawn by Giacomo Gastaldi in 1562 and subsequently appeared on maps by Abraham Ortelius (1564), Bolognini Zaltieri (1567), and Gerardus Mercator (1567). The source of the word *Ania* or *Anián* is not known. Later maps (such as the ones by Herman Moll in 1719 and Johannes van Keulen in 1728) show the strait north of "an island" of California.

9 Cape Mendocino lies at 40°26'N.

10 The manner of Cabrillo's death and his burial site are uncertain. Several historians agree that La Posesión is present-day San Miguel in the southern Channel Islands. See Iris Engstrand and Harry Kelsey, "Juan Rodríguez Cabrillo and the Building of the *San Salvador*," *Mains'l Haul: A Journal of Pacific Maritime Exploration* 45, nos. 1–2 (Winter–Spring 2008): 36–51, for a discussion of Cabrillo's background and voyage to California.

11 See Herbert E. Bolton, "A Summary Account of Juan Rodríguez Cabrillo's Voyage," in *Spanish Exploration in the Southwest, 1542–1706* (New York: Charles Scribner's Sons, 1916), 23.

12 See Harry Kelsey, *Juan Rodriguez Cabrillo* (San Marino, CA: Huntington Library, 1986) for a definitive treatment of Cabrillo's life; see also Engstrand and Kelsey, "Juan Rodríguez Cabrillo," 36–51.

13 López de Legazpi, who sailed well south of the Hawaiian Islands, established the capital city of Manila in 1571.

14 See William Lytle Schurz, *The Manila Galleon* (New York: E. P. Dutton, 1939). The route failed to take ships within sight of the Hawaiian Islands in either direction. Both the English forays into the Pacific have been chronicled in a number of sources. See, for example, Amancio Landin Carrasco et al., *Descubrimientos españoles en el Mar del Sur* (Madrid: Editorial Naval, 1992), vol. 2, chapter 7.

15 O. H. K. Spate, *The Spanish Lake: The Pacific since Magellan*, vol. 1 (Minneapolis: University of Minnesota Press, 1979).

16 See Iris Engstrand, "Seekers of the 'Northern Mystery': European Exploration of California and the Pacific," in *Contested Eden*, ed. Ramon Gutíerrez and Richard Orsi (Berkeley: University of California Press, 1998), 86–87. Both Francisco de Gali in 1587 and Pedro de Unamuno visited the California coast near Morro Bay but made no recommendations for a suitable port. See Henry R. Wagner, *Cartography of the Northwest Coast of America*, vol. 1 (Berkeley: Regents of the University of California, [1937] 1965).

17 The galleon went down near what became known as Drakes Bay in the lee of Point Reyes. Archaeological remains originally thought to be left from Drake's voyage were identified as belonging to Cermeño's *San Agustín*.

18 Spanish voyages of discovery from Peru centered on Pedro Fernandez de Quiros (1565–1614), a Portuguese navigator

who participated in several expeditions originating from Peru—primarily as pilot during the voyage of Alvaro de Mendaña of 1595–96 and as captain of his own voyage of 1605–6, during which he crossed the Pacific in search of Terra Australis.

19 The Dutch East India Company sent Abel Tasman (1603–59) on voyages of discovery in 1642 and 1644, on which he reached Tasmania and New Zealand.

20 Robin Inglis, "Successors and Rivals to Cook," in *Captain Cook: Explorations and Reassessments,* ed. Glyndwr Williams (New York: Boydell and Brewer, 2004), 171. From 1767 to 1795, no less than "eight major Spanish expeditions were engaged in a systematic survey of the Atlantic and Pacific coasts in the region of the Strait of Magellan, signaling its importance as a gateway to the South Sea that merited fuller understanding and control."

21 The adoption of the Linnaean system of binomial nomenclature had encouraged naturalists to classify or reclassify the plants and animals of both Europe and the New World.

22 See Iris H. W. Engstrand, "The Transit of Venus: Launching Pad for European Exploration in the Pacific during the Late Eighteenth Century," *Boletín* (Journal of the California Mission Studies Association) 21, no. 2 (2004): 36–48.

23 Inglis, "Successors and Rivals to Cook," 161.

24 In April 1761, after a five-month journey, the Abbé Jean-Baptiste Chappe d'Auteroche reached Tobolsk in Siberia, east of the Ural Mountains. He set up his wooden observatory on a plateau just outside the town. The observation of the transit of Venus went well, but Chappe had to take precautions against the hostility of the local inhabitants, who thought he was a magician. Chappe led the combined expedition to San José del Cabo in 1769.

25 With the settlement of Nueva or Alta California in 1769, the Spanish government was attempting to establish the northern perimeter of its settlement, as shown by the *Expedición de limites al norte de California de 1792.* There are various manuscript copies in Madrid, Mexico City, the Bancroft Library at the University of California, Berkeley, the Beinecke Library at Yale University, and elsewhere. See Freeman Tovell, Robin Inglis, and Iris Engstrand, *Voyage to the Northwest Coast of America, 1792: Juan Francisco de la Bodega y Quadra and the Nootka Sound Controversy* (Norman, OK: Arthur H. Clark, 2012).

26 The expulsion of the Jesuits from all Spanish dominions, especially Baja California, between 1765 and 1768 gave an added incentive to the efforts of Franciscan friars who had already been working in Mexico and the Spanish southwest for close to 250 years.

27 The *visitador general,* José de Gálvez, planned both activities, first in Mexico City and then on the Baja California peninsula. See Iris Engstrand, *Royal Officer in Baja California, 1768–1770: Joaquin Velázquez de León* (Los Angeles: Dawson's Books, 1976).

28 Bucareli to Julián Arriaga, minister of the Indies, July 27, 1773, quoted in Warren Cook, *Flood Tide of Empire: Spain and the Pacific Northwest, 1543–1819* (New Haven, CT: Yale University Press, 1973), 55.

29 Ibid. See also Christon Archer, "The Political and Military Context of the Spanish Advance into the Pacific Northwest," in *Spain and the North Pacific Coast: Essays in Recognition of the Bicentennial of the Malaspina Expedition, 1791–1792,* ed. Robin Inglis (Vancouver, BC: Vancouver Maritime Museum, 1992), 10–11.

30 Manuel P. Servín, "Instructions from Viceroy Bucareli to Ensign Juan Pérez," *California Historical Society Quarterly* 40 (September 1961): 238.

31 See Herbert K. Beals, ed. and trans., *Juan Pérez on the Northwest Coast: Six Documents of His Expedition in 1774* (Portland: Oregon Historical Society Press, 1989). Spain's claim to this northern boundary was assumed by the United States as a result of the Adams-Onís Treaty of 1819. This voyage and the subsequent one in 1775, under the command of Bruno de Hezeta, are also discussed in Christon Archer, "The Spanish Reaction to Cook's Third Voyage," in *Captain Cook and His Times,* ed. Robin Fisher and Hugh Johnston (Vancouver, BC: Douglas & McIntyre, 1979), 101–5.

32 Arriaga to Bucareli, February 24, 1775, cited in Archer, "Political and Military Context," 12. A list of the items collected from the Haida can be found in Donald Cutter, trans. and ed., *The California Coast: A Bilingual Edition of Documents from the Sutro Collection* (Norman: University

of Oklahoma Press, 1969), 278. The documents include the diaries of Crespí and de la Peña.

33 José Mariano Moziño, *Noticias de Nutka: An Account of Nootka Sound in 1792,* ed. and trans. Iris Engstrand, rev. ed. (Seattle: University of Washington Press, 1991), 14. Moziño spent several months with the Natives and gained firsthand knowledge about their memory of the event.

34 James Caster, "The Last Days of Juan Pérez, the Mallorcan Mariner," *Journal of the West* 2 (June 1963): 19.

35 Michael Thurman, *The Naval Department of San Blas: New Spain's Bastion for Alta California and Nootka, 1767–1798* (Glendale, CA: Arthur H. Clark, 1967), 126.

36 Beals, *Juan Pérez on the Northwest Coast,* 35.

37 Herbert Beals, "Malaspina's Precursors: New Light on Spanish Voyages to the Northwest Coast of America, 1774–1779," in *Malaspina '92: I jornadas internacionales,* ed. Mercedes Palau Baquero and Antonio Orozco Acuaviva (Cádiz: Real Academia Hispano-Americana, 1994), 163.

38 The *San Carlos,* commanded by Vicente Vila, was the first ship to depart for Alta California, on January 9, 1769, but it did not reach San Diego until April—well after the *San Antonio* under Juan Pérez.

39 See Freeman Tovell, *At the Far Reaches of Empire: the Life of Juan Francisco de la Bodega y Quadra* (Vancouver: UBC Press, 2008), part 1, chapter 2.

40 This was no doubt the mouth of the Columbia River, recognized and named by the American merchant captain Robert Gray in May 1792.

41 The Spaniards named the area (Grenville Bay) Punta de los Mártires. See Tovell, *At the Far Reaches of Empire,* 25–29.

42 Mourelle had served in the Spanish navy in the Caribbean before joining the naval staff at San Blas. See Donald Cutter, "California: Training Ground for Spanish Naval Heroes," *California Historical Society Quarterly* 40 (June 1961): 109–22.

43 Herbert Beals, trans. and ed., "Year of 1775 Journal of Exploration Made on the Northern Coast of California Undertaken by Juan Francisco de la Bodega y Quadra in the Schooner *Sonora,*" in *Four Travel Journals: The Americas, Antarctica and Africa, 1775–1874* (London: Hakluyt Society/Ashgate, 2007), 115.

44 Ibid., 115–16.

45 Engstrand, "Seekers of the 'Northern Mystery,'" 94–95.

46 Nevertheless, the Spanish governor of Louisiana, Bernardo de Gálvez, nephew of José de Gálvez (by this time minister of the Indies), supported the American cause and believed that it would benefit Spain to drive the British out of the lands bordering Spain's possessions in the Mississippi Valley.

47 This phrase denoted the entire coast northward from California.

48 W. Cook, *Flood Tide of Empire,* 88–92; Inglis, "Successors and Rivals," 173.

49 James Cook, *The Journals of Captain James Cook on His Voyages of Discovery,* vol. 2, *The Voyage of the* Resolution *and* Discovery, *1776–1780,* ed. J. C. Beaglehole (Cambridge: Cambridge University Press for the Hakluyt Society, 1967), ccxxi.

50 See Tovell, *At the Far Reaches of Empire,* chapters 3 and 4, for an account of the 1779 voyage, its preparations, and results. Mourelle continued to explore in the Pacific and visited Tonga and other islands in 1781. At one point Mourelle petitioned the king to become governor of California but instead was transferred to Spain in 1793. He continued to be promoted in the Spanish naval service and died in 1820 at the age of sixty-four. He is buried in the pantheon for naval heroes in San Fernando, near Cádiz.

51 The illness was probably food poisoning, because even though two men died, the others recovered fully.

52 *The Voyage of the Frigate* Princesa *to Southern California in 1782 as Recorded in the Logs of Juan Pantoja y Arriaga and Esteban José Martínez,* ed. Richard S. Whitehead, trans. Geraldine V. Sahyun (Santa Barbara, CA: Santa Barbara Mission Archive Library, 1982). Pantoja Park in downtown San Diego is named for this Spanish navigator, who drew the best contemporary map of San Diego Bay in 1782.

53 Iris H. W. Engstrand, *Spanish Scientists in the New World: The Eighteenth-Century Expeditions* (Seattle: University of Washington Press, 1981), 45. The Linnaean system, introduced throughout Europe by Swedish students of Linnaeus, served as the basis for classifying the fauna and flora of Spain's New World territories. The botanist Daniel

Solander traveled with Cook to Tahiti in 1769 to assist in classification efforts as well.

54 See Iris Engstrand, "José Moziño and Archibald Menzies: Crossroads of the Enlightenment in the Pacific Northwest," *Columbia: The Magazine of Northwest History* 18 (Spring 2004): 24–28.

55 See Iris Engstrand, "Spain's Role in Pacific Exploration during the Age of Enlightenment," in *Enlightenment and Exploration in the North Pacific, 1741–1795,* ed. Stephen Haycox, James Barnett, and Caedmon Liburd (Seattle: University of Washington Press, 1997); Iris Engstrand, "Of Fish and Men: Spanish Marine Science During the Late Eighteenth Century," *Pacific Historical Review* 69 (January 2000): 3–30.

56 See Daines Barrington, "Journal of a Voyage in 1775," in *Miscellanies* (London: J. Nichols, 1781), 469.

57 See *London Evening Post,* May 29, 1776. The basis for the newspaper report was a "Short Account of Some Voyages made by the Order of the King of Spain, to discover the State of the West American Coast from California Upwards. Dated Madrid 24 March 1776." This account was also reprinted in the appendix to a pamphlet promoting the "prospect of success" in searching for a Northwest Passage: *Summary Observations and Facts collected from Late and Authentic Accounts of Russian and other Navigators, to Show the Practicality and Good Prospect of Success in Enterprises to Discover a Northern Passage for Vessels by Sea, between the Atlantic and Pacific Oceans, or nearly to approach The North Pole; For which Offers of Reward are renewed by a late Act of Parliament* (London: John Nourse, 1776), 28–29.

4

From Russia with Charts

Cook and the Russians in the North Pacific

EVGUENIA ANICHTCHENKO

ON JUNE 19, 1778, THREE UNANGAX̂ KAYAKERS APPROACHED CAPTAIN Cook's *Discovery* off Unga Island, the largest of the Shumagin Islands south of the Alaska Peninsula. After a rope was dropped from the ship, one of the kayakers attached a small wooden object and quickly paddled away. At first the puzzled crew took the object for a bird call, but as no music would come out, they finally untied the string that held it together. The mystery object turned out to be a case containing a document written in Russian with the date 1778 and another year—1776—referenced in the body of the text. This was all the crew could understand, as "no one on board could read it."[1]

Set against the grandeur of Cook's voyages and the imposing seascape of the Arctic, the expedition's encounters with Russians appear almost coincidental. The instructions for the third voyage gave no specific mention about contact with Russians beyond recommendations to winter in Petropavlovsk, Kamchatka, if the Northwest Passage could not be sailed, before trying again the following spring for either the Northwest or Northeast Passage.[2] Cook carried no Russian interpreters or even dictionaries in anticipation of possible meetings: had the expedition succeeded in its main goal of finding the Northwest Passage, these would have

John Webber, *Captain Cook Meeting with the Chukchi at St. Lawrence Bay*, 1778 (detail of fig. 4.4).

been unnecessary. Yet every hint of Russian presence was carefully recorded in the third-voyage narratives, and the geographic features noted on Russian maps were painstakingly compared with Cook's own observations.

The "Russian" maps that Cook carried on the voyage are referenced in his notes and ship logs frequently and with frustration. Occasional allusions to Georg Wilhelm Steller's and Stepan Krasheninnikov's descriptions of Kamchatka indicate that Cook and his officers were familiar with their books. They also carried Gerhard Müller's *Voyages from Asia to America, to complete the Discoveries of the North-west Coast of America, containing accounts of Vitus Bering's and Aleksei Chirikov's discoveries,*[3] and David Crantz's *History of Greenland.* All this information about Russian discoveries and establishments in eastern Siberia and the "New World" was used, however, not to facilitate meetings with the Russians, but more likely to identify "negative spaces," places where Russians were not to be found. Cook ignored the recommendation to winter in Petropavlovsk and displayed little interest in charting the Aleutian Chain, where he would most certainly have met Russian hunting parties. In fact, his only contact with the Russians was initiated by the Russians themselves.

This approach seems consistent with the two major goals of the third voyage: to search for the Northwest Passage and to claim "lands undiscovered by any other European Power" for the British Crown.[4] At the time of Cook's third voyage, Russia was the most prominent European power in the north Pacific and Bering Strait regions, with outposts in Chukotka, Kamchatka, and the Aleutian Islands, and the lands known to the Russians were, in Cook's mind, not available for British claim. Although geographically expansive, the Russian position in the region was far from impervious. The forts and trading posts were meagerly manned, the lands surrounding them remained unexplored, and conflicts with the indigenous peoples of Chukotka and Kamchatka raged with bloody frequency.

For this and other reasons, the prospect of two armed foreign ships cruising Russia's new northeastern borders was alarming to the Russian Crown. Lydia Black, the noted historian of Russian America, has even suggested that Russian officials sponsored publication of the grossly inaccurate map by Jacob von Staehlin to mislead the English, Spanish, and French ambassadors in St. Petersburg about Russian discoveries in the north Pacific (fig. 2.6).[5] But although the state officials in both St. Petersburg and London wanted to keep their empires in the north Pacific separate, the realities of sailing in northern oceans brought English and Russian mariners together. After disappointing side trips into Prince William Sound and Cook Inlet, Cook and his companions sailed southwest along the Alaska Peninsula to find a route to the north, briefly anchoring at Unalaska. In August 1778, heavy fog and shallow water off the Alaska coast drove them northwest across the entrance to Bering Strait to Chukotka. Both in Unalaska and Chukotka they found local

Native peoples who had been in contact with the Russians, but not Russians themselves. Two months later, on their return from the Arctic, a leak in the *Resolution*'s bilges forced them to spend another month on Unalaska Island, where for the first time they met Russian traders. The failure to locate the Northwest or Northeast Passage in 1778 brought about a second attempt in 1779 after the tragic death of Captain Cook in Hawai'i. This time the *Resolution* and *Discovery* visited Petropavlovsk and spent more time with their Russian hosts, both on their Arctic-bound route and on the return journey.

Forced by elements thousand of miles away from their European capitals, these encounters were the first meetings between the British and Russians in the north Pacific. In the ensuing decades, their dual presence in the region would evolve into the uneasy balance of rivals responding to a complex mixture of national and international politics, which eventually led to Russia's decision to sell its Alaskan possessions to the United States. In 1778 and 1779, however, the slate was blank and the encounters fleeting. What, then, was the historical importance of these meetings at the far frontier of northern Asia?

RUSSIANS IN SIBERIA

The meetings between the Russians and the British occurred in two related contexts: the European search for northern maritime routes to Asia and the Russian eastward expansion. The first placed Russia in the middle of international politics; the second was essentially an internal affair, rooted in the history of the country's opposition to the remnants of Tatar-Mongolian invasions and its exploitation of Siberia's natural resources. The beginning of both developments preceded Cook's voyages by two centuries, going back to the time of Ivan IV (the "Terrible"), the first Russian czar whose full title included "lord of all northern shores and all Siberian lands."[6]

It was during his reign that a group of opportunistic British merchants attempted to find the Northeast Passage, a shortcut to China along the northern coast of the Eurasian continent. With the backing of the King Edward VI, three ships sailed northeast from England in 1552. Two of them, under the command of Hugh Willoughby, reached Novaya Zemlya, but all those aboard perished during the difficult Arctic winter. The third ship, commanded by Richard Chancellor, was stopped by ice at the mouth of the Dvina River near the Russian city of Arkhangel'sk. Unable to push farther east, Chancellor entered into a profitable arrangement with the Russian czar and established the Muscovy Company, which thereafter served both as a trading company and an important diplomatic link between Russia and England, providing shipping from and to Russia via the White Sea.[7]

The search for the Northeast Passage continued with slow but persistent progress. By the seventeenth century a continuous sea route was established as far as the Yamal Peninsula, but the ice-choked waters around Taimyr proved impassable for European ships. The regions beyond Taimyr did not, however, remain unexplored. Russian military units and traders reached the northern regions of east Siberia by the middle of the seventeenth century, but theirs was an overland journey by foot and rivers, with only occasional coastal voyages. By the 1640s Russians had reached both the East Siberian Sea in the north and the north Pacific in the east. The discovery of these seas, however, did not have any immediate effect on the general pattern of Russian colonization in the region. Although, as one historian puts it, "the Russian drive across the Urals to the Pacific was a convulsive process propelled by many pressures and forces that varied in purpose, skill, intensity and duration,"[8] the main goals were the annexation of new lands and the collection of furs. The standard mode of operation included building a small fort and forcing the local indigenous people to pay taxes (*yasak*) in furs, predominantly sables. As the physical limit of the continent, the sea was initially viewed not as a source of further opportunity but as the terminus of profit.

By contrast, rivers were transportation arteries, providing inland routes for watercraft in the summer and sleds in winter. Even the first Russian voyage through the Bering Strait was motivated by the search for the entrance to the Anadyr River. In 1648 the Cossack Semyon Dezhnev sailed eastward from the mouth of the Kolyma River, rounded the Chukotka Peninsula, and entered the Anadyr River, becoming the first non-Native mariner to sail through the Bering Strait.[9] Once reported to the authorities, Dezhnev's discovery was incorporated into a series of maps published both in Russia and abroad, including the 1690 map of Siberia by the Dutch cartographer Nicolaas Witsen.[10] Witsen's map confirmed the idea that Asia and America were separated by water and played an important role in the European search for the Northwest Passage.

Dezhnev's voyage had a very different meaning for the history of Siberia. Despite frequent attempts,[11] his sea voyage remained unrepeated for centuries to come, but the fort of Anadyrsk, which he established 750 kilometers inland on the upper Anadyr River, and the land route connecting it with the Russian settlements on the Kolyma, provided footholds for the colonization and exploration of interior Chukotka and Kamchatka.[12] While the attention of other European powers was turning to northern ocean passages, Russia was more concerned with inland resources and transportation routes connecting its subarctic regions. Between 1581 and 1740 the Russian crown added 10 million square kilometers (3.9 million square miles) to its territory and founded several dozen Siberian settlements, but only three of them were located on the coast.

Once called the country's "late" and "lame" approach to the exploration in the north Pacific,[13] this situation in reality demonstrated a careful strategy of investment geared toward a guaranteed return from land resources. Unlike many European countries, Russia did not have to reach overseas in order to expand. Vast territories east of the Ural Mountains had all the lure of the New World: land, forests rich with fur-bearing animals, legends of golden rivers and silver mountains, and indigenous people incapable of resisting Russian weapons. Siberian furs were the major factor behind state and private expansion until the beginning of the eighteenth century, but other resources were also actively and successfully sought. Copper and iron deposits were discovered in the 1660s in the Yenisei region. Silver was found on the eastern slopes of the Ural Mountains, in Nerchinsk, and in the Argun River basin.[14] The first century of Siberian exploration brought riches to the Russian Empire comparable to those Spain found in the New World in the sixteenth century, but without the perils of the seagoing expeditions.

As the Russian Empire expanded toward the Arctic coasts, it reassessed the reasons for colonizing Siberia. This treeless region lacked sables and provided no land-animal furs beyond modest quantities of fox pelts. A substitute was soon found in walrus ivory—"walrus tooth," as Russian documents refer to it—which quickly became a new currency of Siberian taxation and trade. In Yakutsk, one pound of walrus ivory was valued at 226 rubles, the equivalent of one sable skin.[15] Russians obtained walrus ivory through hunting, trade and, when they could manage it, taxation of indigenous peoples. The Chukchi, the native people of Chukotka, ferociously opposed Russian taxation. The interactions between them and the Russians were a complicated network of trade, warfare, and intermarriage, and often depended on relationships between specific Russian officials and tribal leaders.[16] Military conflicts raged in the region from 1649 until 1778, when the Russian commander of the Gizhiginsk fortress, Timofei Shmalev, with the help of a Chukchi interpreter, Nikita Daurkin, reached a peace agreement with Chukchi leaders.[17] Coincidentally, Cook's landing in Chukotka took place in August of the same year.

The influence of the relationship with the Chukchi on the history of early Russian exploration of the Bering Strait is a fascinating and understudied subject. The Russians gained much of their knowledge of the Bering Strait directly from their attempts to either subjugate or avoid these fiercely independent people. As experienced mariners, the Chukchi understood the strategic importance of maritime transportation and repeatedly destroyed the ships of early Russian explorers. Their hostility made wintering off the Chukotka coast impossible for Russian ships, which in turn significantly shortened the navigation season for the early eighteenth-century explorers attempting to sail across Bering Strait. Bering's decision to look for the coast of North America in the southeast during his second voyage to North America was probably influenced by his desire to avoid the dangerous and unstable Chukotka. At the same time, Chukchi knowledge of the lands and people of North America fostered Russian voyages across Bering Strait, and the Chukchi ability to navigate these northern waters was recognized and admired (fig. 4.1).

In 1745 Georg Steller, the famed naturalist on Bering's second voyage, commenting on the

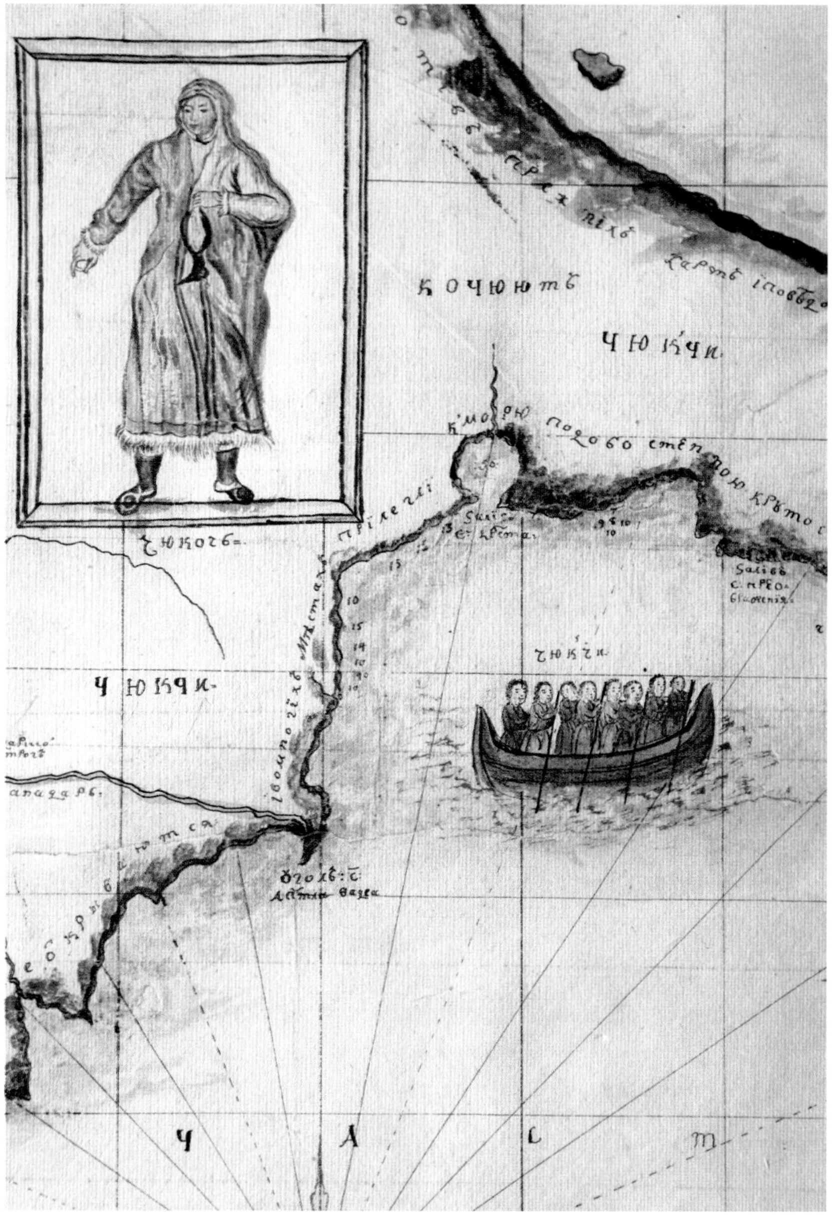

4.1 Detail from a map of northern Siberia to Yakutsk, Kamchatka, and the Asian side of Bering Strait, 1752, with images of Yakut, Tungus, Koryak, Kamchadal, Kuril, and Chukchi peoples. This is one of several versions of a map produced after the first Kamchatka expedition and one of the first depictions of Chukchi people. The captions identify two Chukchi groups, nomadic and maritime. The male figure gives a fairly realistic representation of traditional Chukchi attire. The paddlers in the boat are also identified as Chukchi, but their outfits and the boat itself, which looks like a plank boat instead of a skin-covered umiak, are not representative of Chukchi material culture but rather reminiscent of the traditional depiction of watercraft in medieval Russian manuscripts. State Historical Museum, Moscow, GO 1882/2.

proximity of the Asian and American shores in the Bering Strait region, wrote, "One would long ago have learned this if the pluck and curiosity of the seafarers in their large vessels had been as great as the clamor and courage of the Chukchi, who row from one part to the other in their baidaras and skiffs."[18] Rumors of Chukchi accounts about the land across the strait reached the maritime-minded czar Peter the Great and were a factor in his decision to launch the first state-sponsored expedition to North America.

In 1711 Petr Popov, a Cossack sent to collect taxes from the Chukchi, was entrusted with the difficult task to "find out about the adjacent islands and people inhabiting them." Popov acquired most of his information from Makachkin, a Native of the Chukotka Peninsula. According to Makachkin, a large island that the Chukchi called the "Great Land" was located due east from Anadyrsky Nos and could be reached in one day of traveling either in boats during the summer or by reindeer sledges in winter. This land reportedly abounded with fur-bearing animals, and it was inhabited by people with ivory "teeth" inserted in their cheeks, with whom the Chukchi were at war.[19] Some of this information was reflected in the map compiled in 1711–14 by the Yakutsk nobleman Ivan Lvov. Together with the 1700 "Draft of Kamchadal land," by S. U. Remizov, this is one of the earliest maps depicting the land across the Bering Strait. Although based on the actual voyages of Native seafarers, it reflects Alaska as an island, a misconception that circulated in different charts and maps, including Staehlin's fantastical map, which Cook carried on his voyage to the north Pacific (fig. 2.6). Interestingly, Lvov's map also shows an open sea route along the northern coast of Asia, encouraging hopes for a Northeast Passage.[20]

EIGHTEENTH-CENTURY RUSSIAN VOYAGES IN THE BERING STRAIT AND THE NORTH PACIFIC

The systematic maritime exploration and mapping of Russia's newly acquired eastern coasts began during the reign of Czar Peter I. By his order, the geodesists Ivan Evreinov and Fedor Luzhin charted the Kamchatka Peninsula and the Kuril Islands in 1719. Surprisingly, their instructions also contained the instruction to locate American coasts, which they did not find.[21] Contrary to popular belief, the first Russian voyage of exploration with the sole purpose of reaching North America was not Vitus Bering's 1728 expedition. In 1720, the Anadyrsk navigator Prokopii Nagibin, who had been inspired by stories about the "Great Land," requested two hundred servicemen and funds for a voyage. Although his request was rejected, Nagibin built a ship at his own expense and embarked on the voyage in 1725. He was attacked and killed by Chukchi warriors while sailing down the Anadyr River before reaching the ocean. A similar private attempt was undertaken in 1728 by Afanasii Melnikov. Melnikov's ship was crushed by sea ice, and it took the survivors a year to get back to Anadyrsk.[22]

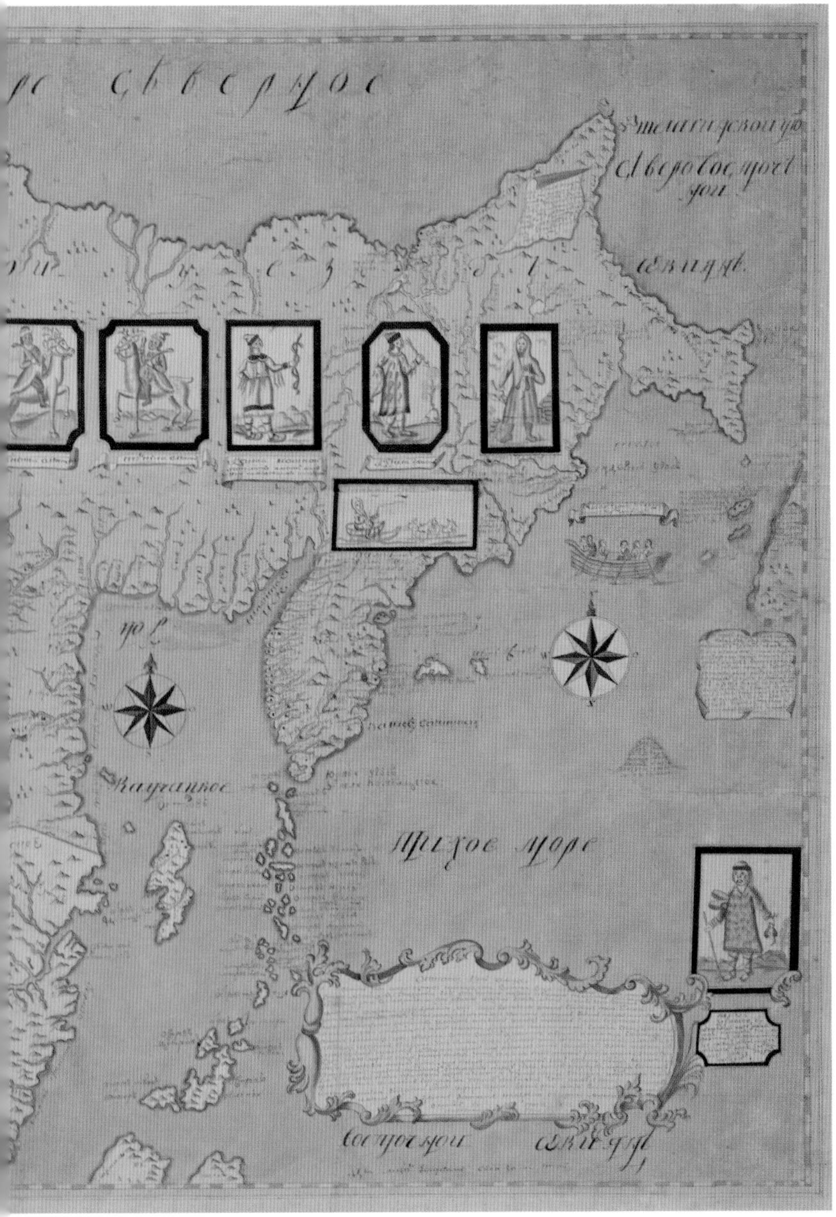

4.2 Detail of an ethnographic variant of the final map from the Kamchatka expedition of 1728. This section of a much larger map of Siberia depicts Chukotka and Kamchatka with the native peoples inhabiting these regions. In addition to its interesting ethnographic images, the map contains detailed place-name information. State Historical Museum, Moscow, GO 7712.

By this time, the first state-sponsored expedition toward the "Great Land" was under way. The narrative of the first and the second Kamchatka expeditions under the command of Vitus Bering is one of the best-known episodes of Russian exploration in the Far East. Less well-known is the fact that Bering's first expedition was initially conceived as a voyage around the world. The czar wanted to dispatch ships from St. Petersburg around Cape Horn to the north Pacific, combining a grand circumnavigation with exploration of the ocean north and east of Kamchatka, which would also have improved the training of Russian mariners.[23] Had such an undertaking been successful, the history of the north Pacific might have been very different. But plans changed, and Bering was instead sent on a grueling, twenty-month-long overland journey to Okhotsk. From there he sailed to Bolsheretsk, where the sixty-foot long *St. Gabriel* was built for the voyage.

On June 13, 1728, the *St. Gabriel* headed northeast in search of the American coast. The expedition sighted St. Lawrence Island and then on August 16 reached 67°24'N, significantly north of what is now known as the Bering Strait. Fearing the approach of winter, and surrounded by fog and ice, Bering turned back. The expedition failed to achieve its major goals: the American coast was not even sighted, much less mapped. However, on the basis of observed ocean depths, driftwood, and seabird routes, Bering was certain that the coast was near.[24] The voyage map, compiled by the midshipman

Peter Chaplin, presented interesting information on Siberian geography along with some of the earliest images of Siberian Native people (fig. 4.2). The map, however, offered little information about the geography of the Bering Strait beyond suggesting the location of Big Diomede Island.[25]

As Bering was returning from his voyage, another expedition sailed north. Three ships and four hundred soldiers were dispatched under the command of the Cossack Afanasi Shestakov and his assistant, Dmitri Pavlutski, to "subjugate the warlike tribes," discover new lands, and bring their population under the Russian Crown.[26] In essence, this was a military assault against the Koryaks (the Native population of Kamchatka) and the Chukchi. In 1731, during one of the battles, Pavlutski captured some "Americans"—Alaska natives, likely captured by Chukchi during one of their raids—which inspired him to send one of his ships across the Bering Strait "to learn more about this distant land and to find and tax the ones that had not previously been taxed." This was Bering's ship, the *St. Gabriel.* Initially the command of the ship was entrusted to Ivan Fedorov, but it was passed to the geodesist Mikhail Gvozdev when Fedorov was overcome by scurvy. Sailing east from Cape Dezhnev, Gvozdev visited Big Diomede Island, discovered Little Diomede and King Islands, and anchored near Cape Prince of Wales, becoming the first explorer to visit continental Alaska.[27]

In the meantime, Bering had returned to St. Petersburg, where a second attempt to discover the American coast was approved as a part of a grand mapping expedition of the far reaches of the Asian coastline. In preparation for the second Kamchatka expedition, the issue of a potential round-the-world voyage was raised and declined once again. This time, two ships, the *St. Peter* and the *St. Paul,* were built in the newly founded settlement of Petropavlovsk in Kamchatka and sailed for America in June 1741. Early in the voyage they separated in a storm and journeyed on independently. Alexei Chirikov, commander of the *St. Paul,* reached the Alexander Archipelago in Southeast Alaska in the vicinity of Takanis Bay, where he lost both of his ship's boats and fifteen crew members when they were sent for water on Yakobi Island. Without landing craft he had little choice but to return to Kamchatka, where he arrived in mid-October.[28]

Bering's first view of Alaska was of Mount St. Elias from the deck of the *St. Peter* on July 16, 1741. Four days later his ship anchored off Kayak Island, where the naturalist Georg Steller obtained the first scientific samples collected in Alaska. Within hours Bering set the vessel on a homeward course, but bad weather and the crew's deteriorating health forced the sailors to winter over on an uninhabited island where the ship was wrecked. During the following months Bering and another two dozen of the expedition's mariners lost their lives to scurvy. Today the island bears Bering's name, and the entire island group is named the Commander Islands in honor of the leader of the first and the second Kamchatka expeditions. The forty survivors built a small boat

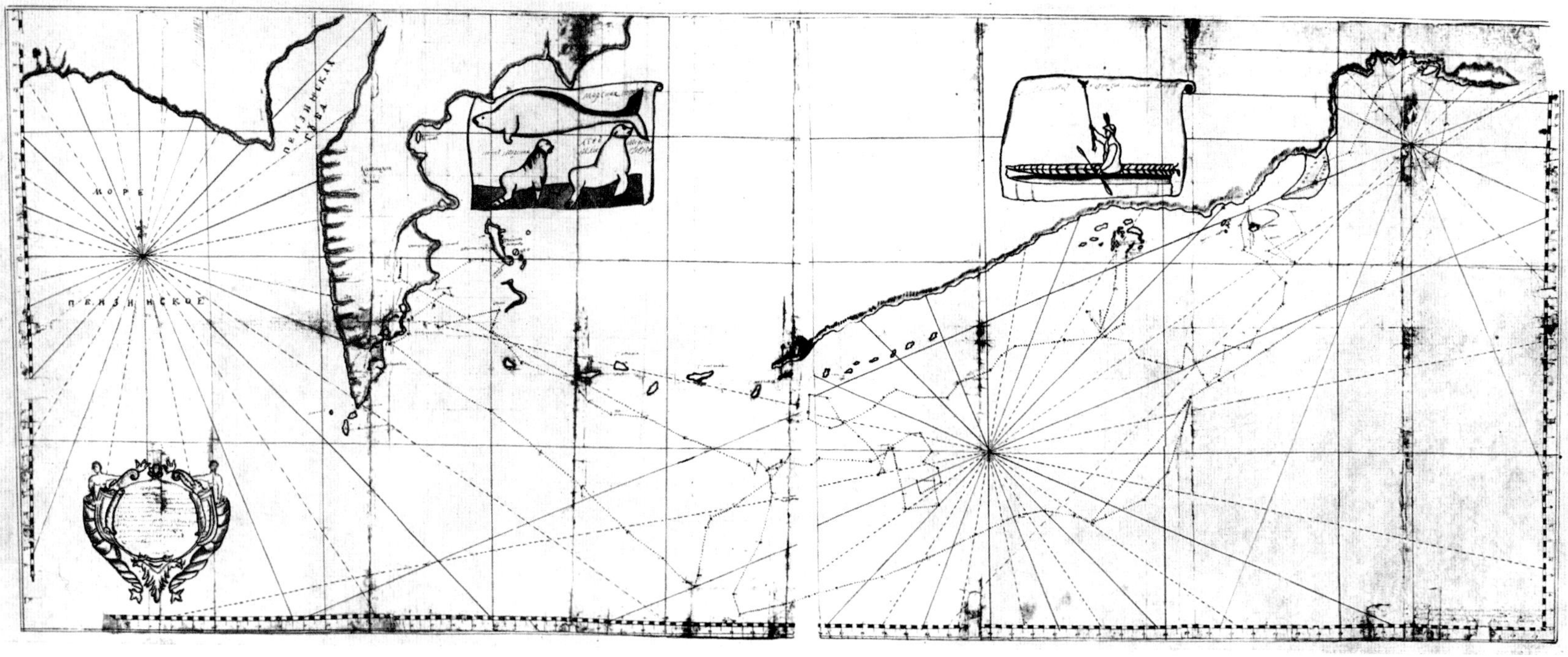

4.3 Sven Waxell, *Chart of the Voyage of the* St. Peter, 1744. From A. Efimov, *Atlas of Geographical Discoveries in Siberia and North-western America, XVII to XVIII Centuries* (Moscow, 1964), map 101. Waxell was fleet lieutenant on Bering's second voyage to North America in 1741. After Bering's death on the island that now bears his name, Waxell assumed the command of a ship built from the wreckage of the *St. Peter* and brought the expedition's survivors to the mainland. His chart, compiled in St. Petersburg from ships' logs and journals of the ships' officers, also features the first depiction of an Alaskan native, an Unangax̂ man in his kayak. Courtesy of Derek Hayes.

from the wreckage of the *St. Peter* and returned to Petropavlovsk in August 1742. They brought with them sea-otter pelts, which were to play a crucial role in promoting future Russian colonization of the Aleutian Islands and mainland Alaska (fig. 4.3). These Russian discoveries, along with information on the islands of Bering Strait and the American coast visited by Gvozdev, were later included in the 1758 map of the academician Gerhard Müller, one of two Russian maps that Cook had at his disposal during his third voyage (fig. 2.3).[29]

Despite Chirikov's expectation that another state-sponsored expedition to North America would soon follow, the new Russian empress, Elizabeth I, was not interested in the exploration of the north Pacific and Bering Sea. For the next twenty years, there were no government-supported voyages of exploration. Finally, in 1766, Captain Ivan Sindt sailed as far as St. Lawrence Island and discovered St. Matthew Island, but he did not succeed in reaching the American coast. According to the modern Russian scholar M. L. Belov, Sindt's map delineated Bering Strait "more precisely than Cook's charts,"[30] but neither the account of Sindt's voyage nor the map was made public. The "Historical Roster of Russian Voyages and Discoveries in the North-east

Sea," compiled in 1790, states that although it is known that Sindt reached islands between 60°N and 65°N, the detailed description of his voyage could not be found in the Irkutsk office.[31] In fact, both Sindt's map and his account were rediscovered by Belov only in the twentieth century.[32]

This lack of publicity for Sindt's voyage was likely a calculated measure, intended to conceal accurate information about the Alaskan coasts from potential rivals in the north Pacific, particularly Spain and Great Britain. By 1763 the Russian Admiralty was planning its own expedition in search of the Arctic Passage. The proposal, submitted by the famous Russian scientist and intellectual Mikhail Lomonosov, suggested either a northeastern route (via the East Siberian Sea and Bering Strait) or the northwestern passage (via Greenland and the northern margins of North America). Although the plan was criticized by such veterans of Arctic seafaring as Fedor Soimonov and Sven Waxell, who warned against the dangers of sea ice in the higher latitudes, the Admiralty went ahead with the idea.

The expedition consisted of two squadrons. The first, under the command of Vasilii Chichagov, was to sail west from the Kola Peninsula and negotiate the Northwest Passage. The other, headed by Petr Krenitsyn and Mikhail Levashov, was to depart from Okhotsk and sail along the Aleutian Chain. The squadrons were expected to meet in Unalaska and swap officers and crews, after which Krenitsyn and Levashov would return to Russia via the Northwest Passage and Greenland while Chichagov sailed to Kamchatka. Chichagov undertook two attempts to sail the westward Arctic routes in 1765 and 1766, and after reaching Spitsbergen, above 80°N, in the summer of 1766, he decided that the route was not feasible and returned to Russia.

Krenitsyn and Levashov sailed separately along the Aleutian Chain in 1768 with the main mission of charting the coasts and collecting information about the local population. Levashov reached the tip of the Alaska Peninsula, but after a difficult winter, the crew's declining health prevented further progress. Both ships returned to Kamchatka in 1769. Again, publication of any expedition materials was restricted, so the first detailed account of the voyage was not published until 1852.[33] Even today, Levashov's hand-drawn atlas has not been published in full. Intelligence about the Russian attempt to negotiate the Northwest Passage, however, reached Great Britain. According to Lydia Black, these efforts were to influence the British Admiralty in its decision to undertake Captain Cook's third voyage.[34]

Bering's voyages of 1728 and 1741, Sindt's exploration of 1764, and Krenitsyn and Levashov's voyage of 1768 were all government-sponsored expeditions, planned by state officials, equipped with European-style ships and navigational instruments, and executed according to detailed instructions. The early exploration of the Aleutian Islands, however, had a very different character. Following the second Bering expedition, the high price of sea-otter pelts in China prompted a wave of short-lived merchant companies, formed with the sole purpose of "enriching themselves through sea otter skins."[35] Between 1743 and 1800, more than forty companies built about eighty ships for voyages to the Aleutian Islands. At first these were not formally incorporated companies but rather groups of people who put their capital together to equip an expedition in the hope of significant returns. Participants were issued shares proportional to their investment and role in the expedition. If the voyage was successful, profits were distributed after the sale of furs. Usually shareholders participated in both shipbuilding and the voyage itself, often serving as ship's carpenters, sailors, hunters, and merchants. In the Russian Far East, these people became known as *promyshlenniki.* They were not a homogenous group. Many came from settlements in eastern and northern Siberia and thus had an understanding of local seafaring.[36] Most were free citizens, but a few were serfs making profits for their noble owners.[37] In addition, Siberian Natives, commonly referred to as Kamchadales, were also often a part of the ship's crews, but the terms and conditions of their engagement are rarely specified in the surviving documents.

The sea-otter hunt was initially conducted in the Near Islands, but the growing number of companies prompted rapid expansion, and by the 1760s, *promyshlenniki* reached as far as the Fox Islands, halfway to the Alaska coast. Once they reached their destination, the hunters would usually stay on the islands for a year, acquiring furs through both trade and forced labor, well within the Siberian expansion paradigm. Unlike the Cossacks' exploits in Siberia, these voyages received no aid from the state. So sharp was the distinction between state-sponsored and privately sponsored journeys in the Bering Sea that when in 1747 the survivors of the merchant vessel *Perkup i Zant,* which wrecked on Bering Island, used the remains of Vitus Bering's ship to build a new vessel, the state authority of Kamchatka confiscated the ship immediately after the crew's return on the grounds that Bering's ship had been funded by the Crown.[38] Despite this, the state exercised a certain amount of control over the Aleutian trading voyages, since each venture had to apply for a state permit to sail to the Aleutians prior to departure and was required to submit an official report upon return. The quantity of pelts collected, along with a list of Native "taxpayers" from each location, was recorded, and a certain percentage of profit was withdrawn in the name of the Crown. The document that the Unangax̂ kayaker delivered to Cook's *Discovery* off Unga Island in 1778 was likely a tax receipt that *promyshlenniki* had issued to the local people of the Shumagin Islands.

The Russian Far East in the second half of the eighteenth century was a classic frontier, a place where the lack of state control and unclear borders left considerable room for personal ambitions and undertakings; where different classes and ethnicities mingled uneasily, and personalities mattered; where the backbone of power was still soft and the wounds of initial colonial encounters still fresh. Like a penciled-in chart, the Russian Far East was present but undefined. Into this mix came Cook and his companions in 1778 and 1779.

CAPTAIN COOK IN CHUKOTKA, AUGUST 1778

Prompted by bad weather and flawed maps, Cook's first venture along the Russian Far East frontier was unintentional. In the beginning of August 1778, the *Resolution* and the *Discovery* left the waters of the Alaskan coast and sailed toward Bering Strait. Despite several earlier Russian expeditions, it was still a region of geographic speculation. A number of features, such as St. Lawrence Island (discovered and named by Vitus Bering fifty years earlier) and King Island (mapped by the Russian navigators Gvozdev and Fedorov in 1732), were absent from both Müller's and Staehlin's charts. Consequently, they were "rediscovered" by Cook. On August 8, Cook sighted a cape on the Alaska coastline, which Müller's map identified as "Coast Discovered by surveyor Gvozdev in 1730." Cook's decision to name this previously discovered land Cape Prince of Wales was not well received in Russia, but the name has remained on the map.[39] Storm and mist forced the ships west of the cape to the Asian side of the strait, and after two days at sea, the *Resolution* and the *Discovery* reached a large bay with an "Indian village."[40] According to Staehlin's map, this should have been the "Island of Alaschka" lying between North America and Russia. Müller's map, however, showed no such land. To resolve these conflicting messages, Cook decided to visit the village.

4.4 John Webber, *Captain Cook Meeting with the Chukchi at St. Lawrence Bay,* 1778. Pencil, pen, and wash, and traces of watercolor. One of six surviving drawings from the historic encounter on the Asian side of the Bering Sea. The visitors are shown watching a dance after their landing at the village of Nunyamo on August 10. Cook noted that the Chukchi refused to trade anything for their spears or bows, which they "held in constant readiness, never once quitting them, excepting . . . four or five laid them down while they gave us a song and a dance." This is an example of Webber's illustrations of key events in Cook's journal. © National Maritime Museum, Greenwich, London, PT2965.

The arrival of the ships sent people of the village "into some confusion or fear." All women, children, and the elderly had retreated inland, and forty or fifty armed men were assembled on the shore. Captain Cook dispatched three armed boats, and he himself went ashore with some officers. The initial reception was tense. David Samwell, surgeon's mate aboard the *Resolution,* reports that a line was drawn on the shore "from one Jaw bone of a whale stuck in the ground to another, and which seemed to have been set up as a boundary between them and our people." The beach was also apparently covered with a great number of dogs that had been killed, "perhaps as an Offering to their Gods to implore their Assistance in defence of their country, which they must have supposed we were going to invade."[41] As the boats drew near the shore, "an old man" with two companions stepped forward and "were so polite as to take off their caps and make a low bow."[42] Cook presented the old man, who he guessed was the leader, with a bead necklace, and received in return a couple of walrus tusks and two fox skins. In return for knives, beads, and tobacco, the Natives brought forward some items of clothing—walrus ivory carvings, quivers, and arrows—but the warriors would not part with their spears and bows "for any considerations." Instead, one of the men demonstrated his archery skills by shooting a dog "at the distance of sixty yards." This show of military prowess was completed with a "warlike exercise which consisted of dancing to the beat of a drum." After a time, the British mariners were allowed into the village, and according to Cook's description, they even gained access to the interior of the houses (fig. 4.4).

Three hours spent among these people convinced Cook that they were not Native Americans but rather inhabitants of Chukotka, on the Asian side of Bering Strait. Both Cook and Samwell remarked that although their boats and bows appeared to be similar, their personal adornments and especially their physical appearance were very different from those of "the Americans." Cook wrote: "All the Americans we had seen before were rather low of stature with round chubby faces and high cheek bones, whereas these are long-visaged stout made men and appeared to be quite a different Nation."[43] Furthermore, the presence of metal spears, the use of tobacco, and the "polite" way in which the men greeted the Englishmen by removing their hats and bowing implied previous contact with Russians. Satisfied with the newly obtained information and the "show of kindness" they delivered to these Native people, Cook and his men returned to the ships.[44]

Unknown to Cook and his company, the inhabitants of the village also "identified" their visitors. In the Chukchi experience, people arriving on large ships and armed with firearms could only be Russians. The offering of walrus ivory was one of the standard currencies of Russian taxation in Chukotka, so the initial response to Cook reinforces the Chukchi interpretation of the ship's visit to their village as a Russian encounter.[45] In an interesting twist to the story, James King turned this mistaken identity into a boastful view of British superiority. According to an account he later received from the governor of Kamchatka, Magnus von Behm, after the 1778 meeting with Cook, a party of the Chukchi arrived at Gizhiginsk, the Russian fort in Chukotka, with proposals of friendship and a voluntary offer of tribute. When asked what caused their sudden peaceful intentions, the Natives explained that "toward the latter end of last summer they had been visited by two very large Russian boats, that they had been treated by the people, who were in them, with the greatest kindness, and had entered into a league of friendship and amity with them; and that relying on this friendly disposition, they now come to the Russian fort, in order to settle a treaty."[46] Since the boats could only have been the *Resolution* and the *Discovery*, King expressed great satisfaction "in having, though accidentally, shewn the Russians true way of collecting tribute, and extending their dominions; and in the hopes that the good understanding, which this event have given rise to may rescue a brave people from the future invasions of such powerful neighbors."[47]

Although we may doubt King's self-satisfied statement that a single moment of amicable trade with two presumed Russian ships had remedied a century of fighting, Russian sources suggest that Cook's visit to Chukotka did help precipitate a change in the Chukchis' status in the Russian Empire. Two important Chukchi leaders, Omylyat Khergyntov and Aoetkin Chymkychyn, had indeed visited the Gizhiginsk fortress in 1778 and signed a peace treaty with the commandant, Timofei Shmalev.[48] This had nothing to do with Cook's 1778 visit but was rather the result of Shmalev's continuous efforts to maintain a peaceful relationship with the Chukchi. Commandant of the fortress since 1776, Shmalev had implemented a policy of fairness and dialogue drastically different from his predecessors' oppressive regime. One of the principal outcomes was the release of Chukchi captives captured by his predecessor three years earlier.[49]

At about the same time, and perhaps even from the same Chukchi leaders, Shmalev had received intelligence about two ships that had visited Chukotka. It is possible that his report to Behm included information about both the peace treaty and the two mystery ships. Behm, in turn, could have mentioned both in his conversation with King, laying the foundation for King's fanciful story. The story, however, did not end there. Making its way through multiple steps of the Russian hierarchy, the account of a treaty with the Chukchi and the mystery ships reached the State Council in St. Petersburg. In September 1779, Duke Vyazemski reported to the council that he had received a letter from the governor of Irkutsk describing a "Chukchi request to become citizens of the Russian Empire, their desire to pay taxes and send hostages to Anadyrsk, and of two ships, which they took for ours." Vyazemski conveyed to the council that Empress Catherine II graciously accepted these people under her rule and, taking into consideration recent epidemics and decline of reindeer herds, excused them from paying taxes for the next ten years. Regarding the ships, Catherine suggested that they might have belonged to the United States of America and ordered that, in case of future visits, the Russian imperial coat of arms should be sent to the Chukchi, "to be displayed on trees in the convenient places along their shores to inform people disembarking from those ships that these lands belong to the Russian empire."[50]

Evidentially, the main reason for accepting the Chukchi as Russian citizens was to solidify Russia's standing in Chukotka in the eyes of potential foreign seafarers. Ironically, therefore, Cook's brief visit to

Chukotka had a truly historic outcome. As a result of the almost comical twist of mistaken identity, Cook's short landing transformed Chukotka—at least theoretically—from an obscure frontier into the official northeastern border of the Russian Empire, marked with proper state insignia and inhabited by Russian citizens. In essence, Catherine's order was a political gesture, designed to set limits for international powers. The directive to hang the Russian coat of arms on trees along the characteristically treeless coast of Chukotka reveals a total lack of understanding of not only the historical but also the physical realities of this region. As a result, most of the decrees existed only on paper. The only Russian coats of arms in the region were those on the walls and buildings of Russian forts, and many Chukchi tribes resisted Russian sovereignty well into the nineteenth century. Nonetheless, Catherine's orders marked the beginning of a new era in the history of the Russian Far East, which was now seen not only as an integral part of the Russian state but also as a place of international importance. Peculiarly, all these changes had been set in motion before Cook's first actual meeting with the Russians.

CAPTAIN COOK ON UNALASKA ISLAND, OCTOBER 1778

Two months after visiting Chukotka, Cook anchored in Samgoonoodha Bay on Unalaska Island. Once again, the stopover was unplanned: the *Resolution* had sprung a leak, and Captain Cook needed a convenient harbor for repairs. Samgoonoodha (now called English Bay), where the British remembered staying for three days on their northbound route, offered an ideal anchorage. Although Cook was aware of the Russian presence on Unalaska during his first visit in June, he did not meet any Russians until this second visit. On October 8, a local Unangax̂ man, Derramoushk, presented Cook with a salmon pie, accompanied by a note in Russian. Unable to read it, Cook dispatched the American corporal John Ledyard to go with Derramoushk "to gain some further information." Two days later Ledyard returned with "three Russian Seamen or Furriers."[51] All three were likely from the *St. Paul,* a ship belonging to the merchants Orekhov, Lapin, and Shilov, "the luckiest of all the Siberian Argonauts."[52] This was the ship's third voyage to the Aleutians, this time under the command of the experienced skipper Gerasim Gregorievich Izmailov,[53] who paid Cook a visit on October 14. Two additional Russian ships, the *St. Vladimir,* which belonged to the same merchants, and the *St. Evpl,* owned by the Vologda merchant Fiodor Burenin, were at the time anchored off nearby Umnak Island.[54] The skipper of the latter, Yakov Ivanovich Sapozhnikov, impressed Cook with his modesty and moderation and later carried the British captain's correspondence to Bolsheretsk, whence it was ultimately transported to London.

Cook found the Russians intelligent and "very ready" to give him all the information he desired.[55] Sharing no common language, but plenty of tea and brandy, they traded information about the whereabouts of different landmarks as well as stories of their adventures. Cook was particularly interested in Russian knowledge of the American coast, the discoveries of Sindt in the Bering Strait, and the extent of the Russian presence in the Aleutians. To satisfy his interest, the well-informed Izmailov, who had been a participant in the Sindt and the Krenitsyn-Levashov expeditions, allowed him to copy two hand-drawn charts. One was supposedly drawn by the naval captain "Wawselee Irkeechoff" and included Kamchatka, the Sea of Okhotsk, the Amur River, Japan, and the Kuril Islands. The second was a chart of the Aleutian Chain, the Alaska Peninsula, and Kodiak Island.

The first chart remains a mystery. The roster of the Russian naval staff for the eighteenth century does not mention "Irkeechoff" or anybody with a similar last name.[56] The description of geographical landmarks is, however, consistent with the map compiled by Ivan Evreinov in 1711, and it is possible that "Irkeechoff" is an attempted transliteration of Evreinov's name. The second chart could have been a chart prepared by Potap Zaikov, skipper of the *St. Vladimir.* He had just returned to Umnak from the Alaska Peninsula, where he had spent three years trapping and conducting topographic surveys. According to Vasilii Berkh, "Skipper Zaikov's chart was the first to give Siberian navigators the true position of the Aleutian Islands."[57]

A keen observer, Cook reached several perceptive conclusions. First, it was evident to him that although the Russian drive across the Aleutians was almost exclusively a private initiative by independent merchants, Russians had a strong hold on the islands. This might explain his lack of any interest in surveying the chain. Second, he became convinced that "no Russian had ever seen any part of the continent to the northward, excepting that part lying opposite the country of the Tchuktschis."[58] And finally, he recorded his growing distrust in Staehlin's map, which he pronounced "a Map that the most illiterate of his illiterate Sea-faring men would have been ashamed to put his name to."[59]

Cook's conversation with Sapozhnikov also convinced him not to spend the winter in Petropavlovsk, which did not appear to be a place where he could obtain necessary supplies and provisions and where he would also be forced to "lay inactive for Six or Seven Months."[60] The visit to Kamchatka was thus postponed until the next year, and on October 26 the *Resolution* and the *Discovery* put to sea, heading to Hawai'i for the winter. Before leaving Unalaska, Cook entrusted to Izmailov's care a letter to the Admiralty, including a chart of all the northern coasts he had visited.[61] In turn, Izmailov gave Cook a letter of introduction to the governor of Kamchatka, Magnus von Behm (fig. 4.5).

Albeit short and informal, Cook's encounter with the Russians in Unalaska was historically significant. Although it was in essence a mariners' exchange, where politics came second to the camaraderie of sailing in uncharted waters, it was nevertheless the first time that representatives of two

4.5 John Webber, *Major Behm,* 1779. Webber drew this portrait of Magnus von Behm, governor of Kamchatka, aboard the *Discovery* when Behm dined with its captain, John Gore, on May 23. Behm was born in Livonia and had an illustrious military career prior to his appointment to Kamchatka. His jurisdiction also included the Izhiginsk region and the Kuril and Aleutian Islands. Behm was at the end of his term when *Resolution* and *Discovery* arrived in Petropavlovsk on their first visit in the spring of 1779, and he generously provided supplies and provisions. Captain Charles Clerke entrusted him with the delivery of charts and reports to St. Petersburg, from where they were forwarded to London. Dixson Library, State Library of New South Wales, Q 77/37.

4.6 John Webber, *A View of St. Peter & St. Paul* (Petropavlovsk), circa 1781–83. Pen, wash, and watercolor. The artist prepared this painting for the engraver from a number of earlier sketches when he was back home in London. It was then published in 1784 as plate 74 in volume 3 of Cook, *A Voyage to the Pacific Ocean.* The little settlement of Petropavlovsk was founded by Vitus Bering in 1740. In 1778 it was Russia's second largest port on the north Pacific, after the seventeenth-century town of Okhotsk. Webber's panorama shows the wide sweep of Avacha Bay with the towering volcanic peak of Viliuchinsky in the distance. Dixson Library, State Library of New South Wales, PXX 2.41.

European countries had discussed their experience in the north Pacific. More important, the almost casual exchange of information and charts marked the beginning of the region's transformation from a natural environment, with its bays, cliffs, and islands, into a political landscape, a chart of economic possibilities and clashing colonial ambitions. In the three weeks they spent in Unalaska, British mariners received not only firsthand accounts of Russian geographical knowledge of the region but also a demonstration of effective fur extraction and a synopsis of Russian interaction with the Native peoples. Soon all of this knowledge would become very useful in organizing British trade along the north Pacific coasts of America.

VISIT TO PETROPAVLOVSK, 1779

The final set of meetings between Russians and the crews of the *Resolution* and the *Discovery* took place in the wake of Cook's death in Hawai'i. Following his plans to return to the Arctic for a second

4.7 Johann Eckstein and Joseph Constantine Stadler, *The Departure of Gore and King from Bolsheretsk with Governor Behm on May 16, 1779,* colored aquatint etching, circa 1780. Gore and King, along with Webber, whose facility in German made effective communication with Behm possible, had crossed the Kamchatka Peninsula from Petropavlovsk to visit the governor. They were treated with the utmost hospitality before Behm accompanied them back to the ships to meet Captain Charles Clerke. King wrote of their raucous send-off, with drums and "people singing . . . a song which the Major told us was a favorite one of the Russian people in taking leave of their friends." © National Maritime Museum, Greenwich, London, A9900.

attempt to find a passage, Clerke, who assumed command of the expedition, brought the ships to Avacha Bay on April 29, 1779 (fig. 4.6). The bay was still under ice, and Clerke dispatched Lieutenant James King and the expedition artist John Webber to the shore with the dubious honor of "opening some communications." In sharp contrast with the reception they received in Unalaska, once King and Webber had crossed the perilous ice, they were met by fifteen armed Russians. Finding themselves once again "miserably unintelligible to each other," they delivered Izmailov's letters and communicated their peaceful intentions and desire to acquire provisions and supplies for their ships and crew.

This initial contact was followed by an invitation to visit the governor of Kamchatka, Magnus von Behm, in his headquarters in Bolsheretsk. Clerke, severely affected by tuberculosis and unable to travel, sent in his stead the captain of the *Discovery,* John Gore, along with King and Webber. Webber's command of German proved to be the only means of effective communication with the Russian. Travel-

4.8 John Webber, *Woman of Kamchatka,* drawing, 1779(?). The woman is dressed in a traditional Russian peasant dress, which makes it difficult to establish her ethnicity. Russian goods and traditions were widespread by the time the expedition visited Siberia. The drawing may have been done on May 8, 1779, in the nearby *ostrog* (fort) of Karatchin, where Gore, King, and Webber were "received by the Kamskadales men & women . . . drest out in their best, & the womens dress was very pretty. . . . The Married women had handsome Silk Handkerchiefs bound round their heads." Captain Cook Memorial Museum, Whitby, UK, C10323.

ing by sled and river rafts, the three British seamen reached the capital of Russian Kamchatka, where they received a warm welcome from Behm. Not only did he pledge to supply the Englishmen with all they requested, but he also refused to accept any payment. Behm entertained his guests with dinners in his house, Kamchadal dancing, and even a ball, which King called "an enchanted scene in the midst of the wildest and most dreary country."[62] After the initial celebrations, the governor joined the Englishmen on their return to Petropavlovsk to meet Clerke (fig. 4.7).

By June 7, 1779, the ships had received 1,800 pounds of rye flour and twenty head of cattle, along with naval stores and 400 pounds of tobacco.[63] The latter pleased the sailors so much that they volunteered to shorten their ration of rum in order to present some quantity of it to the Russians in return for their kindness. Clerke showed his personal appreciation by presenting Behm with a collection of artifacts from Oceania. Later, this ethnographic collection traveled to St. Petersburg and entered the Kunstkamera, the Russian Imperial Museum of Anthropology and Ethnography, where it can still be seen today.[64]

King also reported that Behm "very civilly" showed the Englishmen all the maps he had, but after comparing them to those from Izmailov and their own charts, they determined that they offered no new information.[65] A copy of all Cook's discoveries in America also ended up in the hands of the Russians, through rather mysterious circumstances. According to David Samwell, the expedition's astronomer "exchanged it" for a map of Kamchatka with surroundings.[66] Although Samwell was enraged, the event apparently went unnoticed, or ignored, by Clerke, who had already presented Behm with a simplified version of the British charts.[67] Behm was also entrusted with a package of charts and reports of the voyage, which he promised to deliver to the English ambassador in St. Petersburg.[68]

The ships left Petropavlovsk on June 9, heading north for their second attempt to find the Northwest and Northeast passages, only to find impassable sea ice in the Chukchi Sea. On August 24 they returned to the friendly Russian port, bearing the sad news that Clerke had died two days earlier. Clerke's final wish was to be buried in a church near Petropavlovsk, and a solemn ceremony ensued, involving all the crew and the local Russian soldiers, who marched in procession with the local priest.

Taking advantage of Russian assistance, the Englishmen stayed for seven weeks as they prepared the ships for the long voyage home. The "tedious" stay had little excitement beyond the romantic story of James Holloway, the drummer from the *Discovery,* who tried to desert for the sake of a Kamchadal woman "to whom he had been much attached" (fig. 4.8). The ship's master, Thomas Edgar, wrote, "This man had been long useless to us, from a swelling in his knee, which rendered him lame. Yet this made me more unwilling he should be left behind, to become a miserable burden both to the Russians and himself."[69] Holloway was reclaimed, and on October 10, the *Resolution* and the *Discovery* left Petropavlovsk, sailing from Russia with love, charts, and sea-otter pelts.

Cook's voyage continued to influence the Russian presence in the north Pacific. In 1780, while the *Resolution* and the *Discovery* were still on their way home, the Russian major Mikhail Tatarinov of the Irkutsk navigation school used Cook's and Russian charts to compile a comprehensive map of the north Pacific, Bering Sea, and Arctic Ocean.[70] This map, showing the tracks of Bering, Gvozdev, and Chirikov, was published a year earlier than the official versions of Cook's charts and accounts in London.[71] The Russians were also the first to put Cook's geographical discoveries to practical use. In 1783 three Russian ships hunting in the Fox Islands had a particularly poor catch. The skipper of one of these ships was Potap Zaikov, who had had the opportunity to see Cook's charts and hear from Cook's companions that they had discovered a large bay on the American coast that they called Prince William's Sound.[72] Following this lead, Zaikov reached the sound and became the first Russian *promyshlennik* to overwinter on mainland Alaska, a forerunner of the Russian colonization of the region.

The publication of Cook's charts and accounts provided European powers with a road map, or, to be more accurate, a chart of the economic possibilities in the north Pacific. The first British sea-otter trader, James Hanna, arrived on the Northwest Coast in 1785, and others soon followed. In 1786 the British snow *Lark*, under the command of Captain William Peters, put in to Petropavlovsk in preparation for a fur-trading voyage along the coast.[73] According to Lydia Black, Peters was particularly interested in arranging joint British-Russian trade.[74] For Russia, the arrival of the British traders meant the end of its uncontested presence in the region. The day of the publication of Captain Cook's third voyage journal was, in many ways, the day that the Bering Sea and north Pacific ceased to be Russia's internal affair. The empire was now in need of well-defined and protected eastern borders, and while Cook's visit to Chukotka in 1778 had already transformed the Russian Asian frontier into an international border, the status of the Aleutian Islands and mainland Alaska remained undefined. Cook's claims in Turnagain Arm and Prince William Sound alarmed the Russian Crown, and on December 22, 1786, Catherine II issued a decree that claimed exclusive rights to "all the American coast north of 55°21'," including all the islands along this coast, as well as the Aleutians and the Kuril Islands.[75] This was the first time that the Russian Crown had officially claimed the Aleutian Islands and mainland Alaska as its territory. Catherine's decree not only granted recognition to the private initiatives, but it also prompted more ambitious plans for permanent establishments in Alaska, which were carried through by the merchant Grigorii Shelikhov in the following decade.

Despite the escalation in international rivalry spurred by Cook's account, his unquestionable competence and the scientific results of the third voyage were much admired by the Russians.[76] The Russian Admiralty eagerly hired British mariners for its voyages of exploration, including Cook's former crew member Joseph Billings, who in 1785 was appointed the leader of a Russian geographical and astronomical expedition to eastern Asia, the Arctic, and the north Pacific. The most promising Russian naval cadets were now sent to England to train in the British navy, and in 1801 one such trainee, Urey Lisiansky, became the captain of the *Neva,* the first Russian ship to sail around the world. Accounts of the first and second Cook voyages were published in Russian in 1796, and the third voyage became available to Russian readers in 1805.[77] As often happens with such great undertakings, the effects of Cook's third voyage had a force and intensity that he could hardly have anticipated. For Russia, the meetings with Cook and his companions in 1778 and 1779 signaled the limits of its Far East frontier and fostered the formation of the country's international borders in both the north Pacific and the Arctic. Today, climate change and the consequent opening of the Northeast Passage are once again bringing Russia's Arctic border to the center of international attention.

NOTES

1 *The Journals of Captain James Cook on His Voyages of Discovery,* vol. 3, *The Voyage of the* Resolution *and* Discovery, *1776–1780,* ed. J. C. Beaglehole (Cambridge: Cambridge University Press for the Hakluyt Society, 1967), 383–84.

2 Ibid., ccxxii.

3 Yakov M. Svet and Svetlana G. Fedorova, "Captain Cook and the Russians," *Pacific Studies* 2, no. 1 (Fall 1978): 16–19.

4 Cook, *Voyage of the* Resolution *and* Discovery, ccxxiii.

5 Lydia Black, "The Question of Maps: Exploration of the Bering Sea in the Eighteenth Century," in *The Sea in Alaska's Past: Conference Proceedings,* History and Archaeology Publications Series no. 25 (Anchorage: Office of History and Archaeology, Alaska Division of Parks, 1979), 23–26.

6 Gerhard Friedrich Müller, *Istoriya Sibiri* (Moscow: Vostochnaya Literatura, 2005), 1:202.

7 Alexander Hyde, *The Frozen Zone and Its Explorers: A comprehensive history of voyages, travels, adventures, disasters, and discoveries in the Arctic regions, including recent German and Swedish expeditions; Captain Nare's English expedition; Prof. Nordenskiold's discovery of a northeast passage; the sailing of the Jeannette, etc.* (Hartford, CT: R. W. Bliss, 1880), 40–42.

8 Basil Dmytryshyn, "The Administration Apparatus of the Russian Colonies in Siberia and Northern Asia, 1581–1700," in *The History of Siberia from Russian Conquest to Revolution,* ed. Alan Wood (London: Routledge, 1991), 17.

9 Native oral lore, archaeological data, and historical sources indicate that indigenous peoples frequently sailed through the Bering Strait both before and after the Russian expansion into Siberia. See Don E. Dumond, *The Eskimos and Aleuts* (London: Thames and Hudson, 1977), 118; Christopher Koonooka, trans., *Ungipaqhlanga: Let Me Tell a Story; Legends of the Siberian Eskimos* (Fairbanks: Alaska Native Language Center, 2003), 144–46; Tom Lowenstein, *Ancient Land, Sacred Whale: The Inuit Hunt and Its Rituals* (New York: Farrar Straus and Giroux, 1993), 25–32.

10 M. L. Belov, *Russians in the Bering Strait,* trans. Katerina Solovjova (Anchorage, AK: White Stone Press, 2000), 28–29.

11 According to M. I. Belov, from 1633 to 1689, 177 voyages were undertaken in an attempt to sail between the mouths of the Anadyr and Kolyma Rivers. M. L. Belov, *Russkie Morekhody v Ledovitom i Tikhom Okeanakh* (Moscow-Leningrad: Glavsevmorput, 1952), 328–39.

12 James R. Gibson, "The Exploration of the Pacific Coast," in *North American Exploration*, vol. 2, *A Continent Defined*, ed. John Logan Allen (Lincoln: University of Nebraska Press, 1997), 332.

13 James R. Gibson, "A Notable Absence: The Lateness and Lameness of Russian Discovery and Exploration in the North Pacific, 1639–1803," in *From Maps to Metaphors: The Pacific World of George Vancouver*, ed. Robin Fischer and Hugh Johnston (Vancouver: UBC Press, 1993), 85–103.

14 G. Vernadsky, *A History of Russia*, vol. 5, *The Tsardom of Moscow, 1547–1682* (New Haven, CT: Yale University Press, 1943), 668–71.

15 I. S. Vdovin, *Ocherki Istorii i Etnografii Chukchei* (Moscow-Leningrad: Nauka, 1965), 103.

16 Andrei A. Znamenski, "'Vague Sense of Belonging to the Russian Empire': The Reindeer Chukchi Status in 19th Century Northern Siberia," *Arctic Anthropology* 36, nos. 1–2 (1999): 19–36.

17 Vdovin, *Ocherki Istorii i Etnografii Chukchei*, 137. On the role of Shmalev in Chukchee-Russian relations, see M. B. Grenader, "Poslednie Gody Deyatel'nosti T. I. Shmaleva," in *Letopis' Severa* 7 (1975): 93–94.

18 Georg Wilhelm Steller, *Steller's History of Kamchatka: Collected Information Concerning the History of Kamchatka, Its Peoples, Their Manners, Names, Lifestyle, and Various Customary Practices*, ed. Marvin W. Falk, trans. Margritt Engel and Karen Willmore (Fairbanks: University of Alaska Press, 2003), 191.

19 A. I. Timfeev, ed., *Pamyatniki Sibirskoi Istorii XVIII veka*, vol. 1, *1700–1713* (St. Petersburg, 1882), 458–59.

20 A. V. Efimov, *Is Istorii Velikih Gograficheskih Otkrytii* (Moscow: Nauka, 1971), 152–58.

21 Lydia T. Black, *Russians in Alaska, 1732–1867* (Fairbanks: University of Alaska Press, 2004), 22.

22 Efimov, *Is Istorii Velikih Gograficheskih Otkrytii*, 204–5.

23 N. N. Bolkhovitinov, *Istoriya Russkoi Ameriki, 1732–1867*, vol. 2, *Deyatel'nost' Rossiisko-Amerikanskoi kompanii, 1799–1825* (Moscow: Mezdunorodnye otnosheniya, 1999), 85.

24 Guillaume Delisle, "Memoir Presented to the Senate with Map Which Bering Used Going to America," in Frank A. Golder, *Russian Expansion on the Pacific, 1641–1850* (Cleveland, OH: Arthur H. Clark, 1914), 302–13.

25 M. I. Navrot, "Novyi Variant Itogovoi Karty Pervoi Kamchatskoi Ekspeditsii," in *Letopis' Severa* 5 (Moscow: Izdatel'stvo Mysl', 1971), 173–79.

26 Belov, *Russians in the Bering Strait*, 39.

27 Ibid., 41–44. See also Efimov, *Is Istorii Velikih Gograficheskih Otkrytii*, 215–34.

28 Black, *Russians in Alaska*, 29–50.

29 Ibid., 41–44.

30 Belov, *Russians in the Bering Strait*, 48.

31 Efimov, *Is Istorii Velikih Gograficheskih Otkrytii*, 293.

32 Belov, *Russians in the Bering Strait*, 45.

33 A. P. Sokolov, "Ekspeditsiya k Aleutskim Ostrovam Kapitanov Krenitsna i Levashova, 1768–1769." *Zapiski Gocudarstvennogo departamenta Morskogo ministerstva*, 1852, vol. 10; see also R. G. Lyapunova, "Etnograficheskoe Znachenie Ekspeditsii Kapitanov P. K. Krenitsina i M. D. Levashova na Aleutskie ostrova (1764–1769)," *Sovetskaya Etnografiya* 6 (1971): 67–80; I. V. Glushankov, *Sekretnaya Ekspeditsiya: Ekspeditsiya Krenitsina; Levashova, Poslannaya dlya Otkrytiya, Issledovaniya I Tochnogo Naneseniya na Karty Naibolee Vostochnykh Ostrovov Aleutskoi Gryady* (Magadan, Russia: Magadanskoe Knizhnoe Izdatel'stvo 1972).

34 Black, *Russians in Alaska*, 83–92.

35 V. N. Berkh, *A Chronological History of the Discovery of the Aleutian Islands* (Kingston, ON: Limestone, 1974), 1.

36 Lydia Black, "Promyshlenniki . . . Who Were They?" in *Bering and Chirikov: The American Voyages and their Impact*, ed. O. W. Frost (Anchorage: Alaska Historical Society, 1992), 279–90.

37 Raisa Makarova, *Russians on the Pacific, 1743–1799* (Kingston, ON: Limestone, 1975), 199–206.

38 Berkh, *Chronological History*, 8–9.

39 Y. M. Svet, trans. and ed., *Tretie Plavanie Kapitana Jeimsa Kuka: Plavanie v Tikhom okeane v 1776–1780 gg.* (Moscow: Mysl', 1971), 612.

40 Cook, *Voyage of the* Resolution *and* Discovery, 410.

41 David Samwell, "Some Account of a Voyage to South Sea's in 1776–1777–1778," in Cook, *Voyage of the* Resolution *and* Discovery, 1132–33.

42 Cook, *Voyage of the* Resolution *and* Discovery, 410–11.

43 Ibid., 412.

44 Ibid., 1133.

45 This is supported by Samwell's account of information received during Behm's visit to the *Resolution* on May 21, 1779.

46 James Cook and James King, *A Voyage to the Pacific Ocean . . . in the years 1776, 1777, 1778, 1779, and 1780* (London: John Douglas, 1784), 217–18.

47 Ibid.

48 Russian Central Naval Archive, St. Petersburg, Billings collection, report 14, fols. 101–5.

49 Vdovin, *Ocherki Istorii i Etnografii Chukchei,* 137–38.

50 Arkhiv Gosudarstvennogo Soveta, Tom 1: Arkhiv v Tsarstvovanie Imeratritsy Ekateriny Vtoroi, 1768–1796 [Archive of the State Council, vol. 1: Archive from the Reign of the Empress Catherine II, 1768–1796] (St. Petersburg: Tipografiya Vtorogo Otdeleniya Sobstvennoi E. I. V. Kantselyarii, 1869), 259.

51 Samwell and Edgar identify one of the men as Petr Bnat Rubin. This was likely a Russian sailor, Natrubin. See Svet, *Tretie Plavanie Kapitana,* 616. The other man, whom Cook believed to be master or mate of the vessel, was likely Ivan Lukanin. See Berkh, *Chronological History,* 56.

52 Berkh, *Chronological History,* 56.

53 E. Markova-Dvoichenko, "Shturman Gerasim Izmailov," *Morskie Zapiski* (New York) 13, no. 4 (1955): 14–27.

54 Berkh, *Chronological History,* 50; A. S. Polonski, *Perechen' puteshestvii russkih promyshlennyh v Vostochnom okeane s 1743 po 1800 god*, Archive of the Russian Geographical Society, Manuscript 60–1, p. 132.

55 Cook, *Voyage of the* Resolution *and* Discovery, 449.

56 Svet, *Tretie Plavanie Kapitana*, 617.

57 Berkh, *Chronological History*, 50.

58 Cook, *Voyage of the* Resolution *and* Discovery, 456.

59 Ibid.

60 Ibid., 442.

61 The originals of the letter and chart are in the National Archives, UK, ADM 1/1612 and MPI 1/83.

62 Cook, *Voyage of the* Resolution *and* Discovery, 669.

63 James Gibson suggested that Behm's generosity was in part motivated by "a desire to impress their visitors into believing that Kamchatka (and by implication all of the Russian Far east) was more bountiful and hence formidable than it actually was." James R. Gibson, "The Significance of Cook's Third Voyage to Russian Tenure in the North Pacific," *Pacific Studies* 1, no. 2 (1978): 19–146.

64 For the inventory of artifacts presented to Behm, see Svet and Fedorova, "Captain Cook and the Russians."

65 Cook, *Voyage of the* Resolution *and* Discovery, 672.

66 Samwell, "Some Account," 1248 (May 26, 1779).

67 Black, *Russians in Alaska*, 92.

68 Cook, *Voyage of the* Resolution *and* Discovery, 672.

69 Ibid., 311.

70 Svet and Fedorova, "Captain Cook and the Russians," 11.

71 Black, *Russians in Alaska*, 92.

72 Berkh, *Chronological History*, 62. Berkh's description of the circumstances of Zaikov's acquaintance with Cook's charts is contradictory. According to Berkh, Zaikov saw them on Kamchatka, but his own account of Zaikov's 1772–79 voyage makes it unlikely. In May 1779, when Englishmen visited Kamchatka for the first time, Zaikov was still on Umnak Island. June 12 of the same year finds him on Commander Island, from where he allegedly sailed directly to Okhotsk, arriving on September 6. It is more likely that Zaikov met Cook's companions in October 1778 when he was hunting on Umnak Island, which is only a couple of hours by kayak from Iliuliuk. Russian hunting parties based on Umnak and Unalaska frequently visited each other and exchanged news. Like Sapozhnikov, Zaikov could have come to Unalaska once he heard about the British explorers and obtained information about mainland Alaska in exchange for his chart of the Aleutian Islands.

73 George Dixon, "A voyage around the world, but more particularly to the North West coast of America: performed in 1785, 1786, 1787, and 1788, in the King George and Queen Charlotte, Captains Partlock and Dixon," *The Monthly Review, or Literary Journal* 80 (1789).

74 Black, *Russians in Alaska*, 93.

75 T. S. Fedorova, L. V. Glazunova, and G. N. Fedorova, eds., *Russkie ekspeditsii po izucheniyu Severnoi chaste Tihogo okeana vo vtoroi polovine XVIII v, sbornik dokumentov* (Moscow: Nauka, 1989), 229.

76 On the Russian perception of Cook's voyages, see Terence Armstrong, "Cook's Reputation in Russia," in *Captain Cook and His Times*, ed. Robin Fisher and Hugh Johnston (Vancouver: Douglas and McIntyre, 1979), 121–28, and Simon Werrett, "Russian Responses to the Voyages of Captain Cook," in *Captain Cook: Explorations and Reassessments*, ed. Glyndwr Williams (Durham, UK: Boydell, 2004), 179–97.

77 L. Golenischev-Kutuzov, trans. (from French), *Puteshestvie v juzhnoi polovine zemnogo shara I vokrug onogo, uchinennoe v prodolzhenii 1772, 1773, 1774 i 1775 godov angliiskimi korolevskimi sudami Rezoliutsies i Adventyurom pod nachalstom kapitana Iakova Kuka* (St. Petersburg, 1796); L. Golenischev-Kutuzov, trans. (from English), *Puteshestvie v Severnyi Tihii okean pod nachal'stvom kapitanov Kuka, Klerka i Gora v prodolzhenii 1776, 177, 1778, 1779 i 1780 gg.* (St. Petersburg, 1805).

60
5
10
15
20
25
30
35
40
45
50
55

James Cook and the New Navigation

RICHARD DUNN

5

COOK'S THREE CIRCUMNAVIGATIONS TOOK PLACE IN A REVOLUTIONARY period in which new navigational methods and technologies were developed and put to sea. The voyages themselves had a prominent role in this process, demonstrating that the new techniques could be employed over even the longest distances—by trained and properly equipped navigators at least—and applied to the creation of accurate charts. An event that elegantly symbolized these changes took place in the three weeks during which the *Resolution,* returning home in 1775 after a three-year voyage to the Pacific, made its way from the Cape of Good Hope to St. Helena. John Elliott, a midshipman on board, later recalled with a certain degree of hindsight that:

> having got every thing completed and ready for Sea, we sailed from the Cape of Good Hope on the 27th April, in company of a Spanish and a Danish Frigate, and the Dutton East India Man. The two former ran out on each side of us, and saluted us, Music playing on board the Dane all the time. This was done in compliment to Capt. Cook, and had a pretty effect. We returned the salute, and in this way for some

Marine timekeeper K1, made by Larcum Kendall, London, 1769 (detail of fig. 5.4).

> hours, The Frigates left us, and We steered for St Helena in a straight line, trusting to our Watch and Lunar Observations.
>
> The day before we saw St Helena the Dutton spoke to us and said that they were afraid we should miss the Island, but Capt. Cook laughed at them, and told them that he would run their jibboom on the Island if they chose, and on the 15th May we saw the Land, and anchored in the Bay before the Town in the Evening.[1]

What Elliott remembered can be seen as a turning point in the history of navigation, when two new methods for determining longitude—by chronometer and by lunar observation—came to be applied with confidence to a routine journey. Symbolism aside, the successful arrival of the *Resolution* in St. Helena was part of a longer story that saw a host of academics, practitioners, politicians, and mariners work on and finally crack a problem that had once been thought insoluble. Cook's reputation as an expert navigator and surveyor rested in part on his use of the new navigation, but more remained to be done in the decades following his death to make these techniques truly universal.

NAVIGATIONAL ADVANCES IN THE MID-EIGHTEENTH CENTURY

A good way of understanding the state of navigation in the first half of the eighteenth century is to think about the methods and instruments Cook came across as he began his seafaring career in trading vessels on England's North Sea coast in the 1740s. He learned trusted methods that had barely changed for generations.

Coastal navigation relied on the mariner's ability to understand a ship's movements and read any clues offered by sea and land. First and foremost, this meant measuring how fast the ship was going and in which direction, by the use of the speed log and magnetic compass, and accounting for the effects of tides. Natural and man-made features along the coast—a headland, church tower, or deliberately placed marker, perhaps—gave further clues, as did the depth and nature of the seabed, regularly checked with a lead and line.[2] North Sea sailors, for example, claimed they could tell west from east from the pebbles the lead fetched up: those in the west could be broken with one's teeth. A good lookout (preferably with a telescope) and a memory for local landmarks and lore were a seaman's best guide. Rhymes or other memory devices could help. As they headed north, Whitby sailors recalled that

> *When Flamborough we pass by*
> *Filey Brigg we mayn't come nigh*
> *Scarborough Castle lies out to sea,*
> *Whitby three points northerly.*[3]

This local and contingent knowledge could also be written down and published in books known as pilots or rutters, which included descriptions and sketches of distinctive coastal features.[4]

The tools and techniques Cook learned in his first years at sea would stand him in good stead throughout his life. The lead and line, for instance, with which he became adept on the constantly shifting sand and mud banks of England's east coast, would be indispensable in the great surveys of his later career.

Determining a ship's position in open waters presented significant challenges and required additional methods. Cook studied these after he entered the Royal Navy and rose through its ranks to become a master, or navigating officer, in 1757. The ideal was to fix a position in terms of latitude and longitude. Latitude—the distance north or south of the equator—was straightforward to measure from the maximum angular height of the sun or Pole Star above the horizon.[5] A range of instruments for this purpose had been devised over the centuries. Those still in use in the eighteenth century included the cross-staff, backstaff, and, after its development in the 1730s, the Hadley quadrant or octant. By the time Cook entered the Royal Navy, the octant was becoming the norm (fig. 5.1).[6]

Determining longitude—the ship's east-west position—was a different proposition altogether. Since it was a measure around the Earth's axis of rotation, the longitude difference between two places could be thought of as the difference between their local times, with a difference of one hour of time equating to fifteen degrees of longitude. The local time at the ship's position could be fairly easily worked out from the position of the sun, local noon occurring when the sun is at its highest point in the sky. This could be measured with the instruments used for determining latitude.[7] Ascertaining the time at the reference point at the same moment, however, was not feasible until the 1760s.[8]

Unable to calculate longitude by direct observation, mariners estimated the ship's position by keeping a record of its heading and speed and, having made adjustments for the effects of wind and currents, plotting the results on a chart and noting them in a logbook (see fig. 5.1). This was known as dead reckoning. Latitude determinations from the sun or stars—as long as they were visible—could be used to correct some of the errors.[9]

The knowledge and skills of the mariner making these observations and calculations were clearly crucial, but dead reckoning could work quite well, in particular over short distances and along well-known routes. Cook's logs from his transatlantic voyages on the *Grenville* in the 1760s, for example, show how reliably a skillful navigator could apply it.[10] As European navigators embarked on more ambitious voyages into uncharted and unfamiliar waters, however, dead reckoning could go astray. This became startlingly clear when George Anson was sent to the Pacific at the outbreak of the War of the Austrian Succession (1740–48) with the *Centurion* and five other Royal Navy ships and orders to damage Spanish interests. Anson returned a hero, but the voyage was a series of arduous trials for the crews, most of whom died.[11] The navigational problems began after Anson's fleet passed through

5.1 Archibald Hamilton, *A Seaman Shown Observing with an Octant*, from *A Book of Drafts and Remarks*, 1763. A compass and a log and line (to measure speed) sit to the right of the seaman, with a sounding lead (to measure ocean depth) to the left, and a written log in the background. (NMM, Ms NVP/11). © National Maritime Museum, Greenwich, London, L5870-002.

Le Maire Strait on March 7, 1741, and began the much-feared journey around Cape Horn to reach the Pacific. Severe storms raged for weeks. The ships soon separated—some wrecked in the icy waters—and scurvy began to affect the remaining crew. A month later, the ships' masters estimated that they were well west of Tierra del Fuego and could head north into calmer waters. But just days later, land was unexpectedly and almost disastrously sighted, placing them off Cape Noir, to the west of Tierra del Fuego, over three hundred miles east of their estimated position. The error had arisen from a failure to allow for the effects of wind, currents, and magnetic variation. Although these factors were understood in principle, their specific effects around Cape Horn were unknown.[12]

To mitigate the problems the *Centurion*'s three-hundred-mile displacement exemplified, navigators adopted a practice known as "running down the latitude." Rather than take a direct course to their destination, which would leave them uncertain which way to sail if they found themselves off course, they would aim well to the east or west. Once the ship reached the correct latitude, they would sail directly west or east along that parallel of latitude, confident that their destination lay ahead. It meant sailing farther than on a direct course but offered more certainty of reaching the destination safely.[13] This approach still relied on knowing where the destination lay, however—as Anson discovered when the *Centurion* headed north to meet up with his dispersed fleet. Anson's information placed their rendezvous, the Juan Fernández Islands, closer to the coast of Chile than they really lie. Failing to sight the islands as they headed west along their latitude, Anson lost confidence and turned east again, realizing that he had turned too soon only when the crew sighted the mainland once more. Seventy or eighty men died in the nine days that were lost.[14]

These difficulties stemmed from a lack of the local and contingent knowledge—of tides, winds, currents, and geographical data—that underpinned the navigational practices of the day. What was needed in these unknown waters, most agreed, was a universally applicable form of position fixing based on the determination of longitude (as well as latitude), coupled with accurate charts.

As Cook's naval career progressed, two promising methods were coming to fruition in the wake of the first Longitude Act of 1714. "Nothing is so much wanted and desired at Sea as the Discovery of Longitude," it stated, "for the Safety and Quickness of Voyages, the Preservation of Ships and the Lives of Men."[15] The Act offered rewards of up to twenty thousand pounds to anyone finding a reliable and accurate method for determining longitude to within half a degree, with smaller sums for solutions of lesser accuracy. It also nominated a group of Commissioners (later known as the Board of Longitude) to assess proposals, assign rewards, and encourage research into promising ideas.[16] At the time the act was formulated, a number of approaches seemed possible, of which the four strongest contenders included using the moon, the satellites of Jupiter, artificial timekeepers, and magnetic variation to determine longitude from a ship. On land, accurate surveys were already being made using observations of Jupiter's satellites, whose regular movements meant that they could be used as a celestial clock for finding the reference time. Of these and many other suggestions put forward in response to the act, however, only two methods had proved themselves at sea by the mid-1760s: the lunar-distance method and the use of marine timekeepers. Each aimed to allow mariners to find (or keep) the time at a reference point for comparison with the ship's local time to derive the longitude.

The lunar-distance method used the moon's apparent motion relative to the stars like a clock to find the reference time.[17] It required accurate tables of the moon's future positions: the Observatoire de Paris and the Royal Observatory in Greenwich had been founded to provide them.[18] The moon's motions are so complex, however, that it was not until Tobias Mayer brought together Newtonian gravitational theory with the best lunar observations from Greenwich and elsewhere in the 1750s that accurate predictive tables became available.[19] An important endorsement for his work came in 1761–62, when an up-and-coming astronomer, Nevil Maskelyne, used the tables for longitude determinations while en route to St. Helena (to observe a transit of Venus there).[20] Within a year of returning, Maskelyne began publicizing the method in *The British Mariners' Guide* (1763), as did his assistant on the voyage, Robert Waddington.[21]

The lunar-distance method required an instrument for making accurate observations of the moon from an unsteady deck. This began to seem possible in 1731, when John Hadley and Thomas Godfrey simultaneously announced their invention of an instrument based on the principle of double reflection. Although both men anticipated that their invention might be used to find longitude, initially it was mostly deployed for latitude and local-time observations.[22] Around 1750, by which time it was known as the Hadley quadrant or octant, William Maitland considered it "the best Instrument for finding the Latitude at Sea" (fig. 5.1).[23] Further refinement was needed, however, to produce an instrument completely suited to measuring lunar distances. The octant's scale, which measured up to ninety degrees, was too short for some of the observations, and its wooden frame was insufficiently rigid for precise observation. But in the 1750s, Tobias Mayer devised a circular instrument on the same double-reflection principle. Tests of this with Mayer's tables, under the auspices of the Board of Longitude, led to the creation of the marine sextant in about 1758.[24] Capable of measuring up to around 120 degrees and with a rigid brass frame, the sextant would become the standard instrument for precision measurements at sea (fig. 5.2).

By the 1760s, similarly promising developments had been made in the creation of timekeepers that could keep time on a sea voyage. In 1759 John Harrison completed his famous sea watch (known as H4), which underwent a trial on a voyage to Jamaica in

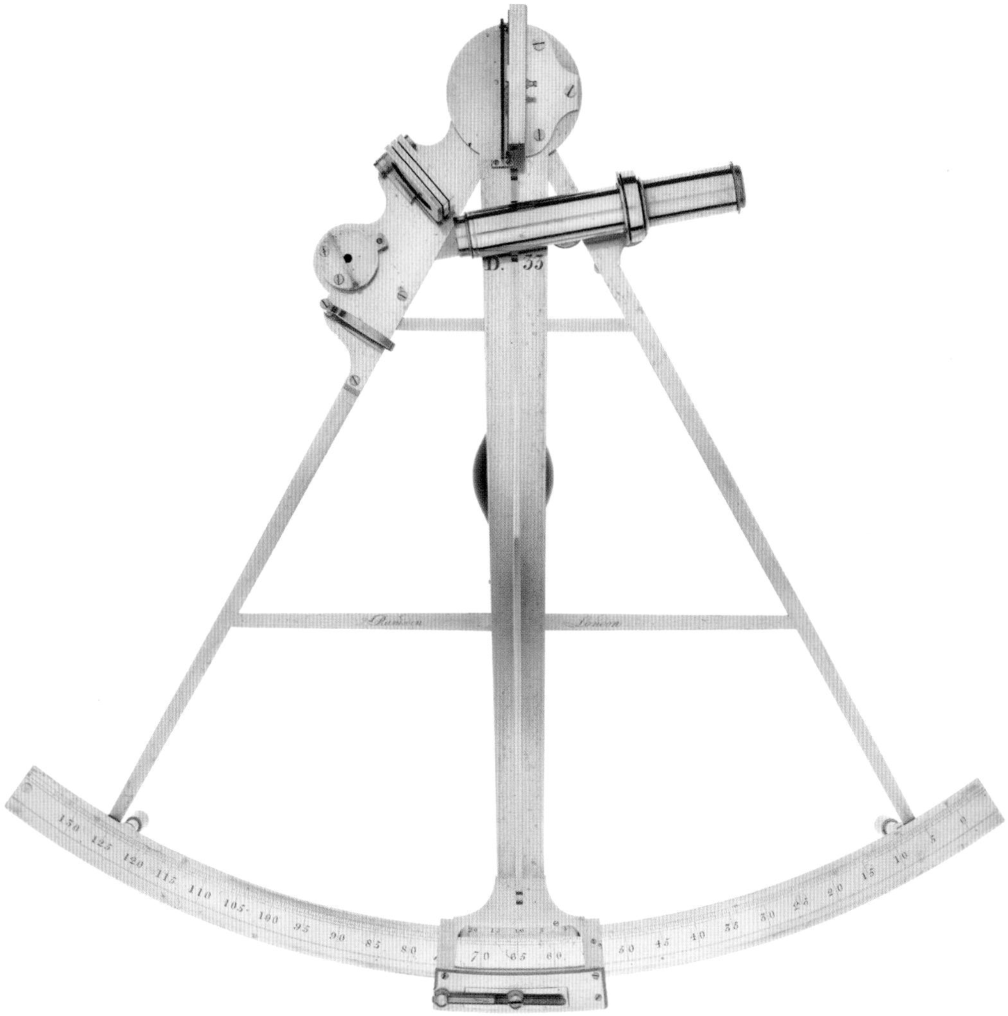

5.2 Sextant made by Jesse Ramsden, London (c. 1772), issued by the Board of Longitude to Cook's third voyage. © National Maritime Museum, Greenwich, London, NAVI236.

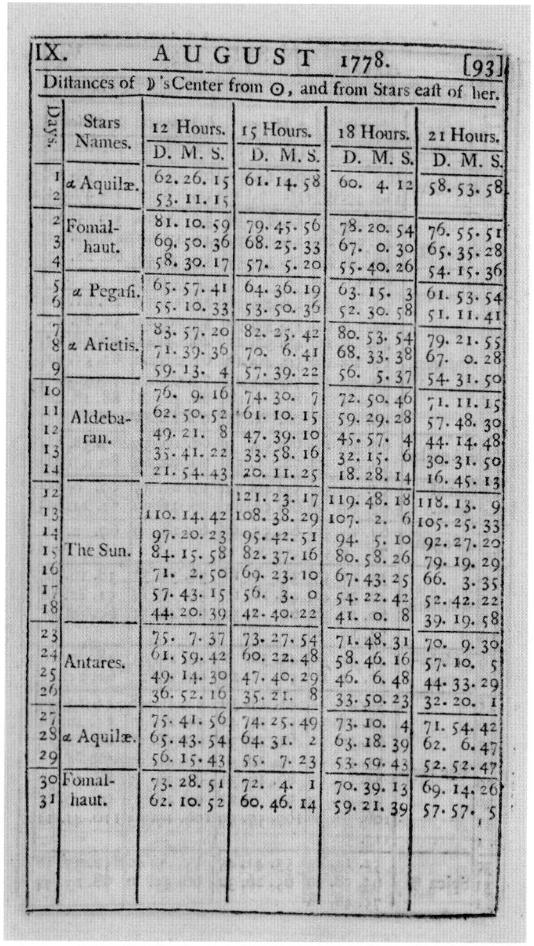

IX. AUGUST 1778. [93]

Diftances of ☽'s Center from ☉, and from Stars eaft of her.

Days.	Stars Names.	12 Hours. D. M. S.	15 Hours. D. M. S.	18 Hours. D. M. S.	21 Hours. D. M. S.
1	α Aquilæ.	62. 26. 15	61. 14. 58	60. 4. 12	58. 53. 58
2		53. 11. 15			
2	Fomal-haut.	81. 10. 59	79. 45. 56	78. 20. 54	76. 55. 51
3		69. 50. 36	68. 25. 33	67. 0. 30	65. 35. 28
4		58. 30. 17	57. 5. 20	55. 40. 26	54. 15. 36
5	α Pegafi.	65. 57. 41	64. 36. 19	63. 15. 3	61. 53. 54
6		55. 10. 33	53. 50. 36	52. 30. 58	51. 11. 41
7	α Arietis.	83. 57. 20	82. 25. 42	80. 53. 54	79. 21. 55
8		71. 39. 36	70. 6. 41	68. 33. 38	67. 0. 28
9		59. 13. 4	57. 39. 22	56. 5. 37	54. 31. 50
10	Aldeba-ran.	76. 9. 16	74. 30. 7	72. 50. 46	71. 11. 15
11		62. 50. 52	61. 10. 15	59. 29. 28	57. 48. 30
12		49. 21. 8	47. 39. 10	45. 57. 4	44. 14. 48
13		35. 41. 22	33. 58. 16	32. 15. 6	30. 31. 50
14		21. 54. 43	20. 11. 25	18. 28. 14	16. 45. 13
12	The Sun.		121. 23. 17	119. 48. 18	118. 13. 9
13		110. 14. 42	108. 38. 29	107. 2. 6	105. 25. 33
14		97. 20. 23	95. 42. 51	94. 5. 10	92. 27. 20
15		84. 15. 58	82. 37. 16	80. 58. 26	79. 19. 29
16		71. 2. 50	69. 23. 10	67. 43. 25	66. 3. 35
17		57. 43. 15	56. 3. 0	54. 22. 42	52. 42. 22
18		44. 20. 39	42. 40. 22	41. 0. 8	39. 19. 58
23	Antares.	75. 7. 37	73. 27. 54	71. 48. 31	70. 9. 30
24		61. 59. 42	60. 22. 48	58. 46. 16	57. 10. 5
25		49. 14. 30	47. 40. 29	46. 6. 48	44. 33. 29
26		36. 52. 16	35. 21. 8	33. 50. 23	32. 20. 1
27	α Aquilæ.	75. 41. 56	74. 25. 49	73. 10. 4	71. 54. 42
28		65. 43. 54	64. 31. 2	63. 18. 39	62. 6. 47
29		56. 15. 43	55. 7. 23	53. 59. 43	52. 52. 47
30	Fomal-haut.	73. 28. 51	72. 4. 1	70. 39. 13	69. 14. 26
31		62. 10. 52	60. 46. 14	59. 21. 39	57. 57. 5

5.3 A lunar-distance table from the *Nautical Almanac* for 1778, which Cook used on the third voyage. The table shows the moon's predicted angular distance from the sun and certain stars at three-hour intervals for August. © National Maritime Museum, Greenwich, London.

1761–62.[25] Although the watch performed well, the Commissioners of Longitude decided that another trial was needed. This would be a voyage to Barbados, with Harrison's device to be tested alongside improved tables by Tobias Mayer and an observing chair devised by Christopher Irwin for viewing the satellites of Jupiter.[26] Traveling to Barbados in 1763, the two astronomers appointed for the trial, Nevil Maskelyne and Charles Green, made lunar-distance and related observations—"which business sometimes was rather too fatiguing," Maskelyne wrote—but found Irwin's chair to be "a mere bauble, not in the least useful for the purpose intended."[27] Harrison's son, William, accompanied H4 to Barbados a few months later, and it performed well. When the Board of Longitude met again to discuss the results in February 1765, the Commissioners agreed to reward Harrison and Mayer. At Maskelyne's suggestion, they also resolved to produce annual tables in support of the lunar-distance method.[28] The *Nautical Almanac and Astronomical Ephemeris,* published annually from 1767, presented the necessary astronomical data for each day of the specified year, simplifying and systematizing the laborious calculations (fig. 5.3).[29]

PROVING LONGITUDE: COOK'S FIRST AND SECOND VOYAGES

With the appropriate tools and tables developed before the *Endeavour* departed in the summer of 1768, the transit of Venus expedition provided an opportunity to test the lunar-distance method in challenging conditions. Expertise came in the person of Charles Green, appointed by the Royal Society to assist with the observations at Tahiti.[30] A short way into the voyage, Green wrote from Rio de Janeiro that at first "no person in the ship could either make an observation of the Moon or Calculate one when made." He must already have begun to pass on his knowledge, however, since Cook was successfully deploying the method by the time they reached Brazil.[31] Having passed through the notorious waters that had caused Anson's fleet such trouble, he was even able to write that "the Longitude of few places in the World are better ascertain'd than that of Strait Le Maire and Cape Horn being determined by several observations of the Sun and Moon, made both by my self and Mr Green the Astronomer."[32]

Convinced of the power of lunar-distance measurements, Cook concluded well before the end of the voyage that "would Sea officers once apply themselves to the makeing and calculating these observations they would not find them so very difficult as they first imagine, especially with the assistance of the Nautical Almanac and Astronomical Ephemeris."[33] The value of the *Nautical Almanac* had become particularly clear by this time. Only the almanacs for the years 1768 and 1769 had been available when the *Endeavour* departed, so for 1770 Cook and Green had to perform the extra calculations that the tables would have obviated. This problem recurred on the third voyage. By August

5.4 Marine timekeeper K1, made by Larcum Kendall, London, 1769, used on Cook's second and third voyages. © National Maritime Museum, Greenwich, London, Ministry of Defense Art Collection, ZAA0038.

1779, James King had brought four mathematically adept midshipmen over to the *Discovery* to help him with the extra calculations.[34]

By the time of the second voyage, the timekeeper method was ready for long-distance trials. This time the expedition had the direct involvement of the Board of Longitude, which directed the astronomical work. This included testing whether Harrison's apparently successful timekeeper could be replicated by another maker.[35] The instrument maker John Bird, one of a special committee before whom Harrison dismantled and explained his "contrivance," was just one of those who doubted how easy it would be to replicate. According to Bird, "several parts are, and must be done by a tentative method, which will always render the execution teadious and difficult."[36] Nonetheless, in 1766 the board commissioned Larcum Kendall, a London watchmaker, to make a near-exact copy. Completed and presented to the board in 1769, Kendall's first marine timekeeper, known as K1 (fig. 5.4), was therefore available for trial on the 1772 voyage, as were three marine timekeepers made by another watchmaker, John Arnold.[37]

Cook was left in no doubt that the four timekeepers must be treated with extreme care. His journal for July 10, 1772, records from Plymouth that

> before we departed the Watches were put in motion in the presence of my self Captain Furneaux, the first Lieutenant of each of the Sloops, the two astronomers and Mr Arnold and afterward put on board: Mr Kendals and one of Mr Arnolds on board the Resolution and the other two of Mr Arnolds on board the Adventure: the Commander, First Lieutenant and Astronomer on board each of the Sloops had each of them Keys of the Boxes which contained the Watches and were allways to be present at the winding them up and comparing the one with the other.[38]

These precautions sometimes posed problems. On one occasion Cook and his first lieutenant were kept on shore, leaving William Wales (astronomer on the *Resolution*) unable to open the box. The watch ran down, and Wales's astronomical observations had to be used to reset it when Cook returned.[39]

The Board of Longitude's instructions to the astronomers, Wales on the *Resolution* and William Bayly on the *Adventure*, stipulated that the watches were to be continually monitored, with their results checked against dead reckoning, lunar-distance observations at sea, and astronomical observations on land. In other words, the astronomers were to compare the full range of available methods for fixing positions. Like Green on the first voyage, Wales and Bayly were also to teach the lunar-distance method to the officers.[40]

The Board of Longitude issued a range of navigational and other scientific instruments, including sextants.[41] The difference in the ways the two technologies for longitude determination were to be treated on the voyage is telling. Sextants were well-established, precise instruments that were being produced in sufficient numbers for some officers to own them personally. Those from the Board of Longitude could be issued without further stipulation as to their handling: in a sense, they and the lunar-distance method were not on trial but rather constituted part of the timekeeper trials. Timekeepers, by contrast, were an emerging, experimental technology. Those on board Cook's ships in 1772 were rare, bespoke items to be kept under lock and key. Determining whether they could be maintained at sea and eventually mass produced was one of the points of the test.[42]

The performance of the timekeepers reflected their experimental nature. Arnold's performed poorly, but Kendall's went very well, with Cook coming to see it as his "trusty friend" and "never-failing guide."[43] By the time he reached the Cape of Good Hope on the return leg in 1775, he was a convert. He wrote enthusiastically to the secretary of the Admiralty that, "Mr. Kendals Watch has exceeded the expectations of its most Zealous advocate and by being now and then corrected by lunar observations has been our faithful guide through all the vicissitudes of climates."[44] For Cook, Kendall's timekeeper was no longer on trial. Setting sail for St. Helena, he opted not for the usual course of "running down the latitude" but put his trust in the mechanism. "Depending on the goodness of Mr. Kendals Watch," he wrote, "I resolved to try to make the island by a direct course, it did not deceive us and we made it accordingly on the 15th of May at Day-break."[45] Cook's words were simple, but they demonstrated that the elusive goal of accurately determining longitude at sea had been achieved.

LONGITUDE TECHNIQUES IN PRACTICE

While Cook's first and second voyages had a significant role in testing the new navigational techniques, all his voyages had other objectives as well. The ships on each expedition carried specialists—astronomers, naturalists, and artists—and attendant equipment to collect data, specimens, and artifacts in support of the Admiralty's exploratory and imperial agendas. In addition to aiding navigation, the new longitude methods had a place in the surveying activities at which Cook was so adept. Deploying them for surveying was crucial, indeed, for what use was fixing a position without complete and accurate charts on which to plot it?

The surveying achievements were astonishing: over five thousand miles of previously unknown coastline were charted on the first voyage, including the coast of New Zealand, the east coast of Australia, and Torres Strait. The second voyage disposed of the myth of a southern continent and carried out further surveys, including New Caledonia and the New Hebrides (Vanuatu). On the final voyage, while searching for the Northwest Passage, Cook's expedition charted over four thousand miles of America's Pacific coast, from Oregon to Alaska, as well as part of the coast of Asia (fig. 11.10).[46] Several modern authors have commended the accuracy that was generally achieved.[47]

Surveying and charting were explicitly mandated in Cook's instructions. Those for the third voyage specified that

> at whatever Places you may touch in the course of your Voyage, where accurate Observations of the nature hereafter mentioned have not already been made, you are, as far as your time will allow, very carefully to observe the true Situation of such Places, both in Latitude & Longitude; the Variation of the Needle; Bearings of Head lands; Height, Direction, and Course of the Tydes and Currents; Depths & Soundings of the Sea, Shoals, Rocks &ca; and also to survey, make Charts, and to take views of, such Bays, Harbours, and different parts of the Coast, and to make such Notations thereon, as may be useful either to Navigation or Commerce.[48]

Cook and the expedition astronomers received more specific scientific instructions as well, from the Royal Society on the first voyage and from the Board of Longitude on the second and third. The Board of Longitude's instructions were particularly explicit about the testing and exploitation of the new techniques for determining longitudes. The observers, they noted, were to make observations for latitude and longitude at sea, comparing longitudes from dead reckoning with those from lunar observations and the timekeepers. They were to "settle the position of Head Lands, Islands and Harbours in Latitude and Longitude, by the Cœlestial Observations; and also to set down what Longitude the Watch gives." This meant periodically making observations on land with larger, more accurate instruments, including an astronomical regulator and astronomical quadrant, which in turn allowed the astronomer to check the "Watch Machine" against the regulator.[49] The scientific instructions, which were largely determined by Nevil Maskelyne as astronomer royal and a commissioner of longitude, also helped to dictate what equipment would be supplied.[50]

As these instructions suggest, the voyages involved both testing the new techniques and applying them in ways that complemented long-established methods and each other. For Cook, surveying an area meant "takeing a Geometrical Plan of it, in which every place is to have its true situation." This was not always possible given the perennial constraints of time and resources.[51] But defining the "true situation" of places was where the new techniques came into their own: the geographical locations established by astronomical means or timekeepers became fixed anchors for running surveys with more commonplace methods and equipment. For instance, Cook discussed his corrections to Russian charts of the northern Pacific, which he found to be riddled with errors: "Oonalaska is one of the principal islands, and the only one in which there is a harbour is not liable to any such errors, as the most of the islands were seen by us, consequently their latitude and longitude pretty exactly determined, particularly the harbour of Samgoonoodha in Oon[a]laska which must be looked upon as a fixed point" (figs. 2.3 and 2.6).[52] Cook's confidence in defining Samgoonoodha harbor as a "fixed point" derived from thirty-four sets of lunar observations taken to establish its position.[53]

Precisely fixing geographical locations was time-consuming, however, and possible only where a ship could be safely anchored for some days and an observatory erected on land. Most of the surveying was done on the move and relied on techniques and instruments with which Cook had become familiar in Newfoundland in the mid-1760s.[54] These combined triangulation from measured baselines on land with running surveys from the ship. J. C. Beaglehole has summarized these surveys: "[Cook] would measure accurately his base-lines and his angles, fix the positions of prominent features, plot them on his paper, plot a net of triangles anchored to fixed positions. . . . He would calculate latitudes accurately with the help of his quadrant. . . . When he had his land features in correct relation, he would go on to his hydrographical work, would sound, take bearings, draw detail."[55]

The instruments used for surveying were the surveyor's chain (often called a Gunter's chain) for measuring baselines, an azimuth compass and sextant (or an octant) for angles, and lead and line for depth soundings.[56] On Porto Praya in the Cape Verde Islands, Wales noted that he went ashore and "measured it both ways, and differed only ten links of the Gunter's Chain. I set the line with the Azimuth Compass both ways, whilst Capt Cook took the Angles subtended by the several points of the Bay from each station, with my Sextant."[57] Over longer distances, an alternative was to measure a base by observing the difference between the sight and sound of firing guns, as Wales and Bayly did in Queen Charlotte Sound in New Zealand.[58]

Where possible, a temporary observatory was set up on land to allow the larger, more accurate clocks and telescopes to be deployed (fig. 5.5). The stability of land also enabled the astronomers to carry out observations that were impossible at sea: for example, observing Jupiter's satellites for fixing longitudes.[59] For the second voyage, William Bayly devised what became the standard observing tent, praised by Wales as "one of the most convenient portable observatories that has yet been made." It was big enough to hold the clocks and instruments when erected, yet packed into a box "six feet and nine inches long, and about twenty inches square" to go into the ship's hold.[60]

One positive spin-off from the development of seaborne methods of determining longitude was that land-based observatories were no longer the sole means of fixing positions with some degree of certainty (although the accuracy of measurements from land remained greater). Lieutenant James King noted of the third voyage that "on the coast of America and Asia greater care was taken to find the difference between Longitudes by Lunar obsns &

5.5 John Webber, detail of Resolution *and* Discovery *in Ship Cove, Nootka Sound,* pen, wash, and watercolor, 1778. The illustration shows the *Resolution* on the right and the astronomers' observing tents on the rocky outcrop in the center left of the picture. © National Maritime Museum, Greenwich, London, PAJ2959.

by T.K. [timekeeper], these comparisons were made at Sandwich Sound, to the N of Cape Newenham & in Norton Sound, from whence I should suppose the Col of Lunar observations on these coasts to be nearly the true situation of the ship in Longitude."[61]

Cook and his officers had been some of the first to use the lunar-distance method routinely in this way on the first voyage. Once timekeepers became available as well, the two could be used to cross-check each other for greater accuracy. During the second voyage, Cook's journal recorded that "the difference of Longitude between the two Ports [Sandwich and Resolution] pointed out by the Watch, and by the [lunar] observations did not differ from each other two miles."[62] But errors could arise: Cook came to realize during the same voyage that much of New Zealand's South Island had been placed too far east during the first.[63]

Just as the new methods and instruments complemented the more traditional approaches, so astronomical and timekeeper methods of longitude determination complemented each other. On the third voyage, the longitude of Ship Cove in Nootka Sound was settled by 134 sets of lunar observations: 20 from the ship before arrival, 90 on land at the temporary observatory, and another 24 from the ship again after departure, those before and after being reduced by the timekeepers (see figs. 11.5 and 5.5).[64] Complementarity could work in other ways, too. Lieutenant King noted: "Lunar observations . . . are absolutely necessary, in order to reach the greatest possible advantage from the time-keeper, since, by ascertaining the true longitude of places, they discover the error of its rate."[65] Conversely, the timekeepers could be used to determine the places that would otherwise have been passed by. Cook was, for instance, fulsome in his praise for William Wales, who "lost no one observation that could possibly be obtained. Even the situation of such islands as we past without touching at are by means of Mr Kendalls Watch determined with almost equal accuracy."[66]

There was nonetheless a hierarchy: astronomical observations were to be regarded as more certain than those made with timekeepers alone. This was clear not only from the need to check the timekeepers' rates by astronomical means but also in the ways in which geographical positions were determined and recorded. In the later parts of the third voyage, indeed, the astronomical observations took on even greater importance when concerns over the timekeepers arose, in particular when K1 stopped shortly after Cook's death and failed to work properly for the rest of the voyage. Hence Charles Clerke's journal note of June 23, 1779: "Towards the evening the Clouds so far dispers'd as to enable us to catch a few sights at the [Moon] & [Sun]: these Observations are now of much more consequence than heretofore to us, as we cannot put that confidence in the performance of our Time Keeper."[67] Six days later, he noted that its performance was "so irregular that I fear very little dependence is to be put upon it." Fortunately, Bayly's lunar observations would be "every way adequate to the adjusting the situation of the various parts of this Coast we have been able to take a look at with sufficient precision."[68] Thereafter, the ships relied on Kendall's third timekeeper, K3 (fig. 5.6), which seems to have performed quite well, though not as well as K1 had.[69]

Astronomical methods could have their problems too. King, for instance, voiced concerns about "the extream errors in different peoples observing with different sextants," which he felt could undermine confidence in the lunar distance method. He was quick to explain that "without much practise, great care in handling the instrument & above all in finding its error, considerable differences will often happen, but it will almost always be found that the mean of many results with different sextants will be very near the truth; and as our sextants were used by all the young Gentlemen who chose to observe, I fancy many of the extream errors in the results put down may be attributed to their passing from one person to another, without a sufficient attention being always paid to the alterations which this might occasion in their adjustment."[70]

This passage highlights a second significant function of the voyages: training officers in the new techniques.[71] This task would have a more subtle and longer legacy, that of embedding astronomical and timekeeper methods of longitude determination within the navy. On the second voyage, for example, William Wales was to "teach such of the Officers on board the sloop as may desire it the use of the Astronomical Instruments & the Method of finding the Longitude at sea from the Lunar

5.6 Marine timekeeper K3, made by Larcum Kendall, London, 1774, used on Cook's third voyage and Vancouver's 1791–95 expedition. © National Maritime Museum, Greenwich, London, Ministry of Defense Art Collection, ZAA0111.

Observations."[72] Cook was highly optimistic. The new techniques could be learned by "any man with proper applycation and a little practice," provided that sufficient instruments could be supplied.[73] King was of the same opinion. In this, one suspects that the abilities of these two mathematically talented officers somewhat blinded them to the problems others had with the lengthy calculations needed for lunar-distance and local-time determinations. Nonetheless, they had shown that astronomical methods and timekeepers could be successfully deployed for navigation and surveying, and that the skills could be learned by others. Over the next decades, the knowledge slowly spread through the navy, becoming formalized in the nineteenth century. By 1802, determining longitude by lunar distances was integrated into the qualifying examinations for lieutenants.[74] By about 1830, all Royal Navy vessels were being issued with chronometers as their main navigational aid.

THE FIRST AMONG NAVIGATORS

It seems fitting to conclude by thinking about Cook's immediate legacy in the context of navigation and cartography. The results of his second voyage alone had prompted the Earl of Sandwich to describe Cook as "the first navigator in Europe." Others made similar statements in the wake of his death, and Cook entered the popular imagination.[75] Bernard Smith and others have, for instance, discussed the influence of Cook's renown on Samuel Taylor Coleridge's "Rime of the Ancient Mariner," the titular seafarer being, significantly, a navigator. This influence seems in part to have come through William Wales, who taught at Christ's Hospital when Coleridge was a pupil there, as well as through the published accounts and visual imagery from the voyages.[76]

Underscoring Cook's legacy as a discoverer, Georg Forster's 1787 encomium noted that "there are no large discoveries left to make." He asked: "Can anyone who looks at a map and sees the changes in geography, achieved through the passionate research of a single man, doubt for a moment that our century could compete with the greatness of any age?" Forster noted how Cook's use of astronomy in navigation assisted him in his "great undertaking."[77] The new navigation, Forster asserted, was inextricable from the achievements of the great explorer.

As Glyn Williams has noted, there was some reluctance to celebrate Cook officially, but seamen and explorers were in awe of his feats of navigation, exploration, and surveying. To the comte de La Pérouse, Cook was "'the first among navigators . . . the real Christopher Columbus of this country [Hawai'i], of the coast of Alaska and of almost all the islands of the South Sea,"while Alejandro Malaspina remarked that he "marvelled at the accuracy of Captain Cook's descriptions. . . . [G]uided as if by his own hand, we put aside any idea of discovery." Only the hydrographer, William Dalrymple, once a contender to head up the transit of Venus expedition, remained

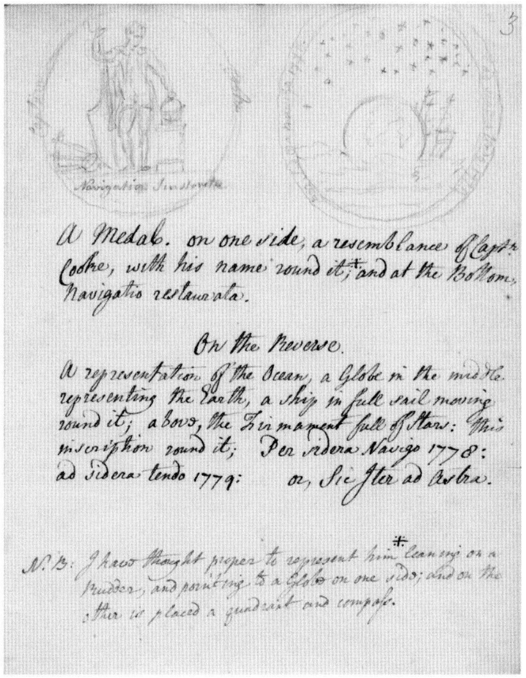

5.7 Lewis Pingo, *Design for the Royal Society's Proposed Cook Medal*, 1784. © National Maritime Museum, Greenwich, London, PAD2899.

5.8 Anonymous design submitted for the Royal Society's proposed Cook Medal, ca. 1784. © The Royal Society, London, #MS/214.

skeptical, writing of Cook that "I cannot admit of a Pope in Geography or Navigation."[78]

Lacking official moves to commemorate Cook, the Royal Society commissioned a medal to honor their late-lamented fellow.[79] The chosen design by Lewis Pingo (fig. 5.7) was somewhat muted—Cook in uniform on one side as "the most intrepid explorer of the seas," and Fortune (sometimes identified as Britannia) on the other with rudder and globe and the motto "Our men have left nothing untried." Some of the other submissions to the Royal Society's competition were more effusive about Cook's place as navigational hero. The most unequivocal had the words *Navigatio Instaurata* (or *restaurata*) beneath the figure of Cook, shown leaning on a rudder and pointing to a globe on one side of him, an octant and compass on the other (fig. 5.8). The reverse was "a representation of the Ocean, a Globe in the middle representing the Earth, a ship in full sail moving round it; above, the Firmament full of Stars; this inscription round it; Per sidera Navigo 1778: ad sidera tendo 1779: or, Sic Iter ad Astra."[80] For this proposer, at least, Cook's reputation rested on his navigational feats and use of the new methods of position-fixing in the restoration of navigation.

By the time of his death, then, James Cook had led a series of voyages that proved that methods of longitude determination could be applied over long distances with considerable confidence. He and the officers and specialists who traveled with him applied those same methods to surveys and the production of charts that would be of lasting benefit. They also began the process of teaching the new techniques to other officers throughout the navy. It was a process that would take some decades to complete, but the revolution had begun.

NOTES

1 Christine Holmes, ed., *Captain Cook's Second Voyage: The Journals of Lieutenants Elliott and Pickersgill* (London: Caliban, 1984), 45.

2 Gillian Hutchinson, *Medieval Ships and Shipping* (Leicester: Leicester University Press, 1994), 165–66, 170–77; D. W. Waters, *The Art of Navigation in England in Elizabethan and Early Stuart Times* (London: Hollis and Carter, 1958), 3–38.

3 John Gascoigne, *Captain Cook: Voyager between Worlds* (London: Hambledon Continuum, 2007), 53–54.

4 See, for example, D. W. Waters, *The Rutters of the Sea: The Sailing Directions of Pierre Garcie; A Study of the First English and French Printed Sailing Directions* (New Haven: Yale University Press, 1967).

5 Latitude is derived from this observation with a few simple calculations, notably to correct for the sun's position in its apparent annual path above and below the equator, for its semidiameter, and for the observer's height above sea level.

6 Gloria Clifton, "The Adoption of the Octant in the British Isles," in *Koersvast: Vijf eeuwen navigatie op zee,* ed. Remmelt Daalder et al. (Zaltbommel: Aprilis, 2005), 85–94; see also D. Fauque, "The Introduction of the Octant in Eighteenth-Century France," ibid., 95–104.

7 For the methods involved, see William J. H. Andrewes, "Finding Local Time at Sea, and the Instruments Employed," in *The Quest for Longitude,* ed. W. J. H. Andrewes (Cambridge, MA: Harvard University Press, 1996), 394–404.

8 See Alan Stimson, "The Longitude Problem: The Navigator's Story," in Andrewes, *Quest for Longitude,* 72–84, and other chapters in the same volume.

9 W. E. May, "Navigational Accuracy in the Eighteenth Century," *Journal of the Institute of Navigation* 6 (1953): 71–73.

10 George Huxtable and Ian Jackson, "Journey to Work: James Cook's Transatlantic Voyages in the *Grenville,* 1764–1767," *Journal of Navigation* 63 (2010): 207–14.

11 Glyn Williams, *The Prize of All the Oceans* (London: HarperCollins, 1999).

12 May, "Navigational Accuracy"; Williams, *Prize,* 39–49.

13 D. W. Waters, "Nautical Astronomy and the Problem of Longitude," in *The Uses of Science in the Age of Newton,* ed. J. G. Burke (Berkeley: University of California Press, 1983), 144.

14 Williams, *Prize,* 54.

15 "An Act for providing a Publick Reward for such Person or Persons as shall discover the Longitude at Sea," 12 Anne, c. 14.

16 Derek Howse, *Greenwich Time and the Longitude* (London: Philip Wilson, 1997), 53–61; Derek Howse, "Britain's Board of Longitude: The Finances, 1714–1828," *Mariner's Mirror* 84 (1998): 400–417; Peter Johnson, "The Board of Longitude, 1714–1828," *Journal of the British Astronomical Association* 99 (1989): 63–69.

17 George Huxtable, "Finding Longitude by Lunar Distance," *Navigation News,* September–October 2007, 22–23; Howse, *Greenwich Time,* 183–85.

18 Howse, *Greenwich Time,* 33–51.

19 E. G. Forbes, *Tobias Mayer (1723–62), Pioneer of Enlightened Science in Germany* (Göttingen: Vandenhoeck und Ruprecht, 1980), 134–50; E. G. Forbes, *The Birth of Navigational Science* (London: National Maritime Museum, 1974); Steven Wepster, *Between Theory and Observations: Tobias Mayer's Explorations of Lunar Motion, 1751–1755* (New York: Springer, 2009).

20 Nevil Maskelyne, "Journal of a Voyage from England to St Helena," Cambridge University Library, MS RGO 4/150; Derek Howse, *Nevil Maskelyne: The Seaman's Astronomer* (Cambridge: Cambridge University Press, 1989), 29–30, 38–39.

21 Robert Waddington, *A Practical Method for Finding the Longitude and Latitude of a Ship at Sea, by Observation of the Moon* (London: W. Richardson and S. Clark, 1763). Waddington also began teaching the lunar-distance method to East India Company officers.

22 John Campbell and James Bradley, third astronomer royal at Greenwich, reportedly succeeded in using a Hadley quadrant for longitude determinations in the late 1740s; see William Wales, *The Original Astronomical Observations, Made in the Course of a Voyage towards the South Pole, and round the World* (London: W. and A. Strahan, 1777), xxxiv.

23 William Maitland, *An Essay towards the Improvement of Navigation* (London: H. Kent, c. 1750), 36; Willem Mörzer Bruyns, *Sextants at Greenwich* (Oxford: Oxford University Press, 2009), 23–36. See also J. A. Bennett, "Catadioptrics and Commerce in Eighteenth-Century London," *History of Science* 44 (2006): 247–87; Silvio A. Bedini, *Thinkers and Tinkers: Early American Men of Science* (New York: Scribner, 1975), 118–23.

24 James Bradley, letter to John Clevland, secretary of the Admiralty, Greenwich, April 14, 1760, in Tobias Mayer, *Tabulae motuum solis et lunae novae et correctae* (London: W. and J. Richardson, 1770), cxi–cxv; Forbes, *Birth of Navigational Science,* 4; Mörzer Bruyns, *Sextants at Greenwich,* 37–38; A. N. Stimson, "Some Board of Longitude Instruments in the Nineteenth Century," in *Nineteenth-Century Scientific Instruments and Their Makers,* ed. P. R. de Clercq (Amsterdam: Rodopi, 1985), 95.

25 Jonathan Betts, *Harrison* (London: National Maritime Museum, 2007); Humphrey Quill, *John Harrison: The Man Who Found Longitude* (London: John Baker, 1966).

26 Albert van Helden, "Longitude and the Satellites of Jupiter," in Andrewes, *Quest for Longitude,* 86–100; see also Richard Dunn, "Scoping Longitude: Optical Designs for Navigation at Sea," in *From Earth-Bound to Satellite: Telescopes, Skills and Networks,* ed. G. Strano et al. (Leiden: Brill, 2011), 141–54.

27 Nevil Maskelyne, letter to Edmund Maskelyne, December 29, 1763, Royal Museums Greenwich, REG09/000037.

28 Maskelyne was by this time a Commissioner of Longitude, having been appointed astronomer royal the day before the meeting. Leonard Euler also received a smaller reward for work relating to the lunar-distance method. Mayer's reward went to his widow, as he had died in 1762.

29 Mary Croarken, "Tabulating the Heavens: Computing the *Nautical Almanac* in 18th-Century England," *IEEE Annals of the History of Computing* 25, no. 3 (2003): 48–61; Howse, *Greenwich Time,* 65–71; D. H. Sadler, *Man Is Not Lost: A Record of Two Hundred Years of Astronomical Navigation with the Nautical Almanac, 1767–1967* (London: HMSO, 1968); see also E. G. R. Taylor, *Navigation in the Days of Captain Cook* (London: National Maritime Museum, 1974), 3. The first *Tables Requisite,* containing data that did not change annually, was published in 1766.

30 Green, an astronomical assistant at the Royal Observatory, had also been Maskelyne's assistant during the Barbados trials of 1763–64.

31 J. C. Beaglehole, *The Life of Captain James Cook* (London: Adam & Charles Black, 1974), 154. Cook took his own sextant on the voyage. The Royal Society also supplied one made by Jesse Ramsden, which was presumably used by Green. See Derek Howse, "The Principal Scientific Instruments Taken on Captain Cook's Voyages of Exploration, 1768–80," *Mariner's Mirror* 65 (1979): 120.

32 *The Journals of Captain James Cook on His Voyages of Discovery,* vol. 1, *The Voyage of the* Endeavour, *1776–1780,* ed. J. C. Beaglehole (Cambridge: Cambridge University Press for the Hakluyt Society, 1955), 52–53.

33 Ibid., 392.

34 Cook and Green used Maskelyne's *British Mariner's Guide* to help them calculate the values normally given in the *Nautical Almanac.* See also Cook, *Voyage of the* Endeavour, 392; James Cook and James King, *A Voyage to the Pacific Ocean* (London: W. and A. Strahan, 1784), 3:286.

35 For a more detailed discussion, see J. A. Bennett, "The Travels and Trials of Mr Harrison's Timekeeper," in *Instruments, Travel and Science: Itineraries of Precision from the Seventeenth to the Twentieth Century,* ed. M. N. Bour-

guet, C. Licoppe, and H. O. Sibum (London: Routledge, 2002), 75–95.

36 John Bird, letter to Thomas Hornsby, August 20, 1765, quoted in J. A. Bennett, "Science Lost and Longitude Found: The Tercentenary of John Harrison," *Journal of the History of Astronomy* 24 (1993): 286.

37 Derek Howse, "Captain Cook's Marine Timekeepers, Part I: The Kendall Watches," *Antiquarian Horology* 6 (1969): 190–93.

38 *The Journals of Captain James Cook on His Voyages of Discovery,* vol. 2, *The Voyage of the* Resolution *and* Adventure, *1772–1775,* ed. J. C. Beaglehole (Cambridge: Cambridge University Press for the Hakluyt Society, 1961), 16–17. Similar conditions would be applied on the third voyage. See *The Journals of Captain James Cook on His Voyages of Discovery,* vol. 3, *The Voyage of the* Resolution *and* Discovery, *1776–1780,* ed. J. C. Beaglehole (Cambridge: Cambridge University Press for the Hakluyt Society, 1967), 1504.

39 Cook, *Voyage of the* Resolution *and* Adventure, 445.

40 Ibid., 724–28.

41 Ibid., 721; Howse, "Principal Scientific Instruments," 120.

42 Cook's second voyage showed that large-scale production of chronometers was possible in theory. It took a number of years for makers like John Arnold and Thomas Earnshaw to make it a reality. For the later history of the chronometer, see Alun C. Davies, "The Life and Death of a Scientific Instrument: The Marine Chronometer, 1770–1920," *Annals of Science* 35 (1978): 509–25.

43 Cook, *Voyage of the* Resolution *and* Adventure, cxii; Derek Howse, "Captain Cook's Marine Timekeepers, Part II: The Arnold Chronometers," *Antiquarian Horology* 6 (1969): 76–280.

44 Quoted in Howse, "Captain Cook's Marine Timekeepers, Part I," 194.

45 Cook, *Voyage of the* Resolution *and* Adventure, 660.

46 Glyn Williams, *The Death of Captain Cook* (London: Profile, 2008), 6; Beaglehole, *Life of Captain James Cook,* 634.

47 See, for example, R. A. Skelton, "Captain James Cook as a Hydrographer," *Mariner's Mirror* 40 (1954): 92–119; Beaglehole, *Life of Captain James Cook,* 409–10 n. 2; Andrew C. F. David, "Cook, James (1728–1779)," *Oxford Dictionary of National Biography* (Oxford: Oxford University Press, 2008), www.oxforddnb.com/view/article/6140, accessed November 26, 2012.

48 Cook, *Voyage of the* Resolution *and* Discovery, ccxxii–ccxxiii. See also Cook, *Voyage of the* Endeavour, cclxxix–clxxxiv; Cook, *Voyage of the* Resolution *and* Adventure, clxvii–clxx.

49 Instructions issued by the Board of Longitude to William Bayly for the third voyage, reproduced in Cook, *Voyage of the* Resolution *and* Discovery, 1500–1503.

50 See, for example, Nevil Maskelyne, draft list of instruments to be lent to Captain Cook, 1776, Royal Museums Greenwich, Ms AGC/8/29; see also Howse, "Principal Scientific Instruments."

51 Cook, *Voyage of the* Resolution *and* Adventure, 509 n. 4.

52 Cook, *Voyage of the* Resolution *and* Discovery, 454–55.

53 Cook, *Voyage of the* Resolution *and* Discovery, 469.

54 Beaglehole, *Life of Captain James Cook*, 60–98.

55 Ibid., 70. Potential sources of error included the difficulty in logging a ship's track with any accuracy, correctly positioning soundings and submerged features, and the masking of some land features by others.

56 Andrew David, "Vancouver's Survey Methods and Surveys," in *From Maps to Metaphors: The Pacific World of George Vancouver,* ed. Robin Fisher and Hugh Johnston (Vancouver: UBC Press, 1993), 51–69; Skelton, "Captain James Cook as a Hydrographer."

57 Quoted in David, "Vancouver's Survey Methods," 53.

58 Ibid.

59 For example, see Cook, *Voyage to the Pacific Ocean*, 2:120.

60 Wayne Orchiston, *Nautical Astronomy in New Zealand: The Cook Voyages* (Wellington: Carter Observatory Board, 1998), 59–60.

61 J. King, "Log and Proceedings," February 12, 1776–February 2, 1778, National Archives (UK), Ms. ADM 55/116, quoted in Cook, *Voyage of the* Resolution *and* Discovery, clxxxi.

62 Cook, *Voyage of the* Resolution *and* Adventure, 524–25.

63 Beaglehole, *Life of Captain James Cook*, 223, 336, 423.

64 Ibid., 589.

65 Cook, *Voyage to the Pacific Ocean*, 3:322–23.

66 Cook, *Voyage of the* Resolution *and* Adventure, 579–80.

67 Cook, *Voyage of the* Resolution *and* Discovery, 682.

68 Ibid., 685.
69 Howse, "Captain Cook's Marine Timekeepers, Part I," 196–99.
70 Cook, *Voyage of the* Resolution *and* Discovery, clxxx–clxxxi.
71 See, for example, Cook, *Voyage of the* Endeavour, 392, 501; Cook, *Voyage of the* Resolution *and* Discovery, 1501.
72 Cook, *Voyage of the* Resolution *and* Adventure, 726.
73 Ibid., 524–25.
74 Charles Consolvo, "The Prospects and Promotion of British Naval Officers, 1793–1815," *Mariner's Mirror* 91 (2005): 140–41.
75 Williams, *Death of Captain Cook*, 6.
76 Bernard Smith, *European Vision and the South Pacific* (New Haven, CT: Yale University Press, 1985), 69; Luke Strongman, "Captain Cook's Voyages and Coleridge's 'The Rime of the Ancient Mariner,'" in *Junctures: The Journal for Thematic Dialogue* 12 (2009): 69–81.
77 Georg Forster, *Cook the Discoverer* (Sydney: Horden House, 2001), 170, 195, 247–49.
78 Williams, *Death of Captain Cook*, 94–95. On Dalrymple and the transit of Venus expedition, see Andrew Cook, "James Cook and the Royal Society," in *Captain Cook: Explorations and Reassessments*, ed. Glyndwr Williams (Woodbridge, UK: Boydell & Brewer, 2004), 37–55.
79 Williams, *Death of Captain Cook*, 14–15.
80 "The Cook Medal Papers," 1784–85, Royal Society, London, MS/214, no. 3.

6

A New Look at Cook

Reflections on Sand, Ice, and His Diligent Voyage to the Arctic Ocean

DAVID L. NICANDRI

OF THE DOZENS OF BOOKS THAT HAVE STUDIED, PRAISED, CRITICIZED, OR debunked the career of Captain James Cook (fig. 6.1), one of the most popular is Tony Horwitz's cleverly titled *Blue Latitudes: Boldly Going Where Captain Cook Has Gone Before,* published in 2002. Horwitz seized upon one of Cook's most famous lines, "Ambition leads me not only farther than any other man has been before me, but as far as I think it possible for man to go" for both his subtitle and his organizing rubric.[1] Horwitz was also, of course, following a bit of popular cultural tradition. Cook's semantic construction was immortalized in the space age of the 1960s when it was adapted by Gene Roddenberry as the epigram for his *Star Trek* TV series. Stylistically, it may have also prefigured what many found to be the idiosyncratic exclamation of Neil Armstrong when he first set foot on the moon, namely, that his was a "small step for man," not "a man," as was commonly supposed to be his narrative intent.

Following Cook to *most* of the places the great navigator had sailed, Horwitz's book is an engaging interpretive travelogue. I emphasize *most* because, though *Blue Latitudes* is a well-written book from a best-selling, Pulitzer Prize–winning author, it still falls comfortably within what I call the "Polyne-

Georg Forster, *Ice Islands with Ice Blink,* 1772–73 (detail of fig. 6.6).

6.1 Nathaniel Dance, *Portrait of James Cook*, 1775. Oil. Though Dance has been deemed a lesser talent than the portraitist Joshua Reynolds, who captured images of many of Cook's contemporaries, this is generally considered to be the best likeness of the several known depictions of Cook. Painted after his return from the second voyage to the Pacific, it shows Cook pointing to his epochal map of the high latitudes of the Southern Hemisphere. © National Maritime Museum, Greenwich, London, BCH 2628.

sian palm-tree paradigm." That is, Horwitz focuses on Cook's visits to the sun-drenched beaches of Hawai'i, Tahiti, and other South Pacific islands—scenes of some celebrated or infamous cross-cultural encounters—while largely ignoring his travels to those parts of the world that are of ever-increasing significance in the twenty-first century: the high, frozen "white" latitudes of the Indian, Pacific, Atlantic, and Arctic Oceans and the ice masses or lands that bound them. Horwitz dismisses these regions, as he considers the notion of following Cook to Antarctica and the Arctic as "the literary equivalent of chewing on ice cubes."[2]

Like Cook's contemporaries, many historians have seized on the most enchanting venues visited by Cook as the essential narrative baseline for his exploration of the Pacific. The famous accounts of his stays in Polynesia became one of the most destabilizing episodes in the history of Western civilization. Tahiti, in particular, became "the standard by which all other places and people were judged," Horwitz observes, "and invariably found wanting, most often in the beauty of their women" and in liberality in the granting of sexual favors.[3] In stark contrast, the icy high latitudes can be uninviting and even deadly. But even if the polar regions are lightly inhabited and infrequently visited compared to the tropics, that should not make them less relevant to students of Captain Cook. In fact, one might now argue the opposite.

There will always be a scholarly interest in Cook's Native encounters, and, concomitantly, the anthropological perspective has always dominated the Cook discourse. But as a facet of environmental history, Cook's experience in the frigid seas can be seen as a compelling indicator as to the pace and effects of global warming. Most travelers today probably share Horwitz's preference for "adventures where I can encounter people, not penguins," but Cook's voyages, in addition to having imprinted the image of Polynesian paradise in the Western mind, serve as important markers in our developing awareness of accelerated climate change.[4]

This is particularly true in regard to the quest that gave rise to Cook's third and final voyage, the search for the Northwest Passage. If Cook had sailed through Bering Strait in August 2013 instead of August 1778, he might well have passed through the Canadian archipelago at the top of North America and emerged in Baffin Bay. Once through Davis Strait, he could have headed home to England across the Atlantic Ocean. In a playful sense, Cook did not fail: he was merely ahead of his time. Even though he is rarely associated with these regions, his third voyage to the far north and much of his second voyage exploring the high southern latitudes give us reason to take a new look at Cook.

Paradoxically, for a man about whom so much has been written in the last half century, the Cook literature is remarkably orthodox. A few examples have deviated from a strict chronological account—notably that of Horwitz himself, the writing of Bernard Smith, and the famous literary exchanges between the anthropologists Marshall Sahlins and

Gananath Obeyesekere over the meaning of Cook's reception and death in Hawai'i.[5] But one element of Cook dogma has remained constant throughout: the assertion that he should never have conducted his fatal third voyage.

Several subelements of this orthodoxy stand out: the claims that Cook was not as diligent, determined, or thorough as he had been on his first two expeditions; that he had a more fractious relationship with his officers and crew; and, most prominently, that he had become complacent, perhaps even careless or cruel, in his relations with Native peoples. This critical indictment started as a mere hint from John Cawte Beaglehole, editor of the definitive four-volume edition of *The Journals of Captain James Cook* (fig. 6.2).[6] There is no small irony here, because Beaglehole often fawned over his subject to such excess that he made it easy for the debunkers to cut Cook down to size. However, as Nicholas Thomas was the first to point out,[7] Beaglehole's first, tentative rhetorical questioning of Cook's fitness for continued duty after his second voyage has become scholarly cant and a literary harbor especially favored by postcolonialist authors and their partisans. In their view, Cook was a violent and irrational man whose compromised judgment brought about the circumstances leading to his death at Kealakekua Bay.

There is certainly a case to be made that Cook, after a decade of almost incessant voyaging, had become fatigued by the demands of regular intercultural encounters. Nevertheless, within a week after the news of his death reached London in January 1780, one sage observer remarked that it was amazing Cook had survived long enough even to lead a third expedition. This anonymous writer, in the London *Morning Chronicle* of January 18, 1780, did not think it "a remarkable circumstance that [Cook] should be killed, but that he should have so often escaped." The author, who gives evidence of having traveled with Cook on one of the first two voyages, professes that Cook was heard to say as much.[8] This has the ring of truth. In addition to risking his life in many contentious encounters on a variety of sandy shores, Cook also tempted fate many times among rocks, reefs, and fields of ice. After barely avoiding running aground in the Society Islands (Tahiti) on the third voyage, in May 1777, Cook averred, "Such risks as thise [*sic*] are the unavoidable Companions of the Man who goes on Discoveries."[9]

However tentatively he may have first planted the seed of doubt, as he delved deeper into the record of the third voyage, Beaglehole seems to have become increasingly convinced of Cook's error in undertaking the third voyage. Following Beaglehole, most historians view the third voyage as a below-par effort and a long prologue to Kealakekua. Inevitably, the failure to find a Northwest Passage and Cook's death cast a pall over scholarly perceptions of the third voyage. But a careful reading of the Cook journals shows that the indictments of Cook's deportment, principally what might be termed his exploratory nonfeasance and his failures

6.2 John Cawte Beaglehole. Few editors or biographers have been so symbiotically linked to their subjects as Beaglehole is to Cook. His monumental annotation of Cook's and related journals, including extensive introductory essays to each Pacific voyage that are nearly books in themselves, have combined to create a lasting imprint on all subsequent Cook historiography. Famously, Beaglehole laid the foundation for the orthodox interpretation that Cook should not have undertaken his third voyage, which was, in his estimation, a disaster. Given the extensive scope and time-consuming nature of Cook's global voyaging, it might be asked whether it was Cook who got tired of his work, or Beaglehole. Photograph by Lynette Corner. J. C. Beaglehole Room. Victoria University of Wellington, 2/103c.

6.3 James Cook, *Chart of part of the NW Coast of America explored by Capt. J Cook in 1778.* Manuscript chart sent home by Cook from Unalaska in October 1778. Though Cook's maps of the west coast of North America contained gaps, a function of his being blown off course and scrupulous adherence to his instructions to look for a passage at 65°N, this was the first realistic depiction of the northwest quadrant of the continent. National Archives, Kew, MPI 83.

in shipboard management, do not hold up under scrutiny.

This contrarian view becomes crystallized in the explications of Cook's pursuit of the Northwest Passage and his foray along the Arctic ice shelf. It became a commonplace among historians of the Pacific Northwest to disparage Cook's competence by noting that the great navigator "missed" the outfall of the Columbia River and the Straits of Juan de Fuca when he sailed up the west coast of North America in the late winter and spring of 1778. The truth is, he was not looking for them. The weather had been stormy on the occasion of the American landfall and barely improved before he reached Alaska; thus the first enduring place name Cook assigned along the Pacific coast was Cape Foulweather, on the Oregon Coast. Even if the atmospherics had been more conducive to exploration, he still might not have pursued those openings beyond the immediate goal, which was to secure sufficient wood and water to reach the more northerly latitudes his instructions demanded. Though Cook's fastidiousness as a navigator and officer have been often remarked upon, one facet of his style of discovery has been almost entirely overlooked relative to the third voyage: his fidelity to mission. Historians following Beaglehole's lead have criticized Cook for not undertaking the explorations they think proper.

Cook's adherence to the strategic purpose of the third voyage, as stipulated in his instructions from the Admiralty, is probative. Other than the "convenient Port," which was envisioned as an intermediate place of refreshment along the "Coast of New Albion" (Sir Francis Drake's place name for the mid-latitude American shore, north of Spain's possessions), Cook was not even supposed to begin looking for his objective—the Northwest Passage—until he had reached "the Latitude of 65°, or farther, if you are not obstructed by Lands or Ice." This specification of latitude was informed by Samuel Hearne's terrestrial exploration of Canada's northern perimeter west of Hudson Bay and north to the Arctic Ocean via the Coppermine River (fig. 2.5). Indeed, Cook was emphatically cautioned "not to lose any time in exploring Rivers or Inlets, or upon any other account until you get into the before-mentioned Latitude of 65°." It was only at that northerly juncture that he was "very carefully to search for, and to explore, such Rivers or Inlets as may appear to be of a considerable extent, and pointing towards Hudsons or Baffins Bay" using "your utmost endeavours to pass through with one or both sloops."[10]

Cook adhered to this charge as scrupulously as wind, weather, and the coastal topography allowed (fig. 6.3). He was also charged to perform a "running survey," so his superiors expected that he would usually be well offshore and occasionally out of sight of land. In hindsight, because he refused to exhaust the recourses that certain inlets availed, he exposed himself to second-guessing, which took form principally in the Vancouver expedition, a survey from San Diego to Cook Inlet conducted over the

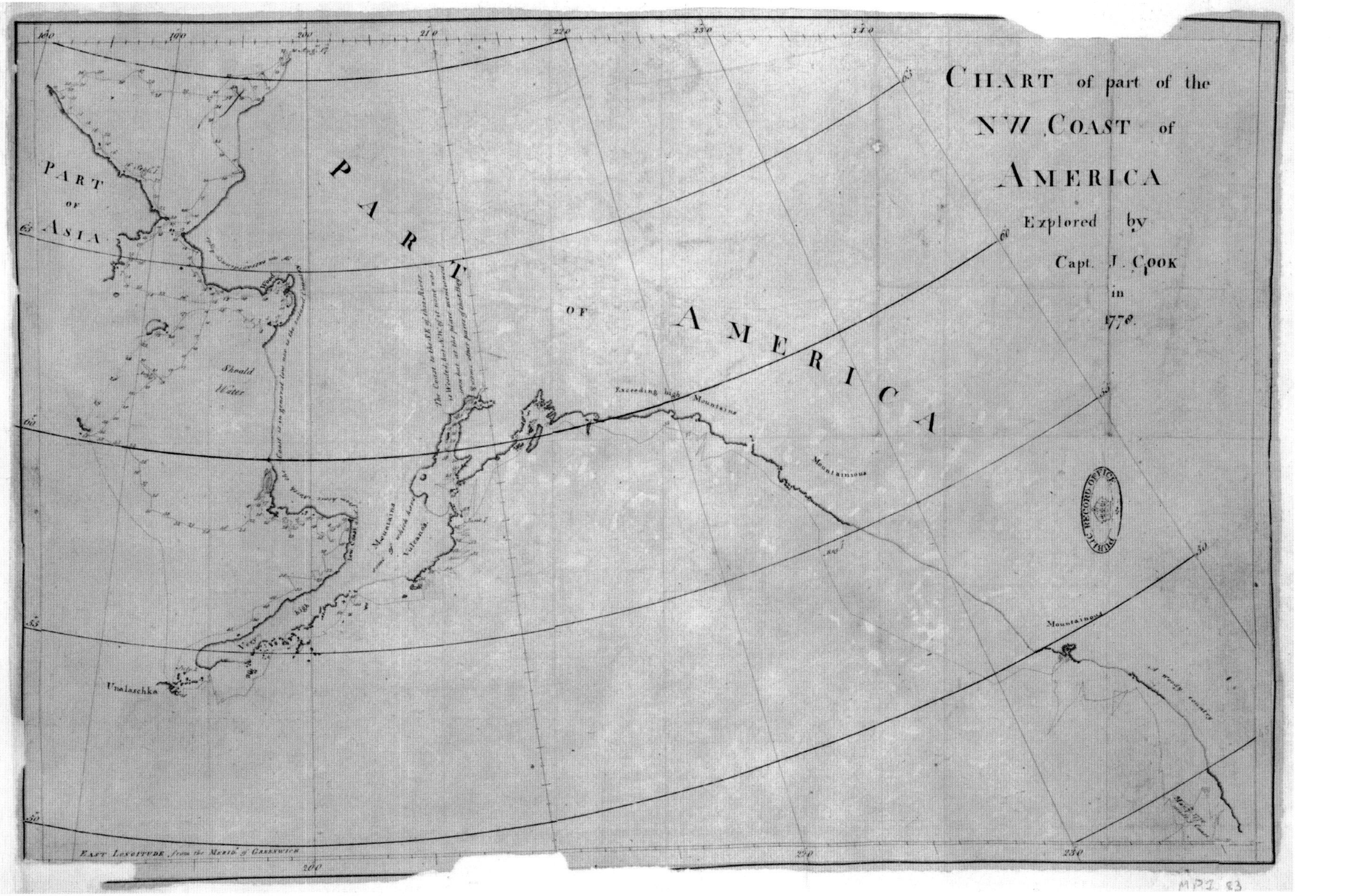

CHART of part of the
N.W. COAST of
AMERICA
Explored by
Capt. J. COOK
in
1778.
PART OF ASIA
PART OF AMERICA
Shoald Water
Exceeding high Mountains
Mountainous
Mountainous
Mountains some of which are Volcanos
Unalaschka
A woody country
PUBLIC RECORD OFFICE
EAST LONGITUDE from the Merid. of GREENWICH

course of 1792 to 1794. It is one of the great ironies of Cook's phenomenal career that his faithful adherence to the main purpose of the expedition, among other means by avoiding attractive nuisances, has cast his third voyage in a poor light. Beaglehole took this initial opportunity to charge, in the familiar refrain, that the Cook of voyages 1 and 2 would not have passed up the opportunities for exploration that the supposedly worn-out Cook of the third voyage ignored so casually.

Beaglehole first raises this argument in his introduction to Cook's third voyage journal. Discussing Cook's unplanned and then prolonged stay in Tonga, Beaglehole proffers the "speculation" that became the seed of scholarly dogma when he argues that in the spring and summer of 1777, Cook passed up a chance to record upward of one hundred additional neighboring islands. Beaglehole admits that many of these were mere reefs and sandy islets, but he expresses shock that the great Cook was now "content to enquire into them no further," not even the more substantial islands we know as Samoa and Fiji. Beaglehole then posed his determinative question: "Can there be any doubt that Cook, on his second voyage, if he had heard of their existence . . . would have been after them, fastened them down securely on his Pacific chart, even at the cost of minor disorganisation to his time plan?"[11] Beaglehole took his cue from the journal of George Gilbert, who could not account for the fact that Cook failed to search for Fiji even though, seemingly, time availed.

Cook concluded that Fiji, from what he could learn of it at a distance, was likely a "very fruitfull island." But the three-day sail that would be required to map it would make no cardinal contribution to the main purpose of the voyage; nor was a visit necessary for refreshment. So he did not pursue the exploration of Fiji. Beaglehole, a New Zealander, seems almost to have taken Cook's third voyage indifference to the southwest Pacific as a kind of regional slight. He then posed one of the most influential questions ever asked about James Cook's career: "Is it possible that, just as unsuspected strain on his mind was beginning to affect his attitude to the human situation, so, in relation to unexpected geographic possibilities, he was beginning to experience a certain tiredness?"[12]

Though Beaglehole was always careful to couch his argument in tentative phrases, historians have since conflated it into the necessary and fundamental premise for understanding the outcome of Cook's last voyage. Beaglehole asserted that the third voyage was "different from the first or second," not only in the obvious sense of object and scope, but more critically, if elusively, "in feeling"; but he posed his entire argument merely as a hypothesis. "Like most hypotheses," he said, "it can be controverted," but it hasn't been for more than half a century. Beaglehole was confident that his theory was "tenable." The temperamentalism that Cook displayed over Tongan theft, and then again over the theft of a goat in Moorea, was roughly concurrent with his decision against charting more islands. These circumstances, taken together, gave the theory its original currency and most credible grounding.[13]

Here I argue and attempt to show in greater detail that Cook as navigator and geographic problem solver, as opposed to beach broker, was as vigorous and thorough in pursuit of the actual mission of the third voyage—finding a passage to Europe via the far north Pacific—than he was at any of his best moments during the first two voyages. Admittedly, any expedition that ends up with its commander dead warrants consideration as "a disaster," as Beaglehole sees it. Charles Clerke's death six months later certainly adds weight to that view. Still, it is arguable whether Beaglehole's supposition that Cook's "faculties had simply been stretched to the uttermost for a long period" applies over the entire extent of his last voyage.[14] I believe there is distinct evidence to the contrary when Cook's time in the high northern latitudes is studied on its own terms and not as an interlude filling in time and delaying his inevitable death in Hawai'i. And besides, with the American War of Independence beginning just as Cook was leaving, is it reasonable to assume that had he not voyaged in search of the Northwest Passage that Cook would have sat out that war in retirement?

Evincing some ambivalence about criticizing Cook's judgment, Beaglehole asked, in contemplation of the chances for the success of the third voyage, "Has one simply come to expect from Cook the superhuman?"[15] There was nothing preternatural about Cook at any point in his career, but historians have failed to acknowledge the economy of effort by which he accomplished his goals. What some viewed as a casual approach, bordering on the lackadaisical, can be viewed from another vantage as evidence of a very experienced navigator who developed a kind of empirical exploratory shorthand. Cook was always conscious of the mission of the third voyage, even if some of his shipboard contemporaries, and many later critics, found fault with the way he executed it. Suffice it to say that Cook, having accomplished both the main and subsidiary goals of the second voyage, considered himself to be "done" with the South Pacific Ocean (figs. 6.4 and 6.5).[16] In the run-up to the venture north of the equator, he clearly was not intending to make major discoveries in the vicinity of Tonga or anywhere else in the Southern Hemisphere. In general terms his deportment in that zone is completely consistent with his viewing of Polynesia as merely a staging area for the run north, plus a few minor considerations such as dropping off Mai, his supernumerary, and some domesticated animals that were gifts from King George and himself.

The crankiness ascribed to Cook on this voyage owed in part to his missing the timeline set forth in his directions by one year, the dilapidated condition of the ships under his command, and a more fractious crew (even though Cook scholarship seems determined in the view that the only shipboard difference between the third voyage and the two before it was the psychological condition of the

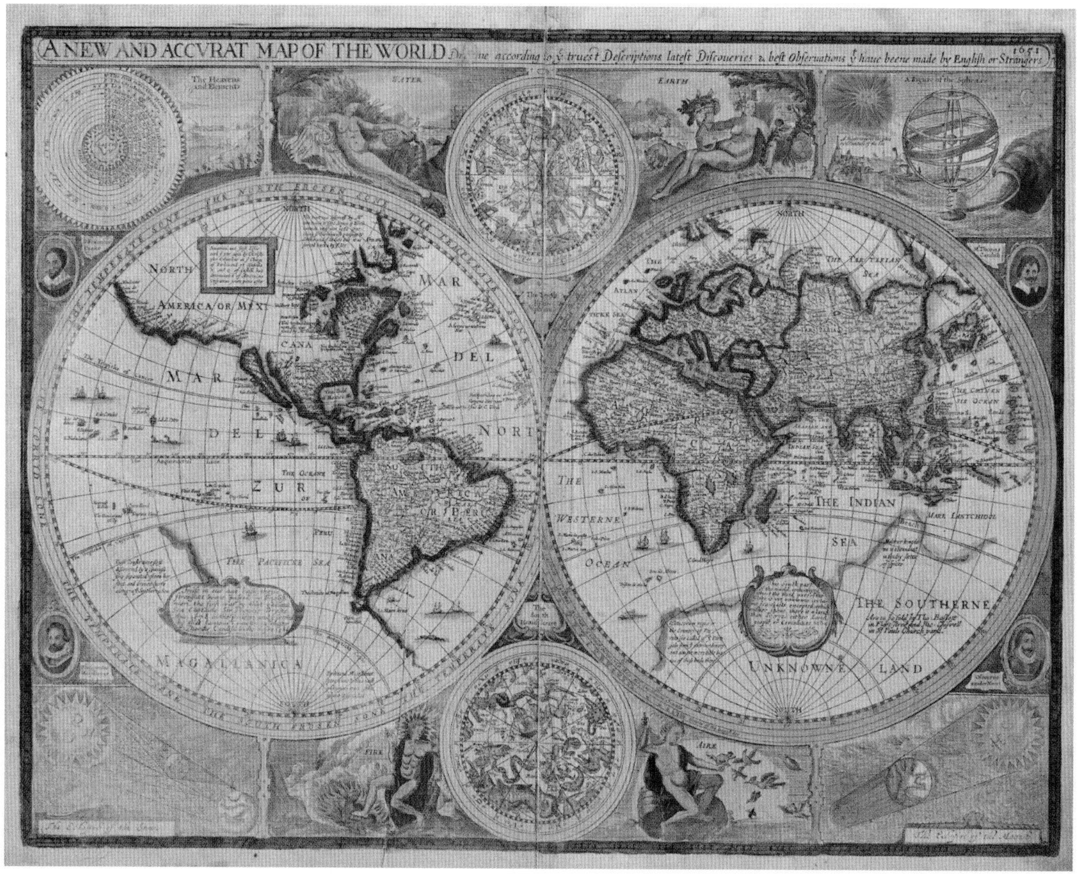

6.4 John Speed, *A New and Accurat Map of the World*, 1651. When Speed's map is contrasted with the master map tracking Cook's several voyages, published a century later (fig. 6.5), one quickly discerns the nature and reliability of Cook's contributions to global geography. Washington State Historical Society, 1975.14.13.001.

6.5 Henry Roberts, *A General Chart Exhibiting the Discoveries made by Captn. James Cook in this and his two preceeding Voyages, with the Tracks of the Ships under his Command*, 1784. Cook's master map, published with the account of his third and last voyage, is arguably the first modern map of the world in the sense that it provides a normative depiction of geographic reality. Roberts's pristine cartographic image is noteworthy for its lack of embellishment, strict reliance on the grid of latitude and longitude, and its placement of the Pacific basin in the center. University of British Columbia Library, Rare Books and Special Collections, G3200.1784.R6.

captain). By chance rather than by an active search he came upon a truly significant find, the Hawaiian Islands, which were charted in a customary fashion. One does not have to be a trumpeter for American exceptionalism to acknowledge that these islands, whose discovery by Cook set in motion a sequence of events that led to their eventual annexation by the United States, were a discovery equal to anything he accomplished on his first voyage and exceeding any like find on the second. In any event, despite having stumbled into Kauai in January 1778, Cook was not diverted from his prescribed mission. He likely made a mental note to return if the search for a Northwest Passage went unrewarded. After securing refreshments and provisions in Hawai'i, Cook immediately proceeded toward his intended goal.

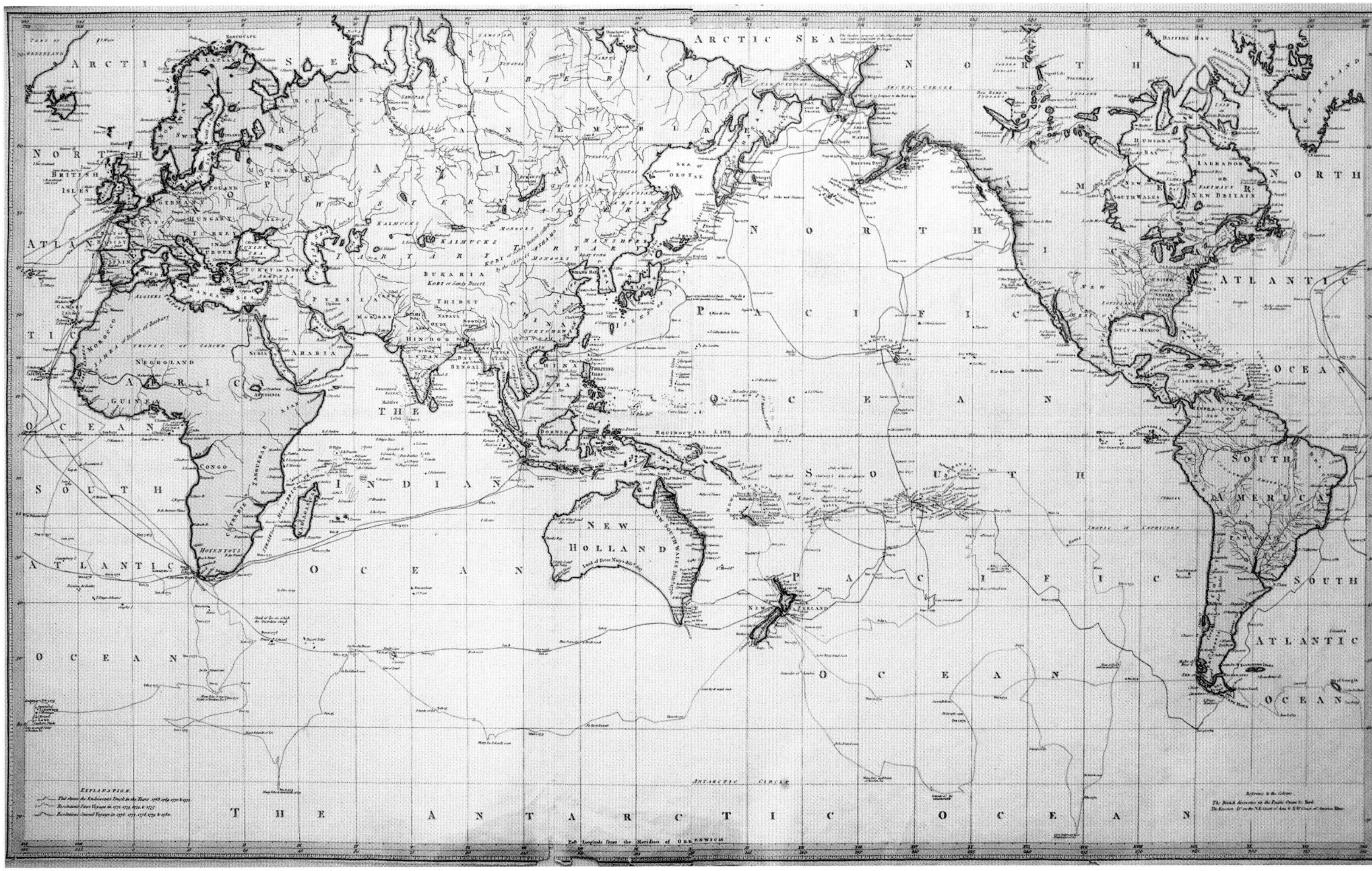
ARCTIC SEA
NORTH BRITISH ISLES
POLAND
GERMANY
HUNGARY
TURKEY
ARABIA
PERSIA
TARTARY
THIBET
BUKARIA
HINDOO
BENGAL
CHINA
NEGROLAND
GUINEA
AFRICA
ABYSSINIA
CONGO
HOTENTOTS
ZANGUEBAR
INDIAN OCEAN
NEW HOLLAND
NEW SOUTH WALES
NEW ZEALAND
BORNEO
PHILIPINE ISLES
SEA of OKOTSK
EQUINOCTIAL LINE
NORTH PACIFIC OCEAN
SOUTH PACIFIC OCEAN
SOUTH AMERICA
GULF of MEXICO
NEW BRITAIN
LABRADOR
HUDSONS BAY
BAFFINS BAY
GREENLAND
NORTH ATLANTIC OCEAN
SOUTH ATLANTIC OCEAN
TROPIC of CANCER
TROPIC of CAPRICORN
ANTARCTIC CIRCLE
THE ANTARCTIC OCEAN
EXPLANATION.
East Longitude from the Meridian of GREENWICH

The quest for the Northwest Passage was probably Cook's most ambitious venture. Finding a way over, around, or through North America had become the holy grail of all exploration after the first great age of American discovery in the fifteenth and early sixteenth centuries. In the end, Cook could not find such a passage. In our day, however incrementally, the fabled passage is slowly becoming manifest, opening the door to commercial access and extractive development 250 years after Cook sailed into the Pacific in search of it.

On March 7, 1778, at a latitude calculated to 44°33'N, James Cook first sighted the western shore of North America in the form of a flat-topped mountain—denominated "Table Mountain" (one of his favorite toponyms) on the charts.[17] It is known today as Mary's Peak, the scenic backdrop to the pretty college town of Corvallis, Oregon. Stormy weather forced a retrograde move to the south, but by March 29, Cook was back in sight of land at 49°29' and soon found an inlet where he "resolved to anchor to endeavour to get some Water, of which [we] were in great want."[18] This inlet would become known as Nootka Sound, a place that would resonate deeply in the regional history of the Pacific Northwest over the next fifteen years. For four weeks, Cook's ships, the *Resolution* and *Discovery,* underwent repair, and having established generally amiable relations with the Native inhabitants, the crew secured provender and replenished their water casks. On the evening of April 26 Cook set off at last, a year later than intended, to find a passage to the Atlantic.[19]

On leaving Nootka a storm wailed for four days, forcing Cook's ships well out to sea and sight of land for six degrees of latitude. The coast did not come into view again until May 1 at 55°N. Cook did not resume naming landmarks until Mount Edgecumbe, near present-day Sitka, at 57°N. Passing the presumed location of the imagined strait of Admiral de Fonte (a mythical seventeenth-century Spanish navigator much touted by French mapmakers), it was not speculative geography that captured Cook's attention so much as the veritable Russian voyages of Vitus Bering and Alexei Chirikov dating back to 1728 and 1741 (fig. 2.3). Cook was flustered trying to reconcile Bering's narrative account and the maps prepared by Gerhard Müller, partly derived and partly inspired by that voyage, with his own seaborne vantage (fig. 2.3). But one aspect of Müller's map proved superior to French cartography. Cook began to notice that the coastline was not bearing east toward the nominal Atlantic outlets for any passage, that is, Baffin Bay and Davis Strait—and neither was it trending due north.[20]

Cook's journals invariably come alive when his voyages intersect with the presumed or real explorations of his predecessors and contemporaries in discovery. On sighting Bering's Mount St. Elias and a coastal inlet that Cook thought was the farthest extent of early Russian voyaging, at almost 60°N, he found himself in previously (if sketchily) charted territory for the first time since leaving Tahiti. Given the idealizations found in the mission statement, Cook might otherwise have supposed he was within a week of reaching 65°N and the point where he would turn east toward Hearne's outfall. Instead, Cook's journal for May 7 and 8 reflects the hard reality of North America's continental architecture. "We now found the Coast to trend very much to the west inclining hardly any thing to the north," Cook wrote, and if that was not troubling enough, the westerly wind pattern, if it did not actively retard progress, brought weather that was too calm. As Charles Clerke noted aboard the *Discovery,* "We continue to have most extra ordinary fine Weather, with such gentle Breezes that we just crawl along the shore."[21] At the time of writing, Cook and Clerke were off Icy Bay, or slightly to the west of the top of the parabolic curve that defines the Gulf of Alaska, just prior to the appearance of what would be named Prince William Sound. The generally fair weather, which lasted well into the summer of 1778 and inspired the naming of mountains in Alaska's panhandle as the Fairweather Range, contributed to the sense of surprise when the ships suddenly met with impenetrable ice in mid-August. At comparably high latitudes in the Southern Hemisphere during Cook's second voyage, far colder temperatures were the norm, and encounters with and discussions about icebergs and fields of ice were common.

Though it initially seemed promising as a prospect for a passage, Prince William Sound proved disappointing.[22] An even larger inlet, later named after Cook, was explored between May 26 and June 5, 1778. Still well south of the latitude targeted in his instructions for any detailed search, Cook was grappling with a troubling juxtaposition: the reality of the land and seascapes visible from the *Resolution*'s deck versus the perplexing cartographic depictions on the charts in the captain's cabin. By this time, Cook was referring to another map, Jacob von Staehlin's infamously misleading image, which was supposedly the most recent map of Russian exploration in North America (fig. 2.6). It may be deduced that Cook was at first seduced into reading the wide entrance to Cook's Inlet as one of the channels "to the north" through Staehlin's fanciful archipelago. In any event, Cook was tempted into exploring the inlet bearing his name as a function of the relative lateness of the season as much as the view through his telescope.

As early as May 17, when still in Prince William Sound, Cook began to fret about traveling far enough north to turn east into the supposed passage on a timely basis. Soon after entering the inlet, Cook concluded he was in another cul-de-sac and only explored it as far as he did "to satisfy other people [more] than to confirm my own opinion." Cook was referring to his junior officers, who had prematurely concluded that this inlet was not merely an access corridor to the north through Staehlin's imaginary island chain but the Northwest Passage proper. Foremost among these optimists was the American Lieutenant John Gore, who would dot his forlorn journal with a litany of geographic prospects gained and lost, such as Gulf of Good Hope, Cape Hold with Hope, and Cape Lost Hope.[23]

The failure to thoroughly explore Cook Inlet is also cited as evidence of Cook's increasing weakness and lack of vigor. This conclusion fails to acknowledge that by June 1778 Cook had been surveying the globe's surface almost continuously for nearly a decade. As the most studious and best-traveled navigator of the age, he was confident in his judgments. It can equally well be argued that Cook was not displaying fatigue or carelessness but rather economy of effort. It is nonetheless true that in calling off the full and final exploration of the inlet, Cook left an opening for other speculators, and this fact became central to Vancouver's later mission to ascertain definitively whether or not it led to an inland sea analogous to Hudson Bay. As Beaglehole pithily put it, "Cook thought he had spared them the trouble." But some dreams die hard. For his part, Cook regretted the amount of time he had spent on this chimera, and by June 6 he was back in the Gulf of Alaska.[24]

Once on the open water again, Cook found that the Alaska Peninsula foreclosed any immediate opportunity to sail north. He must have been mortified to be forced well to the southwest before he found a corridor through the Aleutian Chain between Unalaska and Unalga Islands. After a few days in Unalaska's English Bay, Cook was finally able to forge a route northward toward the Bering Strait and into the Chukchi Sea—which he reached in August, not June as his instructions anticipated.

In making his run toward 65°N, Cook seems not to have entertained the possibility of coming upon ice, despite the fact that on his second voyage, encounters with "Sea Ice Islands" in the low fifties of southern latitude were not uncommon. Once above the Antarctic Circle (66°34'S), contact with icebergs and pack ice was routine. Similarly, icebergs were ubiquitous in the fifties and sixties of the North Atlantic, posing hazards for whalers and other traders heading to and along the shores of Hudson Bay. So there is no reason for Cook not to have expected to see ice islands once he broke through the Aleutian chain, with the possible exception that Bering made no mention of them.[25] If Cook had been on the original June timetable specified for reaching 65°N, the ice might very well have forestalled his transit through Bering Strait. Because of the vagaries of Russian cartography and the perplex of continental geography, he did not get far north until August, a time of year more conducive to the discernment of the Arctic zone.

Any discussion of Cook's travels in the polar regions must take account of the prevailing scientific theory of that age that salt water did not freeze and that sea ice instead resulted from an outflow of frozen masses emanating from freshwater rivers located in high latitudes. A preposterous notion to present-day sensibility (which owes much to Cook's observations in the icy latitudes during the second and third voyages), this doctrine fed a corollary proposition almost more incredible to modern understanding, that the Arctic Ocean was altogether free of ice at the pole (at least seasonally), because no land was thought to be proximate to it.

Daines Barrington, a member of the Royal Society with good connections to the British Admiralty, was the best-known proponent of this theory in the English-speaking world during Cook's era, though its foremost theoretician was a Swiss writer and bibliophile, Samuel Engel. This combination of theory and speculation, complemented by the necessary economic pressures of empire and trade, laid the foundation for Cook's last voyage. The thinking was that the right man, commanding the right ship(s), at the right time of year, could get through from one ocean to the other, maybe by way of the North Pole itself. Anecdotal information from seafarers who ventured into the seventies or higher latitudes in the Atlantic without encountering ice enabled Barrington to marshal support within the Royal Society for a great northern voyage as early as 1773, while Cook was still on his second expedition.[26]

Ironically, it was roughly at this time that Cook and Johann Reinhold Forster, the leading scientist on the voyage toward the South Pole, began to doubt Engel's theory. Forster devoted a whole section of his book *Observations Made during a Voyage round the World* to this subject.[27] Because of the great volumes of ice found in the bergs and pack ice encountered on the second voyage, juxtaposed with the shrinking size of any putative continent at or near the South Pole, Forster was led to conclude, rather emphatically, that seawater did freeze. Although one has to assume that Cook and Forster discussed sea-ice theory between themselves, their published narratives are not entirely in accord on this point. If Cook took a somewhat agnostic posture toward the Barrington-Engel hypothesis, Forster was an atheist, certain that salt water froze. This divergence may have been due to Cook's well-known and oft-demonstrated hesitance to pose as a scientist, particularly since he knew, or could safely surmise, that Forster would address the topic in print.

Cook's Arctic campaign, in Beaglehole's phrasing, "was not to be fought according to the rules laid down by Daines Barrington and Samuel Engel."[28] It did get off to a promising start, though. In thick but temperate weather, Cook made his most northerly landing—Alaska's Sledge Island, off the southwest shore of the Seward Peninsula—near 64°N on August 5, 1778. On August 9, proceeding cautiously in the mist, fog, and drizzle endemic to summers in the Bering Sea, Cook sighted Cape Prince of Wales. Given its exotic location and distance from England, it may seem as odd a place name as can be imagined for North America's westernmost point. But it fittingly reflects Great Britain's reach across the breadth of the continent from Walter Raleigh's landfall at Roanoke Island to James Cook's voyage along the Pacific coast.

After sighting the Diomede Islands, Cook saw and visited more land to the west, that of the Chukchi in eastern Siberia. The entire geographic tableau—the capes on both the American and Asian sides and the water between them—formed the Bering Strait and the anticipated gate providing access to the Atlantic. On the next day, August 10,

6.6 Georg Forster, *Ice Islands with Ice Blink,* 1772–73. Gouache. Drawing on his familiarity with icebergs and pack ice in the high southern latitudes during the course of his second voyage, Cook immediately realized the portent of "ice blink" when he encountered it in the Arctic Ocean during the third voyage. Mitchell Library, State Library of New South Wales, Safe PXD 11: Digital Order #a156042.

prompted by the pleasant weather and exploratory prospects, Charles Clerke wrote euphorically, "We all feel this morning as though we were risen in a new World."[29] After the disappointments and frustrations in Prince William Sound, Cook Inlet, and the long westerly extension of the Alaska Peninsula, the expedition had doubled the tip of North America and was now at the prescribed latitude of 65°N. The season of great discovery was seemingly at hand. Lieutenant James King wrote in his journal, "All our Sanguine hopes began to revive & we already begin to compute the distance of our Situation from known parts of Baffins Bay."[30]

For a week, probing carefully in the fog, Cook sailed into the Arctic Ocean in a northeasterly direction, just off the North American coast. But on August 17 a rare atmospheric phenomenon was seen from the deck: a cream-colored reflection of sunlight off the ice, projected into the sky on and just above the horizon (fig 6.6). Cook called it "ice blink." Here, at the crux of the voyage, Cook inscribed a line in his journal that needs more study than it usually receives. He wrote that no attention was given to the appearance of the blink at first, "from a supposition that it was improbable we should meet the ice *so soon*" (emphasis added). Cook was now at 70°N. As noted earlier, on his circumnavigation of the South Pole, Cook routinely saw ice above 60°S. He was turned back by solid pack ice just above the Antarctic Circle in the Indian Ocean on his first swing south and again high in the South Pacific when he reached his southernmost point (71°10') in the transect of that ocean. Why then was he surprised to find ice at 70°N?

Cook's late spring and summer in Alaskan waters were quite temperate compared to his experience in the high southern latitudes during the second voyage. On his last swing into the southern extremity of the Atlantic Ocean, Cook found South Georgia and the South Sandwich Islands held in an icy grip. At only 60°S (a latitude equivalent to that of Anchorage, Alaska, in the north), these were forbidding, bone-chilling places, even at the height of the southern summer.

Cook also carried with him Captain Constantine John Phipps's account of a voyage into the North Atlantic, which was published in 1774. On another venture promoted by Daines Barrington and the Royal Society, Phipps reportedly reached 80°37' before the ice stopped him just west of Spitsbergen, part of the Svalbard Archipelago north of Norway, effectively on the divide between the Atlantic and Arctic Oceans.[31] Phipps failed to reach the North Pole, but Barrington applied the somewhat promising findings of that voyage to the exploration of the north Pacific, leading ultimately to Cook's last command. Barrington, the Admiralty, and Cook seem to have concluded that Phipps's northerly reach, at the time a record by sail for a European, established the upper limit of an ice-free corridor over the top of North America, bound on the south by Hearne's recorded latitude of 71°34' at the debouche of the Coppermine River. Armed with this theory, Cook's practical objective was to press his way east through those nine degrees of latitude. On August 17, Cook had yet to enter that latitudinal range.[32]

The ice hinted at by the initial appearance of the blink fast became a crushing reality to Cook. He soon found it hard to maneuver north or east because of field ice floating about the ships. A day later he was fully stymied by an ice pack forming a wall as much as twelve feet high. That day, August 18, Cook reached a recorded 70°44' latitude. This was as far north as he would get, not quite matching the southern extreme of latitude he had reached on the second voyage. At this northern apex, Cook was out of sight of land, but as he turned from the face of the ice, the American coast came into view. Cook appropriately named this low point of land Icy Cape. In fact, the ice here began to close in, and Cook was fortunate to evacuate to the south and west before his ships were trapped (fig. 2.7).[33]

At this point in his voyage, twenty-five months after the expedition's launch, and with cold and fatigue compounded by monumental disappointment settling into the bodies and minds of the officers and crew, Cook diligently probed and darted along the ice edge for eleven more grueling days—to the particular annoyance of those crew members who found walrus meat unpalatable. Cook exhausted every prospect for an opening through or around the ice pack, rarely with a clear view of his surroundings because of the Arctic fog, frequently relying for guidance on the incessant barking of the walruses abounding on the ice edge. As Beaglehole notes, this species made for "a very effective foghorn."[34] Yet another challenge was maintaining contact with Clerke on the *Discovery*. It was some of the most vigorous sailing of his career.

Because ice blocked his way toward Baffin Bay, Cook pressed toward the west, with the ice generally, though not always, on his starboard side. Carefully navigating through and along the floes, drawing on the experience gained on the voyage in the Antarctic and from sailing around shoals and reefs during all three voyages, Cook drove an astounding eighteen degrees of longitude west from

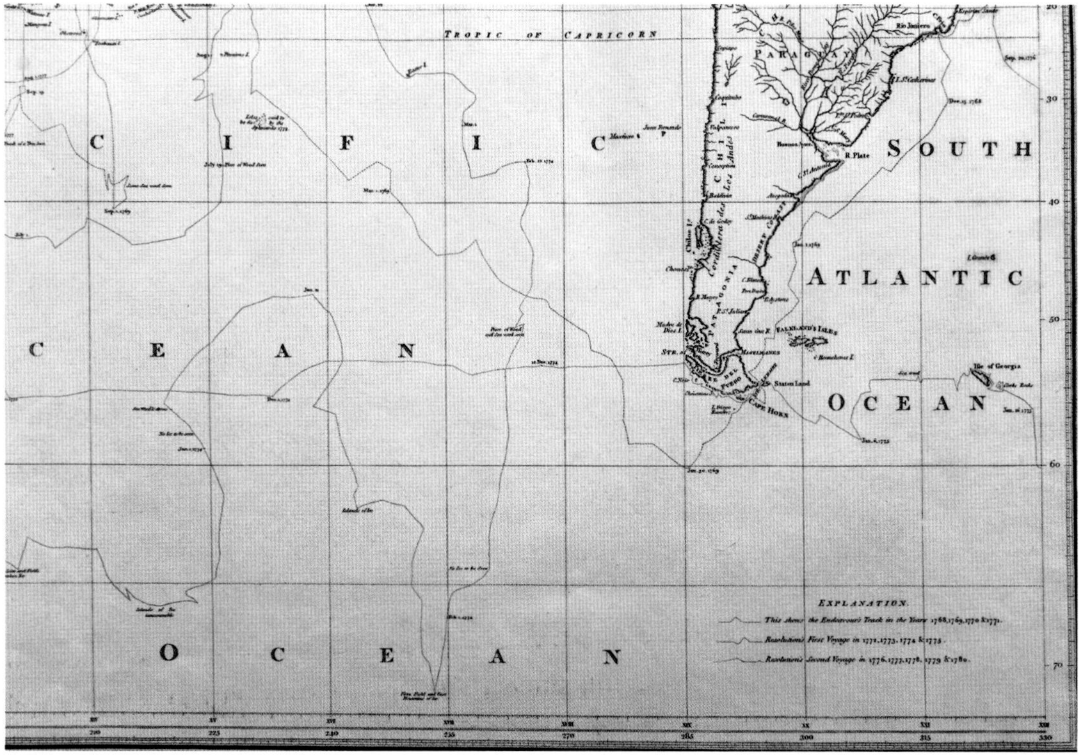

6.7 Detail from the *General Chart* (fig. 6.5), showing Cook's Antarctic probe. This detail shows the needle-nose penetration toward Antarctica southwest of Tierra del Fuego in January, 1774. Cook reached his highest southern latitude on this segment of his second voyage. University of British Columbia Library, Rare Books and Special Collections, FC 3821.241.243. A1 1784.

the point of his first encounter with the blink. This took him a substantial distance above the Asian landmass, whose coast came into view on August 27. Though Cook may have reached higher latitudes on his southern venture, there is no analogue for such an extensive lateral maneuver along the ice edge as accomplished here (figs. 6.7 and 6.8).

Though the Royal Society's geographical theories and the commercial and imperial premises behind Admiralty planning combined to create Cook's preference for a route over North America, a fair reading of his journal for late August 1778 suggests that if circumstances had permitted, he would have made a run for a Northeast Passage back to Europe over the top of Russia. But such a scheme was defeated by rapidly dropping temperatures and snowfall that began to compound the recurrent fog. With the ice north of Siberia now also beginning to close in on Cook, as it had off Alaska's Icy Cape, and the calendar signaling the end of the exploration season, Cook relented. Requiring wood and water to replenish the ships, he set a course toward Bering Strait, determined to return to the north for a second try at the passage the following year.

Cook made his turn at Cape Shmitda, coasting the Siberian mainland in a southeasterly direction, until he repassed the strait on September 2. All the while he and his officers diligently fixed landmarks and looked for a harbor they might use the next spring. Most historians, feverishly anticipating the complicated circumstances that led to his death in Hawai'i, discount or entirely ignore Cook's next maneuver.

Crossing back over to the American side after transecting the strait, Cook made one last attempt to reconcile geographic reality with Staehlin's map, with the underlying goal of preserving every conceivable prospect for a passage over America. Thinking he might have missed a corridor to the Arctic Ocean south and east of Cape Prince of Wales and Icy Cape (Staehlin's map could have been interpreted as showing that these continental promontories were features of islands), after he had broken through the Aleutians earlier in the summer, Cook nosed the *Resolution* and *Discovery* into the waters he named Norton Sound. Here, late in the northern summer, the indefatigable Cook directed a very thoughtful and thorough survey of this inlet, despite the ridicule directed at the effort by some of the officers because of its consistently shallow waters. The irascible William Bligh, master of Cook's flagship, was one of these; perhaps he was still stinging from a harsh or skeptical word from the captain when he tempered Bligh's enthusiasm for the prospects of Prince William Sound and Cook Inlet.

The Seward Peninsula, as it came to be known, proved to be an extension of the larger American land mass and not an island, but this episode reveals the jaundiced view that has dogged Cook since he sailed into those northern waters. If he pulled up short in an investigation, as he did in Cook Inlet, contemporary armchair geographers and later scholars would charge him with not being thorough. If he put stock in Staehlin's insular theory about "Alashka" and spent a week in Norton Sound, he would be seen as gullible. Without the benefit of hindsight, Cook took the time to thoroughly explore the northern latitudes identified in his instructions.

After his return to English Bay, Unalaska, in the early fall, Cook's journal is dominated by his plan to explore the Arctic again (fig. 6.9). This required finding a safe and hospitable anchorage in the Pacific. His decision to return to Hawai'i has inevitably dominated Cook historiography because it turned out to be so portentous. The underlying proposition—that the great navigator was preparing for another run north rather than a return home after a single season in the Arctic—has, however, received far less consideration in assessments of the third voyage. A lesser explorer would have considered the summer of 1778 probe of the Arctic to be sufficient. But Cook was not a one-year wonder like his contemporaries Phipps or Richard Pickersgill. The latter, who had served

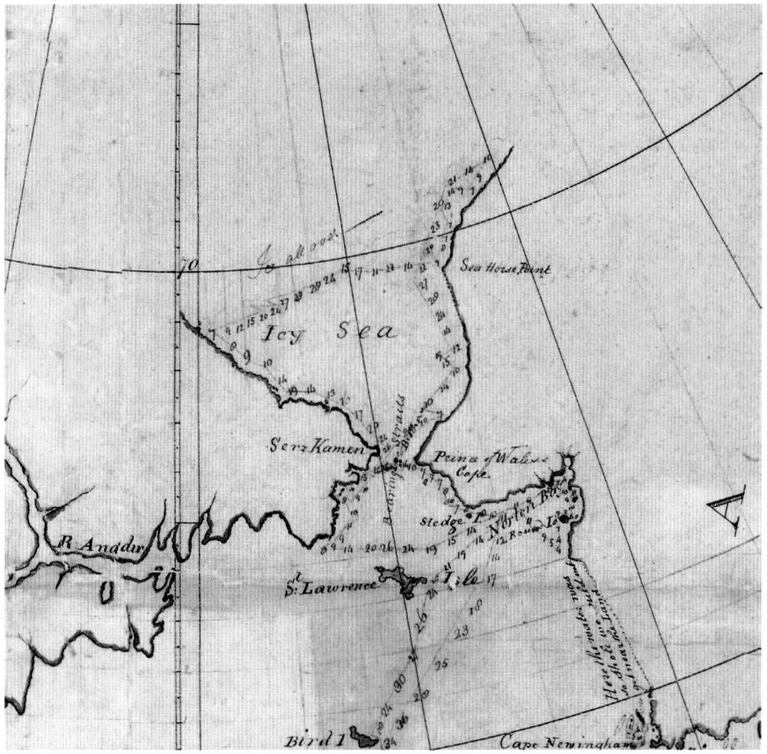

6.8 Detail from William Bayly's chart of the northern Pacific Ocean, 1778. In contrast to his quick, in-and-out forays into the high southern latitudes, this representation of Cook's extended track in the Arctic belies the notion that he had lost his exploratory desire and resolve. Vancouver Maritime Museum, 1991.0018.002.

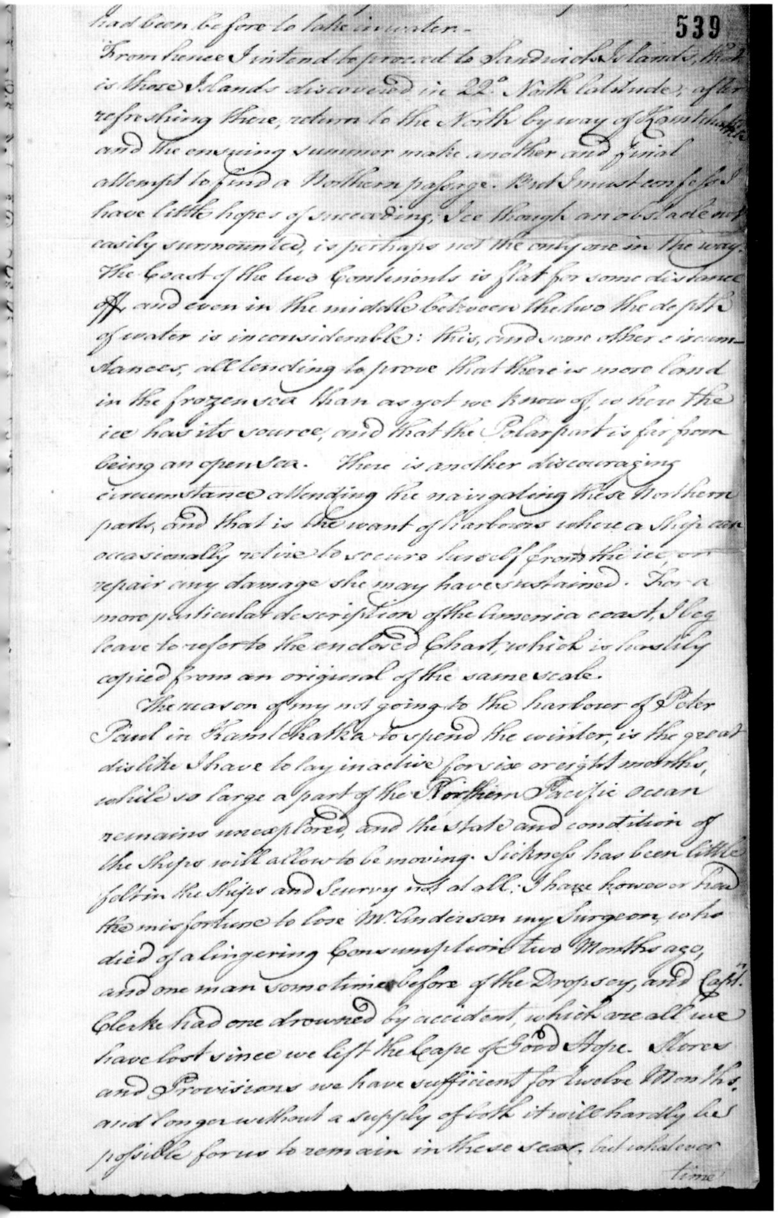
had been before to take in water - 539
From thence I intend to proceed to Sandwich Islands, that
is those Islands discovered in 22° North latitude; after
refreshing there, return to the North by way of Kamtschatka
and the ensuing summer make another and final
attempt to find a Northern passage. But I must confess I
have little hopes of succeeding, Ice though an obstacle not
easily surmounted, is perhaps not the only one in the way.
The Coast of the two Continents is flat for some distance
off and even in the middle between the two the depth
of water is inconsiderable: this, and some other circumstances, all tending to prove that there is more land
in the frozen sea than as yet we know of is where the
ice has its source, and that the Polar part is far from
being an open sea. There is another discouraging
circumstance attending the navigating these Northern
parts, and that is the want of harbours where a Ship can
occasionally retire to secure herself from the ice or
repair any damage she may have sustained. For a
more particular description of the America coast, I beg
leave to refer to the enclosed Chart, which is hastily
copied from an original of the same scale.
The reason of my not going to the harbour of St Peter
and Paul in Kamtschatka to spend the winter, is the great
dislike I have to lay inactive for six or eight months,
while so large a part of the Northern Pacific Ocean
remains unexplored, and the state and condition of
the Ships will allow to be moving. Sickness has been little
felt in the Ships and Scurvy not at all. I have however had
the misfortune to lose Mr Anderson my Surgeon, who
died of a lingering Consumption two Months ago,
and one man sometime before of the Dropsey, and Capt.
Clerke had one drowned by accident, which are all we
have lost since we left the Cape of Good Hope. Stores
and Provisions we have sufficient for twelve Months,
and longer without a supply of both it will hardly be
possible for us to remain in these seas, but whatever
time

6.9 Extract from Cook's letter to the Admiralty from Unalaska on October 20, 1778. Contrary to the reigning orthodoxy that Cook was a fatigued and failing explorer during the third voyage, this letter, written after what he expected to be the first of two seasons exploring in the high north, posits his determination to take a second run at finding the Northwest Passage. The projected sojourn in Hawai'i for rest and refreshment was the obviously correct recourse in the circumstances Cook found himself in, but it was a fateful decision nonetheless. National Archives, Kew, ADM 1/1612, f.539.

with Cook on the first two voyages, conducted a wan attempt at exploring the extremity of Baffin Bay, as the Admiralty naively thought he might meet Cook there and lead him home. Pickersgill never got higher than 68°, ten degrees short of William Baffin himself.[35]

By October 1778, Cook's expedition, according to the original plan, should have been coming to a close. But having come so far and still unsatisfied with his first attempt, Cook planned on extending the voyage into a fourth year. He was so persuasive and had so thoroughly inculcated a practice of observation and testing among his shipboard colleagues that after his death, the new expedition commander, Charles Clerke (who was dying himself), led a demoralized crew on a return to the Arctic in the summer of 1779. Still guided by Cook's logic, the expedition approached from a different direction at an earlier time of year in hopes of achieving different results.

Even after that fruitless attempt in the Arctic, and Clerke's death off the Kamchatka coast shortly thereafter, the surviving leadership team, lieutenants John Gore and James King, dedicated themselves to making further contributions to Europe's understanding of East Asian geography. On their voyage home, a fierce storm blew the *Resolution* and *Discovery* well to the east of Japan, which is why that island group, alone among all the major landforms of the Pacific basin, is shaped oddly in the master map detailing Cook's voyages.

In addition to recording his plans for his second

foray to the Arctic, the other noteworthy aspect of Cook's journal at English Bay is his stinging rebuke of Russian cartography. His attentiveness to Staehlin's map has itself been cited as an example of Cook's deteriorated skills during his last voyage. No fully competent explorer, the argument goes, would have invested so much time in investigating such an illusion. There are two responses to this argument. First, we know today that Staehlin's map was fanciful, but Cook could not have known that until his experience proved it so. Thus, ironically, Cook is scored for attending to fraudulent cartography whose dubiety he proved.

Second, in investigating Staehlin's claims, Cook was attempting to pursue scientific truth. The members of the "Republic of Letters"—scientists, natural philosophers, and explorers of the Enlightenment era—presumed the reliability and credibility of reported findings. Cook had started his career in Enlightenment science as a part of the great international venture that studied the transit of Venus, an experiment that augured an era of international cooperation and respect for scientific endeavor. Staehlin's "Map of the New Northern Archipelago" seemed to lay claim to scientific authority. It was included in a larger work authored by Staehlin, the secretary of the Academy of Science in St. Petersburg, in 1774, with additional external validation in the form of an English-language version published in London and translated by no less a figure than Matthew Maty, secretary of the Royal Society. Indeed, James King consistently referred to it as Maty's map. Thus it had every necessary imprimatur for Cook's studied consideration.[36]

Supplementing his own findings with knowledge about regional geography gleaned from Gerasim Izmailov, the Russian fur trader in Unalaska, Cook cut loose with his criticism of Staehlin's cartographic image. Complaining that it was "so erroneous a map," showing islands strewn about "in regular confusion, without the least regard to truth," Cook deemed it a product that Staehlin or even "the most illiterate of his illiterate Sea-faring men" should have been "ashamed to put his name to." Here Cook was not evincing the intemperance that has become, to some, the defining characteristic of the third voyage. He was instead attempting to enforce the scientific discipline of that age.[37]

Not that any of this truly mattered in the end. As Beaglehole points out, it was not faulty cartography—which Cook in his inimitable way was able to work around—but rather sea ice that ended his quest for the Northwest Passage. Today we might ask whether not finding what was then nonexistent can be deemed a failure. Considering the collateral benefits of Cook's findings in the Northeast Pacific, where indeed does the failure lie? Determining the general outline of the North American coast from southern Oregon to Nootka, the directional trend and scale of the Alaskan landmass, the nature and trajectory of the Aleutian Chain, and the specific location of Bering Strait, and adding the Hawaiian islands to the Pacific map for good measure, constitute an incomparable catalog of accomplishment.

We need a more nuanced, perhaps more even-handed, evaluation of Cook. This new, synthetic view would not reinstitute the hagiography of the imperialist mode. It would recognize the postcolonial critique but move beyond the ideological limitations of that outlook and its endless rehashing of the meanings of beach crossings. As scholars such as Nicholas Thomas, Bernard Smith, and Ian MacLaren have shown, a more fruitful approach to Cook lies in case studies that thoroughly analyze the journals' text, imagery from the published accounts, and the encrustations of orthodoxy that abound in the secondary literature. In the twenty-first century, an age whose hallmark will be massive climate change, perhaps it is time to acknowledge that the environmental backdrop for evaluating the relevance of Cook's discoveries is certainly not a sandy beach, nor even the ocean blue, but a cool summer along that Alaska coastline leading to the Arctic ice pack.

NOTES

1 Tony Horwitz, *Blue Latitudes: Boldly Going Where Captain Cook Has Gone Before* (New York: Picador/Henry Holt, 2002), 219.

2 Ibid., 220.

3 Ibid., 78.

4 Ibid., 217.

5 See, for example, Bernard Smith, *Imagining the Pacific: In the Wake of the Cook Voyages* (New Haven, CT: Yale University Press, 1992); Marshall Sahlins, *How "Natives" Think: About Captain Cook, for Example* (Chicago: University of Chicago Press, 1995); Gananath Obeyesekere, *The Apotheosis of Captain Cook: European Mythmaking in the Pacific* (Princeton, NJ: Princeton University Press, 1992).

6 *The Journals of Captain James Cook on His Voyages of Discovery,* vol. 3, *The Voyage of the* Resolution *and* Discovery, *1776–1780,* ed. J. C. Beaglehole (Cambridge: Cambridge University Press for the Hakluyt Society, 1967).

7 Nicholas Thomas, *Cook: The Extraordinary Voyages of Captain Cook* (New York: Walker, 2003), 332.

8 Arthur Kitson, *Captain James Cook, R.N., F.R.S.: "The Circumnavigator"* (New York: E. P. Dutton, 1907), 493.

9 Cook, *Voyage of the* Resolution *and* Discovery, 119.

10 Ibid., xlii, cxxi–cxxii.

11 Ibid., cvii–cviii, 163.

12 Ibid., cviii, 163.

13 Ibid., vii, viii.

14 Ibid., xxxi.

15 Ibid., cviii.

16 *The Journals of Captain James Cook on His Voyages of Discovery,* vol. 2, *The Voyage of the* Resolution *and* Adventure, *1772–1775,* ed. J. C. Beaglehole (Cambridge: Cambridge University Press for the Hakluyt Society, 1961), 587. This was not a passing shipboard reflection but a point Cook also made with some vehemence in his published account detailing the second voyage.

17 Cook, *Voyage of the* Resolution *and* Discovery, 289.

18 Ibid., 295.

19 Ibid., 297.

20 Ibid., cxxiii–cxxiv; 341 n. 2.

21 Ibid., 340.

22 Ibid., cxxv.

23 Ibid., cxxv, cxxvi, cxxvii.

24 Ibid., cxxvii, cxxviii.

25 Ibid., cxxx.

26 Ibid., xlix.

27 Johann Reinhold Forster, *Observations Made during a Voyage round the World,* ed. Nicholas Thomas et al. (Honolulu: University of Hawaii Press, 1996), 61–78.

28 Cook, *Voyage of the* Resolution *and* Discovery, cxxx.

29 Ibid., cxxxi.

30 Ibid., cxxxii.

31 Ibid., l.

32 Ibid., cxxxii.

33 Ibid.

34 Ibid., cxxxiii.

35 J. C. Beaglehole, *The Life of Captain James Cook* (Stanford, CA: Stanford University Press, 1974), 687.

36 Ibid., 488. An English version was published in England in 1774 and presented to the Royal Society by its secretary, Matthew Maty.

37 Cook, *Voyage of the* Resolution *and* Discovery, cxxxviii.

Encounters

View of the Indigenous People of Nootka Sound from the Cook Expedition Records

RICHARD INGLIS

7

IN THE LATE EIGHTEENTH CENTURY, NOOTKA SOUND ON THE WEST COAST of Vancouver Island was the center of international diplomacy and the commercial maritime fur trade in the north Pacific. The third voyage of Captain Cook to the Northwest Coast of America in 1778 and the reactions of the indigenous peoples of the region did much to set the stage for these later developments. The 1784 official publication of Cook's account of his third voyage became the de facto guidebook to Nootka Sound for subsequent voyages.

This essay focuses on the descriptions and drawings of the indigenous people of Nootka Sound and the artifacts collected from them that constitute the Cook expedition record. It evaluates the identification of the people and their villages as well as the interactions between these people and the crews of the two ships during their one-month stay in April 1778. It examines two features of this encounter in particular: rights of ownership and the nature of trade, including the collecting of "curiosities."

Nootka Sound is the traditional territory of the Mowachaht/Muchalaht First Nation. At the time of contact, the Mowachaht and Muchalaht had numerous villages located throughout the region to which people traced their origins. Archaeolog-

John Webber, *The Inside of a House in Nootka Sound,* circa 1781–83 (detail of fig. 7.9).

7.1 John Webber, *A Canoe of Nootka Indians,* April 1778. Pencil, pen, and wash. This sketch captures the traditional welcome by the Mowachaht, described in various Cook expedition accounts as well as those of later explorers and traders. Oration, singing, and spreading feathers onto the sea were common features of such occasions. There are no earlier sketches of this scene, and the artist never developed it into any other, more finished, paintings. Private collection. Courtesy of Hordern House Rare Books, Sydney, Australia.

ical research has dated the occupation of Nootka Sound to more than four thousand years ago. The arrival of the Cook expedition is remembered in the traditions of the Mowachaht and Muchalaht people:

> When the two ships from the Cook expedition arrived at the end of March, the beach keeper from our village went out in a canoe to greet the newcomers, standing up in the canoe and with his best oration welcomed the ships to our territorial waters and invited them to come to the harbour in front of our village [fig. 7.1].[1]
>
> In our history, the words that the chief was calling out were *nu.tka.ʔičim, nu.tka.ʔičim, nu.tka.ʔičim,* which translates into English as "sail around." Of course there was misunderstanding as the newcomers did not understand our language. The words somehow became the name that was applied to us by the outsiders, the Nootka.
>
> The Cook expedition ships did not come in the direction that our chief was beckoning but instead chose an anchorage that was distant from our villages but still in our territory. We considered the ships as drift on our waters, and according to the traditional ownership rights of our Chiefs they were under our control. This meant that we constantly had to be with the ships to prevent any trespass by our neighbours.
>
> Our dealings with the Cook expedition were on congenial terms. Yes there were misunderstandings, mostly as a result of crew members from the expedition not recognizing the extent of our ownership rights and taking our resources without permission or payment.
>
> The month-long visit of the Cook expedition in our territory established an economic and political relationship. We provided the ships with daily supplies of fish, as well as water, wood, oil, and furs in trade for metal, a rare material of great value to us.[2]

COOK EXPEDITION RECORDS FOR NOOTKA SOUND

The Cook expedition arrived off Nootka Sound, on the west coast of Vancouver Island on March 29, 1778. Two days later, on March 31, the two ships anchored in Ship Cove, now known as Resolution Cove, on the southeast side of Bligh Island, where they remained until April 26 (figs. 7.2 and 7.3). This location was several miles distant from any of the indigenous villages in the region that were recorded later by the expedition (fig. 7.4).

The expedition arrived in Nootka Sound not by intent but out of necessity, as the ships were in need of repairs and Cook wanted to rest the crews. The one-month stay of the expedition introduced Cook to cultural behaviors that were dramatically different from those of the people he had interacted with in the South Pacific on the previous voyages and in Hawai'i on the third voyage.

Interactions with the indigenous population occurred initially off the entrance to Nootka Sound and then daily at the anchorage in Ship Cove. Cook also deployed two launches on a one-day exploration around the sound, a distance of approximately thirty miles. During this trip, he visited three villages, two occupied and one abandoned. He returned to the first village on another day with the expedition artist, John Webber.

There are over thirty extant logs or journals from Cook's third voyage, of which seven complete texts and extracts of another five are published. The rest remain as manuscripts held primarily in the National Archives of the United Kingdom.[3] A number of journals are missing, including that of William Bligh (master on the *Resolution*) and George Vancouver (midshipman on the *Discovery*). The logs and journals vary greatly in length, in subject matter recorded, and in details provided. Some are incomplete, and a few appear to be copied from the ship logs.[4] Some are curt, with little in the way of description, while others provide full descriptions of events.

The difficulty of relying on published official accounts has been well documented by I. S. MacLaren. He identifies four stages in the pro-

7.2 John Webber, *A View in Ship Cove,* April 1778. Pen, wash, and watercolor. Here the artist depicts a common scene of trading at the anchorage, with at least thirteen canoes around the *Resolution.* Midshipman Edward Riou noted that upon their arrival, the visitors were immediately convinced that the Natives were experienced at the business of trade. Once the ships anchored, the activity in Ship Cove can only be described as frenetic and relentless: Cook himself writes of being surrounded by over thirty canoes filled with people and being visited daily by a considerable number of Natives. © British Library Board, MS 15514 f. 10.

7.3 John Webber, *A View in King George's Sound* (Nootka Sound), 1778. Pen, wash, and watercolor. This image likely depicts the waterfront on the southwest side of Ship Cove. The figure is shown kneeling and filling a cup from the stream that was known as a watering place (see fig. 7.8). In a later painting, Webber completely changed the ensemble of the people, replacing the man with the spear with a figure wearing a chief's hat and carrying a bow and a quiver for arrows. The rugged, rocky, and pine-covered landscape in late winter would have been a massive shock to the senses of the explorers who had spent the previous year in Polynesia. © The Trustees of the British Museum, #1859-7-9-102.

duction of an official account: the log or notebook of the recorder; the journal (narrative) written by the recorder based on the first-stage document; a manuscript for a book, often produced by a professional writer (with or without the assistance of the recorder); and the final publication. The products of the third and fourth stages are often edited to meet the expectations of the market and other considerations. MacLaren noted that as an account progresses through the four stages, there is increased distance from the words of the observer and consequently a reduction in the reliability of the publication as an account of what was actually witnessed or experienced.[5]

The large number of accessible original logs and journals provide a valuable resource for developing an understanding of indigenous life in Nootka Sound at the time of contact. The logs recorded events on a daily basis and are generally brief and factual. In many of the records, a descriptive section providing a summary of the land, resources, and manner and customs of the people follows the daily entries for the time in Nootka Sound.

The journal entries on indigenous life are limited to what each writer was able to view from the ships or the shore.[6] As the ships were anchored far from any of the villages, the observations would have been extremely limited if Cook had not undertaken two visits to the village at the western entrance to the sound. Here the officers had free access to the village and the houses, providing them increased opportunities to observe indigenous life.

Rüdiger Joppien and Bernard Smith have identified forty-two drawings from Nootka Sound by the expedition artists.[7] The images include the ships at anchor in Ship Cove, the scenery at the anchorage, the indigenous people, and, in the words of Cook, "drawings of every thing that was curious both within and without doors" at the village at the western entrance to Nootka Sound.[8] The drawings by John Webber in particular are of great documentary value.

As with the written record, there are a number of stages evident in the illustration process that affect the accuracy of the depictions. In the case of the Cook expedition drawings, one original field sketch may yield several finished drawings; and, for some scenes, separate illustrations were prepared for the engraver, the engraving, and any re-engravings for subsequent editions.[9] The engravings and re-engravings are the images that are the most generally known and used. Some are faithful copies of the field sketches, while others show significant changes and embellishments. No reason for the changes has been identified other than the aesthetics of the time.

The "curiosities" (artifacts) purchased by the crews of the ships during the expedition form a third data set. These were not an official collection made by the expedition but the result of individual purchases by crew members. As a result, the various items dispersed quickly upon the return of the expedition to England. Adrienne Kaeppler has identified nearly one hundred artifacts collected by the Cook expedition as coming from Nootka Sound. This is the largest number of artifacts collected from any area visited by the expedition on the Northwest Coast.[10]

THE INDIGENOUS PEOPLE OF NOOTKA SOUND

In review of the journals and logs from the expedition, not a single name of a people, a chief, or a village is recorded. The officers generally agreed that they interacted with different peoples while in Nootka Sound. King wrote, "That they are divided into a number of independent separate communities is certain; & we have given instances that the Contests among them are very frequent."[11] In several of the journals, the term *tribe* is used to describe the different communities that came to trade at the anchorage.[12] The officers also agreed that there were Native chiefs but only speculated on their authority. Cook wrote in his journal of "a Chief named [blank]." Although the name does not appear in the journal, the phrasing suggests that he heard a name for at least one chief.[13]

Five villages are depicted on the expedition chart of Nootka Sound (see fig. 7.4). Cook took two of the ships' launches to visit two of these villages near the end of his stay. The first was a populous village on the western side of the sound, where Cook noted that to most of the inhabitants, "I was known."[14] Charles Clerke described them as "exceedingly civil."[15] At the second village, located on the north shore of Hanna Channel, Cook noted

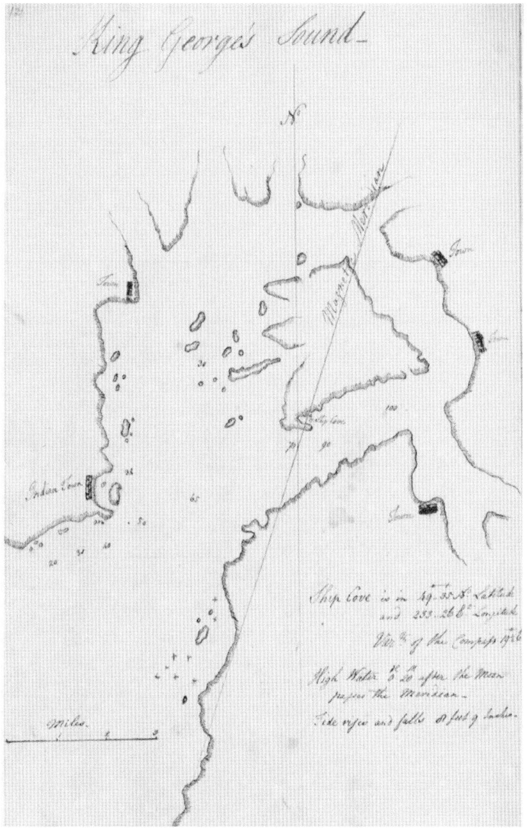

7.4 James Burney, *King George's Sound*, 1778. One of a number of small charts drawn by the visitors, this is noteworthy for the clarity with which the location of the occupied Native village sites are identified. Surveying the entrance to the sound in small boats, the explorers saw other, abandoned villages, but only those with residents were recorded. This chart, and those of the later Malaspina expedition, complement Native oral traditions and have contributed significantly to modern archaeological and other anthropological research in Nootka Sound. Mitchell Library, State Library of New South Wales, Safe 1/64, p. 121.

that "the inhabitants were not so polite as those of the other I had visited."[16] Midshipman Edward Riou of the *Discovery* provided more detail of the visit to the two villages in his journal:

> Monday 20th April: AM At 8—Our Large Cutter with one of the Resolution's boats went to reconnoitre the Sound. They made for the SW point where they arrived in about an Hour—here they found an Indian town situated in the bottom of a Cove to the No. ward of the point, this Cove is a small and excellent Harbour. . . .
>
> The natives seemed not in the least alarmed at the approach of our boats but received them on shore in a very friendly & peacable manner—. . . They never offered to steal one single article but endeavoured to entertain our people in the best manner they could by inviting them to their Houses, satisfying their Curiousity and shewing them the different Commoditys they are furnished with . . .—at 5 in the afternoon went on shore to another Town and were received in a very friendly manner. Here they found more of our old acquaintances than at the Town to So:ward who behaved with great Honesty, but were not so sociable as to ask them into their Houses but on the contrary refused them admittance. However they made up for their impolite behaviour by giving them a Dance and Song.[17]

From this reference it appears that people from both villages traded at the ships, although more came from the second village. Riou noted earlier that "Our neighbours . . . in the night went up the Sound and the next morning and returned with their reinforcements," inferring that the second village controlled the trade.[18] The hostilities at the anchorage that are described in many of the journals may reflect a rivalry between these two villages.

There was no agreement on the size of the population of Nootka Sound in the journals. Cook concluded that they "appeared to be pretty numerous."[19] King estimated the population at 2,600 based on the five villages known to exist: "The two first of these [villages] were visit'd, the number of habitations noted, & from these Observations were suppos'd to contain each 700 souls, the largest we may suppose 1000, & the two small 100 each: which will make 2600 Inhabitants in the whole."[20]

In assessing the descriptions of Native activities in the daily entries and overview summaries in the journals, two features of the indigenous society stand out: the highly developed notion of ownership and the importance of trade and their skill as traders.

Ownership

One feature of the interactions between the two parties that was commonly commented on in the journals was the control of access to the ships by the local population, referred to in the journals as "neighbors" or "landlords." Once the ships were in the anchorage, they were constantly guarded by the local residents. Cook wrote on the fourth day at anchor:

> We at the same time observed that they had people looking out on each point of the Cove and canoes passing to and fro between them and the Main body. At length a party in about a dozen large Canoes, appeared off the South point of the Cove, where they laid drawn up in a body. Some people in Canoes pass'd to and fro between the two parties and there was some speaking on both sides. At length the difference, whatever it was, was compromised, but the Strangers were not allowed to come along side the Ships nor to have any trade or intercourse with us: our first friends, or those who lived in the Sound seemed determined to ingross us intirely to themselves. This we saw on several other occasions, nor were all those who lived in the Sound united in the same cause; the Weakest were frequently obliged to give way to the strong, and were sometimes plundered of every thing they had, without attempting to make the least resistance.

He adds: "If at any time they allowed Strangers to trade with us it was always managed the trade for them in such a manner that the price of their articles was always kept while the Value of ours was lessening daily."[21]

Clerke characterized the management of the trade with the ships:

> These People in whose boundaries or confines of Country we happen'd to lay, look'd upon us [as] so far their property as to be entitled to a right of monopolizing all kind of Exchanges with us to themselves; other parties, desirous of a few hatchets & c and not intirely coinciding with this Plan of monopolization, sometimes endeavoured to break through it; upon these occasions, our landlords always had recourse to Arms. . . . The visiting Party was allowed to trade with us, upon condition that some of these People attended them, that they might take care the market was not hurt by an under sale of Goods; at the same time, they are Witnesses to the acquirements of these Traders, some proportion of which I think there is all reason to suppose they have a claim to, in consideration of granting them the indulgence of trading with us.[22]

The concept of ownership was stronger than Cook had experienced elsewhere:

> Here I must observe that I have no were [*sic*] met with Indians who had such high notions of every thing the Country produced being their exclusive property as these; the very wood and water we took on board they at first wanted us to pay for. . . . [T]he workmen took

> but little notice of their importunities and at last they ceased applying. But made a Merit on necessity and frequently afterwards told us they had given us Wood and Water out of friendship. . . . I sent some to cut grass not thinking that the Natives could or would have the least objection, but it proved otherways for the Moment our people began to cut they stoped them and told them they must Makook for it, that is first buy it.[23]

King later concluded that "No people had higher Ideas of exclusive property."[24]

Trade

During the expedition's monthlong stay, trade with the indigenous people was constant. From the first moment of contact, the people of Nootka Sound showed no fear of the ships and were eager to trade. In the descriptions from the journals, the initial trade between the two parties is exclusively in "curiosities." After the first few days, there is little further mention of "curiosities," suggesting that the exchanges then shifted to other products. Once the indigenous people understood that fresh fish was desired, they traded almost daily enough fresh fish to supply the crews of the two ships.

Cook described the eagerness to trade from the first meeting before the expedition had entered the anchorage: "We no sooner drew near the inlet than we found the coast to be inhabited and the people came off to the Ships in Canoes without shewing the least fear or distrust. We had at one time thirty two Canoes filled with people about us. . . . [They] shewed great readiness to part with any thing they had and took whatever was offered them in exchange, but were more desireous of iron than anything else.[25]

Riou remarked on the arrival of the ships off the coast: "In the Canoe that first came Along side was a Man that stood up and held forth a long while . . . after having finished his harangue he presented it [his woven hat] to Sale as well as several other things, which at once convinced us they were no novice at that business."[26]

Clerke remarked on March 30: "Many Indians in their Canoes about but they bring nothing to sell as yet, but some of their weapons, which are Spears & Bows & [some?] of their cloathing, which consists of very greasy dirty Skins, a Garment made of the bark of trees, & another composed of a kind of Wool."[27]

The trade of curiosities and furs continued at the anchorage for several days. Riou wrote on April 1: "The Natives continue their visits bringing with them apparently everything they are in possession of but nothing is so well received by us as skins, particularly those of the sea beaver or otter, the fur of which is very soft and delicate:—but as is always the case with us for want of certain restrictions respecting trade, everybody is very desirous of purchasing at first, by which conduct the value of the Commoditys are exceedingly enhanced, and these as well as every other people have immediately taken the advantage of our Eagerness."[28]

Subsequent entries in journals, however, pertain almost exclusively to the trade of fresh fish, sometimes train (whale) oil, and occasionally furs. The trade was a daily activity of which a few examples follow:

April 7: "Today I purchased as much fish of the Natives (a kind of Sprat & Bream) as all our People could eat; this is the first time they have brought such abundance to market."[29]

April 14: "Got as much Fish of the Indians as supplied all hands."[30]

April 16: "We had many canoes, with Indians about us, with whom we trafficed for fish and train-oil."[31]

April 22: "They supply us with plenty of wild Onions & flat fish, Spratts & shell fish as usual."[32]

April 25: "We bought much oil of them for our Lamps, which they brought to us in bladders."[33]

David Samwell, surgeon, compared the trade to the fish market in London: "The Indians bring us flat fish [halibut] now enough for us to serve the whole Ship's Company, and they bring the fur of the Sea Beaver & the skins of Bears, Wolves [and] other Animals to sell. . . . [T]hey bring us some Sprats to sell as well as flat fish & it is as common to buy a halfpenny of Sprats here as it is in London, they measure them out to us & give us good pennyworths and are very fine fish."[34]

And Cook noted that even inclement weather did not deter the aboriginal people from trading: "The bad weather which now came on did not however hinder the Natives from Visiting us daily and proving very usefull, as they frequently brought us a tolerable supply of fish, when we could catch none our selves with hook and line and there was no place near us to draw a net. The fish they brought us were either Sardins or a small fish very like them and a small kind of Bream, with now and then a small Cod."[35]

John Williamson, an officer on the *Resolution,* commented on the daily nature of the trade and of the range of products from fresh and dried fish, whale and whale oil, wild onions, and furs: "During our continuance here we were daily visited by the Natives, who brought fresh dry'd Fish, whale & whale Oil, & wild Onions, also the skins of the Sea Otter & many other Animals."[36]

Cook also noted a secondary trade that allowed the indigenous people who controlled the anchorage to continue to supply the demand from the ships: "We also found that many of the principals of those about us carried on a trade with their neighbours with the articles they got from us; as they would frequintly be gone from us four or five days at a time and then return with a fresh cargo of skins curiosities &c."[37]

Metal (in the forms of iron, copper, brass, saws, and hatchets) was the item most desired in the trade by the indigenous people. Cook commented: "Nothing would go down with them but metal and brass was now become their favourate, so that before we left the place, hardly a bit of brass was left in the Ship. . . . Whole Suits of Cloaths were striped

7.5 John Webber, *The Inside of a House in Nootka Sound,* 1778. Pencil, pen, and wash. This is Webber's initial study of the scene that was later engraved and published. The artist depicts a more active place than that portrayed in the more carefully composed painting done for the engraver (fig. 7.9). This field drawing includes little studies of the fire and the racks leaning together above it for cooking sardines and salmon, and of a woman weaving cedar bark cloth, which appears in a separate drawing. Scottish National Gallery, D1453.

of every button, Bureaus & C of their furniture and Copper kettle[s], Tin canesters, candle sticks, & c all went to wreck, so that these people got a greater middly and variety of things from us than any other people we had visited."[38]

DRAWINGS

The second data set from the Cook expedition that provides insight into the life of the indigenous inhabitants of Nootka Sound is the drawings by the expedition's artists.[39] The return visit of Cook, with Webber, to the village at the western entrance produced a particularly valuable set of illustrations (fig. 7.5). Webber wrote later of an incident that occurred during his drawing of the interior of one of the houses:

> While I was employd a man approach'd me with a large knife in one hand seemingly displeas'd when he observ'd I notic'd two representations of human figures which were plac'd at one end of the apartment carv'd on a plank, and of a Gigantic proportion and painted after their custom. However, I proceded, & took as little notice of him as possible, which to prevent he soon provided himself with a Mat, and plac'd it in such a manner as to hinder my having any further a sight of them. Being certain of no further opportunity to finish my Drawing & the object too interesting for leaving unfinish'd, I considered a little bribery might have some effect, and accordingly made an offer of a button from my coat, which when of metal they are much pleas'd with, this instantly produced the desird effect, for the mat was remov'd and I left at liberty to proceed as before. Scarcely had I seated myself and made a beginning, but he return'd & renew'd his former practice, till I had disposd of my buttons, after which time I found no opposition in my further employment.[40]

Eight drawings by Webber depict aspects of the life of the indigenous people in Nootka Sound and provide considerable insight into their culture: *A Canoe of Nootka Indians; Habitations in Nootka Sound; The Inside of a House in Nootka Sound; An Inside View of the Natives Habitations; Natives of Nootka Sound; A Native Prepared for Hunting; A Woman of Nootka Sound;* and *A Man of Nootka Sound.* Two other drawings depict in part some aspect of the life of the indigenous people: *The* Resolution *and* Discovery *in Ship Cove;* and *A View in King George's Sound.*[41] Multiple versions of these drawings were produced, often with slight variations in the scenes.

Analysis of these drawings adds considerable information on elements of the indigenous culture in Nootka Sound. The drawing *Habitations in Nootka Sound* provides details on the layout of the houses in the village as well as locations of platforms and drying racks. *The Inside of a House in Nootka Sound* provides details of house construction, including walls, roof, posts and beams, and location of doorways, interior benches, firepits, and furnishings (storage boxes, etc.). Several activities of the local people are also portrayed, including weaving, cooking and fish drying. The drawings of people provide information on dress and body decoration. Other aspects of the indigenous material culture are depicted in all the drawings.

A number of the images were altered during the transition from sketch to engraving. In *Habitations in Nootka Sound,* Webber changed the image significantly. In the original image, the focus is the village with the houses, drying racks, midden heaps, and a few people and canoes (fig. 7.6). The second image shows changes to the village, mainly the addition of the longboats and sailors interacting with the villagers on the beach (fig. 7.7). Further details of the village structure, not evident in the drawings, are provided in the journals. James Burney, a surveyor and an officer on the *Discovery* and later on the *Resolution,* described the village as having two rows of houses. He also counted ninety-five canoes on the beach.[42] A plan of the village, drawn by Thomas Edgar, depicted three rows of houses (fig. 7.8).[43]

Webber's *Inside of a Nootka House* remains much the same in the different versions, other than the addition of a couple of people around the fire (fig. 7.9). The image provides an understanding of the layout of a house, with benches, firepit, storage boxes, fish hanging from the rafters, and activity areas.

In two drawings of indigenous people, Webber portrayed individuals wearing clothing normally associated with the opposite gender. In *A Woman of Nootka Sound,* Webber changed the flattened top hat worn by women in an earlier drawing (fig. 7.10) to a chief's knob-top hat in a whaling scene (fig. 7.11). The latter image became the engraving. In *A Man of Nootka Sound,* the individual is wearing a short cedar-bark cape with fur around the neck that is described by Williamson as a woman's cape (fig. 7.12).[44] In later editions of the official journal, the illustrations are reengraved based on the images in

7.6 John Webber, *Habitations of the Natives in Nootka Sound,* 1778. Pencil, pen, and wash. This is the initial field sketch from which the artist developed other paintings, and it has a spare authenticity absent in the later works. It depicts the Mowachaht village of Yuquot, across the entrance to the sound from where the expedition's ships were anchored. On his second visit to the village in two days, Cook was accompanied by Webber. It was on this occasion that Cook became aware of the Mowachaht's strong sense of property rights. Not only was he obliged to pay for the privilege of cutting grass to feed the ships' goats and sheep, but Webber had to pay with the buttons from his coat for the opportunity to make an interior drawing. Scottish National Gallery, D1452.

7.7 John Webber, *Habitations in Nootka Sound,* April 1778. Pen, wash, and watercolor. This version of the scene is a more consciously composed painting based on the field sketch of the Yuquot waterfront. The bank leading up to the houses from the beach is steeper, and the skyline of the houses with trees behind is more graduated to present a greater sense of place and context. Two groups of Natives have been added, one surrounding an officer on the beach, the other gathered around the *Resolution*'s launch. Webber prepared the painting for the engraver after the expedition's return to Britain, whose work appears as plate 41 in the portfolio of scenes and people that accompanied the publication of Cook's journal in 1784. Dixson Library, State Library of New South Wales, PXX 2.23.

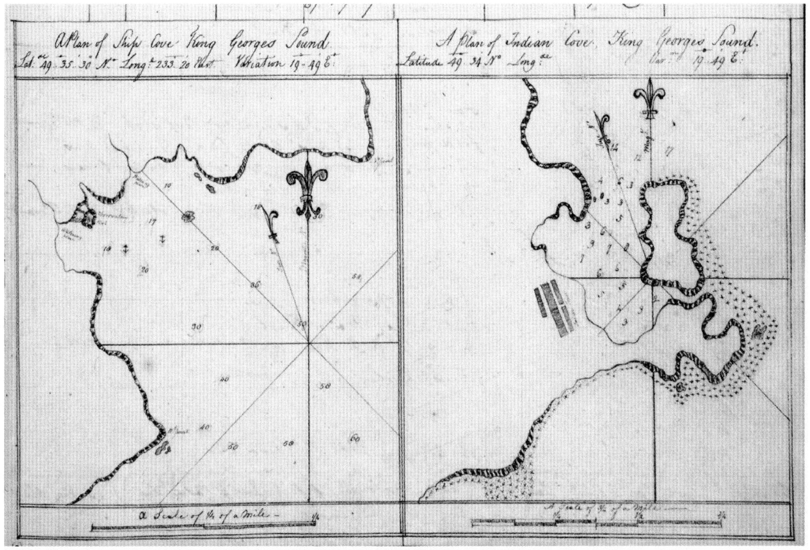

the first edition. This has resulted in images that are reversed as well as in changes to details.

CURIOSITIES

The trade in curiosities dominated the early days of trading at the ships. The crew may have acquired additional objects during the visits to the two villages toward the end of the stay, as Riou implied on April 20: "The natives seemed not in the least alarmed at the approach of our boats but received them on shore in a very friendly & peacable manner—none of them being armed, but most of them bringing their different valuables to sell."[45] Whether any "valuables" were acquired or not at this time was not recorded in any of the journals.

7.8 Thomas Edgar, *Nootka Anchorages,* 1778. This chart by the master of the *Discovery* depicts Ship Cove and Indian (today Friendly) Cove, site of the village of Yuquot. The plan of the former complements John Webber's panorama of the scene and identifies the location of "observatory rock" (see fig. 5.5) and the stream that was the visitors' principal "watering place." Edgar depicts the "Indian Town" visited by Cook as having three rows of houses, which are not apparent in Webber's drawing of the location from the beach. National Archives, Kew, ADM 55/21 f. 153.

7.9 John Webber, *The Inside of a House in Nootka Sound,* circa 1781–83. Pen, wash, and watercolor. This is the artist's second painting of the scene, which was done for the engraving that was published as plate 42 in the portfolio designed to complement Cook's journal. Cook wrote that this was the largest house in the village and described its interior and the activities going on, including the method of boiling water in a wooden trough with red-hot stones. In this description he refers specifically to what must have been Webber's first painting, done in 1778, thus demonstrating the extent to which he looked to Webber throughout the voyage to illustrate key sections of his manuscript account. Dixson Library, State Library of New South Wales, PXX 2.24.

7.10 John Webber, *A Woman of Nootka Sound,* April 1778. Pencil and chalk drawing. A comparison between this drawing, done in situ at Nootka, and the engraving published in 1784 is the most obvious example of how the reading public was presented with a picture of "reality" substantially different from that experienced by the explorers on Cook's third voyage. The familiar image of the engraving (fig. 7.11) presents so dramatic a change from the sketch—in the representation of the facial features and hat—that one might suspect that this is not the same woman at all. Private collection: courtesy of Hordern House Rare Books, Sydney, Australia.

7.11 *A Woman of Nootka Sound,* 1784. Engraving based on a painting by John Webber created specifically for the engraver, circa 1781–83. The chief's hat with the whale-hunt motif is completely out of place here and would never have been worn by a woman. This distinctive hat appears in a number of Webber's drawings from the stopover at Nootka (see, for example, fig. 9.9), and it seems that he was fascinated by it. Its shape, skilled construction, and compelling image would have been different from anything he had seen before he arrived on Vancouver Island. University of British Columbia Library, Rare Books and Special Collections, FC 3821.243.A1 1784—Copy 3.

7.12 John Webber, *A Man of Nootka Sound,* 1778. Pen, ink, and watercolor. This is one of three similar drawings that Webber created while at Nootka. Each of them shows the fur-lined shoulder cape, woven from bark fiber, fitting tightly round the sitter's neck. This garment is usually associated with women in his other works. In the painting he prepared for the engraver after he returned to England, the cape is still in evidence—in contrast to the fur cloaks shown on other male figures—but it is draped over the shoulder. The drawing is also noteworthy for the extensive decoration on the man's face. Courtesy of the Peabody Museum of Archaeology and Ethnology, Harvard University, PM# 41-72-10/497 (digital file #60741396).

The objects traded initially were everyday items that people had with them in the canoes, rather than items purposely selected for trade. A few of the "curiosities" were viewed in use in performances on the canoes (masks, rattles, and whistles) or worn (hats and capes). Riou wrote on the second day of contact: "At Daylight several Canoes came to us, in order to trade which consisted of divers things such as skins of various animals, their Garments, weapons of war, and nick nacks of which in their way they have numbers, but are in general an imitation of the Heads of animals [masks] or birds carved [rattles]."[46]

The "curiosities" acquired were diverse.[47] They included fifteen items of clothing, including nine woven hats (fig. 9.9) and five cedar-bark capes; sea otter robes and a leather apron with deer hooves; eleven human and animal masks, four depicting wolves, three birds, and four human faces (fig. 9.12); twelve musical instruments, including eight bird-shaped rattles (figs. 9.3 and 9.17), two bone and horn rattles, and two whistles; twenty-four weapons, including nine war clubs with stone blades (fig. 9.18), six stone clubs, and nine whalebone clubs (fig. 9.5); nine decorated wooden combs; utensils, including three bowls (fig. 9.15) and three spoons; hunting and fishing implements, including a bow and arrows, two arrow cases (fig. 9.13), two spears, fishing lines and barbs (fig. 9.6), and harpoons with lanyards; three woodworking tools and nine whalebone bark beaters (fig. 9.7). Furs of various animals were also traded. It appears that almost anything was for sale, from chiefly wear to utilitarian items. The only item noted as not being for sale was a type of small crooked knife which "they set too high a value on to part with them."[48]

The descriptions of these items in the various journals provide considerable detail on the material culture of the inhabitants of Nootka Sound, including context for many of the artifacts collected, such as the weapons, fishing implements, clothing, and items used in manufacture.

CONCLUSION

The journals, illustrations, and artifacts collected from the Cook expedition provide a remarkably detailed picture of the life and material culture of the indigenous people of Nootka Sound in the late eighteenth century. Nowhere else had Cook met a people with the notion that everything was owned. The control of access to the trade, the frequency and volume of the trade, and the discerning nature of the trade all indicate that the local indigenous people were experienced and highly skilled traders and that trade was a prominent feature of their society.

Interactions at the ships allowed the expedition to view some aspects of the indigenous material culture—clothing, canoes, masks, musical instruments, and artifacts associated with conflict—and the intertribal relations related to control of the trade. Visiting the village at the western entrance and entering the houses provided expedition members with the opportunity to view the daily lives of the indigenous population and record the sights in drawings.

The published Cook journal, or one of the other contemporaneously published journals from the expedition, was carried by many of the subsequent expeditions to the Northwest Coast of America. That Nootka Sound became the major port of call in the early years of the sea-otter fur trade is a direct result of the knowledge that it was a safe harbor, with an indigenous population that was accommodating and which had supplies to replenish the ships. Subsequent visitors, when describing the indigenous culture of the region, often stated that their observations either confirmed what Cook and others from the expedition described or supplemented what had been recorded.

And finally, it was the friendly reception at the village on the western side of the sound (Yuquot) described in the Cook expedition journals that led one of the first traders to return to that anchorage eight years later, in 1786, and name it Friendly Harbour (Cove), a name that has remained to this day.

NOTES

1 The beach keeper is the chief who has the hereditary responsibility to welcome outsiders to the territory and to invite them ashore.

2 Chief Mike Maquinna, paper presented at colloquium "Arctic Ambitions: Captain Cook and the Northwest Passage," Anchorage Museum, March 15, 2011. Other versions of contact narratives are published in Barbara S. Efrat and W. J. Langlois, eds., "The Contact Period as Recorded by Indian Oral Traditions," in *Captain Cook and the Spanish Explorers on the Coast: Nu tka,* ed. Barbara S. Efrat and W. J. Langlois, (Victoria, BC: Provincial Archives of British Columbia, 1978).

3 *The Journals of Captain James Cook on His Voyages of Discovery,* vol. 3, *The Voyage of the* Resolution *and* Discovery, *1776–1780,* ed. J. C. Beaglehole (Cambridge: Cambridge University Press for the Hakluyt Society, 1967), xxiii–xxvii, clxxi–ccx.

4 Beaglehole studied all the records from the expedition and provided a rigorous analysis of them in his introduction to the third-voyage journals.

5 I. S. MacLaren, "Exploration/Travel Literature and the Evolution of the Author," *International Journal of Canadian Studies* 5 (Spring 1992): 39–68. MacLaren used the journals from Cook's third voyage as an example of the changes that can occur in the different stages of production.

6 Some journal entries also report on what others had witnessed.

7 Rüdiger Joppien and Bernard Smith, *The Art of Captain Cook's Voyages, Volume Three Catalogue: The Voyage of the* Resolution *and* Discovery, *1776–1780* (New Haven, CT: Yale University Press, 1988), 433–69.

8 Cook, *Voyage of the* Resolution *and* Discovery, 306.

9 Webber oversaw the production of the engravings for the official published account of the third voyage.

10 Adrienne L. Kaeppler, *Holophusicon: The Leverian Museum; An Eighteenth-Century English Institution of Science, Curiosity, and Art* (Altenstadt, Germany: ZKF, 2011), 195; see also Adrienne L. Kaeppler, ed., *Cook Voyage Artifacts in Leningrad, Berne, and Florence Museums* (Honolulu, Hawaii: Bishop Museum Press, 1978).

11 King's journal in Cook, *Voyage of the* Resolution *and* Discovery, 1413.

12 Journal of Charles Clerke, April 18, ADM 55/22, National Archives, UK. An extract from Clerke's journal is published as appendix 3 in Cook, *Voyage of the* Resolution *and* Discovery, part 2. Clerke was captain of the *Discovery;* after Cook's death he became captain of the *Resolution,* but he died six months later.

13 Cook, *Voyage of the* Resolution *and* Discovery, 307.

14 Ibid., 303. In later fur-trader accounts, Maquinna is noted as being chief of the village.

15 Clerke's journal in Cook, *Voyage of the* Resolution *and* Discovery, 1327.
16 Cook, in ibid., 304.
17 Journal of Edward Riou, ADM 51/4529, 79a–79. National Archives, UK. Riou was a midshipman on the *Discovery* and later on the *Resolution.*
18 Ibid., 78.
19 Cook, *Voyage of the* Resolution *and* Discovery, 311.
20 King's journal in ibid., 1404.
21 Ibid., 299, 302.
22 Clerke's journal in ibid., 1327.
23 Ibid., 306.
24 King's journal in ibid., 1407.
25 Cook in ibid., 296–97.
26 Riou in ibid., 295–96 n. 5.
27 Clerke, ADM 55/22, 151.
28 Riou, ADM 51/4529, 77.
29 Clerke, ADM 55/22, 153a.
30 Clerke, ADM 55/22, 153.
31 William Ellis, *An Authentic Narrative of a Voyage Performed by Captain Cook and Captain Clerke in His Majesty's Ships* Resolution *and* Discovery *during the Years 1776, 1777, 1778, 1779, and 1780* (London: G. Robinson, 1782; rept. Amsterdam: N. Israel; New York: Da Capo, 1969), 1:203. Ellis was surgeon's mate on the *Discovery* and also one of the expedition artists.
32 David Samwell, part of journal in Cook , *Voyage of the* Resolution *and* Discovery, 1097. Samwell was assistant surgeon to Anderson on the *Resolution* when the expedition sailed in 1786; he became surgeon on the *Discovery* after Anderson's death in 1778.
33 Samwell in Cook, *Voyage of the* Resolution *and* Discovery, part 2, 1103.
34 Ibid., 1096.
35 Cook in ibid., 301. The "small fish" were probably herring.
36 Journal of John Williamson, ADM 55/117, National Archives, UK, 100.
37 Cook, *Voyage of the* Resolution *and* Discovery, 302.
38 Ibid., 302–3.
39 Rüdiger Joppien and Bernard Smith, *The Art of Captain Cook's Voyages, Volume Three Text: The Voyage of the* Resolution *and* Discovery, *1776–1780* (New Haven, CT: Yale University Press, 1988), 80–98; Rüdiger Joppien and Bernard Smith, *The Art of Captain Cook's Voyages, Volume Three Catalogue: The Voyage of the* Resolution *and* Discovery, *1776–1780* (New Haven, CT: Yale University Press, 1988), 433–69.
40 Letter from Webber to John Douglas, quoted in Joppien and Smith, *Volume Three Text*, 86.
41 Joppien and Smith, *Volume Three Catalogue,* 433–69.
42 Journal of James Burney, ADM 51/4528, National Archives, UK.
43 Thomas Edgar, "A Plan of Indian Cove [Yuquot], King George's Sound," 1778, in *The Journals of Captain James Cook on His Voyages of Discovery,* vol. 4, *Charts and Views, Drawn by Cook and His Officers and Reproduced from the Original Manuscripts,* ed. R. A. Skelton (Cambridge: Cambridge University Press for the Hakluyt Society, 1969), plate 50c.
44 Williamson, ADM 55/117, 100.
45 Riou, ADM 51/4529, 79a–79.
46 Ibid., 76–77a.
47 The following discussion relies upon Kaeppler, *Holophusicon.* See also Kaeppler's essay in this volume.
48 King, in Cook, *Voyage of the* Resolution *and* Discovery, part 2, 1396.

The Cook Expedition and Russian Colonialism in Southern Alaska

ARON L. CROWELL

8

THE INDIGENOUS EXPERIENCE OF EUROPEANS DURING THE AGE OF DIScovery began with first contacts that, however brief or benign, presaged the severities of colonial rule. National powers of mercantile expansion into the Atlantic and Pacific spheres—England, France, Spain, Portugal, the Netherlands, Russia, and later the United States—competitively sought to explore and claim territories, extract resources, and profit from global trade.[1] For Native Americans, Western contact and colonization brought decimation by disease, displacement from traditional lands, and the loss of political and cultural autonomy. Yet the arc of colonial history was complex, shaped by indigenous resistance and characterized by cultural and genetic exchanges between colonizers and colonized from which creolized identities and multiethnic New World societies emerged.[2]

James Cook's transit along the southern Alaskan coast during his third and final world voyage occasioned a unique survey of indigenous peoples living on both sides of an encroaching colonial frontier (fig. 6.3). Journals and logs of the expedition from May and early June 1778 report British encounters with the Chugach (Sugpiat) of Prince William Sound (Cook's Sandwich Sound) and the Dena'ina of Cook Inlet, neither of whom had previously been

John Webber, *Man of Unalaska*, watercolor prepared for engraving, 1778 (detail of fig. 8.8).

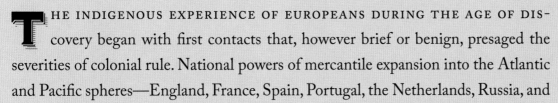

8.1 John Webber, *View of Snug Corner Cove,* 1778. Watercolor. Framed by dramatically rendered peaks and glaciers, the *Resolution* and *Discovery* anchor at Snug Corner Cove in Prince William (Sandwich) Sound. Chugach men and women from nearby villages approach by boat to trade with the British vessels, the first European ships they had seen. © British Library Board, Add MS 15514, fol. 8.

in direct contact with any Western nation (fig. 8.1).[3] Continuing west toward Unalaska Island in late June, Cook's vessels entered the territory of the Unangax̂ (Aleut) and at the same time crossed into a region newly controlled by Kamchatka-based Russian fur traders, the vanguard of their nation's expanding colonial empire. Russian maritime fur companies had extended their operations eastward across the Aleutian Island archipelago during the four decades preceding Cook's arrival, coercing and exploiting Unangax̂ communities to produce annual cargoes of sea-otter pelts for the Chinese market.[4] Unalaska and nearby islands marked the farthest extent of Russian activities in 1778, although penetration into Sugpiaq and Dena'ina regions farther east was imminent.

Records of the Cook expedition depict the very different social and political conditions that obtained to the east and west of this colonial border. The Chugach and Dena'ina were still outside the zone of Russian control, and this independent status was reflected in their response to the appearance of British ships. Armed parties approached the vessels prepared to trade but also to fight, a dual stance that reflected customary interaction among indigenous polities in the region. Cook reacted as he had been instructed by the British Admiralty, that is, to "observe the Genius, Temper, Disposition, and Number of the Natives and Inhabitants, where you find any; and to endeavor, by all proper means to cultivate a friendship with them; making them Presents of such Trinkets as you may have on board, and they may like best; inviting them to Traffick; and shewing them every kind of Civility and Regard."[5] Chugach and Dena'ina leaders, who impressed Cook and subsequent adventurers as shrewd, assured, bold, and aggressive, responded in kind and entered into active trade with the ships, bargaining with sea-otter pelts and other furs for beads, iron, and other desirable goods.

Contrasting impressions of a suborned and politically vitiated Native society were recorded at Unalaska. Cook noted the evident pacification wrought by Russian rule, writing that the "severe examples" which had been made of those who fought against the fur traders in earlier years were "excusable sence the most happy consequences have attended, and one sees now nothing but the greatest harmony subsisting between the two Nations."[6] Unangax̂ resistance had been widespread, including a violent rebellion on Unalaska and neighboring islands in 1763–64 that killed scores on both sides, but it was ultimately overcome.[7] The Russian companies forced Unangax̂ men to hunt sea otters and trap foxes and the women to produce clothing and food. Villages were stripped of arms to prevent further insurrection, and Unangax̂ chiefs were subordinated as "tributaries," that is, payers of *yasak,* or fur taxes. Consistent with this upending of the indigenous economy and social order, Cook engaged almost entirely with Russian rather than Unangax̂ leaders on Unalaska, and the local people had only food to offer in trade, not valuable furs.

The differing circumstances of these neighboring Alaska Native groups in 1778 are all the more striking given their commonalities prior to Western intrusion. The Sugpiat, Dena'ina, and Unangax̂, while linguistically and culturally distinct, followed similar patterns of hunting, fishing, and dwelling in seasonal settlements along the coast.[8] Abundant food resources in the Gulf of Alaska and southern Bering Sea supported large populations in all three cultural areas, particularly in the eastern Aleutians and Kodiak archipelago. Societies were similarly organized by matrilineal descent and divided into elite, common, and slave classes, the latter composed primarily of war captives. Leaders were "rich men" who built wealth and prestige with the support of their kin groups and hosted lavish feasts and religious ceremonies.[9] They led raids on enemy groups, negotiated regional alliances, and undertook seafaring expeditions to trade for precious goods such as copper, iron, amber, and walrus ivory. Trade and war unified southern Alaska into a broad zone of cross-cultural interaction, and the political complexity of its indigenous societies shaped the dynamics of encounter, resistance, and accommodation to Western powers.

COLONIAL AMBITIONS IN THE NORTH PACIFIC

Colonialism in southern Alaska emerged from international competition for the fur wealth of the north Pacific, one of the last parts of the globe to be explored by Western nations. Admiralty instructions for Cook's third voyage reflected Britain's imperial aims: first, to locate the western entrance of the postulated Northwest Passage across North America and thereby to open the Pacific to British navigation and commerce; and second, to lay claim to northern territories that had not already been claimed by other powers.[10] Britain's principal north Pacific rivals were Spain—a hostile competitor in the South Pacific since the early eighteenth century and actively extending its interests into the subarctic—and Russia, whose traders were already established along the thousand-mile Aleutian Island chain.[11]

Vitus Bering's first Pacific voyage for the Russian Crown in 1728 had confirmed the existence of Alaska, the "Great Land" sighted by Semyon Dezhnev in 1648, and Bering's second voyage to Alaska's southern latitudes in 1741 charted parts of the Aleutians and revealed the potential for a rich maritime fur industry. The Russian fur trade that burgeoned in Alaska over the subsequent decades replayed the fifteenth- to seventeenth-century colonization of Siberia, when conquered indigenous peoples were incorporated into the Russian Empire as producers of sable and other land furs. Following Emel'ion Basov's pioneering voyage in 1743, scores of maritime expeditions sponsored by private fur merchants sailed from Kamchatka and overwintered in the Aleutian Chain.[12] In some instances the voyagers or *promyshlenniki* (who were ethnically Russian or Siberian Native) engaged in peaceful trade, but more often they resorted to armed force or hostage taking to coerce island residents.[13] By the early 1780s, all the Aleutian Islands had submitted to Russian control, and the leading edge of trade had advanced to the Alaska Peninsula and Kodiak Island. In 1784, Grigorii Shelikhov subdued the populous and fur-rich Kodiak archipelago, and within another twenty years, Russian outposts extended as far as Sitka (Novo-Arkhangel'sk) in Southeast Alaska. The state-chartered Russian American Company administered the colony from 1799 until 1867, when Alaska was purchased by the United States.

Spain had long claimed the entire west coast of the Americas as part of its New World empire, and Bering's 1741 reconnoiter was at least partially directed toward ascertaining the actual northern limit of Spanish colonial sway.[14] Although Spanish occupation at the time of Bering's voyage extended no farther north than Mexico, news of Russian discoveries and fur profits prompted expansion to California as well as secretive reconnaissance voyages to Southeast Alaska by Juan Pérez in 1774 and Juan Francisco de la Bodega y Quadra in 1775.[15] Cook's published charts and accounts, including notes on Alaskan fur resources and Russian activities, inspired a second wave of Spanish voyages that extended as far north and west as Kodiak Island (led by Ignacio Arteaga in 1779, Esteban José Martínez in 1788, Gonzalo López de Haro in 1788, and Alejandro Malaspina in 1791). British, American, and Spanish competition for Northwest Coast sea otters following Cook's voyage culminated in the Nootka Controversy of 1789, sparked by Spanish seizure of a British trading vessel. Throughout this period, Malaspina and other Spanish explorers vied with Britain in the search for the fabled Northwest Passage and the global trade advantage its discovery would bring.

Cooks' third voyage took place in this thickening atmosphere of international rivalry, although concerns about Spain and Russia did not seem to weigh equally in London. The Admiralty warned Cook against touching on any Spanish dominions in America but made no mention of the Russian territories, despite published maps and accounts by Gerhard Müller, Samuel Engel, and Jacob von Staehlin, which indicated their extent (figs. 2.3 and 2.6).[16] No speakers of Russian were assigned to the British voyage, suggesting that contacts with fur traders in the Aleutians were not anticipated. Cook, however, was well aware of the Russian presence and its significance for potential British trade. He consulted Russian charts (which proved fanciful and inadequate) and observed Alaska Native populations to discern Russian influence. When satisfied (as in Cook Inlet and later at Cape Newenham in Bristol Bay) that neither Russia nor Spain had already established claims, Cook declared ownership for Britain, set up possession monuments, and distributed manufactures to the inhabitants as "Traces and Testimonies" of having been the first to visit the area.[17] Thus, while geographic and scientific discovery were significant elements of Cook's third voyage, another purpose was to lay the groundwork for Britain's colonial agenda in the north Pacific.

PRINCE WILLIAM SOUND, MAY 12–19, 1778

On May 12, the *Resolution* and *Discovery* anchored in a small cove (English Bay) in Port Etches on Hinchinbrook Island at the entrance to Prince William Sound, which Cook named Sandwich Sound. The next day Captains Cook and Clerke sailed their vessels some thirty miles farther into the sound to a more secure harbor at Snug Corner Cove, where the expedition remained until May 17 (see fig. 8.1).[18]

Initial Chugach impressions of Cook's vessels, probably the first sailing ships they had seen (Bering's 1741 track was more than sixty miles to the south), have not been preserved in oral tradition. They may have been similar to those of the Kodiak Island Sugpiat, who thought the first Russian sailing ship was a "giant whale" but on closer inspection "a strange monster, never seen before, whose stench (of tar) made us sick."[19] Cook's construal of the Chugach who approached his ships in Prince William Sound was framed both by the scientific tradition of the Enlightenment and by the strategic objectives of his voyage. He made special note of Chugach watercraft (fig. 8.2), which included one- and two-man kayaks as well as large, open boats (*angyaq* in the Sugpiaq/Sugcestun language). Constructed of sea-mammal skins stretched over wooden frames, they carried ten to thirty paddlers and passengers. Referring to his copy of David Crantz's *History of Greenland* (1767), Cook observed that the Chugach *angyaq* was quite similar to the Greenland Inuit *umiaq* or "women's boat," except for its rounded bow, which bore "some resemblance to the head of a Whale." The Chugach kayaks were also like those of Greenland except for their split, upturned prows. Chugach clothing, hunting weapons, tattoos, and facial jewelry (including lip plugs or labrets) were also much as described by Crantz. From their physical appearance and material culture, it thus appeared that the residents of Prince William Sound (figs. 8.3 and 8.4) had strong Arctic affinities and were not "of the same Nation" as the Mowachaht people of Nootka Sound on Vancou-

8.2 John Webber, *People of Sandwich Sound and their Canoes,* 1778. Field sketch. Above, Chugach Sugpiaq men dressed in seal-intestine parkas and spruce-root hats paddle a two-hatch kayak (*qayahpaq*); below is an *angyaq* with ten paddlers and passengers. Both types of boats were constructed of wooden frames sheathed in seal or sea-lion skin, with distinctive bifurcated bows. The standing man, probably the leader of a trading party, wears a hat topped with woven cylinders (see fig. 8.6) and spreads his arms in a traditional greeting. National Library of Australia, NK7402.

ver Island, where the expedition had recently called. A distinct ethnic border had in fact been crossed between the Northwest Coast cultural region and the southernmost extension of the Inuit world. The suggestion of influence, if not direct intercourse, between Greenland and Prince William Sound fanned British hopes that the western end of the long-sought passage linking the Atlantic and Pacific Oceans had been found, although Cook refrained from endorsing this surmise.[20] In any case, exploration of the inner sound soon proved the conjecture wrong. Modern studies have demonstrated that the ancestral migrations and circumpolar influences that shaped Sugpiaq culture spread anciently along the Alaskan coast from Bering Strait, rather than directly from the eastern Arctic.[21]

At Port Etches, the Chugach hailed the alien ships by spreading their arms wide (as in fig. 8.2), shouting out in their language, and holding aloft a white fur; at Snug Corner Cove, wooden rods were raised, adorned with feathers or bird wings. Other early Russian and European vessels in southern Alaska reported similar greetings,[22] and Cook was later saluted in this manner in Cook Inlet.[23] Nathaniel Portlock, an officer on the *Resolution* who returned to trade at Prince William Sound in 1786, reported that the Chugach greeting spoken on these occasions was *lawle,* meaning "friendship."[24] This was probably from *ilali,* "to make or be friends" in the Sugpiaq (Sugcestun) language,[25] although Sarychev and Merck in 1790 heard the word as *cali* from Chugach people at Nuka Bay on the Kenai Peninsula. Similar words occur in other southern Alaskan coastal languages and dialects (*ilali* also occurs in Eastern Aleut and *idhadi* in Dena'ina), suggesting that the combination of word and gesture was an established regional overture to trade that was extended by custom to the first Western vessels.

Chugach visitors to the British ships eagerly sought to exchange furs for glass and metal goods. As George Dixon would observe on his voyage with Portlock in 1786, the trade was always directed by a single person of authority.[26] At Snug Corner Cove, these leaders were mostly men, but David Samwell also noted one "fair good looking woman very decently dressed & who seem'd to be the Chief of her party."[27] One of the first to board the *Resolution* at Snug Corner Cove was a man of middle age dressed in a sea-otter parka and a woven spruce-root hat decorated with blue glass beads. Although not named in Cook's account, this might have been Sheenawa, chief of the Tatitlarmiut, who were "the most powerful tribe" in the Sound, according to Portlock.[28] The principal Tatitlarmiut village of Kunin was located nearby, hidden by forest from the vantage point of Cook's vessels but revealed by smoke that rose from its houses.[29]

Chugach elders told the anthropologist Kaj Birket-Smith in the 1930s that the Tatitlarmiut were one of eight traditional local groups in Prince William Sound, each with its own headman and territory. Leaders of the richest villages dominated the region and reinforced their influence by hosting the annual Feast of the Dead, an important event of the winter ceremonial cycle.[30] Sheenawa and other headmen built their wealth in large part through local and intersocietal trade, and exchanges with British, Spanish, and Russian vessels were an extension of this traditional role.

The source of blue, white, and green glass beads that some Chugach men and women already owned and wore was debated among the British, in particular since "not a Single bead" had been seen among the Nuu-chah-nulth. Samwell supposed that these had come from Russian traders to the

8.3 John Webber, *Woman of Prince William Sound,* 1778. Pencil and chalk sketch. A young Chugach woman, her brow and cheeks rouged with face paint, is portrayed with nose pin, beaded lip stud, and pierced earrings. The beads appear to be traditional types made of shell, jet, shale, bone, or amber, based on their tubular and tear-drop shapes. The woman's fur cloak may be black bear, her dress soft caribou skin. Anchorage Museum Collection, 2000.029.1.

8.4 John Webber, *A Man of Prince William Sound,* 1778. Pencil and chalk sketch. This Chugach man wears a painted hat woven from spruce roots and decorated with large, wire-wound glass beads, a type that was produced in China for the Russian fur trade. He is dressed for the sea in a seal-intestine parka, its hood tucked up under his hat. A fur or bird-skin coat would have provided warmth beneath this waterproof outer layer. The British admired the perfection of Chugach boats, clothing, and maritime hunting technology, which were clearly of Inuit origin with influences from the Northwest Coast. Collection of William S. Reese.

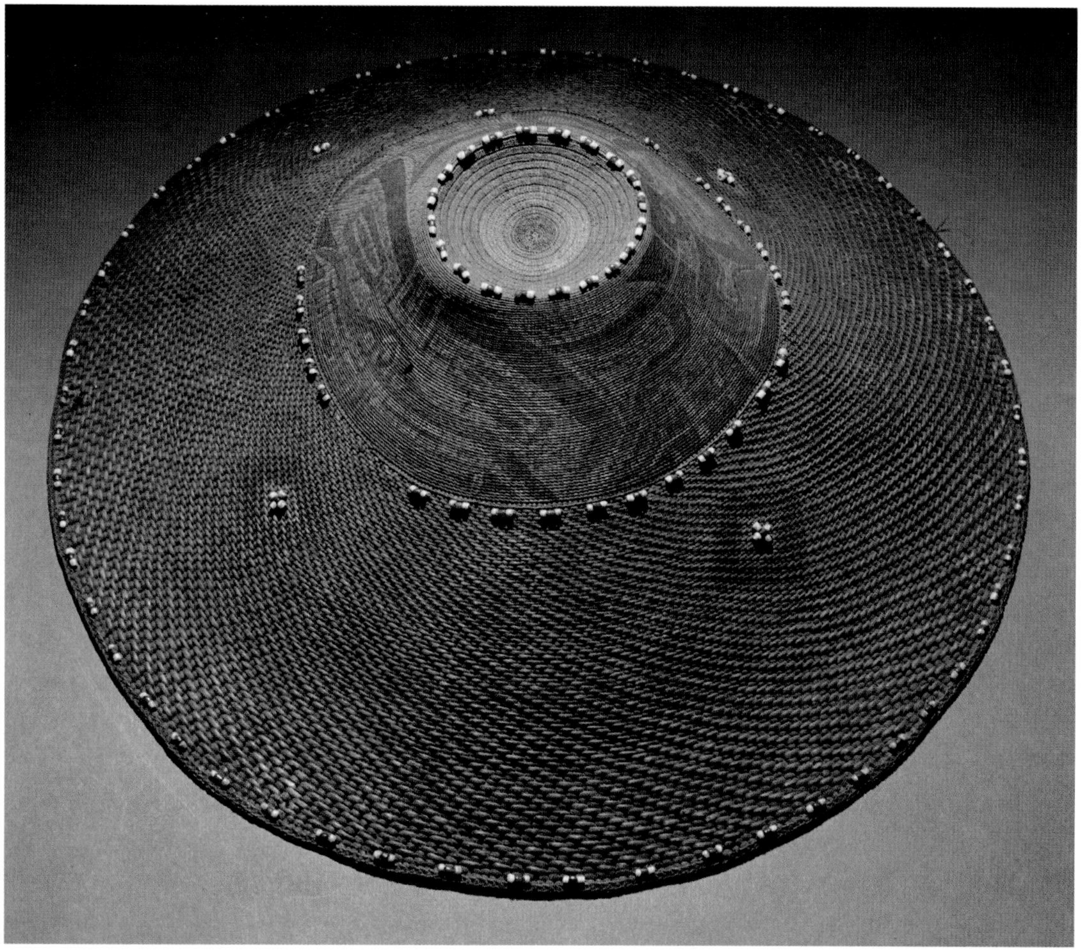

8.5 Spruce-root hat from Prince William Sound with glass beads. This broad-brimmed hat, acquired by the Cook expedition in 1778, has been elegantly woven from spruce root and ornamented with clusters of small blue and white trade beads. A raised, radiating weave pattern makes up the brim, while the crown is flat twined to provide a smooth surface for painting. The abstract representation of a large-eared animal with wide eyes and mouth can be seen. The beauty and iconography of such hats embodied the essential spiritual connection between human and animal beings. © The Trustees of the British Museum, NWC 4.

west,[31] and the varieties seen, including large, blue, wire-wound beads of Chinese manufacture, were in fact typical of Russian imports to the Aleutians.[32] Given the distance from Prince William Sound to the Russian frontier in 1778, it is probable that the beads in Chugach possession had trickled eastward through Sugpiaq and Dena'ina middlemen. Glass beads seem to have been replacing the stone, shell, and bone varieties used before contact, and because of their rarity were regarded as emblems of status and wealth. The elite attached them to their ears and labrets, and "men of the first consequence" used them to decorate bentwood hunting hats and spruce-root hats (fig. 8.5), some topped with woven cylinders ("potlatch rings"), which signified the hosting of memorial feasts (figs. 8.6 and 9.2).[33] White beads were used as well to decorate the rims and handles of utensils used during the winter ceremonies. It would seem that the Chugach were willing to trade substantial quantities of furs for just a few beads because of their local rarity and high value.

Cook and his officers noted that the Chugach men wore body armor made of wooden slats and carried iron or copper spears and fighting knives (fig. 9.21). Contrary to British interpretation at the time, these weapons did not come from Russian traders, who in fact sought to keep armaments of all kinds out of Native hands. Instead, they were the product of a centuries-old local tradition of metalworking. Natural copper nuggets were found in Prince William Sound (one location was Kanaualik, meaning "copper place," in Port Etches) or acquired in trade from Dene (Athabascan) groups who gathered them along the White and Copper Rivers. Iron was obtained via long-distance indigenous trade routes to Siberia or gleaned from Asian vessels that drifted across the Pacific on the Japanese Current.[34] Copper and iron were heated, hammered, and ground with abrasive stones to produce large, fluted blades. The Chugach were especially eager to acquire wrought iron bars ("toes") from the British because these were of a suitable size and shape for making knives.

Chugach armor and weapons were products of indigenous warfare traditions that had originated nearly a millennium earlier.[35] Raids were launched against nearby villages and more distant groups, which for the Chugach included the Dena'ina, Tlingit, Eyak, and Kodiak Island Sugpiat. The objectives were to kill enemy fighters (often in reprisal for earlier attacks), loot valuables, and capture women and children for use as slaves. Raiding alternated with trading as determined by shifting enmities and alliances.

The aggressive side of this balance was exhibited toward the Cook expedition. Led by their chiefs, the Chugach made repeated attempts to steal unattended valuables from the two British vessels (even the ships' boats) and at one point boldly boarded the *Discovery*, threatened the crew with knives and spears, and took items that included the iron-clad rudder.[36] When officers and sailors managed to regain the upper hand without bloodshed, the Chugach reverted to a more peaceable manner, suggesting that they had been testing British resolve. Cook noted that Chugach men were indifferent to the threat of British muskets and concluded that they had never seen one fired, an indication that face-to-face interaction with Russians had not yet occurred.

COOK INLET, MAY 26–JUNE 6, 1778

After leaving Prince William Sound, the expedition traveled west along the Kenai Peninsula. Because their course took them well offshore, they did not see the Sugpiaq villages that existed on this mountainous coast. Delayed by gales alternating with foggy weather and light winds, the ships tacked back and forth at the entrance to Cook Inlet for several days and sighted Cape Elizabeth, the Kodiak archipelago, the Barren Islands, and Cape Douglas. On May 27 the vessels entered the inlet and passed Kachemak Bay to the east and the low, wooded shorelines and the high peaks of the Alaska Range to the north and west. Over the next week Cook and Clerke explored up the inlet to its head, eventually realizing that the decreasing salinity of the water, regular tides, and the mountains closing in around the horizon meant that "we were in a large River and Not a Strait that would communicate with the Northern Seas."[37]

During the ten days spent exploring "Cook's River," the British traded on several occasions with men in kayaks and with parties of men, women, and children in large skin-covered boats.[38] Clothing, beads, and iron from the ships were exchanged for

8.6 Chugach spruce-root "chief's hat," acquired by the Cook expedition at Prince William Sound in 1778. The woven cylinders atop the hat most likely signify that the owner had hosted one or several feasts of the dead. Tlingit leaders adorned their clan hats in similar fashion to celebrate the sponsorship of lavish memorial feasts, or potlatches. The face of an animal spirit is painted on the crown of the hat. Figure 9.2 shows another hat of this type, decorated with glass trade beads that were just becoming available in the region. © The Trustees of the British Museum, NWC 8.

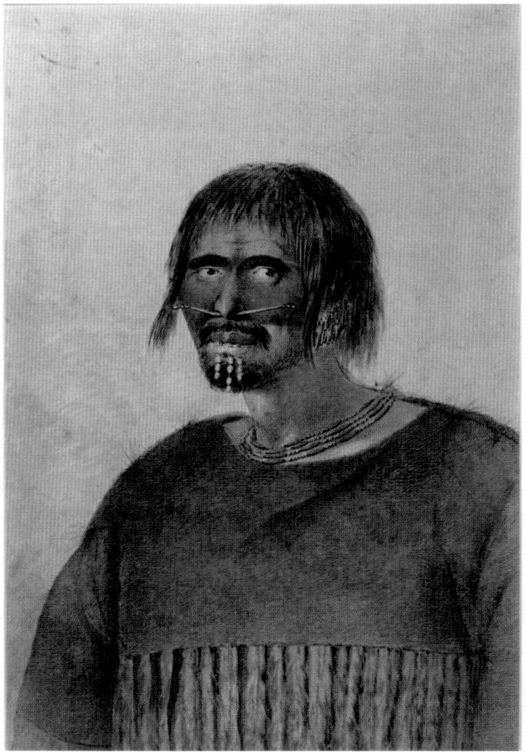

8.7 John Webber, *Man of Turnagain Arm*, 1778. Watercolor. This image shows a Dena'ina man from the shores of Cook Inlet, dressed in a fringed caribou-hide tunic. He wears face paint, a bone nose pin, a labret with pendant glass trade beads, and a bead necklace. From their appearance, technology, and way of life, James Cook thought that the Dena'ina were "of the same Nation" as the Sugpiaq of Sandwich (Prince William) Sound. He failed to perceive the distinctiveness of Dena'ina cultural identity, language, and historical origins. Courtesy of the Peabody Museum of Archaeology and Ethnology, Harvard University, PM# 41-72-10/501 (digital file #60741400).

various furs (sea otter, marten, marmot, hare, and Arctic ground squirrel) as well as fresh and dried salmon and halibut. Cook committed fewer details of these encounters to his journal than in Prince William Sound, but observed that the watercraft, clothing, personal ornaments, and weapons of the people appeared similar in most respects to those of the Chugach (fig. 8.7).

However, his conclusion that "all of the people we have met in this River are of the same Nation as those who Inhabit Sandwich Sound . . . both in their persons and Language" was incorrect.[39] Although some Sugpiat then lived at Nanwalek near Kachemak Bay, and others from Prince William Sound or the outer Kenai coast could have been seen in the inlet, most or all of the individuals whom the British encountered would have been Dena'ina Athabascans. Dena'ina villages lined both sides of the inlet, from Kachemak Bay to Turnagain Arm on the east and from Tuxedni Bay to Kustatan, Tyonek, and Knik on the west, and it was people from these communities who came out to trade with the ships.[40] Cook did not perceive their distinctive cultural identity because Dena'ina who had migrated to the shores of Cook Inlet some centuries before had adopted many elements of Sugpiaq culture, including skin boats, weapons designed for hunting sea mammals, and waterproof clothing made of seal intestines.[41]

Dena'ina interactions with Cook survive in oral tradition, including a story related by Simeon Chickalusion about a Tyonek man who traded with a strange ship that was like "a giant bird with great white wings" and who acquired the uniform of a British sailor.[42] A vocabulary list collected from Native visitors to the *Resolution* by the expedition surgeon, William Anderson, includes words in both the upper and lower Cook Inlet dialects of the Dena'ina language.[43] Dena'ina identity is also indicated by items that the people carried, including iron and copper knives with spiral ends "like the head of a fiddle" and a caribou-skin quiver decorated with dyed porcupine quills purchased from one of the visitors (fig. 9.8).[44]

After confirming that Knik and Turnagain Arms were tidally treacherous dead ends rather than openings to the continental interior, and having decided to depart the inlet for explorations farther west, Cook sent Lieutenant James King ashore with two armed boats to display the flag and to "take possession of the Country and River in his Majesty's name." The party was instructed to bury a bottle containing English coins and a piece of parchment inscribed with the date as well as the names of the captains and ships.[45] King landed at "Point Possession" on the southwest side of the entrance to Turnagain Arm, across from present-day Anchorage (fig. 10.6). The group was greeted on shore by as many as forty Dena'ina men, probably residents of nearby Ch'aghałnikt (Point Possession Village). The encounter began with peaceful trading, but when the British finished the claiming ceremony and climbed a nearby hill to survey the country, the Dena'ina men became alarmed and donned armor and weapons that they had hidden nearby. During the tense confrontation that followed, the British shot a dog to demonstrate the deadly power of their firearms. The Dena'ina men quickly withdrew, and King felt certain that they had never previously seen a musket fired. Dena'ina actions toward the British at Point Possession were similar to Chugach behavior at Snug Corner Cove, a mixture of amity and aggression that reflected regional patterns of shifting intersocietal relations.

One Dena'ina oral tradition about the Cook expedition refers specifically to the incident concerning the dog. The late Fedosia Sacaloff narrated that the First Underwater People (so called because their ships seemed to emerge from underwater as they breasted the horizon) traded at Kustatan, bringing sewing needles and scissors.[46] The Underwater People shot a dog, a small but memorable incident that links the British and Dena'ina narratives.

Like the Chugach, the Dena'ina wore glass beads but did not show signs of direct contact with Russian traders. Cook concluded that the beads had been obtained through neighbors with whom the Russians traded directly, and he wrote that "I will be bold to say that the Russians were never amongst these people, nor carry on any commerce with them, for if they did they would hardly be clothed in such valuable skins as those of the Sea beaver [sea otter]; the Russians would find some means or other to get them all from them."[47]

Cook was correct about limited Russian penetration of the Gulf of Alaska at the time of his voyage, for in 1778 the nearest Russian outpost was Potap Zaikov's on Unimak Island, hundreds of miles to the west.[48] The approximate state of Russian cartographic knowledge at the time is shown on a 1782 chart by Zaikov, which depicts the Aleutian Island chain and Kodiak Island but gives no indication of Cook Inlet.

SHUMAGIN ISLANDS AND UNALASKA ISLAND, JUNE 17–JULY 2 AND OCTOBER 2–26, 1778

After departing Cook Inlet, the ships headed west around Kodiak island and on June 17 arrived at Unga Island in the Shumagin group, part of Unangax̂ territory.[49] Native men came out to the *Discovery* with a wooden box containing a message written in the Russian alphabet, and shouted out a word recorded as "Callikaah."[50] This term—*kalikax̂*—derives from the Koryak (eastern Siberian) *kalíkal,* which means "book, letter, or record." The incident was one indication of the fusion of Russian, Siberian, and Alaska Native languages and cultures that was already under way in the Aleutian Islands. It was later learned that the document was a receipt for hostages and fur tribute provided by local communities to a Russian company.[51] Most likely it was thought that Cook's ships were there to impose similar demands. Cook noted, "This seems to be the farthest east that the Russians trade along the coast of America."

Near Sanak Island another kayaker came out

8.8 John Webber, *Man of Unalaska,* watercolor prepared for engraving, 1778. Webber's watercolor depicts a mature Unangax̂ man in traditional hunting dress. His visor is a thinly shaved piece of wood, softened in hot water and bent into a smoothly curving form, then ornamented with sea-lion whiskers, glass beads, walrus ivory carvings, and paints compounded from volcanic pigments. This style of headgear marks the artist's subject as a commoner in Aleut society; those of higher rank wore large, closed-crowned hats with even more elaborate painting and decorations. He wears a nose pin and an ivory labret in the form of a whale's tail. Dixson Library, State Library of New South Wales, PXX 2.28.

8.9 John Webber, *A Portrait of a Woman of Unalaska,* 1778. Charcoal field sketch. This portrait of an Unangax̂ woman shows her cheeks and chin marked with tattoos and her ears, lower lip, and nose adorned with beads and traditional ornaments. She wears a tunic of white leather or seal esophagus, with a standing collar of dyed esophagus strips and caribou-hair embroidery. The dangles sketched on her collar and tunic probably represent puffin beaks. Museum of the Aleutians 2001.059.001.

to the ships. Dressed in a cap, green cloth pants, and a black jacket under a seal-intestine parka, he bowed in the European manner and otherwise gave the impression of an "acquired politeness" that indicated Russian acculturation.[52]

After a ten-day passage along the coast of the western Alaska Peninsula and a near-shipwreck in fog at Sedanka Island, the *Resolution* and *Discovery* reached safe anchorage on June 28 at Samgoonoodha, later called English Bay, at the eastern tip of Unalaska Island.[53] Because of bad weather, the British stayed until July 2, an interval that afforded opportunities to explore on shore and to meet Unangax̂ residents from nearby villages. Some came out to the ships to trade for tobacco, among them a young man dressed in a beaded bentwood hat, a waterproof parka made of whale intestines, and an inner garment sewn from bird skins and mended with silk patches.[54] An Unangax̂ messenger delivered a second Russian note, to which Cook replied in English and Latin with information identifying his ships.

This first visit to Unalaska was no more than a brief stopover on the expedition's push to the north in search of a transcontinental passage. Cook left Unalaska as soon as the weather cleared, and over the next three months he coasted the Alaska mainland to Bering Strait, touched on the Siberian and Alaskan shores of the Chukchi Sea, and attained the highest northern latitude of the voyage at Icy Cape before being turned back by pack ice on August 18.

Cook returned to Samgoonoodha/English Bay in early October, this time to remain for over three weeks while the ships underwent repairs. Expedition personnel traded almost daily with Unangax̂ residents for fish, berries, and meat, and the men frequented villages in English Bay and Deep Bay, just south of their anchorage (figs. 8.8 and 8.9). They visited Unangax̂ households and, according to Samwell, may have had sexual relations with the women.[55] Cook's personal observations (supported by the accounts of Clerke, Edgar, King, and Samwell) provide descriptions of the Unangax̂ way of life, including their diet, in which salmon, halibut, and seals were preeminent; their finely crafted kayaks (fig. 8.10) and hunting weapons; their modes of dress and personal ornamentation; and the diverse manufactures of the island, including grass baskets and mats that the women wove with "neatness and perfection."[56]

The drawing "Natives of Oonalashka and Their Habitations," by the expedition artist John Webber, which shows inhabitants outside their semisubterranean longhouses, was probably drawn at the head of English Bay, where hills and cliffs match those in the drawing's background (fig. 8.11). An archaeological site with large house pits known as Samgoonoodha Village exists at this location today. Webber's interior view of an Unangax̂ dwelling (fig. 8.12) shows its central communal space surrounded by living areas for individual families. Entrance was gained through the roof, via a log ladder with cutout steps. Some houses of this type were up to 150

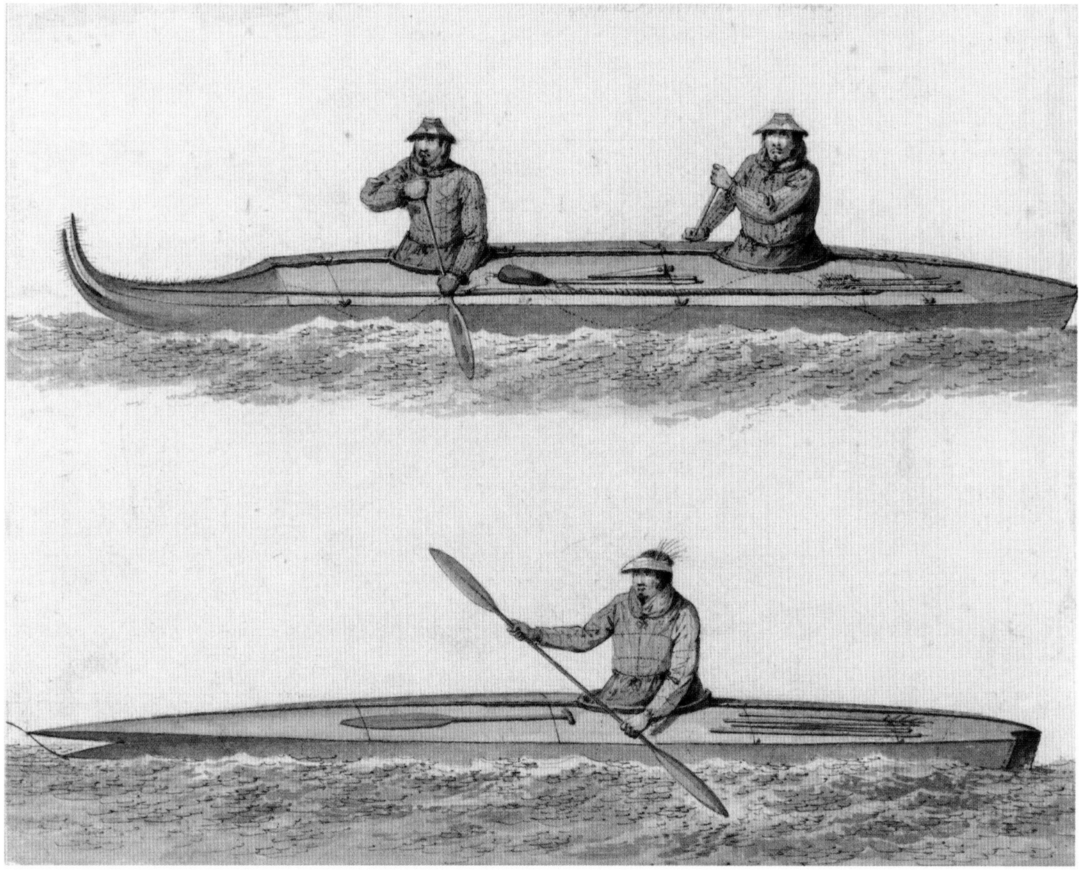

8.10 John Webber, *Kayaks of Prince William Sound and Unalaska,* 1778. Watercolor. The Unangax̂ kayak (at bottom in the figure) was built for survival on the stormy, tide-ripped seas of the Aleutian Island chain. In contrast to the relatively broad Sugpiaq boats of Prince William Sound (top), Aleutian kayaks were so narrow and sharply keeled for speed that they would not float upright without a rider. The divided bow came to a sharp point, and the stern contracted to a narrow, rudder-like tail. Using double-ended paddles, Unalaska kayakers could "go at a great rate and in a direction as straight as a line can be drawn," according to Cook. A single-blade paddle was carried on deck along with hunting harpoons. The Unangax̂ paddler in Webber's illustration wears a bentwood visor and seal-intestine parka, with a spray skirt drawn up around his waist to keep water out of the boat. Dixson Library, State Library of New South Wales, PXX 2.30.

8.11 J. Hall and S. Middiman, *Natives of Oonalashka and their Habitations,* engraving after drawings by John Webber from 1778. From Cook, *A Voyage to the Pacific Ocean* (1784), plate 57. The grass-covered mound at left is the exterior of an Unangax̂ longhouse, with several occupants gathered on the roof. Next to the water are racks for kayaks and drying fish. This settlement was at the head of Samgoonoodha (English) Bay on Unalaska Island, near where the British ships lay at anchor during October 1778. University of British Columbia, Rare Books and Special Collections.

feet long and sheltered one hundred people or more, with members of high-ranking lineages inhabiting the apartments at one end.[57]

As elsewhere, Cook studied Unangax̂ culture for clues to the existence of a Northwest Passage. Referring once again to Crantz and his ethnographic description of Greenland, Cook deduced that the Unangax̂ language, customs, and material culture were of Inuit extraction and concluded that "there can be little doubt that there is a northern communication of some sort by sea between this Ocean and Baffin's bay, but it may be effectually shut up against Shipping, by ice and other impediments."[58] This assessment, now relatively pessimistic about a passable sea route across North America, reflects Cook's failure in previous months to discover any opening to the east along the Alaskan coast, or to penetrate the Arctic sea ice.

The October stay at Unalaska gave Cook an opportunity to gather strategic information about the Russian fur trade. The nearest group of traders, headed by Gerasim Izmailov, was headquartered at Iliuliuk (called Egoochshac or E'chock'suk by the British), located twelve miles west of Samgoonoodha at Unalaska Harbor or "Captain's Harbor" (fig. 8.13). Russian expeditions had overwintered there since 1768, and Izmailov had arrived in 1776.[59] The Russian manager sent baked salmon pies as a gift to Cook and Clerke at Samgoonoodha, and John Ledyard was dispatched on a return visit bearing rum, wine, and porter.[60] Izmailov then came to English Bay with a large retinue of Unangax̂ kayaks, and the two leaders compared charts, managing an informative discussion despite the lack of a shared language. From Izmailov Cook learned that Russian knowledge of the Alaska mainland was limited (in fact, far inferior to his own), and that Russian efforts to explore and trade beyond Unimak Island had been repelled by local residents.[61] Cook gathered additional intelligence from Jacob Ivanovitch, a trader based at Umnak Island who also called on the British ships at Samgoonoodha.

Ledyard and others who visited Iliuliuk (fig. 8.13) reported that thirty to sixty Russians and up to seventy Kamchadals (or Itelemen, from eastern Siberia) lived there in a sod-walled barracks building.[62] The structure was not unlike an Unangax̂ longhouse, although it was provided with a thatched roof, ground-level doorway, and mica-glazed window. About twenty Unangax̂ boys also stayed in the barracks, apparently hostages ceded by elite families of the island. There were two warehouses for supplies and furs and dwellings for Unangax̂ workers. The Russian-Siberian contingent possessed few supplies from Kamchatka and relied heavily on local goods produced by the Unangax̂; they dressed in skin and gut clothing, traveled in kayaks, and ate a diet of fish, berries, and sea-mammal meat. The great difficulty of transporting Russian-made goods across Siberia and the Pacific Ocean to Alaska remained a significant problem in Russian America for many decades.[63]

British observations, supplemented by Russian accounts, describe colonial labor practices on Unalaska Island and their impact on Native residents. Fleets of Unangax̂ kayaks were sent out in spring and summer to hunt sea otters, using a method of surrounding the animals in the water and spearing them with darts.[64] The intensive focus on otter hunting led to winter starvation in the villages because normal subsistence harvesting had to be neglected, and many men were lost at sea during voyages to distant hunting grounds.[65] Unangax̂ leaders such as Cawachcag'nen, reportedly the chief of all Unalaska Island, were responsible to the Russians for fur production, but their authority in other areas was "confined within narrow bounds since the People have been brought into subjection."[66] Unangax̂ women were required to produce food for fur-company personnel, including bundles of dried fish that the British saw them preparing on several occasions.[67] Native workers received token payments in the form of glass beads, tobacco, needles, cloth shirts, and brass kettles. Although adzes and small metal knives were also distributed, Cook noted that "these are the only instruments they had made of iron, for altho the Russians live amongst them they had far less of this Metal, than those who never saw a Russian."[68] Notably the Unangax̂ possessed no fighting knives or spears like those of the Chugach and Dena'ina, because the Russians had confiscated all weapons of war, along with large

8.12 John Webber, *Inside of a House in Oonalaska,* watercolor prepared for the engraver, ca. 1781–83. Details of Unangax̂ culture and family life are depicted in this longhouse interior. The large communal structure has a driftwood frame covered with grass thatching and a floor set several feet below ground level. A log ladder gives access to the rooftop entrance, through which smoke from the cooking fires could also escape. Wooden food and water containers are scattered on the floor, and mats woven of grass provide both seating and privacy screens for family areas. At the time of the Cook expedition, the people of Unalaska Island possessed few Russian goods, and none can be seen in this illustration. Dixson Library, State Library of New South Wales, PXX 2.34.

8.13 *View of Captain's Harbor in 1817.* Lithograph of a drawing by Louis Choris, artist with the Otto von Kotzebue expedition (1815–18), from Louis Choris, *Voyage pittoresque autour du monde* (1822). This is one of two views that the artist created looking into and (as here) out of what is today Dutch Harbor, Unalaska. Some forty years after John Ledyard had been sent by Cook from Samgoonoodha to the fledgling settlement of Iliuliuk to establish contact with the Russian fur traders, it had grown into the Russian American Company's principal establishment in the Aleutian Islands. Rasmuson Library, University of Alaska Fairbanks, B0083—Copy 2, Plate 11.

skin boats formerly used for interisland travel, trade, and warfare.

The paucity of Russian-imported trade goods and their minor importance in the forced labor system meant that Unangax̂ material culture had overall been little altered by contact. As the British observed, traditional forms of clothing, tools, hunting weapons, kayaks, fishing gear, baskets, and other locally made items were still predominant in daily life. Late eighteenth-century archaeological data confirm this pattern. For example, bone and stone tools made up over 80 percent of the artifacts recovered from a longhouse at Reese Bay on Unalaska Island that was occupied from before 1750 to about 1790, and many additional organic items that would have been present were not preserved.[69] Artifacts of Russian origin consisted of glass beads along with a few scraps of glass and metal.[70]

Many of the British observers reported that harsh measures were employed to control the

Unangax̂ population, including "instant death" as punishment for theft. Samwell wrote: "The inhabitants of this Island are in a state of Subjection to the Russians & it should seem from what we observed amongst them that they are made to pay Tribute to their Masters, all of their Arms of every kind are taken from them. The Russians with the Parent's consent take their Children from them when they are young & employ them at their Factory. . . . [T]hey are brought up to speak the Russian language & most probably are baptized & taught something of the Christian Religion."[71]

Other British comments reflect this mix of subjection and acculturation imposed on colonial subjects. Under Russian rule the Unangax̂ had learned to be "peaceable," "inoffensive," and "mild"; they never tried to steal (a capital offense); they were reluctant to trade without permission from their overlords; and many had learned words and phrases in the Russian language, used Western forms of polite address such as bowing, and showed at least nominal reverence for the Russian Orthodox faith.[72] King further remarked that "the whole of their behavior gave us a good Opinion of their Masters, who seem'd to have thought it worth the trouble to Correct their passions, & make them better members of Society, yet there were many appearances of these People being abridg'd in their freedom, & against whom force must have been us'd."[73]

While the Russian and Siberian personnel of the Izmailov company claimed never to have sexual relations with Unangax̂ women, they or their predecessors had evidently introduced venereal infection to the island.[74] In later years both unsanctioned unions and official marriages between Russians and Unangax̂ women were common, and from these families an ethnically creole population would be born, with roots in both cultures.

THE COLONIAL AFTERMATH

The fur wealth of the north Pacific attracted Spanish and French voyagers and scores of British and American fur traders, many of whom followed Cook's track to Canada's northwest coast and southeastern Alaska.[75] Nonetheless it was Russia, a peripheral European power with limited capacity to supply its distant colony, which dominated the Aleutian Islands and the Gulf of Alaska until 1867 and left a lasting cultural imprint.

Under Russian rule, the eastern Aleutian Islands and Kodiak archipelago developed into a core "dependent" region where colonial control was strong, Native populations were initially large, and a mandatory fur-production system similar to what Cook observed in 1778 was enforced under terms of the Russian American Company's several charters. Cook Inlet and Prince William Sound, although incorporated into the fur trade by the 1780s, remained part of a less populous, "semidependent" peripheral zone where the company maintained a more limited presence and acquired furs primarily through voluntary trade.[76]

The pernicious effects of colonization were

most devastating in the core region, where an initial Unangax̂ and Sugpiaq population of perhaps 25,000 plunged to fewer than 4,500 by the late 1830s as the result of harsh punishments, the loss of hunters at sea, epidemics, and malnutrition. Many once-thriving villages were deserted, including the English Bay and Deep Bay settlements that Cook visited on Unalaska Island.[77]

Nonetheless, the harsh conditions that prevailed at the time of Cook's voyage were ameliorated by later reforms. The Russian Orthodox Church began missionary work on Kodiak Island in 1794 and advocated for better treatment of the Alaska Native population, and the Russian American Company moderated its policies.[78] Creoles, defined by the company's second charter in 1821 as the offspring of Russian or Siberian men and Alaska Native women, were recognized as colonial citizens with rights to be paid for their work, to be exempt from taxes, and to receive an education.[79] By the 1850s, creoles comprised about 20 percent of the colonial population.[80] In addition, a large proportion of the populace that was not creole in the official sense was bicultural, bilingual, and Orthodox.[81] Educated creoles became clergy, administrators, clerks, navigators, and artisans.

Cultural influence in Russian America also extended in the opposite direction. As Ledyard and others observed, Russian and Siberian men who worked in the fur trade ate, dressed, and lived almost entirely like their Alaska Native cohorts. Many married into Alaska Native families and chose to stay in the colony rather than return home, becoming permanent bicultural residents of the colony.

Observations by the Cook expedition of indigenous peoples and Russian fur traders in southern Alaska hold significant ethnohistoric value, due in large part to the timing and trajectory of the voyage. The vessels first passed through what was then the faint eastern penumbra of Russian influence at Prince William Sound and Cook Inlet, where no direct Western contact had previously occurred and where Alaska Native societies remained free and independent. It continued into the heart of Russian colonial occupation in the eastern Aleutians, where control over the indigenous inhabitants had been brutally and effectively established. Over the course of just a few months in 1778, the expedition bore witness to Alaska Native peoples at the expanding edge of the capitalist world-system and to the social and cultural transformations that they were undergoing or about to begin.

NOTES

1 Anthony Pagden, *Lords of All the World: Ideologies of Empire in Spain, Britain, and France c. 1500–1800* (New Haven, CT: Yale University Press, 1995); Immanuel Wallerstein, *The Modern World-System III: The Second Era of Great Expansion of the Capitalist World-Economy, 1730–1840s* (New York: Academic Press, 1989).

2 Aron L. Crowell, *Archaeology and the Capitalist World System: A Study from Russian America* (New York: Plenum, 1997); Aron L. Crowell, "Ethnicity and Periphery: The Archaeology of Identity in Russian America," in *The*

Archaeology of Capitalism in Colonial Contexts: Postcolonial Historical Archaeologies, ed. Sarah K. Croucher and Lindsay Weiss (New York: Springer, 2011), 85–104; Charles R. Ewen, "From Colonist to Creole: Archaeological Patterns of Spanish Colonization in the New World," *Historical Archaeology* 34, no. 3 (2000): 36–45; Kurt A. Jordan, "Colonies, Colonialism, and Cultural Entanglement: The Archaeology of Postcolumbian Intercultural Relations," in *International Handbook of Historical Archaeology,* ed. Teresita Majewski and David Gamister (New York: Springer, 2009), 31–49; Eric R. Wolf, *Europe and the People without History* (Berkeley: University of California Press, 1982).

3 *The Journals of Captain James Cook on His Voyages of Discovery,* vol. 3, *The Voyage of the* Resolution *and* Discovery, *1776–1780,* ed. J. C. Beaglehole (Cambridge: Cambridge University Press for the Hakluyt Society, 1967).

4 Vasilii Nikolaevich Berkh, *A Chronological History of the Discovery of the Aleutian Islands, or the Exploits of the Russian Merchants,* trans. Dmitri Krenov, ed. Richard A. Pierce (Kingston, ON: Limestone, 1974); Lydia T. Black, *Russians in Alaska, 1732–1867* (Fairbanks: University of Alaska Press, 2004), 59–77; Raisa V. Makarova, *Russians on the Pacific, 1743–1799,* trans. and ed. Richard A. Pierce and Alton S. Donnelly (Kingston, ON: Limestone, 1975).

5 Cook, *Voyage of the* Resolution *and* Discovery, ccxxiii.

6 Ibid., 459.

7 Black, *Russians in Alaska,* 89.

8 Aron L. Crowell, "Maritime Cultures of the Gulf of Alaska," *Revista de Arqueologia Americana/Journal of American Archaeology* 17, no. 19 (2000): 177–216; Aron L. Crowell, Amy F. Steffian, and Gordon L. Pullar, eds., *Looking Both Ways: Heritage and Identity of the Alutiiq People* (Fairbanks: University of Alaska Press, 2001); James Kari and James A. Fall, *Shem Pete's Alaska: The Territory of the Upper Cook Inlet Dena'aina,* 2nd ed. (Fairbanks: Alaska Native Language Center, 2003); Margaret Lantis, "Aleut," in *Handbook of North American Indians,* vol. 5, *Arctic,* ed. David Damas, general ed. William C. Sturtevant (Washington, DC: Smithsonian Institution, 1984), 161–84; Rosa G. Liapunova, *Essays on the Ethnography of the Aleuts: At the End of the Eighteenth and the First Half of the Nineteenth Century,* trans. Jerry Shelest, ed. William B. Workman and Lydia T. Black (Fairbanks: University of Alaska Press, 1996).

9 Margaret Lantis, "The Aleut Social System, 1750 to 1810, from Early Historical Sources," in *Ethnohistory in Southwestern Alaska and the Southern Yukon,* ed. Margaret Lantis (Lexington: University of Kentucky Press, 1970), 139–311; Joan B. Townsend, "Ranked Societies of the Alaskan Pacific Rim," in *Alaska Native Culture and History,* ed. Yoshinobu Kotani and William B. Workman (Osaka: National Museum of Ethnology, 1980), 123–56.

10 Cook, *Voyage of the* Resolution *and* Discovery, ccxx–ccxxiii.

11 Glyndwr Williams, "'To Make Discoveries of Countries Hitherto Unknown': The Admiralty and Pacific Exploration in the Eighteenth Century," in *Pacific Empires: Essays in Honour of Glyndwr Williams,* ed. Alan Frost and Jane Samson (Vancouver: UBC Press, 2005), 13–32; Glyndwr Williams, *Arctic Labyrinth: The Quest for the Northwest Passage* (Toronto: Viking Canada, 2009), 132–48.

12 Basil Dmytryshyn, E. A. P. Crownhart-Vaughan, and Thomas Vaughan, eds., *To Siberia and Russian America: Three Centuries of Russian Eastward Expansion,* vol. 2, *Russian Penetration of the North Pacific Ocean: A Documentary Record, 1700–1799* (Portland: Oregon Historical Society, 1988); Svetlana G. Fedorova, *The Russian Population in Alaska and California, Late 18th Century–1867,* trans. and ed. Richard A. Pierce and Alton S. Donnelly (Kingston, ON: Limestone, 1973); Petr Aleksandrovich Tikhmenev, trans. and ed. Richard A. Pierce and Alton S. Connelly (Seattle: University of Washington Press, 1978).

13 Black, *Russians in Alaska,* 128–35; Rosa G. Liapunova, *Essays on the Ethnography of the Aleuts.*

14 Raymond H. Fisher, *Bering's Voyages: Whither and Why* (Seattle: University of Washington Press, 1977).

15 Christon I. Archer, "Russians, Indians, and Passages: Spanish Voyages to Alaska in the Eighteenth Century," in *Exploration in Alaska,* ed. Antoinette Shalkop (Anchorage, AK: Cook Inlet Historical Society, 1980), 129–43; Wallace M. Olson, *Through Spanish Eyes: The Spanish Voyages to Alaska, 1774–1792* (Auke Bay, AK: Heritage Research, 2002).

16 Glyndwr Williams, "Alaska Revealed: Cook's Explorations in 1778," in Shalkop, *Exploration in Alaska* (Anchorage, AK: Cook Inlet Historical Society, 1980), 69–87.

17 Cook, *Voyage of the* Resolution *and* Discovery, ccxxiii.
18 Ibid., 344–55.
19 Heinrich Johan Holmberg, *Holmberg's Ethnographic Sketches,* ed. M. W. Falk, trans. F. Jaensch (Fairbanks: University of Alaska Press, 1985), 57.
20 Cook, *Voyage of the* Resolution *and* Discovery, 351.
21 Crowell, Steffian, and Pullar, *Looking Both Ways;* Kaj Birket-Smith, *The Chugach Eskimo* (Copenhagen: Nationalmuseets Skrifter, Etnografiske Raekke, 1953); Don Dumond, "A Re-Examination of Eskimo-Aleut Prehistory," *American Anthropologist* 89, no. 1 (1987): 32–56.
22 For example, George Dixon, *A Voyage round the World: But More Particularly to the North-west Coast of America: Performed in 1785, 1786, 1787, and 1788, in the* King George *and* Queen Charlotte, *Captains Portlock and Dixon,* facsimile ed. (Amsterdam: N. Israel; New York: Da Capo, 1968), 146; Carl Heinrich Merck, "Siberia and Northwestern America, 1788–1792," in *The Journal of Carl Heinrich Merck, Naturalist with the Russian Scientific Expedition Led by Captains Joseph Billings and Gavriil Sarychev,* trans. Fritz Jaensch, ed. Richard A. Pierce (Kingston, ON: Limestone, 1980), 111–12; Nathaniel Portlock, *A Voyage round the World, But More Particularly to the North-west Coast of America, Performed in 1785, 1786, 1787, and 1788, in the* King George *and* Queen Charlotte, *Captains Portlock and Dixon* (London: John Stockdale; facsimile ed., Amsterdam: N. Israel; New York: Da Capo, 1968), 112–13; Gawrila Sarychev, *Account of a Voyage of Discovery to the North-east of Siberia, the Frozen Ocean, and the North-east Sea* (1806; rept. Amsterdam: N. Israel; New York: Da Capo Press, 1969), 11–20; George Vancouver, *A Voyage of Discovery to the North Pacific Ocean and round the World, 1791–1795,* ed. W. Kaye Lamb, 4 vols. (London: Hakluyt Society, 1984), 4:1277.
23 Cook, *Voyage of the* Resolution *and* Discovery, 1115.
24 Portlock, *A Voyage round the World,* 255; confirmed by Vancouver, *A Voyage of Discovery round the World,* 4:1277.
25 Michael Fortescue, Steven Jacobson, and Lawrence Kaplan, *Comparative Eskimo Dictionary with Aleut Cognates* (Fairbanks: Alaska Native Language Center, 1994), 126.
26 Dixon, *Voyage round the World,* 67–69.
27 Cook, *Voyage of the* Resolution *and* Discovery, 1110.
28 Portlock, *Voyage round the World,* 237–38.
29 Cook, *Voyage of the* Resolution and Discovery, 1107.
30 Birket-Smith, *Chugach Eskimo,* 18–22, 112–13.
31 Cook, *Voyage of the* Resolution *and* Discovery, 1108.
32 Barbara E. Bundy, Allen P. McCartney, and Douglas W. Veltre, "Glass Trade Beads from Reese Bay, Unalaska Island: Spatial and Temporal Patterns," *Arctic Anthropology* 49, no. 1 (2003): 29–47; Crowell, *Archaeology and the Capitalist World System.*
33 Cook, *Voyage of the* Resolution *and* Discovery, 1112.
34 Steven Acheson, "The Thin Edge: Evidence for Precontact Use and Working of Metal on the Northwest Coast," in *Emerging from the Mist: Studies in Northwest Coast Culture History,* ed. R. G. Matson, Gary Coupland, and Quentin Mackie (Vancouver: University of British Columbia Press, 2003), 213–29; Birket-Smith, *Chugach Eskimo,* 12; George Quimby, "Japanese Wrecks, Iron Tools, and Prehistoric Indians of the Northwest Coast," *Arctic Anthropology* 22, no. 2 (1985): 7–16.
35 Herbert D. G. Maschner and Katherine L. Reedy-Maschner, "Raid, Retreat, Defend (Repeat): The Archaeology and Ethnohistory of Warfare on the North Pacific Rim," *Journal of Anthropological Archaeology* 17, no. 1 (1998): 19–51.
36 Cook, *Voyage of* Resolution *and* Discovery, 1416.
37 Ibid., 364.
38 Ibid., 361–72, 1114–17.
39 Ibid., 371.
40 Kari and Fall, *Shem Pete's Alaska;* Cornelius Osgood, *Ethnography of the Tanaina* (New Haven, CT: Yale University Publications in Anthropology 16, 1937); Joan B. Townsend, "Tanaina," in *Handbook of North American Indians,* vol. 4, *Subarctic,* ed. June Helm (Washington, DC: Smithsonian Institution, 1981), 623–40.
41 Suzi Jones, James A. Fall, and Aaron Leggett, eds., *Dena'inaq' Huch'ulyeshi: The Dena'ina Way of Living* (Fairbanks: University of Alaska Press, 2013).
42 Kari and Fall, *Shem Pete's Alaska,* 345–48.
43 Ibid., 346.
44 Cook, *Voyage of the* Resolution *and* Discovery, 371 n. 3.
45 Ibid., 368, 1421–22.
46 Kari and Fall, *Shem Pete's Alaska,* 356.

47 Cook, *Voyage of* Resolution *and* Discovery, 371.

48 Franz N. Klichka, "A Report on the Voyage of Potap K. Zaikov to Islands in the North Pacific Ocean between Asia and America, Aboard the Merchant Vessel Sv. Vladimir, as Described for the Academy of Sciences by Franz Nikolaevich Klichka, Governor of Irkutsk," in Dmytryshyn, Crownhart-Vaughan, and Vaughan, *To Siberia and Russian America,* 2:263.

49 Cook, *Voyage of the* Resolution *and* Discovery, 383.

50 Ibid., 383 n. 3.

51 Ibid., 384 n. 1; Klichka, "Report on the Voyage of Potap K. Zaikov," 263.

52 Cook, *Voyage of the* Resolution *and* Discovery, 386.

53 Ibid., 391.

54 Ibid., 392.

55 Ibid., 1141–49.

56 Ibid., 459–68, 1142–46, 1333–40, 1426–28.

57 Georg Heinrich von Langsdorff, *Remarks and Observations on a Voyage around the World from 1803 to 1807,* trans. Victoria Joan Moessner, ed. Richard A. Pierce (Kingston, ON: Limestone, 1993), 13; Liapunova, *Essays on the Ethnography of the Aleuts,* 169–77; Ivan Veniaminov, *Notes on the Islands of the Unalashka District,* trans. Lydia T. Black and R. H. Geoghegan, ed. Richard A. Pierce (Fairbanks: Elmer E. Rasmuson Library, University of Alaska Fairbanks; Kingston, ON: Limestone, 1984), 262.

58 Cook, *Voyage of the* Resolution *and* Discovery, 468.

59 Black, *Russians in Alaska,* 90; Makarova, *Russians on the Pacific,* 72.

60 Cook, *Voyage of the* Resolution *and* Discovery, 448–49; *John Ledyard's Journal of Captain Cook's Last Voyage,* ed. James Kenneth Munford (Corvallis: Oregon State University Press, 1963), 91–100.

61 Cook, *Voyage of the* Resolution *and* Discovery, 451–56.

62 Ibid., 457–58; *John Ledyard's Journal,* 98.

63 James R. Gibson, *Imperial Russia in Frontier America: The Changing Geography of Supply of Russian America, 1784–1867* (New York: Oxford University Press, 1976).

64 Iakov Netsvetov, *The Journals of Iakov Netsvetov: The Atkha Years, 1828–1844,* trans. and ed. Lydia Black (Kingston, ON: Limestone, 1980), 43–44; Veniaminov, *Notes on the Islands,* 329–33.

65 Veniaminov, *Notes on the Islands,* 255.

66 Cook, *Voyage of the* Resolution *and* Discovery, 1146.

67 Ibid., 1140.

68 Ibid., 461–62.

69 Douglas W. Veltre and Allen P. McCartney, "Ethnohistoric Archaeology at the Reese Bay Site, Unalaska Island," in *Archaeology of the Aleut Zone of Alaska: Some Recent Research,* ed. Don E. Dumond (Eugene: University of Oregon Anthropological Papers no. 58, 2001), 87–104.

70 Bundy, McCartney, and Veltre, "Glass Trade Beads," 29–47.

71 Cook, *Voyage of the* Resolution *and* Discovery, 1142.

72 Ibid., 459, 1142, 1426.

73 Ibid., 1427.

74 Ibid., 1337, 1149.

75 James R. Gibson, *Otter Skins, Boston Ships, and China Goods: The Maritime Fur Trade of the Northwest Coast, 1785–1841* (Montreal: McGill-Queen's University Press, 1992).

76 Aron L. Crowell, "Ethnicity and Periphery," 85–104.

77 Donald W. Clark, "Pacific Eskimo: Historical Ethnography," in *Handbook of North American Indians,* 5:161–84; Sonja Luehrmann, *Alutiiq Villages under Russian and U.S. Rule* (Fairbanks: University of Alaska Press, 2008).

78 Black, *Russians in Alaska,* 191–253; Michael J. Oleksa, *Orthodox Alaska: A Theology of Mission* (Crestwood, NJ: St. Vladimir's Seminary Press, 1992).

79 Lydia T. Black, "Creoles in Russian America," *Pacifica* 2, no. 2 (1990): 142–55; Basil Dmytryshyn, E. A. P. Crownhart-Vaughan, and Thomas Vaughan, eds., *To Siberia and Russian America: Three Centuries of Russian Eastward Expansion,* vol. 3, *The Russian American Colonies, 1798–1867* (Portland: Oregon Historical Society, 1989), 360–61, 468–70; Fedorova, *Russian Population in Alaska and California,* 206–15; Luehrmann, *Alutiiq Villages,* 116–23.

80 Dmytryshyn, Crownhart-Vaughan, and Vaughan, *To Siberia and Russian America,* 3:505–6.

81 Michael J. Oleksa, "The Creoles and Their Contributions to the Development of Alaska," in *Russian America: The Forgotten Frontier,* ed. Barbara Sweetland Smith and Redmond J. Barnett (Tacoma: Washington State Historical Society, 1990), 185–96; Veniaminov, *Notes on the Islands,* 229–39.

9

Gifting, Trading, Selling, Buying

Following Northwest Coast Treasures Acquired on Cook's Third Voyage to Collections around the World

ADRIENNE L. KAEPPLER

THE THREE PACIFIC VOYAGES OF JAMES COOK, AND THE NATURAL-HISTORY specimens and ethnographic objects that the expeditions acquired, contributed to and became part of groundbreaking Enlightenment science in the late eighteenth century. The ships from each voyage returned home with significant "natural and artificial curiosities" that were new to the European world, and today these collections include type specimens of animal and bird species, ethnographic treasures, and important works of art. As the third voyage was undertaken to search for a Northwest Passage between the Pacific and Atlantic Oceans, it held promises of many new specimens and objects from parts of the world not previously visited or explored by Europeans. Professional and amateur scientists were especially interested in the natural-history specimens, but they also sought unusual cultural items for their cabinets of curiosities. The objects collected became known through journal descriptions, paintings, and engravings and quickly became coveted. More than two thousand objects from Cook's voyages have been documented, and museums and private collectors still wish to acquire them.[1]

Anthropological and historical research, art history and theory, and scholarship on indigenous

Cloak with Northwest Coast form-line design, Nootka Sound (see fig. 9.9).

identity require knowledge about the ethnographic objects and their biography and history. Important questions include who collected cultural objects during the voyages and to whom and to what institutions were they given or sold. We also need to know about the entrepreneurs—collectors and dealers—who realized that there was money to be made by buying and selling Cook-voyage curiosities.

Now, more than two centuries later, a great deal of research has been done in museums and archives, but not every object yet has its complete "biography." In this essay I focus on cultural objects acquired on the Northwest Coast of America and on the east coast of Asia and their circuitous routes to their present homes.

As Cook's voyages shifted from the South Pacific to the Northwest Coast of America and the coast of Asia, new and different collectibles were found. The surgeon's mate on the *Discovery,* David Samwell, observed of the participants on the third voyage that "instruments of war and dresses of the Natives seem'd the only Cargo they had brought," suggesting that most were not prepared to collect natural-history specimens and instead acquired cultural objects, which they knew would be collectible and marketable.[2] No special knowledge was required to trade such objects. Indeed, by the end of the third voyage, cultural items had shifted from unimportant appendages to natural-history collections to highly desirable objects in their own right. These new collectibles included feather-covered cloaks, capes, helmets, and god figures from Hawai'i, as well as other sculptures, ornaments, bowls, tools, and weapons. On the Northwest Coast of America, the voyagers found a whole new set of objects to collect—masks, tongue clubs (often known as "slave killers"), rattles in the shape of birds, and bone clubs, along with new versions of weapons, fishhooks, cloaks, unusual textiles, cloth beaters, and other tools. Specialized collectors and dealers, such as George Humphrey, were there to meet the ships as they docked and buy whatever they could.

The length of stay in an area and the quality of interaction with the local people influenced how many and what kind of objects were collected. The largest group of important objects came from the area known as King George's Sound, or Nootka Sound, and a significant number also came from Prince William Sound. The routes and journeys the objects took after their arrival in Europe are diverse and fascinating.

Before the ships from the third voyage arrived back in London, some objects had already been given away in Kamchatka and Cape Town. William Anderson, surgeon on the *Resolution,* who died on the voyage, gathered the collection that was presented by Captain Charles Clerke to the governor of Kamchatka, Major Magnus Behm, in appreciation for his assistance in repairing and provisioning Cook's ships.[3] Taken overland to St. Petersburg, these pieces became part of the collection of Empress Catherine the Great, and they are now in the Kunstkamera at the Peter the Great Museum of Ethnography in St. Petersburg. Although the collection was originally thought to include four American cloaks,[4] this claim has been found to be incorrect: there are no American or Asian objects in this collection.[5]

When the expedition stopped in South Africa on the way back to England, a Nootka mask (fig. 9.1), a rattle, and a fishhook were left in Cape Town. After passing through several hands, they are now at the Iziko South African Museum in Cape Town.

It is notable that the two Americans on the voyage—John Gore and John Ledyard—appear to have collected very little. John Gore had been a master's mate with John Byron and Samuel Wallis before he traveled with Cook on his first and third Pacific voyages. On the first voyage, he was especially important to Cook because he had some knowledge of the Tahitian language. On the third voyage, after the deaths of Cook and Clerke, Gore took command of the expedition. Thus when the ships arrived in England on October 4, 1779, an American, ironically, was in command. What Gore may have collected has so far escaped much notice. The only entry that I have found is in the "book of presents" to the British Museum in 1780, which records "several natural and artificial curiosities from the South Seas from John Gore, Esq, Commander of the *Resolution,* James King, Esq. Commander of the *Discovery,* James Burney, Lieut. Phillips, Lieut. Roberts, Mr. William Peckover, and Mr. Robert Anderson, gunners, and Mr. Thomas Waling, quartermaster." A few days later, there was another gift to the British Museum, "of several artificial curiosities from the South Sea from Captain Williamson, Mr. John Webber, Mr. Cleveley, Mr. William Collett and Mr. Alexander Hogg." However, the book does not note how many pieces came from each donor or what they were. We can only conclude that at least one object (whether natural or artificial is not known) came from John Gore. Gore is said to have obtained two Spanish spoons at Nootka Sound, which he gave to Joseph Banks, so it is possible that Gore gave other objects to him as well.[6] John Ledyard was a marine who wrote his own account of the third voyage. Only one Hawaiian piece that he collected has so far been identified.

Which of these objects came from America remains largely a mystery. Even Jonathan King, who worked with the artifacts and documents for several years, was not fully successful in sorting out which objects came from Cook's third voyage, which from Vancouver's voyage (primarily from the surgeon-botanist, Archibald Menzies, and the surgeon's mate, George Hewett, companions on the *Discovery*), and which from other eighteenth-century donations. In fact, King's work sets up a whole series of speculations about from whom objects might have come and where they might be today.[7] The ones in the Anchorage Museum exhibition can reasonably be associated with Cook's voyages (figs. 8.5 and 8.6).

Fortunately, many of the objects held by the British Museum can be traced to Cook's voyage from external documentation.[8] My book *Artificial*

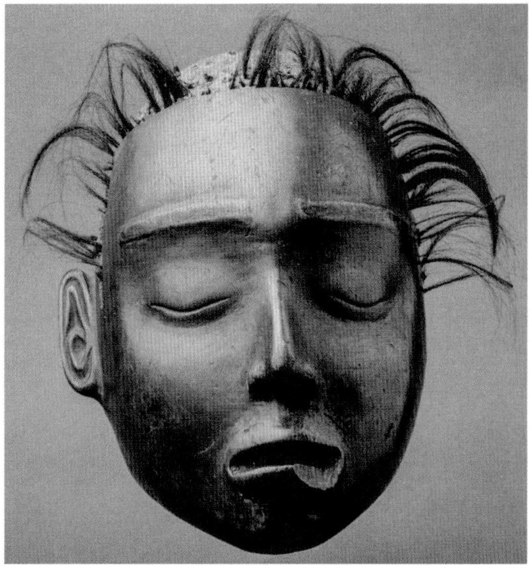

9.1 Anthropomorphic mask, Nootka Sound. Red cedar and hair, acquired by the Cook expedition in 1778. Cook's ships stopped in Cape Town during the second and third voyages. This mask was seemingly presented to the governor of the Cape Colony by Lieutenant James King, along with other curiosities, to form the nucleus of a museum. Found in 1860 in the house of the sexton of the Dutch Reformed Church, the objects were transferred to the South African Museum. Image courtesy of Iziko Museums of Cape Town, SAM 2361, photograph courtesy of the Royal British Columbia Museum.

9.2 *Man of Prince William Sound,* 1794. Watercolor by Philippe Jacques de Loutherbourg for the pantomime *Omai, or, a Trip round the World,* performed in London in 1785, using a libretto by John O'Keeffe and costumes and sets designed by de Loutherbourg. This costume was based on objects collected in Prince William Sound during Cook's third voyage, complemented by the drawings of John Webber, the expedition artist. The model for the quiver is probably the one now in the Museum of Archaeology and Anthropology at Cambridge University. National Library of Australia, pic-an2668176.

Curiosities includes information about many of the important collectors and what happened to their third-voyage pieces, including donations to the British Museum; except for a few additions, this is still relevant today.[9]

IMPORTANT COLLECTORS AND COLLECTIONS OF COOK-VOYAGE AMERICAN OBJECTS

After arriving in London, John Webber, the artist on the third voyage, sent a collection to his ancestral home in Berne, Switzerland. This collection includes a number of important objects from North America. From the Nootka Sound area are a cedar-bark rectangular cloak, a mask, a tongue club, a cedar-bark beater made of whalebone, a scraper, and two harpoons. From the Prince William Sound area are a small, dressed human figure, bow and arrows, spears and a spear thrower, and harpoons. This is one of the few personal assemblages from the third voyage that has been kept together as a "collection." Even so, it does not constitute Webber's entire collection. In addition to objects given to the British Museum, Webber also gave objects to the artist Philippe Jacques de Loutherbourg, who staged the pantomime *Omai, or, a Trip round the World* at Covent Garden.[10] Loutherbourg's collection was sold by a Mr. Coxe in 1812, but I have not located any of the Webber objects from this auction. Loutherbourg's watercolor *Man of Prince William Sound,* now in the National Library of Australia, Canberra, is probably based on Webber's objects or drawings (fig. 9.2).

An important collection not identified until the 1990s was apparently made by Lieutenant James Burney. The son of the renowned musician Charles Burney and brother of the writer Fanny Burney, Burney was first lieutenant on the *Discovery.* Through the auspices of Bishop Benjamin LaTrobe, a good portion of Burney's collection went first to the Moravian Museum in Barby, was then transferred to Niesky, and is now in Herrnhut, Germany.[11] A few pieces were removed from the collection during World War II, and others were sold or exchanged. For example, the collector Harry Beasley is said to have bought objects from the collection when it was in Niesky: "They paid £5 for a Hawaiian godstick £25 Tahiti gorget: £8 2 Tahiti figures etc."[12] The American objects still in Herrnhut include a tongue club (similar to that shown in fig. 9.18), a Nootka mask, and a Nootka hat.

COLLECTIONS WHOSE COLLECTOR OR COLLECTORS ARE NOT KNOWN

Several important objects from America are in the Natural History Museum of Florence, Italy, although it has so far been impossible to sort out who collected them or to trace their journey from London to Florence. Clothing and ornaments from the Northwest Coast and Alaska include a rectangular cloak, a circular cape, a fiber "apron," a pair of slippers made from animal intestines, four hats, a horn bracelet, and two wooden combs. Boating, fishing, and hunting equipment includes paddles, ropes, harpoons, fishhooks, spearheads, and a spear thrower. Weapons include bone clubs, a tongue club (again similar to that shown in fig. 9.18), and a stone club. There is also a human face mask with human hair and a bird-head frontlet.[13]

A collection in the Hunterian Museum, Glasgow, Scotland, includes a bird rattle (fig. 9.3), a bark beater made of bone (fig. 9.7 shows a similar example), a hand adze, a spear thrower (fig. 9.4), and a whalebone hand club (fig. 9.5). The objects came from a variety of sources, which probably included the collection of David Samwell.[14]

The collection in Göttingen, Germany, includes a few pieces from America.[15] Although much of the collection is from Johann Reinhold Forster, natural historian on Cook's second voyage, a large part of the collection came from George Humphrey (1745–1816), a natural-history dealer in London, who specialized in shells but was also a major dealer in artificial curiosities. By 1782 Humphrey had amassed the large collection of ethnographic artifacts that was sold to Göttingen on behalf of King George III of Britain. Humphrey often collected directly from individuals on the ships, but unfortunately he did not usually record and pass on this information. Objects from the Nootka Sound area include a boat-model dish, halibut hooks (fig. 9.6), harpoon points, bows and arrows, an arrow case, and a bark beater (fig. 9.7). Objects from Alaska and the Aleut include a bow and arrows, spear throwers, and ivory ornaments.

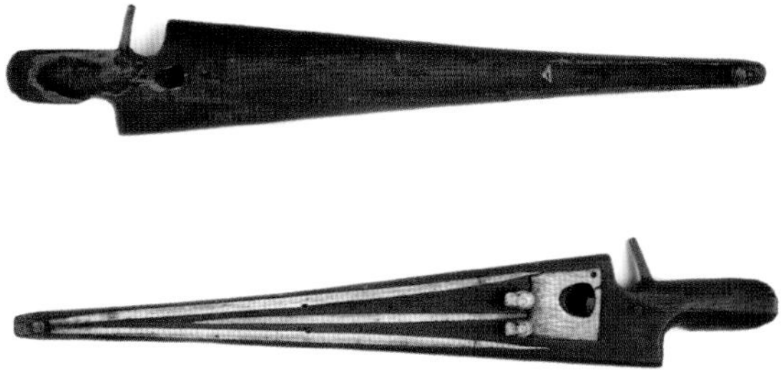

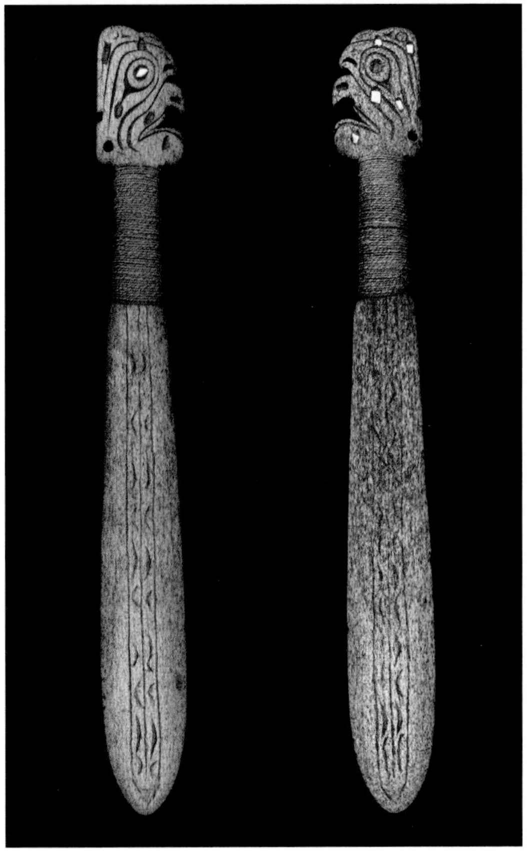

9.3 Bird-shaped rattle, Nootka Sound. Wood and stone. Typical rattles collected at Nootka used the form of a bird in two halves, enclosing a hollow body in which little stones were placed. This rattle has a distinctive motif on the bird's chest. Finely carved rattles such as this were probably used in ceremonies to accompany songs and dances. The exact route of objects from Cook's third voyage to the Hunterian Museum is not known. One possible source was David Samwell, surgeon's mate on the *Resolution,* who attended William Hunter's medical school in 1780–81 and sold the remainder of his collection in 1781. Hunter is noted as a purchaser. © The Hunterian, University of Glasgow 2013, E369.

9.4 Spear thrower, Prince William Sound. Wood and bone. Also called a throwing board, this implement allowed the hunter to extend his reach to throw bone-pointed darts "with great Force and Exactness," as David Samwell noted in his journal. Some were simple and undecorated, but others, such as this one, were decorated with ivory or bone. © The Hunterian, University of Glasgow 2013, E 92/2.

9.5 Sword club, Nootka Sound. Whalebone (dense lower jaw), shell, and fiber. These close-combat weapons, with round-pointed blades, were usually carved with a head in the shape of a bird—often representative of a thunderbird or an eagle. They were carried hidden beneath a cloak. The section tightly wrapped with fiber improved the grip of the bearer. © The Hunterian, University of Glasgow 2013, E97.

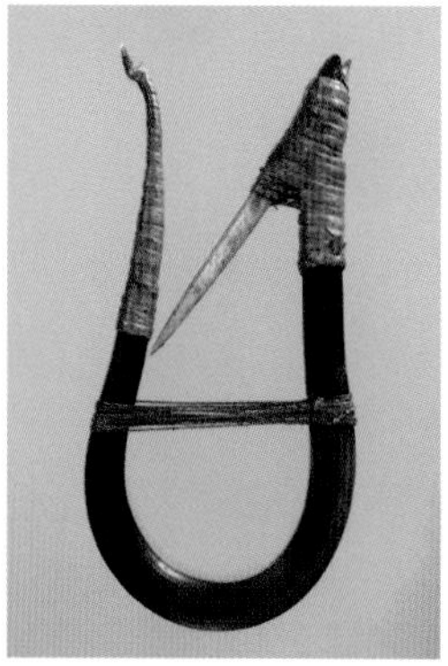

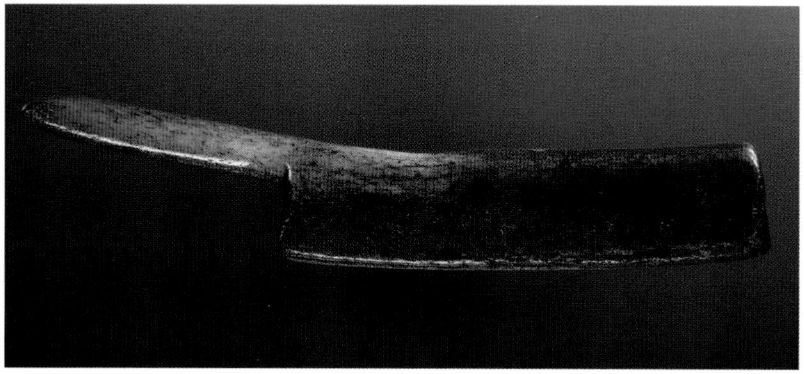

9.6 Halibut fishing hook, Nootka Sound. Wood, bone, and spruce-root splints. A number of these hooks were traded to the explorers by the Mowachaht, along with a variety of other hunting and domestic tools and equipment. Examples exist in most collections that hold a significant number of artifacts from Cook's third voyage. University of Göttingen, AM 618.

9.7 Bark beater, Nootka Sound. Whalebone. These beaters were used to beat the bast of yellow cedar bark into fibers from which a yarn was produced to weave capes and cloaks. Examples from Cook's visit to Nootka still survive in a number of museum collections; this one is noteworthy for its deep thumb groove, the result of sustained use over time. University of Göttingen, AM 620.

Captain Cook's own collection from the third voyage went into the museum of Sir Ashton Lever, known as the Holophusicon or Leverian Museum. Lever also had third-voyage objects from Lieutenant John Williamson, Lieutenant James King, and David Samwell. The latter gathered a large and important collection that was sold at auction in 1781 and from which Lever made purchases. He bought, for example, "an uncommon shaped bone-spoon with a border, and 4 birds carved on it, from the N.W. coast of America." This was depicted by the Leverian Museum artist Sarah Stone but has not been located. One object likely from Cook Inlet that probably came from Samwell's sale is "a singular quiver, curiously ornamented, and 3 arrows pointed with iron, from the N.W. coast of America," now in the Museum of Archaeology and Ethnology, Cambridge (fig. 9.8).[16]

James King, who became commander of the *Discovery* following the death of Clerke, gave objects to the British Museum and to Ashton Lever as well as to the museum of Trinity College Dublin. Items possibly from King's collection now in the National Museum in Dublin include a bird rattle, a chief's hat (fig. 9.9), a bracelet, and a whistle from Nootka Sound, as well as a hunter's visor from Norton Sound (fig. 9.10).[17]

When Clerke bequeathed his collection to Joseph Banks, it probably became part of the so-called Banks collection, along with the portion of Anderson's collection that did not go to Behm. These may be part of the gift that entered the British Museum in 1780 as "a collection of artificial curiosities from the South Sea Islands, the West coast of North America and Kamchatka; lately brought home in His Majesty's ships *Resolution* and *Discovery.*" As with other collections in the British Museum, it is not known how many objects were included, and it is not possible to identify which objects were collected by Clerke or Anderson and given by Banks.

PRIVATE COLLECTIONS AND MUSEUMS

Besides selling objects to dealers such as George Humphrey, individuals on the voyage would have kept some objects and given others away to friends. Documentation for such objects is difficult to find. A number of objects remained with Cook's wife and other members of her family, including the family of her cousin, Rear Admiral Isaac Smith, who sailed on the first and second voyages and resided with Mrs. Cook until she died in 1831. His descendants

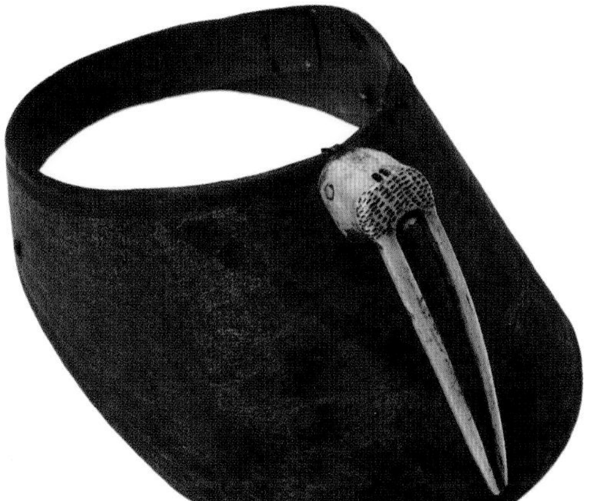

9.8 Skin quiver for arrows, probably Dena'ina from Cook Inlet. Leather, wood, porcupine quill, sinew, and paint. This quiver may be from Cook's own collection, which went to the Leverian Museum in London. It was purchased by "Rowe" at the Leverian sale in 1806 for Arthur Holdsworth, who lived at Widdecombe House, Knightsbridge, South Devon. There it remained until 1922, when it was acquired by curator Louis Clarke for the Cambridge collection. Reproduced by permission of University of Cambridge Museum of Archaeology and Anthropology (1922.981).

9.9 Nootka chief's hat with whaling motif. Twined from cedar bark. This distinctive hat, with its onion-bulb top and whaling-scene motif depicting a harpooner standing in his canoe, signifies chiefly status. Mowachaht chiefs were noted for their skill in the whale hunt, and hats such as this one are still made today and worn by chiefs on ceremonial occasions. A number of examples appear in John Webber's Nootka drawings, and this one was presented to Trinity College Dublin by James King. National Museum of Ireland, AE: 1882.3876.

9.10 Kayak hunter's visor, Norton Sound, Alaska. Wood, ivory, hide, glass, and bead. A distinctive bentwood, "hollow-head" visor, decorated on the front with a carved ivory walrus head, from which protrude two long tusks. It is very similar in general style to visors depicted by John Webber, and as this visor was among the items donated in 1782 to Trinity College Dublin by James King, and thought to contain Cook material, it may well have been collected on the voyage. National Museum of Ireland, AE: 1882.3897.

lent their pieces to the Colonial and Indian Exhibition in London in 1886.

After the exhibition was over, the Government of New South Wales purchased much of the collection, and the objects went to the Australian Museum and the Mitchell State Library in Sydney. The few American objects that were included are a horn scoop, an ivory bird, a comb, and a fishing implement, now in the Australian Museum.[18] Mrs. Cook also gave a small collection to Sir John Pringle, president of the Royal Society before 1781, which included a Northwest Coast whalebone bark beater (fig. 9.7 shows a similar example) now in the National Museum of Scotland in Edinburgh.[19]

A number of private collections that became museums had collections from Cook's voyages, and objects can often be followed through one or more auction catalogues. Five collections that included objects from Cook's third voyage include the Museum of the Duchess of Portland, Richard Greene's museum in Lichfield, Daniel Boulter's museum and sale room in Great Yarmouth, Ashton Lever's museum in London, and William Bullock's museum in Liverpool and London.[20] Margaret Cavendish Bentinck (1714–85), second Duchess of Portland, amassed a large collection at her home in Bulstrode House in Buckinghamshire. She was particularly interested in shells, but she also had a small collection of artificial curiosities, including several from Cook's voyages.[21] None, however, can be associated with the coasts of America or Asia. Richard Greene (1716–93) of Lichfield started collecting at age twenty-six. His collection, exhibited in his home, included geological and other natural-history specimens, arms and armor, and ethnographic objects. In his catalogue of the collection, published in 1786, we find "A Meat dish of Wood, rudely carved from *Otaheite* and A wooden Mask, representing the Head of a Wolf, worn by the natives of *Otaheite*." The latter piece would have been from the Northwest Coast of America (the term *Otaheite* was a catchall used to designate all of the islands and even the Northwest Coast) and thus must have been from Cook's third voyage. A "Quiver, from *Sandwich* Island," must also be from America, as quivers were not used in Hawai'i. After Greene's death, the museum went to his son, who sold some of the contents to W. H. Yate in 1800. Yate moved the museum to Bromesberrow Place near Gloucester, but the catalogue he published in 1801 does not list the American objects. In 1805, Greene's grandson, Richard Wright, purchased the museum and moved it back to Lichfield. Wright died in 1821, and the collection was said to have been sold at auction.[22] I have not been able to trace any objects to Greene's museum.

Daniel Boulter (1740–1802) operated a museum and sale room in the Market Place, Yarmouth (or Great Yarmouth). He is said to have spent a day on Cook's ship after its return and purchased many articles, some of which were from the Northwest Coast of America. Only one (Hawaiian) object has so far been found. Objects listed from the Americas and Asia are "Another [comb], in hard Wood, curiously carved, the Top representing the Head of an Eagle, North-west Coast of America"; a "Harpoon pointed with Shell, Kamschatka"; a "Curious Fish-Spear pointed *with* Bone and barbed, from Onalaska"; and a "Hemp-Beater . . . of Bone, curiously grooved."[23]

As noted above, Cook's own collection from the third voyage went into the museum of Sir Ashton Lever. The collection, dating from 1771, began in Manchester, England, and was the world's first popular museum of science, curiosity, and art. In 1775 the collection was moved to Leicester Square, London, and in 1785 to the Surrey side of Blackfriars Bridge, where it was displayed in the first museum rotunda. In Leicester Square the museum was known as the Holophusicon (from the Greek *holophusikon,* a name coined by Lever, meaning that it embraced all of nature). While in Leicester Square, Lever commissioned a young artist, Sarah Stone, to illustrate objects in his collection.[24] By the time the collection was disbursed in 1806, it contained the largest collection of specimens and artifacts from the voyages of Captain Cook that has ever been assembled in one place, including type specimens of Pacific birds, fishes, shells, and insects, Hawaiian feathered cloaks, Tahitian mourning dresses, and masks and rattles from the Northwest Coast of America. It also contained type specimens of primates from Africa, insects from Malaysia, and famous shells and geological specimens, as well as the Turkish clothing and guns of Edward Wortley Montague (son of Lady Mary Montague), sculptured heads from the Cave of Elephanta in India, Oliver Cromwell's armor, and countless other objects of curiosity, such as a series of monkeys "grotesquely set up."[25]

Unfortunately, after Lever lost the museum in a lottery, the new owner made the mistake of moving the collection to an unfashionable part of London, and in 1806 the contents were sold at auction in some seven thousand lots.[26] At the auction, there were about 140 purchasers, some of whom bought only one or two lots, while others bought several hundred specimens and objects. Some of the purchases at the sale became important parts of well-known British and foreign public and private collections. Leopold von Fichtel bought for the emperor of Austria; Dr. Creichton for the Empress of Russia; Dr. Clift for the Royal College of Surgeons, London; Dr. Laskey for the Hunterian Museum, Glasgow; William Bullock for his Liverpool Museum; and Edward Donovan for his London Museum. The Earl of Derby, Peter Dick, and Richard Cuming bought for their private collections, while the buyers George Humphrey, a Mr. Atkinson, and a Mr. Heslop were natural-history and artifact dealers. From these collections, and many others, specimens and objects have continued to surface in public and private collections. Their history had essentially been lost until I started my detective work in the 1970s, focusing on the drawings of Sarah Stone and other museum artists and the annotated auction catalogues. There were twelve auction catalogues, each annotated differently, with

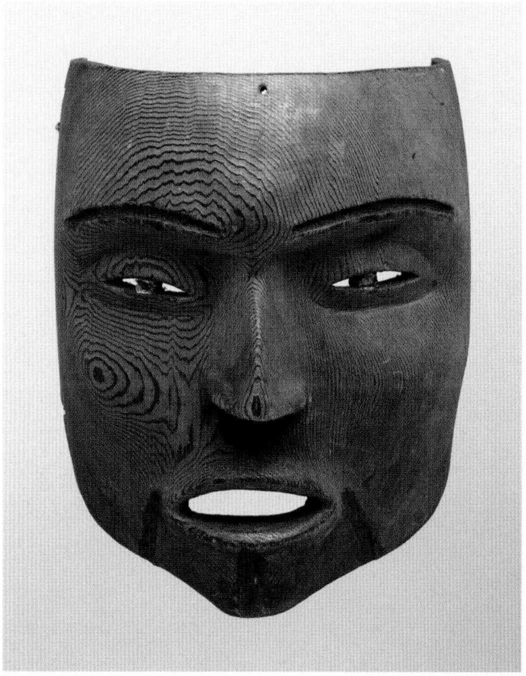

9.11 Cloak with Northwest Coast form-line design, Nootka Sound. Yellow cedar bark, nettle fibers, mountain-goat(?) wool, and fur. This cloak was probably part of Cook's own collection, which went to the Leverian Museum in London. Purchased by Leopold von Fichtel for the emperor of Austria at the Leverian sale in 1806, it is the only known example from Cook's voyage with a design that depicts the human face. Weltmuseum, Vienna, #218.

9.12 Anthropomorphic mask, Nootka Sound. Wood. The Leverian Museum label still attached to this mask notes that it was the "Mask of a dancer from Nootka Sound." The mask was purchased for Francis I, emperor of Austria, at the sale of the Leverian Museum's collections in 1806. Weltmuseum, Vienna, #223.

purchasers' last names. From these I made a master list arranged by purchaser. I tried to identify these purchasers and to associate the individual specimens and artifacts with the drawings by Sarah Stone and other artists as well as with descriptions in the auction catalogue. I then followed the paper trail and physical movements of the specimens and artifacts. All of the American and Asian objects once in the Holophusicon are detailed in the book *Holophusicon: The Leverian Museum; An Eighteenth-Century English Institution of Science, Curiosity, and Art.*[27]

A significant collection of more than two hundred ethnographic objects from Cook's voyages, held by the Leverian Museum, was purchased by Leopold von Fichtel for the emperor of Austria and is now in the Weltmuseum, Vienna. The Leverian auction was the origin of both the ethnographic collection and the natural-history collection from Cook's voyages. The latter is in the Natural History Museum across the street from the Ethnographic Museum. Thirty pieces of the ethnographic collection are from the Northwest Coast of America and Asia. They include the earliest datable Northwest Coast cloak, made of twined mountain goat wool and shredded cedar bark with human faces (fig. 9.11). It also includes two Nootka "masks," one of a human face (fig. 9.12) and the other with an eagle frontlet; a bird rattle; a tongue club (figure 9.18 shows a similar example); two stone daggers—one with a face on the handle end; two bone clubs; two hats twined of spruce root; the upper ring section of a Tlingit hat (described as a "Puff, resembling a powder puff but which is filled with delicate down. The natives of King George's Sound puff the down on their hair by way of an ornament"); two scoops or bowls made of horn; two wooden bowls; a bark beater made of bone (now missing); two carved arrow cases (fig. 9.13); a spear; a Pacific Eskimo basket (fig. 9.14); and seven pieces of fishing and hunting equipment, including a spear thrower of wood and walrus ivory, two model canoes, and a hafted beaver-tooth tool. It is remarkable that after more than two centuries, only one piece is missing.

Another large collection was purchased at the Leverian auction by a buyer named Rowe. After considerable searching, I identified him as John Rowe, a Baptist minister from Bristol, and a man of some means and taste. He bought at the Leverian sale on behalf of his brother-in-law, Richard Hall Clarke, who lived at Bridwell, Uffcumbe, near Exeter, Devonshire. Clarke was so interested in his collection that in 1809 he built a building, known as the chapel, just behind his house to contain it. The beautiful house has retained its original character and much of its exquisite internal decoration, but the chapel-museum is now in ruins.

I identified this collection by making associations between the Polynesian and American Indian materials that had been sold in an auction in Devonshire in the 1960s and the Sarah Stone drawings. After several generations, the materials had completely lost their history and association with

9.13 Arrow case and lid, Nootka Sound. Wood, sea-otter teeth, and pigment traces. These small, purpose-built boxes were used to store arrows. From the Leverian Museum sale of 1806 via Leopold von Fichtel. Weltmuseum, Vienna, #215 ab.

9.14 Basket, Prince William Sound. Spruce root. Probably collected in Prince William Sound, as the cultural origin is thought to be "Pacific Eskimo." It was purchased at the Leverian Museum sale of 1806 via Leopold von Fichtel. Weltmuseum, Vienna, #57.

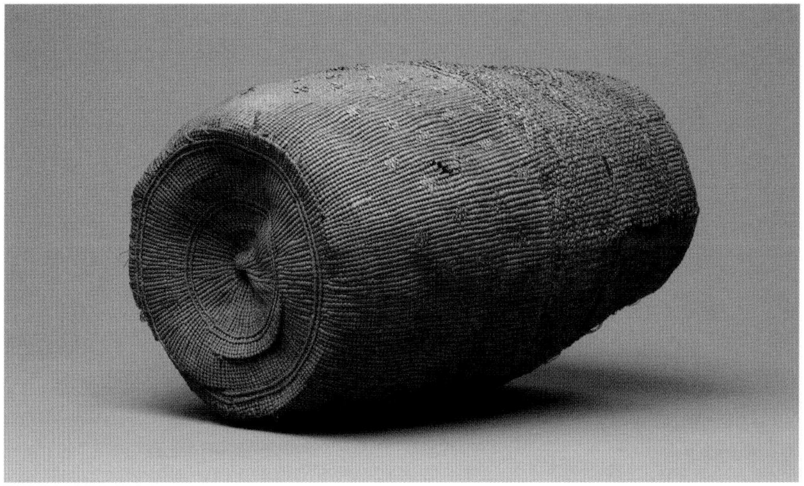

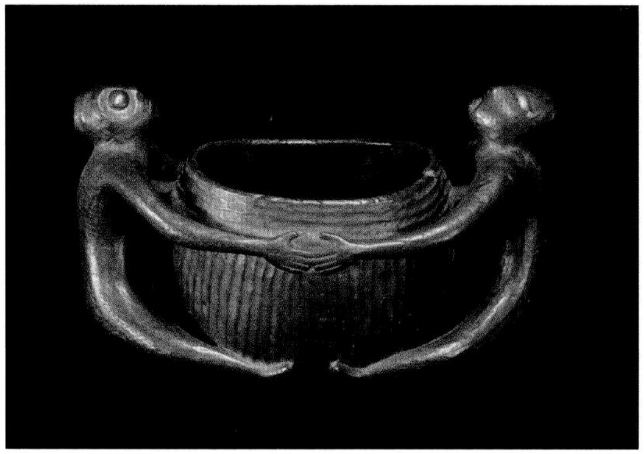

9.15 Bowl, Nootka Sound. Alder wood. This drinking bowl with human figures as handles was purchased at the Leverian Museum sale of 1806 by "Rowe" and became part of the collection of his brother-in-law, Richard Hall Clarke of Bridwell, Uffcumbe, near Exeter, Devonshire. It was handed down in the Clarke family and purchased by the British Museum at auction in Torquay in 1971. The decoration and the fluting design, which was reserved for people with high rank, suggest that it was used on ceremonial occasions. © The Trustees of the British Museum, AM 5.1.

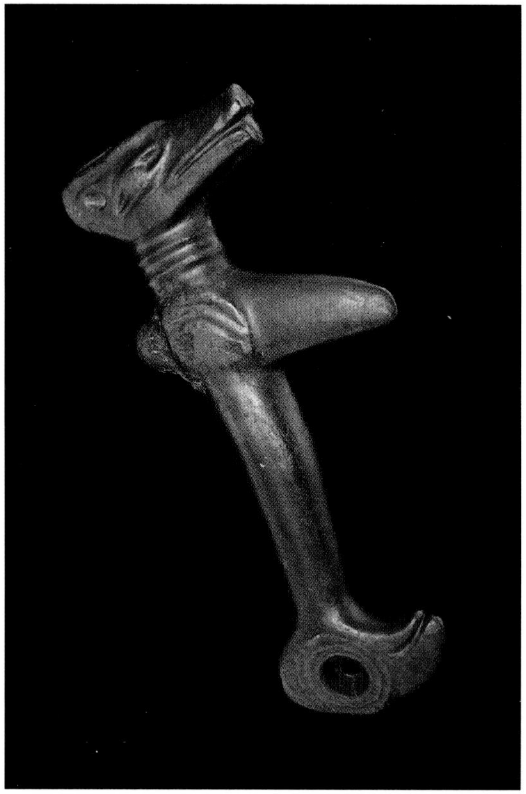

9.16 Ceremonial club, Nootka Sound. Stone. This club was purchased at the Leverian Museum sale of 1806 by "Rowe" and also became part of the collection of Richard Hall Clarke. Sold at auction in Torquay in 1967, it was purchased by the New York dealer John Klejman. He sold it to John H. Hauberg, who donated it to the Seattle Art Museum. According to an eighteenth-century illustration by Sarah Stone, it was at one time decorated with green feathers. Seattle Art Museum, Gift of John H. Hauberg, 91.1.21

the Leverian Museum and Cook's voyages. After I revealed the history to the Clarkes, a few remaining ethnographic specimens were sold at another auction in 1971. These mid-twentieth-century auctions include numerous pieces now in public and private collections, including the Northwest Coast bowl with sculptured human figures now in the British Museum (fig. 9.15); a stone club from the Northwest Coast of America, at one time in the Hauberg collection and now in the Seattle Art Museum (fig. 9.16); a Northwest Coast wolf mask, at one time in the Bennet collection in Chevy Chase, Maryland, and now with a New York dealer; a wooden club in the form of a hand holding a ball, also from the Bennet collection and now in the Museum of Anthropology at the University of British Columbia, Vancouver; and a Nootka mask and comb in the Menil collection in Houston, Texas.

Rowe also bought on behalf of another relative, Arthur Holdsworth of Widdicombe House, South Devon, who had a large museum room set up in his mansion. This collection also lost its association with the Holophusicon and Cook's voyages. Many objects that by then had acquired a spurious history were purchased from the mansion in the 1920s for the Museum of Archaeology and Anthropology in Cambridge, England. My detective work has now associated about sixty of these artifacts from the Leverian auction with Cook's voyages. This collection, along with objects from the first and second voyages, makes the Cambridge collection one of the most important Cook-voyage collections in

9.17 Rattle with double-bird shape, Nootka Sound. Wood and abalone shell, with the handle lashed with cherry bark. Finely made bird-shaped rattles such as this one were likely used to accompany songs and dances on ceremonial occasions. This one is particularly unusual in having two heads. It was purchased by "Rowe" at the Leverian sale in 1806; it then went to Widdecombe House, where it was acquired by curator Louis Clarke for the Cambridge collection in 1922. Reproduced by permission of University of Cambridge Museum of Archaeology and Anthropology (1922.948).

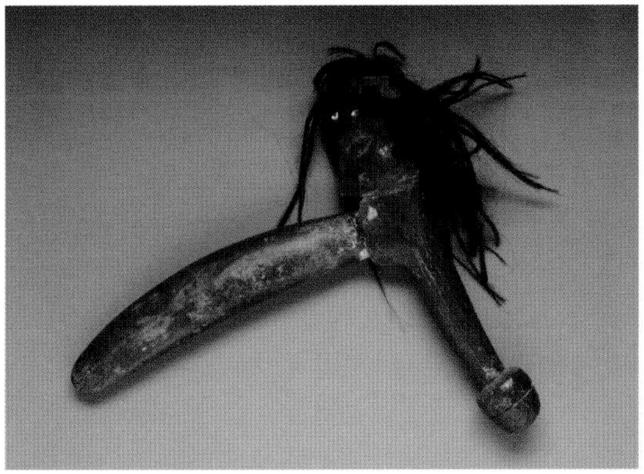

9.18 Tongue club with carved wooden handle in the shape of a human head, Nootka Sound. Wood, stone, human hair, teeth, and shell. Although these clubs are often described as "slave killers" in the early literature, no existing documentation supports their use for this purpose. Their iconic feature is a stone blade that protrudes like a tongue, and they were likely used in close combat as a war weapon. This example was purchased by "Rowe" at the Leverian sale in 1806; it then went to Widdecombe House, where it was acquired by curator Louis Clarke for the Cambridge collection in 1922. Reproduced by permission of University of Cambridge Museum of Archaeology and Anthropology (1925.371).

9.19 Scoop/spoon, Prince William Sound or Cook Inlet. Mountain-sheep horn. The finely incised decoration along the rim and base is rubbed with red ocher. It was purchased by "Rowe" at the Leverian sale in 1806; it then went to Widdecombe House, where it was acquired by curator Louis Clarke for the Cambridge collection in 1922. It retains its "4" label from the Leverian Museum. Reproduced by permission of University of Cambridge Museum of Archaeology and Anthropology (1922.951B).

9.20 Dressed figure, Prince William Sound. Bone, hide, black human hair, and white fur. Although this small figure is sometimes described as a shaman figure, it is not actually known how it was used. It was purchased by "Rowe" at the Leverian sale in 1806; it then went to Widdecombe House, where it was acquired by Baroness von Hügel and given to the Cambridge collection in 1921. Reproduced by permission of University of Cambridge Museum of Archaeology and Anthropology (1921.567.2).

9.21 Slat armor, Prince William Sound. Wood, leather, sinew cords, and pigment. The vertical wooden slats are tied together with cords and painted with formline designs that appear to be Tlingit in origin. Cook specifically mentions this style of armor, which Thomas Edgar noted in his journal "reatches from the shoulders to the lower par of the waist and fastens behind like a woman's stay's." It was purchased by "Rowe" at the Leverian sale in 1806; it then went to Widdecombe House, where it was acquired by curator Louis Clarke for the Cambridge collection in 1922. Reproduced by permission of University of Cambridge Museum of Archaeology and Anthropology (1922.950B).

Britain.[28] Objects from the Northwest Coast and Asia include a double bird rattle (fig. 9.17); a tongue club (fig. 9.18); an Athapaskan horn scoop, which still retains the "4" label (fig. 9.19) that ties it to its description in the Leverian *Companion* of 1790;[29] a skin-dressed bone doll (fig. 9.20); slat armor from Prince William Sound (fig. 9.21); and a Chukchi quiver depicted by Webber from the coast of Asia near St. Lawrence Bay (figs. 4.4 and 12.8).

Other objects from the Leverian collection have been connected through the Sarah Stone drawings to the British Museum, such as a sculpture of a mother and child purchased by a Mrs. Higgins, in the Christy collection by 1865, and a Nootka mallet now in the Museum of Anthropology at the University of Michigan. Its route from the auction to Michigan has not been traced. Other items have disappeared without trace, such as the sledge and dog harness used by members of Cook's third voyage in Kamchatka.

Another purchaser at the Leverian auction whose collections became a museum was Richard Cuming. His son, H. Syer Cuming, made special efforts to obtain objects from the Leverian Museum collection. Following his death, the Cuming Museum was set up in South London, near the area known as Elephant and Castle. This museum retains the only existing example of a "monkey grotesquely set up" that had been featured in the Holophusicon. It also has a beautiful horn bracelet inset with dentalia shells from Prince William Sound, which retains an original Leverian Museum label.

A similar collection was made by Peter Dick and exhibited at his home on Sloane Street, London. He published a catalogue of his collection in 1815, which notes objects that came from Cook's voyages.[30] From this we can trace some of the purchases he made at the Leverian auction. Through a rare auction catalogue of 1821 we can follow a few of the objects to their present homes. Although a number of objects from America were listed, none has so far been located.

A Reverend T. Vaughan purchased some eighty lots of natural-history specimens and ethnographic objects. The Sarah Stone drawings enabled me to trace the ethnographic objects to the Royal Albert Museum in Exeter, to which they were presented in 1868 by Henry Vaughan of Regents Park, London. Some thirty-five pieces have been identified, including an adze or plane with a metal blade, and a Nootka tongue club depicted by Stone, which was stolen from the museum in the 1950s.

Finally, William Bullock, the proprietor of a private museum that was in many ways the successor to the Leverian Museum, acquired objects from several of the purchasers at the Leverian auction.[31] Bullock began his collection in about 1789, and his museum was open to the public from about 1795 until 1819, when it, too, was dispersed by auction. American pieces from this auction include a bark beater made of whalebone, now in the Museum of New Zealand Te Papa Tongarewa, Wellington (purchased by "Winn" at the auction and given by his descendant Lord St. Oswald); and a bird rattle (purchased by H. K. Lichtenstein, director of the Zoological Museum of the University of Berlin), which eventually became part of the collection of the Königlich Preussische Kunstkammer, from which the present Ethnologisches Museum in Dahlem originated.

When the contents of the Leverian Museum were auctioned in 1806, the importance that the ethnographic works of art would hold some two centuries later could not have been imagined—most importantly to the descendants of their makers. Individual ethnographic artifacts that can be traced to the eighteenth century with certainty are relatively few. Those that can be associated with the voyages of Captain Cook have attained a kind of mystique not only because they have the stamp of authenticity but also because each object is acquiring its own biography—some making a full circle back to their homelands.

TWO COOK-VOYAGE OBJECTS AS NATIVE AMERICAN TREASURES

Objects become treasures because they have been designated as valuable by their custodians or the descendants of their custodians. Many objects collected on the voyages had little significance to their first European owners and became treasures only during their ownership by the descendants of the collectors or subsequent owners. Two objects from the South Pacific associated with Cook's voyages have become Native American treasures, but not

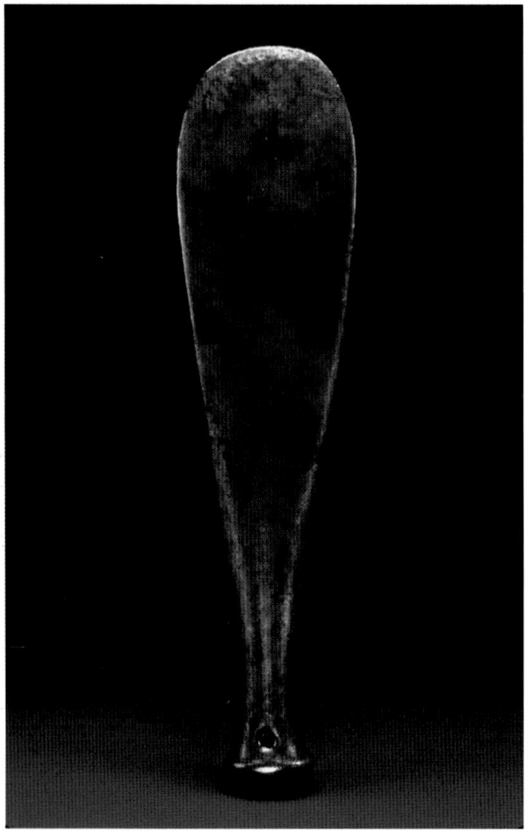

9.22 *Patu,* England. Brass. This British replica of a basalt *patu onewa* is one of six surviving examples of a collection cast for Joseph Banks as trade items for use on Cook's second voyage. Banks did not go on that expedition and gave at least some of them to Charles Clerke for the third voyage. This one was traded to a Native on the Northwest Coast, probably at Nootka, and was subsequently exchanged further, eventually traveling inland to the Columbia River region. In the 1890s it became part of the collection of Helen Kane Kunzie, who sold it to the Smithsonian Institution in 1897. Because it was said to have come from a grave, it was repatriated to the Confederated Tribes of Umatilla in Oregon in 2005. Smithsonian Institution Archives, 2004–16794.

necessarily because of an association with Captain Cook or his voyages. These are a brass *patu* and a Tahitian gorget.

During Cook's first voyage, Joseph Banks acquired from an important Maori individual a basalt hand weapon, called a *patu onewa,* which he took back to England. For Cook's next voyage to the Pacific, Banks had forty brass replicas of his *patu* made to give as gifts to other important Maori. They were made in the brass foundry of Eleanor Gyles in London in 1772 and were engraved by Thomas Orpin of London with his name ("Jos Banks"), the date (1772), and his family's coat of arms. After a disagreement concerning his accommodation on the *Resolution,* Banks did not travel on the second voyage. Before the third voyage, Banks apparently gave some of the brass *patu* to Charles Clerke to use as gifts or trade items.[32] At various stops along the Northwest Coast of America, a few of the brass *patu* were given to or exchanged with Native Americans. Through further exchanges between Native Americans, one of these eventually traveled inland to Umatilla, Oregon, and in the 1890s it became part of the collection of Helen Kane Kunzie, who sold it to the Smithsonian Institution in 1897 (fig. 9.22). In the list of objects that she wished to sell to the Smithsonian, Mrs. Kunzie attributed the majority of her collection, including the *patu,* to "Umatilla graves." Although there was no real evidence that the *patu* was ever in a grave, and it did not have a shared group identity, it was claimed by the Umatilla as an unassociated funerary object and was repatriated to them. Suddenly it became a treasure and is now in the Umatilla Community Center, Tamatslalik.

A treasure of a different sort is the so-called Raven Cape. This is a breast gorget or *taumi* worn in the Society Islands, usually by warriors or high-status men. Although it is not clear exactly how or by whom the *taumi* was transported to the Northwest Coast of America, it is most likely that it arrived on one of Cook's third-voyage ships. At least twenty examples were collected during Cook's visits to the Society Islands. Alternatively, it could have been collected on Vancouver's voyage: George Hewett gave two to the British Museum, and Archibald Menzies gave another.[33] The gorget was said by the Tlingit to have come from the first white man to visit their area, and it became a clan heirloom, passed from generation to generation, and from one clan house to another. It was used at the funerals of chiefs and ceremonial gatherings. In 1923 it was purchased from its owner by Louis Shotridge and is now in the University of Pennsylvania Museum, Philadelphia.[34]

THE IMPORTANCE OF COOK-VOYAGE ARTIFACTS

Objects collected during Cook's voyages have become more and more treasured over time. The descendants of those who made the objects seem to be more interested than ever to know about and see the treasures made by their ancestors. Although, for the most part, individual makers are not known, the objects collected on Cook's voyages were usually made with traditional tools and can be said to capture the style and aesthetics of the people before contact with outsiders. Comparisons of Cook-voyage objects with others from the same areas traceable to the nineteenth century and later reveal differences and continuities. Different carving tools, different paint in different colors, imported beads, and other decorations all influenced the ways objects were made and looked, but often the reasons for making them and how the objects were used remained the same. Little or no paint is found on Cook-voyage objects from the Northwest Coast, whereas objects collected in the nineteenth century often have colorful paint and more stylized, pointed eyes. Observing the wide range of objects from Cook's voyage, we are forced to question the validity of previously accepted notions about precontact cultures. Although only about two hundred objects from Cook's voyages can be traced to collection sites in America and Asia (including nearly one hundred pieces of fishing and hunting equipment), they have become one of the most valuable resources for the study of eighteenth-century material culture from these areas. The objects can be followed through gift and trade exchanges between individuals on Cook's ships and local people who made, used, and traded them from others. Back in Europe, the objects were bought and sold over and over, and these trajectories, too, can be followed. Today, the treasures move around the world and back to their homelands for exhibition in a transformed world.

NOTES

1 Adrienne L. Kaeppler, *"Artificial Curiosities," Being an Exposition of Native Manufactures Collected on the Three Pacific Voyages of Captain James Cook, R.N.* (Honolulu, HI: Bishop Museum Special Publication 65, 1978a).
2 Letter from John White to Mathew Gregson, October 18, 1780, in Liverpool Public Library.
3 Adrienne L. Kaeppler, ed., *Cook Voyage Artifacts in Leningrad, Berne, and Florence Museums* (Honolulu, HI: Bishop Museum Special Publication 66, 1978b), 1–2.
4 L. G. Rozina, "The James Cook Collection in the Museum of Anthropology and Ethnography" (title translated from Russian), *Sbornik Museii Antropologii i Ethnografii* 23 (1966): 234–25, translated in Kaeppler, *Cook Voyage Artifacts.*
5 Adrienne L. Kaeppler, "A Further Note on the Cook Voyage Collection in Leningrad," *Journal of the Polynesian Society* 92 , no. 1 (1983): 93–98.
6 *The Journals of Captain James Cook on His Voyages of Discovery,* vol. 3, *The Voyage of the* Resolution *and* Discovery, *1776–1780,* ed. J. C. Beaglehole (Cambridge: Cambridge University Press for the Hakluyt Society, 1967), 322 n.
7 J. C. H. King, *Artificial Curiosities from the Northwest Coast of America: Native American Artefacts in the British Museum Collected on the Third Voyage of Captain James Cook and Acquired through Sir Joseph Banks* (London: British Museum, Department of Ethnography, 1981).
8 See for example, Adrienne L. Kaeppler, "Tracing the History of Hawaiian Cook Voyage Artifacts in the Museum of Mankind," *British Museum Yearbook 3* (1979): 167–97.
9 Kaeppler, *Artificial Curiosities,* 45–48.
10 [John] O'Keeffe, *Omai, or a Trip round the World.* London: Cadell, 1785.
11 Stephan Augustin, *Kunstsachen von Cooks Reisen: Die Sammlung und ihre Geschichte im Völkerkundemuseum Herrnhut* (Dresden: Museum für Völkerkunde, 1993).
12 Hermione Waterfield and J. C. H. King, *Provenance: Twelve Collectors of Ethnographic Art in England, 1760–1990* (Geneva: Somogy Art Publishers and Barbier-Mueller Museum, 2006), 82.
13 Kaeppler, *Artificial Curiosities,* 156–77; Monica Zavattaro

and Antonio Ferretti, *Sognatori dell'alce: The Elk Dreamers* (Florence: Edifir–Edizioni Firenze, 2010).

14 Adrienne L. Kaeppler, "Ethnographic Treasures from Cook's Voyages in the Hunterian Museum," in *William Hunter's World: The Art and Science of Eighteenth-Century Collecting,* ed. Mungo Campbell, Geoff Hancock, and Nick Pearce (Farnham, UK: Ashgate, 2014).

15 Brigitta Hauser-Schaüblin and Gundolf Krüger, eds., *James Cook: Gifts and Treasures from the South Seas . . . The Cook/Forster Collection, Göttingen* (Munich: Prestel, 1998).

16 *A Catalogue of a Small but Choice Collection of rarities from the New-discovered Places in the South Seas, consisting of the Cloth, garments, Warlike Instruments and other singular Inventions of the Natives (particularly from Owhyjee, the Island where Captain Cook was killed) . . . The Property of an OFFICER belonging to His Majesty's Ship* The Discovery, *lately arrived: Which will be Sold by Auction, By Mr. Hutchins, At his ROOMS in King-Street and Hart-Street, Covent-Garden, On Thursday, June 14, 1781, and the following Day* (London, 1781).

17 J. D. Freeman, "The Polynesian Collection of Trinity College Dublin and the National Museum of Ireland," *Journal of the Polynesian Society* 58, no. 1 (1949): 1–18; Rachel Hand, "Eighteenth-Century Chukchi Quivers in Cambridge, Dublin, and Göttingen," *Journal of Museum Ethnography* 24 (2011): 178; Rachel Hand, "'A Number of Highly Interesting Objects Collected by the Late Captain Cook': The Cook-Voyage Collections of Trinity College Dublin (Now in the National Museum of Ireland) and Their Exhibition, 1777–2006," in *Old Collections, New Knowledge: Cook-Voyage Collections of "Artificial Curiosities" in Britain and Ireland, 1770–2010,* ed. Jeremy Coote (Oxford: Museum Ethnographers Group, Occasional Paper No. 5, 2013).

18 Kaeppler, *Artificial Curiosities,* 281–84.

19 Dale Idiens, "Cook-Voyage Collections in Edinburgh," in Coote, *Old Collections.*

20 See Adrienne L. Kaeppler, "From the South Seas to the World (via London)," in Coote, *Old Collections.* See also W. H. Mullins, "Some Museums of Old London, I: The Leverian Museum," *Museums Journal* 15, no. 4 (1915): 123–29, 162–72.

21 J. Lightfoot, *A Catalogue of the Portland Museum, lately the property of the Duchess Dowager of Portland, deceased: which will be sold by auction . . .* (London, 1786).

22 H. S. Torrens, "Dr. Greene's Museum Lichfield in 1788," *GCG Newsletter of the Geological Curators Group* (1974): 5–10; Richard Greene, *A . . . Catalogue of the Curiosities, Natural and Artificial, in the Lichfield Museum*, 3rd ed. (Lichfield: John Jackson, 1786). See also Richard Greene, *A Catalogue of Curiosities, &c.* (1773); and "A.H.W.", [article on Greene's Museum in Lichfield], *Gentlemen's Magazine* 58, no. 4 (October 1788): part 2; W. H. Yate, *A concise and descriptive Catalogue of all the natural and artificial Curiosities in the Museum of W. H. Yate, Esq, at Bromesberrow-Place near Glocester. Being the extensive and valuable collection of the Late Dr. Greene, of Lichfield, with many additions, collected by the present proprietor* (Gloucester: R. Raikes, 1801).

23 [Daniel Boulter], *Museum Boulterianum: A catalogue of the Curious and Valuable Collection of Natural and Artificial Curiosities in the Extensive Museum of Daniel Boulter, Yarmouth* (Norwich[?], London[?], 1793[?]). See also Thomas Southwell, "Notes on an Eighteenth Century Museum at Great Yarmouth . . . ," *Museums Journal* 8, no. 4 (1908): 110–23.

24 Roland W. Force and Maryanne Force, *Art and Artifacts of the Eighteenth Century: Objects in the Leverian Museum as Painted by Sarah Stone* (Honolulu, HI: Bishop Museum Press, 1968).

25 For a full account of the museum, see Adrienne L. Kaeppler, *Holophusicon: The Leverian Museum; An Eighteenth-Century English Institution of Science, Curiosity, and Art* (Vienna: Museum für Völkerkunde, 2011).

26 [Edward Donovan, George Humphrey, and John Parkinson], *Catalogue of the Leverian Museum . . . The sale of the entire collection (By Messrs. King and Lochee,) will commence on Monday the 5th of May, 1806* (London, 1806).

27 See Kaeppler, *Holophusicon.*

28 Julia Tanner, *From Pacific Shores: Eighteenth-Century Ethnographic Collections at Cambridge; The Voyages of Cook, Vancouver and the First Fleet* (Cambridge: University of Cambridge Museum of Archaeology and Anthropology, 1999).

29 [James Parkinson], *A Companion to the Museum (Late Sir Ashton Lever's)* (London, 1790).

30 [Peter Dick], *A Descriptive Catalogue of a Museum of Antiquities and Foreign Curiosities, Natural and Artificial; including Models illustrative of Military and Naval Affairs, Armour and Weapons, Instruments of Torture, Polytheism, Sepulchres, With the Manner of Depositing the Dead, The Costume of different Nations, Manuscripts, Natural History, Including Anatomy, &c. &c. &c.* (London, 1815?). See also *A Catalogue of the Entire and Valuable Museum of P. Dick Esq. Removed from Sloane Street . . . Which Will be Sold by Auction by Mr. Bullock at his Egyptian Hall, Piccadilly, on Tuesday, 27th of February, 1821* (London, 1821).

31 Adrienne L. Kaeppler, "Cook Voyage Provenance of the 'Artificial Curiosities' of Bullock's Museum," *Man* 9, no. 1 (1974): 68–92; William Bullock, *A Companion to the Liverpool Museum*, 5th ed. (Liverpool, 1819); *Catalogue of the Roman Gallery, of Antiquities and Works of Art, and the London Museum of Natural History . . . which will be sold by Auction . . . by Mr. Bullock . . . on Thursday, the 19th of April* (London, 1807).

32 Adrienne L. Kaeppler, "Two Polynesian Repatriation Enigmas at the Smithsonian Institution," *Journal of Museum Ethnography* 17 (2005): 152–62; Jeremy Coote, "Joseph Banks's Forty Brass Patus," *Journal of Museum Ethnography* 20 (2008): 49–68.

33 J. C. H. King, "Vancouver's Ethnography," *Journal of the History of Collections* 6, no. 1 (1994): 41–51.

34 Adria H. Katz, "The Raven Cape: A Tahitian Breastplate Collected by Louis Shotridge," in *Raven's Journey: The World of Alaska's Native People*, ed. Susan A. Kaplan and Kristin J. Barsness (Philadelphia: University Museum, University of Pennsylvania, 1986), 78–90.

10

The International Law of Discovery

Acts of Possession on the Northwest Coast of North America

ROBERT J. MILLER

> *You are also with the consent of the Natives to take possession, in the Name of the King of Great Britain, of convenient Situations in such Countries as you may discover, that have not already been discovered or visited by any other European Power, and to distribute among the Inhabitants such Things as will remain as Traces and Testimonies of your having been there; But if you find the Countries so discovered are uninhabited, you are to take possession of them for His Majesty by setting up proper Marks and Inscriptions as first Discoverers and Possessors.*
>
> —Admiralty Instructions to Captain James Cook regarding the Northwest Coast, 1776

EUROPEAN COUNTRIES AND THE UNITED STATES USED THE INTERnational law of exploration and colonization in establishing their claims to own the Northwest Coast of North America. Under this well-established international law, today called the doctrine of discovery, two of the most crucial requirements for establishing ownership, sovereignty, and jurisdiction over newly discovered territories were for a representative of the nation making the claim to be the first "discoverer" of the area and then for its representatives to physically settle and occupy the region. In attempting to prove they were the first discoverers, Europeans and Americans engaged in "acts of possession." In the vast majority of these situations, the discovering country was unable to actually occupy and settle the areas for years, decades, or even centuries after a first discovery, so they undertook acts of possession that were designed to establish their legal claims to own the territories under international law. These acts were intended to prove which country had found the area first and to symbolically establish occupation.

Claiming land by engaging in symbolic acts of possession sounds ludicrous today. However, this was deadly serious business in international law and international relations from the mid-1400s until the

John Webber, *Two Views of Kaye's [Kayak] Island*, 1778 (detail of fig. 10.4).

mid-1900s. Conflicts over the ownership of areas newly found by Europeans led to endless diplomatic maneuverings, international arbitrations, court cases, and even wars. Today, we cannot ignore the history, law, and practices of exploration and discovery because, according to another principle of international law called intertemporal law, modern-day territorial titles "are to be judged by the law in force at the time the title was first asserted and not by the law of today."[1] Thus, not only did acts of possession help determine European ownership of newly discovered areas centuries ago, but they continue to determine international boundaries today and have ongoing legal effects. Thus modern-day countries are considered to own various parts of the earth that were claimed centuries ago by first discoveries, acts of possession, actual occupancy, and the law of the doctrine of discovery. Furthermore, in 2007 Russia reminded the world of the doctrine of discovery by planting a flag on the bottom of the Arctic Sea, and China did the same in the South China Sea in 2010, to claim ownership and sovereignty in those areas.

In accordance with international law, the Admiralty's instructions to Captain James Cook, quoted in the epigraph, ordered him to explore the Northwest Coast, to engage in acts of possession, and to leave evidence that he had visited the area. These steps were not the arcane sideshow that they might appear today because Euro-American countries employed these and other facets of the international law of discovery to claim lands. Obviously, in doing so, Euro-Americans completely ignored the preexisting sovereign, property, commercial, and human rights of indigenous nations and peoples. Captain Cook seems to have been aware of the incongruity of Britain's claiming lands already occupied by indigenous peoples, but he nonetheless complied with his orders in modern-day Alaska.

THE DOCTRINE OF DISCOVERY

From the fifteenth to the twentieth century, European countries developed international law to authorize, regulate, and control the acquisition of colonial empires.[2] In the eighteenth and nineteenth centuries, Britain, Russia, Spain, and the United States used this international law to claim rights, assets, and lands along the Northwest Coast of North America.

The United States Supreme Court enshrined the international law of discovery into American law and crystallized the elements of the doctrine in 1823 in *Johnson v. M'Intosh*.[3] *Johnson* has been cited hundreds of times by American courts and dozens of times by courts in Australia, Canada, and New Zealand, as well as by the British Privy Council. The case sets out ten distinct elements or factors that constitute discovery.[4] I list them all here but fully explicate only the first two elements because they constitute the practical acts of possession.

1. *First discovery*. The first Euro-American country to discover land unknown to other Euro-Americans claimed property and sovereign rights over

the land and Native peoples. First discovery alone, however, without permanent physical possession, was considered to create only an incomplete and temporary title by the discovering country.

2. *Actual occupancy and possession.* To perfect a complete title to the land, a Euro-American country had to actually occupy and physically possess the newly found lands within a reasonable amount of time after first discovery. Occupation was usually established by building forts or settlements. But Europeans and the United States also tried to prove "actual occupancy" through symbolic acts of possession.
3. *European title.* Euro-American countries acquired a property right called preemption or European title, giving them the sole right to buy land from Native nations.
4. *Native title.* Indigenous nations were considered by Euro-Americans to have lost the full ownership of land. Indigenous peoples retained only the right to occupy and use land.
5. *Native limited sovereign and commercial rights.* Indigenous nations were considered to have lost aspects of their inherent sovereign powers.
6. *Contiguity.* Euro-Americans claimed a significant amount of land contiguous to and surrounding their actual discoveries.
7. *Terra nullius.* This phrase means "empty land." If lands were not occupied by anyone, then they were considered available for Euro-American claims.
8. *Christianity.* Religion was used as a significant justification for discovery.
9. *Civilization.* European ideals of "civilization" were used to justify colonization.
10. *Conquest.* Euro-Americans claimed title to indigenous lands through military victories. "Conquest" also described the rights Euro-Americans claimed automatically after first discoveries.

It is worthwhile to note that the Admiralty expressly ordered Captain Cook to use six of these elements: first discovery, acts of possession and actual occupation, European title, native title, native sovereignty, and *terra nullius.* It is also worthwhile to set out here how the doctrine developed to better understand its application in North America. In the early 1400s, Portugal, Spain, and the Catholic church began developing international law—the rules and principles countries follow in dealing with each other—to assert sovereignty over non-Europeans and claim their lands and assets. Britain and France helped develop this emerging law when they began claiming rights in the New World. Taking "possession" of land by symbolic acts of possession and by actually occupying newly found lands became key elements in establishing European legal claims over newly discovered lands and indigenous peoples.[5]

In 1436, Pope Eugenius IV issued a papal bull that authorized Portugal to convert the Canary Island Natives to the Christian faith and to con-

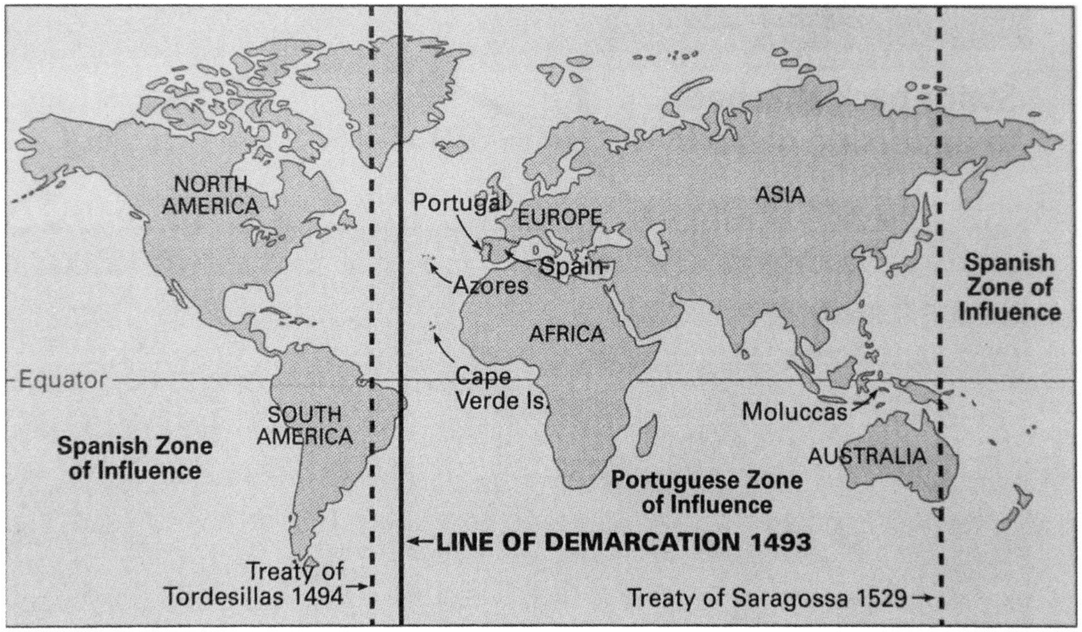

10.1 With the intention of preventing disputes over lands being discovered by explorers from Spain and Portugal at the end of the fifteenth century—disputes that he also believed might undermine the spread of Christianity—Pope Alexander VI divided the Atlantic world between the two nations with a "line of demarcation" in 1493. The Treaty of Tordesillas adjusted the line farther west, which resulted in Portugal's gaining Brazil, and the Treaty of Saragossa in 1529 extended the line around the world. Instituto de Historia del Pacífico Español, Vancouver.

trol the islands for the pope. This bull was reissued to extend Portugal's rights down the west coast of Africa.[6] For example, in regard to Africa, on January 8, 1455, Pope Nicholas V authorized Portugal "to invade, search out, capture, vanquish, and subdue all Saracens [Muslims] and pagans whatsoever, and other enemies of Christ wheresoever placed, and the kingdoms, dukedoms, principalities, dominions, possessions, and all movable and immovable goods whatsoever held and possessed by them and to reduce their persons to perpetual slavery, and to apply and appropriate to himself and his successors the kingdoms, dukedoms, counties, principalities, dominions, possessions, and goods, and to convert them to his . . . use and profit . . . [and to] possess, these islands, lands, harbors, and seas."[7] Pope Nicholas also granted Portugal title to the lands in Africa that Portugal had already "acquired and which shall be acquired in the future."[8]

In 1493, Spain also sought papal approval for its claim to Columbus's discoveries in the New World. Pope Alexander VI issued four bulls stipulating that the lands Columbus discovered, which were "not hitherto discovered by others," belonged to Spain.[9] The pope further granted Spain lands it might discover in the future if they were not "in the actual possession of any Christian king."[10] He also drew a line of demarcation from the North Pole to the South Pole, three hundred miles west of the Azores Islands, and granted Spain title to all the lands "discovered and to be discovered" west of that line and Portugal the same rights east of the line.[11] In 1494, Spain and Portugal signed a treaty moving the demarcation line farther west to give Portugal a claim to part of the New World. In 1529, they extended the line around the globe through the Pacific Ocean (fig. 10.1).

Consequently, under emerging international law, Spain and Portugal possessed the sole rights to colonize the world. They argued that their discovery of new lands and undertaking acts of possession established their ownership. The Portuguese, for example, erected stone and wooden crosses along the coasts of Africa and Brazil, and the Spaniards engaged in similar acts of possession elsewhere in the New World.

Although France and England engaged in acts of possession in claiming lands in North America, English and French legal scholars also developed new theories about the doctrine of discovery that allowed their countries to colonize and trade in the New World. England, for example, decided that it would not be in violation of the papal bulls if it claimed only lands not yet discovered by any other Christian monarch. Later, Queen Elizabeth I and her advisers developed another element of discovery and required any European country claiming land to be in actual occupancy and physical possession of the land. Thus English monarchs instructed their explorers to discover lands "unknown to all Christians" and "not actually possessed of any Christian prince."[12] France concurred. Hence, these countries created a requirement of occupancy for making legal claims to newly discovered lands. But even then, the first step in the process was for a country to make a first discovery and to engage in acts of possession. Consequently, when Europeans conducted symbolic acts of possession, they were engaging in recognized procedures and rituals required by international law in order to establish legal claims.

ACTS OF POSSESSION IN ALASKA AND THE NORTHWEST COAST

Russia, Britain, Spain, and the United States made doctrine of discovery claims to the Northwest Coast of North America and thereafter contested their conflicting rights to these lands. Spain possessed the oldest claim to the Pacific coasts of both Americas under international law and the papal bulls. But starting in 1741, Russia was the first European country to discover the islands and coastline of modern-day Alaska and to begin occupying them and exploiting the indigenous peoples and assets of the region. Captain James Cook commenced the British efforts to claim and exploit the lands and assets in 1778. Although Cook's official mission was to search for the Northwest Passage, the Admiralty also ordered him to engage in acts of possession along the way. He followed those instructions in Alaska and three times used acts of possession to claim the area for the British Crown.

Spanish Acts of Possession

Spain claimed the eastern Pacific Ocean under the line of demarcation drawn in 1493 by Pope Alexander VI and the Spanish-Portuguese treaties of 1494 and 1529. But it also claimed the region by means of numerous acts of possession over several centuries. In 1513, for example, Vasco Núñez de Balboa claimed the Pacific and all its adjoining lands for Spain (fig. 10.2). He engaged in the ceremonies of first discovery and acts of possession: a priest sang the Te Deum, and his men erected a stone monument, cut a tree into a cross, and marked other trees with crosses. In 1536, Hernán Cortés made Spain's first claim to North American Pacific waters, on the west coast of Mexico, and claimed the lands by acts of possession. Spain then occupied several

10.2 Woodcut from Antonio Herrera de Tordesillas, *Historia general de los hechos de los castellanos en las islas i tierra firme del mar oceano,* 1726. Vasco Núñez de Balboa, having crossed the Isthmus of Darien, strides into the Pacific Ocean on September 29, 1513, claiming the "South Sea" for Spain. Although the Netherlands, France, and Britain ignored the concept of the "Spanish Lake," sailed in it at will, and claimed territories for themselves, Spanish government policy—that interlopers were to be arrested—remained firmly in place in 1778, when the viceroy of New Spain was ordered to hamper Cook's voyage to North America by detaining him and withholding any kind of assistance. University of British Columbia, Rare Books and Special Collections, E141.H58.

locations on the west coast of Mexico and engaged in other acts of possession on the coast of Mexico, Baja California, and modern-day California from 1539 to 1602.[13]

Spain reinvigorated its colonization activities on the west coast in the late 1700s.[14] Starting in 1769, missions and forts were established in Monterey Bay, San Diego Bay, and San Francisco, all accompanied by acts of possession. In response to Russian activities in the far north and Cook's voyage in 1776–78, Spain also launched several expeditions to the north Pacific, undertook several acts of possession along the coast, and physically occupied modern-day Nootka Sound, British Columbia, and—briefly—Neah Bay, Washington.[15]

In 1774, Juan Pérez was ordered to 60° north latitude. According to his instructions, in "places adequate for settlement, he should take possession, using the standard form attached to his instructions, and erect a large wooden cross supported by a cairn of stones hiding a glass bottle . . . containing a copy of the act of possession."[16] If Pérez sighted a foreign settlement, he was ordered to go north of it and perform an act of possession.

In 1775, Bruno de Hezeta was instructed to sail to 65°N and on his southward return to search for foreign settlements and "take possession where able to go ashore safely." On the Northern California coast, Hezeta "as testimony of formal possession . . . erected a large cross bearing the inscription: Carlos III, King of Spain by the grace of God."[17] On July 13, 1775, at Point Grenville on the Washington coast, Spaniards performed two formal acts of possession in the presence of the chaplain, accompanied by the planting of a large cross.

The captain of the second ship in the Hezeta expedition named a port at 57°N and engaged in an act of possession by unfurling the flag, erecting a large cross, cutting cross designs on rocks, and taking "possession of these lands with all the required formalities."[18] On June 7, 1775, at Trinidad Bay, he engaged in another act of possession by planting a cross while priests chanted the Te Deum. On August 24, he sailed to Prince of Wales Island

and took possession "with the usual formalities."[19] Spanish officials were convinced that Spain's claims had been secured by these acts of possession.

In 1779, Ignacio de Arteaga was sent to Alaska in response to Captain Cook's voyage. Near Prince William Sound, at 61°N, Arteaga "performed a formal possession, and erected a cross."[20] This was the northernmost Spanish act of possession performed. Arteaga also took possession of a bay at the southern tip of the Kenai Peninsula. He was led to believe that the Russian fur-trading activities were confined to the Aleutian Islands, and this gave Spain a false sense of security that it retained dominion over the mainland.[21]

In 1788, Esteban José Martínez and Gonzalo López de Haro were ordered to sail to at least 61°N to search again for Russian settlements and "to take official possession for Carlos III wherever convenient."[22] In mid-May, they conducted an act of possession in Prince William Sound. López de Haro then sailed to Three Saints Bay on Kodiak Island and Dutch Harbor on Unalaska and encountered Russian outposts. Surprisingly, despite the presence of Russians, Martinez performed a brief ceremony of possession on Unalaska and buried a copy of the official document of possession.

The Spanish performed acts of possession at Nootka and on southern Vancouver Island, where in 1790 Manuel Quimper conducted an elaborate ceremony near modern-day Victoria. In 1791, Spain's heavily religious acts of possession were modified, seemingly to conform more to Captain Cook's secular method. The instructions given by Alejandro Malaspina to his officers Dionisio Alcalá Galiano and Cayetano Valdés in late 1791, as they prepared to embark on their 1792 exploration into the Strait of Juan de Fuca and circumnavigation of Vancouver Island, stated: "It would now be appropriate to substitute for the method thus far followed of taking possession . . . the . . . more universal method of an exact hydrographic determination, and of one coin or another buried in a bottle in which the day, month, and year of discovery is stated, and the vessels which have made it."[23] Malaspina himself performed this simpler and less religious ceremony at the head of Yakutat Bay in July 1791: "Before leaving this bay I buried a bottle containing a record of our survey, the date on which it was made, and the possession taken in the name of His Majesty, confirmed by a coin buried beside the bottle."[24]

Russian Acts of Possession

In 1741, Czar Peter the Great sent Vitus Bering to explore the strait between Russia and North America. This expedition landed in the Aleutian Islands, sighted the mainland of America around 55°N, and named several geographical features. But thereafter, the Russian government apparently arranged only two more official voyages of discovery to North America. In 1764, Catherine II ordered a secret expedition led by Petr Krenitsyn and Mikhail Levashov "to confirm the discoveries already made, to make further discoveries and explorations, to subjugate the inhabitants of newly discovered lands to Russia, and to collect iasak [tax]."[25] After Captain Cook's 1778 arrival in Alaskan waters, followed by other British and Spanish traders and explorers, Catherine II sent another voyage to Alaska in 1786 "formally to affirm the right of Russia to all lands discovered by Russian seafarers and promyshlenniks [private traders] in the Pacific Ocean . . . [and] to be included formally among the possessions of the Russian state."[26] She ordered this expedition to engage in acts of possession on the coast by "placing or fastening of crests and burying of metals inscribed in Russian and Latin in suitable places."[27] She also ordered that "crests and signs of other powers who can possess no right whatsoever to these lands" were to be destroyed, and if any foreign settlements were discovered, she instructed, "You may on the basis of prior discovery by Russia and the authority given you, order those foreigners . . . to leave at once the places belonging to the Russian state," and "you may destroy them and level and destroy the signs and crests." This expedition was also ordered to claim for Russia territory "not previously discovered by any European power."[28]

Although the government only financed a few expeditions, private Russian fur traders actively exploited the resources and indigenous peoples in North America. Between 1745 and 1798, there were no less than eighty private trading expeditions to the Aleutian Islands, and others traveled to the North American mainland.[29]

The traders Grigorii I. Shelikhov and Aleksandr Baranov were probably most responsible for establishing Russian fur activities and posts in the Aleutians and Alaska. By 1796, they had established settlements at Three Saints Bay on Kodiak Island, at Unalaska Bay, at Afognak, and at several locations on the American mainland.[30] Shelikhov claimed that he was working solely for the empress's benefit, to create a Russian empire in America and to bring religion to the indigenous peoples. The government did instruct Shelikhov in 1786 to "pacify the Americans and spread the glory of the Russian state into the unknown lands of America as far as the 40th parallel."[31]

Shelikhov and other merchants were apparently ordered to perform acts of possession. Private traders were given metal plaques and two-headed royal crests to mark the areas Russia claimed by discovery and possession. Ultimately, Russian traders buried as many as thirty numbered bronze possession plates from 1787 to 1811 to "establish discovery and possession."[32] A plate found in the mid-1930s at Sitka states: "Country and possession of Russia."[33]

In 1787, the governor general of Siberia at Irkutsk ordered private traders operating on the American mainland "to discover new islands and bring the Islanders under the power of the Russian Empire, and affirm the acquisition of all the newly acquired part of America, marking the land with signs appropriate and natural to the Might and Name of Russia."[34] In 1788, he ordered Gerasim Izmailov and Dmitrii Bocharov to explore the southern Alaskan coast and "to place copper crests and iron plaques with the inscription 'Russian territory' in the lands discovered by the company."[35] They buried "copper plates with a cross and an inscription reading 'Russian territory,'" numbered 7, 8, 9, and 19, in Constantine Harbor, Yakutat Bay, and Lituya Bay.[36]

As described by the historian Lydia Black, Russians also engaged in an act of possession on July 15, 1799, during the construction of Novo-Arkhangel'sk (Sitka), when they conducted a religious service and a military parade, and fired volleys "to mark the taking of possession and incorporation of the territory under the Russian scepter. A possession plate and crest were buried, together with various folk symbols, as tangible proof of Russian sovereignty."[37] This plate, number 12, was discovered in the 1930s and is on display in Sitka today (fig. 10.3).

Russians engaged in official acts of possession and actual occupancy to claim Alaska and the mainland as far south as San Francisco Bay. These claims under international law were recognized by other countries. Russia signed a treaty with the United States in 1824 that acknowledged Russia's territory as extending as far south as 54°N, Alaska's southern border today. Britain and Russia also signed a treaty in 1825 recognizing the same border and setting the border between Alaska and British Columbia.

British Acts of Possession

Britain engaged in numerous acts of possession on the Northwest Coast and claimed various rights based on international law. Acts were performed by Francis Drake in 1579 in California, three times by James Cook in 1778 in Alaska, twice by Captain George Vancouver in 1792 and 1794 in the Strait of Juan de Fuca and Alaska, once by Lieutenant William Broughton in 1792 on the Columbia River, and once by Alexander Mackenzie of the North-west Company in 1793 on the Dean Channel near present-day Bella Coola, British Columbia.

When Francis Drake sailed around the world in 1577–80, his main purpose was to attack the Spanish, but he was also ordered to explore the Pacific coast of America and to take possession of regions beyond the northern limits of Spanish occupation. He apparently sailed as far north as 44°N (modern-day Oregon) and then landed on the California coast, north of San Francisco Bay, in June 1579, at 38° or 39°N.[38] Drake "proclaimed the territory part of his Queen's realm, naming it Nova Albion . . . [and] accordingly lay claim to the territory on the basis of prior discovery." Drake also claimed possession by setting "on a large post his famous plates of brass," which some historians believe stated "In the name of her Majesty Queen Elizabeth of England and her successors for ever I take possession of this kingdom . . . to be known unto all men as Nova Albion."[39] This alleged first discovery and act of possession were the basis for centuries of British claims to ownership of the Northwest Coast of North America.[40]

In 1776, Britain ordered James Cook to explore the Northwest Coast (starting at 45°N, where Drake

10.3 Possession plaque, Russian Empire, late eighteenth century. Sheet copper. This plaque was found in 1936 on the site of Old Sitka, the original Russian fort in Norfolk Sound. In response to the arrival of British fur traders in the north Pacific in the 1780s, the government issued a number of plaques to be buried and crests to be displayed for placement in various locations down the coast south of Prince William Sound. One crest, identified by its number as having come from Yakutat Bay, entered the native trading system and was found in a grave site on the Columbia River in 1934. National Park Service, Sitka, Alaska, SITK-1650.

allegedly sailed in 1579), to seek the Northwest Passage, and also to engage in symbolic acts of possession. Cook was ordered by the Admiralty "to take possession of [lands] for His Majesty by setting up proper Marks and Inscriptions as first Discoverers and Possessors."[41] Cook ultimately performed three acts of possession in Alaska at Keyes (Kayak) Island, Cook's Inlet, and Cape Newenham.

On May 11, 1778, around 58°N, Cook landed on an island he named Keyes Island (Kayak Island) (fig. 10.4). Here he personally performed his first act of possession in Alaska: "I went in a boat and landed.... At the foot of a tree on a little eminency not far from the Shore, I left a bottle in which an Inscription seting forth the Ships Names, date &c and two Silver two penny pieces (date 1772)" (fig. 10.5).[42]

On June 1, 1778, Cook ordered Lieutenant James King to undertake an act of possession in modern-day Cook Inlet, at 61°N. Cook called the location Point Possession, which is still its name today (fig. 10.6). Cook wrote: "I sent Mr. King again with two armed boats, with orders to land on the northern point of the low land on the SE side of the River, there to desplay the flag, take possession of the Country and River in his Majestys name and to bury in the ground a bottle containing t[w]o pieces of English coin (date 1772) and a paper on which was in[s]cribed the Ships names date &c."[43] King recorded in his own journal: "The captain ... sent me ... to take Possesion of all the Country, in the Name & for the use of his Majesty.... [We] performed the Ceremony of taking Possession, by hoisting Colours &c; & drinking his Majestys health in good English Porter.... [W]e contriv'd to place a bottle that the Captain had given us (with a Parchment Scroll in it)."[44]

Finally, on July 16, 1778, at 58°N, Cook sent Lieutenant John Williamson to a promontory on Cape Newenham to conduct an act of possession. Williamson "climed the highest hill [and] took possession of the Country in His Majestys name, left on the hill a bottle in which was in[s]cribed on a piece of paper, the Ships names date &c and name[d] the Promontory *Cape Newenham.*"[45]

Britain continued performing acts of possession on the Northwest Coast during George Vancouver's expedition. Vancouver, who had served as a midshipman on Cook's second and third voyages, was ordered to survey the entire coast from San Diego to Cook Inlet looking for inlets that might provide communication into the depths of the continent.[46] In his act of possession on June 4, 1792, at 49°N, he applied the principle of contiguity when he claimed the territory as far south as 39°N, where Francis Drake had allegedly conducted his act of possession in 1579.[47]

On June 4, 1792, Vancouver recorded the act of possession he performed in Admiralty Inlet in Puget Sound, arguably his most important "discovery":

> I had long since designed to take formal possession of all the countries we had lately been employed in exploring, in the name of, and

10.4 John Webber, *Two Views of Kaye's [Kayak] Island*, 1778. Grey wash, and wash and watercolor. Webber sketched this island, northwest of Yakutat Bay, as part of his assignment to record coastal profiles for the benefit of future navigators. It was the scene of Cook's first act (of three) of possession in Alaska and noteworthy as the earlier landing place of Georg Wilhelm Stellar of Vitus Bering's expedition in July 1741. Given at least three different names by various explorers, Kayak received its current name from Gavriil Sarychev, a member of the Joseph Billings expedition, who was hydrographer to the Russian navy in the 1820s. © British Library Board, Ms. 15514, fol. 3ab.

10.5 Before he left Britain, Cook was given a quantity of Maundy money—so named from sets of four pennies traditionally given by the monarch to the poor on the Thursday before Easter—by Dr. Richard Kaye, chaplain to George III. Pennies like this, which bore the image of the king, were used in the act of possession on Kayak Island and presumably elsewhere. Cook named it "Keyes Island" (but later in his journal corrected his spelling error and referred to Kayes Island) to acknowledge the gift, but this name did not endure. Private collection, Vancouver, Canada.

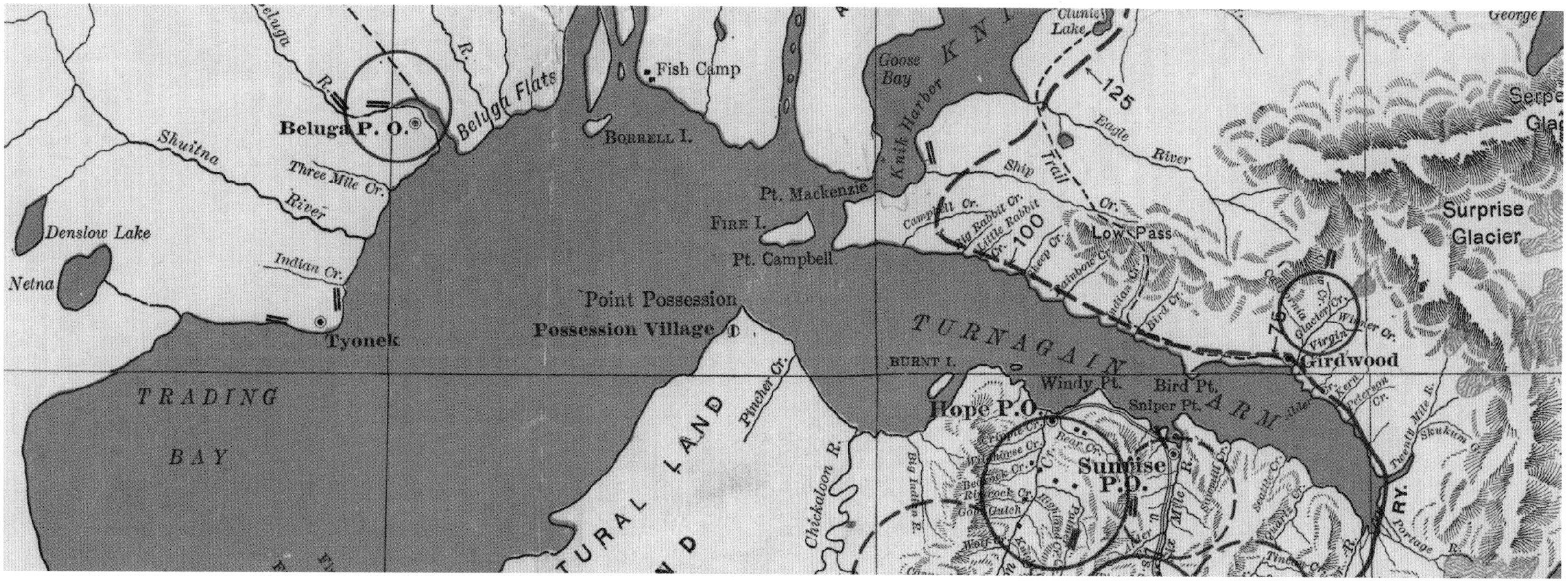

10.6 D. H. Sleem, *Map of Central Alaska* (detail), 1910. The map shows Point Possession in Cook Inlet, across the entrance to Turnagain Arm from Anchorage. Point Possession is clearly marked on the chart of Cook's River in Cook, *A Voyage to the Pacific Ocean* (1784), vol. 2, plate 44, in recognition of the ceremony conducted by King on direct orders from Cook. It is one of a number of names that have survived from Cook's explorations along the coast of Alaska. Anchorage Museum Collection, Map 6/4.

> for His Britannic Majesty. . . . I went onshore . . . pursuing the usual formalities which are generally observed on such occasions, and under the discharge of a Royal salute from the vessels, took possession accordingly of the coast, from that part of New Albion, in the latitude of 39°20' north, and longitude 236°26' east, to the entrance of this inlet of the sea, said to be the supposed straits of Juan de Fuca. . . . This branch of Admiralty Inlet obtained the name of Possession Sound.[48]

After learning from the American Robert Gray that Gray had discovered, sailed into, and named the Columbia River, Vancouver dispatched Lieutenant William Broughton to explore the river. Broughton traveled about 125 miles upriver and on October 30, 1792, at what he called Possession Point, "he formally took possession of the river, and of the country in its vicinity, in His Britannic Majesty's name, having every reason to believe, that the subjects of no other civilized nation or state had ever entered this river before."[49] On August 17, 1794, Vancouver performed another act of possession in Frederick Sound in Southeast Alaska.[50] His men claimed possession of a great extent of territory, raised the flag, fired three volleys, and drank to the king's health.

In 1793, Alexander Mackenzie of the Northwest Company became the first European to cross the continent north of Mexico when he arrived on the

Pacific coast in modern-day British Columbia. On July 22, he undertook an act of possession by painting on a rock: "Alex. Mackenzie from Canada by land 22d July 1793" (fig. 10.7).[51]

United States Acts of Possession

After gaining its independence from Britain, the United States quickly became interested in trade on the Northwest Coast, and American merchants became involved in the sea-otter trade that Cook's third voyage instigated. When Robert Gray discovered the Columbia River in May 1792, he was apparently the first Euro-American to sail into it, and he named the river after his ship, the *Columbia Rediviva* (fig. 14.4). The United States' international law claim to the entire Oregon country (which included modern-day Oregon, Washington, parts of Idaho, and British Columbia) originated from this "first discovery" and the discovery element of contiguity.

President Thomas Jefferson was anxious to strengthen the US claim to the Oregon country, and so he directed the Lewis and Clark expedition of 1803–6 to reach the mouth of the Columbia River.[52] On arriving there, Lewis and Clark built Fort Clatsop and occupied it from December 1805 to March 1806. They engaged in an act of possession when they left a document, called the Fort Clatsop memorial, in the fort and gave copies to Indian chiefs. The memorial was, in essence, a legal document that claimed the Oregon country for the United States. Lewis and Clark also carved and branded their names on trees in the Oregon country as further acts of possession.

In 1811, the American fur trader John Jacob Astor built a permanent trading post, Astoria, at the mouth of the Columbia (fig. 14.5). For more than forty years afterward, the United States claimed the Oregon country under international law in negotiations with Russia, Spain, and Britain. The United States used the elements of discovery to claim the entire watershed of the Columbia River because of its first discovery of the river by Robert Gray in 1792, the occupation of the mouth of the river by Lewis and Clark in 1805–6, and the permanent occupation of the region through the American settlement of Astoria in 1811.

Interestingly, in 1818, President James Monroe and Secretary of State John Quincy Adams ordered an American naval captain and a diplomat to engage in acts of possession on the Northwest Coast near Astoria. The post had been captured during the War of 1812 by Britain and renamed Fort George. When Britain delayed in returning the post to the United States, Monroe and Adams ordered Captain James Biddle and the diplomat John Prevost to travel to the Columbia and undertake symbolic acts of possession to protect America's claim.[53] Adams wrote that the mission was "to resume possession of that post [Astoria], and in some appropriate manner to reassert the title of the United States."[54] Monroe and Adams ordered Biddle and Prevost to "assert there the claim of sovereignty in the name of . . . the United States, by some symbolical or other

10.7 "From Canada by Land," fur trader Alexander Mackenzie's inscription in Dean Channel on the British Columbia coast, 1793, after the first crossing by a European of the North American continent north of Mexico. In 1789, Mackenzie had explored the river now bearing his name all the way to the Arctic Ocean. Four years later, he relied on Native guidance to portage between a number of rivers to cross the Rocky and Coastal Mountains, reaching tidewater by descending the Bella Coola River in a canoe acquired from a Nuxalk village he had visited. Photo courtesy of Derek Hayes.

appropriate mode of setting up a claim of national authority and dominion."[55]

On August 19, 1818, Biddle performed two acts of possession. On the north side of the mouth of the Columbia, he raised the US flag, turned some soil with a shovel, and nailed up a lead plate that read: "Taken possession of, in the name and on the behalf of the United States."[56] He then moved upriver and engaged in another act of possession on the south side and nailed up a wooden sign. Prevost arrived at Fort George/Astoria a month later, and the British cooperated in a ceremony allegedly restoring Astoria to the United States.[57]

The United States also relied on Spanish acts of possession and discovery rights as part of its claim to the Oregon country. In 1819, Adams negotiated a treaty with Spain in which Spain retained title to the lands in North America south of 42°N. Under article 3 of the treaty, Spain granted to the United States all its claims between 42° and 54°N.[58] Thereafter, the United States claimed for decades that it owned the Northwest Coast on the basis of Spain's discoveries, acts of possessions, and rights under international law.

In addition, the United States relied on Russia's discovery claims, acts of possession, and actual occupancy of lands south of Alaska on the Northwest Coast in order to counter British claims. In 1824, the United States signed a treaty with Russia in which Russia ceded all its claims to the west coast of North America south of 54°N (fig. 14.6b).

After these treaties, only the United States and Britain were still disputing who owned the part of the Northwest Coast that is today Oregon, Washington, and British Columbia (ignoring, of course, the indigenous peoples who had lived in these areas since time immemorial). The United States repeatedly argued that it owned the Oregon country.[59] Britain based its claim to the Oregon country on Francis Drake's first discovery of the region and his act of possession in 1579, the cession by Spain to England of trading and settlement rights in the Pacific Northwest in 1790 during the Nootka controversy, Broughton's voyage up the Columbia River to "Possession Point," and the activities of English fur-trading companies in western Canada and in the Columbia River basin.[60] They finally settled their disagreement in 1846 by signing a treaty and drawing the borderline at 49°N (fig. 14.11).

French Acts of Possession

France, as Britain's main imperial rival, was also interested in the Northwest Coast of North America.[61] Seeking to emulate Cook's success, Jean-François Galaup, comte de La Pérouse, was instructed to explore the Pacific and was specifically ordered, in regard to the Northwest Coast, "to take possession at some spot north of Bucareli Sound [in Southeast Alaska], which Paris considered the northernmost point of Spanish territory."[62] On July 1, 1786, he entered Lituya Bay and, in the name of Louis XVI, "set about taking possession of the land with the usual formalities—I buried a bottle that contained an inscription relative to this act of possession at the base of the rock, putting in with it one of the bronze medallions."[63]

SIGNIFICANCE OF ACTS OF POSSESSION

Over many centuries, international law deemed first discovery and acts of possession to be part of the process of acquiring the ownership of newly discovered lands. Europeans operated under this regime from the fifteenth century onward, and these procedures had serious legal consequences. It is a totally different question, however, whether countries could back up their claims with the military, economic, and diplomatic might needed to effect international recognition of their ownership of the lands. But, as the historian Manuel Servin noted, we should not "overlook or ignore the historical importance and significance of the ceremony by which explorers and colonizers lay claim to territory in the New World."[64]

First discoveries and acts of possession had real consequences.[65] Most colonial territories around the world were claimed and acquired by the rituals of taking possession and actual occupancy. Consequently, these rituals helped determine modern-day international borders and thus continue to be important components of international law, international relations, and international affairs.

European countries vigorously pressed their claims to lands based on the elements of the doctrine of discovery and acts of possession in diplomatic affairs, international arbitrations, court cases, and even warfare.[66] They engaged in hundreds of acts of possession from the fifteenth to the twentieth century. Germany, Britain, and the United States claimed and came to own islands in the Pacific even into the 1930s simply by raising flags or posting signs.[67] In parts of Africa, from 1870 to 1914, European countries acquired internationally recognized political and economic rights simply by declaring protectorates over regions they never occupied. In the 1920s, a few British and American explorers flew over islands and dropped flags to establish discovery claims.[68] And in 1955, Britain landed three men on Rockall Island, a speck of rock off the coast of Scotland, to attach a plate claiming to take possession of the island. In 1972, the British Parliament enacted a law certifying that 1955 act of possession.[69] Clearly, Euro-American countries continued to regard acts of possession as legally and diplomatically significant in the twentieth century.

TWENTY-FIRST-CENTURY ACTS OF POSSESSION

Even in the twenty-first century, many countries are still arguing about prior first discoveries, acts of possession, and occupancy in the Antarctic, the Falkland Islands, and other regions around the world.[70] When Russia and China planted their flags under the sea, both countries were claiming the oil and gas resources located under the seabed and dominion over those parts of the ocean.[71] In recent decades,

Canada and Denmark have staked claims to Han Island, off Greenland, by planting flags and engaging in discovery rituals.[72] In 2012, China stepped up its effort to control most of the South China Sea by occupying Yongxing Island.[73] Also in 2012, Japan and China raised international tensions by pushing their competing claims to a group of islands in the South China Sea.[74]

Similar claims are sure to arise in the Arctic with the retreat of the ice pack. In fact, there is now a viable Northwest Passage: since 2009, ships have been able to sail from the Atlantic to the Pacific north of Canada. The United States and Canada have disagreed whether this route is in international waters or, as Canada claims, Canadian internal waters. And the Russian claim to the oil and gas under the Arctic Ocean has also produced a sharp response from other countries that border the Arctic Ocean: the United States, Canada, Denmark, and Norway. NATO declared it would protect its interests in the assets in this region. In 2011, Russia stated it would deploy troops to defend its interests there.[75]

CONCLUSION

The doctrine of discovery and acts of possession were used by Spain, Russia, Britain, and the United States to claim the Northwest Coast of North America from the mid-1700s until at least 1846. These measures were significant both legally and diplomatically in determining the modern-day international boundaries in this region. James Cook engaged in acts of possession here at the express order of the Admiralty.

The nations involved disagreed on exactly what rights each acquired by their acts of possession, but they were unanimous in the view that indigenous nations and peoples would lose the ownership of their lands and assets. While the international borders of the Northwest Coast are well established today, indigenous nations are struggling to preserve their traditional homelands. In the 1867 treaty in which the United States bought Alaska from Russia, Native Alaskans were left to the mercies of the United States, but Russian citizens were protected in their property and religious rights. The indigenous owners of the land, the "uncivilized native tribes," were "subject to such laws and regulations as the United States may from time to time adopt in regard to aboriginal tribes of that country."[76]

The doctrine of discovery and *Johnson v. M'Intosh* remain the law in the United States and in almost all settler societies. As long as that is the case, the doctrine of discovery and its symbolic acts of possession will continue to adversely affect indigenous nations and peoples.

NOTES

Epigraph: *The Journals of Captain James Cook on His Voyages of Discovery,* vol. 3, *The Voyage of the* Resolution *and* Discovery, *1776–1780,* ed. J. C. Beaglehole (Cambridge: Cambridge University Press for the Hakluyt Society, 1967), ccxxiii.

1 John Dugard, *International Law: A South African Perspective* (Cape Town: Juta, 2000), 113–14.

2 Robert J. Miller, *Native America, Discovered and Conquered: Thomas Jefferson, Lewis and Clark, and Manifest Destiny* (Westport, CT: Praeger, 2006); Robert A. Williams Jr., *The American Indian in Western Legal Thought: The Discourses of Conquest* (New York: Oxford University Press, 1990).

3 21 U.S. (8 Wheat.) 543 (1823).

4 Miller, *Native America,* 3–5.

5 Miller, *Native America,* 3; James Muldoon, ed., *The Expansion of Europe: The First Phase* (Philadelphia: University of Pennsylvania Press, 1977), 3–4, 155–56, 186, 191–92.

6 Sidney Z. Ehler and John B. Morrall, trans. and ed., *Church and State through the Centuries* (New York: Biblo and Tannen, 1967), 146–53; Frances G. Davenport, ed., *European Treaties Bearing on the History of the United States and Its Dependencies to 1648* (Gloucester, MA: P. Smith, 1917), 23.

7 Davenport, *European Treaties,* 23.

8 Ibid.

9 Ibid., 9–13, 23, 53–56.

10 Ibid.

11 Charles Gibson, trans. and ed., *The Spanish Tradition in America* (New York: Harper & Row, 1968), 38; Ehler and Morrall, *Church and State,* 156.

12 W. Keith Kavenagh, ed., *Foundations of Colonial America: A Documentary History* (New York: Chelsea House, 1973), 1:18, 1:22–29, 3:1690–98.

13 Warren L. Cook, *Flood Tide of Empire: Spain and the Pacific Northwest, 1543–1819* (New Haven, CT: Yale University Press, 1973), 58; Barry M. Gough, *The Northwest Coast: British Navigation, Trade, and Discoveries to 1812* (Vancouver: UBC Press, 1992), 16, 18.

14 Freeman M. Tovell, *At the Far Reaches of Empire: The Life of Juan Francisco de la Bodega y Quadra* (Vancouver: UBC Press, 2008), 13; Raisa V. Makarova, *Russians on the Pacific, 1743–1799,* trans. and ed. Richard A. Pierce and Alton S. Donnelly (Kingston, ON: Limestone, 1975), 147–51.

15 Thomas Vaughan, E. A. P. Crownhart-Vaughan, and Mercedes Palau de Iglesias, eds. and trans., *Voyages of Enlightenment: Malaspina on the Northwest Coast, 1791–1792* (Portland: Oregon Historical Society, 1977), 4; Tovell, *At the Far Reaches,* 203, 213; Gough, *Northwest Coast,* 126, 138; James R. Gibson, *Otter Skins, Boston Ships, and China Goods: The Maritime Fur Trade of the Northwest Coast, 1785–1841* (Seattle: University of Washington Press, 1992), 14, 18.

16 Cook, *Flood Tide,* 56, 58.

17 Ibid., 56, 58, 72.

18 Ibid., 80; Tovell, *At the Far Reaches,* 33.

19 Ibid., 36.

20 Cook, *Flood Tide,* 97; see also Tovell, *At the Far Reaches,* 71–72, 94–95.

21 Cook, *Flood Tide,* 97–98.

22 Ibid., 120, 122.

23 John Kendrick, trans., *The Voyage of* Sutil *and* Mexicana, *1792: The Last Spanish Exploration of the Northwest Coast of America* (Spokane, WA: Arthur H. Clark, 1991), 42–43.

24 Andrew David, Felipe Fernández-Armesto, Carlos Novi, and Glyndwr Williams, eds., *The Malaspina Expedition,* vol. 2, *Panama to the Philippines* (Cambridge: Hakluyt Society/Museo Naval, 2003), 125–26.

25 Makarova, *Russians on the Pacific,* 3, 166.

26 Ibid., 155–56.

27 Ibid.

28 Gough, *Northwest Coast,* 125; Makarova, *Russians on the Pacific,* 3.

29 Nikolai N. Lolkhovitinov, *The Beginnings of Russian-American Relations, 1775–1815,* trans. Elena Levin (Cambridge, MA: Harvard University Press, 1975), 148.

30 Lydia T. Black, *Russians in Alaska, 1732–1867* (Fairbanks: University of Alaska Press, 2004), 107; Grigorii I. Shelikhov, *A Voyage to America, 1783–1786,* trans. Marina Ramsey, ed. Richard A. Pierce (Kingston, ON: Limestone, 1981), 47; Gibson, *Otter Skins,* 13–14, 18.

31 Makarova, *Russians on the Pacific,* 123.

32 Mary Foster and Steve Henrikson, "Symbols of Russian America: Imperial Crests and Possession Plates in North America," *Concepts* (Spring 2009): 1–2; Basil Dmytryshyn, E. A. P. Crownhart-Vaughan, and Thomas Vaughan, eds. and trans., *Three Centuries of Russian Eastward Expansion,* vol. 2, *Russian Penetration of the North Pacific Ocean, 1700–1797: To Siberia and Russian America* (Portland: Ore-

gon Historical Society, 1988), 349; Eric A. Powell, "Letter from Russian America: Unearthing America's Czarist Heritage," *Archaeology* (September–October 2006): 59, www.archaeology.org/0609/abstracts/letter.html.

33 Foster and Henrikson, "Symbols of Russian America," 6. See also Dmytryshyn, Crownhart-Vaughan, and Vaughan, *Russian Penetration,* 334, 350.

34 Dmytryshyn, Crownhart-Vaughn, and Vaughn, *Russian Penetration,* 334.

35 Makarova, *Russians in the Pacific,* 129.

36 Shelikhov, *Voyage to America,* 84, 86, 98, 102.

37 Black, *Russians in Alaska,* 155–56.

38 Gough, 20–21; Robin Inglis, ed., *Historical Dictionary of the Discovery and Exploration of the Northwest Coast of America* (Lanham, MD: Scarecrow, 2008), xxx.

39 Gough, *Northwest Coast,* 21, 22; Inglis, *Historical Dictionary,* 109.

40 John Logan Allen, ed., *North American Exploration,* vol. 1, *A New World Disclosed* (Lincoln: University of Nebraska Press, 1997), 400; Manuel Servin, "The Act of Sovereignty in the Age of Discovery" (PhD diss., University of Southern California, 1959), 237–38; Gough, *Northwest Coast,* 23, 27, 156.

41 Cook, *Voyage of the* Resolution *and* Discovery, ccxxiii.

42 Ibid., 341–42; see also ibid., part 2 (David Samwell's journal), 1105–6.

43 Ibid., 368.

44 Ibid., 1421.

45 Ibid., 399–400.

46 Gough, *Northwest Coast,* 148. See also George Vancouver, *A Voyage of Discovery to the North Pacific Ocean and around the World, 1791–1795,* ed. W. Kaye Lamb (London: Hakluyt Society, 1984), 1:335–37.

47 W. Kaye Lamb, "Introduction," in Vancouver, *Voyage,* 1:105; Cook, *Flood Tide,* 334–35.

48 Vancouver, *Voyage,* 2:569.

49 Ibid., 2:760–61 n. 1.

50 Vancouver, *Voyage,* 4:1382. See also Inglis, *Historical Dictionary,* 331.

51 Inglis, *Historical Dictionary,* 200.

52 Miller, *Native America,* 99; David L. Nicandri, *River of Promise: Lewis and Clark on the Columbia* (Bismarck, ND: Dakota Institute Press, 2010), 203–17, 239–44.

53 *The Writings of John Quincy Adams, 1816–1819,* ed. Worthington Chauncey Ford (rept., Westport, CT: Greenwood Press, 1968), 4:204–5.

54 *Writings of John Quincy Adams,* 6:366, 6:372–73. See also Frederick Merk, *The Oregon Question: Essays in Anglo-American Diplomacy and Politics* (Cambridge, MA: Belknap Press of Harvard University, 1967), 15–24.

55 Merk, *Oregon Question,* 17–18, 22–23. See also William Earl Weeks, *Building the Continental Empire: American Expansion from the Revolution to the Civil War* (Chicago: Ivan R. Dee, 1996), 50; James P. Ronda, *Astoria and Empire* (Lincoln, NE: University of Nebraska Press, 1990), 310–15, 308–10.

56 Merk, *Oregon Question,* 22–23.

57 Ibid., 23–24.

58 *American State Papers: Documents, Legislative and Executive, of the Congress of the United States* (Washington, DC: U.S. Government Printing Office, 1819), 5:446–47, 5:455, 5:470; Treaty of Amity, Settlement, and Limits, February 22, 1821, article 3, Treaties and conventions concluded between the United States of America and other powers since July 4, 1776 (Washington, DC: Government Printing Office, 1889).

59 *American State Papers,* 3:185, 3:731, 4:377, 4:381, 4:452–57, 4:468–72; Merk, *Oregon Question,* 4, 14–23, 42, 47, 51, 110, 156, 165–66, 399, 403; *American State Papers,* 6:663–66.

60 *American State Papers,* 5:436–37, 5:446–47, 5:449, 5:554–58, 5:791, 6:644, 6:652–53, 6:657, 6:661–70; Merk, *Oregon Question,* 4, 14–35, 42, 47, 51, 68–69, 110, 156, 164–66, 185–88, 395–412.

61 Robin Inglis, "Lapérouse 1786: A French Naval Visit to Alaska," in *Enlightenment and Exploration in the North Pacific, 1741–1805,* ed. Stephen Haycox, James Barnett, and Caedmon Liburd (Seattle: University of Washington Press, 1997), 51–52, 55; John Dunmore, *Where Fate Beckons: The Life of Jean-François de La Pérouse* (Fairbanks: University of Alaska Press, 2007), 205.

62 Cook, *Flood Tide,* 112.

63 Inglis, "Lapérouse," 53–55.

64 Manuel Servin, "Religious Aspects of Symbolic Acts of Sovereignty," *The Americas* 13, no. 3 (January 1957): 255–67.

65 See generally Patricia Seed, *Ceremonies of Possession in Europe's Conquest of the New World, 1492–1640* (New York: Cambridge University Press, 1995), 9 n. 19, 69–73, 101–2; A. S. Keller, O. J. Lissitzyn, and J. E. Mann, *Creation of Rights of Sovereignty through Symbolic Acts, 1400–1800* (New York: Columbia University Press, 1938).

66 See, for example, Lynn Berat, *Walvis Bay: Decolonization and International Law* (New Haven, CT: Yale University Press, 1990), 8–9; E. Hertslet, *The Map of Africa by Treaty,* ed. R. W. Bryant and H. L. Sherwood (1909; rept., London: Frank Cass, 1967), 3:988–89, 3:991–93; Servin, "Act of Sovereignty," 280–81, 305; The Island of Las Palmas, 2 R. I. A.A. 829, Hague Court Reports 83 (1928); M. F. Lindley, *The Acquisition and Government of Backward Territory in International Law: Being a Treatise on the Law and Practice Relating to Colonial Expansion* (London: Longmans, Green, 1926), 66, 149, 157, 301–2; Western Sahara Advisory Opinion Int'l Court Justice Rep. 12 (1975); Berat, *Walvis Bay,* 8.

67 Servin, "Act of Sovereignty," 270, 274, 275, 280.

68 Ibid., 296–97.

69 Island of Rockall Act 1972.

70 Servin, "Act of Sovereignty," 283, 290, 291–93; Lindley, *Acquisition and Government,* 50.

71 William J. Broad, "China Explores a Rich Frontier, Two Miles Deep," *New York Times,* September 12, 2010; Robert J. Miller, "Finders Keepers in the Arctic?" *Los Angeles Times,* August 6, 2007, http://articles.latimes.com/2007/aug/06/news/OE-MILLER6.

72 "Canada Island Visit Angers Danes," *BBC News,* July 25, 2005, http://news.bbc.co.uk/2/hi/europe/4715245.stm.

73 Jane Perlez, "China Asserts Sea Claim with Politics and Ships," *New York Times,* August 12, 2012.

74 Martin Fackler, "Dispute over Islands Reflects Japanese Fears of China's Rise," *New York Times,* August 21, 2012, www.nytimes.com/2012/08/22/world/asia/dispute-over-islands-reflect-japanese-fear-of-chinas-rise.html?pagewanted=all&_r=0.

75 Alan Cullison, "Russia to Deploy Troops to Defend Interests in Arctic," *Wall Street Journal,* July 2, 2011, http://online.wsj.com/article/SB10001424052702303763404576419862777063804.html.

76 1867 Treaty with Russia, article 3, *Statutes at Large,* 539, available online at Library of Congress, http://memory.loc.gov/cgi-bin/ampage?collId=llsl&fileName=015/llsl015.db&recNum=572.

THE
NOR
Cape Prce of Wales
Kings I.
Cape Rodney
NORTON SOUND
Bald-head
Cape Darby
Sledge I.
Cape Denbigh
Besborough
Stewarts I.
Cape Stephens
Andersons Isle
Point Shallow-water
Aug. 1, 1779
Augt 1, 1778
SHOAL WATER
Shoal Ness
60
Cape Newenham
Calm Point
Round I.
Bristol River
BRISTOL BAY
July 24
Foggy Cape
Pinnacle Pt.
Foggy I.
Two Headed Pt.
Cape Trinity
Trinity I.
June 14th
C. St. Barnabas
Cape Greville
June 10th
C. Whitsunday
Whitsuntide Bay
I. St. Hermogenes
Cape Douglas
Smokey Bay
Point Banks
Barren Isles
Mt. Augustine
Cape Bede
Cape Elizabeth
Anchor Pt.
Vulcano
COOKS RIVER
Riv. Turnagain
Pt. Possession
PRINCE WILLIAM'S SOUND
Snug Corner Bay
C. Hinchinbroke
Montagu I.
Green I.
COMPTROLLERS BAY
C. Suckling
Kayes I.
Track
May 12
May 8th
May 22
May 23
Oct. 1.
1778

Cook on the Coasts of the North Pacific and Arctic America

The Cartographic Achievement

JOHN ROBSON

11

THE MAIN PURPOSE OF JAMES COOK'S THIRD VOYAGE TO THE PACIFIC WAS to search for the Northwest Passage, the supposed link between the Pacific and Atlantic Oceans in high latitudes.[1] If it existed, its discovery would allow the British to sail between the two oceans without passing through waters claimed or controlled by the Spanish. Cook was asked by the British Admiralty to take command of this expedition, but little persuasion was necessary, as Cook saw it as a further opportunity to pursue his passion for charting newly discovered coasts.

When the voyage was completed and HMS *Resolution* and HMS *Discovery* returned to Britain in late 1780, the reaction to the voyage was significantly affected by news of the deaths of both expedition commanders, James Cook and Charles Clerke. There was also disappointment that the expedition failed to locate the passage despite having searched a huge stretch of coastline. Cook and his men had been foiled by pack ice and cold that prevented progress beyond Icy Cape on the north Alaska coast at 71°N (where, over a hundred years later, a route was located). However, the ships brought with them a huge store of information, including artifacts, specimens, and new charts to add to the material assembled on the earlier voyages.[2]

Chart of the NW Coast of America and the NE Coast of Asia, Explored in the years 1778 & 1779. Engraved and colored after Henry Roberts (detail of fig. 11.10).

The creation of new charts had become Cook's raison d'être, and by the time of the third voyage, he had become a brilliant hydrographic surveyor and cartographer. The search for the Northwest Passage took him into new and largely unexplored waters in the north Pacific Ocean, thereby providing a new canvas on which to work.

PRIOR CARTOGRAPHIC KNOWLEDGE OF THE NORTHWEST PACIFIC OCEAN

In preparation for the voyage, the Admiralty obtained copies of all the available charts to assist in determining routes to follow and locations to investigate. A number of texts existed describing past voyages, but doubts existed as to their credibility and accuracy.

Francis Drake ventured some way into the north Pacific in 1579 during his voyage around the world, but there was considerable doubt as to how far north he had sailed.[3] The British used the name *New Albion,* a moniker coined by Drake, to refer to the coast north of California, but Drake's expedition had brought back no precise details to assist Cook. No other British sailors were known to have sailed the North American coast after Drake, but Samuel Hearne had more recent reports about the interior from his explorations of the continent west from Hudson Bay.[4] In 1771, Hearne reached the mouth of the Coppermine River, reducing the likelihood that a navigable passage lay south of 70°N along the Northwest Coast (fig. 2.5).

The British were aware that both Russian and Spanish ships had visited the region, but the way these countries shared their information varied considerably. Russia had made available details of most of its expeditions, and many accounts had been translated and published in London; the Spanish were secretive, and only a small amount of information had leaked out about their movements.

Charts were included in the Russian cartographer Gerhard Müller's *Voyages from Asia to America,* published in Britain in 1761.[5] These charts proved most important and influenced the plans for Cook's voyage adopted by the Admiralty. For example, *A Map of the Discoveries made by the Russians on the North West Coast of America* was published by the Imperial Academy of Sciences at St. Petersburg and then republished by Thomas Jeffreys (fig. 2.3). It showed the results of several Russian explorations, including those of Vitus Bering in 1728 and 1741 and that of Mikhail Gvozdev in 1732. This chart showed tracks of ships following a vague outline of the southern side of the Aleutian Islands and the Alaska Peninsula into the Gulf of Alaska. Overall, it bore more than a passing resemblance to a true representation of the region, even if it gave only a hint of the Alaska coastline. The east side of the Bering Sea is poorly depicted, but both shores of the Bering Strait are shown, indicating that America and Asia are separated. The coast trending south toward California has little confirmed detail.

Whereas these maps were vague, a later chart produced in 1774 by Jacob von Staehlin, secretary of the Russian Royal Academy of Sciences, proved dangerous.[6] This chart, *A Map of the New Northern Archipelago discovered by the Russians in the Seas of Kamtschatka and Anadir,* was drawn to show the northeastern part of the Asian continent, including the Bering Strait and some of what lay beyond (fig. 2.6). But it was filled with errors, depicting Alaska as a large island with a wide strait separating it from America at about 165°west of Greenwich. This chart gave Cook nightmares as he explored the Alaska coastline in 1778. He was, though, prepared to forgive the explorers while criticizing the cartographers, as he wrote on September 4, 1778: "In justice to Behrings Memory, I must say he has delineated this Coast very well and fixed the latitude and longitude of the points better than could be expected from the Methods he had to go by. . . . The more I was convinced of being up the Asia Coast the more I was at a loss to reconcile Mr Staehlins Map of the New Northern Archipelago with my observations."[7] He also wrote on September 16, 1778: "Haveing now fully satisfied myself that Mr Staehlin's Map must be erroneous and not mine it was high time to think of leaving these Northern parts."[8]

When the Admiralty assembled maps for the voyage, they also had access to two other, rather suspicious maps of Spanish origin. One chart, "A General Map of the Discoveries of Admiral De Fonte and other Navigators, Spanish, English, and Russian, in quest of a Passage to the South Sea, By Mr. De l'Ille Sept. 1752," showed the places supposedly visited by two explorers, Bartholomew de Fonte and Juan de Fuca, who had sailed into the region on behalf of Spain (fig. 2.2).[9] De Fonte, who was later proved fictitious, was supposed to have sailed up the coast in 1640, discovering an inlet he called Rio de los Reyes at 53°N. Cook was very suspicious of the de Fonte report, and on April 30, 1778, soon after he left Nootka Sound, he wrote: "I continued the same course until the 30th at 4 AM when I steered NBW in order to make the land, regretting very much that I could not do it sooner especially as we were passing the place where Geographers have placed the pretended Strait of Admiral de Fonte. For my part, I give no credet to such vague and improbable stories, that carry their own confutation along with them."[10]

Juan de Fuca, who was said to have lived from 1536 to 1602, claimed to have sailed along the American coast in 1592, discovering a large inlet at about 48°N. He then sailed eastward through the inlet for twenty days to reach the Atlantic before he returned to Mexico. De Fuca probably existed, but doubts remain about his claimed voyage, though the discovery in the 1780s of the strait that now carries his name in the same latitude gives it some credence. Cook, though, was as scathing about de Fuca as he was about de Fonte. As he sailed north along the Washington coast, he wrote: "It is in the very latitude where we now were that geographers have placed the pretended Strait of Juan de Fuca but we saw nothing like it, nor is there the least probability that iver any such thing exhisted."[11] Unfortunately for Cook, he was too far off the coast to observe the strait. If he had, he would have confirmed its existence, though it was certainly not de Fuca's claimed passageway back to Europe.

Not long before Cook's expedition left Britain in 1776, news reached London of recent Spanish activity in the north Pacific. The Spanish, aware of Russian movements, had been keen to assert themselves north of their California colonies. Juan Pérez led an expedition in 1774 north from San Blas in Mexico that reached Langara Island, the northernmost of the Queen Charlotte Islands in British Columbia, before returning south.[12] He briefly entered Nootka Sound but did not land. The next year, Juan Francisco de la Bodega y Quadra, who commanded the sloop *Sonora,* was part of a larger expedition led by Bruno de Hezeta.[13] Bodega and his pilot, Francisco Mourelle, deliberately separated from Hezeta when the commander decided to turn south, and they sailed the *Sonora* farther north to 57°N, reaching Kruzof Island, west of modern-day Sitka, before sickness forced them to return. Bodega produced a chart, and Mourelle wrote the story of their remarkable expedition.[14] While an early version of Mourelle's narrative quickly reached London, it is most probable that these Spanish charts were not available to Cook before he left on the third voyage (fig. 3.8).

During the voyage, Cook met Gerasim Izmailov on Unalaska in October 1778. Izmailov was the Russian factor in charge of the sea-otter pelt trade in the area but had also sailed on several expeditions in the Bering Sea. As a result, he was able to comment on and correct Cook's charts, as well as to share charts of his own. Cook recorded on October 16, 1778, that "Mr Ismyloff . . . brought with him the Charts Afore mentioned which he allowed me to Copy. There were two of them both Manuscripts and every mark of being Authentick."[15]

SURVEYING AND CARTOGRAPHY ON THE THIRD VOYAGE

Because Cook was late in leaving Britain in 1776, he spent more time than originally planned in the South Pacific so that he might arrive on the northwest Pacific coast in early spring. This gave him nearly another year in the South Seas. En route he visited several new islands and revisited old favorites. He also returned Mai, whom Captain Tobias Furneaux had taken to Britain in 1774, to his homeland in the Society Islands.

Although he charted Prince Edward Island and Kerguelen Island in the southern Indian Ocean on this voyage, Cook did not spend time remapping places already visited, so New Zealand and Tahiti hardly feature on the new charts. And although Cook was aware of nearby Fiji and Samoa while at Tonga, he did not investigate them, so the expedition's principal surveys in the South Pacific were limited to the Cook Islands, Moorea, and some of the Ha'apai Group in Tonga. In December 1777, Cook left Tahiti for North America, passing and charting Christmas Island and the western Hawaiian Islands en route. By March 1778, Cook had reached Drake's "New Albion" on the American coast, where the exploration for the Northwest Passage began.

To produce his charts, Cook conducted running surveys at sea combined with land-based surveys.[16] Running surveys were carried out as the ships sailed between anchorages and while in sight of land. As the ship sailed along a coast, intersecting cross-bearings were taken of features on the land using compass and sextant, all the while keeping a record of the course and measuring the distance sailed with the ship's log. Such charting was prone to errors, partly from the difficulty of fixing the ship's true position and partly from problems in sighting the land features.

On Cook's previous voyages, whenever the ships anchored, he surveyed the inlet or harbor. He set up an observatory to take sightings of the sun, moon, and stars by which to determine the location's latitude and longitude. A baseline was set down on land and, using a theodolite and the triangulation method, the surrounding area was surveyed. Survey parties also took depth soundings and recorded rocks and islands and any other information that would be useful to fix the ship's position. This information produced a base chart onto which the features obtained in the running surveys along the neighboring coast could be more confidently added.

However, James Cook behaved differently on this voyage than on his earlier ones. While he maintained the overall control of the surveys and even carried out some early in the voyage, he increasingly entrusted this task to his ships' masters, William Bligh and Thomas Edgar. Bligh later wrote that he had carried out many of the surveys on which the charts were based. Surveys were normally led by one of the established surveyors, who left the ship in a small boat, rowed by a group of seamen. Two or three junior officers would assist the surveyor and, in the process, learn how to use the equipment and perform the survey.

Henry Roberts, a master's mate on the *Resolution,* was entrusted to coordinate the production of charts after the surveys were finished. The raw data were collated and rough charts drawn, which were then transformed into more orderly and complete versions for retention. Gradually, information from smaller charts was combined to produce larger regional charts. After the voyage, Roberts produced the final versions for the voyage narrative.

Cook recognized the value of instructing his junior officers, his "young gentlemen," in the skills of navigation, surveying, and cartography. He had benefited from similar guidance from John Simcoe, who had encouraged Cook early in his career on HMS *Pembroke.* At Louisbourg in eastern Canada in 1758, Samuel Holland had taught Cook the rudiments of surveying and instilled in him the passion for chart making. So on the three voyages, Cook took the time to instill this same passion in his younger colleagues. They were more than grateful, as learning from the master mariner would be an advantage for their future naval careers. Cook wrote: "I had several young men amongst my sea-officers who, under my direction, could be usefully employed in constructing

11.1 *Views on the West Coast of America.* Coastal profiles engraved after drawings by John Webber and William Bligh. University of British Columbia, Rare Books and Special Collections, FC 3821.243.A1 1784 Copy 3.

charts, in taking views of the coasts and headlands near which we should pass, and in drawing plans of the bays and harbours in which we should anchor. A constant attention to this I knew to be highly requisite, if we would render our discoveries profitable to future navigators."[17]

Cook employed the midshipmen in copying charts, which had benefits for all concerned. As well as teaching the midshipmen about cartography, it provided extra copies of the charts, which could be sent home to Britain. Late in the voyage, for example, charts were included in the material sent to London from Kamchatka. This was common practice on most European voyages of exploration. If Jean-François de La Pérouse had not sent records across Siberia in 1785 during his Pacific voyage, scholars would know little of the French expedition before its destruction in a hurricane in the Solomon Islands in 1788.[18]

The production of charts was only one of the survey tasks undertaken on the voyage. Cartographers also prepared coastal views and sailing directions so that sailors who returned to these locations would know how to enter and leave harbors and inlets. Such information included sight lines, hidden rocks, and the best places to anchor. John Webber, the *Resolution*'s artist, drew many coastal views during the third voyage (fig. 11.1). Few sailors were accomplished artists, so having an artist of Webber's skill on board was a bonus. The *Discovery* carried no trained artist, but William Ellis, the surgeon's mate, filled the role admirably. His coastal views improved during the voyage, probably as a result of Webber's influence (fig. 11.2). William Bligh, William Bayly, and Mathew Paul (a young midshipman fresh from Christ's Hospital School) also contributed views of the American coast (fig. 11.3).

Cook and other British sailors of the time benefited from the advancements made by instrument makers in the eighteenth century. Existing instruments were improved, and new ones were introduced. Sextants and diffracting telescopes enabled sailors to take astronomical sightings, and the recently developed marine chronometer allowed longitude to be calculated easily and with certainty. More exact readings made resulting charts more credible.

But improved instruments required trained and accomplished officers to use them effectively. William Bayly, astronomer on the *Discovery,* and James King, one of the lieutenants, were more than able. The best evidence of improving instruments and officers can be seen by comparing the readings for latitude and longitude at places visited during the three voyages. For example, Cook anchored at Ship Cove in Queen Charlotte Sound, New Zealand, six times, at least once during each voyage. By the third voyage, the longitude fixed by the survey was only 6'34" different from the known longitude today. The latitude set on the voyage varied just by just five

11.2 William Wade Ellis, *Isanotski Volcano, Unimak Island,* 1778. Pencil and color wash sketch. Alexander Turnbull Library, Wellington, New Zealand, A-264-043-1.

11.3 Mathew Paul, *The Peaked Hill [Mount Fairweather] as seen on May 7, 1778.* Ink and color-wash sketch. National Archives, Kew, ADM 51/4560/209 f. 392v.

seconds from the figure determined using modern instruments today.

Throughout the voyage, observatories were set up at strategic locations to obtain exact coordinates. Multiple sightings over a period of days would be made and an average result calculated for both latitude and longitude. This enabled readings taken at sea between observations on shore to be regarded with more authority. Just two observatories were established in North America. The first was set up at Ship Cove in Nootka Sound, the expedition's first landfall on the American coast. The coordinates established were 49°36'N and 126°42'W (233°18'E on the chart). This compares with 49°36'15"N and 126°32'00"W as measured today.

The second observatory was set up at Samgoonoodha (now known as English Bay) at Unalaska, the expedition's last landfall before sailing to Hawai'i for rest and recuperation in October 1778. The coordinates established were 53°36'N and 166°30'W (193°30'E on the chart). This compares with 53°56'N and 166°15'W as measured today, demonstrating in both cases that the surveyors were skilled in surveying techniques. In addition to the use of observatories, sets of lunar distances were obtained while the ships were at sea, and longitude was obtained using the chronometers in order to fix the locations of features they had observed.

THE VOYAGE CARTOGRAPHERS

The most accomplished of the cartographers on the voyage was James Cook himself. He had already produced a marvelous portfolio of charts during his first two Pacific voyages and his earlier surveys in Quebec and Newfoundland. He carried out some of the surveys during the earlier parts of the third voyage but entrusted the compilation of the charts to others.

After Cook, William Bligh was the most important cartographer on the voyage. Appointed master on the *Resolution,* Bligh was an accomplished surveyor who carried out countless surveys and prepared many charts. Unfortunately, because few of his charts have survived, it is difficult to

Coordinates for Queen Charlotte Sound

	LAT. AND LONG.	COOK'S	MODERN	DIFFERENCE
First voyage	Lat.	41° 05' 08" S	41° 05' 43" S	00° 00' 35" to the N
	Long.	175° 28' 59" E	174° 14' 02" E	01° 14' 57" to the E
Second voyage	Lat.	41° 05' 54" S	41° 05' 43" S	00° 00' 11" to the S
	Long.	174° 30' 11" E	174° 14' 02" E	00° 16' 09" to the E
Third voyage	Lat.	41° 05' 48" S	41° 05' 43" S	00° 00' 05" to the S
	Long.	174° 20' 36" E	174° 14' 02" E	00° 06' 34" to the E

properly assess his contribution. Bligh later stated that he had lost many of his own charts during the mutiny on the *Bounty* in 1789. He made it quite clear after the voyage that he was unhappy that the master's mate on the *Resolution,* Henry Roberts, was asked to prepare the charts for publication, and Bligh was not given credit for having drawn the originals. He annotated a copy of King's published voyage journal, exclaiming in the margin in his own hand: "None of the Maps and Charts in this publication are from the original drawings of Lieutenant Henry Roberts; he did no more than copy the original ones from Captain Cook, who besides myself was the only person that surveyed and laid the coast down, in the *Resolution.* Every plan & Chart from C. Cook's death are exact Copies of my Works."[19]

Bligh was born at St. Tudy, Cornwall, in 1754. He was only twenty-two years old when he was appointed master of the *Resolution.* He would gain notoriety in 1789 after a mutiny while he was in command of the *Bounty.* His commitment to chart making was demonstrated when, cast adrift in the longboat after the mutiny, Bligh still drew charts, including one of Fiji as they passed through those islands. Subsequently, he had an interesting career, being lauded for bravery at the Battle of Camperdown in 1797 but enduring a controversial tenure as the confrontational governor of New South Wales in 1808. He died in 1817.

Henry Roberts was born in 1757 at Shoreham, Sussex, into a seafaring family. He had sailed with Cook on the second voyage before serving as master's mate on the third. In addition to conducting or assisting with surveys, Roberts was entrusted with drawing the fair-copy charts (figs. 11.4 and 11.5). He was later given the task of preparing final versions for publication. He wrote a letter from Shoreham in Sussex on May 18, 1784 describing his role:

> Soon after our departure from England, I was intrusted by Captain Cook to complete a map of the world as a general chart, from the best materials he was in possession of for that purpose; and before his death this business was in a great measure accomplished; That is, the grand outline of the whole was arranged, leaving only those parts vacant or unfinished which he expected to fall in with and explore. But on our return home, when the fruits of our voyage were ordered by the Lords Commissioners of the Admiralty to be published, the care of the general chart being consigned to me, I was directed to prepare it from the latest and best authorities; and also to introduce Captain Cook's three successive tracks, that all his discoveries, and the different routes he had taken might appear together, by this means to give a general idea of the whole.[20]

After the death of Clerke, John Gore was given command of the expedition until it returned to Britain. From Deptford, he wrote to Philip Stephens about Roberts immediately after the voyage, on October 7, 1780: "I herewith send for Their Lordships inspection The remainder of the Mapps

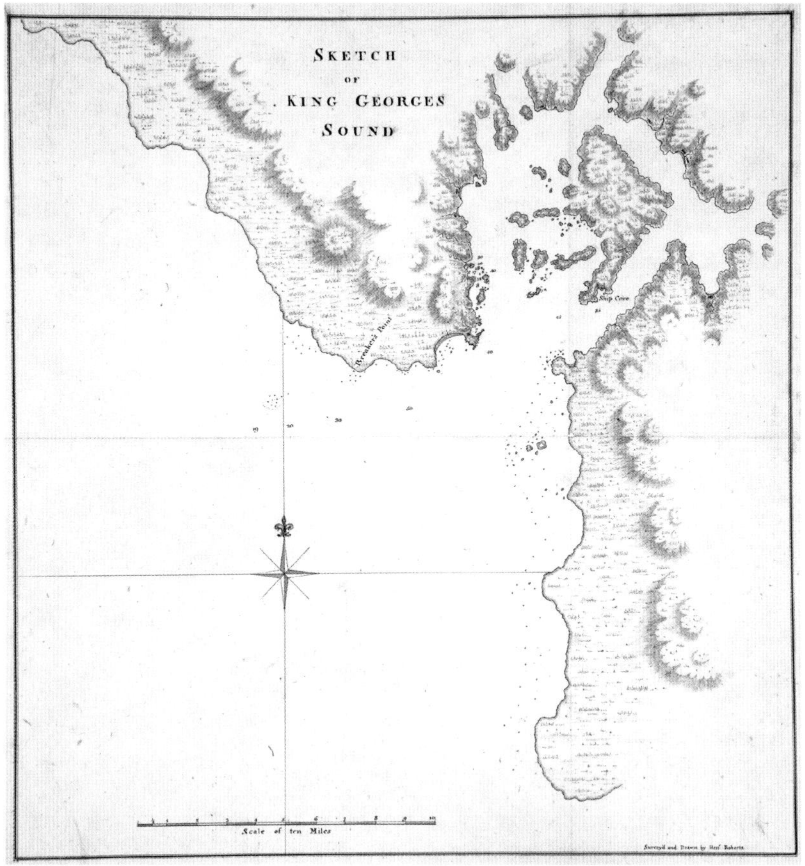

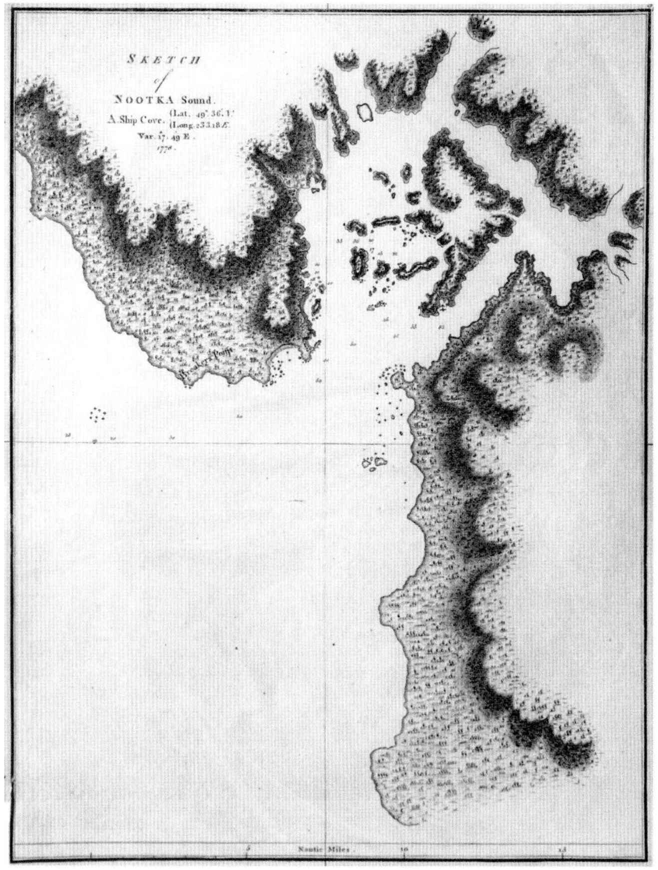

11.4 Henry Roberts, *Sketch of King Georges [Nootka] Sound,* manuscript chart, 1778. National Archives, Kew, MPI 81.

11.5 *Sketch of Nootka Sound.* Engraved version of fig. 11.4. From Cook, *A Voyage to the Pacific Ocean* (1784), atlas, plate 37. University of British Columbia, Rare Books and Special Collections, ARC 1677 C1784N.

and Journals on board the Resolution. Mr Roberts is Charg'd with the Care of Them And bears you This. He was principal assistant Hydrographer to Capt. Cook and is most certainly a very Deserving young Man."[21]

Roberts was appointed lieutenant in 1780 and commander in 1790. He was given the command of an expedition to the Northwest Coast of America, but the expedition was postponed, only to be later given over to Vancouver. Promoted to captain in 1794, Roberts died of yellow fever in 1796 when he was captain of HMS *Undaunted* in the West Indies.

Thomas Edgar, master of HMS *Discovery,* was another accomplished surveyor. Information on his charts often varies from the published versions, suggesting he carried out independent surveys or drew his own charts. Edgar was born in 1746 at Woolwich, where his father, Thomas, worked in the dockyard. He joined the navy as a boy, becoming captain's servant to Hugh Palliser on the *Shrewsbury.* In 1764, while Palliser was governor of Newfoundland, Edgar followed Palliser to the *Guernsey.* Joseph Gilbert, who was master of the *Resolution* on Cook's second voyage, became master of the *Guernsey,* where he taught Edgar the fundamentals of surveying. Palliser's patronage continued throughout Edgar's career, and it is likely he arranged Edgar's appointment to the *Discovery.* His log contains many fine charts (fig. 11.6). After the voyage, Edgar was finally promoted to lieutenant and later joined the *Hope,* a merchant ship that visited the Falkland Islands in 1786 and 1787. His survey and chart of West Falkland Island was published by Arrowsmith in 1797.[22] Edgar died in 1801.

James Burney, who had sailed on the *Adventure* as a lieutenant during Cook's second voyage, began the third on HMS *Discovery* as first lieutenant and ended it, after a spell on *Resolution,* as commander of the *Discovery.* Burney produced a large number of charts in a rather minimal but unique style (figs. 7.4 and 11.7). He was born in London in 1750, the son of the musicologist Charles Burney. His sister was the popular novelist and playwright Fanny Burney. His active naval career ended in 1784, when he retired and became a historian of Pacific exploration. He also became a man about town in London, where he was a friend of literary figures such as Charles Lamb, William Hazlitt, and Robert Southey. In 1821, six months before his death, he was promoted to rear admiral on the retired list.

Edward Riou was born about 1759, the second son of Stephen and Dorothy Riou. He joined the *Discovery* as a midshipman and soon became an active member of the survey team, producing many charts. His charts, among the best from the voyage, had good detail and attractive embellishment, suggesting that he was not merely copying the work of others (fig. 11.8). Riou went on to have an illustrious but short naval career, which ended with his death in 1801 at the Battle of Copenhagen. A memorial to him stands in St. Paul's Cathedral, London.

Throughout the voyage, other men on both ships also produced charts. Astronomer William Bayly and midshipman George Vancouver contributed a few covering the American coast, while Nathaniel Portlock and John Williamson prepared maps from other parts of the voyage. Interestingly, no charts survive from the other commanders of the expedition: Charles Clerke, John Gore, and James King.

The total number of charts from America is surprisingly small.[23] It was normal practice on Cook's voyages for all journals, logs, and charts to be handed over to the commanders before the ships reached home. This was partly to stop them falling into the wrong hands, for example French or Spanish, and partly to prevent private publication ahead of the official accounts. However, not all men obliged: some held on to their material. Some charts may have been lost. Soon after the return to Britain, a parcel containing "Capt Cook's Journals Log Books, & loose

A Plan of King Georges Sound.

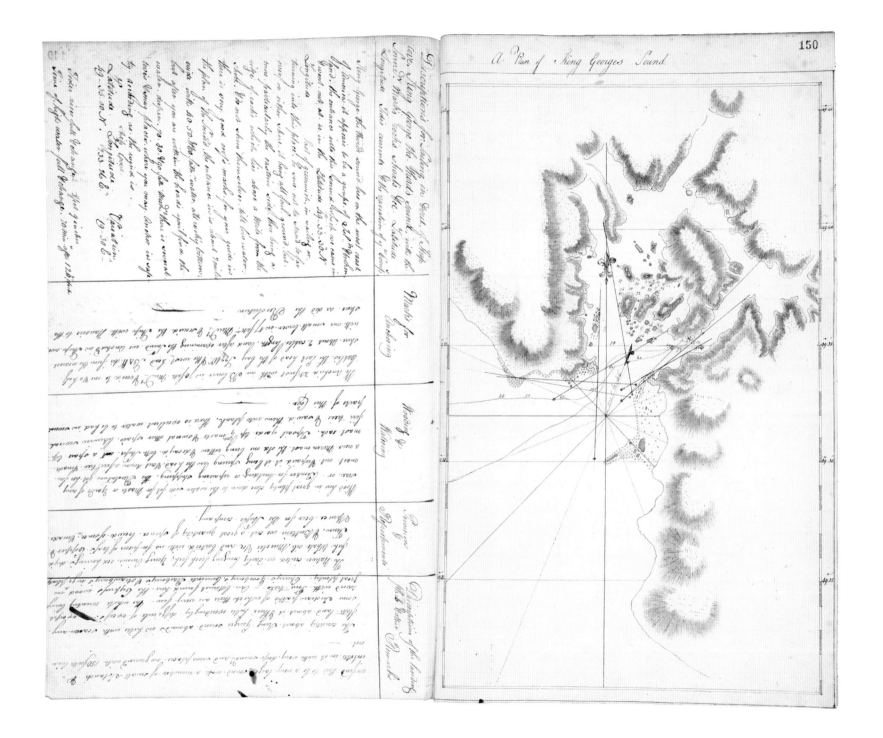

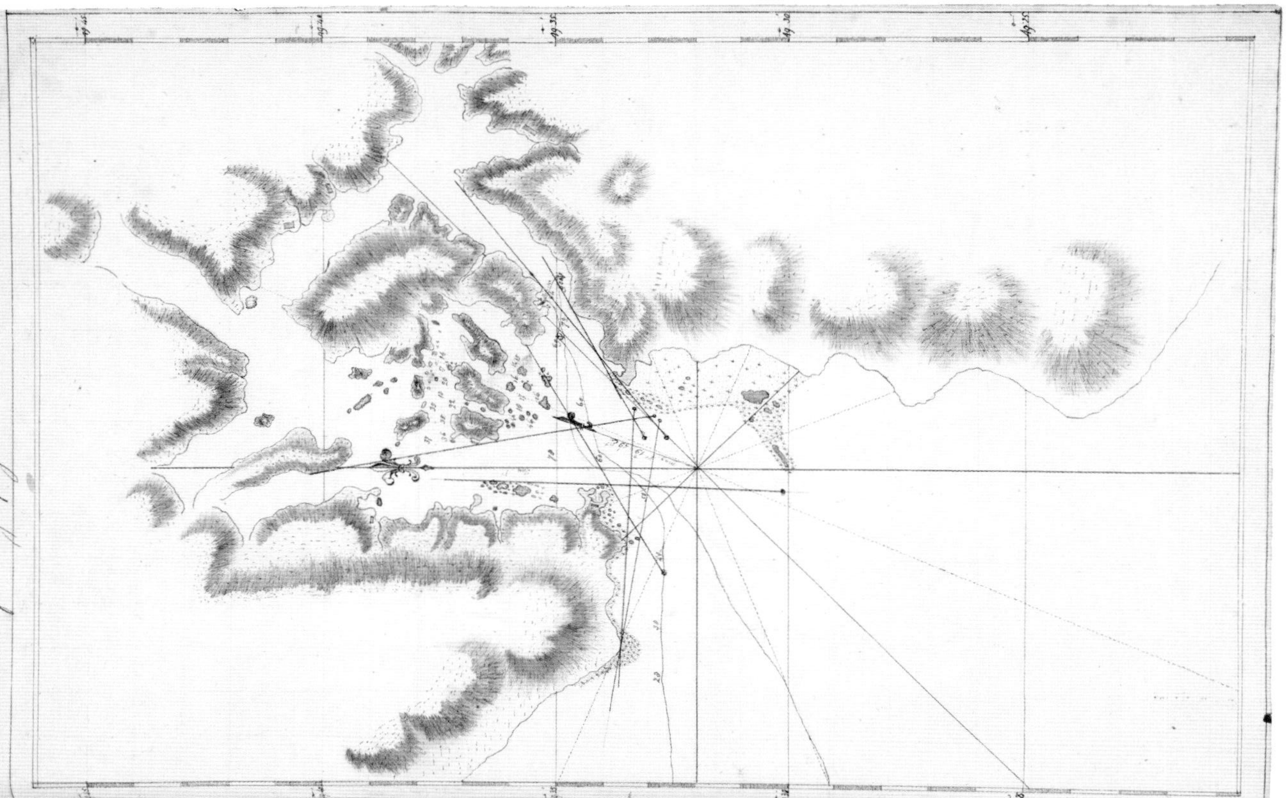

Discriptions for Sailing in & out of Ship cove. King George the Third's sound, with the Sound^gs Marks rocks shoals &c. Latitude Longitude Tides currents & the variation of y^e Comp^s

King George the thirds sound lies on the west coast of America it appears to be a groupe of Isl^ds & broken land. the entrance into this sound which we came in & went out at is in the Latitude 49..33..30 N Longitude East of greenwich, in sailing or turning into this place be sure not to stand to far over on either shore it being all foul ground but more particularly the eastern side there being a ridge of rocks which lies above a Mile from the shore & do not shew themselves till low water. there is very good cross marks for your guide in the plan of the Sound. the entrance in is about 2 miles wide with 40.50 & 60 fath^m water. all rocky bottom, but after you are within the heads you'l find the water deepen. 70.80 & 90 fath Mud^y there is several coves & snug places where you may Anchor in safety according as the wind is.

Latitude	Ship Cove. Longitude	Variation
49-35.00 N.	233.16 E^t	19-30 E^t

Tides rises full & change 8feet 9 inches

Time of high water full & change. 20 Min after 12 O'clock

Marks for Anchoring

We Anchor'd at first with our B. bower in 70 fath Mud^y & veer'd to one & a half Cables. the East head of the bay S22W. the west head S58W. dis^t from the nearest shore About 2 cables length. & and after examining the Sound we Anchor'd in Ship cove with our small bower in 17 fath^m Mud^y & moor'd the Ship with Hausers to the shore as did the Resolution

Wooding & Watering

Wood lies in great plenty close down to the water side fit for Masts or Yards of any size or Timber for building or repairing shipping. the Resolution got her fore mast out & repair'd it it being sprung in the head & cut down a tree & made a new Mizen mast the old one being rotten & decay'd. both Ships cut a spare top mast each. Topsail yards top g^t masts & several other spars likewise several fir trees & saw'd them into plank. there is excellent water to be had in several parts of this Cove.

Provisions & Refreshments

The Natives visited us Daily bringing fresh fish. Young Onions. red herrings. dry'd fish. Whale oil. Muscles &c. and barter'd with us for pieces of brass. Copper & Tinn. & Buttons we cut a great quantity of spruce. brew'd spruce. Smoke Spruce. beer for the Ships company.

Discriptions of the landing place & other Remarks

we find this to be a very large sound with a number of small Islands & inlets in it with very deep soundings and some places no ground with 150 fath line out. —

The country about King Georges sound abounds in hills with scarce any flatt land about it & these hills exceedingly difficult of access & some Indians paths of which there are very few. the whole country being cover'd with Pine trees. — An Botonist found here the Cypress wood in great plenty. Cherry's. Gooseberry's. Currents. Rasberry's & Strawberry's in great plenty

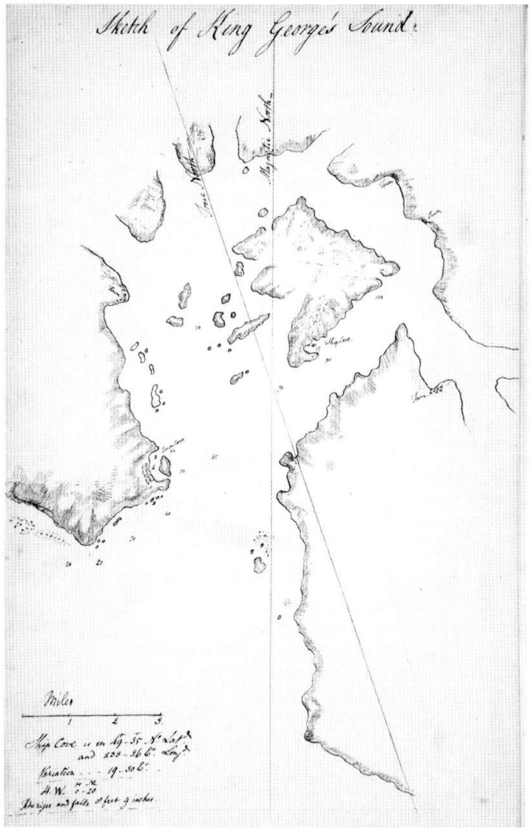

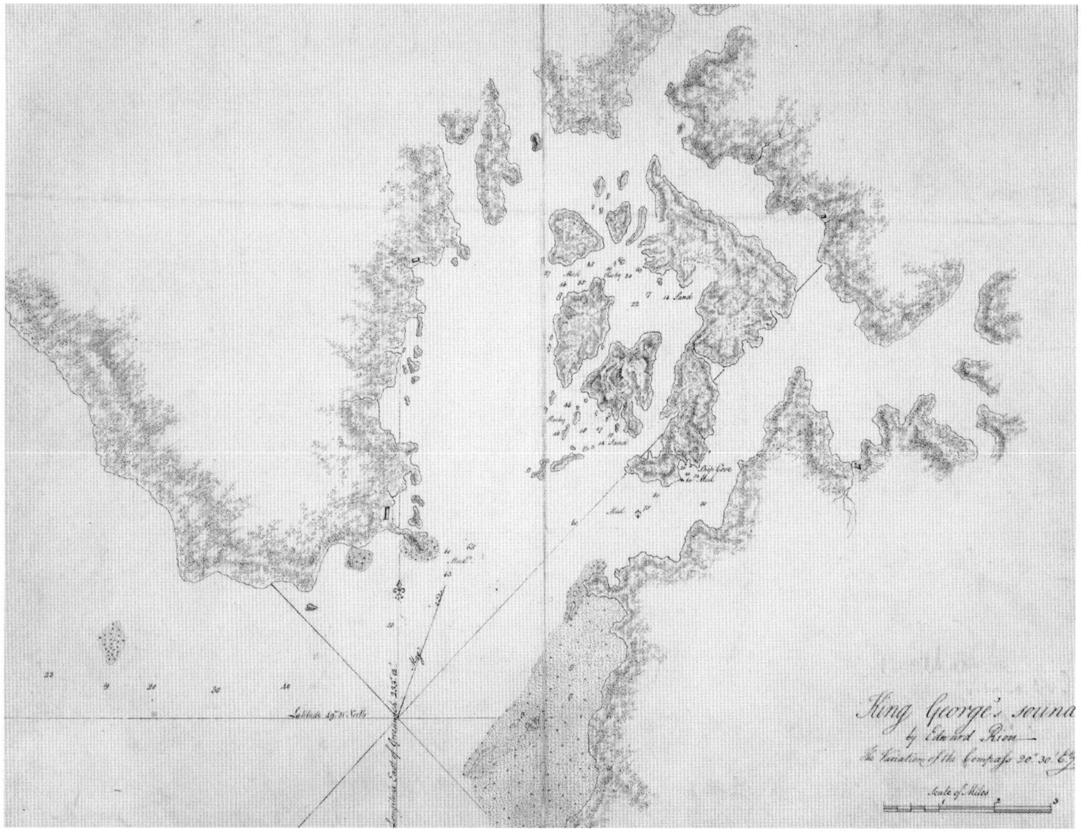

Manuscripts relative to this voyage" went missing and was never found. The loose manuscripts may have included maps. James King wrote that he had "made all the enquiries but without effect for Capt. Cook's loose papers, they are not at the Admiralty, Mrs Cook has not got them & the Clerke knows nothing of them, C. Gore is out of town but it seems unlikely that he can give any account; however on my return I will make another search."[24]

Additionally, some manuscript charts may have been destroyed after they had been used to prepare final versions, either during the voyage or when Roberts was preparing material for publication. It is intriguing that many more charts survive from the *Discovery* than from the *Resolution,* suggesting that Roberts relied on or had better access to originals from Bligh and Cook, who were on the command ship with him. Periodically the Admiralty

11.6 Thomas Edgar, *A Plan of King Georges Sound,* manuscript with accompanying sailing directions, 1778. National Archives, Kew, ADM 55/21 f. 150.

11.7 James Burney, *Sketch of King Georges [Nootka] Sound,* manuscript chart, 1778. National Archives, Kew, ADM 51/4528/45 f. 225v.

11.8 Edward Riou, *King Georges [Nootka] Sound,* manuscript chart, 1778. National Archives, Kew, ADM 352/334.

returned charts to men after the voyage narrative had been published. John Elliott, a midshipman on the second voyage, reported that some time after his voyage, he had breakfast with Cook, who returned charts to him: "I attended to his invitation, and did receive my Chart etc., with my Name, Elliott's Chart and Ship's Track, written on it in his own hand."[25] There is no evidence, however, that any crew members were given their charts after the third voyage journal was published.

CARTOGRAPHIC ACHIEVEMENTS ON THE VOYAGE

The charts of Nootka Sound are described here in order to demonstrate the approaches and styles adopted by Cook's cartographers and the quality of charts they produced. The work of four different men has survived, allowing comparisons of technique and competence. The expedition put into this inlet at 49°36'N on March 29, 1778, and anchored in a cove (Ship Cove, later called Resolution Cove) on the east side of an island later named Bligh Island after the *Resolution*'s master. The inlet was also called King George's Sound, so all the manuscript charts carry that name. The British remained in Nootka Sound until April 26 while they replaced the masts, replenished water and firewood stocks, and traded with the local Nuu-chah-nulth people. After some communication, the British erroneously believed the local name for the region to be *Nootka,* and that name was adopted for the sound.

The British began by setting up their observatory on the shore of Ship Cove to establish the latitude and longitude, which would serve as the basis for future surveys (fig. 5.5). Near the time to leave, Cook set out with two of the ships' boats on April 20 to explore the sound and make a survey. They returned the next day after circumnavigating the island. On April 22, Cook returned to the village at Friendly Cove, now called Yuquot, near the entrance to the sound. One of the surveyors, James Trevenen, explained that some readings taken on the first visit to the village were erratic: "In making a sketch of the Sound I had been employed in taking the necessary bearings the last time we were here, and on our return nothing could be made of them. . . . But on this second visit, going to the same place, and placing the compass in the old station, it was found that there was some magnetic quality in the rocks which threw it quite out of its proper direction."[26]

The records state that Cook led the survey. In his memoirs, Trevenen describes the captain's participation, but the other members of the survey party are not named, so it is unknown whether Bligh or Edgar accompanied Cook. The charts show that the survey party carried out only a basic reconnaissance. Side channels were noted, but none was explored to any great distance, and few depth soundings were taken. At another time, a different survey party apparently examined the many small islets on the west side of Bligh Island, as they are depicted in detail on the charts, together with soundings between them.

No original sketches by Cook and Bligh during the Nootka surveys have survived. Instead we have two versions by Henry Roberts from the *Resolution,* as well as two by James Burney and one each by Thomas Edgar and Edward Riou from the *Discovery.* The three cartographers on the *Discovery* may have shared the same raw data, but their charts are very different in appearance, so it is likely they were not copying each other. Edgar's chart is the most authoritative of the three, perhaps reflecting his superior position on the ship and his considerable experience. His chart was drawn in his log opposite sailing directions, and it includes sight lines to be used with those directions. The tracks of the ships in and out of the sound are shown. The whole chart is given a border. Latitudes but not longitudes are shown. By contrast, Burney's charts are little more than sketches of the shoreline. As with Burney's other charts from the voyage, the simplistic style is still effective. The most interesting of the *Discovery* charts, though, is that by Riou. In this attractive chart, Riou spent more time than his colleagues showing the terrain on the islands and shoreline of the sound.

Meanwhile, on the *Resolution,* Henry Roberts prepared two charts. The first, located in his log book, is a basic representation of the sound. His second version was prepared for inclusion in John Gore's log book and was probably drawn after Gore assumed command of the expedition in September 1779. It is a tidier chart, with a border, scale, and north point, but it does not include latitudes and longitudes. Interestingly, it carries the statement "surveyed and drawn by Henr Roberts," suggesting that Roberts was part of the April 20 survey party that went to Yuquot with Captain Cook. Roberts appears to have used his second chart as the basis of the engraved chart included in the atlas that accompanied the narrative of the voyage. By this time the name of the inlet had been changed to Nootka Sound.

Cook was conservative in the place names he bestowed, which have been generally retained on modern maps of the Pacific Northwest, British Columbia, and Alaska. Royalty, the nobility, and senior members of the Admiralty and Royal Navy were honored as they had been on previous voyages. Efforts were made, however, though not always successfully, to determine local names. Nootka Sound was a case in which the local people misunderstood Cook's question, and Cook misunderstood their response. Cook had more success in learning local names from Polynesians, with whom he had already established a degree of understanding.

Cook rarely mentioned his own religious beliefs in his writings and only infrequently used religious names for coastal features. However, he used the calendar more on the third voyage, and several saints and other religious events were commemorated, especially on the American coast. For example, describing reaching the Oregon coast, he wrote: "The Northern one [headland] was the same which we had first seen on the 7th; and, on that account, I called it Cape Perpetua. . . . The

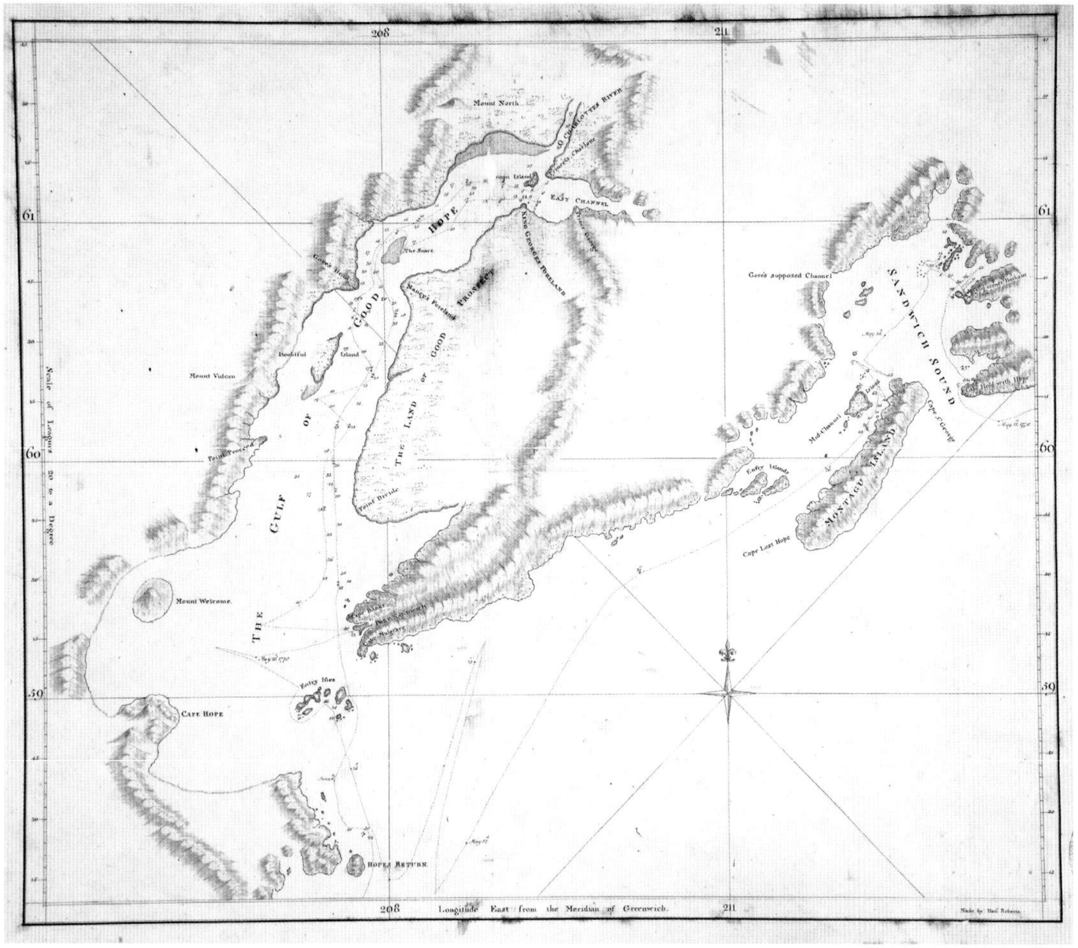

11.9 Henry Roberts, *Chart of Prince William Sound and Cook Inlet,* manuscript chart for insertion in John Gore's journal, 1778. National Archives, Kew, MPI 82.

southern extreme before us, I named Cape Gregory. . . . In our calendar, the 7th of March is distinguished by the name of Perpetua M, and the 12th by that of Gregory B."[27]

Some of the names he bestowed were changed after the voyage, such as Prince William Sound, which Cook originally called Sandwich Sound (fig. 11.9). Some of his other names lapsed as local names were restored. In some cases, names honoring Cook and his colleagues were applied after the voyage. For example, Nootka Sound now has several features with names alluding to the voyage, including Bligh Island, named by Commander George Richards in 1862.[28] Cook Inlet was not so named until after the voyage returned to Britain, and it became known as an inlet only after Vancouver's definitive survey in 1794.

Cook's instructions specified that he should reach the North American coast at about 45°N and put into the first available harbor for restocking and repairs, which he did at Nootka Sound. After this, he was to proceed quickly to 65°N before beginning his survey proper. When Cook left Nootka, he kept away from land. As a result, he largely ignored the coast north between Vancouver Island and Kruzof Island. Running surveys could never be very precise, depending as they did on being able to sight the coastline. Nighttime, fog, haze, and stormy weather were just some of the factors that hindered such a survey, so some features were missed (such as the Strait of Juan de Fuca), others misinterpreted, and some not located in their true position.

Time was another factor hindering the voyage's surveys. Cook knew the surveying of the imagined passageway in the far north would require as much time around high summer as possible. Thus he could not afford to spend too much time checking all the features he encountered on the way. Speed and fatigue led to errors. Bligh pointed out after the voyage that Cook had mischarted an island in the north Bering Sea: approaching St. Lawrence Island on three occasions from different directions, he had failed to realize it was the same island. Instead he gave it three different names: Anderson's Island on August 3, 1778; St. Lawrence Island on September 4, 1778; and Clerke's Island on September 5, 1778. Bligh wrote: "Here is a gross mistake for Anderson's Id & the East end of Clerk's Id is one and the same land & how they have blundered to lay them down as two I cannot conceive."[29]

After slow and methodical preparation, the official publication of the voyage was released in 1784. Given the importance of the North American section of the voyage, it is curious that it was represented by only five charts. There are two small-scale charts for the harbors in which observatories were set up (Nootka Sound and Samgoonoodha, Unalaska). Two larger-scale charts cover the areas where more detailed searches took place for the Northwest Passage (Bering Strait to Norton Sound and Prince William Sound to Cook Inlet). The fifth chart is a regional one covering the stretch of coast from Oregon to Kamchatka and north to Icy Cape (fig. 11.10). Another chart of the whole Pacific Ocean, drawn by Henry Roberts at Cook's behest after Cook's death, is a fine testament to Cook's achievements over the preceding ten years (fig. 6.5). The tracks of all three voyages were depicted, and the coastlines and virtually all the Pacific island groups were located in their true positions.

In six months in 1778, James Cook charted much of the Northwest Coast of America, from 45°N in Oregon to 71°N at Icy Cape in northern Alaska, an incredible feat. However, while Cook's expedition had produced a much clearer representation of this coast than previous expeditions, it was by no means perfect, and there were still gaps and detail to be filled in. The time allowed for the survey and the sheer size of the area to be explored meant that only a quick examination was possible. Weather conditions, the state of the ships, and the condition of the men also affected the quality of the charts produced.

The news of Cook's presence on the coast caused the Spanish to renew their efforts, and soon their ships were sailing north again. The British also returned through government-sponsored and commercial expeditions. The British and American sea-otter pelt trade, a by-product of Cook's voyage, soon brought sailors to the region who would begin to fill in the gaps. Several of these sailors had learned their trade with Cook. Nathaniel Portlock and George Dixon (from the third voyage) and James Colnett (from the second) drew charts for stretches of the American coast. However, it fell to George Vancouver, another of Cook's protégés, to lead an expedition from 1791 to 1795 that delineated the coast in detail (fig. 13.13).[30] Even after Vancouver's survey, it could not be stated with absolute certainty that a Northwest Passage did not exist. However, Cook's and Vancouver's work showed that if it did exist at all, it was most probably located north of 70°N in cold and inhospitable territory.

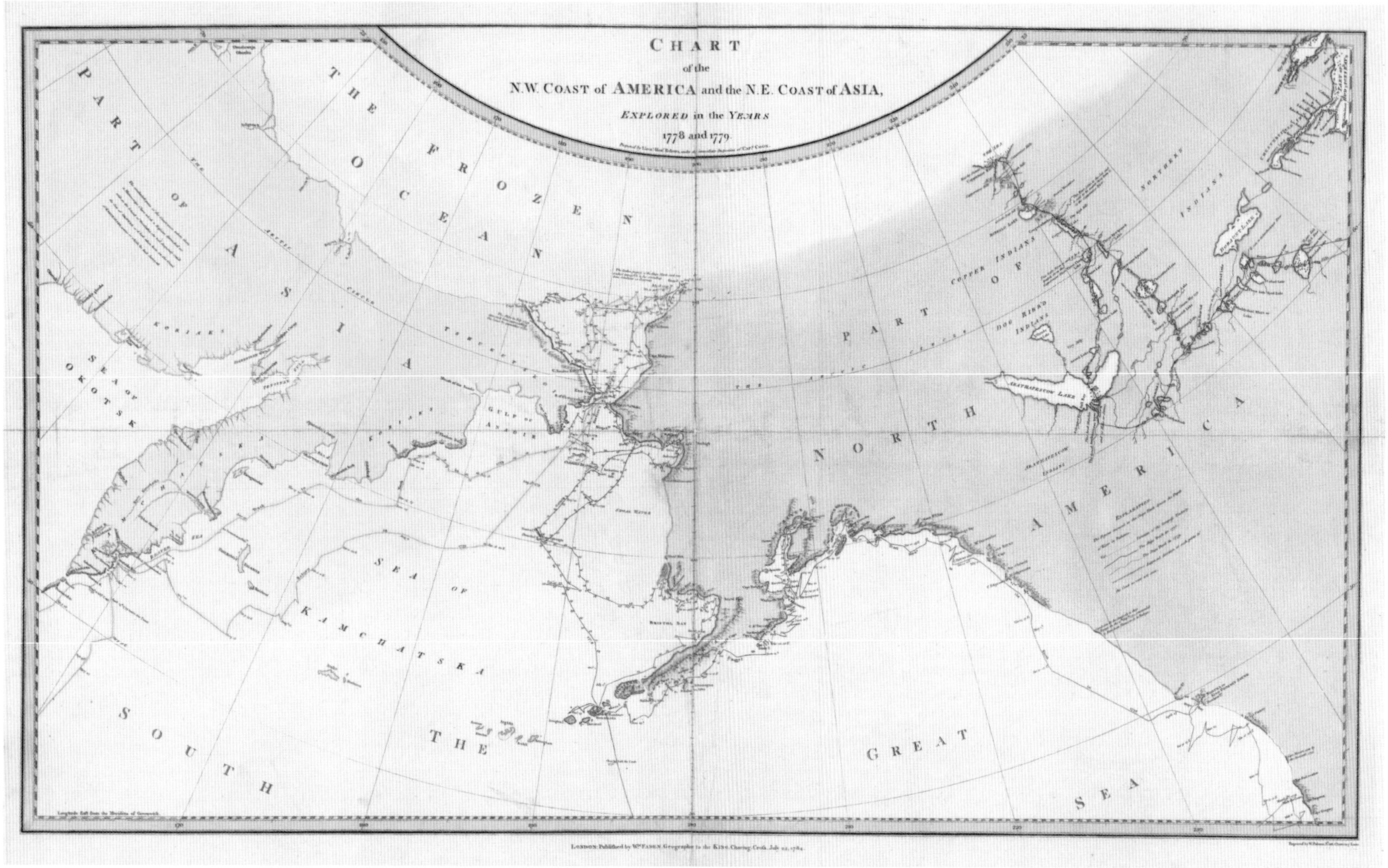

11.10 *Chart of the NW Coast of America and the NE Coast of Asia, Explored in the years 1778 & 1779.* Engraved and colored after Henry Roberts. Engraved by W. Palmer; published by W.m Faden. University of British Columbia, Rare Books and Special Collections, G9235.1779.R65 1784.

NOTES

1 Cook's instructions are reproduced in *The Journals of Captain James Cook on His Voyages of Discovery,* vol. 3, *The Voyage of the* Resolution *and* Discovery, *1776–1780,* ed. J. C. Beaglehole (Cambridge: Cambridge University Press for the Hakluyt Society, 1967), ccxx–ccxxiv.

2 A full account of the voyage, prepared by James King, appeared in 1784 as James Cook and James King, *A Voyage to the Pacific Ocean . . . in the years 1776, 1777, 1778 1779 and 1780,* 3 vols. and atlas (London: John Douglas, 1784). An edited version of the journal appeared in 1967 as Cook, *Voyage of the* Resolution *and* Discovery.

3 Harry Kelsey discusses Drake's route and how far north he sailed in his *Sir Francis Drake: The Queen's Pirate* (New Haven, CT: Yale University Press, 1998).

4 Samuel Hearne, *A Journey from Prince of Wales's Fort in Hudson's Bay to the Northern Ocean in the Years 1769, 1770, 1771 and 1772* (London: A. Strahan and T. Cadell, 1795).

5 Gerhard Müller, *Voyages from Asia to America, for Completing the Discoveries of the North West Coast of America* (London: T. Jeffreys, 1761).

6 J. Von Staehlin, *An Account of the New Northern Archipelago, Lately Discovered by the Russians in the Seas of Kamtschatka and Anadir* (London: C. Heydinger, 1774).

7 Cook, *Voyage of the* Resolution *and* Discovery, 433.

8 Ibid., 441.

9 The map was included in Müller, *Voyages from Asia.*

10 Cook, *Voyage of the* Resolution *and* Discovery, 335.

11 Ibid., 293.

12 Herbert K. Beals, ed., *Juan Pérez on the Northwest Coast: Six Documents of His Expedition in 1774* (Portland: Oregon Historical Society, 1989).

13 Herbert K. Beals, ed., *For Honor and Country: The Diary of Bruno de Hezeta* (Portland: Oregon Historical Society, 1985).

14 Francisco Antonio Mourelle, *Prospectus for Voyage of the Sonora in the Second Bucareli Expedition to Explore the Northwest Coast* (San Francisco: Thomas C. Russell, 1920).

15 Cook, *Voyage of the* Resolution *and* Discovery, 452.

16 Cook's surveying methods are discussed in G. S. Ritchie, "Captain Cook's Influence on Hydrographic Surveying," *Pacific Studies* 1 (1978): 78–95, and R. A. Skelton, "Captain James Cook as a Hydrographer," *Mariner's Mirror* 40, no. 2 (1954): 92–119.

17 Cook and King, *Voyage to the Pacific Ocean,* 1:5.

18 *The Journal of Jean-François de Galaup de La Pérouse, 1785–1788,* 2 vols., ed. and trans. John Dunmore (London: Hakluyt Society, 1994).

19 This annotation appears in ink on the title page of Bligh's own copy of Cook and King, *Voyage to the Pacific Ocean,* vol. 1. The volume is now held as item Sb 170 in the Admiralty Library, Royal Navy Naval Historical Branch, HM Naval Base, Portsmouth, UK. Bligh's comments are detailed in Rupert T. Gould, "Bligh's Notes on Cook's Last Voyage," *Mariner's Mirror* 14, no. 4 (1928): 371–85.

20 Cook and King, *Voyage to the Pacific Ocean,* 1:lxxxv.

21 John Gore to Philip Stephens, October 7, 1780, British Library, Adm. 1/1839.

22 Thomas Edgar, *Chart of West Falkland Island, from an Actual Survey by Lieut. Thos. Edgar of the Royal Navy, in the Years 1786 & 1787* (London: A. Arrowsmith, 1797).

23 The five charts were reproduced in the atlas accompanying Cook and King, *Voyage to the Pacific Ocean.* They and all the other surviving charts were reproduced in Andrew David, Rüdiger Joppien, and Bernard Smith, eds., *The Charts and Coastal Views of Captain Cook's Voyages,* vol. 3, *The Voyage of the* Resolution *and* Discovery, *1776–1780* (London: Hakluyt Society, 1997).

24 British Library, Egerton MS 2180, fol. 21. Reproduced in David, Joppien, and Smith, *Charts and Coastal Views,* 3:xciv.

25 John Elliott, *The Memoirs of John Elliott,* in *Captain Cook's Second Voyage: The Journals of Lieutenants Elliott and Pickersgill,* ed. Christine Holmes (London: Caliban Books, 1984), 46.

26 Christopher Lloyd and R. C. Anderson, eds., *A Memoir of James Trevenen* (London: Navy Records Society, 1959), 21.

27 Cook and King, *Voyage to the Pacific Ocean,* 2:260–61.

28 John T. Walbran, *British Columbia Coast Names, 1592–1906* (Ottawa: Government Printing Bureau, 1909).

29 This annotation appears in pencil in the margins of page 467 of Bligh's copy of Cook and King, *Voyage to the Pacific Ocean,* vol. 3.

30 George Vancouver, *A Voyage* of *Discovery to the North Pacific Ocean and round the World, 1791–1795,* ed. W. Kaye Lamb (London: Hakluyt Society, 1984).

12

Narrating an Alaskan Cruise

Cook's Journal (1778) and Douglas's Edition of A Voyage to the Pacific Ocean *(1784)*

I. S. MacLAREN

WHAT WAS JAMES COOK *NOT*? AN EVANGELIST MISSIONARY, A NATURALIST, a man of wealth, a reader, a democrat, a pacifist, a "natural-born writer."[1] He was not ornate, baroque, romantic, affected, sentimental, religious, diffident, unsociable, intolerant, or remarkably splenetic. In most respects, he was not reliant on others any more than he was short, stout, sickly, silly, vivacious, or craven. He was not well bred, but he was respectable. In the words of his most famous biographer, J. C. Beaglehole, "He was not original."[2] From a young age, Cook worked diligently as a mariner, thereafter a naval captain, to become an explorer successful in navigating and in charting geography and, as far as *any* imperialist's sense of diplomacy extends, diplomacy. He was rigorous, thorough, and seldom improvident. "Geography," Beaglehole maintained, "provided him with the imaginative, Navigation with morals."[3]

Although he sired six children with his wife, Cook was not home sufficiently often or long to be a dedicated husband or father, and his death left Elizabeth a widow for five decades. (Their children unluckily also meeting death early, she spent her last four decades as an ex-mother, as well.)[4] Although his geographical discoveries of both presence and absence were colorful, he himself was not colorful.

John Webber, *Sea Horses*, circa 1781–83 (detail of fig. 12.10).

After he achieved distinction in the Atlantic in the late 1750s and 1760s, his three voyages to the Pacific in the 1770s amply extended his naval reputation for geopolitical and commercial pursuits, from cartography of the known to discovery of the unknown. He plotted his way around an ocean bigger than all the planet's land mass. Bent on dispelling Europe's illusion of a sort of Grendel's Mere, he transformed the Pacific into, if not Lord Cobham's lake at Stowe Park (eighteenth-century England's most touted splash), then a much more clearly comprehended body of water and islands than Europe could imagine. As a cartographer, so as a writer: Beaglehole (fig. 6.2) finds that the many deletions and interlineations in Cook's manuscripts testify to a dogged pursuit of accuracy.[5] But, however much he wrote, Cook did not pretend to be an author.[6]

In December 1775, five months after his second voyage to the Pacific Ocean concluded with his arrival at Spithead on July 30, Britain's parliament tightened the conditions of its 1745 Northwest Passage Act, which offered twenty thousand pounds for the discovery of a navigable route around North America: the act now stipulated that the route must lie north of 52°N latitude. At the age of forty-seven (in an era when a British male thought of a long life as extending beyond the age of sixty), Cook was accomplished and celebrated. Yet the geographical challenge and reward enticed him. Meeting the former would secure his fame forever; claiming the latter would secure his family for generations.[7]

Cook was bringing into focus an image of himself that aligned with that of George Anson earlier in the century. Anson had completed an arduous circumnavigation in the early 1740s. This achievement, together with his capture of more than one million pieces of eight (worth about four hundred thousand pounds)[8] from a Spanish galleon on the Mexico-Manila run, and his subsequent appointment as first lord of the Admiralty until his death in 1762, provided British naval captains with their model: not a martinet but a hero, one who was, as one London weekly effused, "a brave, humane, equal-minded, prudent commander . . . his temper . . . so steady and unruffled that the men and officers [would] all look on him with wonder and delight."[9] The delayed publication of his *Voyage round the World* until May 1748, four years less a month after the return of his ship, HMS *Centurion,* did not dampen public anticipation for it; nor did the title page's announcement that it had been compiled by the voyage's chaplain, Richard Walter, in the tradition of the armchair-traveler churchman editors Richard Hakluyt and Samuel Purchas.[10] In the flourish of a quarto (roughly speaking, nine by eleven inches) that contained forty-two copperplate engravings, it offered a template; thereafter, the launching of the quarto of the official version of a voyage signaled to armchair travelers that the expedition was complete.[11]

In 1773, John Hawkesworth earned six thousand pounds, "one of the most lucrative literary contracts of the eighteenth century,"[12] as the writer of *An Account of the Voyages . . . in the Southern Hemisphere,* the three-volume quarto that narrated Cook's first Pacific voyage (fig. 12.1). The book was known in some quarters as *Hawkesworth's Voyages*.[13] In 1777, Canon John Douglas (fig. 12.2) served as Cook's unacknowledged editor for *A Voyage towards the South Pole,* the two-volume quarto of the second Pacific voyage. It is likely that Anson served as Douglas's model for his persona of Cook. Cook was not the near aristocrat that Anson, "the younger son from a minor county family," actually was.[14] Douglas had to render Cook worthy of his discoveries and his predecessor's stature.

Because, as Jonathan Lamb has identified them, to "mak[e] the unfamiliar plausible" and to produce "probable narratives of Pacific discovery" were Cook's challenges, they became Douglas's. For explorers, many of the "anxieties and confusions" anticipated in the contact zone between peoples foreign to one another—that is, manifestations of "the principle of uncertainty"—had to be narratively countered if not entirely allayed.[15] Control had been lacking from Hawkesworth's liberal handling of the narrative of Cook's first voyage. In a letter to Douglas on January 10, 1776, Cook instructed his editor of the published account of the second voyage to render the "Amours of my People at Otaheite & other places . . . in such a manner as might be unexceptionable to the nicest readers."[16] Having, he thought in March 1775, "neither Natural, nor acquired abilities, for writing,"[17] Cook confided in a friend on June 22, 1776, that anything like the narrative "flourishes" in which Hawkesworth had indulged must be avoided.

12.1 *John Hawkesworth, L.L.D.*, 1776, after a portrait by Sir Joshua Reynolds. Mezzotint. A writer, poet, and playwright, in the 1750s Hawkesworth was a member of Samuel Johnson's literary circle, literary editor of the *Gentleman's Magazine,* and editor of the works of Jonathan Swift. The famed musician and historian Charles Burney recommended him as editor of the 1760s Pacific journals of John Byron, Philip Carteret, Samuel Wallis, and Cook. *An Account of the Voyages undertaken by the Order of His Present Majesty for making Discoveries in the Southern Hemisphere* was published in three volumes in 1773. It became a best seller, but Hawkesworth was attacked for excessive tampering with the captains' texts, for publishing descriptions of sexual freedom in the South Seas, and for challenging the doctrine of providential intervention. This vilification seemingly hastened his death within months of its publication. © National Portrait Gallery, London, 35615.

12.2 *The Right Reverend John Douglas D.D., Lord Bishop of Carlisle and Dean of Windsor*, 1790, after a portrait by William Beechey. Mezzotint. Educated at Oxford, ordained in 1747, and ultimately consecrated bishop of Salisbury, Douglas enjoyed the patronage of William Pulteney, first Earl of Bath, whose wealth and connections proved highly beneficial in political and literary circles. Well read in history and literature, he had earned a reputation as an incisive ecclesiastical polemicist and astute political commentator when chosen by the Earl of Sandwich to edit the journals of Cook's second and third voyages to the Pacific. His introduction to the latter drew wide European and American attention to the resources of the northwest Pacific coast. © National Portrait Gallery, London, 35372.

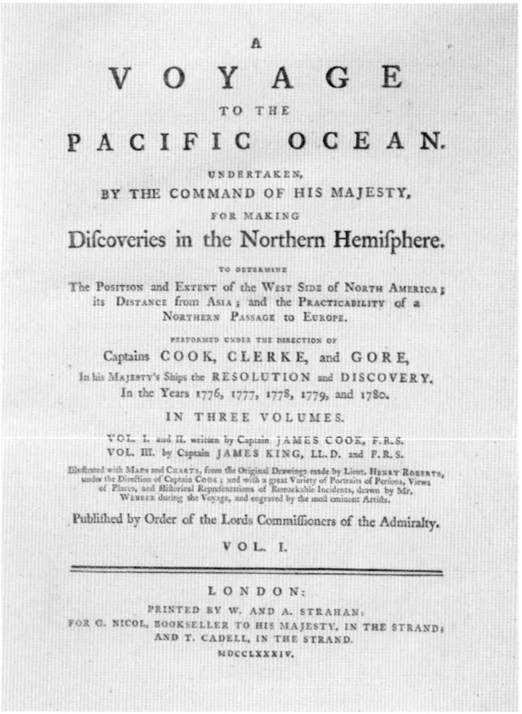
A

VOYAGE

TO THE

PACIFIC OCEAN.

UNDERTAKEN,

BY THE COMMAND OF HIS MAJESTY,

FOR MAKING

Difcoveries in the Northern Hemifphere.

TO DETERMINE

The Position and Extent of the West Side of North America; its Distance from Asia; and the Practicability of a Northern Passage to Europe.

PERFORMED UNDER THE DIRECTION OF

Captains COOK, CLERKE, and GORE,

In his Majesty's Ships the RESOLUTION and DISCOVERY.

In the Years 1776, 1777, 1778, 1779, and 1780.

IN THREE VOLUMES.

VOL. I. and II. written by Captain JAMES COOK, F.R.S.

VOL. III. by Captain JAMES KING, LL.D. and F.R.S.

Illuftrated with Maps and Charts, from the Original Drawings made by Lieut. Henry Roberts, under the Direction of Captain Cook; and with a great Variety of Portraits of Perfons, Views of Places, and Hiftorical Reprefentations of Remarkable Incidents, drawn by Mr. Webber during the Voyage, and engraved by the moft eminent Artifts.

Publifhed by Order of the Lords Commiffioners of the Admiralty.

VOL. I.

LONDON:

PRINTED BY W. AND A. STRAHAN:

FOR G. NICOL, BOOKSELLER TO HIS MAJESTY, IN THE STRAND; AND T. CADELL, IN THE STRAND.

MDCCLXXXIV.

12.3 Title page of *A Voyage to the Pacific Ocean . . . for making Discoveries in the Northern Hemisphere* (1784). The work was edited by John Douglas, canon of St. Paul's Cathedral. Douglas used the journals of William Anderson, surgeon on the *Resolution,* who died in August 1778 in the Bering Sea, to expand on Cook's accounts in the earlier part of the voyage and those of James King for an account of events after Cook's death. As was the custom with the names of silent editors or ghostwriters, Douglas's did not appear on the title page. Rasmuson Library, University of Alaska Fairbanks.

"The Journal . . . must speak for itself. I can only say that it is my own narrative, as it was written during the voyage."[18]

Douglas was bound to oblige Cook to a degree that had not interested Hawkesworth, fascinated as that author had been by the challenge of presenting the public with the "intractable novelty" of "unprecedented things" from the other side of the world in the first-person voice of a Cook whom he represented as the judicious, virtuous, well-mannered agent of "civilized" Britain.[19] Not until the last months of the second Pacific voyage—long after Hawkesworth's demise—did a copy of the ghostwriter's book find its way to Cook, so it cannot be said that he was responding to Hawkesworth's editing between July 1772 and July 1775, when, by Beaglehole's count, he wrote "a million words or so" in the "drafting and redrafting, expanding, abbreviating and recasting, correction, substitution, [and] interlineation" of his account of the second voyage.[20] He must have returned home thinking of himself more capable than at any earlier point of narrating his way round the world, even if he still did not consider himself an author: "An unliterary man he might be," concedes Beaglehole, before claiming too much: "but there was little the literary man could teach him about the conscientious shaping of a text."[21]

It was logical for Douglas, derided as "meddlesome" by Glyndwr Williams but regarded by Beaglehole as an "admirable editor indeed!," to repeat his role in the official narrative of the second Pacific expedition for the official narrative of the third. In the event, *A Voyage to the Pacific Ocean . . . for Making Discoveries in the Northern Hemisphere* comprised three volumes in quarto plus atlas (and engravings) folio (fig. 12.3).[22] It appeared "by Command of His Majesty" on June 14, 1784, three years and nine months after HMS *Resolution* and *Discovery* reached a dismayed England without their captains, James Cook and Charles Clerke. By June 17, all two thousand sets of the first edition had sold.[23]

Douglas faced a different challenge with the next narrative. By the time he launched his third voyage to the Pacific on July 12, 1776, Cook had become the agent of the European yearning to identify the South Pacific not only as the haunt of neoclassical longings for the exotic, earthly paradise, but also as the seat of Enlightenment reading of the vast book of nature.[24] To serve English high culture thus was challenging when the epoch's rationalist urges had also assigned one who "was not a savant of science" the role of geographical fact seeker par excellence.[25] This would surely have been a heavy mantle for Cook to bear when alive, as it was for his persona to bear in print thereafter. Daniel Clayton has helpfully placed on view Edmund Burke's remark that, although Lieutenant James King never spoke of Cook "but with respect and regret," he "lamented the Roughness of his manners and violence of his temper."[26] With the demise of the captain, Douglas had recourse to the journal of the twenty-eight-year-old King (fig.

12.4). Himself very well schooled, he could wield a finer pen than Cook, so his journal served well Douglas's occasional need to refine the persona of the captain with what Glyndwr Williams has called the lieutenant's own "busy editorial pen."[27] Moreover, King survived the expedition, and although he died on November 16, 1784, five months after *A Voyage to the Pacific Ocean* appeared, King had been able to draft the first version of the narrative's third volume. His "mildness gentleness and persuasion" of character informed his registration of the "facts"

12.4 John Webber, *James King,* 1782. Oil. In 1773, after eleven years in the navy and still only twenty-three years old, King was granted leave on half pay and studied in Paris; later he attended science lectures at Oxford, where he met Thomas Hornsby, Savilian Professor of Astronomy, who recommended him for Cook's upcoming voyage. He joined the *Resolution* as second lieutenant and "Nautical and Astronomical Observer." The astronomical observations by Cook, King, and William Bayly were published in 1782. After Cook's death, King wrote the final part of the narrative that formed volume 3 of the 1784 publication of *A Voyage to the Pacific Ocean.* National Library of Australia, 2292701.

12.5 *The Death of Captain Cook,* engraving after a painting by John Webber, 1784. Engraved by Francesco Bartolozzi and William Byrne; published by J. Webber and W. Byrne. Needless to say, the depiction of Cook's death demanded heroic dimensions. It had to show something grander than an intemperate skirmish in which Cook was but one casualty. Thus Cook is positioned in the center of the scene. His figure dominates by its height and the brighter light shone on it. By the gesture to his own men in a grand last effort of forbearance, even as he is about to be stabbed, it is also emphatically humane. The fact that he is upright rather than supine symbolizes his heroic stature at the moment of death. Dixson Library, State Library of New South Wales, DL Pf.61, #6914001.

12.6 Monument to Captain James Cook in Kealakekua Bay, Island of Hawai'i. This obelisk was erected in 1874 with the inscription: "In memory of the great circumnavigator Captain James Cook, R.N. who discovered these islands on the eighteenth of January, 1778, and fell near this spot on the 14th of February, 1779." In 1877, the land at the monument was ceded by the United States to Great Britain, and the British consul in Los Angeles is responsible for the maintenance of the site, which, fittingly, can be reached more easily by water than by land. Photo courtesy of James Barnett.

of the Pacific Northwest's peoples and geography.[28] This would have been all the more important to an editor determined to control a narrative whose readers obviously anticipated the violent death of the protagonist in Kealakekua Bay on February 14, 1779 (fig. 12.5).

DOUGLAS'S TASK

Looking down on a hitherto unknown group of people speaking a foreign language rendered them smaller than the agent of an eighteenth-century empire, smaller than life. It was much less the case that Europeans had never known of them or their lands than that the foreigners had never known Europeans. Of native Sandwich Islanders, who, long before the official account appeared, would have been known as murderers first and foremost and their land as the grave of Britain's hero (fig. 12.6), Douglas ascribed to Cook the observation that he had "never before met with the natives of any place so much astonished, as these people were, upon entering a ship. Their eyes were continually flying from object to object; the wildness of their looks and gestures fully expressing their ignorance about every thing they saw, and strongly marking to us, that, till now, they had never been visited by Europeans."[29] Mariners would descend to meet and trade with them; for their part, they would have to climb up from their watercraft to meet and trade with the visitors (fig. 7.2). The sense of superiority would have been difficult to ignore even if, defying Linnaeus, one resisted dividing humans into, on the one hand, varieties of *Homo sapiens* and, on the other, the catch-all taxon of *Homo monstrosus.* This stark division was one that Cook could not afford to ignore, but his acknowledgment of it also occasionally permitted him to overlook it. In taking increasing control of his own persona in his journals of exploration, he understood by the mid-1770s how to present himself in the Ansonian image, how to project pacific mercantilism as the diplomatic hallmark of his command, and how, despite this awareness, to give final-version authorship over to an editor rather than guard it jealously, even if doing so required his tacit surrender of the authority of the eyewitness.

Narratives of exploration comprised story, geographical intelligence, maps, lists, taxonomies, tables, appendixes, and illustrations; they both constructed and bore witness; they were published to sell as much as to testify, document, and memorialize.[30] They exerted control over the foreign from the point of view of a polished imperial agent.[31] Their publication effected geographical claims on territory. When, in early February 1778, Cook discovered Hawai'i by landing on the island of Kauai at Waimea, he took the surgeon and botanist William Anderson and the artist John Webber ashore with him: emphatically, Douglas had Cook state that "the former . . . was as well qualified to describe with the pen, as the latter was to represent with his pencil, *every thing* we might meet with worthy of observation."[32] The foray ashore would leave nothing unreported or untold: British modes of documenting and processing information could comprehend (that is, both encompass and understand) all there was to be observed. The idea that ways of seeing have blind spots occurs to few imperialists, for their understandable panoptic aim is survey. That the account of Cook's explorations of the Pacific Northwest succeeded news of his death only intensified the pressure on Douglas to shape the persona and first-person voice in a way that both exerted firm control and would be found "unexceptionable to the nicest readers." About the narrative of the second voyage, Douglas, "on Condition of Secrecy," had exerted the necessary order structurally, grammatically, and stylistically: "I did a great deal to ye Capt's Journal to correct its Stile; to new point [punctuate] it; to divide it into Sentences, & Paragraphs, & Chapters & Books. Tho little appears to be done by me, the Journal if printed as the Captain put it into my Hands, would have been thought too incorrect, & have disgusted the Reader."[33] Douglas would continue in the same vein and to at least the same extent in preparing the narrative of Cook's third voyage.[34] In the event, *A Voyage to the Pacific Ocean* proved a highly successful narrative. It singlehandedly publicized geographical intelligence in a story that rendered Pacific North America British. (An entire parcel of nineteenth-century tomes would be needed to put the same stamp on Arctic North America.)[35]

DEFINITIVELY NARRATING APPARENT LANDFALL ON THE PACIFIC NORTHWEST COAST

On Saturday, March 7, 1778, "the long-looked for coast of New Albion*" (North America) hove into view.[36] The Oregon coast, however, proved a chimera, looming in and out of "thick and hazy" weather, which included sleet.[37] It disappeared but "made its appearance" again; like a coy partner, it danced with *Resolution* and *Discovery*. Arising unforeseen, departing unbidden, it "veered" and "extended" as the ships "tacked and stretched," tacked and "stood off" in and through the mists, with no harbor offering itself up to the newcomers for over two weeks of "unsettled" wind and weather.[38] On March 22, in the midst of frustrating uncertainty, Cape Flattery received its name, and Cook chose that baptismal moment to cut through the fog of sea and journal to conclude categorically that there was no Strait of Juan de Fuca, "nor is there the least probability that iver any such thing exhisted" (fig. 12.7).[39] He did so just when the apparition of the cape that flattered him faded away, and with it the entrance to the fifteen-mile-wide strait between Vancouver Island and the Olympic Peninsula. For his part, Douglas trailed the captain word for word through the vaporous mists, failing in any literarily convincing sense to resolve the dichotomy between atmospheric uncertainty and thundering denunciation of theoretical cartography.[40]

In both journal and book, the narrative diverts

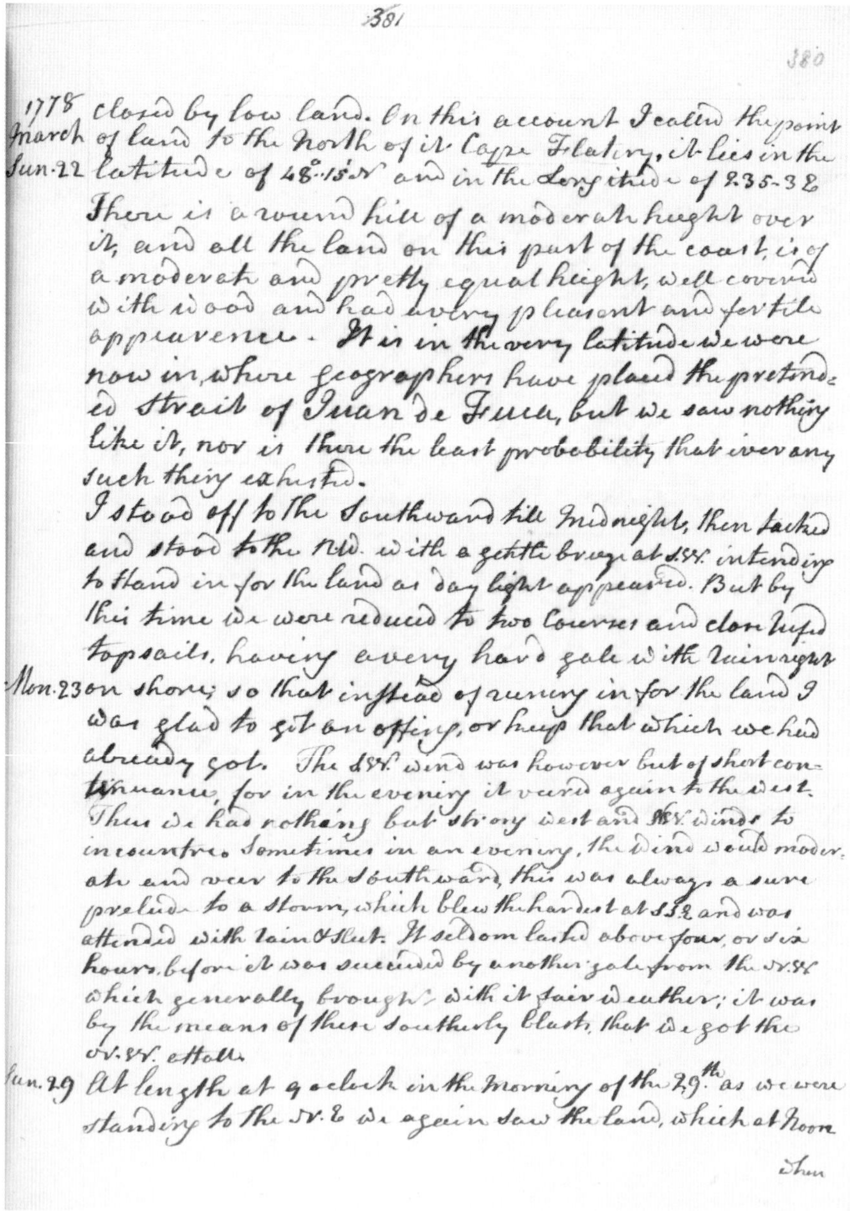

381

380

1778 March Sun.22 closed by low land. On this account I called the point of land to the North of it Cape Flattery, it lies in the latitude of 48°.15' N and in the longitude of 235.38 E
There is a round hill of a moderate height over it, and all the land on this part of the coast, is of a moderate and pretty equal height, well covered with wood and had every pleasant and fertile appearence. It is in this very latitude we were now in, where geographers have placed the pretended Strait of Juan de Fuca, but we saw nothing like it, nor is there the least probability that ever any such thing exhisted.
I stood off to the Southward till Midnight, then tacked and stood to the NW. with a gentle breeze at SW. intending to stand in for the land as day light appeared. But by this time we were reduced to two Courses and close reefed topsails, having every hard gale with rain right
Mon.23 on shore; so that instead of running in for the land I was glad to get an offing, or keep that which we had already got. The SW. wind was however but of short continuance, for in the evening it veered again to the West. Thus we had nothing but strong west and NW. winds to incounter. Sometimes in an evening, the wind would moderate and veer to the Southward, this was always a sure prelude to a Storm, which blew the hardest at SSE and was attended with rain & sleet. It seldom lasted above four, or six hours, before it was succeeded by another gale from the NW. which generally brought with it fair weather; it was by the means of these southerly blasts, that we got the NW. at all.
Sun.29 At length at 9 oclock in the Morning of the 29th. as we were standing to the NE we again saw the land, which at Noon
then

12.1 Extract from Cook's manuscript journal for March 22, 1778, in which he dismissively insists that, because he did not see "the pretended Strait of Juan de Fuca"—for reasons of storm and darkness, not because its entrance, at least, was not there—it therefore did not exist. © British Library Board, Egerton MS 2177A, p. 380.

attention from Cook's being duped or flattered—"there appeared to be a small opining in the land"—by dismissing "in the very latitude we were now in" the "geographers [who] have [there] placed the pretended *Strait of Juan de Fuca*."[41] The illustrious captain finds nothing, but, rather than leave himself bathetically with nothing to discover, he uncovers falsehood. It is a vivid exculpatory moment in *A Voyage to the Pacific Ocean:* nothing could be seen; ergo, nothing was there to see; ergo, sixteenth-century English speculator Michael Lok's claim was meretricious rather than meritorious, and Cook's contemporaries, such as Alexander Dalrymple, who had maintained the existence of the strait as credible, had misled the world.[42]

In both journal and book, the statement's use of litotes, a rhetorical device that emphasizes what it affirms by denying its opposite ("nor is there the least probability") might have vaguely reminded readers of a remark in *A Voyage towards the South Pole* (1777)—a book, it is worth remembering, that Cook himself never saw—to the effect that Douglas's Cook had traversed the southern Pacific Ocean "in a manner as to leave not the least room for the possibility of there being a continent, unless near the pole, and out of reach of navigation." It had "been a favourite theory amongst the geographers of all ages,"[43] not least Dalrymple, who fantasized that humans by the millions inhabited its 5,323 square miles.[44] Certain denunciation thereby renders secure the landfall of Douglas's downright emphatic Cook in northwestern North America.

The tale of establishing contact with the continent is devoid of uncertainty or anxiety; the act of not discovering a strait is clothed in confidence, assurance, control.[45]

NARRATIVELY MAPPING COMPLICATED COASTS UP TO ICY CAPE

Although one would be mistaken to treat the Pacific Northwest Coast as playing but a spectral, merely suggestive role in Cook's journal and Douglas's book, in both it appears as more mysterious than straightforward, its exploration more trial than achievement. All Douglas could do after this denunciation was what Cook had done: break off, begin a fresh paragraph, sail away from the scene of uncertain presence and allegedly certain absence. Thereby, the narrative preserves control over the unknown. As with his dismissal of a southern continent, so Cook achieved with resolution the discovery of absence on the Northwest coast. Thereafter, however, both journal and book produce further uncertainty by taking a week's lacunar leap, from March 23 to 29. By the latter date, according to Cook, "the Country had a very different appearence to what we had before seen." Syntax excepted, Douglas observed it identically: "the appearance of the country differed much from that of the parts which we had before seen."[46]

As the geography sharpens into focus, it also springs to life with the first people encountered since February 2, fifty-four days earlier, at Waimea. The crews must have been delighted, all the more because the Mowachaht of Nootka Sound were, at least initially, regarded as "mild inoffensive people."[47] Moreover, they were agreeable to Cook because they were traders of the first water. Here, the persona developed by Douglas feels as if it has again found terra firma. Douglas's Cook remarks that the hosts "behaved very peaceably, and could not be suspected of any hostile intention,"[48] but only after a lengthy greeting ceremony. At the point where the journal is altogether silent on the moment of contact, the book creates a grand stage for this reception, a stage on which roles are acted in both speech and song. The journalist concerned himself with locating a good anchorage (Ship Cove), but his published persona plays diplomat in act 1, scene 1 of twenty-nine days of ritual theater. Substance now seemed to take over: the mists rolled back, life gained focus with not only individual characters—one person "played the orator" while "others acted their part"—but also a confident assertion of comprehension.[49] Cook had arrived on the continent on whose shores he had last toiled ten years earlier.[50]

But this was hardly the South Seas, by the late 1770s "a receptacle" for what Jonathan Lamb calls "all that was most charming in the [European] imagination, and all that was conceivable for the perfection of society."[51] The Pacific Northwest coast was never a destination for the captain. It stood in his way to a theorized continental thoroughfare. A Northwest or Northeast Passage needed to be an absence, not a presence, of land and people, as it had throughout its imagined existence.[52] Whoever discovered it would launch Britain beyond whatever Spain and Portugal had managed to claim by sailing to and through Drake Passage and round the Horn. Six decades of a lucrative sea-otter trade notwithstanding, no one lusted after the Pacific Northwest any more than, except for the Grand Banks' treasure chest of fish, anyone lusted after Newfoundland. Fog and cold predominated. After Nootka, few individual Native personalities took the stage. No sustained time was shared with Native people; the plot did not thicken. The presence of Russians further compromised the setting's novelty. Moreover, because of ice, it risked being a dead, and deadly, end. So Cook's readers find themselves in rather cooler waters of ambition: like Cook, they are less delighted and more perplexed by what presents itself to him—a tortuous coastline and infuriatingly shallow coastal waters. Perfect for George Vancouver's tireless appetite for fact, this setting offered Cook less than the South Pacific in all respects. And yet he did some of his finest sailing in its waters and around its baffling, sublime outcroppings, exercising what Beaglehole calls his "professional devotion" to the process of reducing "hypothesis and myth or vagueness to facts."[53] He was, after all, Vancouver's mentor.

As Cook's stay at Nootka has received comparatively abundant discussion,[54] it may be of greater profit to cruise with him north, to his encounters with other coastal phenomena and peoples. Rough weather precluded his detailed inspection of the coast on April 30 at 53°N, that is, near "the place where Geographers have placed the pretended Strait of Admiral de Fonte." In his journal, Cook expressed regret at being unable conclusively to refute "such vague and improbable stories, that carry their own confutation along with them."[55] Such decisive remarks suit Douglas's Cook; the editor merely repeats them.[56] The same seems to be the case one month later. On June 1, after completing his search north and east up what he called Turnagain River (Cook Inlet), Cook wrote that he "had traced it . . . 70 leagues or more from its intrance without seeing the least appearance of its Source."[57] Douglas trims his sails identically, retaining the superlative—"without seeing the least appearance"—and continues on Cook's tack:

> If the discovery of this great river*, which promises to vie with the most considerable ones already known to be capable of extensive inland navigation, should prove of use either to the present, or to any future age, the time we spent in it ought to be the less regretted. But to us, who had a much greater object in view, the delay thus occasioned was an essential loss. The season was advancing apace. We knew not how far we might have to proceed to the South; and we were now convinced, that the continent of North America extended farther to the West, than, from the modern most reputable charts, we had reason to expect. This made the

existence of a passage into Baffin's or Hudson's Bays less probable; or, at least, shewed it to be of greater extent.

*Captain Cook having here left a blank which he had not filled up with any particular name, Lord Sandwich directed, with the greatest propriety, that it should be called *Cook's River*.[58]

Douglas simply repeats this crucial statement from the journal even though the sentence structure and even the logic produce an awkward chop. Cook set his course with what Beaglehole calls "seriousness, simple integrity, a perfectly unassuming and primary wish to tell the truth."[59] And Douglas follows him often, even occasionally unto stylistic awkwardness.

Every so often, however, the editor diverges from the journal to lower the boom on theoretical cartographers, as on June 1: "It was a satisfaction to me, however, to reflect, that, if I had not examined this very considerable inlet, it would have been assumed, by speculative fabricators of geography, as a fact, that it communicated with the sea to the North, or with Baffin's or Hudson's Bay to the East; and been marked, perhaps, on future maps of the world, with greater precision, and more certain signs of reality, than the invisible, because imaginary, Straits of de Fuca, and de Fonte."[60]

Perhaps he was motivated by speculations bruited between the time of the expedition's return to Britain and his edition's appearance, but Douglas evidently determined to throttle any inclination to expand Cook's estuary (renamed an inlet by Vancouver in 1794) into a strait. He did so, however, in a way that taunted the speculators, and this extension seems unwarranted. Cook might have been declarative and assured, but he rarely employed irony to the degree evinced in this passage, however implicit. Similarly, Cook seldom drew attention to himself in the way that the phrase "it was a satisfaction to me" does in order to provide context for the subsequent rapier's worth of wit. The complex construction "invisible, because imaginary, Straits" also refines the irony by having the otherwise straightforward statement suspend its completion with parenthesis. Such suspension dramatically underscores the irony of the remark because it introduces both delay in the completion of the principal clause ("than the invisible Straits of de Fuca, and de Fonte"), and it occasions the presentation of the proof ("because imaginary") of the refutation. It is as if the persona of Cook were simultaneously authoring his narrative and anticipating the pleasure it would give its reader by conjuring up fanciful straits and passages only to expunge them from the map in a consummately declarative and fatal parry. This rhetorical flourish, it need hardly be added, formed part of the Cook persona for nearly two centuries, the interval between the publication of Douglas's book and of Beaglehole's vast edition of Cook's journals.[61]

Of the people (Chugach) whom he met and with whom he traded in May while exploring Prince William Sound, Cook wrote that he had "nowhere seen Indians that take more pains to ornament, or rather disfigure themselves."[62] He refers to piercings of the septum ("cartilage that divides the nostrils from each other"), the rim of the ears, the lips, and the upper chin (figs. 8.3, 8.4, and 9.2). Douglas's Cook finds the effect "truly grotesque" and "unsightly" but fails to repeat Cook's comparison between Chugach ornamentation and that of other peoples.[63] He also ignores Cook's disqualification of himself as a judge of how nearly Chugach resemble Greenlandic Inughuit. While he retains Cook's mention of his source (David Crantz's *History of Greenland,* first published in English in 1767) and notes much later in the summer that "one or two on board . . . had been in Greenland,"[64] he does not repeat in any form Cook's self-deprecation: "But as I never saw either a Greenlander or an Esquemaus, who are said to be of the same nation, I cannot be a sufficient judge and as we may very probably see more of them I shall reserve the discussion of this point to some other time."[65] Douglas's Cook modifies or qualifies an observation, remark, or judgment less often than the explorer-journalist.

Watching out at all times for shoals on which Cook might founder, Douglas forbears inclusion of the stereotypical representation of Russians as sharp traders in the explorer's assertion that Russians "were never amongst these people"[66] of Cook Inlet and Prince William Sound, "for if they did they would hardly be clothed in such valuable skins as those of the Sea beaver; the Russians would find some means or other to get them all from them."[67] Instead, Douglas deploys only implication: "for if that had been the case [that is, had Russians had contact with these people], we should hardly have found them clothed in such valuable skins as those of the sea-otter."[68] But when Cook rises to the occasion by scaling the narrative heights decreed by Douglas as apposite, the canon leaves him alone. In 1778, Cook opined that "unless a northern passage is found," the northern Pacific Northwest coast "seems rather too remote for Great Britain to receive any emolument from it."[69] Despite evidence to the contrary by 1784, Douglas evidently concurred; sticking by his captain, he has him muse, "unless a Northern passage should be found practicable, it seems rather too remote for Great Britain to receive any emolument from it."[70] The subordinate clause of the syntax and Cook's diction appeal to Douglas in this case. Cook sounds more authoritative than speculative, so Douglas presents him in his own words, merely heightening Cook's discernment in requiring that a Northwest Passage be "practicable."[71]

When the expedition stood off Unga Cape on June 19 after exhausting Cook Inlet, and days before discovering the way offered by Unimak Pass through the easternmost of the Aleutian Islands to what Cook named Bristol Bay, Charles Clerke, commander of the *Discovery,* showed Cook a note in Russian delivered by native canoes. The account of it receives interesting handling by Douglas:

> No one on board her [*Discovery*] had any suspicion that the box contained any thing till after the departure of the canoes, when it was accidentally opened, and a piece of paper was found, folded up carefully, upon which something was written in the Russian language, as was supposed. . . . Not learned enough to decypher the alphabet of the writer, his numerals marked sufficiently that others had preceded us in visiting this dreary part of the globe, who were united to us by other ties besides those of our common nature; and the hopes of soon meeting with some of the Russian traders, could not but give a sensible satisfaction to those who had, for such a length of time, been conversant with the savages of the Pacific Ocean, and of the continent of North America.[72]

By contrast, Cook had reported in his journal that "no one on board either ship could read it [Russian]." The active verb "could read" plays truthfully up against Douglas's demurral in the passive voice, "as was supposed," which steers attention away from the expedition members' ignorance of Russian to the implicit lack of clarity in the "something" that was written on the paper.[73] The implication of Cook's or the Admiralty's negligence in failing to supply the expedition with someone fluent in Russian is thereby averted. After all, the note's writer, far from being a naval commander, was likely to be a mere "Furrier," and a foreigner at that, worthy of little notice by Douglas's Cook.[74] So Douglas transfers the deficiency to the prose and its author by means of an agent-absent dangling construction: "Not learned enough to decypher the alphabet of the writer, his numerals . . ." This deferral possibly even prompts the reader to infer that the document's poor author, not its ignorant reader, is insufficiently learned.[75] A different pair of peoples—both Caucasian—meet in this narrative contact zone, but Douglas subtly registers the same sort of inequality of stature that is present in accounts of Native and newcomer contact.

Meanwhile, Cook the journalist mentions a preoccupation that Douglas excludes: the unpublished captain, rather than be detained by inquiring further into the matter, is keen to persevere while the wind remains favorable and so to endeavor to understand better why a coast that ought to be trending north to Bering Strait keeps running southwest (fig. 11.10). By contrast, Douglas's captain ignores the mariner's interests in order to dwell on those of the merchant in search of further intelligence about possibilities for trade, and subsequently he turns Clerke into a sentimental traveler—"impressed with humane sentiments, on such an occasion"—who worries that the note might have come from some shipwrecked Russians in need of rescue.[76] As a foil to the unfleeceable captain, his inferior officer provides no match.

Douglas continues to tidy and dignify his captain on the journey up the Pacific coast. When, on June 21, some of the crew catch halibut ranging in weight from twenty to one hundred pounds, Cook describes them as "a very great refreshing to us," but to the composed, published captain, they amount modestly to "a very seasonable refreshment to us."[77] By contrast, Douglas does not edit out Cook's allowance for the possibility that mispronunciation explains why a man met on June 21 does not understand what is said to him by Britons using words learned from Natives they met in Prince William Sound: "perhaps this might be owing to our not pronu[n]cing them properly," Cook's journal reads. "But, perhaps, our faulty pronunciation, rather than his ignorance of the dialect, may be inferred from this," is the book's rendering.[78] Although one can imagine Douglas muttering under the felt obligation to include this qualification, he nevertheless produces it, but he does so through a pronounced aporia (suggestion without commitment) by gilding the lily of "perhaps" with the equivocation "may be inferred."

Douglas does remain faithful to the little credit that Cook pays God for incidents of good fortune. Navigation without incident through fog and low early-morning light to a secure mooring seemed nearly a miracle to Cook on June 26. When conditions improved, he and Clerke found themselves between Sedanka Island's Outer Signal and Inner Signal rocks. "There were several breakers about them," wrote Cook, "and yet Providence had conducted us through between these rocks where I should not have ventured in a clear day, and to such an anchoring place that I could not have chosen a better." Douglas repeats even Cook's syntax and turn of phrase.[79] Perhaps his fidelity to the original issued from the canon's belief that oaths of thanksgiving and witness deserved faithful quotation.

Bristol Bay, the next sector of this vast coastal rock garden, now frustrated the navigator and editor both. Wanting clear sailing north, Cook kept raising only land in that direction. He spent much of July baffled both navigationally and geographically. The frustration of the same observations awaited him off the Seward Peninsula, which he did not reach until the first days of August. Given that a gelid sea rebuffed him at Icy Cape, the expedition's farthest point, on August 18 (as it would rebuff the two ships again on July 9, 1779), one can gather just how quickly Cook sailed in the first half of the last dependable month of summer. On August 10, he met Chukchi (or Siberian Yup'ik) on their eponymous Asian peninsula (figs. 12.8 and 4.4). Douglas's rendering of Cook's summary assessment of them follows the explorer's wording closely. That a Yorkshireman states so flatly his surprise that people can live in more than primitive circumstances at 65°N is itself notable, given that it is about the latitude of Reykjavik, Iceland, well known to late eighteenth-century sailors and whalers from the northern parts of Britain: "Several other things, and, in particular, their clothing, shewed that they were possessed of a degree of ingenuity, far surpassing what one could expect to find amongst so Northern a people." It read similarly in Cook's fist.[80] Snow had lately "fell" in the journal, "fallen" in the book. The brightness seen on the horizon at noon on August 17 denotes the same "blink," "Gloomyness"/"gloominess" of the preceding days' weather; incidental commas alone distinguish the versions. At the geographical northeastern limit of the voyage's explorations, both the journal and book spend August 19 on an interlude about walruses, and those aboard who had been to Greenland assure Cook that "no one ever eat of Sea horses" (Douglas's "sea-horses"). These, the unpublished and published captain both think, because of the "snout," resemble less the horse than the sea cow, as Cook knows the latter to be called over on the Atlantic Ocean's Gulf of St. Lawrence (figs. 12.9 and 12.10).[81] When it comes to the probability of there being a permanent ice pack—"that there is always a remaining store, none who has been upon the spot will deny and none but Closet studdying Philosiphers will dispute"—Douglas attempts an improvement on the fine balance of Cook's syntax. However, if it does anything, the alteration weakens the sentence by robbing it of the repetition ("none") as he shifts from a declarative to a negative: "But that there is always a remaining store, every one who has been upon the spot will conclude, and none but closet-studying philosophers will dispute."[82]

NARRATIVELY MAPPING COMPLICATED COASTS DOWN FROM ICY CAPE

Douglas follows Cook in not thinking "it consistent with prudence to make any farther attempts to find a passage" in 1778.[83] Upon his turning back to the Asian coast, Cook and his editor regard Gerhard Friedrich Müller's knowledge of it from Vitus Bering's voyage as "very imperfect."[84] Moreover, where passages from Cook's daily log offer greater drama, color, or decisiveness than his retrospective journal, Douglas remains aboard the more staid journal. In the versions for August 18, for example, Cook's *log* best dramatizes the crisis of a narrowing breadth of sea between the ice and Icy Cape (fig. 2.7), akin to the dilemma with which the Great Barrier Reef had confronted him at the beginning of the decade

12.8 John Webber, *Two Chukchi*, August 1778. Pencil sketch. Summer huts are depicted to the right of the two principal figures armed with bows and arrows, one also carrying a spear. A third figure, seen from the back, carries a quiver slung across his back. The quivers are of interest because a fine example survives in the collection of the Museum of Archaeology and Anthropology, Cambridge, UK. Cook described the Chukchi huts as "pretty large, and circular . . . covered with the skins of sea animals." A more permanent, semisunken winter habitation (left background), covered with sod and soil, was similar to those the explorers had seen in Unalaska. © British Library Board, MS 15514, fol. 16.

12.9 John Webber, *Shooting Sea Horses on an Ice Flow,* field sketch, August 1778. Pencil, pen, charcoal, and wash. This drawing records one of a series of encounters with walruses that fascinated the explorers and merited substantial discussion in the journals about the quality of their meat for eating. Cook suggested that it was preferable to preserved, salted meat. The sketch suggests that Webber went out in the *Resolution*'s launch to witness the slaughter. Nine walruses were dragged on board the *Resolution* for food, oil, and the use of their thick hides "about our rigging" (Cook, *Voyage of the* Resolution *and* Discovery, 420). Library and Archives Canada, MK 2909378.

12.10 John Webber, *Sea Horses,* circa 1781–83. Pen, wash, and watercolor, prepared by Webber for the engraver. The subsequent engraving was published as plate 52 in the official Admiralty account of Cook's last expedition, *A Voyage to the Pacific Ocean* (1784). The artist worked on a number of similar paintings of this event, including a large oil on canvas exhibited that same year at the Royal Academy. Dixson Library, State Library of New South Wales, PXX 2.32.

off Cape Tribulation (June 11–18, 1770): "We found that the Ice had drifted near five leagues from half past two AM to noon. This was what I expected and most feared, and was not a little alarming, for we must inevitably be forced ashore, if we could not get without the Ice, and we had but a bad prospect as the wind was right in our teeth; the only chance we had was the ice taking the ground before us, for we had no reason to expect a harbour on so flat and shallow a coast as this."[85]

In another instance, when Cook meets an Iñupiaq on September 10 off Cape Denbigh, the southern limit of Norton Bay in uppermost Norton Sound (fig. 12.11), he does not repeat in his journal the log's detail that the man gave him "three red foxes skins that were sewed together, so as to make a kind of dress" in return for "a knife and a few Beads with which he seemed well pleased." Because Douglas does not dig this detail out of the log, the fact of the *exchange* of gifts remains in only that version; the latter versions describe only the bestowal of a gift by the newcomer on the well-pleased native.[86] Nor does the book lift from the log the categorical statement that Cook wrote when at the mouth of Koyuk River on September 19: "in all these Northern parts we have not found such a thing as a harbour, or even a well sheltered bay."[87] Douglas remains faithful to the extent that he works almost entirely with his chosen base text—Cook's retrospective journal—despite the multiple manuscripts available to him written in the navigator's hand.

Why the Chukchi do not come to trade with Cook's ships on September 3 baffles the explorer, who found the disinclination "a little extraordinary as the Weather was favourable enough and those we had visited had no reason that I know of to des-like our company." If anything, Douglas's addition of a pair of commas around the subordinate clause keeps his navigator even more emphatically in irons: the absence of traders "seemed a little extraordinary, as the weather was favourable enough; and those whom we had lately visited had no reason, that I know of, to dislike our company."[88] This marks as good a demonstration as any that Douglas's version often differs from the captain's only to an extent similar to the difference between John Webber's dozens

12.11 John Webber, *Inhabitants of Norton Sound and their Habitations*, circa 1781–83. Pen, wash, and watercolor. Although the expedition spent the best part of ten days in Norton Sound, only one scene captured by Webber has survived. The initial watercolor sketch he made in September 1778 was later recreated in this second painting as the basis for the engraving that appeared in 1784 as plate 54 in the portfolio published with *A Voyage to the Pacific Ocean.* Dixson Library, State Library of New South Wales, PXX.2.33.

of drawings and the published engravings of them by "the most eminent Artists," as the title page of *A Voyage to the Pacific Ocean* puts it.[89] As the regularized engravings catch the English eye more consistently than do the sketches, so the punctuation and syntax provided by Douglas catch the English ear.[90] Some of the substantive differences that one finds in the journal and book versions of the twenty-nine days spent off Yuquot, Nootka Sound, are not so apparent in the narrative accounts for the succeeding months. It would appear that Douglas thought of himself chiefly as tidying, not as altering.

Still, tidying could occasionally extend to substantive revision, by both deletion and addition. Douglas will not permit his Cook to go as far as the captain himself does in his description of one of the people, probably an Iñupiaq, with whom he traded four knives "made out of an old iron hoop" for four hundred pounds of char and whitefish on September 13 in Norton Bay. Both the journal and the book cast the man as "the most deformed cripple I either ever saw or heard of"/"had ever seen or heard of," but Douglas omits Cook's further remark, "so much so that I could not even bear to look at him: this state he seemed to have been in from his birth."[91] And when Cook satisfies himself in mid-September that he has exhausted the possible reasons for crediting as accurate the map of Jacob von Staehlin (see fig. 2.6), whose island of "Alascha," imposed off the Chukotkan coast of Asia, bemused Cook for many weeks until he discovered the Koyuk River, Douglas does not resist heaping greater scorn on the German polymath: there is no warrant in the journal for the published Cook's "having restored the American continent to that space which he [Staehlin] had occupied with his imaginary island of Alaschka."[92] But when Cook reaches the height of his vilification, although Douglas follows him, only the book takes the precaution of both quoting and, in a footnote, citing page 15 of Staehlin's *Account of the New Northern Archipelago* when repeating Cook's reference to the claim that Staehlin furnishes "*a very accurate little map.*"[93] Finally, in the report on August 3 of the death of William Anderson, the surgeon aboard the *Resolution,* Douglas uses Cook's wording as far as it extends, but there is no warrant in the journal for this sentence in the book: "The reader of this Journal will have observed how useful an assistant I had found him in the course of the voyage."[94] Meanwhile, this sentence's exact identification of the text of *A Voyage to the Pacific Ocean* as Cook's own journal insists that the posthumously published book is utterly Cook's work.

In another case of addition, one that Glyndwr Williams has discussed,[95] Douglas makes his Cook more clever by having him sort out the geography of northeasternmost Asia and northwesternmost North America on his way through Bering Strait *to* Icy Cape rather than on his way back *from* the cape. On September 1, Cook the journalist wrote only that he "was now well assured that this was the Coast of Tchuktschi, or the NE Coast of Asia." Douglas's Cook, by contrast, supposed as much all along, for he was "now well assured, of what I had believed before, that this was the country of the Tschutski, or the North East coast of Asia."[96]

In his journal, Cook indulged in a digression that is part encomium of Vitus Bering, part political speculation. Douglas renders the prose more diplomatically. It follows the journal's declaration that "its probable the Russians would never have thought of making further discover[ie]s on the America Coast, as indeed Goverment did not for what has been sence done, has been by traders," but it renders the declaration in a more politic, polished phrasing that would have disgusted no readers: "Indeed, after his [Bering's] time, government seems to have paid less attention to this; and we owe what discoveries have been since made, principally to the enterprising spirit of private traders, encouraged, however, by the superintending care of the Court of Petersburg."[97]

When Cook meets the fur-trade factor Gerasim Grigoriev Izmailov on October 14 at Unalaska, the narratives of both journal and book concentrate on geographical and cartographical questions, implicitly downplaying the captain's inveterate mercantile interests. Russian-Alaskan cuisine suits Cook and Douglas's Cook all but identically: "I have eat whale's flesh of their dressing [cooking], which I thought very good; and they made a kind of pan-pudding of salmon roe, beaten up fine, and fried, that is no bad *succedaneum* for bread." But Douglas demurs when Cook writes of the Russians' "purpose of furing"; "collecting furs" is the editor's choice.[98]

How then does the tidying by Douglas remain faithful to Cook's journal? Both versions speak of the Unangax̂ as being under "great subjection" by the Russians, as being "the most peaceable inoffensive people," and as dwelling in the "greatest harmony" with the Russians. Unangax̂ mats and grass baskets are "beautiful and strong" in both journal and book; indeed, all the women's manufactures, in faulty parallelism, "neither want for engenuity nor perseverance." Both the unpublished and published Cook swear that the Unangax̂ "canoe" can "go at a great rate and in a direction as streight as a line can be drawn." Both the unpublished and published urine trough in the middle of the typical Unangax̂ house emit "a stench," which is not a bit "mended" by the leather hides steeped in it. Both Cooks wonder why there are no penguins on the coast of North America, and both note that the "chatterer" (magpie) abounds. Cook wonders in both journal and book, "May not Nature have denied to some soil the power of raising trees without the assistance of art?" and implies lassitude in both: "And the Soil in many parts [places] seemed Capable of producing grain, roots and vegetables but at present, Russians as well as Indians seem satisfied with what nature brings forth." Having seen no one who appeared as old as sixty, both Cooks conclude that "probably thier hard way of living may be the means of shortening thier days." Only in Cook's geographical conclusion, based on ethnicity, does Douglas step in to provide some slight clarification. Where Cook wrote that "there is great reason to believe that all these nations are of the same extraction, and if so there can be little doubt but there is a northern communication of some sort by sea between this Ocean and Baffins bay, but it may be effectually shut up against Shipping, by ice and other impediments, such at least was my opinion at this time," Douglas provides his reader with a more secure geographical orientation: "A Northern communication of some sort, by sea, between this West side of America and the East side, through Baffin's Bay; which communication, however, may be effectually shut up against ships, by ice, and other impediments. Such, at least, was my opinion at this time."[99]

VOYAGING POSTHUMOUSLY INTO PRINT

At Petropavlovsk in May 1779, Clerke entrusted Cook's journal to Magnus von Behm, governor of Kamchatka (fig. 4.5).[100] Behm delivered it to St. Petersburg. On January 10, 1780, about equidistant in time between the navigator's death in Kealakekua Bay and the reappearance of the *Resolution* and *Discovery* in the Thames, the Admiralty opened it.[101] Although the nation was spending most of its international attention on the revolution of thirteen of its North American colonies, the British Enlightenment quickly fastened on the figure of a deceased Cook, who would be made to vindicate its humanist values and imperial ambitions. As he had penetrated the latitudes and longitudes of the entire world, the mortal and temporal realm seemed insufficiently ample to be worthy of him (fig. 12.12).

The burden of literary expectation placed by Enlightenment readers on explorers, whose writing skills were not what qualified them for expeditions of geographical exploration, should not be underestimated. In about 1814, Sir Walter Scott, recollecting a conversation with the explorer Mungo Park in 1804, wrote that Park "freely mentioned many singular anecdotes and particulars" that did not find their way into *Travels in the Interior Districts of Africa* (1799), because Park "scrupled to admit [them] to the jealous eye of the critical public."[102] Park self-censored his narrative as well as submitting it to others (including Bryan Edwards, secretary to the African Association) so that it could be readied for publication.[103] Glyndwr Williams has argued that the same had been true of Cook. Picking up on Beaglehole's description of Cook's journal as a remorseless compression of the ship's log, he writes of Cook's self-censure as he converted entries for his ship's "log and proceedings" to a journal.[104] The Arctic explorer Samuel Hearne went to his grave in November 1792 without hazarding the publication of a narrative of his pedestrian journeys in the early 1770s. Although Douglas quotes Hearne in his introduction to *A Voyage to the Pacific Ocean,* Hearne's *Journey . . . to the Northern Ocean* did not appear until 1795.[105] George Vancouver was in his grave in mid-May 1798 before his brother John could get *A Voyage of Discovery to the North Pacific Ocean* published (it appeared later that year). Alexander Mackenzie, who reached Dean Channel, fifty kilometers (thirty-one miles) west of Bella Coola,

British Columbia, on July 22, 1793, forty-seven days after Vancouver had charted and named it (fig. 10.7), had his *Voyages from Montreal* published in 1801 with the help of the writer William Combe. Its introduction included a familiar rhetorical device—*atechnos*—to deter readers from assigning blame or even suspicion to the narrative and its author: "When, at length, the opportunity arrived, the apprehension of presenting myself to the Public in the character of an Author, for which the course and occupations of my life have by no means qualified me, made me hesitate in committing my papers to the Press; being much better calculated to perform the voyages, arduous as they might be, than to write an account of them. However, they are now offered to the Public with the submission that becomes me."[106]

It may be that, accustomed as twenty-first-century readers are to professional travel writing, we underestimate how intimidating venturing into print might have seemed to a nonauthor in an age

12.12 *The Apotheosis of Captain Cook,* 1794. Engraving from an earlier design by Philippe de Loutherbourg, with landscape reference to John Webber. Because Cook was long dead by the time his ships arrived home, the work of immortalizing him was already well under way when *A Voyage to the Pacific Ocean* appeared in 1784. This image, bestowing divinity, was lowered as the final curtain for Loutherbourg's 1785 pantomime *Omai, or, a Trip around the World.* Particularly noteworthy is its exaltation of Cook by the transformation of smoke at the scene of the crime into clouds of glory in the heavens above. Still in his naval attire, Cook holds his sextant rather than his rifle or sword, and it correlates with the angel's trumpet. His next grand achievement, this symbolism suggests, will be charting the firmament. National Library of Australia, 7678295–1.

of ultra-critical readers. Even the well-educated Park felt terribly alone as he composed for an expectant public. How could a narrative rise to the occasion, given the press reports of exotic peregrinations? There is evidence on both sides of the argument that Cook came nearer in the journal of his third voyage than he had previously to sounding like an author. J. C. Beaglehole averred that in his journal of the third Pacific voyage, by contrast to those of the first and second voyages, "Cook set out deliberately to write a book," if only in order, upon his return to England, not "to be faced again by the labours that afflicted him after his second voyage in producing something that the ordinary man could read."[107] Probably *A Voyage to the Pacific Ocean* gives its reader more of Cook than do *An Account of the Voyages . . . in the Southern Hemisphere* and *A Voyage towards the South Pole,* but the publication in 1967 of Cook's own journal of the third voyage revealed the extent of Douglas's toil to turn the captain of an Alaskan cruise from something he was—a writer of a six-hundred-page journal—into something he was not—an author of an official narrative that enjoyed nearly two hundred years of uncontested authority.

NOTES

1 J. C. Beaglehole, *Cook the Writer: The Sixth George Arnold Wood Memorial Lecture* (Sydney: Sydney University Press, 1970), 6. Thirteen years earlier, after the appearance of the first volume of his edition of Cook's journals for the Hakluyt Society, Beaglehole wrote that he "would not call [Cook] a conscious literary artist" (J. C. Beaglehole, "Some Problems of Editing Cook's Journals," *Historical Studies: Australia and New Zealand* 8, no. 29 [November 1957]: 22.)

2 Although this manner of defining Cook in negatives initially seemed an original and efficient means of encircling the vast historicized character of the man, readers of J. C. Beaglehole, *The Life of Captain James Cook* (London: Hakluyt Society, 1974) will know that it is indebted, like so much of Cook studies, to Beaglehole, himself a sophisticated stylist (698). The quotation is from page 702 and is repeated on 703.

3 Beaglehole, *Life,* 713.

4 John Robson, ed., *The Captain Cook Encyclopaedia* (London: Chatham, 2004), 19.

5 Beaglehole, *Cook the Writer,* 8.

6 This assertion does not mean that Cook did not *aim* to be an author. During his third voyage, he must have had in mind a book rather than a report to the Admiralty, for he wrote up his journal in civil, not nautical, time. The latter marks the noon hour rather than midnight as the beginning of a day. See Beaglehole, *Cook the Writer,* 14. I thank Glyndwr Williams for this point.

7 For a colorful recent version of Cook and the reprise in 2001 of his Pacific voyages, see Tony Horwitz, "A Week before the Mast: Hooked on Cook," *New Yorker,* July 22, 2002, 42–55.

8 Glyndwr Williams, *The Prize of All the Oceans: The Triumph and Tragedy of Anson's Voyage round the World* (London: HarperCollins, 1999), 216.

9 *Universal Spectator* (London), 25 August 1744, reprinted in *Documents Relating to Anson's Voyage round the World, 1740–1744,* ed. Glyndwr Williams (London: Navy Records Society, 1967), 242; quoted in Glyndwr Williams, "George Anson's *Voyage round the World,*" *Princeton University Library Chronicle* 54, no. 2 (Winter 2003): 296.

10 *A Voyage Round the World, in the Years MDCCXL, I, II, III, IV. By George Anson, Esq; Commander in Chief of a Squadron of His Majesty's Ships, sent upon an Expedition to the South-Seas. Compiled from Papers and other Materials of the Right Honourable George Lord Anson, and published under his Direction. By Richard Walter, M. A. Chaplain of his Majesty's Ship the* Centurion, *in that Expedition* (London: John and Paul Knapton, 1748).

11 The relation between the actual voyage and its subsequent narrative, often titled *Voyage,* and other aspects of the genre are treated in I. S. MacLaren, "In Consideration of the Evolution of Explorers and Travellers into Authors: A Model," *Studies in Travel Writing* 15, no. 3 (September 2011): 221–41. The question of the involvement by Benjamin Robins, not just Richard Walter, in the writing of Anson's book is treated in Williams, "George Anson's *Voyage,*" 303–8.

12 Helen Wallis, "Publication of Cook's Journals: Some New Sources and Assessments," *Pacific Studies* 1, no. 2 (Spring 1978): 165.

13 "Paradoxically," notes Wallis, "Hawkesworth's literary reputation, which had been the equal almost of Dr. Johnson's, was destroyed by the book which also preserved his name for posterity" (ibid., 173.)

14 Williams, *The Prize of All the Oceans,* 9.

15 Jonathan Lamb, "Introduction," in *The South Pacific in the Eighteenth Century: Narratives and Myths; Papers from the Ninth David Nichol Smith Memorial Seminar,* ed. Jonathan Lamb, Robert P. Maccubbin, and David F. Morrill, special issue of *Eighteenth-Century Life* 18, no. 3 (November 1994): 5, 4, 1, and 2, respectively. Concerning Cook's uncertainty and anxiety, for a less problematical interpretation than Lamb's, namely that Cook denies the novelty of the unknown by interpreting the new in terms of the familiar, see Nathalie Zimpfer, "Domestication de l'autre et création de soi: *The Voyage of the* Resolution *and* Adventure, *1772–1775,* by Captain James Cook," in *De Drake à Chatwin: Rhétorique de la découverte,* ed. Frédéric Regard (Lyon: ENS, 2007), 99 ff.

16 James Cook to John Douglas, 10 January 1776, British Library, Egerton MS 2180; quoted in Beaglehole, *Life,* 464; quoted in part by Lynne Withey, *Voyages of Discovery: Captain Cook and the Exploration of the Pacific* (New York: William Morrow, 1987), 311.

17 Cook, "Explanation," March 22, 1775; National Archives, UK, ADM 55/108. This remark was excised from the passage by the time that it appeared as the last paragraph of Douglas's general introduction in *A Voyage towards the South Pole, and round the World. Performed in His Majesty's Ships the* Resolution *and* Adventure, *in the Years 1772, 1773, 1774, and 1775. Written by James Cook, Commander of the Resolution . . . ,* 2 vols., ed. John Douglas (London: W. Strahan and T. Cadell, 1777), 1:xxxvi. Confessing that "one sighs in vain for" the very first draft of this note, Beaglehole quotes the 1775 version in *The Journals of Captain James Cook on His Voyages of Discovery,* vol. 2, *The Voyage of the* Resolution *and* Adventure, *1772–1775,* ed. J. C. Beaglehole (Cambridge: Cambridge University Press for the Hakluyt Society, 1961), cxxvii (hereafter [Cook], *Voyage of the* Resolution *and* Adventure); and so does Wallis, "Publication," 175. Beaglehole also quotes the subsequent version in [Cook], *The Voyage of the* Resolution *and* Adventure, 2, and in *Life,* 471.

18 James Cook to William Wilson, June 22, 1776, quoted in George Young, *Life and Voyages of Captain James Cook* (London: Whittaker, Treacher, 1836), 305; quoted in [Cook], *Voyage of the* Resolution *and* Adventure, cxliii.

19 The challenge for Hawkesworth has received fine identification and analysis by Jonathan Lamb, "Circumstances Surrounding the Death of John Hawkesworth," in *The South Pacific in the Eighteenth Century,* 100. It is well to remember Beaglehole's adjuration: whether or not Hawkesworth "died of chagrin, as was widely noised about, we have no real means of knowing" (*Cook the Writer,* 11).

20 Beaglehole, *Cook the Writer,* 12.

21 Ibid., 16.

22 Glyndwr Williams, "Cook, James," *Dictionary of Canadian Biography,* vol. 4, *1771–1800,* ed. George W. Brown, David M. Hayne, and Francess G. Halpenny (Toronto: University of Toronto Press, 1979), 167; Beaglehole, *Cook the Writer,* 17.

23 Beaglehole, *Life,* 464; Wallis, "Publication," 188. The price of the set was probably £3/5/0, though perhaps more: see Rüdiger Joppien and Bernard Smith, *The Art of Captain Cook's Voyages,* vol. 3, *The Voyage of the* Resolution *and* Discovery, *1776–1780* (New Haven, CT: Yale University Press, 1988), 168–69. "Five additional English editions were published that year [1784] alone and an additional 14 editions were printed by 1800" (Daniel J. Slive, curator, *'A Curious Variety of Mazes and Meanders': The Voyages of Captain James Cook in the Global Eighteenth Century,* Dept.

of Special Collections, Young Research Library, UCLA, November–December 1999; http://unitproj.library.ucla.edu/special/cookmenu/cookcheck3.htm, accessed February 2013).

24 On this idea, see, for example, Luke Strongman, "Captain Cook's Voyages and Coleridge's 'The Rime of the Ancient Mariner,'" *Junctures: The Journal of Thematic Dialogue* 12 (June 2009): 69–81, http://www.junctures.org/index.php/junctures/issue/view/14/showToc, accessed April 2014.

25 Daniel Clayton, "Captain Cook's Command of Knowledge and Space: Chronicles of Nootka Sound," in *Captain Cook: Explorations and Reassessments,* ed. Glyndwr Williams (Woodbridge, UK: Boydell, 2004), 118.

26 P. J. Marshall and John Woods, eds., *The Correspondence of Edmund Burke,* vol. 7, *January 1792–August 1794* (Cambridge: Cambridge University Press, 1968), 589; quoted in Clayton, "Captain Cook's Command of Knowledge," 112 n. 11.

27 Glyndwr Williams, "King, James," in Brown, Hayne, and Halpenny, *Dictionary of Canadian Biography,* 4:412. The most recent biography is by Steve Ragnall, *Better Conceiv'd than Describ'd: The Life and Times of Captain James King (1750–84), Captain Cook's Friend and Colleague* (Leicester: Troubador, 2013).

28 James Trevenen, another officer on Cook's third Pacific voyage, quoted in Williams, "King, James," 413.

29 *A Voyage to the Pacific Ocean. Undertaken by Command of His Majesty, for Making Discoveries in the Northern Hemisphere. To Determine the Position and Extent of the West Side of North America; its Distance from Asia; and the Practicability of a Northern Passage to Europe. Performed under the Direction of Captains Cook, Clerke, and Gore, in His Majesty's Ships the* Resolution *and* Discovery. *In the Years 1776, 1777, 1778, 1779, and 1780. Vol. I. and II. Written by Captain James Cook, F.R.S. Vol. III. by Captain James King, LL.D. and F.R.S.,* 3 vols. and atlas (London: G. Nicol and T. Cadell, 1784), 2:194 (January 20, 1778). (Hereafter [Douglas, ed.], *A Voyage to the Pacific Ocean.*) It would be the better part of two hundred years before the reader of books could hear Cook's own voice: "I never saw Indians so much astonished at the entering a ship before, their eyes were continually flying from object to object, the wildness of thier [*sic*] looks and actions fully express'd their surprise and astonishment at the several new o[b]jects before them and evinced that they never had been on board of a ship before" (*The Journals of Captain James Cook on His Voyages of Discovery,* vol. 3, *The Voyage of the* Resolution *and* Discovery, *1776–1780,* ed. J. C. Beaglehole [Cambridge: Cambridge University Press for the Hakluyt Society, 1967], 265, hereafter [Cook], *Voyage of the* Resolution *and* Discovery.)

30 Clayton, "Captain Cook's Command of Knowledge," argues insightfully for the need to decenter the narratives, both European and Native, of Cook's one-month stay at Nootka Sound in order to understand how description is shaped, composed, and presented.

31 On the elevation of Cook's persona by Douglas and on Douglas's ways of erecting a discursive barrier between civilized agent of empire and savage, see I. S. MacLaren, "Exploration/Travel Literature and the Evolution of the Author," *International Journal of Canadian Studies/Revue internationale d'études canadiennes* 5 (Spring/Printemps 1992): 39–68, esp. 46–48.

32 [Douglas, ed.], *A Voyage to the Pacific Ocean,* 2:200; emphasis added. No correlative statement occurs in Cook's journal ([Cook], *Voyage of the* Resolution *and* Discovery, 269).

33 John Douglas, "Autobiography," 1776–96, British Library, Egerton MS 2181, f. 42v; quoted by Beaglehole in [Cook], *Voyage of the* Resolution *and* Adventure, cxliv. Notwithstanding this attestation, Beaglehole thought Douglas "had an acute mind, wrote well himself, and respected Cook" as "Cook respected him" (Beaglehole, *Cook the Writer,* 17.)

34 Aiming to do so in anonymity, Douglas was outraged when the January 18, 1783, issue of the *Morning Chronicle* correctly identified him as the editor of the forthcoming *Voyage to the Pacific Ocean* and, in his view, misidentified his role. In a letter of January 19, 1783, to his publisher and friend William Strahan, Douglas bristles at being "announced to the Public as employed in *finishing grammatically* Capt. Cook's Voyage. After all my Care & Study to have my Name kept back, it equally mortifys & surprises me, to be thus made the sport of News Papers."

He also growled at having Cook "supposed" to be "incapable of writing a Journal, by saying I had *digested* that of his former Voyage & am now *finishing* that of the last" (British Library, Egerton MS 2180, f. 68; quoted in Wallis, "Publication," 182).

35 It is noteworthy that Spain's disinclination to publish its explorers' reports precluded the declaration of a Pax España on the territory; Russians worked the Northwest Coast, but few explored it in the name of their monarch; and China's interest, chiefly in trade, attended no imperial or colonial ambitions.

36 [Douglas, ed.], *A Voyage to the Pacific Ocean,* 2:258. The asterisk refers to a footnote by Douglas—"This part of the West side of North America, was so named by Sir Francis Drake"—which, following Cook's own reference ([Cook], *Voyage of the* Resolution *and* Discovery, 289), serves to remind his reader just how long before the advent of Cook this far-off land had been anglicized in British cartography.

37 [Douglas, ed.], *A Voyage to the Pacific Ocean,* 2:259.

38 Ibid., 2:259, 2:260, 2:261. Cook did not experience particular misfortune. Modern sailors are advised that "sea fog is sometimes very dense in the vicinity of [Juan de Fuca] strait and may last for days at a time. It is usually accompanied by calms or light airs from the NW. . . . Occasionally, the fog stands before the entrance like a wall. Fog occurs with almost equal frequency over the strait from October through July" (*Sailing Directions [Enroute]: British Columbia,* 10th ed. [Bethesda, MD: National Geospatial-Intelligence Agency, 2007], 3. www.uscg.mil/d13/docs/cvts/Pub154bk.pdf, accessed November 2012.)

39 [Cook], *Voyage of the* Resolution *and* Discovery, 294. Twenty-six kilometers (sixteen miles) separate Tatoosh Island, Washington, from Carmanah Point, British Columbia.

40 [Douglas, ed.], *A Voyage to the Pacific Ocean,* 2:263. Barbara Belyea discusses Cook's, George Vancouver's, and in her view most historians' hostility to theoretical cartography in another register in "Just the Facts: Vancouver and Theoretical Geography," unpublished paper, 1992. See also Barbara Belyea, "Myth as Science: The Northwest Passage," *Dark Storm Moving West* (Calgary, AB: University of Calgary Press, 2007), 1–13.

41 [Cook], *Voyage of the* Resolution *and* Discovery, 293–94 (italics in original); [Douglas, ed.], *A Voyage to the Pacific Ocean,* 2:263: "But we saw nothing like it; nor is there the least probability that ever any such thing existed." Douglas here opens a footnote to refer his reader to "Michael Locke's apocryphal account of Juan de Fuca, and his pretended strait, in Purchas, Vol. iii. p. 849–852. [*sic*] and many later Collections." As to Cook's own use of litotes, one may note Beaglehole's contention that "from the form in which the journal is cast, we may judge that Cook set out deliberately to write a book—or at least an account of the voyage that would need the minimum of editing by another hand, or of rewriting by his own, before it appeared as a book" ([Cook], *Voyage of the* Resolution *and* Discovery, clxxii). For his part, Douglas contended in his autobiography that he had used Cook's journal only as his "Ground work," but he later deleted that claim and substituted the following: "The Public never knew, how much they owe to me in this work. The Capt's M.S.S. was indeed attended to accurately, but I took more Liberties than I had done with his Acct of the second Voyage; and while I faithfully represented the facts, I was less scrupulous in cloathing them with better Stile than fell to the usual Share of the Capt." John Douglas, "Autobiography," ff. 48–49v; quoted in [Cook], *Voyage of the* Resolution *and* Discovery, cxcix.)

42 On Lok and Dalrymple, see James McDermott, "Lok, Michael (*c.*1532–1620x22), Mercer, Merchant Adventurer, and Traveller," and Andrew S. Cook, "Dalrymple, Alexander (1737–1808), Hydrographer," *Oxford Dictionary of National Biography* (Oxford: Oxford University Press, 2004–14), accessed online March 2014.

43 *A Voyage towards the South Pole,* 2:239.

44 All the greater, then, is the irony that the preparation of the third voyage's engravings involved Cook's nemesis: "Banks and Webber supervised the engraving of the drawings while Alexander Dalrymple (none other) 'at Lord Sandwich's desire,' had direction of the charts and coastal views, with the exception of the general chart" (Wallis, "Publication," 180).

45 It goes almost without saying that, as a cartographic geographer, Cook felt himself on stable ground. His ethno-

graphic observations, by contrast, ranged from speculative to decided. Consider James Boswell's report of Cook's remarks when the two dined with some members of the Royal Society at the Mitre, 39 Fleet Street, London, on April 18, 1776: "I must observe that he candidly confessed to me that he and his companions who visited the south sea islands could not be certain of any information they got, or supposed they got, except as to objects falling under the observation of the senses; their knowledge of the language was so imperfect they required the aid of their senses, and any thing which they learnt about religion, government, or traditions might be quite erroneous. He gave me a distinct account of a New Zealander eating human flesh in his presence and in that of many more aboard, so that the fact of canibals is now certainly known." *Private Papers of James Boswell from Malahide Castle; In the Collection of Lt.-Colonel Ralph Heyward Isham,* vol. 11, *His Jaunts to London, Oxford, Birmingham*[,] *Lichfield, Ashbourne, Bath and Bristol and His Meeting with Margaret Caroline Rudd*[,] *Spring, 1776,* ed. Geoffrey Scott and Frederick A. Pottle (n.p. [United States], 1931), 256.

In his journal entry for Tuesday, April 2, the thirty-five-year-old Boswell had sketched Cook, twelve years his senior, as "a plain, sensible man with an uncommon attention to veracity . . . a man of good steady moral principles, as I thought, [who] did not try to make theories out of what he had seen to confound virtue and vice" (11:218), but this often quoted and cited remark (as in Beaglehole, *Life,* 451) needs the context of Boswell's susceptibility to such a quality in others at a point in his life when he himself was in the throes of remorse over a "fit of debauchery" and, being married, adultery with the prostitute Nancy Cooms as well as afraid of having contracted a venereal disease from another prostitute named Smith, and when he felt implicitly chastised at meeting the bookseller and actor Tom Davies and his wife, whose "strict conjugal union secretly reproached [Boswell's] licentiousness" (11:216).

46 [Cook], *Voyage of the* Resolution *and* Discovery, 294; [Douglas, ed.], *A Voyage to the Pacific Ocean,* 2:264.

47 [Cook], *Voyage of the* Resolution *and* Discovery, 296.

48 [Douglas, ed.], *A Voyage to the Pacific Ocean,* 2:267.

49 Ibid., 2:266.

50 This sounds triumphal; in fact, Cook was on continental islands (Newfoundland and Vancouver Island) ten years apart.

51 Jonathan Lamb, "Pacific: Literary Representations," in *The Oxford Companion to World Exploration,* ed. David Buisseret (New York: Oxford University Press, 2007), 2:132.

52 One exception occurred with Martin Frobisher's three voyages (1576–78), their "discovery" of fool's gold, and the subsequent short-lived, fanciful characterization of the North American Arctic as an El Dorado.

53 Beaglehole, *Cook the Writer,* 20.

54 See MacLaren, "Exploration/Travel Literature"; Clayton, "Captain Cook's Command"; Noel Elizabeth Currie, *Constructing Colonial Discourse: Captain Cook at Nootka Sound* (Montreal: McGill-Queen's University Press, 2005); and, most recently, Glyn Williams, *The Death of Captain Cook: A Hero Made and Unmade* (Cambridge, MA: Harvard University Press, 2008).

55 [Cook], *Voyage of the* Resolution *and* Discovery, 335.

56 [Douglas, ed.], *A Voyage to the Pacific Ocean,* 2:343.

57 [Cook], *Voyage of the* Resolution *and* Discovery, 367. Beaglehole's note at the end of this sentence quotes the remark in the posthumously published narrative of George Vancouver after his survey of Turnagain Arm in May 1794: "Thus terminated this very extensive opening on the coast of North West America, to which, had the great and first discoverer of it, whose name it bears, dedicated one day more to its further examination, he would have spared the theoretical navigators, who have followed him in their closets, the task of ingeniously ascribing to this arm of the ocean a channel, through which a north-west passage existing according to their doctrines, might ultimately be discovered." (George Vancouver, *A Voyage of Discovery to the North Pacific Ocean, and round the World in which the coast of North-West America has been carefully examined and accurately surveyed. Undertaken by his Majesty's Command principally with a view to ascertain the Existence of any navigable Communication between the North Pacific and North Atlantic Oceans and Performed in the Years 1790, 1791, 1792, 1793, 1794 and 1795 in the* Discovery *and* Chatham *under the Command of Captain George Vancouver,*

ed. John Vancouver, 3 vols. and atlas [London: G. G. and J. Robinson and J. Edwards, 1798], 3:125.)

58 [Douglas, ed.], *A Voyage to the Pacific Ocean,* 2:396–97.

59 Beaglehole, *Cook the Writer,* 20.

60 [Douglas, ed.], *A Voyage to the Pacific Ocean,* 2:397. It is notable that other editions than the first, even though published in the same year (if not the same month), did not alter this wording substantively but made other changes quite regularly. For example, in the impressively inferior four-volume edition printed in London in 1784, Cook's superlative is tempered; the commodore "saw no appearance of its source." This edition is notable for its use of the first-person plural to refer, presumably, to other officers of the expedition, and the third-person singular for the persona of Cook:

> The time we spent in the discovery of this great river ought not to be regretted. . . . But the delay . . . was an essential loss to us, . . . [I]t was now evident that the continent of North America extended much farther to the west, than we had reason to expect from the most approved charts. The Commodore, however, had the satisfaction to reflect, that, if he had not examined this very large river, speculative fabricators of geography would have ventured to assert, that it had a communication with the sea to the north, or with Hudson's or Baffin's bay to the east; and it would probably have been marked, on future maps of the world, with as much appearance of precision, as the imaginary straits of de Fuca, and de Fonte.

A Voyage to the Pacific Ocean; Undertaken by Command of His Majesty . . . Illustrated with Cuts. In Four Volumes, 4 vols. (London: John Stockdale, Scatcherd and Whitaker, John Fielding, and John Hardy, 1784), 2:331–32. The reason for this choice is unclear, except perhaps as an effort to evade conviction for producing an unauthorized edition. This aesthetically wretched and thus doubtless cheaper publication appears never to use the first-person singular voice for Cook. It bewilders its reader not only by substituting "the Commodore" for the paragraph's use of the first-person plural in its first three sentences, but also by referring to "Captain Cook," in the next paragraph, for example. Yet, although it jibes and jostles its reader, it offers no different content.

In February 1774, seventeen months before Cook returned from his second Pacific voyage, a famous legal case, *Donaldson v. Beckett,* by ruling against the legality of the principle of copyright unto perpetuity, appeared to loosen the stranglehold that a cartel of London publishers exerted on the book trade. In the wake of that decision, but also because the rising middle class in the last quarter of the century demanded more and cheaper books, the publication in 1784 of the narrative of the third voyage was very quickly pirated both in London and in Dublin. (For differing views on the significance of the 1774 legal ruling, see William St. Clair, *The Reading Nation in the Romantic Period* [Cambridge: Cambridge University Press, 2004], 107–18; James Raven, *The Business of Books: Booksellers and the English Book Trade* [New Haven, CT: Yale University Press, 2007], 231; and Ronan Deazley, "What's New About the Statute of Anne? Or Six Observations in Search of an Act," in *Global Copyright: Three Hundred Years since the Statute of Anne, from 1709 to Cyberspace,* ed. Lionel Bently, Uma Suthersanen, and Paul Torremans [Cheltenham, UK: Edward Elgar, 2010], 26–53.)

61 [Cook], *Voyage of the* Resolution *and* Discovery, 368 n. 2. Despite the wealth of research into the third expedition and the publication of the official narrative of it under the names of Cook and King, it remains unclear *precisely* which manuscripts the editor Douglas had before him. Williams raises this matter in *Death of Captain Cook,* 54. In an address given in 1957 ("Some Problems of Editing Cook's Journals"), Beaglehole did not clarify the confusion. In a lecture given in 1970 on completion of the publication of his enormous edition and biography, he described the journal as "a sophisticated document" (*Cook the Writer,* 18). In his biography, he stated that Douglas worked with "Cook's journal, with considerable interpolations from Anderson's" (*Life,* 691). Anderson's journal as edited by Beaglehole ([Cook], *Voyage of the* Resolution *and* Discovery, 725–986) does not extend beyond September 1777 and thus does not cover the northwest Pacific coast.

There is no reason to doubt this attestation. Douglas records Cook as writing that on the third voyage the captain "reasonably expected to derive considerable assistance from [Anderson] in recording our new proceedings" ([Douglas, ed.], *A Voyage to the Pacific Ocean,* 1:5); and in the published account of the stay at Yuquot, Douglas has his Cook state that he has "occasionally blended Mr. Anderson's observations with my own; but I owe every thing to him that relates to their language" ([Douglas, ed.], *A Voyage to the Pacific Ocean,* 2:334). But what else of Cook's, if anything, did Douglas use?

Beaglehole clarifies that Philip Stephens, secretary of the Admiralty, wrote to Douglas on November 14, 1779, saying that he was about to post "in three parcels 'Captain Cooks Journals Log Books & loose Manuscripts relative to this Voyage'" ([Cook], *Voyage of the* Resolution *and* Discovery, clxxi, quoting British Library, Egerton MS 2180, f. 19). Thereafter, Beaglehole quotes a letter by James King to Douglas of December 16, 1780: Cook's "loose papers" are not to be found anywhere ([Cook], *Voyage of the* Resolution *and* Discovery, clxxi, quoting British Library, Egerton MS 2180, f. 21). Beaglehole does not specify what King means. Are we to understand that King's "loose papers" and Stephens's "loose Manuscripts" are one and the same, or do the "loose papers" comprise everything—including "Log Books"—mentioned by Stephens *except* the "journals" (whatever they in the plural comprised)? Beaglehole was likely unable to answer this question to his own satisfaction: "We can guess at the nature of loose papers, but guessing provides us with no evidence" (*Cook the Writer,* 18). He does assert that Cook's journal, which "remorselessly compressed" log entries for long days at sea "to a sentence or two of narrative" ([Cook], *Voyage of the* Resolution *and* Discovery, clxii), is the 605-folio quarto bound in the British Library as Egerton MS 2177 A (clxxi). But then there is "an earlier stage of journal-log" (clxxi), housed in the National Archives as ADM 55/111–112 and 113. This is likely the "Log and Proceedings" to which he refers elsewhere (*Cook the Writer,* 18). Or is it? Williams notes that "there is a reference to 'two Volumes of the Log' after the ships returned to London. We know that Douglas had this in his possession while he was preparing Cook's journal for publication, for in a marginal note in his own edited copy of the journal he refers to Cook's 'Log Book', and takes information from it which is not in the journal" (*Death of Captain Cook,* 52).

Respecting the "journal-log," Beaglehole states that a note in Douglas's hand misidentifies it as "a faithful Copy of the Journal in Capt Cooke's own handwriting" when in fact at least some of it is one version of Cook's log, with ADM 55/112 and 113 covering the months spent on the Northwest Coast of North America and up to January 6, 1779 ([Cook], *Voyage of the* Resolution *and* Discovery, clxxiv, clxxv). Beaglehole states elliptically that from this journal-log "we learn that Cook's MS log did survive the voyage, whatever happened to it afterwards" (clxxv). The journal-log is only a copy, which he confusingly describes as both an "original document" and, notwithstanding Douglas's identification of it as being "in Capt Cooke's own handwriting," "all in the same hand, that of a very intelligent clerk, who does not hesitate to improve on Cook's spelling and punctuation" (clxxiv). In what sense was it original if not in Cook's hand and if "improve[d]" by another?

Meanwhile, one wonders what, if anything, Douglas made of this journal-log. Beaglehole supposes not much: Douglas "cannot have read very far either, however faithfully the paragraphs he did read were found to correspond with the quarto journal, or he would certainly have come upon the log entries" in this journal-log (clxxv). Apparently, the editor read enough to satisfy himself that there was no reason to collate passages from it into his revision of the journal (Egerton MS 2177 A). Clearly, he had decided that the journal was his base text. In accomplishing his aim of representing the captain's last intentions for the narrative, perhaps Douglas reached the decision that an edition of it ought not to have collated into it details that are found only in the journal-log, even though he considered it written "in Capt Cooke's own handwriting." But if Douglas felt so strongly about remaining loyal to Cook's journal, why does *A Voyage to the Pacific Ocean* make extensive use of Anderson's journal? It is difficult to say. All in all, one is left wondering whether the reader of Beaglehole's edition, which quotes selected passages from the log in footnotes, knows more than Douglas could have known, more than Douglas cared to know, or as much as Douglas knew but chose not to collate? Wallis's otherwise enlightening essay is content to paraphrase Beaglehole's not altogether satisfactory account ("Publication," 177). At the very least, there is an undeniable need for a chronology of the manuscripts with their provenance, assembled by an accomplished bibliographer.

62 [Cook], *Voyage of the* Resolution *and* Discovery, 350.

63 [Douglas, ed.], *A Voyage to the Pacific Ocean,* 2:369.

64 Ibid., 2:457.

65 [Cook], *Voyage of the* Resolution *and* Discovery, 351. The anticipation in this sentence—"we may very probably see"—offers one of a number of instances clarifying that Cook wrote up his journal from his log at periodic points during the voyage.

66 The Tlingit suggestion is offered by Nicholas Thomas, *Cook: The Extraordinary Voyages of Captain James Cook* (New York: Walker, 2003), 369. Tlingit are more properly identified at the coast no farther north than Yakutat, well east of Prince William Sound. The expedition encountered Chugach on the eastern side of the sound.

67 [Cook], *Voyage of the* Resolution *and* Discovery, 371. As he advanced north, Cook was now following not Spaniards but Russians. Alexei Chirikov (aboard the *St. Paul* with seventy-six men) and Vitus Bering (aboard the *St. Peter* with seventy-five men) left Petropavlovsk, on the Kamchatka Peninsula, on June 4, 1741. The ships were separated within days: Chirikov made landfall at Prince of Wales Island and Bering at Kayak Island (fig. 10.4). At the latter, Bering named Mount St. Elias (fig. 13.11). Chirikov lost his ship's two boats and fifteen men. He arrived back at Kamchatka on October 8, 1841, and died of tuberculosis after returning to Russia. Bering's ship wrecked on Bering Island, off Kamchatka Peninsula, and he died there. Others, including the naturalist Georg Wilhelm Steller, survived the winter, built a ship from the remains of the *St. Peter,* and arrived back at Petropavlovsk in September 1742. Upon their return to Russia with pelts of sea otter that they had acquired on the Aleutian Islands, Russia's interest in Alaska began. Although further state-sanctioned expeditions did not materialize, *promyshlenniki* quickly established themselves on the Aleutians and, not being adept at ocean hunting, subjugated the Unangax̂ to their enterprise. The richer the harvest, the farther east it needed to extend, until it reached the mainland at the Alaska Peninsula, near where Cook encountered these contract workers in October 1778. By that decade, "three merchants—Grigory Ivanovich Shelikhov, Pavel Sergeyevich Lebedev-Lastochkin, and G. Panov—monopolized the harvest" (Claus M. Naske and Herman E. Slotnick, *Alaska: A History of the 49th State* [Grand Rapids, MI: William B. Eerdmans, 1979, 28].)

68 [Douglas, ed.], *A Voyage to the Pacific Ocean,* 2:401; bracketed text added.

69 [Cook], *Voyage of the* Resolution *and* Discovery, 371.

70 [Douglas, ed.], *A Voyage to the Pacific Ocean,* 2:401.

71 Another instance of Douglas's following Cook almost verbatim occurs with the captain's effort at an aesthetic description on June 21 off Mount Shishaldin, Unimak Island. In this case, even Cook's syntax is preserved and only punctuation, parentheses, and one grammatical correction supplied: "We seldom saw this or any of the other mountains wholly clear, when a narrow cloud, sometimes two or three one above the other, would embrace the middle like a girdle, with which the Column of smoke rising perpendicular to a great height out of it[s] summit and spreading before the wind into a tail of vast length, made a very picturesque appearances" ([Cook], *Voyage of the* Resolution *and* Discovery, 385–86; compare [Douglas, ed.], *A Voyage to the Pacific Ocean,* 2:416).

72 [Douglas, ed.], *A Voyage to the Pacific Ocean,* 2:414.

73 [Cook], *Voyage of the* Resolution *and* Discovery, 384, 449 (entry for October 8, 1778); [Douglas, ed.], *A Voyage to the Pacific Ocean,* 2:495.

74 [Cook], *Voyage of the* Resolution *and* Discovery, 458; [Douglas, ed.], *A Voyage to the Pacific Ocean,* 2:509.

75 Mitigating this instance of Douglas's meddling is the narration of a similar subsequent incident: on June 28, "an Indian brought on board such another note as was brought to Captain Clerke; which he presented to me; it was in the same Russian Language which as I have before observed none of us could read" ([Cook], *Voyage of the* Resolution *and* Discovery, 392). This time, Douglas

handles the deficiency straightforwardly: "He presented it to me; but it was written in the Russian language, which, as already observed, none of us could read" ([Douglas, ed.], *A Voyage to the Pacific Ocean,* 2:423–24).

76 [Douglas, ed.], *A Voyage to the Pacific Ocean,* 2:414.

77 [Cook], *Voyage of the* Resolution *and* Discovery, 386; [Douglas, ed.], *A Voyage to the Pacific Ocean,* 2:417.

78 [Cook], *Voyage of the* Resolution *and* Discovery, 386; [Douglas, ed.], *A Voyage to the Pacific Ocean,* 2:418.

79 [Cook], *Voyage of the* Resolution *and* Discovery, 389; [Douglas, ed.], *A Voyage to the Pacific Ocean,* 2:420.

80 [Douglas, ed.], *A Voyage to the Pacific Ocean,* 2:449; [Cook], *Voyage of the* Resolution *and* Discovery, 412.

81 [Cook], *Voyage of the* Resolution *and* Discovery, 414, 416–17, 419, 421; [Douglas, ed.], *A Voyage to the Pacific Ocean,* 2:452, 455, 457, 459.

82 [Cook], *Voyage of the* Resolution *and* Discovery, 425; [Douglas, ed.], *A Voyage to the Pacific Ocean,* 2:464. Like Cook, Douglas ends a paragraph with this sentence and thereby renders the conclusive tone of its claim consummate.

83 [Cook], *Voyage of the* Resolution *and* Discovery, 427; [Douglas, ed.], *A Voyage to the Pacific Ocean,* 2:466: "I did not think it consistent with prudence, to make any farther attempts to find a passage."

84 [Cook], *Voyage of the* Resolution *and* Discovery, 429; [Douglas, ed.], *A Voyage to the Pacific Ocean,* 2:470. For a version of Müller's map, see fig. 2.3.

85 Quoted in [Cook], *Voyage of the* Resolution *and* Discovery, 418 n. Compare this passage and [Douglas, ed.], *A Voyage to the Pacific Ocean,* 2:456. Beaglehole discusses which version of the log Douglas consulted, could have consulted, or ought to have consulted and "regrets the omission from the journal occasionally of some entertaining detail" ([Cook], *Voyage of the* Resolution *and* Discovery, clxxv). A good example is the wit of the log's description of the wooden, crownless cap worn by Aleut, the circular hole of which admits the head, "for which reason one would think it designed to shade the face from the Sun, but as this luminary does not, I apprehend, often trouble them, I rather think it is intended to confine the hood of the upper garment close to the head" ([Cook], *Voyage of the* Resolution *and* Discovery, 459 n.).

86 [Cook], *Voyage of the* Resolution *and* Discovery, 437; [Douglas, ed.], *A Voyage to the Pacific Ocean,* 2:478.

87 [Cook], *Voyage of the* Resolution *and* Discovery, 444 n.; contrast [Douglas, ed.], *A Voyage to the Pacific Ocean,* 2:490–91.

88 [Cook], *Voyage of the* Resolution *and* Discovery, 431; [Douglas, ed.], *A Voyage to the Pacific Ocean,* 2:472.

89 Wallis notes that publishing all the engravings in the fourth volume rather than inserting them at the most pertinent points in the three volumes of narrative was "an arrangement contrary to [James] King's wish and advice" but consistent with the decision of the publisher, George Nicol ("Publication," 182). In all, the publication of the eighty-seven plates was the work of twenty-five London engravers, who were exhorted to improve on the engravings published in *A Voyage towards the South Pole* seven years earlier (Joppien and Smith, *The Art of Captain Cook's Voyages,* 3:162 n., 3:163).

90 Wallis notes that Webber, not being an engraver, was not responsible for the published engravings but was responsible for supervising their preparation ("Publication," 190), so the evolution of image and the evolution of text into published form are not identical. That said, there is some similarity. As figures 12.9 and 12.10 indicate, Webber's method was to work up his initial sketch (fig. 12.9) into a watercolor (fig. 12.10), from which the engravers then worked. But, as Joppien and Smith have noted, the walrus was subject matter that apparently fascinated Webber or at least afforded him both dramatic and didactic opportunities, for he reworked his depiction several times (*The Art of Captain Cook's Voyages,* 3:115–18). The sketch is a far looser composition; as he proceeded toward an engraving-readied rendition, the scene grew more constructed and formal, more controlled and staged in ways that resemble Douglas's tidyings of the verbal record.

91 [Cook], *Voyage of the* Resolution *and* Discovery, 438; [Douglas, ed.], *A Voyage to the Pacific Ocean,* 2:481.

92 [Douglas, ed.], *A Voyage to the Pacific Ocean,* 2:486; compare [Cook], *Voyage of the* Resolution *and* Discovery, 441.

93 [Douglas, ed.], *A Voyage to the Pacific Ocean,* 2:506 (emphasis in original); [Cook], *Voyage of the* Resolution *and* Discovery, 456.

94 [Douglas, ed.], *A Voyage to the Pacific Ocean,* 2:440; compare [Cook], *Voyage of the* Resolution *and* Discovery, 406.
95 Williams, *Death of Captain Cook,* 46.
96 [Cook], *Voyage of the* Resolution *and* Discovery, 429; [Douglas, ed.], *A Voyage to the Pacific Ocean,* 2:469–70.
97 [Cook], *Voyage of the* Resolution *and* Discovery, 450 (bracketed text is Beaglehole's); [Douglas, ed.], *A Voyage to the Pacific Ocean,* 2:497 (bracketed text added).
98 [Douglas, ed.], *A Voyage to the Pacific Ocean,* 2:508 (bracketed text added), 509; [Cook], *Voyage of the* Resolution *and* Discovery, 458.
99 [Cook], *Voyage of the* Resolution *and* Discovery, 458, 459, 461, 461–62, 463, 465, 465, 466, 467, 468, 468; [Douglas, ed.], *A Voyage to the Pacific Ocean,* 2:509, 510, 512–13, 513–14, 516, 518, 518, 519, 520, 521, 522.
100 Webber's portrait of Behm is also reproduced in color in Joppien and Smith, *The Art of Captain Cook's Voyages* 3:137, plate 164.
101 Beaglehole, *Life,* 689. Williams notes that Lieutenant John Gore sent another copy of Cook's journal to London by fast frigate when the expedition arrived at the Cape of Good Hope in May 1780. The original, however, remained with Gore until he reached London (Williams, *Death of Captain Cook,* 52–53).
102 Walter Scott to John Whishaw, ca. 1814; affixed as letter 10 in the copy of Mungo Park, *Travels in the Interior Districts of Africa: Performed under the Direction and Patronage of the Africa Association, in the Years 1795, 1796, and 1797* (London: G. and W. Nicol, 1799) held by Selkirk Library Archives (Borders Council), SC/5/56, f. 2; quoted in Charles W. J. Withers, "Geography, Enlightenment and the Book: Authorship and Audience in Mungo Park's African Texts," in *Geographies of the Book,* ed. Miles Ogborn and Charles W. J. Withers (London: Ashgate, 2010), 208.
103 For Edwards's involvement, see Olwyn M. Blouet, "Bryan Edwards, F.R.S . . . 1743–1800," *Notes and Records of the Royal Society of London* 54 (2000): 215–22. Blouet notes that Edwards kept Sir Joseph Banks informed of "his progress in editing Park's journals" (222 n. 39).
104 Williams, *Death of Captain Cook,* 48.
105 Samuel Hearne, *A Journey from Prince of Wales's Fort in Hudson's Bay, to the Northern Ocean. Undertaken by Order of the Hudson's Bay Company, for the Discovery of Copper Mines, a North West Passage, &c. In the Years 1769, 1770, 1771, & 1772* (London: A. Strahan and T. Cadell, 1795).
106 Alexander Mackenzie [with William Combe], *Voyages from Montreal, on the River St. Laurence, through the Continent of North America, to the Frozen and Pacific Oceans; in the Years 1789 and 1793. With a Preliminary Account of the Rise, Progress, and Present State of the Fur Trade of that Country* (London: T. Cadell, Jun. and W. Davies, and W. Creech, 1801), iii–iv. The proliferation of atechnos in narratives of exploration receives treatment in MacLaren, "In Consideration," 224. It goes almost without saying that Cook's remark from March 1775, that he possessed "neither Natural, nor acquired abilities, for writing," marks another such example, although he did not write it for publication and it appeared in print only after Douglas polished it somewhat (see note 17, above).
107 [Cook], *Voyage of the* Resolution *and* Discovery, clxxii.

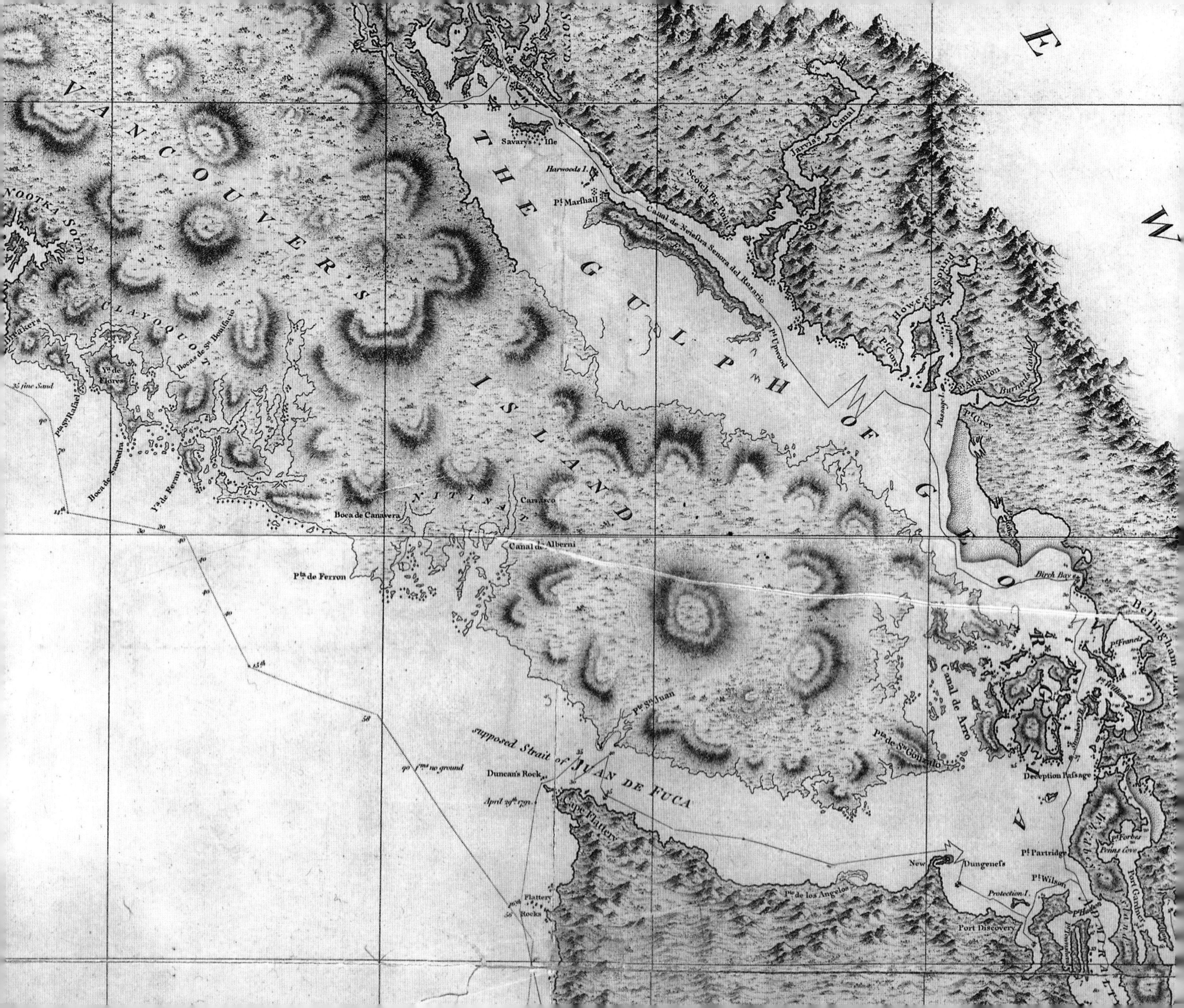
VANCOUVER'S ISLAND
THE GULPH OF GEORGIA
NOOTKA SOUND
CLAYOQUOT
Breakers
35 fine Sand
Pta Sn Rafael
Yla de Flores
Bocas de Sn Bonifacio
Boca de Saavedra
Yla de Ferron
Boca de Canavera
NITINAT
Carrasco
Canal de Alberni
Pta de Ferron
Savary's Isle
Harwoods I.
Pt Marshall
Canal de Nuestra Senora del Rosario
Pt Upwood
Scotch Fir Point
Jarvis's Canal
Howe's Sound
Pt Gore
Passage I.
Pt Atkinson
Burrard's Canal
Pt Grey
Birch Bay
Bellingham Bay
Pt Francis
Canal de Arro
Pta de Sn Gonzalo
Pta Sn Juan
supposed Strait of JUAN DE FUCA
90 fms no ground
Duncan's Rock
April 29th 1792
Cape Flattery
Flattery Rocks
Deception Passage
New
Dungeness
Pta de los Angelos
Pt Partridge
Pt Wilson
Protection I.
Port Discovery
Pt Hudson
Port Townshend
Pt Forbes
Penns Cove
Port Gardner

13

The End of the Northern Mystery

George Vancouver's Survey of the Northwest Coast

JAMES K. BARNETT

CAPTAIN COOK'S FINAL VOYAGE WAS CRITICAL TO THE EUROPEAN EXPLORATION of the Northwest Coast of North America. He was the first to sail the full reach of the coast from Oregon to the Arctic and record its principal features, setting the standard for those who followed. In the two subsequent decades, the coast became a virtual crossroads of empires, as most of the major European seafaring countries, as well as the fledgling American nation, sent ships to assert claims of sovereignty, pursue scientific and ethnographic inquiries, and harvest furs for commercial gain.

The French were the first to follow Cook to Alaska with the ill-fated voyage of Jean-François Galaup, comte de La Pérouse. Emulating Cook's voyages, the expedition had a dozen scientists and artists on board, all fueled by a fervent desire to promote science, explore nature, and meet the inhabitants of newfound lands. The expedition left France in August 1785, a little over a year after Cook's third voyage journal was published. Although his principal geographic discoveries were near Japan, La Pérouse was the second European to command an expedition to Hawai'i and the first foreigner to visit the fledgling Spanish colonies of Alta California.

La Pérouse came to the Gulf of Alaska from Hawai'i in July 1786, eleven months after leaving

A Chart Shewing Part of the Coast of NW America (Vancouver Island, Puget Sound, and Columbia River), 1798 (detail of fig. 13.6).

France. Although surrounded by whales, seals, sea otters, ducks, and other marine creatures, he was disappointed by the imposing view of glaciers and snowbound peaks surrounding Mount St. Elias. He wrote: "The sight of land, after a long voyage, usually excites feelings of delight; but on us it had not this effect. The eye wandered with pain over masses of snow, covering a barren soil, unembellished by a single tree. The mountains appeared to be a very little distance from the sea, which broke against the cliffs of a table-land . . . totally destitute of greenery."[1]

The expedition coasted to the east, where tidal rips nearly capsized the vessels as they entered Lituya Bay, which the French called Port des Français. They set up observatories and began considerable trade with the local Tlingit people, who lived nearby in large, well-hewn wooden homes. The Natives had extensive skill in wood carving, building canoes, and even working with iron and copper. One of the voyage objectives was to learn whether there were geographic connections between the coast and the American interior. The sailors surveyed the shoreline and charted nearby glaciers, but they could not penetrate the massive mountains that surrounded the bay.[2] As they prepared to leave, disaster struck. Two longboats were overcome by the tidal rip at the outlet of the bay, and twenty-one French sailors drowned. The local people observed the disaster from shore but were powerless to help. In profound despair, the crew erected a monument with the inscription: "Twenty-one brave sailors perished at the entrance to this harbor; whosoever you may be, mingle your tears with ours."[3]

Overcome by the tragedy and stymied by constant fog, La Pérouse sailed for California without searching anymore for the imagined passageways. In a month the expedition reached Monterey Bay, where the French were surprised by the modest structures and the small number of Spaniards in the colony. They were also disturbed by the drudgery imposed on the Indians within the mission enclaves, wishing that the friars cared as much for their charges' material welfare as for their salvation.[4] The expedition then sailed across the Pacific for China, arriving in Macao in January 1787. There they found forty-one foreign ships at anchor, most of them British ships in the sea-otter trade. Sailing north, the expedition passed Japan and the Kuril Islands and in September reached Petropavlovsk, the humble village Charles Clerke had visited a decade earlier, which was still made up of a few dozen ill-made cabins. The crew replaced the plaque at Clerke's tomb, visited a nearby volcano, and attended a modest ball held in their honor. They also dispatched a member of their crew to carry the voyage journals back to France. It was a fortunate decision, repeated again at their brief stop at Botany Bay. Leaving Australia in 1788, the sailors planned to reconnoiter Tonga and other islands in the South Pacific before returning home the next year. But the expedition vanished in a hurricane at the remote Vanikoro Island, probably after just a few months at sea. They were never seen again, but the incomplete journals were published posthumously in 1797.[5]

While the French made only one desperate attempt to stake their claim to the Northwest Coast, the Spanish considered the region to be part of their domain and sailed these waters many times. However, most of their voyages were kept secret, according to Spanish naval tradition. Made aware of Cook's departure from England in 1776, Viceroy Antonio de Bucareli of New Spain was ordered to intercept him as he reached America. In 1779 Bucareli sent two frigates north from Mexico, commanded by Lieutenant Ignacio de Arteaga, with Juan Francisco de la Bodega y Quadra as his second in command. When Captain Charles Clerke was in Kamchatka and tested the Arctic ice pack, the Spaniards sailed along coastal Alaska, reaching Prince William Sound and the Kenai Peninsula. When they observed Afognak Island, they gave up the search for Cook's expedition. Despite Cook's presence in these waters the previous year, neither fleet was aware of the other, and the Spanish returned to California believing that Cook had not reached the coast and that the Russians were still confined to the Aleutians.[6]

After the official account of the Cook expedition was published and La Pérouse visited Spain's California colonies, the Spanish decided to mount their own circumnavigation under the command of Alejandro Malaspina. His royal expedition was probably even better outfitted for coastal examinations than the Cook or La Pérouse voyages, with botanists, cartographers, astronomers, and artists gathered aboard to conduct a massive inquiry in the name of science. Malaspina left Cádiz, Spain, at the end of June 1789. Rounding Cape Horn, the voyagers enjoyed a grand tour of the major ports along the west coast of South America before they arrived at Mexico in early 1791. There Malaspina received a dispatch ordering him to change his route and sail for Alaska to look for the rumored Northwest Passage. In three months they reached Port Mulgrave, now called Yakutat Bay, where hundreds of Tlingit residents overwhelmed the sailors in wooden canoes to conduct trade. The local people offered fresh provisions, fishing implements, and domestic articles in exchange for European clothing, nails, buttons, beads, and anything metal. The scholars aboard studied the local people and their surroundings, returning with many drawings and journal entries recording their language, economy, warfare methods, and social practices.

Like the explorers before him, Malaspina searched in vain for the elusive passage to Europe. He later reflected in his journal that modern readers would be surprised by the seriousness Europeans gave to these imagined straits and waterways, believing Cook's survey in 1778 had already settled the matter. He then sailed for Nootka Sound and California, observing but not entering the Strait of Juan de Fuca and the Columbia River. Arriving at Monterey, he visited several missions, writing a generous and superficial report of California Indian life with the Franciscans. The expedition then crossed the Pacific Ocean to investigate the Philippines,

Australia, and Tonga before returning home via South America. The scientific data collected during the expedition probably surpassed the findings of Cook's third voyage, but after he returned to Spain, Malaspina was embroiled in political intrigue, convicted of treason, and imprisoned. The manuscripts of his expedition languished, and Spain's scientific momentum came to an abrupt end.[7]

Although the Russian occupation of the north Pacific was limited to the Aleutian Islands at the time of Cook's voyage, the Russians soon repositioned to Kodiak Island to expand operations along the Alaska mainland, employing fleets of captive Aleutian and Kodiak Island hunters to annihilate sea-otter populations in Kodiak, Cook Inlet, and Prince William Sound.[8] At the same time, the Russian government undertook expeditions to their newfound colonies, although it is unclear whether these journeys were for the lofty objectives of the Enlightenment or simply to assure the collection of tribute. The most notable voyage was by an Englishman, Joseph Billings, who sailed with Cook as a seaman on the *Discovery.* Although authorized in 1785, the overland march from the Baltic delayed the expedition's departure until 1790, when it sailed for the Russian fortifications at Unalaska and Kodiak. Billings was disturbed by the coercive and rapacious manner of Russian commerce, writing that he once observed over six hundred kayaks in a single hunting party in the waters around Kodiak Island, decimating the populations of sea otters, sea lions, and fur seals.[9]

In 1784, when the official publication of Cook's last voyage was released, merchants and traders from a host of nations were inspired to launch expeditions to the West Coast in search of sea-otter furs. In May 1785 Richard Cadman Etches, a prosperous London merchant, formed the King George's Sound Company. Joseph Banks, interested in both commercial and scientific investigations, was one of his partners. They hired Nathaniel Portlock and George Dixon, who had sailed with Cook: both left England in companion trading vessels in the same month that La Pérouse left France. Later, Captains James Hanna and James Strange were dispatched from China, and John Meares departed Bombay in a race for furs.

Hanna was the first and most successful. Dixon and Portlock found little fur in two summers in Alaska and had the good sense to spend the winter in Hawai'i. But Meares, unaware of the severity of Alaskan winters, unwisely decided to stay in a cove in Port Fidalgo in Prince William Sound. He built a cabin on shore, anticipating an idyllic time in the woods, but by early spring the deep snow and bitter cold prevented the sailors from hunting game or even getting off the ship. By spring the crew was overcome by scurvy, and twenty-four men died, nearly half the vessel's complement. Their desperate condition made it clear that the traders needed a more temperate port on the coast, at a distance from the Russian settlements.[10]

Like other merchants in the sea-otter trade, Meares, Portlock, and Dixon were primarily concerned with commerce. Exploration and charting were secondary. However, each captain published his own voyage journal, and at least Portlock's and Dixon's accounts were credible, as they included many landmarks of Southeast Alaska on their charts that Cook bypassed in the stormy weather encountered in the spring of 1778. Meares's journal is not only tainted by his misguided decision to spend a winter in Alaska but also offers an improbable map of the north Pacific that boldly depicts a waterway from the Great Slave Lake with three imagined outlets into Prince William Sound and Cook Inlet. More improbable, halfway between the lake and the outlets Meares inserted in his legend: "Falls said to be the Largest in the Known World."[11]

The traders and captains centered their activities on Nootka Sound. The local chieftain, Maquinna, became a virtual gatekeeper of the trade, as his Mowachaht people acquired the treasures of Europe in exchange for sea-otter furs. Captain Hanna was the first trader to enter the harbor in 1785; soon others followed. Although most of the trading vessels were British, before long American, Spanish, Portuguese, and even Swedish vessels stopped at Yuquot, the Native village at the entry to Nootka Sound. The irrepressible Meares decided to construct a small warehouse on a beach near Yuquot. The first Americans in the fur trade were John Kendrick and Robert Gray, who reached Nootka Sound in 1788, staying until late 1789, when they returned to Boston via China with a considerable treasure of sea-otter furs. Robert Gray was the first to circumnavigate the world flying the Stars and Stripes.[12]

The Spanish launched an expedition in 1788 to determine the extent of the English fur trade and Russian occupation of the coast. Esteban José Martínez sailed past California to coastal Alaska, reaching the Russian outposts in Kodiak and Unalaska and mapping seven Russian outposts with 460 inhabitants. In Unalaska, Martínez learned of the growing British merchant fleet in the China-Nootka trade. These reports alarmed the new viceroy, Manuel Antonio Flores, so in early 1789 he sent Martínez to establish permanent buildings at Yuquot, which the Spanish called Santa Cruz de Nutka. They also established a fort on a nearby island, called Fort San Miguel. Like the Russians to the north, the Spanish reasoned that the best way to establish sovereignty over the region was to construct fortifications along the coast and enter into peaceful relations with the local people. While the Spanish captain Juan Pérez briefly touched at Nootka Sound in 1774, four years before Cook, he did not land or take possession of the region for Spain. Having already erected missions and presidios in Alta California, the Spanish asked Martínez to occupy Nootka Sound and establish similar buildings and settlements.[13]

Captain James Colnett, a partner of Meares, entered the bay a month after Martínez. He was unwilling to accept the Spanish fort and claim to sovereignty, and the captains quarreled bitterly. Colnett was finally arrested. Maquinna was amazed that Europeans were so erratic, but he was soon drawn into the conflict when the Spanish killed a local chief who disputed the Spanish claim. When Martínez returned to Mexico that fall, he took Colnett and two British ships with him. The British government was outraged by the seizure. Etches, who stood to gain if Nootka was available for his trading ships, goaded the English prime minister, William Pitt, into a propaganda campaign over the Spanish arrests. John Meares was so agitated by the arrest that he came to London to plead his case, publishing an inflated account of the Nootka "incident" that enraged the British public.

The Nootka crisis then broke onto the international scene. War was imminent. While the Spanish may have had a prior right to Nootka, they kept their many expeditions secret, so they had little choice but to agree to a truce. In the Nootka Convention of 1790, Spain gave up its claim that it alone could establish settlements in the Pacific Northwest and agreed to restore Meares's land and building at the port. The treaty assured merchants of all nations free access to the harbor as a center of fur operations along the unoccupied stretch of coast north of California.[14]

Unaware of the diplomatic agreements being made in Europe, in 1790 the latest viceroy, the second count of Revillagigedo, and Bodega decided to refortify Nootka, so they sent all their ships and senior captains to the north. One surveyed the Strait of Juan de Fuca, and another, under the command of Salvador Fidalgo, surveyed Prince William Sound and Cook Inlet, naming the two largest communities in Prince William Sound, Cordova and Valdez.[15]

As the accounts and maps of the British traders and the La Pérouse voyage arrived in Europe, the theoretical geographers began to dream again of imagined passageways along the Northwest Coast, focusing on the island maze of Southeast Alaska as well as Cook Inlet and Prince William Sound. Alexander Dalrymple, hydrographer to the East India Company (and later first hydrographer of the British Admiralty), was a well-regarded Scottish geographer who speculated about such routes even before Cook's voyage. The latest reports suggested to him that there might still be a connection between Hudson Bay and the Pacific, perhaps a river system connecting Alaska with lakes in the Canadian interior, and he urged the Admiralty to search for it.[16] At the same time, English merchants implored the Admiralty to send Australian prisoners and settlers to colonize the Queen Charlotte Islands to advance British sovereign and commercial interests. With the adoption of the Nootka Convention, the Admiralty had yet another reason to undertake a return voyage after Cook, since supervision was required to restore Meares's possessions.

The new expedition was entrusted to Cook's favorite chart maker, Henry Roberts, who selected George Vancouver as his second in command. Roberts and Vancouver were chosen because, having sailed with Captain Cook on both the second and third voyages, they had experience with the meticulous techniques required to survey the tempestuous and intricate Northwest Coast. But the controversy at Nootka Sound delayed the expedition's departure, and Roberts was reassigned to the West Indies. When the Nootka Convention was finally signed, the voyage was reinstated as an exploratory expedition. The plan to settle the coast was deferred, and Vancouver was elevated to command (fig. 13.1). He was instructed to receive restitution of the land and buildings at Nootka and then undertake a detailed survey from Baja California to Cook's River in Alaska, from 30° to 60° north latitude.[17]

Vancouver was just fifteen years old when he was chosen as a midshipman on Cook's second voyage. While little is known about his service with Cook, he claimed he had been nearer to the South Pole than any other man. When Cook decided that they could go no farther than 71°10's, Vancouver climbed out on the bowsprit to position himself farther south than any of the crew aboard. On the third voyage, Vancouver's name does not appear in the journals at all, except that he and Thomas Edgar, master of the *Discovery,* took part in a well-reported melee with Hawaiians over stolen armorer's tongs on February 13, 1779, the day before Cook's death at Kealakekua Bay.

Now on his own voyage, Vancouver sailed in a vessel named after Cook's consort, the *Discovery.* Like Cook, he believed that reports of a passage from the Northwest Coast or Alaska to the Canadian interior were unlikely, but he was instructed to resolve the matter once and for all. He selected officers who had served with him in the West Indies, among them Peter Puget, Joseph Baker, Joseph Whidbey, and Zachary Mudge, accompanied by the most capable surveyors, astronomers, and mapmakers of the day. In prosecuting the search, his ship was escorted by the armed tender *Chatham,* commanded after the first year by Puget. The two ships carried 145 men, 40 fewer than on Cook's final voyage. They were periodically supported by a supply ship. This formidable task was intended to take two summers but ultimately required a third season.[18]

The ships sailed on April 1, 1791, following Cook's third-voyage route around the Cape of Good Hope to Australia, New Zealand, Tahiti, and finally Hawai'i, which was reached in eleven months. During the first survey season, they made landfall in North America in April 1792, north of San Francisco Bay. Following the coastline to the north, the sailors saw the flooded entrance to what would soon be named the Columbia River, but the volume of water from the spring runoff kept them from approaching. They continued north to Cape Flattery and the Strait of Juan de Fuca, where they met the Boston trader *Columbia Rediviva,* commanded by Robert Gray, now on the coast in his second voyage. Gray had spent several days in the strait, but now he was heading south. He waited for the floodwaters of the Columbia River to subside and made the first entry over treacherous sandbars guarding the river on May 11, 1792. Gray named the great river after his ship.[19]

When Vancouver reached the end of the Strait of Juan de Fuca, the coastline led past Port

13.1 *George Vancouver,* circa 1800. Oil painting; artist unknown (variously attributed to Lemuel Abbott and William Bright Morris). The authenticity of the portrait is uncertain. A globe with the track of Cook's voyage in the background suggests that this oft-reproduced eighteenth-century portrait is probably George Vancouver after his return from the epic voyage. The likeness has been used many times: it appears both on the dome of the legislative building in Victoria, British Columbia, and as a statue in front of the city hall in Vancouver. © National Portrait Gallery, London, NPG 503.

13.2 John Sykes, *View of the Boat Encampment, Pugets Sound,* 1792. Watercolor and pencil on paper. Vancouver's expedition had no official artist, so three midshipmen, including Sykes, drew plans of bays and landscapes—but no portraits—during the voyage. This view is among the first, showing a boat encampment and observatory tents in Discovery Bay, as the expedition entered Puget Sound. Courtesy of the Bancroft Library, University of California, Berkeley: Robert B. Honeyman Collection, BANC PIC 1963.002.1112—ffALB.

13.3 John Landseer, *Mount Rainier from the South Part of Admiralty Inlet [Puget Sound],* 1798. Engraving after a 1792 sketch by John Sykes. In George Vancouver, *A Voyage of Discovery to the North Pacific Ocean,* vol. 1, plate 3. This engraving is based on Sykes's drawing of the iconic mountain from the area near modern-day Tacoma, south of Seattle. University of British Columbia, Rare Books and Special Collections, FC 3821.25.A1 1798a—Copy 3.

Townsend into the inner reaches of the series of islands and channels that make up today's Puget Sound. His crew went to work in the shore boats conducting the first of forty-six coastal surveys, some of them lasting weeks at a time. Joseph Whidbey, master of the *Discovery,* and James Johnstone, master of the *Chatham,* were usually in command of the survey parties. Vancouver led some of the surveys himself. These were not "running" surveys, like those performed by Cook, where the ships coasted in and out of storms away from the shore. Instead, the sailors rowed and sailed the smaller shore boats along every waterway, following each inlet to its head. They landed frequently to take astronomical observations and establish their positions by triangulation at prominent coastal points until each coastal feature was surveyed and added on to the expedition's master maps (fig. 13.2). The longest survey took twenty-three days and charted seven hundred miles of shoreline in the area north of the Queen Charlotte Islands and into southern Alaska. In this way the expedition's meticulous survey settled all doubts about the principal bays and inlets on the serrated Northwest Coast.[20]

As Puget was in command, his name was bestowed upon one of the inlets they surveyed. The name *Puget Sound* was intended at the time to identify the inland waters south of the Narrows near Tacoma but is now used to identify the shoreline of the greater Seattle metropolitan area. In less than a month, the voyagers found and named Whidbey and Vashon Islands, Mount Rainier (fig. 13.3), Mount Baker, Hood Canal, Port Orchard, Port Discovery, Possession Sound, Restoration Point, Deception Pass, Bellingham Bay, and Admiralty Inlet, some of the most prominent landmarks in modern-day Washington State. Vancouver bestowed more than three hundred names on mountains, headlands, waterways, and islands along the coast, most of which continue in use today. As a part of his remarkable journey, Vancouver took formal possession of the region on June 4 at Tulalip Bay, near the modern-day city of Everett, Washington. The expansive area he claimed for Britain encompassed the stretch of coastline and the internal bays and inlets from Oregon to southern Canada, a land he called "New Georgia" after the British monarch, George III.[21]

By mid-June Vancouver's expedition had passed the San Juan Islands and explored what is now downtown Vancouver, Canada. The channel dividing modern-day British Columbia mainland from Vancouver Island he named the Gulf of Georgia (called Georgia Strait today). A week later they encountered the smaller Spanish schooners *Sutil* and *Mexicana,* commanded by Dionisio Alcalá Galiano and Cayetano Valdés. Looking for a site to replace their Nootka fortifications, the Spaniards had sailed through the Strait of Juan de Fuca and entered the north arm of the Fraser River, the first Europeans to do so. Cordial relations were established, and the four ships moved together through the narrows that separate Vancouver Island from the mainland surveying the coastline in tandem and sharing the results (fig. 13.4). Ultimately the Spaniards fell behind and reached Nootka Sound three days after Vancouver.[22]

In the days after the parties separated, after exiting Johnstone Strait, the *Discovery* ran aground in Queen Charlotte Strait in a fogbank near Fife Sound (fig. 13.5). It was driven by the tide onto sunken rocks shortly after high tide, so the sailors spent anxious hours as the ship was slowly exposed

13.4 John Landseer, *Cheslakee's Village in Johnstone Strait,* 1798. Engraving after a 1792 sketch by John Sykes. In Vancouver, *Voyage,* vol. 1, plate 5. Vancouver's description of this Kwakwaka'wakw village on the northeast coast of Vancouver Island provided readers with one of his rare commentaries on the Native peoples encountered during the voyage. The illustration shows a substantial settlement. A trail across the island linked this village with European settlements and other, larger settlements in Nootka Sound. The trail was used for social and commercial purposes, as evidenced by Vancouver's comment that he observed Spanish muskets and "other European commodities" at the village. University of British Columbia, Rare Books and Special Collections, FC 3821.25.1798a—Copy 3.

13.5 Zachary Mudge, *The* Discovery *on the Rocks in Queen Charlotte Sound,* 1792. Watercolor. After exiting Johnstone Strait in the inland waters north of Vancouver Island, the *Discovery* ran aground in Queen Charlotte Strait in a fog bank. After anxious hours, the ship was finally floated free at high tide. Dixson Library, State Library of New South Wales, PD 695: #a7764001.

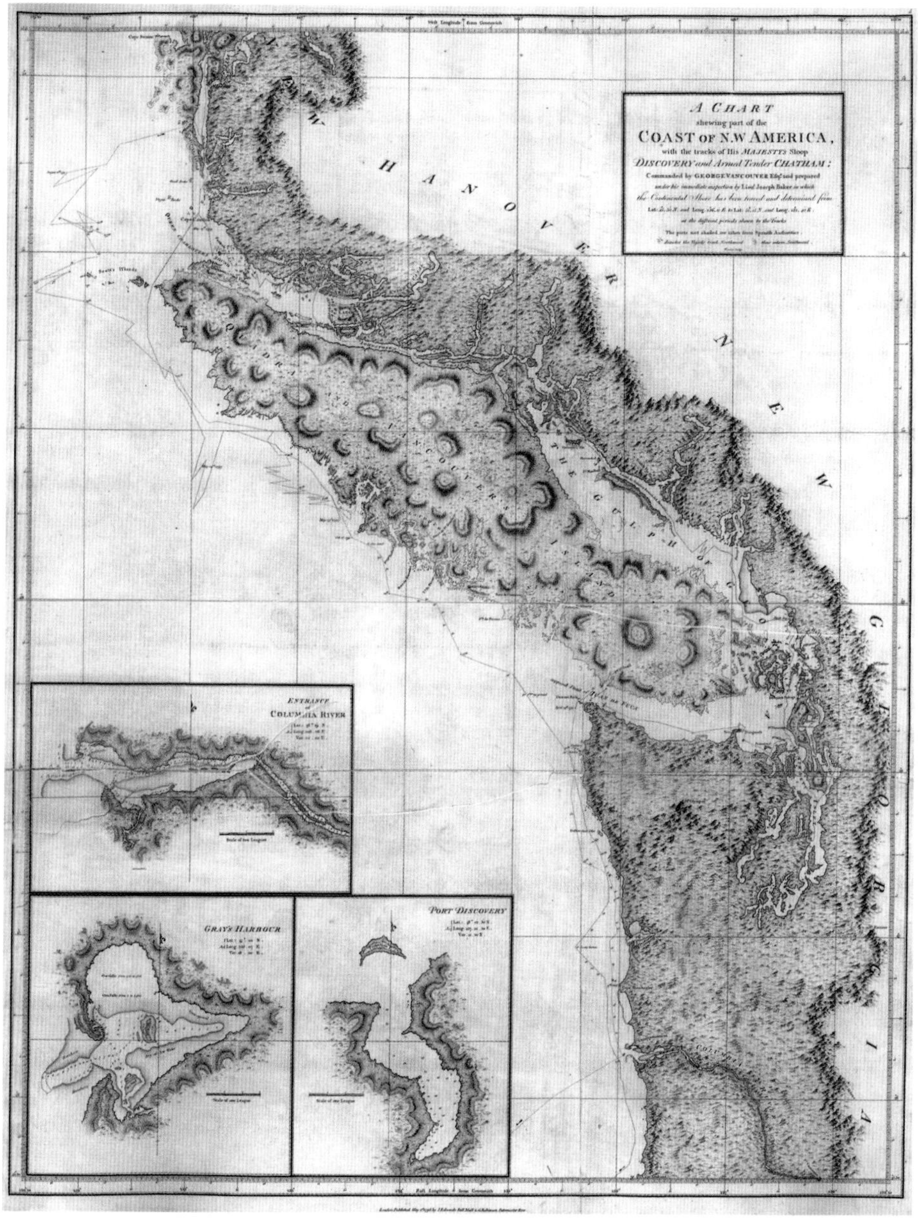

13.6 *A Chart Shewing Part of the Coast of NW America* (Vancouver Island, Puget Sound, and Columbia River), 1798. This engraved chart, included in the atlas to Vancouver's *Voyage,* offers the first complete and reasonably accurate map of a key section of the Pacific Northwest coast. It records the British discovery of Puget Sound, which earlier Spanish voyages had missed, and confirms the insularity of Vancouver Island after Vancouver's circumnavigation. Courtesy of Derek Hayes.

at low tide, nearly foundering. Fortunately there was no swell, but soon the ship was at a dangerous and precarious angle in a few feet of water. "Her situation, for a few seconds, was alarming in the highest degree," Vancouver wrote. Luckily at high tide the ship floated free. A day later the *Chatham* also ran aground. It too reached an oblique angle before being freed during the next high tide. After the vessels were freed of these snares, they entered the Pacific on August 9, 1792, earning their crews the distinction of being the first Westerners to circumnavigate the island (fig. 13.6).[23]

The expedition then sailed south to Nootka Sound to supervise the restoration of Meares's meager possessions and to rendezvous with the store ship *Daedalus*. The store ship had had its own harrowing journey. Arriving in Waikiki Bay after a passage from Cape Horn and the South Pacific, the commander of the *Daedalus,* Lieutenant Richard Hergest, and two of the crew were killed in a fracas in Hawai'i. Hergest, who had been with Cook in Kealakekua Bay, was already apprehensive about the volatile Hawaiians. Nevertheless, he, the astronomer William Gooch, and a seaman foolishly wandered, unarmed, away from a watering party to examine a Native village. When a needless fight broke out at the watering place, they were killed in a melee reminiscent of Cook's death on the Big Island. In retribution, when he reached Oahu the following winter, Vancouver sought justice for the murders. Three Hawaiians were identified as the killers, probably just to appease Vancouver, but the captain conducted a thorough investigation before accommodating chiefs dispatched the three men.[24]

By 1792 Nootka had expanded to a small colony of two hundred Spaniards with as many as fifty homes, some with gardens (figs. 13.7 and 3.9). It also served as an international gathering place, where, in the short summer, five Spanish, eleven British, two Portuguese, one French, and eight American vessels anchored.[25] In this scene, Vancouver, as British commissioner appointed to receive the reparations, met with Captain Bodega y Quadra, who as the senior naval officer in Mexico represented Revillagigedo (fig. 3.6). They were hosted by Maquinna (fig. 14.3), who lived intimately with the Spanish and regulated trade between Natives and traders throughout the region. Negotiations were so amicable that out of mutual respect, the two captains named the large island the four ships had just circled to be "Quadra and Vancouver Island." But neither captain was given adequate instructions to negotiate the restitution of British property in the cove, or discretion to find common ground, so Vancouver abandoned the talks and wrote for further directions from the diplomats in Europe. After several pageants ashore with the local people, Vancouver left Nootka for California.[26]

While Vancouver sailed ahead, his consort entered the mouth of the Columbia River, struggling past dangerous breakers and a sand bar. When Gray had entered the river mouth in May, he had traveled twenty miles upriver. Now the *Chatham* anchored, and its shore boats went one hundred

13.7 James Heath, *Friendly Cove, Nootka Sound,* 1798. Engraving after a 1792 drawing by Henry Humphrys, another midshipman on Vancouver's expedition. In Vancouver, *Voyage,* vol. 1, plate 7. This engraving shows the extent of the Spanish establishment in Friendly Cove in 1792. Vancouver and Juan Francisco de la Bodega y Quadra met here to negotiate the transfer of the settlement under the terms of the 1789 Nootka Convention. However, Bodega offered only "Meares Cove," on the right of the picture, signified by the letters A and B along a short stretch of the shoreline, which Vancouver thought was too small. As a result, the transfer was never concluded. University of British Columbia, Rare Books and Special Collections, FC 3821.25.1798a—Copy 3.

miles upriver to the location of modern-day Vancouver, Washington. Meanwhile, in November Captain Vancouver was warmly received upon entering San Francisco Bay, the first foreign ship to visit the mission and presidio there. As he entered the vast harbor, he would have gazed eastward to the rolling hills and verdant oak of coastal California, the scenic backdrop to what would later become the pretty college town of Berkeley. After ten days, he sailed south to Monterey, where he was shocked by the deplorable conditions of the missions and the treatment of the Indians. Even more, he was amazed by the undermanned presidio garrisons and speculated how they might be easily conquered.[27]

In January he sailed to Hawai'i, where the crew spent two months refitting the vessels while the captain advised King Kamehameha of the benefits of combining the warring tribes into a single nation and then ceding the islands to Great Britain for their protection. In early March 1793, after resolving the murders of Hergest and Gooch at Waikiki Bay, the expedition spent a week at Kealakekua Bay, receiving a tumultuous welcome that rivaled the first visit by Cook. The British, nonetheless wary of the surly and unpredictable nature of Hawaiian crowds, posted a continuous guard.

Vancouver returned with some trepidation to the place where Cook was murdered in 1779 and even met with the Hawaiian who was said to have thrust the fatal dagger into the captain. Although he was sorry about Cook's death, the killer expressed no remorse. Vancouver wrote that he visited "first of all the fatal spot, where Captain Cook so unexpectedly, and so unfortunately for the world, was deprived of his valuable life. This melancholy, and ever to be deplored event, the natives are at much pains exactly to represent, to produce reasons for its taking place, and to shew that it fulfilled the prophecies of the priests, who had foretold this sad catastrophe."[28]

In April the expedition returned for a second season on the Northwest Coast with surveys commencing from Vancouver Island and extending into Southeast Alaska. During the next four months, boat parties surveyed the maze of islands and inlets that make up this part of the coast while the ships periodically repositioned farther offshore. Observatory tents were set up at Restoration Bay at the end of Burke Inlet, British Columbia, and two hundred miles north at Salmon Cove at the head of Observatory Inlet, along the Canadian border with Southeast Alaska (fig. 13.8).

At the same time that Vancouver sailed from England, a young Scottish explorer, Alexander Mackenzie, undertook the second of his great expeditions for the North West Company to explore the Canadian Shield from Hudson's Bay to the Arctic and north Pacific. In his first expedition, in the modern-day Northwest Territories of northern Canada, he followed the river that now bears his name, reaching the Arctic Ocean on July 14, 1789. Influenced by the earlier reports of Peter Pond and armchair geographers in London, he was disappointed that the river emptied to the north and did not lead him to Cook Inlet. After returning to England to consult with the geographers about other possible routes across the continent, he traveled to Canada again in 1792 to find a route to the Pacific. He followed the Peace River to the Rocky Mountains and crossed the Coast Mountains along the Bella Coola River to Queen Charlotte Sound, reaching the Pacific near Bella Coola, British Columbia, on July 20, 1793 (fig. 10.7). Vancouver had just mapped the same inlet on June 5, so the two explorers had missed each other at Bella Coola by just forty-eight days. They never met, but the coastal people told Mackenzie of the British ship that had been in the same waters earlier in the summer.[29]

Leaving Salmon Cove on July 23, Vancouver was in charge of a prolonged survey party that reached Revillagigedo Island in southern Alaska on August 12, 1793, when a large group of Tlingit Indians surrounded the small boats in a surprise attack reminiscent of Cook's demise at Kealakekua Bay. Vancouver attempted to fend them off with trinkets and shouts, then fired over their heads, but finally he gave orders to shoot to kill. As many as ten Natives died. In this case, unlike the Hawaiian

13.8 James Fittler, *Salmon Cove, Observatory Inlet,* engraving from a 1793 sketch by Thomas Heddington. In Vancouver, *Voyage,* vol. 2, plate 9. This engraving, depicting a bay on the British Columbia coast south of the current border with Alaska, is based on a drawing by yet another midshipman on the voyage. The ships anchored in the cove as Vancouver took charge of a prolonged survey party in the ships' launches at the end of the second survey season. The explorers rowed and sailed into Alaskan waters where, in the Behm Canal at a place Vancouver called "Traitor's Cove" (near modern-day Ketchikan), they suffered a treacherous attack by Tlingit Natives. As many as ten local people were killed. This was the only hostile encounter on the Northwest Coast during the expedition's three survey seasons. University of British Columbia, Rare Books and Special Collections, FC 3821.25.1798a—Copy 3.

encounter, the other Natives broke off the attack. Vancouver was disheartened by the attack, writing at length about the deaths in his journal and his reluctance to order his men to shoot. He blamed the confrontation on "civilized commercial people" (probably American traders) who fomented discord among warring tribes to increase the demand for guns, or "destructive engines," as he called them. While there were other threats and confrontations, particularly in their encounters with the Tlingit, this was the only bloodshed during the expedition's three years' charting of the Northwest Coast.[30]

When the season was spent, Vancouver left Alaska, returning to San Francisco and Monterey. The ships then sailed south to Santa Barbara, Ventura, and San Diego, becoming the first foreign expedition to visit Southern California. In late December Vancouver reached Hawai'i again. In two months he achieved the Hawaiian cession, confirmed by King Kamehameha and his ruling council. Although the British government capitalized on the Vancouver voyage to secure broad ownership of western Canada, it did not follow up on this agreement to annex Hawai'i as a British colony.[31]

In February 1794 Vancouver sailed from Hawai'i to begin his third and final survey season, reaching Cook Inlet while winter weather still gripped the land. The Admiralty required that Vancouver resurvey Cook's River, as both Meares and Dalrymple speculated that it might still be the outlet of the same lakes and rivers that had inspired Mackenzie's quest to the Arctic. When they arrived in mid-April, the vista of snow-capped mountains was awe-inspiring, and a wisp of volcanic steam rose from Mount St. Augustine. Snow fell frequently, and temperatures dropped to 7°F. Maneuvering was difficult, as ice floes drifted in the ebb and flow of the tide, crashing into the sides of the ships. After landing in the estuary off Eagle River for water, Vancouver repositioned his ships to Fire Island, near modern-day Anchorage, Alaska, as Cook had done eighteen years earlier. From this vantage Vancouver is credited as the first European to view Mount McKinley (Denali), North America's highest peak. Joseph Whidbey left with two shore boats on April 28 to explore the eastern arm that Cook named "Turnagain River," and in two days he returned to report it closed farther east, so "this can be no longer considered a river."[32]

Vancouver and his biologist, Archibald Menzies, then surveyed the northern branch of the river in a yawl and small cutter. Vancouver found that the shoals in the middle of the arm were dry at low tide, and that the two shores came together. They waited for high tide, as Vancouver wanted to end all the speculation: "I resolved to continue our researches as far as it might be found navigable for the boats." The shores gradually converged, and soon they sighted the end of Knik Arm. They landed near the end of an arm and climbed a small hillock to look to the north, viewing the tall peaks of the Alaska Range in the distance. "[We] had a good view of the Banks & sandy shoals which seemed to extend across the inlet about 3 or 4 miles above the ship,

& backd one another to the very head of the arm," Menzies wrote. "Our station at this time was little more than a league [three miles] above where Capt Cooks boats returnd, & had they come up this far what a satisfactory view they would have had of the termination of this great inlet, where they could behold the impossibility of navigating it higher up, & consequently preventing the indulging of those chimeral speculations concerning its spacious & unbounded extent."

Having proved that this inlet was not the estuary of a great river, let alone a connection to the Atlantic Ocean, Vancouver decided to substitute the name *Cook's Inlet* for *Cook's River.* He was frustrated that Cook had been so careless, since Cook's failure to spend a few more hours examining the inlet, particularly Turnagain Arm, meant that the British had to send a second expedition to confirm these waters reached a dead end (fig. 13.9). In a blunt rebuke of both Cook and Dalrymple, Vancouver wrote: "This terminated this very extensive opening on the coast of North West America, to which, had the great and first discoverer of it, whose name it bears, dedicated one day more to

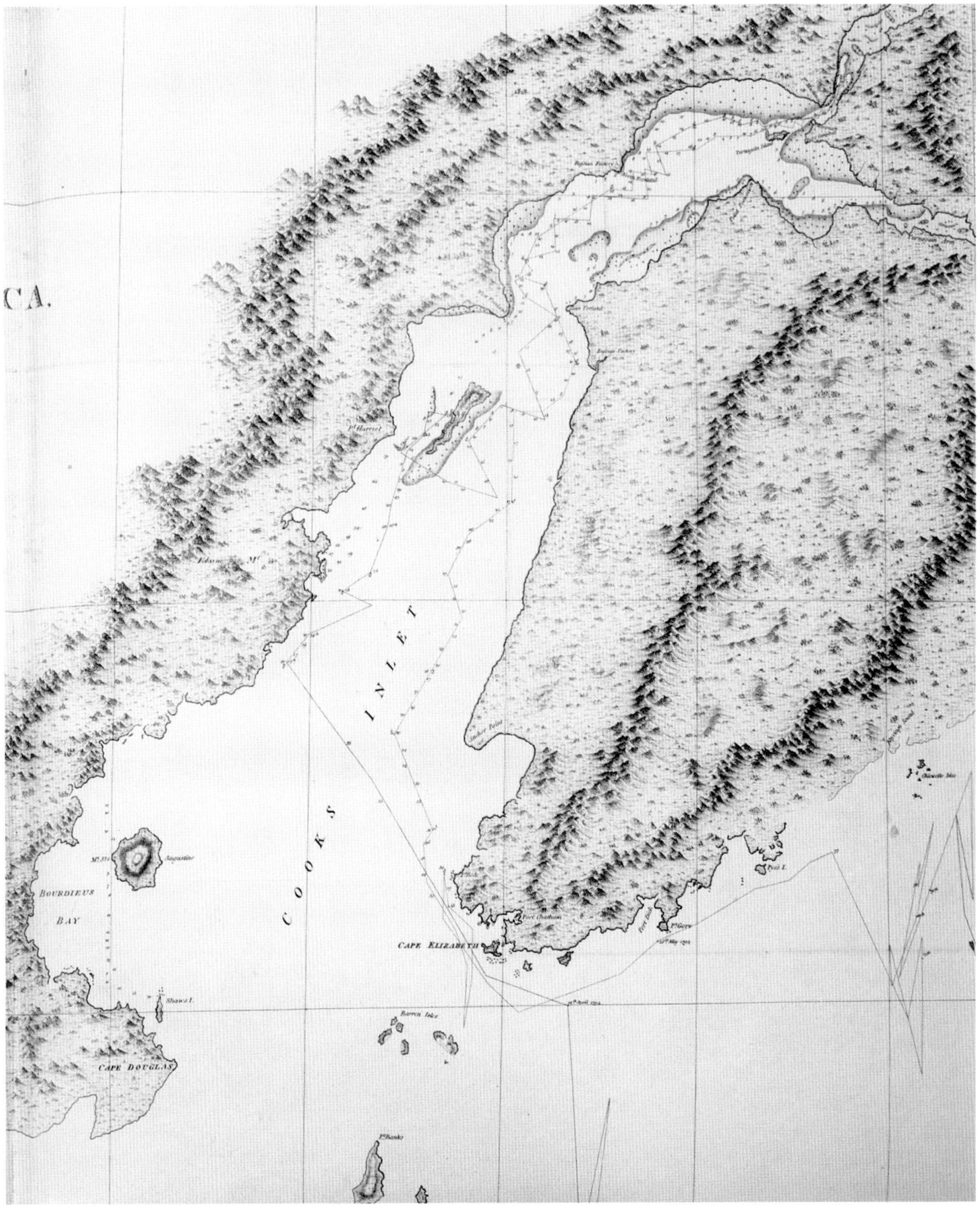

13.9 *Chart Shewing Part of the NW Coast of America* (Kodiak Island and Cook Inlet), included in the atlas to Vancouver's *Voyage.* This engraved chart offers a more detailed and accurate map of the area of Cook Inlet after Vancouver had confirmed that "Cook's River" was not in fact the estuary of a great river. The inlet, as Cook himself had believed, was not connected to any waterway leading into Alaska's interior, nor to any imagined passageways across the top of North America to the Atlantic and Europe. Courtesy of Derek Hayes.

13.10 B. T. Pouncy, *Port Dick, near Cook's Inlet,* engraving after a sketch by Henry Humphrys. In Vancouver *Voyage,* vol. 3, plate 13. Port Dick is located on the southern Kenai Peninsula at the mouth of Cook Inlet, which the expedition encountered at the beginning of the third survey season in 1794. The original drawing has no ethnographic detail; the engraver was apparently instructed to add the Native hunters in their kayaks to show the expedition's contact with a group hunting sea otters in the area. University of British Columbia, Rare Books and Special Collections, FC 3821.25.1798a—Copy 3.

its further examination, he would have spared the theoretical navigators, who have followed him in their closets, the task of ingeniously ascribing to this arm of the ocean a channel, through which the north-west passage existing according to their doctrines might ultimately be discovered." Menzies wrote that the inlet should be called "by the name of Cook's Gulph, as it no more resembles a river than any other great Inlet on this coast."[33]

Vancouver often came in contact with the local Dena'ina people, who frequently paddled to the ships in their skin canoes. On April 26, over twenty Natives spent the night aboard the *Discovery,* Vancouver's flagship. Russians first arrived a week later. After completing the survey that disproved the imagined passageway, Vancouver went with some of his officers to meet with Russian traders at the mouth of the Kenai River. They had erected a crude fort and factory, which housed several dozen Russian hunters, next to a Native village overlooking the river. He told the Russians he wanted to meet their manager, Aleksandr Baranov, the highest-ranking Russian official on the coast. Having no interpreter, Vancouver finally gave up hope of the meeting after several days and left Cook Inlet. Passing Port Dick at its outlet, the British observed a fleet of four hundred kayaks filled with Native sea-otter hunters (fig. 13.10). Because of his earlier visit to Unalaska with Captain Cook, Vancouver knew they were hunting against their will. The Russian technique was to exact tribute from the Natives and to threaten their families to assure their maximum effort in hunting sea otters.[34]

Passing Resurrection Bay, the expedition entered Prince William Sound. Local fur hunters told them there were just 466 Russians in all of Alaska at the time, dispersed in three forts at Kenai, Port Etches (Prince William Sound), and Bristol Bay. The hunters also seemed well acquainted with the geography of the region, explaining the proximity of the sound to Turnagain River, and told them that the Kenai Peninsula was almost an island, but for a short portage. "The two extensive inlets appeared," according to Vancouver, "to be separated from each other by a narrow isthmus of mountainous land." Later the British learned that the local people regularly portaged their canoes over the isthmus. Vancouver surveyed the area in considerable detail, giving names for the principal landmarks, all of which survive to this day. The area features the popular receding glacier, Portage Glacier, and the adjacent Portage Pass, east of Anchorage. It is just a few miles from Passage Canal, named by Vancouver, and the small community of Whittier, at the western extremity of Prince William Sound.[35]

The expedition next sailed for Mount St. Elias, where in late June they entered Yakutat Bay (fig. 13.11). Here they found a Russian hunting party of over nine hundred Kodiak Islanders hunting sea otters in kayaks. Vancouver was surprised at the massive size of this expedition, certain that it would anger the local Tlingits and destroy the sea-otter population. Later the expedition entered Icy Strait, where Whidbey began a survey eastward from the entrance to Cross Sound. At first the survey was hampered by ice calving from the glacier that extended to the entrance of Glacier Bay. Today this strait is ice free. In two centuries, the glacier has retreated an astounding sixty miles into smaller tideland glaciers occupying the separate fjords and inlets of the bay.

After examining Lynn Canal, leading north from modern-day Juneau to Skagway, Whidbey proceeded down Chatham Strait between Baranov and Admiralty Islands. While the instructions required that Vancouver concentrate on the continental shore, all the coastal features of Southeast Alaska's island maze were carefully charted. By late August the three-year coastal survey was finally finished at a place they called Port Conclusion, on the inner coast of Baranov Island. In his penultimate journal entry, Vancouver spoke of the finality of his work. Despite Meares's fanciful map, no passage through the continent had been found: "I trust the precision with which the survey of the coast of North West America has been carried into effect, will remove every doubt, and set aside every opinion of a north-west passage, or any water communication navigable for shipping, existing between the North Pacific, and the interior of the American continent, within the limits of our researches. The

13.11 *Icy Bay and Mount St. Elias,* 1794. Proof engraving set into a copy of Vancouver's *Voyage,* vol. 3, after a drawing by Thomas Heddington. This early engraving shows *Discovery* and *Chatham* off Yakutat Bay, unlike the engraving in the first edition of the work, plate 14, which presents only one ship. It is likely that the original sketch had no ships and that the engraver experimented with placing them in the picture. DeGolyer Library, Southern Methodist University, Dallas, Texas, Folio-2G420.V22.1798.

discovery that no such communication does exist has been zealously pursued, and with a degree of minuteness far exceeding the letter of my commission or instructions."[36]

Unlike Cook, Vancouver and his crew found the local people to be an ever-present distraction, but they did little to investigate or report Native languages, habits, or cultures. The sailors encountered the full range of people who lived on the coast: Salish, Kwakiutl, Nuu-chah-nulth, Haida, Tlingit, Alutiiq, and Dena'ina. They must usually have established a good rapport with the people, as the exhaustive survey would not otherwise have been possible, but the captain's journal does little more than describe each encounter. Unlike Cook, Vancouver was not captivated by the life and customs of the local people or the differences in cultures along the coast. Instead he regarded his contacts as just one element of risk in the daily grind of coastal surveying, and now that the examination was complete, the people of the coast were left in peace.

The journals suggest a great deal of sensitivity to Native interests, even after the clash at Behm Canal during the second survey season. For example, during the investigation of an Alaska burial site, Vancouver insisted that the explorers leave the area undisturbed. He often noted his outrage with unscrupulous Western traders who provided guns to Natives along the coast and in Hawai'i. He said the British did not offer weapons in trade with the local people. Unfortunately, since there was no official artist on board, the expedition relied on three amateur artists—John Sykes, Henry Humphreys and Thomas Heddington—to record the voyage outcomes. None of them being accomplished ethnographers, they did not draw the local people or their customs—a disappointing oversight.

Over one hundred drawings were available to Vancouver when he assembled his journal for publication. Most were coastal views, so the majority of significant depictions of the Northwest Coast show erected observatory tents in Puget Sound (fig. 13.2), several views of distant snow-capped mountains (fig. 13.3), the anchorages in Nootka Sound (fig. 13.7), Salmon Cove (fig. 13.8) and Behm Canal, and two drawings of headlands with distant Native homes surrounded by forested hillsides (see fig. 13.4). Ironically, the original Humphrys drawing of Port Dick, at the outlet of Cook Inlet, showed water and hillsides with no ethnographic detail. In the published version, the engraver added dozens of Natives hunting sea otters in kayaks, presumably at Vancouver's behest. This is perhaps the most noteworthy portrayal of inhabitants in the published account (fig. 13.10).[37]

After leaving Alaskan waters, the expedition proceeded south, anchoring in Nootka Sound. They attempted one last time to resolve the requirements of the Nootka treaty, but they were not successful. Vancouver was saddened to learn that the esteemed Captain Bodega y Quadra had died that spring.[38] The voyagers then sailed to Monterey, California (fig. 13.12), before returning to England the following September, completing a circumnavigation of the world. At four years and six months, the expedition was the longest in the annals of British exploration, covering an estimated 65,000 miles. The small boat surveys probably added another 10,000 miles. By comparison, Cook's second expedition covered 55,000 miles, and his third voyage lasted four years and three months. Despite minor outbreaks of scurvy and a few skirmishes with natives, Vancouver and the sailors who accompanied him suffered just six fatalities, one-third the normal mortality rate in all of Britain at the time.[39]

The accuracy and completeness of Vancouver's survey were critical to future commerce and coastal navigation in the region (fig. 13.13). William Dall, an Alaskan explorer, stated in 1870 that Vancouver's explorations "have not been excelled by any other navigator," and he found in the 1880s that Vancouver's charts were still the most trusted authority on Alaskan waters. Indeed, these charts were still the official maps of the coast well over a century after their initial publication. They were consulted for determining the boundary in the Anglo-Russian Convention of 1825, the Oregon boundary dispute in 1846, and the San Juan Islands arbitration in 1872. The numerous names that Vancouver bestowed on places along the coast are a lasting memorial to his expedition.[40]

When Vancouver left North America in 1794, he concluded twenty years of intense exploration on the Northwest Coast. Although fur-trading expeditions continued for several more decades, and many vessels followed Vancouver's charts, they usually had only commercial objectives. It was mostly the Russian navy that continued the spirit of scientific observation in expeditions that circumnavigated the globe in the early nineteenth century and gave further certainty to the outlines of the Alaska coastline. While the consequences of Vancouver's voyage were unmatched, neither the captain nor his published journal received much attention. The published journals of his mentor James Cook, it seems, cast a long shadow.

On his return Vancouver was in poor health due to a life at sea, and he labored in obscurity in the quiet village of Petersham preparing the voyage journal. Like any stern commander, he had detractors among his crew, and they spoke often about his

13.12 John Sykes, *The Mission of San Carlos near Monterrey,* watercolor, 1792, in Sykes, *Sketches of Scenery on the NW Coast of America.* Sykes prepared this iconic drawing, one of the first depictions of a mission in California, in 1792 at the end of the first survey season. The expedition returned to Monterey in 1794 before sailing back to England. This mission, better known as Mission Carmel, was the favorite of Father Junípero Serra, who founded the missions of Alta California. When he died in 1784, Serra was interred beneath the chapel floor. UK Hydrographic Office, HO 20/NO/50: View 64.

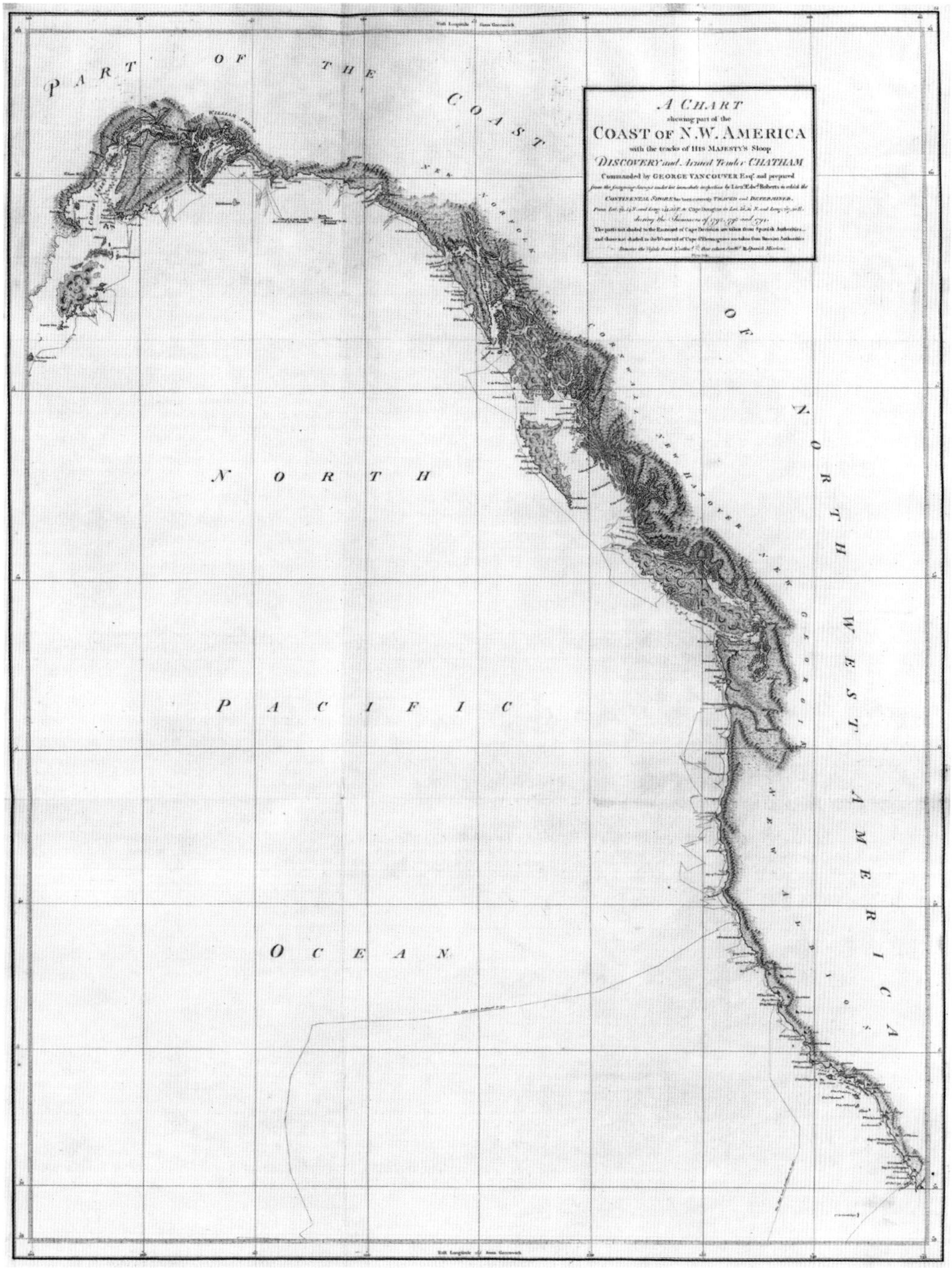

temper when they got back to England. Much is made of his temperament and record of discipline on the voyage, even though the number of floggings he administered was not remarkable in comparison to other commanders, including Cook, and he was devoted to the health of everyone aboard. Most of the crew served with distinction and without complaint. Seven were later promoted to flag rank, with Puget ascending to rear admiral in 1821. Recent investigations suggest that Vancouver died of hypothyroidism, a complication that may have followed the malaria he contracted while serving in the Royal Navy in Jamaica, which plagued him for the rest of his life. This illness probably explains both his record of periodic rages and passions on the voyage and his early death.[41]

Nonetheless, in his remaining years, Vancouver was embarrassed and dishonored by his critics. A sixteen-year-old midshipman on the voyage, Thomas Pitt, was frequently disciplined and finally sent home for irascible and insolent conduct on the voyage. He was a cousin of the prime minister

13.13 *A Chart Shewing Part of the Coast of NW America* (San Diego to Cook Inlet). In the atlas to Vancouver's *Voyage,* plate 14. Vancouver's unprecedented three-year survey encompassed the area from California to Alaska. For more than a century after the expedition, its voyage charts were the most trusted authority on the waters of the Northwest Coast, including coastal Alaska into Cook Inlet. Vancouver's sectional and summary charts of the coast, published in 1798, incorporated not only the results of his own survey but also information received from the Cook expedition, Spanish navigators, and British and American fur traders. Courtesy of Derek Hayes.

and, with the death of his father, the midshipman became Lord Camelford. Resenting his treatment on the voyage and his humiliating return, Pitt harassed Vancouver publicly and privately. He challenged him to a duel, published unflattering letters, and even attacked him with a cane on a London street. This battering led to a newspaper cartoon caricature that disgraced the captain.

Just as important, because Vancouver gave insufficient deference to Menzies and his scientific work on the voyage, Joseph Banks, the powerful and influential president of the Royal Society, rebuked Vancouver. Banks and Menzies were longtime friends, and Banks sponsored Menzies to be naturalist on the voyage. Haughty and aloof, he was in regular conflict with Vancouver, particularly after Menzies was appointed surgeon. When Menzies told Banks of the conflict, Banks complained, with the result that the Admiralty procrastinated over making good Vancouver's pay and allowances until after his death.[42]

In addition to demoralizing Vancouver, these events maligned the voyage record. Now considered one of Britain's greatest explorers, Vancouver was abandoned by his friends and labored over the voyage journal in obscurity for the last two years of his life. He died impoverished and in despair a month before his forty-first birthday. After his death his brother John completed the journal, which was published in 1798. Called *A Voyage Of Discovery to the North Pacific Ocean, and round The World, in the Years 1791–95*, it appeared in three text volumes with a separate folio atlas. Although there were two editions, it was not as popular as other contemporary expedition journals, particularly the journals of Captain Cook's three voyages. Today it is quite valuable and difficult to find at any price.[43]

George Vancouver was laid to rest in a modest Petersham churchyard near a bend in the Thames River, his simple headstone a stark contrast to the imposing white obelisk erected for Captain Cook on the north shore of Kealakekua Bay.[44] Nonetheless, Vancouver's voyage ranks among the most significant achievements in Western exploration. He helped implement the Nootka Convention, asserted claims of British sovereignty, secured the cession of Hawai'i, and concluded a meticulous survey over thirty degrees of latitude along the Northwest Coast. And because most of the surveys conducted by the Spanish were kept secret, Vancouver's charts, place names, and conclusions about the coastal topography were retained as the final word about the Northwest Coast into modern times. But all of that knowledge was mostly lost in Britain for at least a century after his death.

In the spirit of the European Enlightenment, Captain James Cook initiated the campaign of discovery in his peripatetic survey of coastal Alaska in 1778. His map was incomplete, but it was the first to depict realistic coastal trends from Oregon to the Arctic. Ships from a host of nations then followed, and each in its own way considered the geography, ethnography, and commercial opportunities of this farthest temperate shore from Europe, the so-called backside of America. But none of them undertook a thorough survey until Cook's former midshipman, the determined George Vancouver, completed three seasons of painstaking investigation to reveal the coastal outline from Cook Inlet to San Diego, particularly the intricate tapestry of Puget Sound, coastal British Columbia, and Southeast Alaska.

NOTES

1 Jean-François Galaup, comte de La Pérouse, *A Voyage round the World Performed in the Years 1785, 1786, 1787 and 1788 by the Boussole and Astrolabe* (Paris: A. Hamilton, 1799), 358–59.

2 Julius S. Gassner, *Voyages and Adventures of La Pérouse,* translation of 1839 edition of F. Valentin (Honolulu: University of Hawai'i Press, 1969), 27–43; John Dunmore, *Pacific Explorer: The Life of Jean François de La Pérouse, 1741–1788* (Palmerston North, New Zealand: Dunmore Press, 1985), 229–31. See also Robin Inglis, *La Pérouse 1786: A French Naval Visit to Alaska,* in *Enlightenment and Exploration in the North Pacific, 1741–1805,* ed. Stephen Haycox, James Barnett, and Caedmon Liburd (Seattle: University of Washington Press, 1997), 49–64. The voyage instructions are discussed on p. 58. See also Glyndwr Williams, *Voyages of Delusion: The Search for the Northwest Passage in the Age of Reason* (London: Harper Collins, 2002), 340–48.

3 La Pérouse, *Voyage round the World,* 387; Gassner, *Voyages and Adventures,* 33–34.

4 Gassner, *Voyages and Adventures,* 43–51; Dunmore, *Pacific Explorer,* 232–43.

5 Gassner, *Voyages and Adventures,* 135–56; Dunmore, *Pacific Explorer,* 276–95, 307. The journals were published in English two years later, in 1799.

6 Warren L. Cook, *Flood Tide of Empire: Spain and the Pacific Northwest, 1543–1819* (New Haven, CT: Yale University Press, 1973), 93–98.

7 Cook, *Flood Tide of Empire,* 306–20; Williams, *Voyages of Delusion,* 371–85; Iris H. W. Engstrand, *Spanish Scientists in the New World: The Eighteenth-Century Expeditions* (Seattle: University of Washington Press, 1981); Andrew David, Felipe Fernández-Armesto, Carlos Novi, and Glyndwr Williams, eds., *The Malaspina Expedition,* vol. 2 (London: Hakluyt Society, 2003), 100–160, 468–80. On July 26, 1791, Malaspina was convinced there was no undiscovered passageway along this part of the Alaska coastline, concluding that earlier Spanish voyages, and the earlier Cook expedition, were dispositive. "If our present survey, being subsequent to that of the distinguished English navigator, does not allow us the complacency of considering it as important for the progress of geography, let us hope at least it will put to an end in the future to new speculations on the existence of a passage in these latitudes, and not risk so many lives and fortunes in such investigations."

8 In order to preserve the fledgling Kodiak Island colony, the Russians went to war with the local people . This conflict was described from the conqueror's perspective in Shelikhov's personal accounts, found in Basil Dmytryshyn, E. A. P. Crownhart-Vaughan, and Thomas Vaughan, *Russian Penetration of the North Pacific Ocean, 1700–1797: A Documentary Record* (Portland: Oregon Historical Society, 1988), 296–320, 326–33, 352–53; See also P. A. Tikhmenev, *A History of the Russian-American Company,* ed. R. A. Pierce and A. S. Donnelley (Seattle: University of Washington Press, 1978), 410–14.

9 Martin Sauer, *An Account of a Geographical and Astronomical Expedition to the Northern Parts of Russia* (London: T. Cadell, 1802), 148–209. See also G. Sarychev, *Voyage of Discovery to the Northeast of Siberia, the Frozen Ocean, and the North-east Sea,* vol. 2 (London: Richard Phillips, 1806), 19–28.

10 Cook, *Flood Tide of Empire,* 100–106; Derek Pethick, *The Nootka Connection: Europe and the Northwest Coast, 1790–95* (Vancouver, BC: Douglas & McIntyre, 1980), 12–23; George Vancouver, *A Voyage of Discovery to the North Pacific Ocean and round the World, 1791–95,* ed. W. Kaye Lamb, 4 vols. (London: Hakluyt Society, 1984), 1:15–27; Williams, *Voyages of Delusion,* 348–62. See also J. Richard Nokes, *Almost a Hero: The Voyages of John Meares, R.N., to China, Hawaii and the Northwest Coast* (Pullman: Washington State University Press, 1998), 7–17.

11 John Meares, *Voyages Made in the Years 1788 and 1789 from China to the North West Coast of America* (London: J. Walter, 1790). His notes from the earlier voyage (describing the winter in Prince William Sound) and speculation about the Northwest Passage are in the introductory pages, i–lxvi. See also Barry Gough, *The Northwest Coast: British Navigation, Trade and Discoveries to 1812* (Vancouver: University of British Columbia Press, 1992), 87–95.

12 Cook, *Flood Tide of Empire,* 119–45; Gough, *Northwest Coast,* 96–115.

13 Frederic W. Howay, ed., *Voyages of the "Columbia" to the Northwest Coast* (Boston: Massachusetts Historical Society, 1941). The first voyage log of Robert Haswell, first mate of the *Columbia,* is at pp. 3–107. J. Richard Nokes, *Columbia's River: The Voyages of Robert Gray, 1787–1793* (Tacoma: Washington State Historical Society, 1991), 59–79.

14 Cook, *Flood Tide of Empire,* 160–249; Gough, *Northwest Coast,* 127–45; Nokes, *Almost a Hero,* 155–60.

15 Cook, *Flood Tide of Empire,* 271–84; Pethick, *Nootka Connection,* 32–33.

16 The Admiralty's voyage instructions recognized the advancing knowledge of the Canadian interior and how that might change possible connections along the Pacific coast. By the time Vancouver left England, the maps from the 1783 Peter Pond exploration of Lake Athabasca and the 1789 Alexander Mackenzie expedition to the Arctic Ocean were known in London. While Pond guessed that the interior lakes connected to the Pacific, Mackenzie proved that they emptied into the Arctic. In his third voyage, Cook was sent to find a broad passageway to Europe. Over a decade later, the Admiralty instructed Vancouver to examine possible river connections to known Arctic lakes and rivers. See Vancouver, *A Voyage of Discovery,* 1:41–43.

17 Williams, *Voyages of Delusion,* 362–70; Glyndwr Williams, *Arctic Labyrinth: The Quest for the Northwest Passage* (London: Harper Collins, 2009), 152–55. While on the voyage in 1792, Vancouver gave the name Point Roberts to the point that separates modern coastal Washington from British Columbia.

18 Vancouver, *A Voyage of Discovery,* 1:5, 1:27–54; The purposes and consequences of the Vancouver voyage are described in Glyndwr Williams, "George Vancouver, the Admiralty, and Exploration in the Late Eighteenth Century," in Haycox, Barnett, and Liburd, *Enlightenment and Exploration in the North Pacific, 1741–1805,* 38–48. See also Glyndwr Williams, "Myth and Reality: the Theoretical Geography of Northwest America from Cook to Vancouver," in *From Maps to Metaphors: The Pacific World of George Vancouver,* ed. Robin Fisher and Hugh Johnston (Vancouver: University of British Columbia Press, 1993), 35–50; Williams, *Arctic Labyrinth,* 156–66.

19 Vancouver, *A Voyage of Discovery,* 2:502–3; Howay, *Voyages of the "Columbia."* John Boit's log of the entry into Columbia River is found at pp. 393–97, and Haswell's second voyage log is found at pp. 293–359. Nokes, *Columbia's River,* 179–91; Williams, *Voyages of Delusion,* 386–88.

20 Andrew David, "Vancouver's Survey Methods and Surveys," in Fisher and Johnston, *From Maps to Metaphors,* 51–69; Vancouver, *A Voyage of Discovery,* 1:137–38.

21 Vancouver, *A Voyage of Discovery,* 2:569.

22 Ibid., 500–687. This covers the expedition's exploration of Puget Sound and the circumnavigation of Vancouver Island. There is a separate voyage journal for the two Spanish ships: see John Kendrick, ed., *The Voyage of the* Sutil *and* Mexicana *in 1792* (Spokane, WA: Arthur H. Clark, 1991). Their first meeting with Vancouver, on June 21, 1792, is described at pp. 130–31. Vancouver's report of the meeting is recounted in Vancouver, *A Voyage of Discovery,* 2:591–93. See also Gough, *Northwest Coast,* 156–63; Williams, *Voyages of Delusion,* 386–95.

23 The grounding of the *Discovery* occurred on August 6. Vancouver, *A Voyage of Discovery,* 2:640–47. Lieutenant Zachary Mudge drew a compelling view of the near disaster, showing the *Discovery* floating askew nearly out of the water with the *Chatham* upright nearby. More than a dozen Native people in two dugout canoes observe nearby. Williams, *Voyages of Delusion,* 394.

24 Vancouver's description of the murders is found in Vancouver, *A Voyage of Discovery,* 2:785–86. For his account, see ibid., 3:875–81. Vancouver and Hergest were close friends, and the loss of Gooch, the only voyage astronomer, probably affected the accuracy of expedition surveys, as astronomical observations were essential to the determination of longitude.

25 José Mariano Moziño, *Noticias de Nutka: An Account of Nootka Sound in 1792,* ed. Iris H. W. Engstrand (Seattle: University of Washington Press, 1991), xli, 87.

26 Yvonne Marshall, "Dangerous Liaisons: Maquinna, Quadra and Vancouver in Nootka Sound, 1790–5," in Fisher and Johnston, *From Maps to Metaphors,* 160–75.

27 Cook, *Flood Tide of Empire,* 362–82. Ultimately the Spanish withdrew from Nootka of their own accord (397–433); Pethick, *Nootka Connection,* 135–43; Gough, *Northwest Coast,* 163–65. See Vancouver, *A Voyage of Discovery,* 2:688–746, recording Vancouver's impressions of the Spanish fortifications and missions of California, and 2:747–70, giving Lieutenant Broughton's account of the Columbia River voyage.

28 Vancouver, *A Voyage of Discovery,* 3:797–898. Vancouver revisits the death of Cook at pp. 831–32. See also 1164 n., where Lamb notes that several Hawaiians claimed to have struck the fatal blow.

29 *The Journals and Letters of Sir Alexander Mackenzie,* ed. W. Kaye Lamb (London: Hakluyt Society, 1970), 375–77. The Bella Coola people told him "with an air of insolence" that "a large canoe had lately been in this bay." Mackenzie was dubious at the time, but later understood this was a garbled report of Vancouver's ships transiting the channel. The natives apparently told Mackenzie they had a confrontation with Vancouver, but such an incident is not mentioned in any of the surviving journals.

30 Vancouver, *A Voyage of Discovery,* 3:931, 1005–19, offers Vancouver's recollections of the survey at Elcho Harbour, where Mackenzie soon appeared. Mackenzie could not reach the open ocean because of hostile Natives, so was satisfied inscribing a rock in view of the ocean on the water's edge of Dean Channel, now within British Columbia's Mackenzie Provincial Park. Vancouver was horrified by the deaths on Behm Canal and frustrated that the Tlingit were so insistent on trading for firearms, which the British would not provide. The site of the fatal encounter, called Traitor's Cove, is described in Vancouver's journal at pp. 1012–15.

31 Vancouver, *A Voyage of Discovery,* 3:899–1135, which chronicles Vancouver's second survey season, including his travels in Southern California, and 1136–1205, which narrates the final visit to Hawai'i.

32 Vancouver, *A Voyage of Discovery,* 4:1243.

33 Ibid.; Williams, *Voyages of Delusion,* 401–2. Weather conditions in Cook Inlet were reported by Archibald Menzies, the botanist on the voyage, in *The Alaska Travel Journal of Archibald Menzies, 1793–94,* ed. Wallace M. Olson (Fairbanks: University of Alaska Press, 1993), 91, 101.

34 See *The Journals of Captain James Cook on His Voyages of Discovery,* vol. 3, *The Voyage of the* Resolution *and* Discovery, *1776–1780,* ed. J. C. Beaglehole (Cambridge: Cambridge University Press for the Hakluyt Society, 1967). Cook wrote, "I never thought to ask how long it was sence they got a footing upon Oonalaska and the neighbouring isles, but to judge from the great subjection the Natives are under, it must have been some time" (458). Other crewmen were more critical. David Samwell wrote, "The Russians have been obliged to use harsh Methods to bring the Natives of Nawanalaska & the other Islands about into subjection & to make them honest. They told us that they never forgave a Theft but always punished it with instant death. . . . [T]he inhabitants of this Island are in a state of Subjection to the Russians and it should seem from what we observed amongst them that they are made to pay Tribute to their Masters, all their Arms of every kind are taken from them" (1142).

35 On Vancouver's third and final survey season on the coast, including time in Cook Inlet, see Vancouver, *A Voyage of Discovery,* 3–4:1206–1391. On contacts with George Purtov in Yakutat Bay, see 1313, 1329–31. Baranov apparently sent three messages to Vancouver via Purtov suggesting they meet, but Baranov never kept the appointments (1259–60).

36 Vancouver, *A Voyage of Discovery,* 4:1390. The final survey at Port Conclusion is described by Vancouver in 4:1371 ff. Vancouver and his crew were more than amused at the failure to find a passageway, writing, "No small portion of facetious mirth passed among the seamen. In consequence of our having sailed from ole England on the first of April, for the purpose of discovering a north-west passage, by following up the discoveries of De Fuca, De Fonte, and a numerous train of hypothetical navigators." See also Pethick, *Nootka Connection,* 188–93; Williams, *Voyages of Delusion,* 401–5.

37 Kesler E. Woodward, "Images of Native Alaskans in the Work of Explorer Artists, 1741–1805," and Robin Fisher, "George Vancouver and the Native Peoples of the Northwest Coast," in Haycox, Barnett, and Liburd, *Enlightenment and Exploration,* 161–75, 198–209. Behm Canal was named by Vancouver after Major Magnus Behm, the governor of Kamchatka, who lent considerable assistance to Cook's third expedition when it was under the command of Charles Clerke in 1779. In bestowing Behm's name on a prominent landmark, Vancouver likened him to Quadra in his journal: both were worthy foreign dignitaries whose "general conduct seems to have been actuated by the same motives of benevolence, and governed by principles of similar magnanimity" (Vancouver, *A Voyage of Discovery,* 2:743).

38 "The death of our highly valuable and much esteemed friend Senr Quadra," Vancouver wrote, "who in the month of March had died at St. Blas, universally lamented. Having endeavoured, on a former occasion, to point out the degree of admiration and respect with which the conduct of Sen'r Quadra toward our little community had impressed us during his life, I cannot refrain, now that he is no more, from rendering that justice to his memory to which it is so amply intitled, by stating, that the unexpected melancholey event of his decease . . . produced the deepest regret for the loss of a character so amiable, and so truly ornamental to civil society." The 1794 discussions were also fruitless. In the end another British captain was sent to the sound in 1795, after the treaty was amended. In the Convention for the Mutual Abandonment of Nootka, the two countries agreed that no permanent structures would be erected in Nootka Sound. The five-year-old Santa Cruz de Nutka, the first European colony in British Columbia, and its adjacent fort were demolished. Within months the Spanish buildings were replaced by Maquinna's lodge, and Yuquot changed back to a modest Native village after twenty years of Western domination. Barry Gough, "Rising Tides of Empire," *Columbia* 22, no. 2 (Summer 2008): 36–43.

39 Bern Anderson, *Surveyor of the Sea: The Life and Voyages of George Vancouver* (Toronto: University of Toronto Press, 1960), 213. Like Cook, Vancouver had a passionate devotion to the diet of his crew, ensuring that they dined on fresh provisions, ate citrus fruit, and drank at least two pints of spruce beer each day. Scurvy was virtually unknown, and when observed, it was quickly cured. So, despite his critics, Vancouver had no complaints from the crewmen about their diet when they returned to England. John M. Naish, "The Health of Mariners: Vancouver's Achievement," in Haycox, Barnett, and Liburd, *Enlightenment and Exploration,* 79–87.

40 Anderson, *Surveyor of the Sea,* 232; William H. Dall, *Alaska and Its Resources* (Boston: Lee and Shepard, 1870), 316.

41 Vancouver, *A Voyage of Discovery,* 1:210–12, 1:250. Another detractor was George Hewett, surgeon's mate on the *Discovery.* His comments were limited to constant complaints on the voyage and marginal notes in his version of the voyage journal, so they were not made public until well after the captain's death.

42 W. Kaye Lamb, "Banks and Menzies: Evolution of a Journal," in Fisher and Johnston, *From Maps to Metaphors,* 227–44. Vancouver did not know before the voyage of the long association of Banks and Menzies. In facing down Banks, the Admiralty agreed with the captain that Vancouver's journal would be the only official voyage record.

43 Vancouver, *A Voyage of Discovery,* 1:240–45.

44 Vancouver's simple headstone reads: "Captain George Vancouver. Died in the Year 1798, Aged 40." The gravesite is located in the London borough of Richmond-upon-Thames, fifteen miles southwest of Central London, in St. Peter's churchyard, Petersham, Surrey. It was restored in the 1920s by the Native Sons of British Columbia and is now maintained by the city of Vancouver, British Columbia. The twenty-seven-foot high Captain Cook Monument is a white obelisk surrounded by an ornate, heavy chain railing, constructed in Kealakekua Bay in 1874. The site was ceded in 1877 to Britain, which has maintained the property as sovereign territory ever since.

From Discoveries to Sovereignties

The Imperial Scramble for Northwestern North America

BARRY GOUGH

14

IN A REMARKABLY SHORT INTERVAL, A MERE FLOURISH IN THE HISTORY OF the modern world, sovereignty was established by rival imperial powers on the Northwest Coast of America. The period covered here is essentially 1821 to 1846, with a glance at precursor developments. The Northwest Coast is specifically defined here as that territory including Alaska and the Pacific cordillera lands south to 42°N—that is, the border of Alta California, then a province of Mexico. The western waters of Alaska—the Bering Strait, Kotzebue Sound, and the Arctic Sea leading eastward to Point Barrow—enter our story only marginally, in two aspects: the rivalry for the discovery of the Northwest Passage, and the fight for the navigational rights on the coast, especially in the area now designated as Southeast Alaska.

Taken together, these waters and coasts were locales of a great and simmering conflict of empires. The personalities and characteristics of the lead agents in this rivalry are the stuff of legend. Their commercial promoters and backers were hard-driving masters with little sympathy for the safety or comfort of the officers and men who did their bidding. The assumptions made by these corporate and governmental agents of empire in the line of duty may seem in our own time unacceptable: on

Steve Mayo, *Captain Robert Gray's Ship* Columbia Rediviva *Crossing the Bar of the Columbia River, May 11, 1792,* 1996 (detail of fig. 14.4).

reflection, historians are struck by the rapaciousness of those seeking wealth in this area of vast marine resources. At the same time, we are driven to conclude that commercial impulses lay at the root of empire building. Marine surveys were harbingers of commerce and claims to empire. The borders established in consequence of the rivalries here described reflect the aspirations and abilities of the contenders. Taken altogether, these factors provided the necessary preliminaries to the final division of the continent of North America.

Concepts of international law changed mightily from the fifteenth to the nineteenth century. For the earliest European empires overseas—those of Portugal and Spain—it sufficed merely to proclaim sovereignty. Later, sovereignty was proclaimed in one instance and bargained for in another by rival powers. In Alaska, Russia proclaimed dominion without international let or interference; however, farther south, beyond the limits of Russian dominion, Great Britain and the United States vied for sovereign control and in the end divided the Oregon country. Voyages of discovery added mightily to the information gathered about this hitherto remote locale, but it was commercial activity and rivalry that drove home the arguments for sovereign control, and not least of these factors was the search for land for settlement. Human occupation, not priority of discovery, became the determinant in the final divisions of territory.

All of this happened in the space of fifty years—from the rapacious times of the sea-otter trade, beginning in about 1785 and ending in the 1820s, through the rise of the land-based fur trade and the evolution of coastal trading to the final climax brought about by the infusion of American settlers into Oregon in the early 1840s. Mariners had come not only to make discoveries but also to exploit marine resources: this was a time and place of shifting frontiers, the introduction of new diseases, the despoliation of Native peoples, and the importation of new plants and animals, steam power, arms and ammunition, and spirituous liquor. Because the area was weak in self-sustaining agriculture, the Natives were crucial to the ability of the Europeans and Americans to hunt and to survive. During this violent and potent period in the history of the Northwest Coast, indigenous slavery, intertribal warfare, and cross-cultural violence flourished. Against this background the corporate and international rivalries played themselves out.

This last quarter of the North American continent to be explored witnessed an international rivalry as important as the scramble for Africa or the Pacific islands. The prospect of finding a Northeast or Northwest Passage initially promised benefits to navigation and the imperial pursuits of trade and dominion. Hunting sea otter, seals, and whales provided a recurring economic motivation. British maritime zeal was in the ascendant, the Russians were extending their continental dominions to the Pacific shore and beyond, and Canadian fur traders (followed by the Americans under John Jacob Astor and others) were pressing westward in expectation of establishing transcontinental commercial networks and developing new opportunities in the north Pacific. It was an era of remarkable economic growth on the coasts and littoral of the Asian and American continents, but it was also an era when corporate wars for control were being waged, and the two great powers in this contest were the Russian American Company and the Hudson's Bay Company. These two corporate giants were major players in the contest for empire, and, with the backing of their parent states, they were the important figures in the assertion of influence, formal and informal.

In the summer of 1778, when Captain James Cook was sailing in the north Pacific and its annex, the Bering Sea (thought to be the conduit to the Northwest or Northeast Passage), these waters were already known to Russian mariners. Indeed, Cook's journals make clear this fact. But by accurately charting this broad and geographically complex area, with its many islands, shallow coastal waters, and icy limits, and by documenting the tracks of his own ships into these seas, Cook was revealing to the wider world one of the last unknown corners of the globe. The publication of the authorized account of his third voyage to the Pacific, in 1784, and the further distribution of engraved charts of the north Pacific littoral created a baseline for subsequent historical examination.[1] Semyon Ivanov Dezhnev, Vitus Bering, Alexei Chirikov, and other Russian explorers who were precursors of Cook in these endeavors did not reveal their general discoveries in the same rapid fashion as did Cook's account. However, in 1761, Gerhard Müller, the herald of Russian activities in eastern seas, had revealed the particulars of Dezhnev's determination of the separation by seawater of Asia and America. Details of Russia's expansion across the north Pacific to Kamchatka, the Aleutians, and Kodiak Island, were largely revealed by an English curate, William Coxe, in his sizeable book of 1780, *Account of Russian Discoveries between Asia and America*.[2] That work appeared in French translation the next year. Once geographical particulars, as revealed in Cook's voyage account, were released to the public, Coxe wrote another work, *A Comparative View of Russian Discoveries with those made by Captains Cook and Clerke: And a Sketch of what remains to be ascertained by Future Navigators* (1787). James Burney, who had sailed with Cook on the master mariner's last voyage, published another work on comparative perspectives in 1819 (fig. 14.1).[3] Burney held that the year 1778 had been one of unremitting activity, with enormous gains to geography.[4] The Spanish, British, and Americans, for differing reasons, kept a watch on Russian activities in the north Pacific and marked Russian progress with more fear than admiration. At one level they were fascinated with discoveries; at another, they were concerned about sovereignty.

The Russian government fitted out a number of voyages of discovery, notably the expedition of Ivan Kruzenshtern and Iurii Lisianski, which added much to the knowledge of inlets and islands. Langs-

A

CHRONOLOGICAL

H I S T O R Y

OF

NORTH-EASTERN

VOYAGES OF DISCOVERY;

AND

OF THE EARLY EASTERN NAVIGATIONS OF
THE RUSSIANS.

BY

CAPTAIN JAMES BURNEY, F.R.S.

LONDON:
Printed by Luke Hansard & Sons, Lincoln's-Inn Fields,
FOR PAYNE AND FOSS, PALL-MALL;
AND
JOHN MURRAY, ALBEMARLE-STREET.
1819.

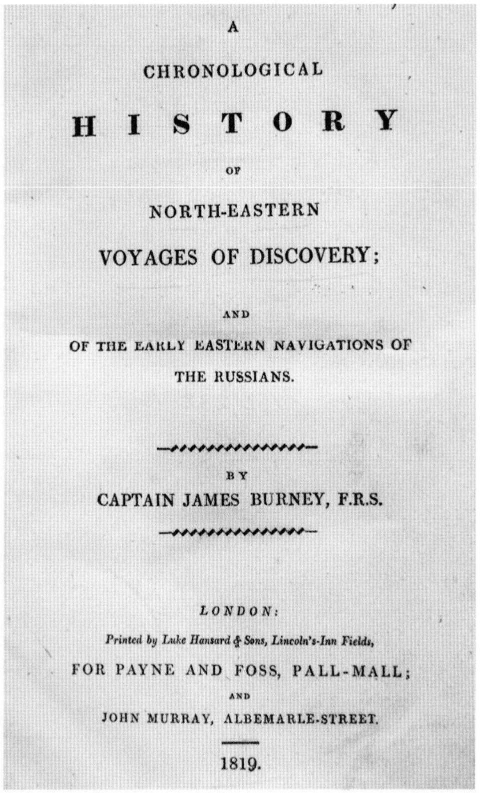

14.1 Title page of James Burney, *A Chronological History of North-Eastern Voyages of Discovery; and of the Early Eastern Navigations of the Russians*, 1819. Burney was a young officer on Cook's second and third voyages, but his active naval career was ended by ill-health and his outspoken republican views on his return to England. A fellow of the Royal Society, he was a distinguished historian and published major works on early exploration in both the southern and the northern Pacific Ocean. This important work documented the Russian advance across Asia and on to America before the formal establishment of Russian America. University of British Columbia Library, Rare Books and Special Collections, G680.B9.1819.

14.2 Luka Voronin, *Islands of Unalaska: The Captain's Harbor [Dutch Harbor], in 1790*, drawing. Voronin was the artist on the Joseph Billings expedition (1785–93). The settlement of Iliuliuk, deeper in the bay to the left, had become a permanent Russian fur-trading post four years before it was visited by members of the Cook expedition in 1778. Billings's *Slava Rossjii* is seen riding at anchor, and on shore an observatory and tents have been set up in front of some dwellings and storage huts. University of Washington Libraries, Special Collections, UW35921.

dorff visited the Aleutians; Golovin followed. Otto von Kotzebue visited Bering Strait, and later Lutke, Wrangell, Etholen, Lazarev, and others discovered islands, observed volcanoes, and described the flora and fauna of the region. Almost the only one among them to give an outsider's view was Joseph Billings, an Englishman who had served under Cook (fig. 14.2). His expedition, under imperial orders, for "A Secret Astronomical and Geographical Expedition for navigating the Frozen Sea, describing its Coasts, and ascertaining the Situation of the Islands in the Seas between the two Continents of Asia and America," begun in 1785 (and stimulated by the report of the departure of a French expedition under Jean-François Galaup, comte de La Pérouse, on the same errand), added somewhat to the geographical knowledge of these regions at the initial stage. Its more remarkable result was to expose the abuses the traders inflicted upon the Natives, and this had the effect of encouraging government authorities to advance a scheme for bringing the various traders into an association known as the Russian American Company in 1799.[5] Taken together, however, these Russian discoveries by sea added significantly to geographical knowledge. The findings of the Russian navigators and scientists were made readily available in English, German, and French translations.

At the British Admiralty, these reports gave rise to an uneasy awareness that a rival was making discoveries uncomfortably close to British possessions and British spheres of influence. In 1817, John Barrow, the Admiralty undersecretary, gave warning that the Russians were strongly impressed with the idea of opening a passage around America, that is, from Bering Strait east to the Atlantic. He thought it would be mortifying if the British were forestalled by the Russians, for the British had been searching for a passage to Cathay since Tudor times. Barrow's views were taken up. In brief, the Russian voyages spurred the British to action, and Captain John Franklin, conversant with Russian achievements by sea and learning of Russia's exertions to increase the fur trade and extend its dominions in the northern part of America, became active in advancing plans that would keep the Russians out of the Mackenzie River valley.[6] In other words, though the British Arctic expeditions of the early nineteenth century have always been cloaked in high-minded scientific language promising benefit to humankind, behind them was an imperial intent (of consolidation or defense).[7]

Apart from the three expeditions of Franklin, Royal Navy activities in the north Pacific are less well-known than the Russian voyages. Principal among these is the voyage of Frederick William Beechey. Although this expedition is invariably mentioned in connection with its attempt to link up with Franklin coming west from the mouth of the Mackenzie River (they missed each other by 160 miles on the Arctic coast of Alaska), Beechey conducted a much more complete survey of the western waters of Alaska than Cook had done (or Billings, for that matter) (fig. 15.3). His examination of Norton Sound, for instance, was outstanding as a contribution to hydrographical science.

On the ethnographic front, and in terms of cross-cultural relations, many studies and inquiries have advanced our knowledge of the Native worlds that had proto-imperial or precursor status in Alaska and on the Northwest Coast of North America at the time that mariners from far away came to plant imperial markers on these shores. This was not a vacant land, and these were not vacant seas but already habitats and places of marine exploitation.

Given these features of the historical geography of this part of the world, it is fascinating to consider how quickly it passed under sovereign control by certain nations, often to the exclusion of others. France, embroiled in revolution and continental war, posed no serious sovereignty threat, though the single voyage of La Pérouse accounted for much geographical knowledge gained. The Americans, having acquired sovereign status independent of Great Britain, had no imperial ambitions in such distant seas and littorals until the North West Company under Alexander Mackenzie alerted them to a transcontinental rival on the northern frontiers of Louisiana, then under faltering French control. Thomas Jefferson, when secretary of state, had awakened to this threat, but United States sovereignty did yet not exist over Louisiana; and until that purchase from France, in 1803, Jefferson could only hope that some associate republic and potential ally might exist on the Pacific coast. But time favored American designs and Jefferson's expectations, and when the Mississippi watershed was offered to him, he could not decline it. This brought Spain's dominions in the Southwest and Mexico, as well as its claims and activities on the Northwest Coast, one step closer to association with Jefferson's vision. The Nootka crisis, and Captain George Vancouver's resistance to the expedient claims put forward by Juan Francisco de la Bodega y Quadra at Nootka in September 1792, made clear that Britain would not step down in its claims, which essentially sought to protect rights of trade and navigation from interference by Spain or any other power (fig. 14.3). But the British preference for trade over

14.3 José María Vásquez, *An Interior View of Maquinna's house,* September 1792. Pen and ink wash. The chief is seen dancing for his visitors, Juan Francisco de la Bodega y Quadra and George Vancouver. The visit to Maquinna took place during a break in the Spanish-British negotiations at Yuquot in Nootka Sound that attempted—unsuccessfully—to implement the terms of the Nootka Convention of 1790. Breaching Spain's assumed sovereignty, this convention formally established a British presence on the Northwest Coast of America. Archivo y Biblioteca, Ministerio de Asuntos Exteriores, Madrid, Ms 146–27.

dominion was becoming less clear as the territorial designs of rival powers became more evident.

Thus we have four contenders: Russia, which under imperial edict was exerting sovereign control over Alaska and the American continent to some then-unforeseeable limit; Britain, which was coming by sea and mainly for commercial interests, such as the possibilities of the trade in sea-otter skins advertised by Cook's account; and Spain, which had an interest in these northern waters by virtue of the rights granted by the Treaty of Tordesillas of 1494, which were limited if not denied in principle by the Russians and the British (fig. 10.1). This circumstance also created an opening for the United States, the last power to come into play. Claims grounded in acts of possession and development were the means of acquiring sovereignty, which in effect requires the consent of the international community.

All of this was happening against a much larger backdrop of historical movements. Britain went to war against France in 1793 and then against Spain. In 1812 came a war between Britain and the United States, one in which, for the first time, historical claims to the Columbia River and its entrance and watershed became a substantial issue (fig. 14.4). Astor's Pacific Fur Company had projected a transcontinental reach into the Columbia country from New York and St. Louis, but after 1813 its faltering maritime department fell essentially under North West Company dominance (fig. 14.5).[8] In these circumstances, various merchant interests in the sea-otter and sandalwood trades, linking the Northwest Coast to Canton (now Guangzhou) via the Hawaiian Islands, were the prevailing interests of the United States in these seas. The Russian American Company had come to depend heavily on the foodstuffs, ships, arms, ammunition, and more that the Yankees supplied to them at Sitka and elsewhere. The eyes of the State Department were on the Columbia River as a promising germ of empire, transforming Jefferson's idea of a potential satellite republic into the goal of outright incorporation into the federal union. The War of 1812 had revealed the new reality of trade war at the mouth of

the Columbia River, the whole great watershed of which was rich in furs and important to the Indian trade, and a new intensity came into American official thinking about the possibilities of a transcontinental state. Immediately after that war, rival "sloop diplomacy" took place, with the United States and Great Britain deploying warships to lay down claims or to counter those of rivals.[9] The diplomatic files are thick from 1818 onward on this matter of rival claims, British and American, to Oregon. In 1819, by the Adams-Onís Treaty, the United States acquired claim to Spain's moribund empire north of Mexico and thereby acquired Spanish claims to priority of discovery in the area. In short, Spain's coastal explorations, which date to the 1770s, could now be added to the American legal file for a claim to an empire fronting on the north Pacific.

Here we see the overlaying claims to empire by all the principal contestants, with that of Spain attaining magisterial status in the historical record. In fact, however, Spanish claims faced innumerable difficulties and came to a quick end with the Nootka crisis and its diplomatic aftermath. News of Russian advances, real or imagined, spurred Spanish voyages of discovery from the west coast of Mexico. Official Russian voyages of 1766, 1767, and 1768 were interpreted as threats. Missions were planted after 1769 at San Diego, Monterey, San Gabriel, and San Francisco. In 1774 Juan Pérez sailed north, intending to explore to 60°N; he reached 54°N (fig. 3.5). The following year, Bruno de Hezeta and Bodega y Quadra defined the coastline, though scurvy and indigenous responses forced their retreat (fig. 3.8). By 1776, Alaska was within the realm of Spanish

14.4 Steve Mayo, *Captain Robert Gray's Ship* Columbia Rediviva *Crossing the Bar of the Columbia River, May 11, 1792*, 1996. Watercolor. Although the Spanish explorer Bruno de Hezeta, in 1775, had recorded the existence of the mouth of a river that later turned out to be the Columbia, Gray is credited with its formal discovery. This event, coupled with the arrival overland of the Lewis and Clark expedition in 1805, established the United States' claim to a "window onto the Pacific" and thus to a significant portion of the Oregon Territory. Courtesy of the artist.

14.5 *Astoria, As It Was in 1813*. Based on a drawing by Gabriel Franchère, this lithograph was published in his *Narrative of a Voyage to the North West Coast of America during the Years 1810–1814*. With other Canadians from Montreal, Franchère worked for John Jacob Astor's Pacific Fur Company. He arrived on the Columbia aboard the *Tonquin* in 1811 and helped establish Fort Astoria. Although the fort came under the control of the Northwest Company in 1813 and was abandoned in favor of Fort Vancouver in 1824, Astoria was later held up as an early American "presence" in the struggle with Britain for the Oregon Territory. University of British Columbia Library, Rare Books and Special Collections: The Wallace B. Chung and Madeline H. Chung Collection, F5819.2.F81.1854.

knowledge, and there was a civilizing mission at work, too. At Nootka Sound, the Spanish put up extensive structures, including a bastion, a battery, an observatory, a commandant's house, a hospital, and several dwellings. They also laid out nine gardens of varying dimensions (figs. 3.9 and 13.7). Spain's presence at Nootka was, however, withdrawn under the third Nootka agreement, or convention, and the settlement reverted to Native land and occupation. At present-day Neah Bay, the Spanish hurriedly put up a short-lived base in 1792, intending it to be the last line of defense against British claims that had been revived following the Nootka crisis and diplomatic demands for freedom of navigation and rights of trade.[10] Captain George Vancouver of the Royal Navy (fig. 13.1) saw through this obfuscation, and he made clear to his Spanish counterpart that Britain considered it unacceptable in international law.[11] Even so, the Spanish retreat to Alta California had already commenced, driven by difficulties of provisioning, costs of maintenance, and ill-health. Spain could not contain Russia, and it could not contain Britain. Thus, in 1819, Spain's interests, based mainly on priority of discovery, passed to the United States. Its claims of sovereign possession had been declared formally at Nootka, Neah Bay, Sooke (Vancouver Island), and elsewhere, but imperial overstretch and decay in administration, plus the ravages of war and revolution in Europe, spelled the end of one of history's most remarkable imperial edifices.

Spain's effective withdrawal from the Northwest Coast significantly reduced the questions of sovereign control. Two subsequent battles would become the central features of the quests for sovereignty that ended, for all intents and purposes, in 1846. That was the famous year of decision, when Oregon south of the forty-ninth parallel, though excluding Vancouver Island, became part of the sovereign United States, and Alta California, which bordered old Oregon at 42°N, became American territory by conquest. The purchase of Louisiana in 1803 and the acquisition of Texas in 1845 rounded out, as it were, the continental United States, concluding the first of the battles between Britain and the United States in the years after Spain's imperial demise.

The second was the compound battle between Russia and Britain, and Russia and the United States, in 1824 and 1825. Britain and the United States did not act in concert against Russia, but almost at the same time, within months of one another, they signed treaties with Russia to limit southern expansion at 54°40'N and to permit international shipping in these waters (fig. 14.6a–c).

The Spanish had gone to Nootka Sound in the late 1780s expecting, on the basis of widespread rumors, to find the Russians there. We also know, from recent sleuthing, that the Russians attempted to establish a naval base at the Columbia River entrance in March 1806 but were thwarted by the difficulties of passing the bar there. We also know that the Russians, under Nikolai Rezanov's direction, pressed south to establish Fort Ross in northern California in 1812; and that the Russians were sustained in their commercial activities in Alaska

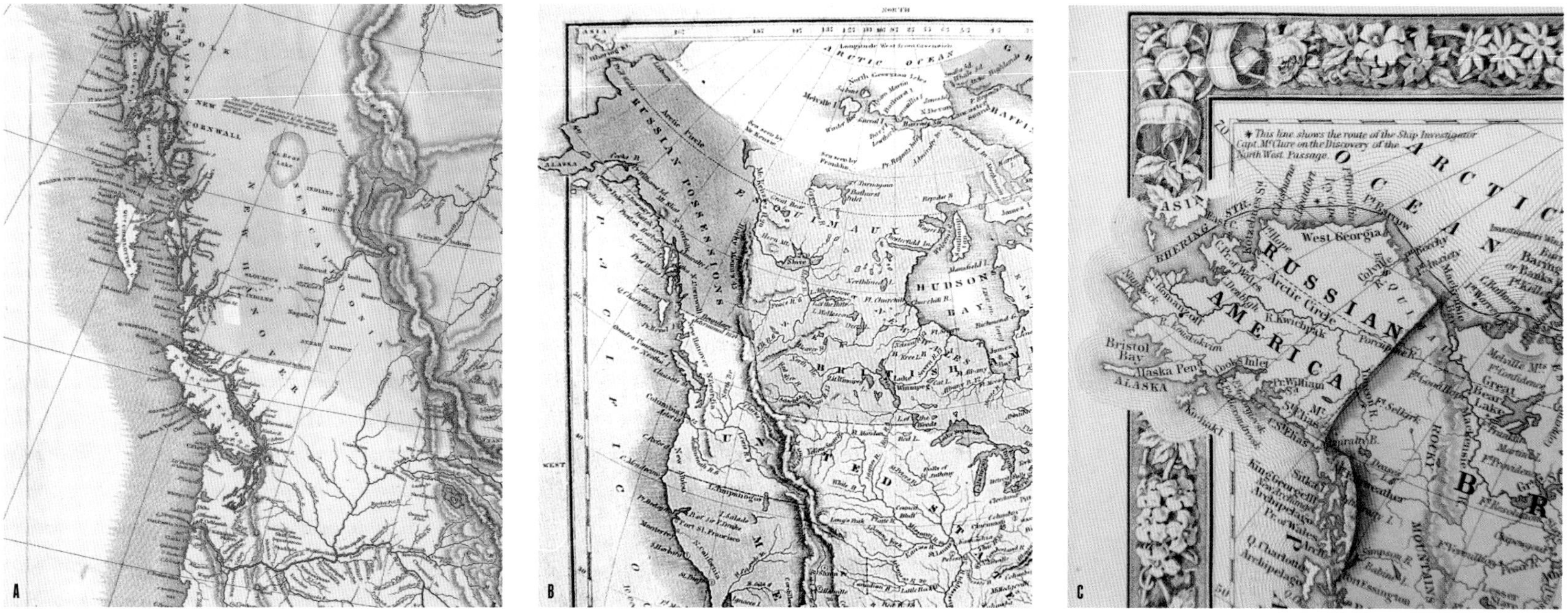

by independent American mariners who sold them food, supplies, and even ships. In short, Russian designs on expansion in North America strangely paralleled those of the United States. (The Russians also cast covetous eyes on the Hawaiian Islands.) The British, the preeminent traders in early years of the sea-otter trade with China, lost their primacy to the mariners of Boston, who found themselves in casual commercial alliance with first the Spanish and then the Russians.

As noted previously, Mackenzie's remarkable overland expedition to Pacific tidewater in 1793, against formidable geographical obstacles, and the subsequent publication of his *Voyages from Montreal* in 1801 had alerted the United States government to the fearful possibility of a British claim to sovereignty on the Pacific shore in these latitudes. Mackenzie's achievement (which was watched closely by Jefferson and informed his own responses to this threat on the northern and western reaches of United States influence)[12] had the accumulated effect of building on previous British claims: first, the claim to Nova Albion made by Sir Francis Drake at Drakes Bay "by the grace of God and in the name of her Majesty Queen Elizabeth of England and her successors forever" on June 17, 1579; second, Cook's act of possession for George III at Point Possession, Cook Inlet, on June 1, 1778;

14.6 The evolution of the boundaries of Russian America, 1821–25. (a) In 1821, Czar Alexander I declared 51°N as the southern limit of Russian sovereignty, but this claim was immediately challenged by the United States, which had inherited the Spanish claim to 54°40'N. (b) This latitude became the coastal boundary agreed upon by St. Petersburg and Washington in 1824. To protect the interests of the Hudson's Bay Company, Britain was principally interested in the still ill-defined eastern boundary. (c) By treaty in 1825, this was pushed west from the Russian-assumed Mackenzie River to the coastal mountains and, in the north, along longitude 141°W to the Arctic Ocean. Maps courtesy of Derek Hayes and University of British Columbia Library, Rare Books and Special Collections, G1019.M6.1865.

and, third, the somewhat similar act of possession of June 4, 1792, near present-day Everett, Washington, by Vancouver, to the territory from Nova Albion north to the Strait of Juan de Fuca and adjacent interior lands. Mackenzie had his eye on the China market, and his scheme of establishing a commercial empire was the origin of the arrangement for taking furs from the Columbia River and adjacent watersheds, including the Yukon and the Snake, directly to Canton, then still under the restrictive monopoly control (as far as British commerce was concerned) of the East India Company.

Severe and brutal trade rivalry along the river courses of what are now Manitoba, Saskatchewan, and Alberta, and even up to the Northwest Territories, between Mackenzie's North West Company and its rival, the Hudson's Bay Company (which held the royal charter), had led to an intervention by the British government and, in effect, the forced union of the two firms in 1821 under the name of the HBC. This corporate merger was designed to end the violence on the frontier and limit its effects on the Indian nations and the Métis, the descendants of the mixed marriages of the fur trade. British imperial statesmen, guided by aspects of trusteeship that were a powerful force in political affairs of that time, saw in the Hudson's Bay Company a useful instrument. In effect, the company was the British Empire in northwestern North America, and so close was this identification that its corporate leaders worked hand in glove with the British foreign and colonial offices, which oversaw these imperial quests for commerce and formal control. Mackenzie's triumphant expedition of discovery and Vancouver's complementary discoveries that no Northwest Passage existed gave the British the priority of discovery in these latitudes. But it was the Hudson's Bay Company that became the willing instrument of British statecraft and from time to time found the backing of the Royal Navy useful.

Mackenzie was the first outsider to trace the course of the river that now bears his name to its mouth. Equally significant, he was the first to cross the Continental Divide to Pacific tidewater (at Dean Channel), in 1793 (fig. 10.7). He had this to say in comparing British and Russian positions in Canadian fur trade geopolitics: "Our situation . . . is in some degree similar to theirs; the non-existence of a practical passage by sea, and the existence of one through the continent, are clearly proved; and it requires only the countenance and support of the British Government, to increase in a very ample proportion this national advantage, and secure the trade of that country to its subjects."[13]

Mackenzie told his cousin Roderick Mackenzie that he hoped his travels would bring him to the court of Catherine the Great. The trader Peter Pond, who had perhaps set in motion the whole project for reaching the Russians on the Pacific coast, had told an acquaintance in Montreal in 1789 that Mackenzie had been ordered to go from Slave River "down the River, and from thence to Unalaska, and so to Kamskathsha, and then to England through Russia."[14] As Mackenzie made clear in his *Voyages from Montreal,* and as he attested in several well-crafted memoranda that he placed before Canadian governors and British statesmen, British government aid was necessary to effect the grand design of Canadian fur traders, by which he meant the North West Company. Otherwise they could have no protection against British corporate rivals, American free traders, or other interlopers.[15] For the time being, Mackenzie's lobbying was ineffective. It was not until 1821, with the merger of the North West Company with the Hudson's Bay Company, that Mackenzie's wish was granted.[16]

After the union of the two warring firms in 1821, the Hudson's Bay Company became the dominant force in northwestern North America. Under the stern leadership of Sir George Simpson, "the little emperor," the firm set its sights on keeping the Russians at a distance, ousting any American coastal traders from the Pacific shore, pushing back American mountain men in such places as the Snake and Sacramento Rivers, and diversifying its resource trades on the Pacific (fig. 14.7). These actions were consistent with Mackenzie's vision that government backing was essential to success against foreign rivals. To a certain extent, the Russians had done the same in 1799 in awarding government charters to various merchant firms. In a way, then, commercial rivalry had long since moved past priorities of discovery and setting down markers of possession. The British firm was less interested in trade development on the Pacific coast, for neither the quantities nor the values of the furs were impressive, and, moreover, the lure of the China market was not yet revealed. The company was still sending its beaver and otter furs to St. Petersburg by the time-honored route through Hudson Bay to London. Rather, the company aimed to consolidate its trade in New Caledonia via the North American Pacific coast.[17] In the early 1820s, all these views augured a reversal of Russian fortunes.

The Russian American Company had been proclaimed under government requirement in 1799 out of a cluster of other merchant firms, with full privileges of trade for a period of twenty years on the Northwest Coast of North America, extending as far south as 55°N on the American continent and including the island chains from Kamchatka eastward toward America and southward to Japan. The charter also authorized the company to expand its control south of Alaska into any territory not already occupied by any other state. This vast sweep of imperial control reached a new state of formality with the establishment of ice-free Sitka (later Novo-Arkhangel'sk) (fig. 14.8). With the founding of Sitka, Aleksandr Baranov was shifting the center of empire southeast (fig. 14.9).[18] But the reform-minded, all-seeing naval officer Vasilii Golovnin, who had harsh words for Baranov, rang alarm bells about affairs on the Russian coast of North America that were heard in St. Petersburg. In 1811 the Ministry of the Interior assumed preliminary supervisory powers over the company.

In 1821 a much more extensive and permanent scheme of empire, recognizing the existing influ-

14.7 William Notman, *George Simpson, circa 1857.* Photograph of an earlier daguerreotype portrait. After the merger of the Northwest Company and the Hudson's Bay Company in 1821, Simpson emerged as the architect of a long period of stability and profitability for the company in western North America. Known as the "little emperor" for his obsession with economy, he spent the years 1824–29 on the Pacific coast, aggressively challenging the operations of the Russians and Americans. With the United States opposition to the designation of the Columbia River as the final boundary between US and British interests in Oregon in the 1820s, Simpson determined to "hunt out" the Columbia before what he saw as an inevitable division of the territory that would move HBC operations north. Hudson's Bay Company Archives, Archives of Manitoba, HBCA 1987/363-S-25/7.

14.8 Georg Heinrich von Langsdorff, *View of the Establishment at Norfolk Sound in 1805*, watercolor. Langsdorff was the artist with the Ivan Kruzenshtern and Iurii Lisianskii expedition (1803–6). The first Russian settlement was created by Aleksandr Baranov in 1799, but it was destroyed by the Tlingit in 1802. Rebuilt two years later on the site of modern-day Sitka, Novo-Arkhangel'sk (New Archangel) upheld Russian sovereignty over the far Northwest Coast of America until 1867. Courtesy of the Bancroft Library, University of California, Berkeley, BANC PIC 1905.06217-06222; #4-0620.

14.9 *Aleksandr Baranov.* Engraving after a portrait in oil by Mikhail Tikhanov. Baranov was manager for the Russian American Company (RAC) from 1799 to 1818. A towering figure in the early history of Alaska, he was employed by Grigorii Shelikhov in 1790 to manage his affairs on Kodiak Island. During the 1790s he oversaw expansion of the activities of the Shelikhov-Golikhov Company into Cook Inlet, Prince William Sound, and down the coast to Yakutat Bay. With the formation of the RAC in 1799, and despite the hostility of the Tlingit, Baranov was able to consolidate the company's primacy in the maritime fur trade on the far Northwest Coast during the first two decades of the nineteenth century. Alaska State Library Photograph Collection, Baranov-1, P01-2603.

ence of the Russian American Company in the north Pacific and intended to protect the company against free traders (British and mainly Americans), was proclaimed upon the renewal of the charter. This was done by an imperial edict of September 4, 1821, under which the whole Northwest Coast of North America above 51°N was declared Russian territory (fig. 14.6a). It also closed the surrounding waters (of which the most important was Bering Strait) to the commercial shipping of other powers. In short, Russia had proclaimed a formal empire, supplanting the informal empire already in existence. The second charter stipulated that that the chief manager be a captain of the Imperial

Navy, and other positions in colonial administration were occupied by naval officers.

The Russians, in effect, had drawn a line in the sand, but restricting coastal trade in an open maritime zone was bound to attract complaints from the Americans and from the British. Czar Nicholas's edict, which proclaimed territorial sovereignty over the lengthy arc extending from Siberia along the coasts of North America, ran counter to the western continental claims of Britain and the United States. The War of 1812 between those two powers had ended with the Treaty of Ghent in 1814, which laid the basis for an international boundary, to be determined, west of the Lake of the Woods. By the subsequent Convention of 1818, that boundary was pressed along the forty-ninth parallel to the Continental Divide. West of that divide, the British and the Americans agreed to recognize each other's claims to trade and occupation without in any way admitting to the other's absolute sovereignty. The edict of 1821 stood in the face of this arrangement, for it decreed Russian property to include all islands and waters north of 51°N; that is, it claimed Russian dominion almost as far as the northern tip of Vancouver Island. It also warned foreigners not to approach within 115 miles of the coast. Britain could hardly accept the latter claim of a *mare clausum,* for, in consequence of the Nootka crisis (and subsequent conventions), the British cabinet of the day in London had obliged the Spanish to accept freedom of navigation as an essential characteristic in the application of international law here. The Foreign Office could not agree to either the territorial or maritime claims of the czar.[19]

The Hudson's Bay Company, British whaling interests, and Sir John Barrow, the influential Admiralty secretary and promoter of polar exploration, all objected to the fact that recognition of the Russian intrusion would end free navigation on the coast. Accordingly, London expressed stiff diplomatic opposition. The foreign secretary, Lord Castlereagh, and his successor, Lord Canning, made clear to Russian envoys in London that both the Russian "pretensions" to territory and the restrictions on trade were unacceptable, the main objection being the exclusionist maritime policy. Legal opinion sought by the British government confirmed against "this infringement on the rights of commerce and navigation."[20] Once again we see that priority was given, in this early age of Pax Britannica, to trade over territory. And the British had something more expansive in mind. Canning wrote privately to the prime minister, Lord Liverpool: "The trade between the Eastern and Western Hemispheres, direct across the Pacific, is the trade to the world most susceptible of rapid augmentation and improvement."[21] This was a view to which British commercial and shipping interests could subscribe.

It was in this context that plans for British exploration in the Arctic were undertaken, and Hudson's Bay Company activities in what is now the Yukon Territory developed apace. The company, the Colonial Office, and the Admiralty cooperated to advance the Franklin expedition of 1825–27, which brought Captain Beechey to make extensive discoveries along the Alaskan coast and in the high Arctic beyond Cook's Icy Cape (fig. 15.3).[22] Extending a track that Cook might have followed, Beechey laid out the prospect that a Northwest Passage might run east of Point Barrow, the northernmost tip of continental North America.[23] This second-generation British search for the Northwest Passage contributed much to science and geographical knowledge and enhanced British claims to priority of discovery and sovereignty in these latitudes.[24]

Meanwhile, the Hudson's Bay Company had advanced its own campaign for checking Russian aspirations. Beginning in 1822, the company determined to keep the Russians at a distance north and west of where, in the first decade of the nineteenth century, Simon Fraser had established for the North West Company posts in the central interior of what is now British Columbia: McLeod's Fort, near the Continental Divide in the fifty-fifth parallel; Fort St. James, south of Stuart Lake; and Fort George, where the Fraser and Stuart Rivers meet. The Hudson's Bay Company sent Samuel Black to explore waters west of the Mackenzie River and the Rocky Mountains with a view to drawing off the Indian trade from the Russians on the coast.[25] Thus began the company's policy of stabilizing and pushing back rival trade by sea and land in these latitudes.[26]

The period marks a remarkable epoch in commercial development on the Northwest Coast and in the Pacific Ocean. The Hudson's Bay Company ascendancy so dominated Russian traders that agreement over trading in the Russian panhandle came to benefit the British firm. In addition, the Hudson's Bay Company diversified its resource development of Vancouver Island and the mainland by putting up a number of trading posts, including some on Russian territory; it also created an agricultural corporation, the Puget's Sound Agricultural Company, to supply foodstuffs to company personnel and to foreign purchasers.[27]

Inadvertently, the Russian foreign office assisted British designs by signing an arrangement with the United States, the Russian-American Convention of April 17, 1824, which stayed Russian progress southward by virtue of the rights American diplomats obtained for their citizens to fish in colonial waters and trade on the coastal strip for a ten-year period (fig. 14.6b). The official historian of the Russian American Company, P. A. Tikhmenev, makes clear that his company was on the losing end of the arrangements. Angry protests were made, but to no avail.[28] (St. Petersburg often acted as unmindful of the Russian American Company: by contrast, the British Foreign Office always attended to the wishes of the Hudson's Bay Company, the latter in most cases taking the lead in policy formulation and even direct diplomacy.)

But the internal difficulties between the imperial ministry and the Russian American Company were less than half the story. Upon the edict of 1821 being proclaimed, company ships had been armed and fitted out to ward off foreign shipping; in addition, the Russian frigate *Apollo* had sailed into Norfolk Sound and then on to the coast to capture all intruders and carry them to Kamchatka for trial. Boston vessels, such as the brig *Pearl,* received orders to leave immediately or face seizure. "I hope our government will not suffer our valuable trade on the North-West Coast to be taken from us," wrote a worried American agent in Honolulu to a Boston trading firm, "by a nation who but a few years since were but a race of barbarians."[29] The United States secretary of state, John Quincy Adams, an unheralded advocate of the expansion of the republic, protested against the Russian right to any territorial establishment on the North American continent and, going further, declared that the American continents were no longer subject to any European colonial establishments.[30]

The Monroe Doctrine had been proclaimed in President James Monroe's message to Congress in 1823 in an attempt to ward off further European colonization in America. It may have been aimed at Russia, although Washington's primary cast was southward to the Caribbean and Latin America. Richard W. Van Alstyne has written, "The Monroe Doctrine is really an official declaration fencing in the 'western hemisphere' as a United States sphere of influence. . . . It was a first-rate expression of the statecraft of a rising imperial republic."[31] London took the diametrically opposite view that colonization of the unoccupied portions of America was open, as before. Besides, British and Canadian claims were strong, resting on Mackenzie's and Vancouver's actions and priority of discoveries. As for the United States' strategic position, the American diplomat Henry Middleton had made clear to both Russia and Great Britain that negotiations without United States participation would lead to a strong protest from his government: the American view was that Britain had "no settlement or possession upon any part of the Northwest Coast of America," its only claims deriving from the Nootka Convention with Spain of October 28, 1790. And since the United States had inherited Spain's claims by the treaty of 1819, any territorial agreement was invalid without the consent of the United States. He went further in explaining that "the United States, by their discovery of the Columbia River and by their subsequent possession of a district on the same part of the Northwest Coast of America [Astoria, or Fort George], have perfected their right of sovereignty to that territory."[32]

In the wake of American diplomatic success, British statesmen pressed their Russian opposites to curtail their southerly quest for dominion. Success crowned their efforts. The two powers signed a convention in February 1825 that established the southern boundary of Russian America at 54°40'N, and thence by the height of mountains parallel to, but no nearer than ten leagues from, the coast to the 141st meridian (Canada's westernmost boundary), on which line it would run clear to the Arctic Ocean (fig. 14.6c). Thus, for the first time, Russian America had an eastern boundary, a real advance over the provisions of the treaty with the United

States. The Russians acknowledged British rights of navigation on the coast and, equally significant, on rivers cutting through the Russian coastal strip. By doing so, the Russians effectively invited the Hudson's Bay Company to cut off, by interior posts, a substantial Russian trade that had been based in the interior. Indeed, this treaty provision encouraged the Hudson's Bay Company to develop its interest in the maritime fur trade, which had previously been minimal.[33] The agreement also allowed British trade at Sitka and on the Russian coast south of Mount St. Elias for a ten-year period.

Many difficulties ensued in the relations of the Russian American Company and the Hudson's Bay Company, most notably an incident in the lower reaches of the Stikine River in 1833, when the Russian American Company's chief manager, Baron Ferdinand Petrovich Wrangell, sent a company ship to build an armed redoubt at the river entrance so as to watch for and bar British traders. The ensuing affair, sometimes known as the *Dryad* incident (named for the HBC brig commanded by Peter Skene Ogden), led to strong Foreign Office complaints, and the Russian government acquiesced. George Simpson, the North American manager of the Hudson's Bay Company, now became prominent in arranging an agreement, concluded in February 1839, that gave the Hudson's Bay Company the privilege of supplying the Russian American Company with foodstuffs and other requirements, in effect giving the British firm a monopoly on the Russian coastal strip.[34] This arrangement allowed for the elimination of American traders on that coast and the discontinuance of the sale of arms, ammunition, and liquor. This was a triumph for the Hudson's Bay Company, though it did not spell the ruin of the Russian trade. The company subsequently relinquished its damage claims for the *Dryad* incident; the firm had gained something far better. In 1840 the British firm built Fort Durham at Taku on Russian territory and took over the post at Point Highfield, which they named Fort Stikine.[35] A later rationalization of trade, made possible by steam navigation, allowed for Fort Durham and other posts without diminishing the dominance in trade.

Before closing, we need to look one more time at the difficulty over Oregon. By terms of the Convention of 1818, a sequel to the Treaty of Ghent, Great Britain and the United States accepted expansive terms with regard to western territories. The northwest boundary between the United States and British North America was fixed along the forty-ninth parallel from the Lake of the Woods to the crest of the "Stoney Mountains" (the Rocky Mountains), thus limiting the northern extent of the Louisiana Territory. No boundary was established for the region west of the Continental Divide, but the two powers agreed that claims by either power would not be prejudicial to the claims of the other until sovereignty could be determined. Diplomatic discussions failed to bring a result, though in 1827 the agreement was renewed for an indefinite period. According to the terms of the new arrangement,

14.10 *Fort Vancouver.* Hand-colored lithograph based on an earlier sketch (1844) by Henry James Warre and published in his *Sketches in North America and the Oregon Territory* in 1848. Established in 1824, the fort served for two decades as the chief trading post and supply depot for the Hudson's Bay Company's Columbia Department. Through this major presence in the Oregon Territory, the company consolidated and expanded its trade "beyond the mountains" to and from Russian America, Alta California, Hawai'i, and the wider Pacific. Oregon Historical Society, 83437.

HBC

it could end one year after notification was given by either power. These were delicate circumstances, as the instructions to Captain Belcher of the Royal Navy's surveying ships *Sulphur* and *Starling* indicate:

> Political circumstances have invested the Columbia River with so much importance that it will be well to devote some time to its bar and channels of approach, as well as to its inner anchorages and shores; but you must be exceedingly careful not to interfere in any manner with the subjects of the United States who live on its banks; neither admitting nor contesting their claims, respecting which there is a distinct understanding between the two Governments, and if necessary you will find some prudent pretext for desisting from the survey, rather than risk any collision or even remonstrance.[36]

Belcher conducted his assignment in 1837 and again in 1839. He concluded that the Americans did not possess an atom of land on the Columbia, for the Hudson's Bay Company dominated the trade there and had erected a new base at Fort Vancouver, on the north shore of the Columbia River (fig. 14.10).[37]

British policy, it may be concluded, was adaptive in nature and entirely reserved. Trade was preferred to dominion. Britain did not seek accretions of formal empire, and it was content to let the Hudson's Bay Company serve as its imperial agent. The company liked it that way and did the government's bidding. Although the British sought to avoid being drawn into any wasps' nests, they were drawn into one imbroglio after another—in the Society Islands, the Hawaiian Islands, Alta California, and Oregon—and only in Oregon did a definite policy emerge. Even then, the United States had the advantage, for the tide of American settlement was sweeping into the Willamette and Columbia Valleys, and Congress was hot for American territorial expansion. But British policy deterred the United States from taking territory up to 54°40'N, and the Oregon Treaty gave Great Britain full possession of Vancouver Island—an important consideration, for it had become the marine depot of the Hudson's Bay Company (in succession to Fort Vancouver, which lay upriver from the notoriously difficult Columbia River bar) (fig. 14.11). In the end, too, the tally of British acquisitions was not long: the Americans took Alta California, the French ran up their flag at the Society Islands, and, for the moment, no clear power had control over the Hawaiian Islands—though on three occasions the British were offered sovereignty there and declined it.

The reluctance of the British to extend their formal dominions in places where they had commercial advantages, backed by their immense maritime and naval strength, was evident throughout these early years of the Pax Britannica. It may be said to have begun with Captain Vancouver's visits to the Hawaiian Islands. James Cook had pointed out that the value of the archipelago was strategic. If British shipping could resort there for water, provisions, and rest, that was all that mattered. It was rights of trade and navigation, once again, that preoccupied Britain on the coast of Alaska when Russia seemed to have an overbearing attitude. And rights of trading in the Columbia River were the subject of the last statement of this sort agreed to by the British in the Oregon Treaty. In so many places where the British could have claimed paramount or even sovereignty on the basis of prior discovery or by acts of possession, they chose not to do so, instead exercising a self-denying ordinance. This attitude allowed the Russians to take a firm hold in Alaska and also permitted the Americans to take Alta California and secure their interests in Oregon. British discoveries on the northwest Pacific coast during and after the sea-otter trade had brought national attention to Nootka Sound and Vancouver Island, however, and it was in this region where the British Foreign Office made its last stand. The czar's actions of 1821 brought the American and British responses that curtailed Russian territorial ownership south of $54^\circ 40'$N. That northern limitation was the first, essential step in the final division of the fourth corner of the continent.

And what of the final disposition of territory on the northern Pacific coast and in Alaska? On March 5, 1841, as the United States and Great Britain were making the final dispositions on rights of trade and navigation in the Oregon Treaty, the Imperial Council at St. Petersburg, after examining the conditions of Alaska, determined to renew the Russian American Company charter once more. The main

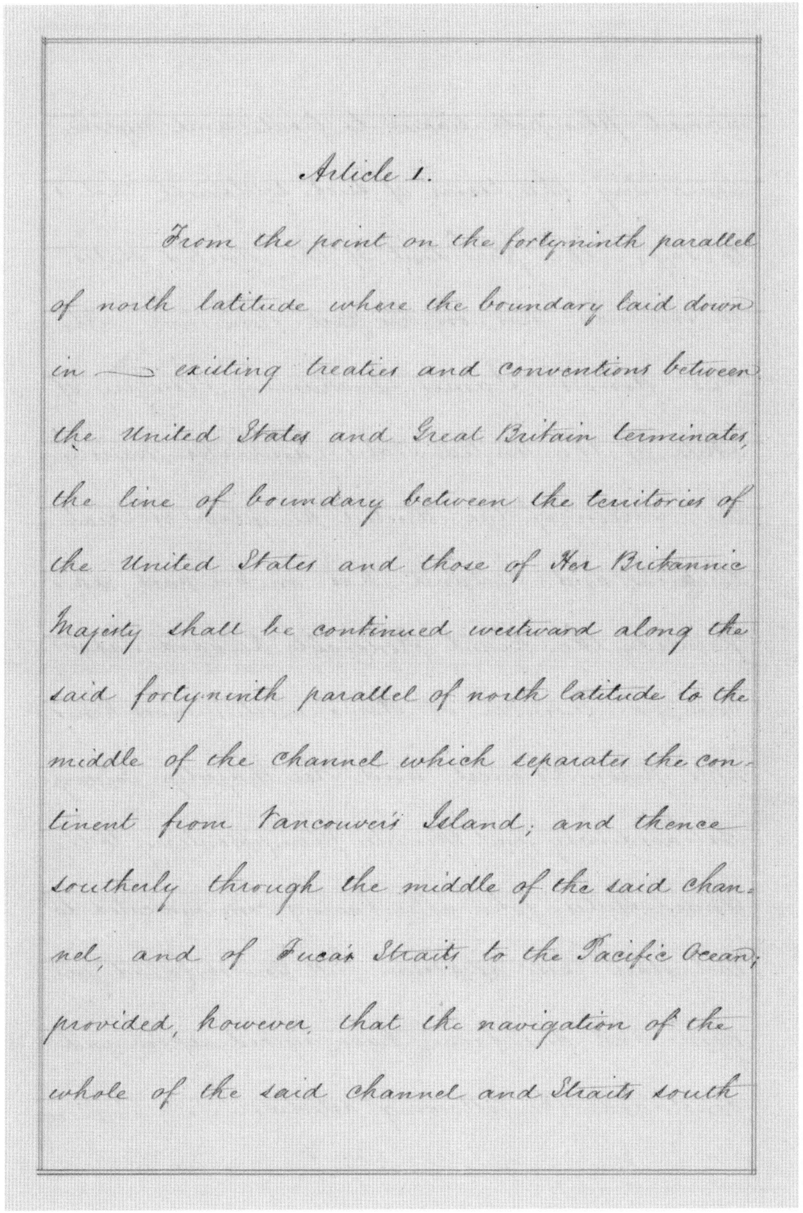

Article 1.

From the point on the fortyninth parallel of north latitude where the boundary laid down in existing treaties and conventions between the United States and Great Britain terminates, the line of boundary between the territories of the United States and those of Her Britannic Majesty shall be continued westward along the said fortyninth parallel of north latitude to the middle of the channel which separates the continent from Vancouver's Island; and thence southerly through the middle of the said channel, and of Fuca's Straits to the Pacific Ocean; provided, however, that the navigation of the whole of the said channel and Straits south

14.11 Article 1 of the Oregon Treaty of 1846, which divided the Oregon Territory between the United States and Britain at the forty-ninth parallel. After Spain had withdrawn from the Pacific Northwest in 1818–19 and treaties in the mid-1820s had defined the southern boundary of Russian America, Britain and the United States agreed to joint occupancy of the region. Twenty years later, increasing American settlement south of the Columbia and the disinclination of the British government to support the monopolistic Hudson's Bay Company north of the river led to a treaty, which averted hostilities that neither side wanted. National Archives and Records Administration, Washington, DC, #299808.

consideration was that in all its various operations, the government had invested the company with a commercial and industrial monopoly under powers for governing a vast and distant territory. If the charter were withdrawn, apart from the fact that the government would have to resume control of the colony at great expense and trouble, throwing open Russian ports to all hunters would be a death blow to the fur trade. For the moment, it was best to leave the Russian colonies in America under corporate control.

The boundaries of Alaska were adjusted in accordance with the British and American treaties already referred to. It would take until 1867 to tidy up these affairs and at last solve the Russian imperial problem by the sale of Alaska to the United States. The 126-year Russian possession of Alaska, claimed by right of discovery from Siberia and enacted by the occupation of the land for the pursuit of seals and sea otters, had come to an end. Right up to this time, the Hudson's Bay Company remained the predominant business power in Southeast Alaska, and even when Russia and Great Britain went to war in 1854, during what is now called the Crimean War, it was business as usual on the Northwest Coast, the Russian American Company and the Hudson's Bay Company having negotiated an arrangement to continue the trade and to have no part in hostilities that indeed might involve Petropavlovsk at Kamchatka or actions at the mouth of the Amur River. All the boundaries established by 1846, save for the Alaska boundary dispute between Britain (acting for Canada and British Columbia) and the United States, which inherited the Russian rights and claims, remained as agreed.

NOTES

1 The chart by Captain Henry Roberts, who had sailed with Cook, was of central importance to the history of cartography. The overland expeditions of Samuel Hearne, Mackenzie, and others can be traced in the various editions of Aaron Arrowsmith's maps of North America. These charts and maps seem impressively detailed for their time, but much remained to be added: the work of hydrographic surveyors and departments, geological surveys, and various travelers. A complete view of terrestrial features was not available until aerial photography became possible in the early twentieth century.

2 William Coxe, *An Account of Russian Discoveries between Asia and America; to which are added, The Conquest of Siberia and the History of the Transactions and Commerce between Russia and China* (London: T. Cadell, 1780). This work passed through four editions (the last appearing in 1804) and as many enlargements. In the 1787 edition, a supplement was included. Concurrently this was also issued separately, by the same publisher, as *A Comparative View of the Russian Discoveries with Those Made by Captains Cook and Clerke: and a Sketch of what remains to be ascertained by Future Navigators.*

3 James Burney, *A Chronological History of North-eastern Voyages of Discovery, and of the Early Eastern Navigations of the Russians* (London: Payne and Foss and John Murray, 1819).

4 Ibid., 251.

5 Hubert Howe Bancroft, *History of Alaska* (1886, rept., Darien, CT: Hafner, 1970), 282–304, esp. 297–98.

6 John Franklin to John Barrow, November 26, 1823, no. 1, letter book, vol. 1, MS. 248/281/1, Scott Polar Research Institute, Cambridge, England.

7 John Barrow, *Voyages of Discovery and Research within the Arctic Regions, from the Year 1818 to the Present Time* (Lon-

don: John Murray, 1846), 12. This work is an explanation of all the various voyages, written by the mastermind who steered the projects through Board of Admiralty meetings and worked with various scientific bodies of the age. See also "Lists of Admiralty Ships Employed on Missions of Discovery, etc., 1669–1860," R.3/34, pp. 5–19, National Archives, Kew, UK.

8 James P. Ronda, *Astoria and Empire* (Lincoln: University of Nebraska Press, 1990), and especially John Denis Haeger, *John Jacob Astor: Business and Finance in the Early Republic* (Detroit, MI: Wayne State University Press, 1991).

9 The most recent review of this subject, based on British Foreign Office papers (specifically F.O. 5/107, 123, 147, and 1470), Colonial Office (C.O. 42/164) and Admiralty (ADM 1/22 and others)—all in the National Archives—is to be found in Barry Gough, *Fortune's a River: The Collision of Empires in Northwest America* (Madeira Park, BC: Harbour Publishing, 2007), chs. 14 and 15. Also still of value is Alfred L. Burt, *The United States, Great Britain and the British North America from the Revolution to the Establishment of Peace after the War of 1812* (New Haven, CT: Yale University Press, 1940).

10 For the most recent discussion of this incident, see Freeman M. Tovell, Robin Inglis, and Iris H. W. Engstrand, eds., *Voyage to the Northwest Coast of America, 1792: Juan Francisco de la Bodega y Quadra and the Nootka Sound Controversy* (Norman, OK: Arthur H. Clark, 2012). Bodega y Quadra specifies "Fuca" (though Núñez Gaona was the Spanish place name given to it at the time, honoring a Spanish admiral) in his letter to George Vancouver, August 29, 1792, cited in ibid., 137.

11 Vancouver cleverly and correctly deduced that the Spanish establishment at Fuca ("in the mouth of Fuca [Strait]") had been made no earlier than the previous May, because he had passed that very point on his own meticulous surveys in late April 1792. He concluded that the port must come under the designation of a port of free access, in conformity with the Nootka Convention. George Vancouver to Juan Francisco de la Bodega y Quadra, September 1, 1792, cited in George Vancouver, *A Voyage of Discovery to the North Pacific Ocean and Round the World, 1791–1795*, ed. W. Kaye Lamb, 4 vols. (London: Hakluyt Society, 1984), 4:1571.

12 David L. Nicandri, *River of Promise: Lewis and Clark on the Columbia* (Washburn, ND: Dakota Institute Press, 2010), 203–17.

13 *The Journals and Letters of Sir Alexander Mackenzie*, ed. W. Kaye Lamb (Cambridge: Hakluyt Society, 1970), 415.

14 Quoted in ibid., 453.

15 The culmination of these urgent and astute memoranda is Alexander Mackenzie to E. Cooke, March 10, 1808, enclosing a letter from Mackenzie to Lord Castlereagh, March 10, 1808, B.T. 1/59, fols. 62–67, National Archives. This is printed in Mackenzie, *Journals and Letters*, 516–19. In his reasoning, Mackenzie foreshadowed the establishment of the Canadian transcontinental state, but it would take the Oregon crisis and the determined position of the Hudson's Bay Company as imperial factor to bring this about. Throughout, the British government was reluctant to add territories to its already large empire, and such accretions were invariably out of some sort of fatal necessity or a desperate measure to keep rival nations from gathering spoils or gaining strategic advantage.

16 Barry Gough, *First Across the Continent: Sir Alexander Mackenzie* (Norman: University of Oklahoma Press, 1997), 180–98, discusses the relations of Mackenzie and the Colonial Office. Significantly, the merchant sector was demanding official recognition and government material support to its trading schemes. This is a demonstration of how the merchant sector, as led by Mackenzie, the agent for the North West Company, was in advance of official thinking as to the projection of commercial and imperial interests in northwestern North America and the Pacific. In effect, Mackenzie's actions were an extension of those of the early partners of the North West Company who lobbied government for protection in the face of challenges from American traders. Mackenzie and his associates were to be frequently disappointed. Lacking the protection of a charter such as the Hudson's Bay Company had enjoyed right from its corporate inception in 1670, the Nor'Westers invariably found themselves at a disadvantage (one overcome only by the union of the two companies in 1821). During the War of 1812, however, the

North West Company did receive support for its trade at the mouth of the Columbia River. British warships convoyed the company trading ship *Isaac Todd* part of the way from England, and in 1813 the British sloop-of-war *Racoon* [*sic*] ran up the Union Flag at Astoria and called it Fort George. The post reverted to American traders by terms of the Treaty of Ghent, though American trade was extinguished. See Gough, *Fortune's a River,* passim, on the evolution and implementation of the Canadian fur traders' success in the face of American and Russian rivalry.

17 Here I follow the official company history: Edwin E. Rich, *Hudson's Bay Company, 1670–1870,* 3 vols. (Toronto: McClelland and Stewart, 1960), 3:610.

18 Lydia T. Black, *Russians in Alaska, 1732–1867* (Fairbanks: University of Alaska Press, 2004), 155–65, describes the difficulties with the Tlingit at this time. This was a significant event in Alaska history and for the Russian American Company's fortunes, to say nothing of its effects on the aboriginal peoples, but it does not deal with the subject of how discoveries came to be translated into empires. Black's history is an excellent treatment, based on many newer, mainly Russian, sources. Russia's adventure to Hawai'i in these years stands outside this subject, though the matter is of undoubted imperial effect. See Peter R. Mills, *Hawaii's Russian Adventure: A New Look at Old History* (Honolulu: University of Hawai'i Press, 2002).

19 Castlereagh to Charles Bagot, January 19, 1822, F.O. 181/48. Castlereagh said "he would not admit either the exclusive sovereignty or the exclusive navigation of Russia in these waters or seas." For discussion of how he saw Russian designs, see H. V. Temperley, *The Foreign Policy of Canning, 1822–1827* (London: Bell, 1925), 64–65, 104–5.

20 Quoted in John S. Galbraith, *The Hudson's Bay Company as an Imperial Factor, 1821–1869* (Berkeley: University of California Press, 1957), 120. My analysis here follows Galbraith (119–23). His main argument is that British policy was reactive to Russian activities and pretensions and that in this particular instance the Hudson's Bay Company "had no cause to complain of governmental lack of attention to its interests" (121).

21 Canning to Liverpool, July 7, 1826, in Edward J. Stapleton, ed., *Some Official Correspondence of George Canning,* 2 vols. (London: Longmans, Green, 1887), 2:73–74.

22 The masterful application of corporate, scientific, and strategic interests exhibited by the British at this time (and designed to counter Russian plans for finding a Northwest Passage and extending its empire in these seas and adjacent lands) is examined in Barry Gough, "British-Russian Rivalry and the Northwest Passage in the Early 19th Century," *Polar Record* 23, no. 144 (September 1986): 301–17; reprinted in Barry Gough, *Britain, Canada and the North Pacific: Maritime Enterprise and Dominion, 1778–1914* (Aldershot: Ashgate Variorum, 2004), ch. 9 (original pagination retained).

23 Revised instructions to Captain Beechey, May 11, 1825, Special Minutes, no. 4, ADM 3/263; Frederick William Beechey, *Narrative of a Voyage to the Pacific and Bering's Strait, to Co-operate with the Polar Expeditions, performed in His Majesty's Ship Blossom . . . in the years 1825, 26, 27, 28,* 2 vols. (London: H. Colburn and R. Bentley, 1831). For further particulars on the genesis and prodigious scientific achievements of this expedition, see Barry M. Gough, ed., *To the Pacific and Arctic with Beechey: The Journal of Lieutenant George Peard of H.M.S. "Blossom," 1825–1828* (Cambridge: Hakluyt Society, 1973), introduction. This latter work reprints the 1830 British Admiralty chart "Part of the North West Coast of America from Point Rodney to Pont Barrow," Beechey's great survey of western Alaska.

24 George S. Ritchie, *The Admiralty Chart: British Naval Historiography in the Nineteenth Century,* rev. ed. (Edinburgh: Pentland, 1995), 153–74.

25 Edwin E. Rich and A. M. Johnson, eds., *A Journal of a Voyage from Rocky Mountain Portage in Peace River to the Source of Findlay's Branch and North West Ward in Sumer 1824* (London: Hudson's Bay Record Society, 1955). See the introduction by R. M. Patterson, which describes British motivations to check Russian traders.

26 Governor and Committee to George Simpson, February 27, 1822, A. 6/20, Hudson's Bay Archives, Province of Manitoba Archives, Winnipeg. Printed in R. Harvey Fleming, ed., *Minutes of Council of the Northern Department of Rupert Land, 1821–31* (London: Hudson's Bay Record Society, 1940), 303.

27 The best study of HBC commercial expansion and consol-

idation, which involved the exploration of watersheds, the building of new posts and the closing of others less profitable, the rationalizing of trade, the introduction of shipping (including steam navigation), the promotion of agricultural enterprises to provide foodstuffs, and the expansion of trade to the Hawaiian Islands, is Richard Somerset Mackie, *Trading beyond the Mountains: The British Fur Trade on the Pacific, 1793–1843* (Vancouver: University of British Columbia Press, 1997). The HBC was acutely aware of Russian rivalry on the north and American rivalry on the south of its trading sphere. See also Galbraith, *Hudson's Bay Company,* especially 135–76, 192–232.

28 See P. A. Tikhmenev, *A History of the Russian American Company,* trans. Richard A. Pierce and Alton S. Donnelly (Seattle: University of Washington Press, 1978), 164–67. This work was first published in Russian in two volumes in 1863.

29 John Coffin Jones Jr. to Marshall & Wildes, November 16, 1822, quoted in Samuel Eliot Morison, *By Land and by Sea: Essays and Addresses* (New York: Alfred A. Knopf, 1953), 95.

30 See, among various studies, Mary E. Wheeler, "Empires in Conflict and Cooperation: The 'Bostonians' and the Russian-American Company," *Pacific Historical Quarterly* 40 (November 1971): 428–29; Howard I. Kushner, *Conflict on the Northwest Coast: American-Russian Rivalry in the Pacific Northwest, 1790–1867* (Westport, CT: Greenwood, 1975); and especially Stephen W. Haycox, "Merchants and Diplomats: Russian America and the United States," in *Russian America: The Forgotten Frontier,* ed. Barbara Sweetland Smith and Redmond J. Barnett (Tacoma: Washington State Historical Society, 1990), 55–71.

31 Richard W. Van Alstyne, *The Rising American Empire* (Oxford: Basil Blackwell, 1960), 98–99.

32 Henry Middleton to Count Karl Nesselrode, February 23, 1824, in *Alaska Boundary Tribunal* (Washington, DC: U.S. Government Printing Office, 1903), 46.

33 Galbraith, *Hudson's Bay Company,* 131.

34 The provisions of the contract of 1839, the diplomacy leading up to it, and its consequences are examined in ibid., 144–55.

35 Rich, *Hudson's Bay Company,* 3:712–13.

36 Hydrographic instructions to Captain F. W. Beechey, n.d., S.L. 21, item 6, Hydrographic Office Archives, Ministry of Defence (Navy), Taunton, Somerset.

37 Edward Belcher to Rear Admiral C. B. H. Ross, December 17, 1839, copy in Colonial Office 6/14, National Archives, UK.

The Continuing Quest

The Lure of the Northwest Passage in the Nineteenth and Twentieth Centuries

JAMES P. DELGADO

15

THE QUEST FOR THE NORTHWEST PASSAGE WAS SET ASIDE IN THE LAST quarter of the eighteenth century as Britain, most of Europe, and the Americas were plunged into a series of wars that continued into the new century. The American Revolution, the French Revolutionary Wars, the Wars of the First and Second Coalitions, and the subsequent Napoleonic Wars continued through 1815, involving widespread conflict on land and sea. Britain was also engaged in conflicts with the United States from 1812 through 1815. Even if war had not intervened, the ostensible "gates" to the far Arctic were barred by ice not only in Baffin Bay but also in the Bering Strait, as Cook had documented in 1778.

The end of decades of war coincided with a warming climate that heralded the end of the "Little Ice Age." The gates to the Arctic were opening, a fact observed by whaling masters pushing farther north in search of prey. As the nineteenth century dawned, whalers encountered increasingly ice-free seas at the fringes of the Arctic. One whaling master, William Scoresby Jr., reported that "I observed on my last voyage (1817) about two thousand square leagues (eighteen thousand square miles) of the surface of the Greenland seas . . . perfectly devoid of ice."[1] Reports such as Scoresby's were read with

Roald Amundsen [left] *and companions, Gjøa expedition, 1903–6,* lantern slide image, in *Cold Recall: Reflections of a Polar Explorer* (2009), edited by Geir O. Klover (detail of fig. 15.7).

15.1 Samuel Drummond, *William Edward Parry,* 1820. Oil on canvas. Less well-known to a modern reader than some of his contemporaries, Parry was one of the most successful British Arctic explorers. During his second voyage into the Canadian Arctic Archipelago, he navigated nearly the entire length of the Northwest Passage before stopping short because of severe pack-ice conditions.

interest by John Barrow (1764–1848), the energetic secretary of the Admiralty. With the end of decades of tension and wars, the Royal Navy was in search of new missions, and Barrow was eager to send the ships on renewed voyages of exploration. From the reports of the whalers and fur traders, and the accounts of earlier exploration, Barrow was convinced that "the water supplied through the Strait of Behring . . . into the Polar Sea, was discharged, by some opening, or other, yet to be discovered, into the Atlantic."[2]

Barrow pushed to renew the quest for the Northwest Passage. Beginning in 1818, the navy mounted a series of expeditions to the Arctic's shores. Slowly and tortuously over the next two decades, sailor-scientists and explorers mapped the northern edges of the North American continent, and some of the islands in the Arctic archipelago gradually revealed a tortured landscape of land, sea, and ice that suggested not one but many possible Northwest Passages.

The initial British approach was an Arctic probe that reconnoitered the coasts of Greenland in 1818. The ships *Dorothea* and *Trent* tried to reach the North Pole via the east coast, while HMS *Isabella,* under the command of John Ross, and HMS *Alexander,* under the command of W. Edward Parry, entered Baffin Bay in obedience to Barrow's instructions that "an attempt should be made to find a passage, by sea, between the Atlantic and Pacific . . . by way of Davis' Strait" (fig. 15.1).[3] Although the eastern ships were stopped by ice, Ross and Parry were not, and under Ross's command, they pushed into Lancaster Sound before turning back. Ross claimed that a line of mountains on the coast that he alone had seen had blocked further progress, but this assertion only infuriated Barrow, who saw in it only "a pitiable excuse for running away home."[4] Barrow dispatched Ross's second-in-command, Parry, on an immediate return to Lancaster Sound, believing, as did Parry and his men, that "this must be the north-west passage."[5]

Parry's orders were to enter Lancaster Sound, and, "in the event of its proving a strait opening to the westward, you are to use all possible means . . . to pass through it . . . and if it should be found to connect itself with the northern sea, you are to make the best of your way to Behring's Strait."[6] Sailing from Britain in two ships, HMS *Hecla* and HMS *Griper,* in May 1819, Parry pushed past the imaginary line of Ross's mountains and into an arctic vastness never before penetrated by Europeans. Parry was guardedly enthusiastic, noting in his journal that "we now began to flatter ourselves that we had fairly entered the Polar Sea."[7] Passing 110°W on September 4, 1819, the expedition met the goal set by Parliament, which was offering a prize of five thousand pounds for the first to reach that geographic landmark, although the men of *Hecla* and *Griper* could not know that they were nearly out of the Arctic archipelago and halfway through the passage.

The British quest for the passage could have ended then with a successful transit, but ice stopped *Hecla* and *Griper* less than two weeks later at 112°51'w. Instead of turning back, Parry decided to moor his ships in a cove on Melville Island. Named Winter Harbour, the cove was home to the two ships and their crews for a year during which Parry tented over the decks, sheathed the ships in ice blocks, and organized regular programs of exercise, entertainment, and exploration (fig. 15.2). Breaking out of the ice with the summer's aid on August 1, 1820, *Hecla* and *Griper* retraced their tracks and returned to Britain by early November.

Parry's successful voyage coincided with a less fortunate exploration of the Arctic coast by Lieutenant John Franklin of the Royal Navy in 1819–22. Ordered to follow the Coppermine River to the northern shores of the continent, Franklin and a land party were then to chart the Arctic coast. The 5,500-mile expedition was harrowing and ended disastrously with a maddened member of the expedition killing and eating some of his companions, a winter of starvation in which the survivors ate scraps of leather and old bones, and finally rescue by one intrepid member of the crew, George Back, who left to find help and returned with local people and food. The commander, John Franklin, survived and returned to Britain to find himself a macabre celebrity, the "man who ate his boots."

While Franklin and his party were still in the midst of their travails, Parry returned to the Arctic with *Hecla* and HMS *Fury* to again try for the passage in May 1821. Wintering at Repulse Bay, Parry spent part of it visited by local Inuit, who freely interacted with their strange visitors. Among the exchanges were hand-drawn maps of their world which they created when the Britons gave them pencil and paper. When the ice freed *Fury* and *Hecla,* Parry followed the Inuit maps south to the top of the Melville Peninsula and a new strait that led to a body of water that the ice kept them from entering. A second winter passed, but as sickness set in, Parry turned home in 1823 rather than spend a third winter trying to force through the ice-choked passage.

Back in London, John Barrow decided that a massive push from four expeditions, which would

15.2 W. Westall, *H.M. Ships* Hecla & Griper *in Winter Harbour,* engraving after a sketch by Lieutenant Frederick William Beechey, 1819. Published in William E. Parry, *Journal of a Voyage for the Discovery of a North-West Passage* (London, 1821). Parry's successful strategy of "freezing in" and housing over his ships, as well as a regular program of physical and mental exercise for his crews, proved highly successful and helped Britain's Arctic explorers survive in an extreme environment. However, no amount of strategy or adherence to Parry's methods would save John Franklin's expedition when it was caught by ice for a lengthy period. University of British Columbia Library, Rare Books and Special Collections, G650.1819. P51.

enter the Arctic through Lancaster Sound, the newly found strait at the Melville Peninsula, the Mackenzie River, and the Bering Strait, would at last conquer the Northwest Passage. John Franklin would again lead a land expedition, tackling the Mackenzie. Parry would sail west through Lancaster Sound, while his lieutenant from his last voyage, George Lyon, would again try the new strait in HMS *Griper.* Another Parry lieutenant, Frederick William Beechey, would push east through the Bering Strait. Barrow hoped some of the expeditions would converge in the passage.

In the summer of 1825, Franklin descended the Mackenzie and reached the Arctic coast, splitting his forces to follow the coast and map it east and west. The eastern party headed for the Coppermine, while the western headed to a hoped-for rendezvous with Beechey and his crew in HMS *Blossom,* who they hoped had pushed past Cook's Icy Cape to reach farther east than Cook had. When Franklin reached his westernmost point on August 16, 1826, he and Beechey were separated by only 160 miles, but they never met. Beechey, meanwhile, named his easternmost position Point Barrow for his patron. Beechey and Franklin both retreated from the Arctic with their crews intact and healthy, and their maps charted the Alaskan coastline as well as the Arctic coast of the future Canada. As Franklin noted in his account of his expedition, "Each succeeding attempt has added a step towards the completion . . . and it is sincerely to be hoped that Great Britain will not relax her efforts until the question of a north west passage has been satisfactorily set at rest" (fig. 15.3).[8]

The Lyon and Parry expeditions, however, had faced great hardship and near disaster. Lyon and the crew of *Griper* were nearly lost to a terrible winter storm, and freezing weather led them to retreat, arriving home early, to the shock of the Admiralty. Publicly praised but privately condemned, Lyon never again commanded a ship. Parry, meanwhile, had also retreated when his expedition in *Fury* and *Hecla,* which sailed in May 1824, encountered an Arctic gripped in bad ice. Wintering on the shores of Prince Regent Inlet, Parry lost some of the good cheer that had carried him through the previous expeditions and long winter "nights" that lasted for months. "All is dreary monotonous whiteness," Parry wrote. "Not merely for days or weeks, but for more than half a year together. Which-ever way the eye is turned, it meets . . . inanimate stillness . . . that motionless torpor. . . . In the very silence there is a deadness with which a human spectator *appears out of keeping.* The presence of man seems an intrusion on the dreary solitude of this wintry desert."[9]

The expedition broke free of the ice in the summer of 1825, and the ships pushed southeast along the shores of Somerset Island. There, caught by ice, they were driven toward shore, and finally *Fury* went into the rocks near shore and was badly damaged. The crew managed to free the ship, but it was clear it could not be saved. Grounding *Fury* on a narrow beach, Parry and his men stripped the stranded hulk, cached its supplies on the beach,

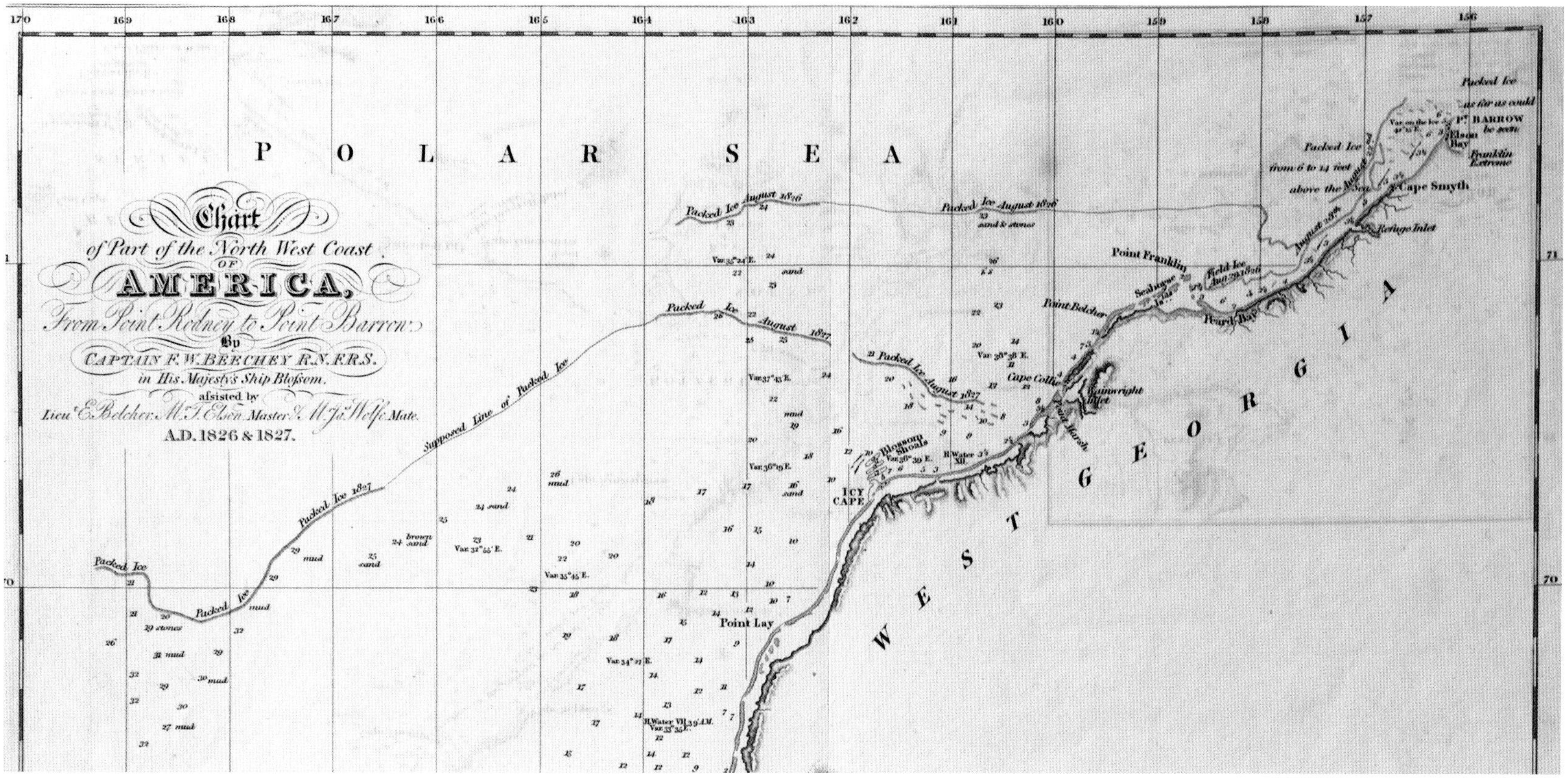

and retreated into an overcrowded *Hecla* to head home. They arrived around the same time as the storm-ravaged *Griper*. The success of Beechey and Franklin notwithstanding, these expeditions seemingly ended British enthusiasm for finding the passage. In 1828, Parliament repealed the 1776 act that offered a twenty-thousand-pound reward for discovering a Northwest Passage.

In 1829, John Ross, the disgraced former commander of the 1818 expedition to Lancaster Sound, mounted a private expedition sponsored by the gin distiller Felix Booth. He took a small steamship, *Victory,* into the Arctic in an attempt to find and navigate the passage and redeem his reputation. Among Ross's crew was his nephew, James Clark Ross, a veteran of Parry's voyages. Departing Britain in June 1829, Ross and *Victory* disappeared into the Arctic for nearly four years. Pushing past the wreck of HMS *Fury,* they headed into a dead end, the Gulf of Boothia, where *Victory* froze in.

15.3 *Chart of Part of the North West Coast of America from Point Rodney to Point Barrow by Captain F. W. Beechey in His Majesty's Ship* Blossom, 1826. Detail showing Arctic Alaska coast. Beechey's expedition successfully charted the Arctic coast of Alaska, advancing far beyond Cook's Icy Cape, but did not make the planned rendezvous with John Franklin's expedition, which had pushed west from the Canadian coast. University of British Columbia Library, Rare Books and Special Collections: Verner Collection, RBSC-ARC-1766: 1830:B.

Despite short moves over the next years, it never fully escaped the grip of the ice. Interacting with the local Netsilik Inuit, Ross and his party explored the Boothia Peninsula, which Ross named for his patron, and they located and marked the site of the magnetic North Pole at 70°5'17"N 96°46'45"W on June 1, 1831. "Nature had erected here no monument to denote the spot which she had chosen as the centre of one of her great and dark powers," Ross wrote, so "amidst mutual congratulations," he and his party "fixed the British flag on the spot, and took possession of the North Magnetic Pole, and its surrounding territory, in the name of Great Britain."[10]

They also charted what Ross believed was a series of islands, not the mainland. The pace and extent of their explorations pushed the men to the limit of their endurance, however. Coated with frost and locked into the ice, *Victory* clearly could not break free. By the spring of 1832, hunger and scurvy were setting in, and so Ross and his companions abandoned their ship on May 28. They nailed the British flag to the mast and began a harrowing, desperate dash over land and ice to reach Fury Beach, where Parry's cached supplies remained. They arrived on July 1, too weak to go farther and with winter quickly descending. They needed to build a camp and rebuild their strength.

Wintering at Fury Beach in a shelter made from the wrecked ship's timber and canvas, Ross and his men repaired *Fury*'s abandoned boats. With the next summer's retreat of the ice, they sailed into Lancaster Sound in August 1833, where through luck they encountered whalers who rescued them. In a touch of irony, the ship that effected the rescue was Ross's old command from 1818, *Isabella*, now whaling where it had once explored. Ross's brave but failed effort nonetheless restored his reputation, brought him a knighthood, and revived Britain's enthusiasm for seeking the Northwest Passage. In 1836, the Admiralty dispatched HMS *Terror*, under the command of George Back (who had just returned from a government-sponsored voyage to the Arctic to find and rescue Ross), to go back to the Arctic to again try for the passage. He was to try by way of the frozen strait found by Parry, the waters that had nearly sunk HMS *Griper*.

Making his way to the strait, Back forced his way in, only to be stuck in ice in Repulse Bay. The resulting hellish, ten-month ordeal nearly wrecked the ship and broke Back's health. When finally freed from the ice, *Terror* limped back to Britain in the summer of 1837, its pumps constantly working to keep the ice-cracked hull from sinking. It was the last Royal Navy expedition into the Arctic for several years. The fur-trading explorers Peter Dease and Thomas Simpson, working with small groups of Inuit guides, covered significant ground and mapped more of the coast, but much of the presumptive passage was marked by blank spaces on the charts. Suggestive leads might end in a trap, while others might be the correct way through what was now clearly a maze of ice, shoals, and islands.

Barrow argued for a renewed push in 1844:

> The discovery of Baffin, which pointed out, among others, the great opening of Lancaster on the Western coast of that bay which bears his name, has in our time been found to lead into the Polar Sea through which the North-West Passage from the Atlantic to the Pacific will one day be accomplished, and for the execution of which we are now contending, and which if left to be performed by some other power, England by her neglect of it after having opened the East and West doors should be laughed at by all the world for having hesitated to cross the threshold.[11]

In response, an expedition was authorized. Commanded by the veteran explorer John Franklin, who was joined by a number of other seasoned Arctic hands, the expedition sailed in May 1845 in HMS *Erebus* and *Terror* with orders to follow Parry's course of 1819–20 and try for the Bering Strait (fig. 15.4).

The expedition vanished after leaving Baffin Bay in early July. Years later, after dozens of searches by numerous expeditions, it slowly emerged that the ships had successfully wintered, moved farther into the passage, and finally been caught and trapped for years by ice to the north of King William Island. After abandoning *Erebus* and *Terror* in April 1848, the surviving crew had headed south. Not one of them made it out of the Arctic alive.

Search and rescue expeditions beginning in 1849 and 1850 found scattered relics, including some graves on Beechey Island, where the expedition first wintered. The fur trapper and explorer John Rae returned from an 1853–54 expedition with Inuit guides and reported Inuit tales of trapped ships, starving men who turned to cannibalism, and disaster. From the Inuit, Rae also gathered relics of the lost expedition, including a medal that had belonged to Franklin and the personally engraved silverware of the expedition's officers. His tales were not widely believed, but it became clear that something had indeed gone terribly wrong at the top of the world. In 1858, Franklin's wife, Lady Jane Franklin, sponsored a search expedition led by Francis Leopold M'Clintock, who took the steam yacht *Fox* north. M'Clintock returned in 1859 with more relics and a final note from the expedition which explained that Franklin had died in 1847; *Erebus* and *Terror* had been abandoned on April 22, 1848; and the survivors had embarked on their final, fatal march. On that route, M'Clintock and his men had found only a trail of abandoned gear and bodies.

By the time M'Clintock returned to Britain, thirty-two separate expeditions had sailed in search of Franklin. In doing so, they exhaustively covered most of the region, mapping the archipelago and showing the various means, when or if the ice cleared, by which a passage might be navigated. One of them, commanded by Robert McClure in HMS *Investigator,* had pushed in from the Bering Strait, followed the Alaskan coast, and then headed north through Prince of Wales Strait between Banks and Victoria Islands and reached a point just

15.4 James Thompson, *Sir John Franklin,* engraving, 1840. Britain's most famous Arctic explorer was also its most unfortunate: two expeditions ended disastrously, the second in the 1840s with the loss of Franklin's two ships and the death of every man on the expedition. Franklin's disappearance spurred a concerted rescue effort that spanned decades. Once it was clear that he had not survived, the quest turned to recovering what records or other precious relics remained. © National Maritime Museum, Greenwich, London, PAD 4408: Reproduction ID: PU 4408.

15.5 S. Gurney Cresswell, *H.M.S.* Investigator *Running through a Narrow Channel, in a Snow Storm, between Grounded and Packed Ice,* plate 5 from *Dedicated, by Special Permission, to her Most Gracious Majesty, the Queen, a Series of Eight Sketches in Colour* (1854). In disobedience of his orders, the expedition of Robert McClure in HMS *Investigator* came close to where Parry's expedition had ended in the ice in 1819. After ice trapped the *Investigator,* McClure and his men, rescued and trekking overland, were credited as the discoverers of "a northwest passage." The intact wreck of the *Investigator* was discovered by Parks Canada archaeologists in 2010. Rasmuson Library, University of Alaska Fairbanks, c 0051 Rare.

thirty miles from Parry's Barrow Strait in the summer of 1850 (fig. 15.5). McClure seemingly had little interest in finding Franklin, having ignored orders to rendezvous with other ships farther south. Writing in his journal, he noted that "I cannot describe my anxious feelings. . . . Can it be possible that this water . . . shall prove to be the long-sought Northwest Passage? Can it be that so humble a creature as I am will be permitted to perform what has baffled the talented and wise for hundreds of years!"[12] After wintering in the Arctic, in the summer of 1851, McClure, having explored on foot and knowing he was close to Parry's old position of 1819–20, again pushed on, only to be stopped by ice. Wintering at a site he named Mercy Bay, McClure trapped his ship forever. The ice never released it, and another Arctic disaster was averted only by the timely arrival of a land-trekking British naval officer from another expedition. He came onto the scene in June 1853, just as McClure was about to abandon *Investigator,* and led the men of the trapped ship to safety on an eastward hike of several hundred miles.

On their return to Britain, McClure and his men were rewarded for the discovery of a Northwest Passage. It was clear that Franklin had also probably "discovered" a passage, as indeed had another search expedition led by McClure's superior officer in HMS *Enterprise.* The awards and the posthumous near canonization of Franklin and his men, who had "forged the last link" of the passage "with their lives," allowed Britain to declare the centuries-long quest for the Northwest Passage over, with glory and no doubt relief (fig. 15.6). It was for some a hollow victory: as one participant, Johann Miertsching, wrote in his diary, the passages "are without significance and useless for navigation as long as the climate in these parts is so severe and the sea covered with ice 50 to 60 feet thick."[13] In 1876, a private attempt by one of M'Clintock's second in commands, Allen Young, to sail the passage in a private yacht, *Pandora,* closed out Britain's attempts to navigate the passage by ship, one hundred years after James Cook had gazed at the ice-locked western gates of the passage at the edges of the Bering Strait.

The twentieth century brought renewed interest in the Arctic and the Northwest Passage. Long settled by the Inuit, the region was also home to fur-trading enterprises such as the Hudson's Bay Company, and whalers regularly worked the waters of the eastern and western Arctic. The passage was divided between two nations when the Dominion of Canada was formed and Britain ceded its Arctic claims to the new nation, and the United States purchased Alaska. In the years that followed, in addition to those who came for commercial opportunity, explorers returned to the Arctic. They circumnavigated and explored the coasts and waters around the northern islands in the Arctic archipelago, beginning with the 1902 expedition of Norway's Otto Sverdrup. In the next decades, Banks, Ellesmere, Axel Heiberg, Amund Ringnes, Ellef Ringnes, Borden, Brock, Bathurst, Longheed, and Melville Islands were probed and mapped.

The centuries-old dream of sailing through the Northwest Passage revived and was completed in the early twentieth century by another Norwegian, Roald Amundsen (fig. 15.7). Rejecting his mother's plans for a steady career at home, Amundsen dedicated himself to a strict physical regimen and spent his early years preparing for the life of an explorer, learning science as well as navigation and participating in Arctic voyages, including serving as mate on a Norwegian sealing vessel. He also gained

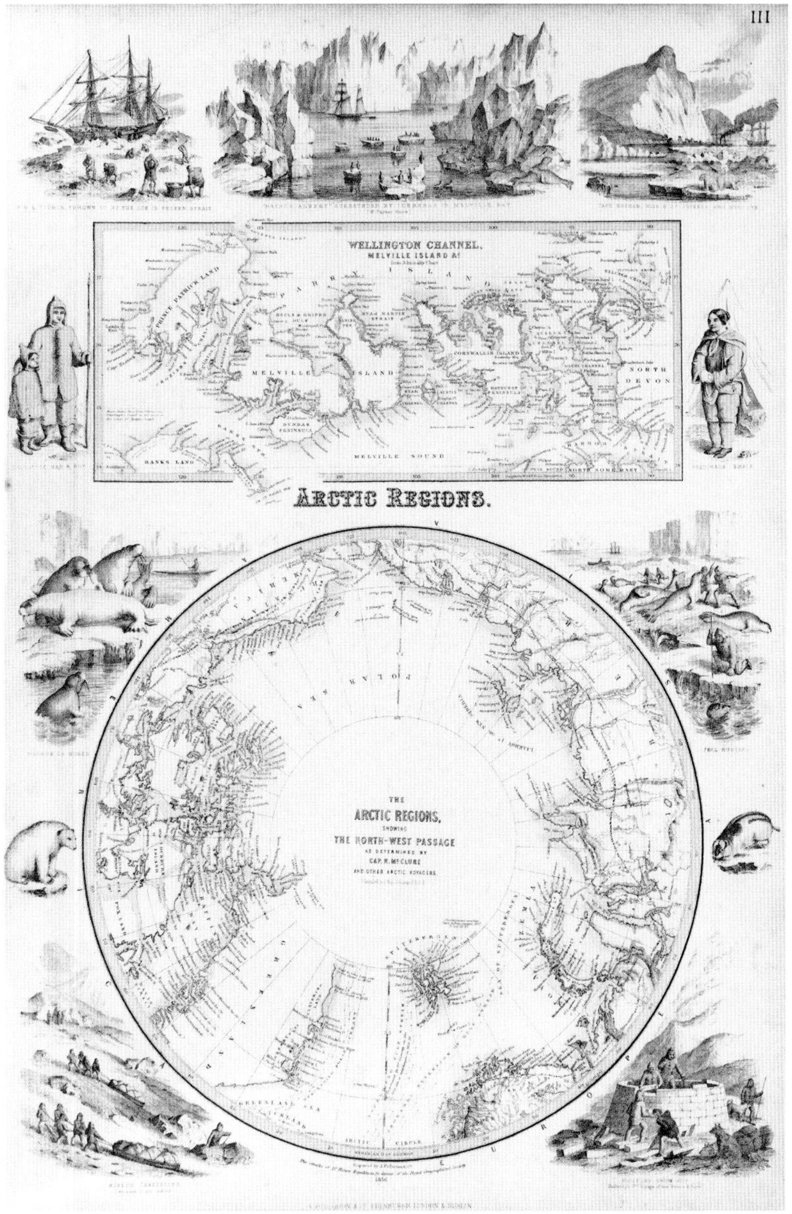

15.6 *Map of the Arctic Regions,* A. Fullarton & Company, London, 1856. A summary chart with illustration motifs of thirty-eight years of Arctic exploration. Thanks to the diligent, often arduous, and occasionally heartbreaking work of Arctic explorers, many of them British, the intricacies of the Canadian Arctic Archipelago and the existence of several possible Northwest Passages had emerged by the middle of the nineteenth century. No ship, however, had yet navigated the length of any passage from either side of the continent. University of British Columbia Library, Rare Books and Special Collections, G3271.S12.F84.1856.

15.7 *Roald Amundsen* [left] *and companions, Gjøa expedition, 1903–6,* lantern slide image, in *Cold Recall: Reflections of a Polar Explorer* (2009), edited by Geir O. Klover. Norway's greatest polar explorer made his reputation by learning from the experiences of past explorers and using a small ship and Inuit knowledge to become the first to navigate the Northwest Passage. Fram Museum, Oslo, Norway.

invaluable experience as mate on Adrien de Gerlache de Gomery's 1897–99 *Belgica* expedition to Antarctica.

Amundsen's plan for a Northwest Passage expedition involved more than the transit itself. It required, he said, "a scientific purpose as well as the purpose of exploration." Otherwise, "I should not be taken seriously and would not get backing." So Amundsen pursued "studies in magnetic science and . . . the methods of taking magnetic observations."[14] His plan was to reestablish the location of the magnetic North Pole, plotted for the first (and until Amundsen's time) last time by James Ross on King William Island in 1831.

Amundsen selected a small vessel for his expedition: *Gjøa,* a seventy-two-foot-long fishing boat working out of Norway's Arctic port of Tromsø (fig. 15.8). "She was forty-seven tons and of the same age as myself."[15] With its shallow draft and small size, *Gjøa* seemed well suited for the shallow and ice-choked straits of the Northwest Passage. "What has not been accomplished with large vessels and main force I will attempt with a small vessel and patience," Amundsen noted.[16] He had the shipyard add a thirteen-horsepower diesel engine that drove a small iron propeller. Amundsen would later write, "Our successful negotiation of the North West Passage was very largely due to our excellent little engine."[17]

Provisioning for five years, Amundsen organized his expedition down to every small detail, adding sleds and dogs to spare the crew the weary labor of hauling sledges in the British tradition of Arctic exploration. With a hand-picked crew of six, Amundsen and *Gjøa* slipped out of Oslo harbor on June 16, 1903, leaving by night to avoid an angry creditor who had threatened to have the vessel seized. "The ruin of my years of work seemed imminent," wrote Amundsen, and so "I resolved upon a desperate expedient."[18] After loading his dogs in Godhavn, on the west coast of Greenland, Amundsen followed Franklin's track into the Arctic archipelago.

Gjøa arrived at Beechey Island, Franklin's old winter quarters and the rendezvous point for many of the expeditions that had searched for him, on August 22, 1903. "The heaviness and sadness of death hang over Beechey Island," Amundsen wrote. "I was on holy ground." In his mind's eye, he imagined *Erebus* and *Terror* at anchor, with Franklin coming ashore, and he decided that this would have been where they wintered. "Let us raise a monument to them, more enduring than stone; the recognition that they were the first discoverers of the Passage."[19]

After leaving Beechey, *Gjøa* entered Peel Strait. Pushing farther south, "our voyage now assumed a new character. Hitherto we had been sailing in safe and known waters. Now we were making our way through waters never sailed in . . . and were hoping to reach still farther where no keel had ever ploughed."[20] When *Gjøa* reached the De la Roquette Islands, it reentered known waters, but this was the limit of sailing knowledge, as *Pandora* had been stopped by ice there in 1876. Without an understanding of the currents and shoals, the

Gjøa's crew proceeded cautiously. Amundsen faced a warmer Arctic, though, and "the water to the south was open. . . . I cast my eyes over our little *Gjøa* from stem to stern, from the deck to the mast top, and smiled."[21]

Pushing on, Amundsen contended with groundings, an engine-room fire, and a near shipwreck before reaching King William Island. Anchoring in a small cove they named Gjøahavn (today's Gjoa Haven), Amundsen and his men were back in known waters, as this area had been charted by the British. "The Northwest Passage was therefore open to us. But our first and foremost task was to obtain exact data as to the Magnetic North Pole, and so the Passage, being of less importance, had to be left in abeyance."[22] *Gjøa* therefore remained in place through 1904 and 1905 as Amundsen explored the region and again pinpointed the magnetic North Pole at latitude 70°30'N and longitude 95°20'W. The earth's shifting magnetic fields had moved the pole some forty miles northeast from the point where Ross had first located it in June 1831.

Amundsen also interacted with the local Netsilik, whose forebears had greeted and worked with John Ross. Soon a community of Inuit was living alongside *Gjøa*. This allowed Amundsen to document them as an amateur anthropologist, collecting tools, weapons, clothing, and other implements of everyday life. His interest was driven by pragmatism as much as ordinary curiosity: he had concluded that to survive in the Arctic, explorers needed to adapt the ways of the Inuit.

Leaving Gjoa Haven on August 13, 1905, Amundsen pushed past King William Island and into Victoria Strait, the last "unsailed link in the North West Passage," and reached Cambridge Bay, where HMS *Enterprise* had wintered five decades earlier. *Gjøa*'s small size and draft and Amundsen's steady eye had been key to reaching this point. "The lead," Amundsen wrote, "flew up and down, down and up, and the man at the helm had to pay close attention and keep his eye on the look-out man who jumped in the crow's nest like a maniac, throwing his arms about for starboard and port."[23] Farther on, *Gjøa* was greeted by the San Francisco whaler *Charles Hansson*. Both ships stopped to spend the winter on the Yukon coast. Breaking free in July 1906, *Gjøa* pushed through the drifting ice along the Alaska coast, stopping at Nome, where the Norwegian explorers were feted as conquering heroes. From there *Gjøa* sailed through the Bering Strait on August 30, 1906. The ship then sailed south to San Francisco, where Amundsen drove *Gjøa* up onto the sands of Ocean Beach to berth his hard-worked craft as a memorial. She was moved to Oslo in 1972.

Following Amundsen's feat, Canada gradually realized that foreign interest in the passage and its resources—in those days defined as whales and seals—would likely come into conflict with Canadian sovereignty. When the Klondike gold rush of 1896–98 introduced both the concept of mineral resources and American interest, Canada began to strengthen government presence in the Arctic through the Northwest Mounted Police, soon to

15.8 *Gjøa* at Frognerkilen, Norway, 1903, before its departure to complete the first traverse of the Northwest Passage. Amundsen's ship, a tiny fishing smack, proved equal to the task of navigating the Northwest Passage. Its sturdy construction and shallow draft, the occasional use of its engine, and Amundsen's courage and stubbornness also played a role. *Gjøa* is now enshrined at the Norwegian Maritime Museum in Oslo. Wilse/Norsk Folkemuseum.

be renamed the Royal Canadian Mounted Police (RCMP). The first RCMP patrol came to Herschel Island, ninety miles from the US–Canada border, in August 1903, and it was followed in the next two decades by increased patrols and the creation of police outposts throughout the Arctic. Many of these were in or near posts established by fur traders. Inuit, either willingly or, later, through direct government intervention, relocated to these outposts, which became more fully established Arctic communities at locations such as Cambridge Bay and Coppermine.

In 1904, as part of a national plan by the government of Wilfrid Laurier to assert sovereignty in the Arctic, the Canadian Polar Expedition, under the command of Joseph Elzear Bernier, was diverted from its intended three-year exploration of the maritime approaches to the North Pole. Instead, Bernier and his vessel, *Arctic,* were placed under the command of the RCMP superintendent J. D. Moodie and sent north to "show the flag" and serve as a base for patrols and treks through the region in a series of three voyages (1906–7, 1908–9, and 1910–11). The "eastern Arctic Patrol" of the RCMP and Bernier left a series of plaques and cairns proclaiming Canada's ownership of the Arctic archipelago. In the 1908–9 expedition, ice conditions were such, in Bernier's opinion, that "if our instructions had included the making of the North West Passage, I feel confident that it could have been made."[24]

As events turned out, it would take three decades before the passage was attempted—and navigated—again. The vessel that made that epic second transit, and the third, was an RCMP ship specifically built for Arctic work. The RCMP leadership made the decision in 1927 to build their own ship to connect the four police detachments in the western Arctic. The vessel would be designed to freeze into the ice and become a fixed detachment of its own in the winter, from which protracted patrols by dogsled would cover hitherto unpoliced areas.

The RCMP vessel, in part copied from Roald Amundsen's Arctic exploration ship *Maud,* which Amundsen had used to try and drift in ice to the North Pole from 1917 through 1926, was launched from North Vancouver, British Columbia, in May 1928. Named for the Quebec parish of St. Roch in east Quebec, the riding of the federal minister of justice, Ernest LaPointe, the schooner was quickly fitted out, provisioned, and readied for her first trip north. Among the crew was the newly recruited RCMP constable Henry Asbjorn Larsen, a fourteen-year veteran of the sea. A recent arrival in Canada, the Norwegian-born Larsen had grown up reading the accounts of Arctic explorers, including Amundsen. Larsen joined the RCMP to go north; he aspired one day to repeat Amundsen's feat. Larsen told his superiors, "I'd very much like to put this ship through the Northwest Passage. She's built to take it and I believe she could do it."[25]

From 1928 to 1939, *St. Roch* was confined to western Arctic waters, supplying RCMP outposts, freezing in for winter patrols, and serving at times as the only representative of the Canadian government in the far north. In 1936, Larsen again pitched his superiors, in this case the commissioner of the RCMP, on navigating the Northwest Passage. "I was told that our role was not to be explorers," Larsen wrote in his autobiography. "But the Commissioner added that he also hoped that the opportunity to navigate from one side of the Arctic to the other would present itself one day."[26]

Then, in September 1939, in response to a perceived threat of German occupation of Greenland and a Nazi seizure of the icy land's cryolite mines (a vital source of aluminum), Larsen was summoned to RCMP headquarters and told to plan to take *St. Roch* to Halifax via the Northwest Passage. "Here it was, my great moment. Canada was at war and the government had realized the need to demonstrate the country's sovereignty over the Arctic islands."[27] After refitting, *St. Roch* departed Vancouver in June 1940 and slowly made its way into the western Arctic. Larsen chose to follow Amundsen's route in reverse.

St. Roch reached Point Barrow on July 23. It was a bad year for ice, and Larsen had a difficult time dodging ice floes as he pushed past Barrow and on to Herschel Island. From there, he sailed to Cambridge Bay, the ship's usual winter quarters. Larsen had hoped to reach Gjoa Haven, but it was too late in the season. Retreating west, Larsen wintered at Walker Bay on the western shores of Victoria Island.

Breaking out of the ice on July 31, 1941, *St. Roch* could not proceed east. New orders had it return west to ferry supplies to western communities. With that task accomplished, Larsen turned east again and pushed past Gjoa Haven in late August. In the face of increasing ice, he motored as far as Pasley Bay on the Boothia Peninsula and anchored. Heavy ice and wind nearly swamped *St. Roch* and threatened to drive it ashore. Hitting an offshore shoal, the ship pivoted and rocked on both beams. Ice began to climb up the starboard side. "I wondered if we had come this far to be crushed like a nut on a shoal and then buried by the ice," Larsen wrote.[28] The ship had nearly rolled on to her side, dragging her anchors, when she suddenly popped free, thanks to Larsen's lassoing a nearby boulder and using his winch to pull his ship off the shoal.

The winter at Pasley Bay brought tragedy when one of the crew, Constable Albert "Frenchey" Chartrand, died of an apparent heart attack in February 1942. Larsen and an Inuk guide, Equalla, made a 1,140-mile dogsled journey to bring a priest back to the ship for a funeral service. Chartrand was buried on a nearby hill overlooking the bay, with a fifteen-foot stone cairn to mark the spot. It stands there still. Fearing another winter, Larsen broke out of his winter quarters in early August 1942 by blasting the ice with black powder bombs and ramming it with the ship's steel-reinforced bow. The hard work cracked one of the engine cylinders, but by blocking it off and moving on partial power, *St. Roch* and its crew were able to motor on, passing through the ice-choked Bellot Strait. "I got the feeling that I had constantly to match wits with the moving

15.9 *St. Roch,* the Royal Canadian Mounted Police (RCMP) Arctic patrol vessel, in Vancouver, having successfully navigated the Northwest Passage from east to west in 1944. The second ship to navigate the passage was a doughty RCMP motor schooner. *St. Roch* made history as a regular presence in the Canadian Arctic, as the second to make the passage, and as the first ship to navigate the passage in both directions. Hauled ashore in 1958 and later housed over, the ship is a national historic site and the centerpiece of the Vancouver Maritime Museum. Vancouver Maritime Museum, #5130.

pack ice," Larsen later recalled. "Many a time did I head for an opening in the ice only to watch it crash together just ahead of me, as if it were a living thing deliberately trying to keep me from reaching open water. On other occasions the ice would snap shut behind me, as if it held me in a trap. But it also happened that when things looked hopeless and I was almost resigned to giving up, the ice would suddenly open up . . . [and] the leads would gradually get wider and wider and allow us to slide through the cracks for mile after mile."[29]

After a difficult transit through the strait, *St. Roch* anchored at the Hudson's Bay Company outpost of Fort Ross and from there, hopping from one Arctic outpost to another, finally reached Halifax on October 11, 1942. "It had not been an easy trip," Larsen reported.[30] The three seasons he had just spent in the Northwest Passage were the worst years he had seen in the Arctic, and "without hesitation I would say that most ships encountering the conditions we faced would have failed."[31] The second transit of the Northwest Passage had been no easy feat, as the scarred sides and worn-out machinery of *St. Roch* attested.

After rebuilding *St. Roch*'s deckhouse and adding a new, more powerful engine, the RCMP ordered it home to Vancouver in 1944. Larsen decided to take "the more northerly route, through Lancaster Sound and west to Melville Island and then across McClure Strait to Prince of Wales Strait. This was the real Northwest Passage, I felt, and it had never before been navigated."[32] Only Parry had come close in 1819. With a new crew, save for two old hands, Larsen set out on July 26, 1944, from Halifax. Picking up the guide and hunter Joe Panipakuttuk in Pond Inlet, along with his six-member family and seventeen dogs, Larsen and crew now headed into the passage.

By the end of August, *St. Roch* stood off the entrance to McClure Strait, "now in waters never before sailed by any vessel."[33] *St. Roch* carefully wove through the ice, down the Prince of Wales Strait, and within a few days reached Walker Bay, its winter quarters in 1940–41. Rather than stop, Larsen kept going, landing the Panipakuttuk family at Herschel Island before racing the ice to get past Point Barrow. On September 27, *St. Roch* passed through the Bering Strait. On October 16, 1944, it arrived in Vancouver harbor after an absence of four years (fig. 15.9). Larsen, the first man to traverse the passage in two directions, had also made the northern run in an amazing eighty-six days. He, his crew, and *St. Roch* were feted in the press and awarded numerous honors and medals.

St. Roch returned to the Arctic in 1945–46 to find that a new age had arrived. In the winter, the majority of the ship's crew were flown out of the Arctic. *St. Roch* was also visited by troops participating in Operation Muskox, a combined Canadian-American operation testing military equipment in Arctic conditions. The Cold War brought substantial change to the north. Starting in the late 1940s, the formerly clear Arctic skies filled with the contrails of long-range bombers. Later, the tracks of intercontinental ballistic missiles (ICBMs) made the far north a strategic frontier. In 1955, construction of the Defense Early Warning system (the DEW line) began. The arrival of the military brought even more changes as bases were built and the military personnel settled into formerly small and isolated settlements.

The next ship through the Northwest Passage was HMCS *Labrador,* a warship under the command of O. C. S. Robertson. *Labrador* made the trip in 1954, basically following Larsen's track of ten years before. This voyage was a harbinger of things to come, for, as its commander noted, "we must now look to the Arctic, not just as a source of future resources, but as an immediate defence against possible aggression. We must define the place that the Arctic could, or might have to play in the defence of the North American Continent."[34]

The strategic frontier of the Arctic was dominated not by surface vessels, however, but by submarines. The idea of submarines running under the ice cap dated to the nineteenth century, when Jules Verne's *Nautilus* did so in his novel *20,000 Leagues Under the Sea.* Early efforts at submarine navigation were hampered by the need for diesel electric submarines to surface, which prevented them from making a prolonged voyage under ice. The development of the nuclear-powered submarine in the 1950s solved that problem. USS *Nautilus,* the first nuclear submarine, reached 90°N on August 5, 1958. The nuclear submarine USS *Skate* was the next north, followed by USS *Sargo.* Then, in 1960, USS *Seadragon,* with Commander George W. Steele II in command, transited the Northwest Passage. It was not a routine voyage; Steele, much like earlier navigators, had to feel his way through at spots, using only sonar.

Robertson, the captain of the *Labrador,* sailed with *Seadragon* on this first submerged transit of the passage. In his confidential report, Robertson noted that "the nuclear submarine has demonstrated its ability to traverse the Arctic Ocean at will. . . . It has also demonstrated its ability to transit narrow and shallow channels submerged under the seas' ice cover. . . . The borders for which nature had previously provided a sure defense are no longer protected. The Arctic is a highway if we will but have the wit to use it."[35] Military and naval planners agreed: to this day, the Arctic is regularly patrolled by nuclear submarines.

The strategic frontier has given way, especially in an age of global warming and retreating ice, to a commercial passage. The commercialization of the Arctic and the Northwest Passage is not a new concept. The quest for the passage was spurred by the dream of a more direct and faster route to Asia's markets. When the ice proved impenetrable, the region's pelagic resources, especially whales, became a commodity to be exploited. The postwar discovery of rich natural resources in the north spurred development and new settlements. A rich oil discovery in 1968 at Prudhoe Bay, on Alaska's North Slope, inspired the Humble Oil & Refining Company to attempt the first commercial voyage through the

15.10 The oil supertanker SS *Manhattan* in the Northwest Passage in 1969. The dream of mariners since the fifteenth century for a commercially viable Northwest Passage was seemingly achieved with the 1969 voyage of the *Manhattan*, but it was more of a trial run than a regular voyage, and merely proved that the passage was not actually a viable commercial corridor. In the twenty-first century, however, global climate change and an increasingly ice-free passage will enable regular commercial voyages through a land and seas once described as "wild and savage." Royal Geographical Society, London, S0000091.

Northwest Passage and to find a relatively short, fast route from the oil fields to eastern US refineries.

The 150,000-ton tanker SS *Manhattan* was refitted as an icebreaker and sent through the Northwest Passage in 1969 (fig. 15.10). Escorted by the Canadian icebreaker *John A. Macdonald*, *Manhattan* made it through. The ice of McClure Strait thwarted the huge ship, though, and *Manhattan* instead sailed through Prince of Wales Strait, reaching open water on September 13, 1969. The achievement was heralded as a "forerunner of a fleet of icebreaker-tankers that might make use of Arctic waters a commonplace within less than a decade."[36] While that has yet to happen, predictions of dwindling ice might well make the passage regularly navigable not only for tankers but also for other vessels. An essentially ice-free passage would make an attractive route for northern European and American vessels seeking to avoid the Panama Canal. Thus the dream of four centuries, and the reason James Cook pushed to the gates of the Arctic, might well be fulfilled within the next few decades.

NOTES

1 John Barrow, *Voyages of Discovery and Research in the Arctic Regions from the Year 1818 to the Present Time* (London: John Murray, 1846), 2–3.
2 Ibid.
3 John Ross, *A Voyage of Discovery . . . for the Purpose of Exploring Baffin's Bay, and Inquiring into the Probability of a North-West Passage* (London: Longman, Hurst, Rees, Orme, and Brown, 1819), iii.
4 Barrow, *Voyages of Discovery,* 49.
5 Ibid., 43.
6 W. E. Parry, *Journal of a Voyage for the Discovery of a North-West Passage from the Atlantic to the Pacific Performed in the Years 1819–20 in His Majesty's Ships* Hecla *and* Griper, *under the Orders of William Edward Parry, R.N., F.R.S.* (London: John Murray, 1821), 53.
7 Parry, *Journal of a Voyage,* 101.
8 John Franklin, *Thirty Years in the Arctic Regions* (New York: H. Dayton, 1859), 235–36.
9 W. E. Parry, *Journal of a Second Voyage for the Discovery of a North-West Passage . . .* (London: John Murray, 1824), 148.
10 John Ross, *Narrative of a Second Voyage in Search of a North-West Passage . . .* (London: A. W. Webster, 1833), 557.
11 John Barrow, as quoted in R. J. Cyriax, *Sir John Franklin's Last Arctic Expedition* (London: Methuen, 1939), 19.
12 Sherard Osborn, ed., *The Discovery of the North-West Passage by H.M.S.* Investigator (London: Longman, Brown, Green and Longmans, 1856), 179.
13 Roald Amundsen, *My Life as an Explorer* (Garden City, NY: Doubleday, Doran, 1928), 33.
14 Ibid.
15 Ibid., 35.
16 Roald Amundsen, *The North West Passage* (London: Archibald Constable, 1908), 1:9–10.
17 Ibid.
18 Amundsen, *My Life as an Explorer,* 36.
19 Amundsen, *North West Passage,* 1:48.
20 Ibid., 1:55.
21 Ibid., 1:57.
22 Ibid., 1:80.
23 Ibid., 2:119.
24 Capt. J. E. Bernier, *Report on the Dominion of Canada Expedition to the Arctic Islands and Hudson Strait on Board the D.G.S.* Arctic, *1908–1909* (Ottawa: Government Printing Bureau, 1910), 38.
25 Henry A. Larsen, Frank R. Sheer, and Edvard Omholt-Jensen, *The Big Ship* (Toronto: McClelland and Stewart, 1967), 113.
26 Ibid., 141.
27 Ibid.
28 Ibid., 153.
29 Ibid., 98.
30 Ibid., 178.
31 Ibid.
32 Ibid., 181.
33 Ibid., 189.
34 O. C. S. Robertson, "The Arctic as a Theatre of War" (unpublished ms., Submarine Force Library and Museum, Groton, CT, 1960), 1.
35 Ibid., 2.
36 Bern Keating, *The Northwest Passage: From the* Mathew *to the* Manhattan, *1497 to 1969* (New York: Rand McNally, 1970), 151.

Sea Ice in the Western Portal of the Northwest Passage from 1778 to the Twenty-First Century

HARRY STERN

16

ON AUGUST 11, 1778, CAPTAIN JAMES COOK SAILED NORTH THROUGH Bering Strait into the Arctic Ocean in search of the Northwest Passage. Working his way along the coast of Alaska, his progress was halted a week later by "ice which was as compact as a Wall and seemed to be ten or twelve feet high at least."

This marked Cook's farthest north, at 70°44'N latitude, just west of present-day Wainwright, Alaska. Retreating southward six leagues (about eighteen miles), Cook encountered "a point which was much incumbered with ice for which Reason it obtained the name of *Icey Cape.*" He continued, "Our situation was now more and more critical, we were in shoald water upon a lee shore and the main body of the ice in sight to windward driving down upon us. It was evident, if we remained much longer between it and the land it would force us ashore" (fig. 2.7). Cook steered southwest to extricate his ships from danger, then turned westward, and for the next eleven days sailed close to the ice edge, trying to find an opening to the north. On August 29, having reached the coast of Siberia at 69°N without finding a break in the ice, he abandoned the search, since "so little was the prospect of succeeding," but he resolved "to return to the North in further search of a Passage the ensuing summer." He sailed south

Detail from *The* Resolution *beating through the Ice, with the* Discovery *in eminent danger in the distance*. Hand-colored soft-ground etching, published by I. Webber in 1792, after a drawing by John Webber, August 1778 (see also fig. 2.7). National Library of Australia, pic-vn 3683642.

through Bering Strait on September 2, having spent three weeks in the Arctic.[1]

On July 8, 2009, the sixty-four-foot cutter *Ocean Watch,* with a crew of seven, sailed north through Bering Strait into the Arctic Ocean on a circumnavigation of North and South America. Four days later, they "turned the corner at Icy Cape . . . and headed east towards Barrow" in clear seas. Twenty-five miles before Barrow, they entered "a maze of ice." Picking their way through the ice floes, they reached the town of Barrow on July 13 and anchored offshore. But as they relaxed in the cockpit, a shout came from shore: "The ice is coming in! Your boat will sink in ten hours!" They quickly motored to safer waters near Elson Lagoon. Seven weeks later they were in Baffin Bay, having transited the Northwest Passage.[2]

Cook encountered impenetrable pack ice in mid-August 1778 and was forced to retreat, but 231 years later, a sailboat cruised beyond Cook's northernmost point a full month earlier in the summer and made the Northwest Passage. Yet Cook's ships and the modern-day *Ocean Watch* were similarly threatened with imminent destruction by the advance of the pack ice against the shore. What, then, is different about sea-ice conditions today compared to Cook's day?

In this essay, we consider the nature and evolution of sea ice in the western Arctic, from early explorers' accounts to the modern era of satellite data. We examine what was known about sea ice in Cook's day and what is known today. How much has the ice retreated, and is it still a barrier to shipping? Would Cook have discovered the Northwest Passage in 1778 if sea-ice conditions had been as they are today? How are sea-ice conditions predicted to change in the twenty-first century? Are there parallels to 1778 in today's resurgence of interest in the Arctic? We begin with a brief primer on the two forms of large-scale ice in the Arctic.

SEA ICE AND GLACIAL ICE

Sea ice forms from freezing seawater. While freshwater freezes at 32°F, seawater freezes at about 29°F because of its salt content. During the freezing process, most of the salt drains out of the ice through brine channels, but some salt remains in the ice.

Newly formed sea ice, called *first-year ice,* grows to about six feet thick over the course of the Arctic winter. The ice floats with about one-eighth of its thickness above the waterline (termed *freeboard*) and seven-eighths below the waterline (termed *draft*).

Sea ice circulates around the Arctic Ocean, driven by wind and currents. The forces acting on the ice sometimes cause it to fracture and split apart, creating *leads* (openings) that are typically long and narrow. New ice then begins to grow in the leads. The forces acting on the ice may also cause it to converge and press against itself, or against the coast, thrusting large blocks of ice up into jumbled *pressure ridges* that can reach fifteen feet or more in height and extend one hundred feet below the waterline. If the water is shallow enough, these jumbled features become grounded on the bottom.

Sea ice and the snow on top of it begin to melt in early summer. The melting snow collects in *melt ponds* on the surface of the ice. The ice continues to decrease in thickness and extent until sometime in September. Sea ice that survives the summer melt becomes *multiyear ice.* It is typically thicker, less salty, and stronger than first-year ice. Sea ice may survive for several years, but eventually most of it drifts out of the Arctic and into warmer water, where it melts. This does not raise sea level, because the ice was already floating in the ocean.

Glacial ice forms on land. As snow falls and accumulates, the weight of the snow on top compresses the snow underneath, which turns into ice. With each year of snow accumulation, the ice grows thicker. For example, the ice in the middle of Greenland is about ten thousand feet thick, and at the bottom of the ice sheet it is one hundred thousand years old. If glacial ice melts and the water runs into the ocean, sea level rises.

Glacial ice flows slowly downhill, or spreads out under its own weight. If a glacier or ice sheet flows all the way to the ocean, the pieces that break off and float away are called *icebergs.* This process also raises sea level. Note that icebergs are made of freshwater ice, because they originate from snowfall.

A glacier or an ice sheet may also flow out across a bay or other body of water and float in place, still attached to its upstream extension. This is called a floating *ice shelf.* If a piece of an ice shelf breaks off and floats away, it is called a *tabular iceberg* or an *ice island.* Ice islands in the Arctic originate from the floating ice shelves of the northern Canadian Arctic Archipelago. The most famous ice island in the Arctic was Fletcher's Ice Island, also called T-3. It was used as a manned scientific research station in the 1950s. Measuring three miles by seven miles in extent and 125 feet thick, it rose only 10 feet above the surrounding pack ice and so could not be distinguished from sea ice at a distance. In 1983, it drifted into the North Atlantic and melted.

The ice that Cook encountered on August 18, 1778, "which was as compact as a Wall and seemed to be ten or twelve feet high at least," was most likely ridged sea ice at the edge of the continuous pack ice, more densely packed than in figure 2.7 but with a similar jumbled nature.

Antarctica also contains sea ice and glacial ice. The sea ice in the Southern Ocean surrounding Antarctica is mainly first-year ice: it forms during the Antarctic fall and winter and melts during summer. The massive glacial ice sheet covering the Antarctic continent—larger in area than the United States and over two miles thick in the middle—flows out toward the edge of the continent into vast floating ice shelves, which calve gigantic tabular icebergs into the Southern Ocean. Cook had much experience in Antarctic waters on his second voyage (1772–75), sailing south of the Antarctic Circle on three separate occasions and recording in detail the impressive scenes of ice. For example, on February 24, 1773, he noted, "The Ice Islands were now so

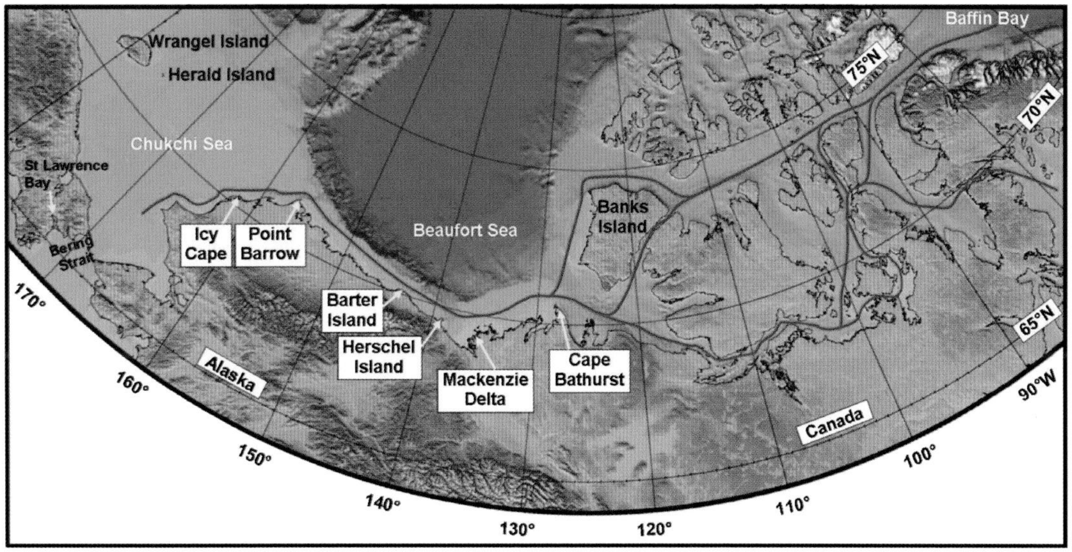

16.1 Routes of the Northwest Passage (in red), with landmarks labeled along the north coast of Alaska and western Canada. Light blue denotes the shallow continental shelf; dark blue denotes the deep ocean. Drawn by H. Stern on a base map adapted from M. Jakobsson, et al., *The International Bathymetric Chart of the Arctic Ocean (IBCAO)*, version 3.0, *Geophysical Research Letters* 39 (2012), L12609, http://dx.doi.org/10.1029/2012GL052219.

numerous that we had passed upwards of Sixty or Seventy sence noon many of them a mile or a mile and a half in circuit, increasing both in number and Magnitude as we advanced to the South. . . . [The scene] at once fills the mind with admiration and horror, the first is occasioned by the beautifullniss of the Picture and the latter by the danger attending it, for was a ship to fall aboard one of these large pieces of ice she would be dashed to pieces in a moment."

THE NORTHWEST PASSAGE

The Northwest Passage is a sea route between the Atlantic and Pacific Oceans that threads its way through the Canadian Arctic Archipelago and along the north coast of Alaska to Bering Strait (fig. 16.1). The portion through the Canadian islands branches into several different routes. The southern routes pass through narrow, shallow straits containing numerous hazards to navigation such as small islands, submerged rocks, and complex currents. The northern routes are more suitable for deep-draft vessels but are more susceptible to blockage by ice.

Sea ice solidly packs the waterways of the Canadian islands from November through June. In July and August, the southern route through the islands begins to melt out, but the northern route typically remains clogged with ice. Sea-ice coverage reaches its minimum in September, but several bottlenecks within the passages may still hold enough ice to block ships from passing. In addition, thick multiyear ice from the Arctic Ocean or from the channels between the northern Canadian islands may drift south and plug up the southern passages. Thus even if the local sea ice melts out completely, the southern passages may still be blocked during summer by imported ice. Sea-ice coverage expands rapidly during October, and by November the Canadian islands are again solidly packed with ice.

A similar annual cycle occurs along the northern coast of Alaska. The sea ice melts back from the coast in June, July, and August, and the ice edge typically recedes to its farthest north in September. Before the mid-1990s, there were some years when sea ice remained up against the coast all summer. Over the past fifteen years, the ice has been receding farther offshore during summer, but onshore winds may still bring the ice pack right up to the coast at times, presenting a barrier to coastal shipping. Although many small boats have successfully navigated the Northwest Passage (mostly since 2007), an ice-free transit of the passage cannot necessarily be expected in any year.

Distinct stocks of bowhead whales inhabit opposite sides of the Northwest Passage, in the Bering Sea and in Baffin Bay. The distribution and radiocarbon ages of bowhead whale remains indicate that the stocks became separated about 8,900 years ago. Thus a year-round sea ice barrier must have become established at that time in the central part of the Northwest Passage.[3] This ice barrier is now breaking down: in August 2010, two bowhead whales from opposite sides of the Northwest Passage spent ten days in the same area of the central passage, documenting overlap between the two populations.[4] Thus the opening of the Northwest Passage has ecological as well as commercial and geopolitical implications.

Early expeditions in search of a Northwest Passage (e.g., by John Cabot, 1497; Martin Frobisher, 1576; John Davis, 1585; and Henry Hudson, 1610) approached from the Atlantic side and tried to work westward. On the Pacific side, Vitus Bering sailed north through the strait that bears his name in August 1728, but he did not sight the eastern shore, and he was not searching for a passage to the Atlantic. Cook was the first explorer to search for a Northwest Passage starting from its western portal. How have sea-ice conditions changed there since the time of Cook?

SEA-ICE OBSERVATIONS OVER THE CENTURIES

Early Explorers

The logbooks and journals of explorers are a rich source of descriptive material about sea ice and the natural environment. Ships' captains typically made daily entries in journals, and often the ships' officers kept their own journals. At the end of an expedition it was customary for the commanding officer to publish a book about the voyage. Here we look at the experiences of several explorers who ventured north of Bering Strait after the time of Cook.

Otto von Kotzebue (1787–1846) circumnavigated the globe in 1815–18 in the *Rurick,* under the Russian flag. On July 30, 1816, he wrote, "We penetrated through Beering's Straits to the north" and discovered Kotzebue Sound.[5] He spent the first two weeks of August exploring the sound "and several points, lying a few minutes farther to the north, on the shores of this sound," before returning south through Bering Strait on August 20. There is no mention in Kotzebue's account of sighting ice during this time. We can conclude that the ice edge was farther north than 67°N in mid-August 1816, although we cannot know whether it was north or south of the latitude where Cook met with ice in mid-August 1778.

The British naval officer Frederick William Beechey (1796–1856) commanded HMS *Blossom,* a ship dispatched to the Bering Strait region to provide relief for John Franklin's voyage down the Mackenzie River to the Beaufort Sea. Beechey's expedition (1825–28) discovered and named Wainwright Inlet (Alaska), Point Barrow, and Elson Lagoon, among other landmarks. On July 30, 1826, Beechey sailed out of Kotzebue Sound and headed north. On August 16 he was off Icy Cape. He wrote, "This cape, the farthest point reached by Captain Cook, was at the time of its discovery very much encumbered with ice, whence it received its name; none, however, was now visible." Here, soundings revealed a series of shallow banks parallel to the coast, known today as Blossom Shoals. Beechey had on board the *Blossom* a small decked launch, which he now put under the command of Thomas Elson, with a crew of nine men, "to trace the shore to the north-eastward as far as it was possible for a boat to navigate, with a view to render the earliest possible assistance to Captain Franklin, and to obtain what information he could of the trending of the coast and of the position of the ice." At midnight on August 17, Elson "commenced his interesting expedition" along the coast. *Blossom* continued north, but only four hours later they sighted "the main body [of ice] in latitude 71°07'N. . . . It was loose at the edge, but close within, and consisted of heavy floes." Thus on the same day of the year that Cook reached his farthest north, Beechey was also stopped by ice only twenty-three miles north of Cook's position.[6]

On August 23 the launch reached Point Barrow (71°23'N), "a low neck beyond which it was impossible to proceed to the eastward, in consequence of the ice being attached to the land, and extending along the horizon to the northward." Soon "the wind changed to south-west, and set the whole body of ice in motion toward the land." Elson tried to retreat, but "the ice continuing to press against the shore, his vessel was driven upon the beach." After several tense days, "a change of wind loosened the ice" and they "succeeded in affecting their escape."[7] They reunited with *Blossom* on September 10. Once again, disaster had been narrowly averted on a lee shore pressed by ice. But the boat voyage had demonstrated that it was possible to navigate north in open water close to the coast, even with ice offshore (fig. 15.3).

In 1848 the British naval vessels HMS *Herald* (commanded by Henry Kellett) and HMS *Plover* (commanded by Thomas Moore) were dispatched to Bering Strait to provide relief for Franklin (again!) on his attempt to sail through the Northwest Passage from east to west. (Little did they know that Franklin's ships had been locked in the ice since 1846, nearly two thousand miles east of Bering Strait; that Franklin was already dead; and that his entire crew would soon perish.) *Herald* and *Plover* spent several summers cruising the waters north of Bering Strait. On July 26, 1849, *Herald* reached the ice edge at latitude 71°05'N, but proceeding "in a series of steps westerly and northerly," attained 72°51'N two days later.[8] On August 17 they sighted (and named) Herald Island, which is at the same latitude as Point Barrow but more than four hundred miles farther west, in the western Chukchi

Sea. In the meantime, a party from *Plover,* traveling in two boats and taking advantage of shore leads, coasted around Point Barrow and east along the Alaskan coast to the mouth of the Mackenzie River.[9] Also at this time, a private yacht, the *Nancy Dawson,* rounded Point Barrow and proceeded fifty miles farther east, leaving a cache of provisions for Franklin. "The Nancy Dawson will ever be remembered in the history of navigation as the first yacht that . . . penetrated to the eastward of Point Barrow." It was not without risk. "The Nancy Dawson . . . had many escapes: she was pressed on shore once, ran on shore on another occasion to the eastward of Point Barrow, when she was only got off by the assistance of the natives, who manned her capstan and hove with great good-will."[10] Thus the ice edge in August 1849 was considerably farther north than in 1778, by at least 40 miles in the eastern Chukchi Sea and 120 miles in the western Chukchi Sea.

The British sent two more ships to Bering Strait in 1850, this time for the purpose of sailing east through the Northwest Passage in search of Franklin: *Investigator* (commanded by Robert McClure) and *Enterprise* (commanded by Richard Collinson). In his book *Arctic Hell-Ship,* historian William Barr describes in detail the expedition of *Enterprise* (1850–55), in which Collinson confined several of his officers to the brig for the better part of the voyage, thereby burdening himself with all the navigational duties.[11] Having become separated from *Investigator* in the Pacific Ocean, *Enterprise* sailed north and reached the entrance to Wainwright Inlet on August 15, 1850. Working her way north and east in loose ice, "on the 20th she was 25 miles due north of Point Barrow, and although the edge of the main pack was in sight to the north, stretching from horizon to horizon, there was no ice to the eastwards."[12] Thus the ice edge in the third week of August 1850 was more than sixty miles north of where Cook had encountered it in 1778, with enticingly clear seas beckoning eastward from Barrow.

Indeed, unbeknownst to Collinson, *Investigator* had rounded Point Barrow two weeks earlier and continued eastward, taking advantage of a strip of open water along the coast that is kept clear by grounded ice farther offshore (fig. 15.5). Collinson, however, insisted on staying at least 15 miles offshore, to the frustration of his officers, and even tried to push north in the hope of finding a clear lane to the east. He abandoned the search on August 28 at 73°23'N, more than 150 miles north of Cook's farthest north.

Enterprise returned to the Arctic in summer 1851. On July 18, abeam of Icy Cape, Second Master Francis Skead described the scene:

> Several heavy grounded floes were passed & the shoals off Icy Cape were crowded with enormous masses of Ice 40 to 50 feet high. Some of them consisted of Floes forced up by pressure, others were small berg masses perfectly clean, with sharp angles, & some of their faces perpendicular as if totally broken

> from some parent berg, but where to find parents for such masses as these I know not; we never saw any that could bear such offspring. Some of the grounded masses lay in 15 fm, but they were small in extent in comparison to their neighbours which crowned the shoals off Icy Cape. The Cape must have been similarly crowned with ice when seen by Cook since, if I remember rightly it was named Icy Cape in consequence. When we visited it last year in Septr. not a particle of Ice was to be seen, & yet to judge from its present state one would say that it could scarcely ever be clear of it. So little are conclusions which are drawn from partial observations to be relied on, particularly where Ice is concerned."[13]

Two days later, *Enterprise* was beset in the ice, drifting northeast. As Barr describes it, "To landward of the drifting ship lay a ridge of grounded floes, rising to a maximum height of 60–80 feet, with a lane of water between it and the shore. As the ship passed Point Barrow in the early hours of the 25th [July], she was carried along alarmingly close to this grounded barrier." Finally on July 31, after eleven days locked in the ice, they were released into the coastal strip of open water east of Point Barrow. Skead wrote: "As it is we are fortunate, but it is the result of an experiment that few men would try at all, & none I fancy attempt a second time. Besides the risk of being crushed against the grounded ice, there is the great probability of being detained in the Pack for an indefinite period of time & carried no one knows whither."[14] Indeed, the latter fate did befall *Jeannette* in 1879 and *Karluk* in 1913, as will be seen below.

By the end of August 1851, *Enterprise* had pushed beyond Cape Bathurst and into Amundsen Gulf, the gateway to the intricate channels of the Northwest Passage. It would be three years before she returned by the same route, having navigated hundreds of miles of uncharted, treacherous waterways but having failed to penetrate the ice that blocked the central portion of the Passage. On August 7, 1854, *Enterprise* rounded Point Barrow heading west, leaving the ice astern. Barr wrote: "By Collinson's calculation, 1164 days had passed since they had first sighted ice on the way north in the summer of 1851, during which time there had been no ice in sight on only 38 days!"[15] The historian Jeannette Mirsky wrote: "Collinson's modest work stands out as one of the greatest feats in Arctic navigation."[16] And Roald Amundsen, the first explorer to successfully navigate the Northwest Passage, wrote: "Sir Richard Collinson appears to me to have been one of the most capable and enterprising sailors the world has ever produced. He guided his great, heavy vessel into waters that hardly afforded sufficient room for the tiny *Gjøa* [Amundsen's ship]. But, better still, he brought her safely home."[17]

Numerous explorers attempted to complete the Northwest Passage during the nineteenth century. The scientists Kevin Wood and James Overland analyzed data from forty-four expeditions to the

Canadian Arctic between 1818 and 1910.[18] Figure 16.2 shows ship tracks and winter-over locations of these expeditions through 1859, together with the frequency of occurrence of sea ice on September 10 (the usual date of minimum extent) for the reference period 1971–2000. Wood and Overland wrote: "On a number of occasions, expeditions came within 150 km of completing the Northwest Passage, but even in years with unfavorable ice conditions, most ships were still able to reach comparatively advanced positions within the Canadian archipelago. By 1859, all possible routes comprising the Northwest Passage had been discovered."[19] Furthermore, they found that ice conditions in the Canadian Archipelago during the nineteenth century were remarkably similar to those during 1971–2000. The Little Ice Age, which brought slightly colder temperatures to Europe and eastern North America between about 1450 and 1850, apparently did not have a big effect on the Canadian Arctic during the nineteenth century. There were cold years and warm years, but according to Wood and Overland, temperatures and ice conditions were not inconsistent with those of the twentieth century. As will be seen, however, summer sea ice has declined dramatically in the twenty-first century, especially at the western portal of the Northwest Passage.

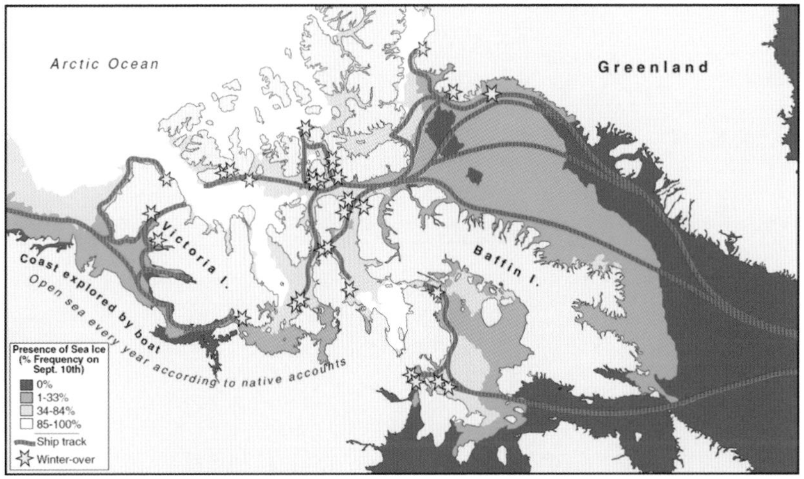

16.2 Ship tracks and winter-over locations of Arctic discovery expeditions, 1818–59, from Wood and Overland, "Accounts." White and shades of blue represent the percent frequency of sea ice on September 10 for the reference period 1971–2000. The ship tracks are consistent with ice conditions during the reference period. Map reproduced with the permission of John Wiley & Sons, Inc.

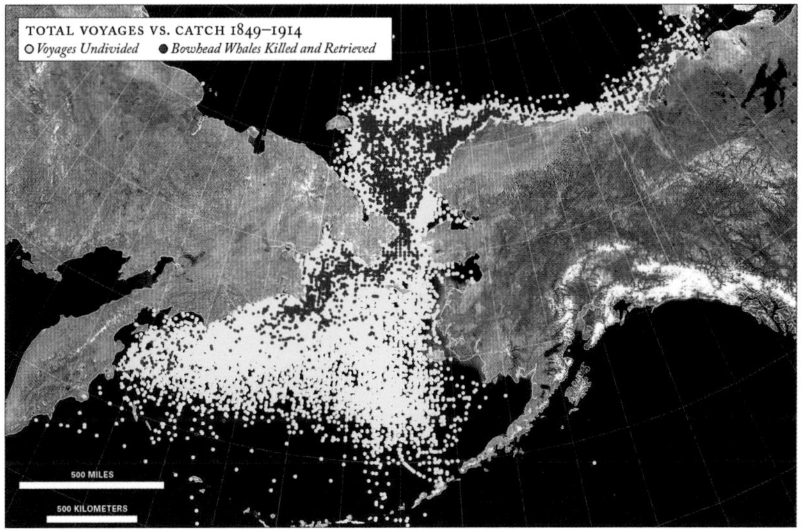

16.3 Whaling-ship positions (yellow) and bowhead whale catches (red), 1849–1914, from Bockstoce, et al., "The Geographic Distribution of Bowhead Whales" (2005). Map used with the permission of *Marine Fisheries Review.*

Whaling Records

On July 23, 1848, the whaling ship *Superior* (under Captain Thomas Roys) sailed through Bering Strait and "made the greatest whaling discovery of the century," sighting vast numbers of bowhead whales and setting off a "gold rush" of whaling that lasted for decades.[20] The whales tended to congregate near the ice edge, so the whaling ships were often near the ice edge too, and the captains recorded the ice conditions in their logbooks. Figure 16.3 shows the locations of whaling ships and bowhead whale catches from 1849 to 1914.[21] Clearly, large numbers of whaling ships managed to navigate along the northwest coast of Alaska in summer and continue eastward beyond Point Barrow. What ice conditions, and dangers, did they encounter?

The comprehensive work by John Bockstoce, *Whales, Ice, and Men,* gives a history of the bowhead whale fishery in the Bering, Chukchi, and Beaufort seas, including notes on ice conditions gleaned from ships' logbooks.[22] Only three years after Roys's discovery, in 1851, more than 170 whaling ships went north. It was an icy year compared to the previous three, and seven ships were lost in the Bering Strait region. The whalers were undeterred, sending 220 ships the following year. As the catches declined in subsequent years, the whalers pushed farther into the Arctic. The first whaling ships reached Point Barrow in 1854. However, not until the 1870s did they regularly venture east of there.

Bockstoce calls the 1870s the "Disastrous Decade" and refers to the coast from Icy Cape to Point Barrow as "a 150-mile ships' graveyard."[23] Consider, for example, the disaster of 1871. In early September, as the whaling fleet waited in a strip of open water along the shore north of Icy Cape for the ice to retreat and open the way to Point Barrow, the wind shifted, driving the ice pack toward shore and trapping the ships. The situation worsened as the ice pressed tighter, crushing one ship after another. On September 12, with no hope of extricating themselves, and with insufficient provisions to last the winter, the captains resolved that all hands should abandon the vessels and work southward in the whaleboats to reach the seven remaining ships not yet trapped near Icy Cape. Thus over 1,200 whalers from thirty-two ships fled in small open boats, sailing for several days under harsh and dangerous conditions to reach the rescue ships. Miraculously, not a single life was lost.

The following year the whalers were back. By the middle of August the fleet was assembled at Point Barrow. It was another icy year, and on August 18 the ice surrounded one ship and dragged it north into the pack, where it was abandoned. Several other ships were damaged that season. But 1873 was a relatively light ice year: by the end of July, twenty ships were at Point Barrow. When no whales were found, they continued east for 150 miles. The next year was similar, and 1875 was even more favorable: some ships reached Barter Island, 250 miles east of Point Barrow.

By 1876 the Arctic whaling fleet had dwindled to twenty ships, the result of overfishing combined with the rise of the petroleum industry, which supplanted the demand for whale oil. Offshore winds in August of that year allowed fourteen whaling ships to reach Point Barrow. But on August 18 the wind shifted, pushing the ice toward shore. The fleet tried to escape to the south, but ten ships became locked in the ice and drifted north with the pack. Twenty miles offshore, the captains decided to abandon the ships. Dragging whaleboats full of supplies across the ice for two days, three hundred men finally reached shore, but more than fifty others had chosen to stay on the ships and take their chances. The three hundred made their way south and were eventually rescued. The pack ice, it turned out, was hard ashore all the way to Icy Cape. The following season, only one of the trapped ships was found, and only three men are known to have survived.

From these and other accounts, two essential facts emerge: first, it was often possible to reach Point Barrow by sailing ship in summertime in the mid-1800s, and second, such a voyage was always accompanied by the prospect of entrapment and destruction in the ice. The relatively warm current that runs north through Bering Strait and follows the coast of Alaska acts to clear the ice from shore in spring and summer, while a wind blowing from the north or west will drive the main ice pack against the shore. Thus the normal year-to-year variability in ice extent due to factors such as a warm or cold spring, combined with the vagaries of weather, conspire to create unpredictable ice conditions along the northwest coast of Alaska in summer.

Taking a systematic approach to the information contained in whaling ships' logbooks, Mahoney and colleagues analyzed more than fifty-two thousand daily observations from logbook entries spanning the period 1850–1909.[24] They grouped the sea-ice sightings by month and by decade, and compared the results to average ice conditions depicted in a US Navy atlas for 1972–82, which predates the rapid sea-ice decline of recent decades. They found "some indication" that summer ice conditions in the 1850s and 1860s were "more severe" than those in 1870–1909, which resembled conditions in 1972–82.

And so in the 1850s, even under "more severe" ice conditions, several ships reached Point Barrow in summertime. Yet in 1871, the entire whaling fleet was still waiting for the ice to open up along the coast in September, and it never did. One may reason, based on cases like these, that the year-to-year variability in summer sea-ice conditions is greater than any decadal climate shifts that may have occurred from the 1850s to the 1970s. It is entirely plausible that Cook's progress would have been halted at Icy Cape on August 18 by sea-ice conditions that occurred in many of the years between 1850 and 1980.

Historical Data, 1850–1940

Sea-ice data for the years from the mid-nineteenth to the mid-twentieth century are found in journals, publications and official reports, maps, and photographic collections. Sources include US Coast Survey data, US North Pacific Expedition records, Bering Sea Patrol data, US Hydrographic Office maps, observations made during the First International Polar Year (IPY) at Point Barrow (1882–83) and in the ensuing decades, logbooks from whaling ships (1850–1910), the Russian Hydrographical Expedition to the Arctic (1910–15), the Second IPY (1932–33), logbooks from US Navy, Coast Guard, and Coast Survey ships (1855–1940), Danish ice charts (starting in 1901), and Russian maps (starting in 1933). These data have not been synthesized into a single homogeneous record of sea-ice conditions in the western Arctic. However, efforts are under way to scan hundreds of thousands of pages from logbooks of US Navy, Coast Guard, and Coast Survey ships, from which millions of Arctic weather and sea-ice observations are being transcribed to digital format by thousands of volunteers for future use in climate studies.[25] This ambitious undertaking will result in much-improved knowledge of the Arctic climate between 1850 and 1940.

It is worth noting two disastrous ice entrapments that occurred during this period: the *Jeannette* in 1879 and the *Karluk* in 1913. The USS *Jeannette,* under the command of George W. DeLong of the US Navy, departed San Francisco in July 1879. The goal of the expedition was to reach the North Pole and make scientific observations; for that purpose, *Jeannette*'s hull had been reinforced to withstand the Arctic pack ice. Her last communication to the outside world was on August 27 from St. Lawrence Bay (in Siberia), about fifty miles southwest of Bering Strait, where Cook had also landed (on August 10, 1778) on his way north. Eight days later, *Jeannette* was beset in thick pack ice near Herald Island. On September 6, DeLong wrote: "This is a glorious country to learn patience in. I am hoping and praying to be able to get the ship into Herald Island to make winter quarters. As far as the eye can range is ice, and not only does it look as if it had never broken up and become water, but it also looks as if it never would."[26] The ship drifted with the ice for twenty-one months. On June 12, 1881, the ice began crushing the ship. The crew unloaded supplies and boats onto the ice. She sank the next day. They began the long trek across the ice toward the Lena River delta in Siberia, hauling their supplies in the boats. Three months later, on the final stretch across open water, a storm sank one of the boats. The other two reached the delta at separate locations, but only thirteen of thirty-three men survived; DeLong was not among them. Three years later, wreckage from *Jeannette* was found on an ice floe near the southern tip of Greenland, roughly three thousand miles from where she was abandoned. This discovery inspired Fridtjof Nansen to hypothesize that sea ice in the Arctic Ocean constantly drifts from the Siberian side across the Pole and into the North Atlantic. To test this idea, Nansen launched an expedition in 1893 in which the ship *Fram* was purposely frozen into the ice and allowed to drift across the Arctic Ocean, confirming his hypothesis.

The Canadian Arctic Expedition, led by the explorer Vilhjalmur Stefansson, left Nome in July 1913 on the *Karluk,* bound for Herschel Island, 350 miles east of Point Barrow. The captain of the ship,

Robert Bartlett, is perhaps the most famous ice pilot ever to have navigated Arctic waters, having guided Robert Peary's North Pole expeditions of 1905–6 and 1908–9 to northern Ellesmere Island on the *Roosevelt.* Although *Karluk* was sheathed with thick planks and equipped with a coal-fired steam engine, Bartlett had reservations about its ability to withstand ice pressure and to power through the ice. On August 13, about 150 miles east of Point Barrow, *Karluk* became trapped in the ice. It drifted west, away from its destination. On September 19, Stefansson left the ship with a small party on a hunting trip. The ship drifted rapidly in a storm, and Stefansson never returned (there is speculation that he never intended to return), instead making his way to land and continuing his exploration of the Canadian Arctic for the next five years. In the meantime, *Karluk* continued to drift. On January 10, 1914, the ice began crushing the ship. The crew unloaded supplies onto the ice. It sank the next day. Four members of the expedition set off to reach Alaska; they were never seen again. The rest of the party made for Wrangell Island. From there, Bartlett and one Inuit hunter traveled seven hundred miles on foot to Bering Strait, where they reached safety and mounted a rescue expedition. In September 1914 their ship arrived at Wrangell Island and rescued eleven survivors, including an Inuit girl named Mukpie, age three. She died in 2008 at the age of ninety-seven.

What are the lessons from these two disasters? In both cases, ice-strengthened ships were crushed by the ice. In the case of the *Karluk,* even an experienced ice captain and a motorized vessel could not prevent the ice from taking the ship. More than 130 years after Cook, ship travel through ice-infested waters remained dangerous and unpredictable.

Sea-Ice Charts and Satellite Data

In the twentieth century, sea ice charts were compiled by the US, Russian, and Danish governments from a variety of sources: ship observations, aerial reconnaissance flights, shore-based observations, scientific expeditions, and, in later years, satellite imagery. The charts typically showed the location of the sea-ice edge and were compiled weekly or monthly, often only during the summer navigation season, for the purpose of safety of navigation, mission planning, and other operational and scientific needs. Collections of sea-ice charts are available from the National Snow and Ice Data Center (NSIDC) in Boulder, Colorado.

Continuous satellite coverage of the polar regions began in October 1978 with the Defense Meteorological Satellite Program's series of satellites carrying sensors that detect the natural emission of electromagnetic radiation from the Earth's surface in the microwave range (roughly 1–100 GHz in frequency), termed *passive microwave* sensors. Since ice and water have different microwave emissions, it is possible to calculate the fractional coverage of sea ice in each 15 × 15 mile patch of polar ocean. This is known as the *sea-ice concentration,* and it ranges

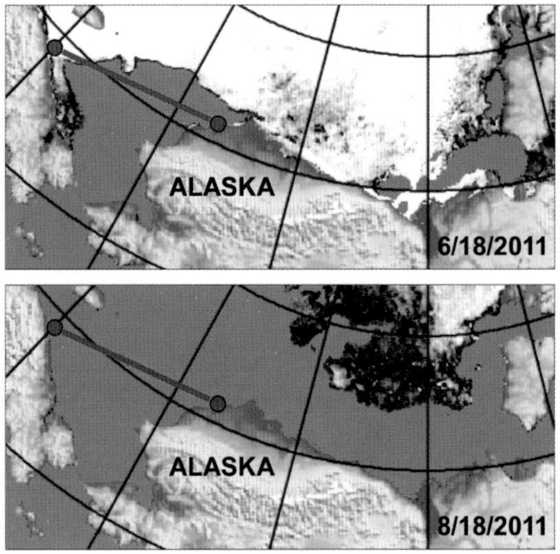

16.4 Sea-ice extent north of Alaska on June 18, 2011 (top), and August 18, 2011 (bottom), from satellite data. White indicates continuous pack ice; black indicates looser ice; blue indicates open water. The red dots show Cook's position on August 18, 1778 (eastern dot) and on August 29, 1778 (western dot), with the approximate ice edge drawn as a red line. Drawn by H. Stern from a base map courtesy of the Centre for Marine and Atmospheric Sciences, University of Hamburg, Germany, found in G. Spreen, L. Kaleschke, and G. Heygster, "Sea Ice Remote Sensing Using AMSR-E 89 GHz Channels," *Journal of Geophysical Research* 113 (2008), C02S03, http://dx.doi.org/10.1029/2005JC003384.

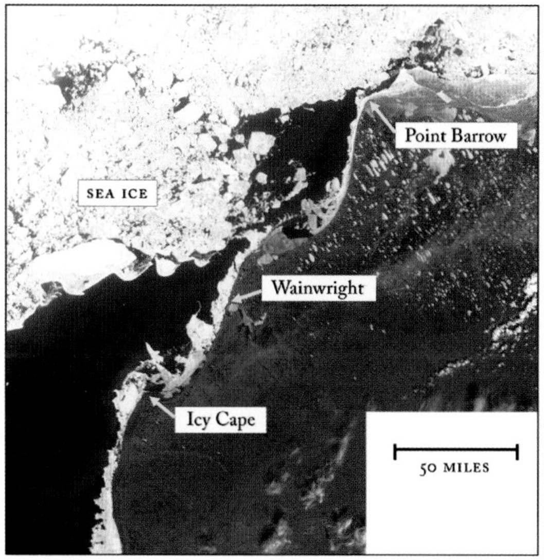

16.5 Satellite image of the northwest coast of Alaska on June 20, 2012, showing sea-ice conditions similar to what Cook must have seen in mid-August 1778. Note the ice along the shore and protruding from Icy Cape. Drawn by H. Stern, based on Rapid Response imagery from the Land Atmosphere Near-Real Time Capability for EOS (LANCE) system operated by the NASA/GSFC/Earth Science Data and Information System (ESDIS), with funding provided by NASA/HQ.

from 0 percent (no ice within a 15 × 15 mile patch) to 100 percent (completely ice-covered). (Note that these data tell us nothing about the thickness of the ice, only its area.) The satellites overfly both polar regions every day of the year, and the sensors are not unduly affected by clouds or darkness. Thus we have a daily record of sea-ice extent in the Arctic Ocean at fifteen-mile spatial resolution from October 1978 to the present day.

Figure 16.4 shows maps of sea-ice concentration north of Alaska based on satellite data. The white areas are close to 100 percent sea ice, and the black areas (which tend to be near the ice edge) are about 50 percent sea ice. Since the maximum concentration in which sailing ships can maneuver is about 30 percent,[27] sailing ships would be restricted to the blue areas in the figure. The upper panel shows data for June 18, 2011, and the lower panel shows data for August 18, 2011. The red dots show Cook's position on August 18, 1778 (eastern dot), and August 29, 1778 (western dot), with the approximate ice edge drawn as a red line. In recent years the summer retreat of sea ice along the north coast of Alaska has been occurring about two months earlier than during Cook's expedition.

Many other types of satellite data have been used to view the polar regions over the past thirty-five years. Optical sensors (like cameras) take high-resolution pictures of the Earth's surface, such as figure 16.5 from NASA's Terra satellite, which shows sea ice near the coast of Alaska on June 20, 2012, in a configuration similar to what Cook must have experienced on August 18, 1778. But since the Arctic is dark all winter and cloudy for much of the summer, optical sensors can give only an intermittent indication of sea-ice conditions. Similarly, infrared sensors are hampered by clouds. Active radar sensors are unaffected by clouds or darkness and produce high-resolution images of sea ice, but their limited spatial and temporal coverage has made them unsuitable for long-term monitoring. Thus the satellite passive microwave data provide the best continuous (in time) and complete (in space) coverage of sea ice over the past thirty-five years.

Satellite data, together with field programs and computer modeling, have given us a precise geographic and physical understanding of Arctic sea ice. What did Cook know about the forms of ice in the sea in the 1770s?

COOK'S KNOWLEDGE OF ICE IN THE SEA

In the early 1770s, Daines Barrington, vice president of the Royal Society, persuaded the British Admiralty to send an expedition to the Far East via the North Pole. Barrington believed that ice in the Arctic Ocean came from northward-flowing rivers that discharged their frozen waters into the sea, and that this ice must necessarily be confined to a band within some distance of land. Cook echoed this idea on his second voyage when he wrote in January 1773, "It is a general recieved opinion that Ice is formed near land." If a ship could penetrate the band of ice, it would find an open polar sea, clear to the North Pole.

In 1773 the Admiralty dispatched two ships under Captain Constantine John Phipps to penetrate this band of ice and pass across the top of the world. Phipps sailed along the west coast of Spitsbergen as far as 80°48'N, where he was stopped by ice. After exploring eastward and becoming trapped in the ice, he managed to reach open water and returned south. Phipps published a book about the expedition in 1774, and Cook would certainly have become familiar with it between the end of his second voyage (July 1775) and the start of his third (July 1776). Perhaps this accounts for Cook's surprise on August 17, 1778, when he wrote, "Some time before Noon we perceived a brightness in the Northern horizon like that reflected from ice, commonly called the blink; it was little noticed from a supposition that it was improbable we should meet with ice so soon."[28] The next day they encountered the wall of ice described in the first paragraph of this essay, a full six hundred nautical miles south of the latitude where Phipps had been stopped. (Today we know that the northern extension of the Gulf Stream keeps the west coast of Spitsbergen ice free in summer).

Clearly Barrington did not believe that the ocean itself could freeze, but Cook was not so sure. On his second voyage, Cook and his men saw many "Islands of Ice" (tabular icebergs), and on January 9, 1773, they collected fifteen tons of floating ice "which had broke from the Main Island." They melted it, and "the Water which the Ice yeilded was perfectly well tasted." They filled their storage casks, with Cook noting, "This is the most expeditious way of Watering I ever met with." Four days later, he wrote, "Some curious and intresting experiments are wanting to know what effect cold has on Sea Water in some of the following instances: does it freeze or does it not? if it does, what degree of cold is necessary and what becomes of the Salt brine? for all the Ice we meet with yeilds Water perfectly sweet and fresh."[29] Thus Cook held out the possibility that the sea might freeze if it became cold enough, but the ice he had collected could not be of such origin, unless somehow the salt had drained out. Of course today we know the difference between sea ice and glacial ice, but Cook was puzzling it out and questioning the "general recieved opinion" of the day.

A further perspective is given at the time of Cook's second foray to the Antarctic Circle, in December 1773, when he wrote, "This feild or loose ice is not such as is usually formed in Bays or Rivers, but like such as is broke off from large Islands."[30] Thus he recognized that tabular icebergs are not made of river ice.

Based on latitude and time of year, most (if not all) of the ice that Cook encountered in the Antarctic on his second voyage was of glacial origin (icebergs), not sea ice. On his third voyage, in the Arctic, it was just the opposite: most (if not all) of the ice was of marine origin. On August 27, 1778, the ships were in the western Chukchi Sea, close to the ice edge. Cook wrote, "Having but little wind, I went with the boats to examine the state of the ice." Cook was a keen observer; he found that "it appeared to be intirely composed of frozen Snow and had been all formed at sea, for setting side the improbability or rather impossibility of such masses floating out of River[s] in which there is hardly Water for a boat, none of the productions of the land was found incorporated, or fixed in it, which must unavoidably have be[en] the case had it been formed in Rivers either great or small." This is remarkable. Cook realized that the ice had formed at sea, and he rejected Barrington's notion of riverine origin. As for the observation that the ice was entirely composed of frozen snow, by this late-summer date, the snow on top of the sea ice might have gone through several melt-freeze cycles, masking the saline ice underneath and giving the impression that the entire mass was frozen snow. Furthermore, Cook wrote, "It appeared to me, very improbable that this ice could be the produce of the preceding Winter alone, but rather that of a great many."[31] Indeed, it was undoubtedly multiyear ice. Cook continued with a detailed explanation of how waves, driven by the wind, eroded the ice, and concluded, "Thus it may happen that more ice is distroyed in one Stormy Season, than is formed in several Winter[s] and an endless accumulation prevented, but that there is always a remaining store, none who has been upon the spot will deny and none but Closet studdying Philosiphers will dispute." Cook's biographer J. C. Beaglehole notes: "There can hardly be a doubt but the particular 'Closet studdying Philosipher' in this case must be Daines Barrington."[32] Thus although Cook still did not grasp that frozen seawater was the source of ice in the Arctic Ocean, he understood that the ice formed at sea, that it could persist year after year, and that Barrington was wrong. If only he had attempted to melt and drink a chunk of that ice, he would surely have noticed the salty taste and realized its origin. But there is no such entry in his journals.

The confusion over polar ice was still not cleared up by Kotzebue's time. In 1821, he wrote:

> Blocks of rock, which are frequently observed on floating ice-bergs of the north, and other indications, teach us that these ice-bergs were originally formed next the land, and it has been attempted to prove, by scientific reasoning and experiments, that ice cannot be formed, except in the contiguity of land, and that an open deep sea, without land or islands, cannot freeze, but must be found open and navigable at all times. We have to oppose only one fact against this notion, which, in our opinion, has been too little regarded; it is the state of the sea round the south pole, unless, by a very arbitrary supposition, to which nothing entitles us, we should represent the southern fields of ice, as attached to an undiscovered, inaccessible continent.

And therefore, "We cannot attach any belief to an open north polar sea."[33]

This is very interesting logic! Kotzebue asserts that the existence of icebergs in the Southern

Ocean refutes the idea that ice at sea originates near land, because there is no known southern continent to give rise to such icebergs. Thus he arrives at the right answer—no open north-polar sea—for the wrong reason, revealing a perfect confusion of the mechanisms of ice formation. A continent does indeed exist in the south, its ice sheets giving rise to the icebergs observed there; a continent does not exist in the north, but the sea does indeed freeze, giving rise to the sea ice observed there.

By the mid-nineteenth century, there is a hint of understanding: with *Enterprise* near Cape Parry on September 1, 1851, Barr notes: "A boat was sent ashore to get some more water, since the water derived earlier from floes was somewhat brackish."[34] Thus the marine origin of the ice must have been apparent.

ARCTIC SEA ICE AND THE NORTHWEST PASSAGE TODAY

Arctic sea ice grows over the course of the winter to a maximum extent of about 6 million square miles by March, then melts back to its minimum extent in September. From the beginning of the satellite record until the early 2000s, the area of Arctic sea ice in September declined slightly, from about 3 million to 2.5 million square miles, with large year-to-year variations (fig. 16.6). Since the early 2000s, summer sea ice has declined sharply, reaching a record low of less than 1.5 million square miles in September 2012. The greatest loss of summer sea ice has occurred in the region north of Bering Strait, exactly where Cook ventured in 1778 (fig. 16.6, lower panels). The sea ice in that region is retreating earlier in the summer by about a week per decade, and advancing later in the fall by about a week per decade, as measured over the satellite era, leading

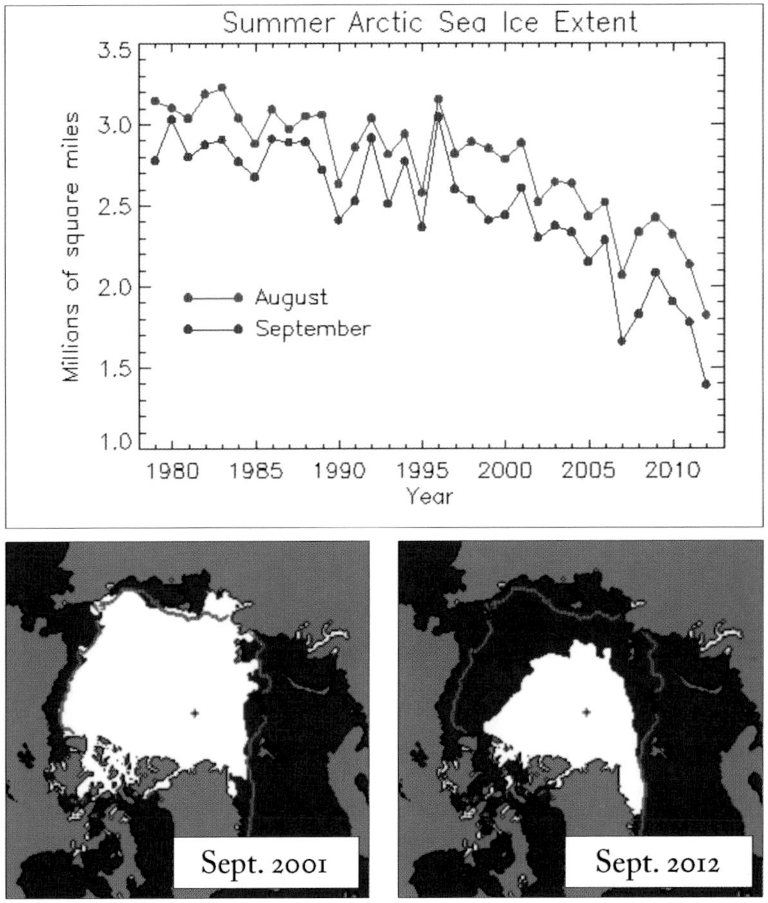

16.6 Arctic sea-ice extent. Top: August and September, 1979–2012. Bottom: September 2001 (left) and September 2012 (right). The purple curve is the median September sea-ice extent over the period 1979–2000. The region with the most rapid loss of summer sea ice is the Chukchi Sea, north of Bering Strait. Data and maps from F. Fetterer, K. Knowles, W. Meier, and M. Savoie, *Sea Ice Index* (Boulder, CO: National Snow and Ice Data Center, 2002, updated 2012).

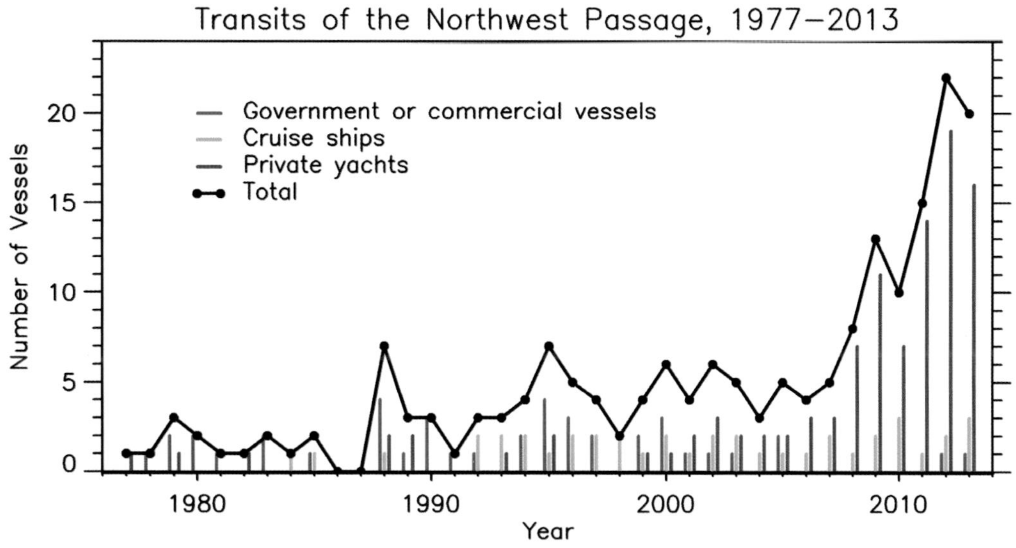

16.7 Transits of the Northwest Passage, 1977–2013, by vessel type and total number. Before 1977 there were just seventeen transits. The total number of transits for 1903–2013 is 203, half of which have occurred since 2004. Graph drawn by H. Stern from data courtesy of R. K. Headland, Scott Polar Research Institute, University of Cambridge.

to an ice-free season that is about six weeks longer now than in the early 1980s.[35]

Moreover, Kinnard and colleagues found that "the pronounced decline in summer Arctic sea ice cover that began in the late twentieth century is unprecedented in both magnitude and duration when compared with the range of variability of the previous roughly 1,450 years."[36] Similarly, Polyak and colleagues concluded that "the current reduction in Arctic ice cover started in the late 19th century, consistent with the rapidly warming climate, and became very pronounced over the last three decades. This ice loss appears to be unmatched over at least the last few thousand years and unexplainable by any of the known natural variabilities."[37]

Tivy and colleagues examined trends and variability in the summer sea-ice cover in the Canadian Arctic and along the routes of the Northwest Passage from 1960 to 2008.[38] They found significant decreases in sea ice along the southern routes but not along the northern routes, where thick multiyear ice from the Arctic Ocean drifts into the channels (see fig. 16.1). Multiyear ice is stronger than first-year ice, presenting a formidable barrier even to icebreakers.

What is the history of transits of the Northwest Passage? As of October 2013, only 146 vessels have ever made the transit.[39] Many of these are icebreakers that have made multiple transits, bringing the total number of transits to 203. Figure 16.7 shows the number of transits from 1977 through 2013 by vessel type. Before the early 1990s, transits were made primarily by icebreakers and other government vessels. Since then, one or two cruise ships per year have consistently made the transit, carrying paying passengers. The number of private yachts did not exceed three per year until 2008, when seven made the transit, followed by a rapid increase thereafter, as the southern route of the Northwest Passage has more consistently melted out in summer. Until 2010, only eleven transits of the northern routes had ever been made, all by icebreakers. Since 2010, five of the seven transits of the northern routes have been by private yachts (fig. 17.5). The Northwest Passage is rapidly opening to adventurous individual mariners.

COOK'S PROGRESS UNDER SEA-ICE CONDITIONS OF THE PAST THREE DECADES

Approaching from the west, the first geographic objective in the conquest of the Northwest Passage is to attain Point Barrow (see fig. 16.1). From there, the coast of Alaska falls off to the southeast for 400 miles, and the first island of the Canadian Arctic Archipelago (Banks Island) lies 650 miles distant. If Cook had attained Point Barrow, he surely would have held out the possibility that he had discovered the western portal of the Northwest Passage.

Cook's progress was halted by sea ice near Icy Cape on August 18, 1778. How would he have fared under the sea-ice conditions of the past three decades? Figure 16.8 (top) shows the date of the first opening of the sea route to Point Barrow, as determined from satellite passive microwave data, for each year from 1979 through 2012 (solid black line). In some years, the ice closed in against the coast after the initial opening (vertical dashed lines). In 1983 and 1988, the sea route to Point Barrow never opened. The colored dots across the figure indicate the status of the sea route to Point Barrow on August 18 of the given year: red for blocked, green for open. In the first half of the record (1979–95), the sea route was blocked in eight of the years and open in nine of the years. In the second half of the record (1996–2012), the sea route was blocked in just one year and open in sixteen. In all years, it was possible to advance at least as far as Icy Cape at some point during the summer.

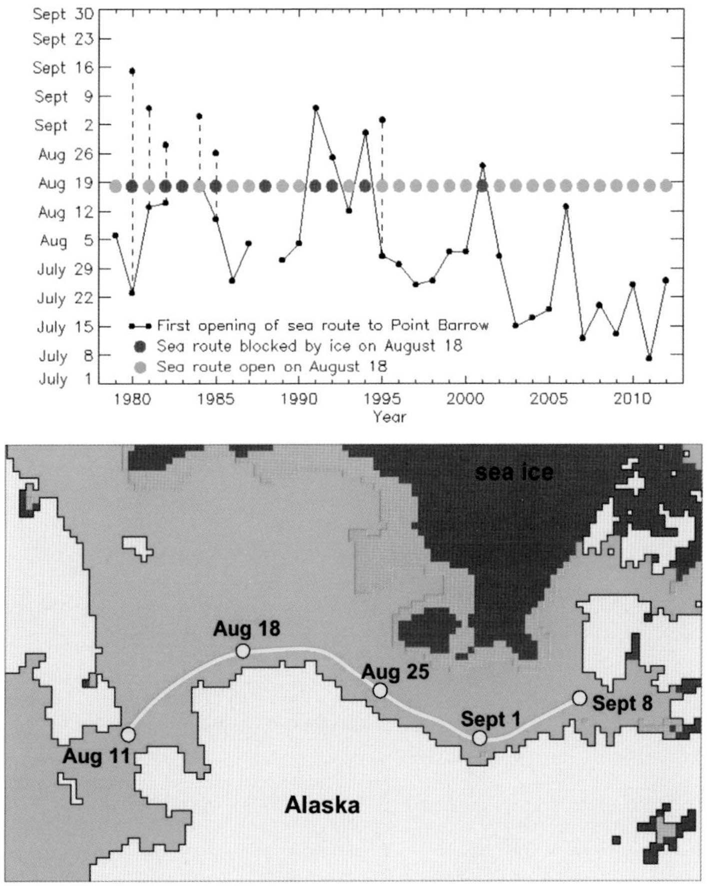

16.8 Top: Date of the first opening of the sea route to Point Barrow, as determined from satellite data, 1979–2012 (solid black line). The vertical dashed lines indicate periods when the sea ice closed in against the coast after initially opening. In 1983 and 1988, the sea route to Point Barrow never opened. Graph drawn by H. Stern. Bottom: Cook's hypothetical progress along the coast of Alaska and northern Canada under sea-ice conditions of 2002 or later. The sea-ice coverage is shown for August 18, 2011, with red indicating dense pack ice, orange loose ice, and blue open water. Map drawn by H. Stern based on sea-ice data from D. J. Cavalieri, C. L. Parkinson, P. Gloersen, and H. Zwally, *Sea Ice Concentrations from Nimbus-7 SMMR and DMSP SSM/I-SSMIS Passive Microwave Data, 1979–2012* (Boulder, CO: NASA DAAC at the National Snow and Ice Data Center, 2013).

We have seen that summer sea-ice conditions from the 1850s to the mid-1990s varied from year to year and probably from decade to decade, but without a major trend. August 1826 was apparently also typical, based on Beechey's account. If we assume that summer sea-ice conditions in the second half of the eighteenth century were no different from those of the nineteenth and twentieth centuries (up to 1995), then, based on the analysis of figure 16.8 above, it appears that Cook had about a fifty-fifty chance of arriving at Icy Cape in an August that would permit a sailing ship to reach Point Barrow. In his bid to discover the Northwest Passage, it seems that Cook simply lost a coin flip.

The situation clearly changed after the mid-1990s. Since then, the sea ice has generally been retreating from the coast of Alaska earlier in the summer. Figure 16.4 (top) shows sea-ice conditions on June 18, 2011, which resemble conditions on August 18 of the 1980s. If Cook had arrived at Icy Cape on August 18 with conditions similar to those of any year since 2002 (for example, as in figure 16.4, bottom), he would not have even seen any sea ice. He would have rounded Point Barrow three days later—but then what?

Figure 16.8 (bottom) shows Cook's hypothetical progress along the coast of Alaska after August 18, given sea-ice conditions as in 2002 or later. On September 1 he would have reached the mouth of the Mackenzie River, and before mid-September he would have entered the Canadian Arctic Archipelago. Here he might have retreated, knowing that he was still far from Baffin Bay, to avoid becoming locked in the ice for the winter. He would have rounded Point Barrow heading west in early October, about two to three weeks before the coastal waters east of Point Barrow typically freeze nowadays, confident that he had found a navigable western approach to the Northwest Passage.

CLERKE'S ARCTIC FORAY OF 1779

After Cook retreated from the Arctic in September 1778, he proceeded south to Hawai'i. Tragically, he was killed there in February 1779. Command of the expedition passed to Charles Clerke, who faithfully returned to the Arctic in summer 1779 to continue the search for the Northwest Passage. The ships sailed north through Bering Strait on July 6, more than a month earlier than in the previous year. The next day they encountered an "immense body of Ice to which we could see no bounds from our Masts Head" at 68°12'N, so they turned westward to follow the ice edge in search of an opening to the north.[40] Did Clerke know that July was *less* likely to have favorable ice conditions than August? On July 10, James King (second lieutenant on the *Resolution*) wrote: "Such being the state of the ice, Capt Clerke, nor any one else, could see any prospect of getting any further to the N°Ward, till the Season was somewhat more advanced; he therefore intends I believe to stand to the S°ward."[41] Similarly, James Burney (first lieutenant on the *Discovery*) wrote: "Captain Clerke intending to . . . return to the Northward again towards the end of the month when we might expect to find the Sea clearer of Ice." Clerke himself wrote: "I run away to the SE:ward." And yet by July 13 they had pushed north to 69°29'N, close to the ice edge, with Clerke writing: "I would certainly wish to avail myself of ye first opportunity if it should break up to make a push to the N°ward before the Season is too far advanc'd upon us."[42] Perhaps Clerke did not understand after all that August would be more favorable than July, even though his officers had that impression. On July 19 they reached their farthest north, 70°33'N, just 11 miles south of the previous year and yet a month earlier in the season. By July 21 they had traced the ice edge back toward the east and found that it attached to the coast, with Clerke writing: "This Sea is now so Choak'd with Ice that a passage I fear is totally out of the question."[43] (This was Clerke's last journal entry. He died a month later from tuberculosis.) Nevertheless, they turned westward and traced the ice edge until they sighted the coast of Siberia on July 27. Here, Burney wrote: "It was judged fruitless to make any more attempts"[44] On July 30 they sailed south through Bering Strait, finished with the Arctic.

Confusion over the Arctic navigation season arose again seventy-one years later. Barr wrote:

> By 15 August [1850] *Enterprise* had reached Cape Collie, a low headland at the narrow entrance to Wainwright Inlet. At this point Skead noted that the officers, on the basis of the reports of experienced arctic captains such as Parry and Ross, anticipated that they still had five or six weeks before freeze-up would end navigation in the Arctic for the season, in striking contrast to Collinson, who insisted that only June and July were suitable for arctic navigation. This view of Collinson's seems to have been derived from his interpretation of a comment by Sir Edward Parry in a memorandum solicited by the Admiralty to the effect that "Every exertion should be made to reach the ice to the northward of Behring's Straits by the 1st of August." Parry was suggesting that ice conditions for getting past Point Barrow would be optimal from that date onwards, quite the opposite of Collinson's interpretation![45]

Both Clerke in 1779 and Collinson in 1850 misread the climatological timing of sea-ice retreat and so missed an opportunity to make further discoveries. Collinson rectified his miscalculation the following season, but Clerke did not have that option.

LOSS OF ARCTIC SEA ICE IN THE TWENTY-FIRST CENTURY

The scientists James Overland and Muyin Wang addressed the question, "When will the summer Arctic be nearly sea-ice free?" They examined published scientific results based on three different approaches: extrapolation of current trends, statistical methods, and global climate models (GCMs).[46] All three approaches give a range of years for the disappearance of summer sea ice, but the approximate mid-range estimates are 2020, 2030, and 2040 for the extrapolation methods, the statistical methods, and the GCMs, respectively. On average, however, the GCMs are believed to be too conservative because the actual (observed) downward trend in summer Arctic sea ice over the past decade (as shown in fig. 16.6) is steeper than the mean model trend. Overland and Wang do not settle on a "best" prediction but conclude that a sea-ice-free Arctic Ocean in summer is very likely to occur in the first half of the twenty-first century, and possibly within a decade or two.

This prospect has sparked intense interest in the Arctic among political, industrial, and military leaders because of the shorter shipping routes between Europe and Asia, the potential oil and gas deposits beneath the newly accessible seafloor, the loss of polar bear (and other marine mammal) habitat, the effect of sea-ice loss on mid-latitude weather, the disputed status of the Northwest Passage as either an international strait or Canadian internal waters, and the rights of the indigenous people to determine their own future in the face of impending development. Some of these issues are discussed elsewhere in the present volume.

CONCLUSIONS

From the 1850s to the mid-1990s, summer sea-ice conditions along the northwest coast of Alaska were highly variable from year to year, but with no discernible long-term trend. There were heavy ice years and light ice years, and there may have been some variability from decade to decade, but a long-term trend is not apparent. During the mid-1800s it was often possible to sail to Point Barrow in mid-August, but an ice-free passage was by no means guaranteed, and it was always attendant with the danger that the ice pack would close in against the coast. The same general conditions seem to have prevailed all the way into the mid-1990s. Since then, however, the sea ice has been retreating earlier in the summer, especially since 2002.

Cook was surprised to encounter impenetrable ice at 70°N latitude. Knowledge of sea-ice extent in Cook's day was derived from experience in Baffin Bay and the North Atlantic, where the summer ice edge melts back to 75°N or even farther. Cook did not expect to be stopped by ice at 70°N.

Cook was unlucky. His progress was blocked by ice in mid-August 1778. This was probably *not* due to colder conditions associated with the Little Ice Age that affected Europe and eastern North America until about 1850. Wood and Overland wrote: "It is clear that the first-hand observations of 19th-century explorers are not consistent with the hypothesized severe conditions of a multi-decadal Little Ice Age" in the Canadian Arctic.[47] Therefore, if the Little Ice Age did not affect the Canadian Arctic in the first half of the nineteenth century, we have no reason to believe that it did so in the last half of the eighteenth century, and therefore no reason to believe that ice conditions in the Canadian Arctic (or farther west along the coast of Alaska) were more severe in the late 1700s than in the early 1800s. It seems that Cook hit a relatively heavy ice year, but one that was not outside the range of natural variability as we know it from the 1850s to the mid-1990s. Cook was simply unlucky. This view is reinforced by Clerke's experience in 1779, when he found the ice edge to be in approximately the same location as in 1778 but a full month earlier in the season.

Cook was impatient. If he had waited just southwest of Icy Cape, the ice pack probably would have receded from the coast by early September, allowing him to continue northeast to Point Barrow. From there, he would have seen the coastline trending east-southeast indefinitely far, and he would have surmised that he had found the western portal of the Northwest Passage. But instead of waiting, he turned westward, away from the direction he ultimately needed to go. He must have felt a need to keep moving, to keep exploring, in search of a break in the ice that might lead to the (mythical) open polar sea.

Cook was lucky. If the ice had retreated away from the coast and Cook had proceeded northeast, he would have exposed his ships to the very real danger of becoming trapped or crushed in the ice in the event of an unfavorable wind shift—a danger that has had fatal consequences for other mariners. Figure 16.8 (top) shows that in any of the years 1980, 1981, 1982, 1984, or 1985, a ship proceeding along the coast beyond Icy Cape after the initial sea-ice retreat would have been subject to episodes of sea-ice advance against the coast (black vertical dashed lines). Figure 16.5 shows a sea-ice configuration similar to what Cook described in his journal. It is not hard to imagine a slight retreat of the ice that would create a wedge of open water up to Point Barrow, followed by a slight advance that would trap or crush a ship. Cook's ships were not built to withstand ice pressure, and he was not prepared to winter over in the Arctic. In that sense, he was lucky that the ice did not retreat and tempt him to go farther.

Finding and navigating the Northwest Passage was a much more difficult undertaking than originally imagined. The western portion of the Northwest Passage was not pioneered until the 1850s, seventy-five years after Cook. Between 1818 and 1879, dozens of expeditions explored the intricate channels of the Northwest Passage, many of them in search of Franklin. The first successful transit was not until 1903–6 (by Roald Amundsen, from east to west in *Gjøa*). The second transit, from west to east, took three summer navigation seasons (1940–42) in the ice-strengthened *St. Roch,* a Canadian schooner with a diesel engine. The captain, Henry Larsen, wondered at one difficult moment "if we had come this far only to be crushed like a nut on a shoal and then buried by the ice."[48] (See chapter 15 in this volume.) It is hardly surprising that Cook, 162 years earlier, did not penetrate very far into the Northwest Passage. Without benefit of charts, auxiliary propulsion, or an ice-strengthened hull, Cook prudently elected not to endanger his ships in the ice. If he had pushed them harder, they might well have been crushed like nuts.

Cook did not fail. Beaglehole wrote, in reference to Cook's third voyage: "In the main stated object of the instructions to its commander—the discovery of the North-West Passage—it failed utterly."[49] This is an unfair assessment. The Admiralty's instructions were to proceed to 65°N or beyond and search for a Northwest Passage. If a passage could not be found, Cook was to try again the following year. The instructions use the words *search* and *explore,* not *discover.* Cook (and Clerke after him, the following year) did exactly as instructed to the best of their abilities, but they were repulsed by an impenetrable barrier of ice. On Cook's second voyage, at his farthest south (71°10's) on January 30, 1774, he wrote: "I whose ambition leads me not only farther than any other man has been before me, but as far as I think it possible for man to go." And so it was in the Arctic: Cook did go farther than any explorer had gone before, mapping the coast of Alaska and Bering Strait, and setting the stage for Beechey's expedition to attain Point Barrow nearly fifty years later. Cook (and Clerke) may not have understood that the Arctic navigation season lasted until late September, but they certainly could calculate the distance from Bering Strait to Baffin Bay across a hypothetical open polar sea or through a shortest-possible Northwest Passage, and deduce that it would have been impossible to reach Baffin Bay before winter set in. Had they become trapped and crushed in the ice, the expedition could certainly be labeled a failure. But the *Resolution* and *Discovery* returned home.

Arctic sea ice is changing rapidly; an ice-free Arctic summer is likely to occur within decades. In addition to the overall decline in summer Arctic sea-ice extent shown in figure 16.6, the Arctic has also been losing more and more of its older, thicker, multiyear sea ice (ice that has survived at least one summer melt season).[50] The average sea-ice thickness is also decreasing.[51] Furthermore, as the sea ice melts back earlier in the spring, the newly exposed ocean absorbs more heat from the sun, leading to more melting—a positive feedback. In the fall, the ocean must give up this extra heat before it can freeze, delaying the formation of sea ice and contributing to a thinner winter sea-ice pack—another positive feedback abetting the disappearance of sea ice. These processes are partly responsible for the fact that the Arctic surface air temperature is rising at nearly twice the global average rate, a phenomenon known as Arctic amplification.[52]

There are parallels between the British Admiralty's interest in the Arctic in Cook's day and the world's interest in the Arctic today. Cook mapped the unknown Arctic coastline of Alaska to support future sovereignty claims, resource extraction, and trade. Today, the five countries bordering the Arctic Ocean are mapping the unknown seafloor to support future sovereignty claims under the United Nations Convention on the Law of the Sea treaty (UNCLOS). Cook's explorations in 1778 were followed seventy years later by the opening of a commercial whale fishery in the western Arctic. Today, the new whale oil is crude oil and natural gas beneath the Arctic seafloor, whose exploitation is poised to begin. In the 1770s, the British Admiralty envisioned a shorter trade route with the Far East through a Northwest Passage. In November 2010, the chief naval officer in charge of oceanography for the US Navy testified before Congress that "the Navy's Maritime Strategy identifies that new shipping routes have the potential to reshape the global transportation system. For example, the Bering Strait has the potential to increase in strategic significance over the next few decades as the ice melts and the shipping season lengthens."[53] Thus, more than two centuries after the British Admiralty dispatched Cook to Bering Strait, its strategic significance still commands the attention of naval leaders, and a dependably navigable Northwest Passage may finally be realized in the next decade or two because of climate change.

NOTES

The author thanks Dave Nicandri for encouragement, Kevin Wood for discussions and the use of his material, and the National Snow and Ice Data Center for sea-ice data.

1 *The Journals of Captain James Cook on His Voyages of Discovery*, vol. 3, *The Voyage of the* Resolution *and* Discovery, *1776–1780*, ed. J. C. Beaglehole (Cambridge: Cambridge University Press for the Hakluyt Society, 1967), 417, 418, 427.

2 Quotations in this paragraph are taken from H. McCormick, *One Island, One Ocean* (San Francisco: Weldon Owen, 2011), 37.

3 D. Fisher, A. Dyke, R. Koerner, J. Bourgeois, C. Kinnard, C. Zdanowicz, A. de Vernal, C. Hillaire-Marcel, J. Savelle, and A. Rochon, "Natural Variability of Arctic Sea Ice over the Holocene," *Eos, Transactions* 87, no. 28 (2006): 273, 275.

4 M. P. Heide-Jørgensen, K. L. Laidre, L. T. Quakenbush, and J. J. Citta, "The Northwest Passage Opens for Bowhead Whales," *Biology Letters* 8, no. 2 (April 23, 2012): 270–73, http://dx.doi.org/.org/10.1098/rsbl.2011.0731.

5 Otto von Kotzebue, *A Voyage of Discovery, into the South Sea and Beering's Straits, for the purpose of Exploring a North-East Passage* (London: Longman, Hurst, Rees, Orme, and Brown, 1821), 3:264.

6 Frederick William Beechey, *Narrative of a Voyage to the Pacific and Beering's Strait* (Philadelphia, 1832), 237–39.

7 Ibid.

8 B. Seemann, *Narrative of the Voyage of H.M.S.* Herald *During the Years 1845–51 under the Command of Captain Henry Kellett* (London: Reeve, 1853), 108.

9 W. Barr, *Arctic Hell-Ship: The Voyage of HMS* Enterprise, *1850–1855* (Edmonton: University of Alberta Press, 2007).

10 Seemann, *Narrative*, 129, 118.

11 Barr, *Arctic Hell-Ship*.

12 Ibid., 30.

13 Quoted in Barr, *Arctic Hell-Ship*, 87.

14 Ibid., 89.

15 Ibid., 218.

16 J. Mirsky, *To the Arctic!* (New York: Knopf, 1948), 147.

17 Quoted in Barr, *Arctic Hell-Ship*, 240.

18 K. Wood and J. Overland, "Accounts from 19th-Century Canadian Arctic Explorers' Logs Reflect Present Climate Conditions," *Eos* 84, no. 40 (2003): 410, 412.

19 Ibid., 410.

20 J. R. Bockstoce, *Whales, Ice, and Men* (Seattle: University of Washington Press, 1986).

21 Figure from J. R. Bockstoce, D. Botkin, A. Philp, B. Collins, and J. George, "The Geographic Distribution of Bowhead Whales, *Balaena mysticetus*, in the Bering, Chukchi, and Beaufort Seas: Evidence from Whaleship Records, 1849–1914," *Marine Fisheries Review* 67, no. 3 (2005): 1–43.

22 Bockstoce, *Whales, Ice, and Men*.

23 Ibid.

24 A. R. Mahoney, J. R. Bockstoce, D. B. Botkin, H. Eicken, and R. A. Nisbet, "Sea Ice Distribution in the Bering and Chukchi Seas: Information from Historical Whaleships' Logbooks and Journals," *Arctic* 64, no. 4 (2011): 465–77.

25 See Arctic Rediscovery Project, www.pmel.noaa.gov/

arctic/rediscover/; "Volunteers Use Historic U.S. Ship Logbooks to Uncover Arctic Climate Data," *UW Today*, March 28, 2013, www.washington.edu/news/2013/03/28/volunteers-use-historic-u-s-ship-logbooks-to-uncover-arctic-climate-data/.

26 Emma DeLong, ed., *The Voyage of the* Jeannette: *The Ship and Ice Journals of George W. DeLong,* 2 vols. (Boston: Houghton, Mifflin, 1883), 116.

27 I. Shapiro, R. Colony, and T. Vinje, "April Sea Ice Extent in the Barents Sea, 1850–2001," *Polar Research* 22, no. 1 (2003): 5–10.

28 Cook, *Voyage of the* Resolution *and* Discovery, 416.

29 *The Journals of Captain James Cook on His Voyages of Discovery,* vol. 2, *The Voyage of the* Resolution *and* Adventure, *1772–1775,* ed. J. C. Beaglehole (Cambridge: Cambridge University Press for the Hakluyt Society, 1961), 74, 77.

30 Ibid., 305.

31 Ibid., 424, 425.

32 Cook, *The Voyage of the* Resolution *and* Discovery, 425 n. 2.

33 Kotzebue, *Voyage of Discovery,* 276–77.

34 Barr, *Arctic Hell-Ship*, 96.

35 K. Laidre et al., "A Circumpolar Assessment of the Status of Arctic Marine Mammals, Sea Ice Loss, and Conservation Challenges in the 21st Century," *Conservation Biology*, forthcoming, 204.

36 C. Kinnard, C. M. Zdanowicz, D. A. Fisher, E. Isaksson, A. de Vernal, and L. G. Thompson, "Reconstructed Changes in Arctic Sea Ice over the Past 1,450 Years," *Nature* 479 (November 24, 2011): 509–12, http://dx.doi.org/10.1038/nature10581.

37 L. Polyak, R. B. Alley, et al., "History of Sea Ice in the Arctic," *Quaternary Science Reviews* 29 (2010): 1757–78.

38 A. Tivy, S. Howell, B. Alt, S. McCourt, R. Chagnon, G. Crocker, T. Carrieres, and J. Yackel, "Trends and Variability in Summer Sea Ice Cover in the Canadian Arctic Based on the Canadian Ice Service Digital Archive, 1960–2008 and 1968–2008," *Journal of Geophysical Research* 116 (March 2011), http://dx.doi.org/10.1029/2011JC007248.

39 R. K. Headland, "Ten Decades of Transits of the Northwest Passage," *Polar Geography* 33 (2010): 1–13. Updated in 2013.

40 Clerke's journal, quoted in Cook, *Voyage of* Resolution *and* Discovery, 689.

41 King's journal, quoted in ibid., 691 n. 1.

42 Burney's journal, quoted in ibid., 691 n. 1; Clerke's journal, quoted in ibid., 691, 693.

43 Burney's journal, quoted in ibid., 697.

44 Ibid., 698.

45 Barr, *Arctic Hell-Ship*, 30.

46 J. E. Overland and M. Wang, "When Will the Summer Arctic Be Nearly Sea Ice Free?" *Geophysical Research Letters* 40, no. 10 (May 28, 2013): 2097–101, http://dx.doi.org/10.1002/grl.50316.

47 Wood and Overland, "Accounts," 410, 412.

48 J. P. Delgado, *Across the Top of the World: The Quest for the Northwest Passage* (Vancouver, BC: Douglas & McIntyre, 1999).

49 Cook, *Voyage of* Resolution *and* Discovery, v.

50 J. A. Maslanik, C. Fowler, J. Stroeve, S. Drobot, J. Zwally, D. Yi, and W. Emery, "A Younger, Thinner Arctic Ice Cover: Increased Potential for Rapid, Extensive Sea-Ice Loss," *Geophysical Research Letters* 34, no. 24 (December 2007), http://dx.doi.org/10.1029/2007GL032043.

51 A. Schweiger, R. Lindsay, J. Zhang, M. Steele, H. Stern, and R. Kwok, "Uncertainty in Modeled Arctic Sea Ice Volume," *Journal of Geophysical Research* 116, no. C8 (August 2011), http://dx.doi.org/10.1029/2011JC007084.

52 J. A. Francis and S. J. Vavrus, "Evidence Linking Arctic Amplification to Extreme Weather in Mid-latitudes," *Geophysical Research Letters* 39, no. 6 (March 2012), http://dx.doi.org/10.1029/2012GL051000.

53 Statement of Rear Admiral David Titley, Oceanographer of the Navy, Director, Task Force Climate Change, before the House Committee on Science and Technology, Subcommittee on Energy and Environment, on the Navy's Climate Change Interests, November 17, 2010, http://gop.science.house.gov/Media/hearings/energy10/nov17/Titley.pdf.

HANSEATIC
HAPAG - LLOYD
EXPEDITION CRUISES

Marine Navigation in the Arctic Ocean and the Northwest Passage

LAWSON W. BRIGHAM

17

THERE IS MUCH SPECULATION TODAY ABOUT THE POSSIBILITIES OF ARCtic navigation, just as there was intense interest during Captain Cook's day in the Northwest Passage as a potential waterway between the Atlantic and Pacific Oceans. Captain Cook well understood that he needed to sail north into the Arctic Ocean through Bering Strait when the sea ice would be at its summer minimum. He hoped that open water might appear to the east and perhaps even as far as the North Pole, but he observed an impenetrable barrier of sea ice ahead in August 1778, while exploring the Chukchi Sea off northwest Alaska.[1] Today, tugs with barges follow the retreat of sea ice in summer along the Alaskan coast to resupply coastal communities. An armada of drilling and support ships also awaits the retreat of sea ice through the Bering Strait so that exploratory drilling can be conducted in open-water (ice-free) operations in the Chukchi and Beaufort seas.

The Arctic sea-ice cover is undergoing a profound transformation—decreasing in extent in all seasons, thinning extensively, and changing in character from multiyear ice (ice that survives more than one season) to a mostly seasonal, first-year sea ice.[2] These changes, driven by regional and global anthropogenic warming, are creating new oppor-

The Hapag-Lloyd cruise ship MV *Hanseatic* in the Arctic during the summer of 2010 (detail of fig. 17.3).

tunities for greater marine access and potentially longer seasons of navigation. However, the most significant drivers of Arctic marine operations early in the twenty-first century are Arctic natural resource developments and the greater linkage of the Arctic to the global economy. With this new globalization of the Arctic has come a general increase in the summer presence of a wide variety and sizes of ships around the Arctic Ocean basin. A few highly capable icebreakers now venture into the central Arctic Ocean in summer, principally for scientific research and exploration of the outer continental shelf. The central point of this essay is that the future of Arctic navigation is tied to global economics and commodities prices. While marine transportation systems are being facilitated by increasing marine access, and larger areas of the Arctic Ocean are becoming ice-free in summer, the primary drivers for the global shipping enterprise remain economic considerations.

CURRENT ARCTIC MARINE OPERATIONS

The maritime Arctic is seeing an expanding range of operations in polar waters: new marine fleets supporting summer offshore hydrocarbon exploration and development; scientific voyages by icebreakers in the central Arctic Ocean; marine tourism in remote Arctic coastal seas; increased fishing in more northerly coastal waters, such as Baffin Bay and Davis Strait; year-round operations by icebreaking carriers in the Pechora (the southeast corner of the Barents Sea) and Kara Seas; and summer use of the Northern Sea Route (NSR) across the Russian maritime Arctic for vessels carrying hard minerals and hydrocarbons to markets in the Pacific. The vast majority of these voyages and operations are considered "destinational," meaning that a ship sails into the Arctic to perform an activity (for example, supporting drilling or loading a cargo of resources, bulk hard minerals, or hydrocarbons), and then sails south out of the region. Notable increases in cruise-ship voyages to Svalbard and the west coast of Greenland are all considered destinational and seasonal voyages to the Arctic (occurring during two to three months in summer). Very few full transarctic voyages are made that use Arctic waterways as a new connection between the Atlantic and Pacific Oceans (fig. 17.1).

Two mining complexes in Alaska and Siberia use marine shipping to carry Arctic resources to global markets. The Red Dog mine in northwest Alaska is one of the largest zinc mines and zinc-concentrate producers in the world. Since 1989, large bulk carriers have sailed ice-free waters in summer to load the products and carry them to markets throughout the Pacific. The Siberian complex at Norilsk, the world's largest nickel and palladium mine (and a top producer of copper and platinum) is linked to domestic and international markets by a marine transportation system to the port of Dudinka on the Yenisei River.[3] Year-round navigation has been maintained since 1979, and in recent years a fleet of advanced icebreaking cargo

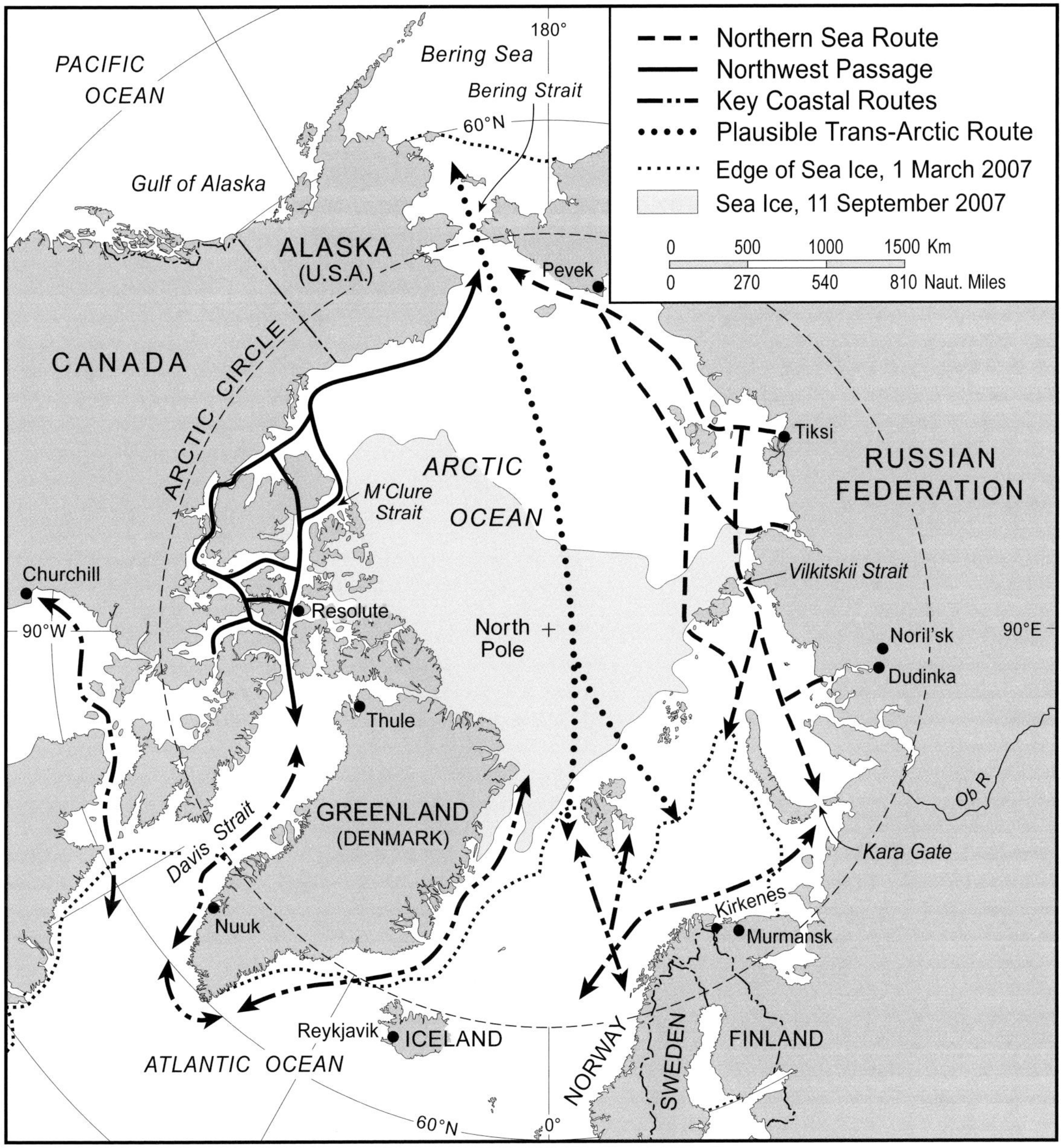

17.1 Arctic marine routes, including the Northwest Passage, Northern Sea Route, and associated coastal routes. A possible future transarctic route is shown for the central Arctic Ocean. Courtesy of Lawson W. Brigham.

Impressions of the Passage Cook Never Made

GUDRUN BUCHER

TOURISM IN THE NORTHWEST PASSAGE started in 1984 when the *Lindblad Explorer,* under Captain Hasse Nilsson, managed the transit for the first time. The *Explorer* was not an icebreaker but rather a reinforced passenger ship that was able to push thin ice out of the way. Once the ice was broken, literally and figuratively, by Lindblad, other passenger ships followed. In 1985 the *World Discoverer* under Captain Heinz Aye mastered the route, and, after the collapse of the Soviet Union, small Russian icebreakers, such as the *Kapitan Khlebnikov,* were chartered by Westerners for ice cruises.

Until the mid-1990s, voyages through the Northwest Passage were risky. One was never quite sure whether it would be possible to get through. When the MS *Hanseatic* ran aground in 1996 in the shallow Simpson Strait and had to evacuate all the passengers, tourism in the Northwest Passage experienced a major setback. However, during the next year the passage was successfully navigated again. Now, in the twenty-first century, more and more private yachts are meeting the challenge.

Ironically, the major problem for tourist voyages now is that passengers complain that they do not see enough ice! It is precisely the prospect of encountering ice and polar bears that makes tourists want to voyage through the Northwest Passage.

My own experience with the Northwest Passage started in 2006, while I was working as lecturer on one of the ice-strengthened passenger ships. The voyage was conducted to commemorate the hundredth anniversary of Roald Amundsen's successful crossing (1903–6). Like Amundsen, we started from the west coast of Greenland. Our farthest north was the little settlement of Upernavik, and from there we entered Lancaster Sound. We cleared Canadian Customs in Pond Inlet (Baffin Island) before we visited Dundas Harbour—an old and long-abandoned post of the Royal Canadian Mounted Police—in the southeast of Devon Island. Next, we visited Beechey Island to see the place where John Franklin spent his first winter and the graves of Franklin's men. Our captain made a speech, and, following tradition, we left some information about ourselves in the little cairn used by many ships since 1956. Following Amundsen's route, we fortunately did not repeat his running aground near Matty Island, thanks to our much better charts. We stopped in Gjoa Haven, where Amundsen overwintered in September 1903.

Amundsen needed three years to navigate the passage. He spent two winters in Gjoa Haven because he could not get out of the ice after the first one. In Amundsen's time, there was no settlement at Gjoa Haven. The Netsilik came to the bay occasionally to hunt, and Amundsen met them there. Together they developed a mixture of Inuktitut and Norwegian languages to communicate. Amundsen observed their lifestyle and copied many survival techniques that later helped him conquer the South Pole. He marveled at Franklin's having perished in a region so abundant in food during the summertime.

The Canadian Coast Guard icebreaker *Sir Wil-*

frid Laurier met our ship in Gjoa Haven and provided some assistance. After leaving Gjoa Haven, we sailed alone but still in contact with the *Sir Wilfrid Laurier.* The water on the Amundsen, or southern, route is quite shallow, especially in Simpson Strait, and therefore not navigable for big tankers or cargo ships. Our little cruise ship, with about 140 passengers, managed without difficulty.

One highlight of the cruise was a visit to the place of Amundsen's third overwintering: King Point, a few miles east of Herschel Island. We had an early-morning landing there with red skies during sunrise. We climbed up the little rise and found the cross that commemorates Gustav Wiik, Amundsen's machinist, who died there. After this highly emotional moment, we went on to Herschel Island, the former place of overwintering for whalers, Hudson's Bay Company traders, and a Royal Canadian Mounted Police post.

We soon became worried by the ice situation in the Beaufort Sea. The ice was moving toward the coast, and we had to slip past before it moved south and blocked our way. These were tough times for the captain but very exciting times for the passengers. Needless to say, the captain managed to cross the Beaufort Sea before the ice bore down on us, and we even went ashore in Barrow, which is often not possible because of high swells on the coast. Barrow offered our first opportunity for resupply: to obtain more beer, for example. It was not an easy task to calculate what the passengers would consume in one month, and the Northwest Passage is a challenge for the provision master on board of a ship of our size. We carried the maximum load of provisions possible and used all available storage space, including an additional container on deck.

And then off we went to Nome, where Amundsen had finished his famous passage in August 1906. We were there exactly one hundred years after him. Traversing the North West Passage had taken us a little less than one month.

My second experience with the Northwest Passage was in 2009. We passed through without any problems and got to see many polar bears. We learned on this voyage that the less ice there is, the more this ice is driven by wind. This makes route planning a challenge. Crossings of Bellot Strait (separating Somerset Island from the Boothia Peninsula) are entirely ice-dependent. One week the strait can be free of ice and easy to pass, and the next week it might be completely blocked. This is the reason why Fort Ross, the Hudson's Bay Company post on the south coast of Somerset Island at the east entrance (or exit) of the strait, was given up in 1947: ice conditions made it too difficult to supply regularly. The Inuit working for the company there were settled farther south, at Spence Bay (today Taloyoak). We were lucky to visit this small settlement and were cordially received.

By 2009 the risk of getting through the passage was already minimized, and therefore my company decided to send its two expedition ships through the Northwest Passage—one from the north Atlantic and the other from the north Pacific. The two ships met in Gjoa Haven and had a great party there on one of the ships. How times have changed from those of Franklin and Amundsen!

In 2011 the two expedition ships sailed the passage in opposite directions again, but this time they met in Cambridge Bay. In 2011 again there was minimal ice in the passage, and for the first time, we went around the north end of Banks Island, with special permission from the Canadian Coast Guard. We visited Mercy Bay, the place where Robert McClure spent one winter and where he was rescued by sledge, making him the first person to traverse the entire passage, although he had to walk part of the way over the ice.

In 2012, the ice was at a modern record minimum. A cruise that year was my fourth experience in the passage. In the past, companies had to allow for extra travel time in case the vessel was hindered by ice. Now they still have to allow a few spare days, but for different reasons: with the retreat of the ice, ships need additional time to go farther north to look for ice and for polar bears. On this voyage we even saw walruses, a species that Cook and his men alternatively marveled at, relied upon, and were disgusted by, when we sailed north around Cornwallis Island, a route not possible in previous years. Traveling the passage is still exciting because one never knows what new possibilities might occur from one year to the next.

17.2 The Sovcomflot tanker SCF *Baltica* transiting the Northern Sea Route in 2010. The ship carried light-oil products from Murmansk to Ningbo in China. The NSR was more than 50 percent shorter than the route via the Suez Canal during the summer navigation season, with minimal ice. During other seasons with significant ice cover, however, the NSR voyage may take longer than the Suez Canal route, and in winter, the eastern NSR is impassable for commercial ships. Courtesy of Sovcomflot and Navigate PR, London.

carriers have operated between Dudinka and Murmansk without dedicated icebreaker support. Several experimental voyages have been conducted in summer carrying nickel plates from the Russian Arctic to China eastbound along the NSR.

Hydrocarbon developments in offshore Greenland, Alaska, northern Norway, and the Russian Arctic have substantially increased marine operations in Arctic waters. A fleet of drilling ships and offshore support vessels has operated during the summers of 2010 and 2011 in lease areas off the west coast of Greenland. In late summer 2012, Shell Oil conducted operations in leased areas off northwest Alaska in the Chukchi and Beaufort Seas; a fleet of two drill ships and sixteen support ships, including ice-management support icebreakers, operated in the US maritime Arctic north of Bering Strait. In the Norwegian Arctic, gas has been pumped from the seabed complex Snøhvit to the port of Hammerfest; liquefied natural gas (LNG) has been produced ashore and shipped to markets in Europe and North America. In the eastern reaches of the Barents Sea, two tanker shuttle systems—one to an offshore oil terminal at Varandey and a second to a new, offshore production platform (Prirazlomnoye)—are designed to carry oil year-round to Murmansk.[4] The three-ship icebreaking tanker fleet operating from the Varandey terminal has delivered twelve million tons of oil annually to Murmansk.

The expansion of operations along Russia's NSR has attracted the most visibility in the maritime community and around the globe (fig. 17.2). The NSR has been used as a summer waterway for carrying Arctic natural resources from the Russian Arctic and northern Europe to markets in the Pacific, principally to China and southeast Asia. During the 2012 summer navigation season, forty-six vessels sailed the NSR with approximately 1.26 million tons of cargo (71 percent of the total was petroleum products). The most notable voyage was of the LNG ice-class carrier *Ob River*, which delivered a cargo of 66,342 tons of LNG from Hammerfest, Norway, to Tobata, Japan. This operation was conducted in November, late in the operational season, with nuclear icebreaker escort. Two voyages during the 2011 NSR summer season also illustrate the new connections between the Russian Arctic and Pacific markets: during August 2011 an ice-class supertanker, *Vladimir Tikhonov,* carried 120,000 tons of gas concentrate from Murmansk across the NSR (under icebreaker escort) to Bangkok, Thailand; during September 2011 the ice-class bulk carrier *Sanko Odyssey* carried 66,000 tons of iron ore from Murmansk to Beilun, China, along the NSR. The Danish firm Nordic Bulk Carriers has also been active in using the NSR in summer, with six voyages conducted during 2012.[5] The missing element has been the use of the NSR for container-ship operations on transarctic voyages between European and Pacific ports during the short summer navigation season.

ARCTIC MARINE SHIPPING ASSESSMENT

The Arctic Marine Shipping Assessment (AMSA), released by the Arctic Council (the intergovernmental forum of the Arctic states) in April 2009, provides key insight into current and future Arctic marine activity with a focus on Arctic marine safety and environmental protection.[6] AMSA is a policy document that creates a framework for the Arctic states to address the many challenges of protecting Arctic peoples and the marine environment in an era of expanding resource use and transport in the north. AMSA can be viewed from three perspectives: as a baseline assessment of Arctic marine activity (an early twenty-first-century database and historic snapshot of Arctic marine use in 2004–5); as a strategic guide for a host of Arctic and non-Arctic stakeholders and actors; and as an Arctic Council policy document, since the AMSA recommendations were the result of a consensus of the eight Arctic states of the Arctic Council. The seventeen AMSA recommendations are presented in three interrelated themes: *enhancing Arctic marine safety* (mandatory application of International Maritime Organization [IMO] rules for Arctic ships, a mandatory polar code), *protecting Arctic people and the environment;* and *building the Arctic marine infrastructure.* Several key findings of AMSA are listed in table 17.1.

One of the important challenges for the authors of the AMSA was to identify the major uncertainties in the future of Arctic marine use. A planning process was employed in which scenarios, or plausible futures, were created for Arctic marine navigation in 2020 and 2050. A team of eighty experts worked to identify nearly 120 factors and forces that could influence the future of Arctic marine activities. Included are such key factors as global oil prices; new resource discoveries; world trade patterns; a major Arctic shipping disaster; a radical change in global trade dynamics; escalation of Arctic maritime disputes; limited windows of Arctic operations (economic considerations for shipping); global agreements on construction rules and standards for Arctic ships; a stable legal climate; the

Table 17.1 Key findings of the Arctic Marine Shipping Assessment

Global climate simulations predict a continuing retreat of Arctic sea ice through the twenty-first century; all simulations predict that an Arctic sea-ice cover will remain in winter.
Most Arctic shipping today is destinational, moving goods into the Arctic for community resupply or moving natural resources out of the Arctic to world markets. Nearly all marine tourist voyages are destinational as well.
Marine shipping is one of many factors affecting Arctic communities, directly and indirectly. The variety of shipping activities and the range of social, cultural, and economic conditions in Arctic communities mean that shipping can have many effects, both positive and negative.
A large number of uncertainties define the future of Arctic marine activity.
Natural resources development and regional trade are the key drivers of increased Arctic marine activity. Global prices for oil, gas, hard minerals, coal, and other commodities are driving the search for Arctic natural resource wealth.
Release of oil in the Arctic marine environment, through either accidental release or illegal discharge, is the most significant threat from shipping activity.
Certain areas of the Arctic region are of heightened ecological significance, and many will be at risk from current or increased shipping.
For significant portions of the primary Arctic shipping routes, adequate hydrographic data, and therefore charts, are not available to support safe navigation. The operational network of meteorological and oceanographic observations in the Arctic, essential for accurate weather and wave forecasting for safe navigation, is extremely sparse.
Increased marine traffic in the central Arctic Ocean for scientific exploration and tourism is a reality.
The law of the sea, as reflected in the 1982 United Nations Convention on the Law of the Sea (UNCLOS), sets out the legal framework for the regulation of Arctic shipping according to maritime zones of jurisdiction.
The lack of major ports and other maritime infrastructure, except for those along the Norwegian coast and northwest Russia, is a significant factor (limitation) in evolving and future Arctic marine operations.

Source: Arctic Council, *Arctic Marine Shipping Assessment (AMSA) 2009 Report* (Arctic Council, 2009).

emergence of new Arctic maritime nations such as China, Japan, and Korea; a global shift to nuclear energy; the safety of other global marine routes; transit fees; maritime insurance industry engagement; and rapid climate change.[7]

This effort identified two primary drivers and uncertainties: (1) the level of demand for Arctic natural resources and trade; and (2) the degree of stability of rules for marine use both within the Arctic and internationally. The framework or axis of uncertainty for the AMSA scenarios was bounded by these two factors.[8] The roles of climate change and continued Arctic sea-ice retreat are fully considered. Arctic sea-ice changes are assumed to provide for improved marine access throughout the Arctic Ocean basin and for potentially longer seasons of marine navigation. But for AMSA, the globalization of the Arctic and development of Arctic natural resources are the primary drivers of increased marine use and the need for marine operations. Greater access as a result of retreating sea ice facilitates marine use, but global economic factors (and linkages to Arctic natural resources) are the most influential factors in the potential expansion of Arctic marine navigation.

LACK OF ARCTIC MARINE INFRASTRUCTURE

A critical concern identified in AMSA is the general lack of marine infrastructure in the Arctic, except for areas along the Norwegian coast and coastal regions of northwest Russia. Deficiencies include inadequate hydrographic data and marine charts, environmental monitoring for weather and icebergs, search and rescue (SAR) capability, environmental response capacity, aids to navigation, complete and adequate communications coverage, salvage, ports and port services (for example, reception facilities for ship-generated waste), and places of refuge. This infrastructure deficit hampers marine safety and environmental protection throughout the Arctic. AMSA makes clear that the vastness and harshness of the Arctic marine environment make marine emergency response (both SAR and environmental response) more difficult.[9] Most notable is the fact that the Arctic Ocean's charting database is not adequate in most areas to support current, let alone future, marine operations. And AMSA calls for a comprehensive and effective monitoring and tracking system for all marine activity—an Arctic marine traffic-awareness system—that will require enhanced data sharing in near–real time among all the Arctic states. Such a system will require improved Arctic satellite and shore-based communications. The funding of most of this new and needed infrastructure will require the development and application of public-private partnerships among non-Arctic states and a host of maritime users and stakeholders as potential partners.

CHALLENGES CONFRONTING FUTURE ARCTIC NAVIGATION

Despite the profound changes in Arctic sea ice during the past five decades (or longer), the practical fact remains that the Arctic Ocean remains fully or partially ice covered in winter, spring, and autumn. Global climate model simulations of Arctic sea ice predict that these conditions will persist through the end of the twenty-first century and beyond.[10] Importantly, the simulations also indicate the disappearance of multiyear or old ice by midcentury or earlier.[11] This would mean that the Arctic Ocean might be entirely ice free for a short period each September; all ice in ensuing months would be first year, and old, or multiyear, ice would no longer pose its greater challenges for naviga-

TABLE 17.2 System of Polar-Class Ships

POLAR CLASS	GENERAL DESCRIPTION
PC1	Year-round operation in all Arctic ice-covered waters
PC2	Year-round operation in moderate multiyear ice conditions
PC3	Year-round operation in second-year ice, which may include multiyear ice inclusions
PC4	Year-round operation in thick first-year ice, which may include old ice inclusions
PC5	Year-round operation in medium first-year ice, which may include old ice inclusions
PC6	Summer/autumn operation in medium first-year ice, which may include old ice inclusions
PC7	Summer/autumn operation in thin first-year ice, which may include old ice inclusions

NOTE: Adopted by the 2002 IMO Guidelines for Ships Operating in Arctic Ice-Covered Waters and the Unified Requirements of the International Association of Classification Societies. The Unified Requirements apply to polar ships of member associations constructed on or after March 1, 2008.

tors. However, the continued presence of sea ice of whatever type for much of the year during the decades ahead is a significant factor in the development of navigation regulations. Ships operating in most regions of the Arctic will be required to have some level of polar- or ice-class capability to survive and sail safely and efficiently; the need for polar ships designed for at least limited ice operations is obvious. Table 17.2 shows the system of polar-class (PC) ships adopted by the IMO and the ship classification societies.[12] Each of the classes relates to Arctic sea-ice conditions for both year-round ships (PC1 to PC5 ships) and seasonal or summer (PC6 and PC7 ships) operations. All of these PC ships have higher costs (because of strengthening and additional propulsion requirements) than normal open-water vessels.

With the Arctic Ocean being ice-covered in some form for much of the year today and in the future, the challenges for transarctic navigation are many. Although ice-class bulk carriers and tankers have recently sailed the length of the NSR in summer, container traffic has been minimal on the NSR and elsewhere in the Arctic. One of the key questions is whether Arctic routes can be reliable and safe while also being economically viable, especially for container traffic. If PC ships are mandatory, how might they be integrated with global fleets for the eight or nine months each year when they are not operating in the Arctic Ocean? Will ships operating along the NSR and other Arctic routes be independently operated, or will they be escorted in convoy by icebreakers, requiring additional fees? On most container routes around the globe, a network of ports are serviced as ships sail from the Pacific to North America and Europe. There are few networking ports in the Arctic. Although the Arctic distances are significantly shorter than the Suez route (for example between Europe and China), the presence of sea ice for as much as two thousand nautical miles might negate any savings because of slower ship speeds, even under escort. Shippers may also face a number of risks associated with schedule disruptions and reliability issues inherent in the vagaries and uncertainties of Arctic marine navigation. There remain significant practical, operational, and technical challenges to transarctic shipping. Comprehensive economic evaluations (cost-benefit-risk analyses) are required for planning, especially for container shipping, to determine the economic benchmarks for seasonal and year-round transarctic operations.

MARINE OPERATIONS IN THE CANADIAN ARCTIC AND NORTHWEST PASSAGE

Because this anthology is focused on the Northwest Passage and Captain James Cook's 1778 foray into the Arctic Ocean, it is important to note the context in which the Canadian Arctic is seen today for marine navigation. It is remarkable that since Roald Amundsen's first transit of the passage in 1903–6, as of the end of the 2012 navigation season, only 185 complete transits of the route had been made (fig. 16.7).[13] A majority of the recent voyages have been made by adventurers in small vessels, which were able to make a full transit in summer along the coast in minimal ice conditions (fig. 17.5).[14]

Observations in the Canadian Arctic have shown negative trends in sea-ice coverage during the past three decades, but the region also exhibits a high year-to-year variability, a key factor when considering regulations, setting marine insurance rates, and planning investments in transportation systems.[15] In addition, projections show sea ice through the winter and nine months of coverage through the year. The unique geography of the Canadian Archipelago, with many of its northernmost channels oriented north-south, adds to the complexity of the sea-ice regime (because mobile sea ice can be swept from the central Arctic Ocean into the more southerly routes of the Northwest Passage). Access to the Northwest Passage will continue to be controlled by the prevailing sea-ice conditions. Additionally, the Canadian Arctic is projected to be one of the regions where multiyear ice will be present until sometime near midcentury. The complexity of the various routes of the passage, draft restrictions, highly variable and difficult sea-ice conditions (for nine or ten months each year), lack of marine infrastructure, lack of comprehensive charting, and high operational costs (including marine insurance) make regular commercial traffic through the Canadian Arctic (and between the Atlantic and Pacific) uncertain at best.[16]

Commercial shipping in the Canadian Arctic today is focused on four activities: community resupply during summer; bulk shipments of natural resources out of the region; support to exploration

17.3 The Hapag-Lloyd cruise ship MV *Hanseatic* in the Arctic during the summer of 2010. Recent cruise-ship sailings in the Arctic are allowing more people to experience the polar environment and Arctic indigenous cultures. Courtesy of Hapag-Lloyd Cruises.

17.4 Aerial view of the Mary River iron-ore site on Baffin Island. Mary River is one of the largest high-grade iron-ore sites in the world and one of the largest mining developments in Canada. In the future, it may have year-round shipping connections to European markets, using icebreaking bulk carriers. Courtesy of Baffinland Iron Mines Corporation.

and resource development; and, marine tourism. The only vessels that regularly transit the Northwest Passage in summer are a number of small, specialized cruise ships (fig. 17.3). The Mary River iron-ore mine complex (on Baffin Island) in the eastern Canadian Arctic has been sending ore by bulk carriers to European ports, and occasionally wheat is shipped to the east from the Hudson Bay port of Churchill, Manitoba, during the summer (fig. 17.4). During the drafting of the AMSA, discussions of the outlook for the Canadian Arctic noted that the Northwest Passage is not expected to become a viable transarctic route. However, destinational shipping is expected to increase, including dry bulk carriage related to mining developments, increasing resupply shipments to growing populations in northern communities, increases in shipments of equipment and supplies supporting resource exploration, and a modest but unpredictable growth of marine tourism (fig. 17.5). Significantly, any future oil and gas production from the Beaufort Sea would be expected to be carried by pipeline out of the Arctic to southern markets, not by tankers.[17] Anticipated increases in marine shipping are related to future mining developments in the region and thus linked to global commodities prices; both seasonal shipping and year-round shipping to the Mary River mine are plausible in the future. The summer 2013 voyage of the M/V *Nordic Orion* (the highest commercial ice-class ship), carrying 73,500 tons of

coal eastbound across the Northwest Passage from Vancouver to Pori, Finland, indicates a potential for bulk cargoes to be carried by capable, icebreaking carriers in a limited Northwest Passage navigation season—estimated by Nordic Bulk Carriers A/S to be two months each summer (fig. 17.6).[18]

CONCLUSION

Navigation in the Arctic Ocean is undergoing significant changes during the early decades of the twenty-first century. More ships will likely use the Arctic Ocean, and a more diverse set of marine operations will be carried out in polar waters than during any other period in history. Most of these new uses are clearly driven by economic interests and the evolving linkages of Arctic natural resources to global markets. The retreating Arctic sea-ice cover provides for greater marine access and potentially longer seasons of navigation, albeit using polar-class ships. Recent voyages along the NSR during summer by bulk carriers and tankers illustrate the possibilities of a marine connection and flow of natural resources from the Russian Arctic and northern Europe to China and other Pacific markets. The potential length of the NSR navigation season for these full voyages has yet to be determined, but for polar-class commercial carriers assisted by icebreakers (in convoy), it could be as long as six months.

17.5 The MV *Stary* near the striking cliffs of Beechey Island in the Canadian Arctic in late summer 2006. With ice conditions on the coastal routes becoming more favorable to shipping, increasing numbers of adventurers in small vessels are transiting the Northwest Passage in summer. Photograph courtesy of Dominik Bac.

17.6 The bulk carrier *Nordic Orion* (Danish-owned but flying the flag of Panama) in Peel Sound, following the Canadian Coast Guard icebreaker *Louis S. St-Laurent* in September 2013. The first ice-strengthened bulk-cargo vessel to transit the Canadian Arctic, and the largest ship to make a Northwest Passage voyage, it was carrying fifteen thousand tons of coal from Vancouver to the port of Pori in Finland. Photograph by Jacques Collin, courtesy of Environment Canada.

Destinational voyages will continue to dominate operations in all Arctic regions, especially those that support offshore oil and gas development, mining development, and marine tourism. The opening of the Arctic Ocean is not likely to revolutionize global trade routes, particularly for container trades (as many have speculated), primarily because of the presence of sea ice for eight to nine months of the year and the uncertainties and vagaries of Arctic operations. A recent commentary in the Russian press noted that the NSR is not a rival to the Suez Canal but a seasonal complement for global traffic, a refreshingly accurate view of current use of the Arctic Ocean for trade.[19] However, these views do not suggest that all container trades will be excluded from use of possible Arctic routes; niche markets and shipping opportunities during summer windows of operation along the NSR are possible. The potential for a Pacific-to-Europe container route during summer along the NSR might be feasible. While bulk carriers and tankers have made profitable voyages across the NSR in recent summers, the economics and costs of container trades using PC ships in ice-covered waters have yet to be fully analyzed. Importantly, the Northwest Passage is receiving less attention as an international waterway from shippers than the NSR. Because of the constraints previously mentioned, the Northwest Passage is not considered a viable route for regular, transarctic commercial traffic, despite the 2013 voyage of the *Nordic Orion*.

I sense Captain Cook would have understood the complexities of the new maritime Arctic. He surely would have appreciated that Arctic sea ice remains a significant constraint to voyaging across the top of the world. More than two centuries after his short but extraordinary voyage north of Bering Strait, a vast majority of the Arctic Ocean has yet to be charted to international navigation standards. A huge challenge remains before the Arctic states and the international maritime community on how to adequately protect Arctic peoples and the marine environment while using this once-inaccessible ocean in sustainable ways.

NOTES

1 Frank McLynn, *Captain Cook: Master of the Seas* (New Haven, CT: Yale University Press, 2011), 359.

2 Arctic Council, *Arctic Climate Impact Assessment* (ACIA) (Arctic Council, 2004).

3 L. Brigham, "Arctic Marine Transport Driven by Natural Resource Development," *The Future of the Arctic,* special issue of *Baltic Rim Economies* 2 (2013): 13–14.

4 L. Brigham, "Arctic Marine Transportation," in *McGraw-Hill 2012 Yearbook of Science and Technology* (New York: McGraw-Hill, 2012), 8–11.

5 Brigham, "Arctic Marine Transportation."

6 Arctic Council, *Arctic Marine Shipping Assessment (AMSA) 2009 Report* (Arctic Council, 2009).

7 Ibid.

8 Ibid.

9 Ibid.

10 J. Stroeve et al., "The Arctic's Rapidly Shrinking Sea Ice Cover: A Research Synthesis," *Climatic Change* 110 (2012): 1005–27.

11 Scott R. Stephenson, Laurence C. Smith, Lawson W. Brigham, and John A. Agnew, "Projected 21st Century

Changes to Arctic Marine Access," *Climatic Change* 118 (2012): 885–99.

12 International Maritime Organization, *Guidelines for Ships Operating in Arctic Ice-Covered Waters* (London: International Maritime Organization, 2002).

13 R. Headland, *Transits of the Northwest Passage to the End of the 2012 Navigation Season* (Cambridge: Scott Polar Research Institute, University of Cambridge, 2012).

14 R. Headland, "Ten Decades of Transits of the Northwest Passage," *Polar Geography* 31 (2010): 1–13.

15 *AMSA,* 2009.

16 Ibid.

17 Ibid.

18 Nordic Bulk Carriers A/S press release, September 19, 2013.

19 "Northern Sea Route Slated for Massive Growth," *Moscow Times,* June 4, 2013.

The Arctic in Focus

National Interests and International Cooperation

GUDRUN BUCHER AND ROBIN INGLIS

18

AS GLOBAL WARMING CONTINUES TO CHANGE THE FACE OF THE ARCTIC, it has become a region of both sharpening national interests and unparalleled international cooperation—diplomatic as well as scientific—and of expanded communications among the indigenous peoples who live across the five polar states of Russia, Canada, the United States, Norway, and Denmark (which has sovereignty over Greenland). The rapid and accelerating melting of sea ice has brought into ever-sharper focus a number of political, economic, social, and environmental issues, making these discussions much more urgent than in the past. Renewed attention on the Arctic, however, is global as well as national because the main factors contributing to the growing interest in the region have international implications, such as the mitigation of the effects of climate change on environments and peoples, the opening of new shipping routes, resource development, and geopolitical maneuvering.

Different nations have widely differing concerns regarding the Arctic. The United States, for example, in addition to concerns about responsible resource management and environmental protection, has major security concerns, as unprotected northern shores make it vulnerable to the intrusion

The Arctic community of Gjoa Haven in Nunavut, Canada (detail of fig. 18.3a).

from the north of organized crime, drug traffickers, terrorists, and potential enemy states.[1] For Russia, paramount concerns are resource exploitation and realization of the potential of the Northeast Passage (more commonly known today as the Northern Sea Route) for shipping between Europe and Asia. For Canada, the main concerns are twofold: upholding Canadian sovereignty over the several possible routes through its northern archipelago and resolution of the boundary dispute with the United States in the eastern Beaufort Sea. Canada is also interested in addressing environmental threats to the region and its Inuit peoples as shipping routes become open for longer periods each year, thus encouraging increased exploration and exploitation of resources, including tourism in off-continental locations.[2] All the Arctic states have now recognized the need for serious discussion about stewardship and environmental regulation to make possible a future that brings to the region practical plans for sustainable development and the protection of its aboriginal peoples. For countries in Europe, and such nations as Japan, Singapore, South Korea, China, and India, the major interests are resource development; the potential for new, shorter, and cheaper transportation routes within the Arctic Ocean; and the development of new technologies, such as those relating to gas and methane extraction, so as to partake of the economic benefits of greater Arctic development.

THE LAW OF THE SEA

Unlike the Antarctic, which is a continent surrounded by oceans, the Arctic region is an ocean surrounded by continents. Thus, under international law, the major part of the Arctic falls under the Law of the Sea, a number of unwritten but nevertheless binding set of rules of customary international law that were codified into the 1982 United Nations Convention on the Law of the Sea (UNCLOS).[3] UNCLOS has been ratified by 164 states as well as the European Union. These include four of the five Arctic Ocean coastal states: Canada, Denmark (Greenland), Norway, and Russia. The United States has not yet ratified UNCLOS but has recognized it as a framework for future discussion about the Arctic.[4]

Under UNCLOS, a nation's maritime rights (meaning jurisdiction and the full application and enforcement of laws and regulations over persons, goods, and activities) are defined by "maritime zones," which are measured initially from a "baseline" at a coast's low-tide mark. Each coastal state is sovereign over a twelve-nautical-mile (twenty-two-kilometer) zone called its *territorial sea.* This zone encompasses water, air space, seabed, and subsoil, and it can be extended to include internal waters where a coast is extensively indented with bays or has adjacent islands. Coastal states can draw straight, simplified baselines across the entrances to the bays and between islands and claim as sovereign *internal waters* all those waters to the land side of the baseline. The key exception to sovereignty in a nation's territorial sea and internal waters is the right of *innocent passage* to be enjoyed by ships of other nations. Innocent passage is essentially transit toward and away from a coast, port, or harbor without engaging in activities deemed prejudicial to peace and order by the host nation, and it includes commercial navigation. Submarines must surface when passing through another state's territorial sea and internal waters. Beyond the twelve-nautical-mile territorial sea is an area called the *contiguous zone*. Here a country can enforce the controls necessary to safeguard its territory or territorial sea from infringement in four specific areas: customs, taxation, immigration, and pollution.

Beyond these two near-coast zones, UNCLOS allows each coastal state an additional 200 nautical miles (370 km) as an *exclusive economic zone* (EEZ), in which the state holds exclusive exploitation rights over all natural resources in the water column (primarily fish) and along and under the ocean floor and seabed. Yet farther, beyond the EEZ, article 76 of the convention provides for the possibility of a coastal state's possessing limited rights over a fourth zone, the *continental shelf*, which is defined as the natural geological extension of a nation's land territory, a clear connection to the continental crust, to the continental margin's outer edge. This means that if a coastal state's claims are accepted, based on proven scientific evidence, some regions that are at present under the sea and governed by international law would be governed by that state's national laws, and the state would hold exclusive rights to exploit the resources in the seabed.

There are two different ways for identifying the limits of this extended continental shelf. To make matters more complicated, a state can use both methods in combination and then choose the more favorable option. The extended continental shelf can be up to 350 nautical miles (648 km) from the Territorial Sea baseline, or 100 miles (185 km) beyond the first bathometric line measuring 2,500 meters in depth. As a starting point, geologists first have to determine the location of the foot of the continental slope, which is the point of maximum change of gradient at its base, meaning the point where the descending shelf flattens out and fades into the abyss below.[5] To identify this point requires bathymetric, geomorphological, geological, and geophysical data and may also incorporate the analysis of sediments from rivers deposited millions of years ago, which have been extended across the ocean floor by the action of currents and hardened over time.

HIGH STAKES: DEFINING THE CONTINENTAL SHELF

When it became clear that a combination of easier access, abetted by global warming, and the development of new technologies and higher prices for oil and gas could lead to the possible exploitation of resources beyond the EEZ, article 76 of UNCLOS became of the utmost importance in the Arctic context. In terms of economic development and the exploitation of the Arctic's energy reserves, the stakes are enormously high. If a state wants to register its claims to what it believes to be its extended continental shelf, it has to do so within ten years after its ratification of UNCLOS. Since the research for the enforcement of a claim is extremely expensive and complicated, a nation wishing to claim an extension of its EEZ has to choose carefully the year of ratification. The criteria for the extension of the EEZ are not entirely straightforward. If the foot of the slope is located within the two-hundred-mile EEZ, no extension is possible. If the foot of the slope is found to be outside this zone, however, an extension is possible under certain circumstances. This is especially relevant in the Arctic, because the ocean floor has huge and flat shelf areas crossed by significant ridges.

As of the beginning of 2014, the analyses of overall claims within the Arctic Ocean under article 76 are still in their early stages. Three nations—Norway in November 2006, Russia in December 2001 and Canada in December 2013—have submitted claims, within their ten-year limit, to the Commission on the Limits of the Continental Shelf (composed of twenty-one eminent scientists chosen by those states that have ratified UNCLOS). The commission does not make binding decisions: rather it makes recommendations that assist neighboring states, whose claims may overlap, in negotiating any resolutions necessary. However, as the recommendations are based on geographical and geological facts, they are considered authoritative. The commission basically upheld Norway's claims, as a result of which a forty-year-old dispute with Russia over their boundary in the Barents Sea was resolved in 2010.[6]

The Russian claim has highlighted the fact that paragraph 6 of article 76 of UNCLOS, containing the definition of the continental shelf, is both complicated and controversial. It says that the outer limit of the continental shelf shall not exceed 350 nautical miles from the baselines from which the breadth of the territorial sea is measured. The problem is that the paragraph does not apply to submarine elevations that are seen as natural components of the continental margin, such as plateaus, rises, caps, banks, and spurs. There are three big submarine ridges in the Arctic: the Lomonosov Ridge, Mendeleev Ridge, and Alpha Ridge—and it is difficult to determine whether they are ridges or elevations.[7] If they are considered submarine elevations, the upper limit of 350 nautical miles does not apply, and a huge amount of undersea territory may be claimed using the 2,500-meter line plus 100 nautical miles and the analysis of sediment. In 2001, Russia brought forward such a claim of extension, which included the Lomonosov Ridge (defining it as an elevation), which reached to the North Pole and encompassed 1.2 million square kilometers.[8] The science behind this claim was not considered adequate as the basis for any recommendation, however, and further analysis was deferred until 2014, with Russia requested to provide more and better-focused data to corroborate its claim.

The Russian claim shows how much more research, analysis, discussion, and difficult negotiation lie ahead for the five Arctic states, primarily because deposits of oil, and especially gas, are located in the huge shelf areas in dispute.[9] At the end of 2013, Canada submitted its claim,[10] which consisted of over one million square kilometers of the Arctic region, and reserved the right to continue its mapping of the Lomonosov Ridge, which it considers an extension of Ellesmere Island, expecting to extend the claim all the way to the North Pole. Denmark will follow with its submission before the end of 2014. As with the Russian and Canadian claims, any contentious aspects of the claim are expected to involve the Lomonosov Ridge, which Denmark maintains is an extension of Greenland. Whatever the findings in the recommendations of the Commission on the Limits of the Continental Shelf, it is reasonable to conclude that Russia, Canada, and Denmark will negotiate in a relatively short period of time—by 2020 perhaps—a resolution of the ridge dispute. As surveying to collect the necessary data is so expensive and so difficult, the three nations and the United States have found it in their best interests to cooperate by having their ships and scientists work together. In the summers of 2006 and 2007, for example, Danish and Canadian scientists worked together researching the ridge question north of both Ellesmere Island and Greenland, and in 2008 the US and Canadian icebreakers *Healy* and *Louis S. St-Laurent* worked together in support of scientists in the Beaufort Sea.[11] Results and differing interpretations will undoubtedly continue to be reflected in submissions to the commission. Despite a Russian expedition's symbolic gesture of planting a titanium replica of the nation's flag at the bottom of the ocean at the North Pole in 2007, largely derided as an unhelpful stunt by its neighbors and particularly roundly denounced in Canada, it is likely that any resolution of the boundary issues in the Arctic will leave the North Pole itself outside any one nation's jurisdiction as the "common heritage of mankind"—a technical term used to designate "those deep seabed areas . . . that are beyond national jurisdiction and are administered by the U[nited] N[ations]."[12]

DISPUTES IN THE NORTH AMERICAN ARCTIC

US and Canadian sovereignty in the Arctic date from the purchase of Alaska from Russia by the United States in 1867 and the transfer of British colonial "authority" to the Dominion of Canada in 1880 of "all British territories and possessions and all islands adjacent of such territories or possessions," with the exception of the colony of Newfoundland. Given that Britain's actual control of the Arctic Archipelago was more assumed than real at that time, however, and that until well into the twentieth century there was a relative absence of any Canadian presence in the high Arctic, the region was vulnerable to challenges from other nations, particularly the United States and Denmark. In 1925,

Canada made a declaration of its Arctic boundaries, and by the 1930s Canada's rights to the archipelago had essentially been accepted by the other Arctic states.[13] The issue of a legitimate presence continued, nevertheless, to concern the Canadian government, as throughout global history the principle of occupation has been a key to establishing sovereignty. The presence of the Royal Canadian Mounted Police and particularly the supply voyages to Inuit villages and police detachment settlements of the *St. Roch* in the 1930s, as well as that ship's separate transits of two of the Northwest Passage routes in the early 1940s, were seen as vital in this regard. In addition, in the mid-1950s, the Canadian government relocated a number of Inuit families from northern Quebec and Baffin Island to Ellesmere Island, largely in response to the overwhelming American military presence in Arctic Canada (supported by the government in Ottawa because the United States was a NATO ally, but not without attendant tensions) as a result of the Cold War.[14]

Today there are four active disputes in the North American Arctic. In the eastern Arctic, Denmark and Canada have two apparently solvable issues, one concerning the boundary in the Lincoln Sea north of Greenland and Ellesmere Island and the other concerning the ownership of Hans Island, a tiny (1.3-square-kilometer) rock in Nares Strait, between the same two islands. In 1973 the two countries agreed on the boundary separating Canada and Greenland but stopped short at the Lincoln Sea, leaving the boundary between their respective EEZs unclear and important fishing rights unresolved. They agreed to disagree about Hans Island. The agreement excluded the island and adjacent waters from rights to seabed mining, and no exploratory licenses have yet been issued on or around the island because of the possibility that there might be hydrocarbon resources in the vicinity, and Hans Island might be useful as a drilling platform.[15] In the spirit of the Ilulissat Declaration of 2008 (see below), Denmark and Canada have continued their discussions, and they agreed in principle in November 2012 on a resolution of the Lincoln Sea issue. The dispute over Hans Island, however, appears more intractable: it has been the subject of competing official visits and flag plantings, notably in 2004–5, and despite joint efforts to scientifically map the seabed since 2006 and intermittent official talks as recently as 2012, any resolution will likely have to await analysis of the two countries' submissions to the Commission on the Limits of the Continental Shelf in 2013 and 2014. The possibility that Hans Island belongs to the geology of *both* Ellesmere Island and Greenland suggests that the boundary in Nares Strait could ultimately be drawn right through the middle of the island. However, the issue became a little more clouded in 2008, when premier Hans Enoksen of Naalakkersuisut, the Greenland government that operates under the auspices of the Danish constitution, declared that the island belonged to the Inughuit people, who discovered, named, and occupied the island long before the arrival of Europeans.[16]

But without archaeological evidence of permanent settlement, this claim is unlikely to derail any final agreement between Denmark and Canada.[17] The issue of Hans Island demonstrates how complicated Arctic matters can become when differing interests are involved in even a single, seemingly simple question.

The other two disputes have created a standoff between the United States and Canada in the eastern Beaufort Sea, and between Canada and numerous other nations, especially the United States, over the question of sovereignty over all of the Northwest Passage, which Canada maintains is in its internal waters.

The dispute in the Beaufort Sea revolves around the extension of the land boundary between Alaska and the Yukon into the ocean (fig. 18.1). Once again, the stakes are high because the area is considered rich in oil and natural gas reserves (and because this is the location of the Arctic National Wildlife Refuge). The disagreement dates from the 1970s, when the American government protested the boundary line that Ottawa was using to issue oil and gas concessions and the delineation of different lines to set out exclusive fishing zones in the nations' respective EEZs.[18] The United States reiterated its approach to the issue in President George W. Bush's national security directive of January 9, 2009, which underlined recognition of "a boundary . . . based on equidistance."[19] The principle of equidistance—tracing a line at equal distance from the closest land point of each state—is a well-established method of maritime boundary delineation, but the American position has been challenged by Canada, which maintains that the maritime boundary should follow the 141°w meridian that defines the eastern border of Alaska (previously Russian America), originally established in the 1825 treaty between Russia and Britain, "in its prolongation as far as the frozen ocean." Canada asserts that continuing the meridian beyond the land involved would be consistent with the treaty's "object and purpose," criteria that have traditionally been recognized as guiding principles in both customary international law and the 1969 Vienna Convention on the Law of Treaties.[20]

Initially the dispute isolated a wedge-shaped sector of approximately 21,000 square kilometers (8,100 square miles) as the area of disagreement, but the joint United States–Canada seabed surveys of 2008 and 2009 showed that each country's claims could extend much farther toward the North Pole than previously imagined. As a result, a University of British Columbia Arctic expert, Michael Byers, pointed out in 2010 that farther to the north, the US position actually works to its detriment. Under the American formula for determining the boundary, the looming presence of Canada's Banks Island on the Beaufort Sea's eastern perimeter radically alters where the border between the two countries would be drawn in areas farther out to sea. According to the US position, Alaska's northward-sloping coastline means that the sea's southern maritime boundary veers slightly eastward of the Yukon-Alaska

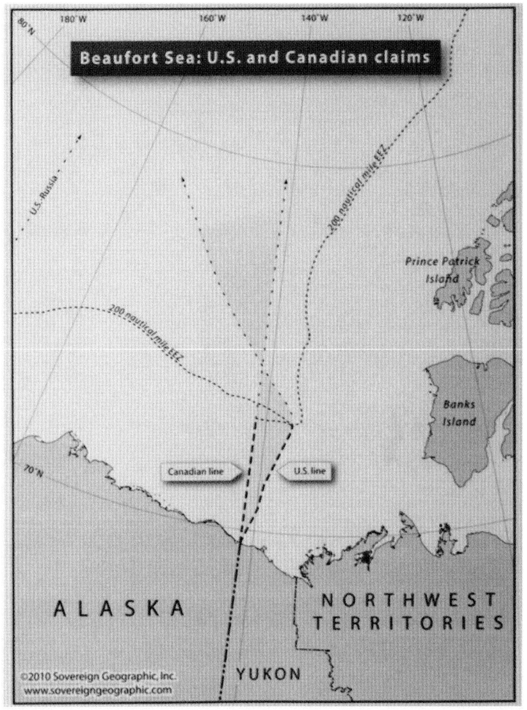

18.1 Disputed boundary claims involving the United States and Canada in the Beaufort Sea. Ironically, each nation would both lose and gain rights over the seabed if its position on the disputed boundary were settled in its favor. Courtesy of Sovereign Geographic, Inc.

land boundary, giving the US a greater amount of marine jurisdiction. However, the overlap in the northerly expanse of the Beaufort would be much larger and reversed, with the boundary under the US formula swinging far to the west because of Banks Island, giving Canada a greater share of the potentially resource-rich seabed. Meanwhile, Canada's longitude-line formula for determining the boundary would give the US more seabed territory in the outer Beaufort.[21] With scientific research and diplomatic debate ongoing, and in the absence of formal US ratification of UNCLOS and the start of the ten-year window for the US to submit a claim for sovereignty over the continental shelf, a resolution could be many years away. On the other hand, the dispute will ultimately have to be resolved in bilateral negotiations anyway, and if the science is clear, and the benefits and disadvantages in the inner and outer Beaufort waters are taken into consideration, pressure from corporations with potential oil and gas interests in the disputed areas might lead to agreement sooner rather than later.

The issue of the Northwest Passage—whether it should be considered international strait or internal Canadian waters—is perhaps the highest-profile and most contentious of the sovereignty disputes in the Arctic. There are in fact seven different routes through the archipelago that separate Davis Strait and Baffin Bay in the east from the Beaufort Sea and Bering Sea in the west.[22] A perception has developed (and this was certainly true in the mind of Henry Larsen, commander of the *St. Roch* in her 1944 east-to-west transit) that the "true" Northwest Passage is the northernmost of the routes running through Parry Channel, because it alone, due to the shallow waters found between the various islands farther south, is potentially suitable for deep-draft cargo ships.[23] However, any navigable route between Baffin Bay and the Beaufort Sea can legitimately be regarded as a true passage, and in fact the Parry Channel remains the least viable because of the heavy sea ice, particularly in McClure Strait. Indeed, there has been only one transit (as of 2010) through the entire northern route, the handful of others (including that of the *St. Roch*) following the easier variant by negotiating Prince of Wales Strait south into Amundsen Gulf.[24] Sometimes, depending on annual fluctuations, conditions are better or worse in the Parry Channel, but it will be many years before it becomes in any way a regular route, and many, many decades more before it is of any real value for commercial transits. Essentially, most marine activities in the Arctic for the foreseeable future will be destinational and will not involve transits.[25] At present, the complete northern route is valuable only for submarines because of its depth.[26]

Nevertheless, the sovereignty issue is a key national policy matter for Canada, and it has invoked two legal arguments to support the contention that the waterways constitute internal waters: historic title and the fact that they lie on the landward side of straight baselines drawn around the entire Arctic Archipelago in 1985.[27] The second is considered the stronger argument, as straight baselines have already been employed in the Arctic by Denmark, Iceland, and Russia,[28] and if indeed the Canadian claim is ultimately successful (wherever it might be decided), Canada would have the right to regulate all activities in the passages and to enforce its laws therein.[29]

The opposing view, shared by at least ten nations and with the United States as the most vocal disputant, considers the principal passages, at least, to be international straits.[30] Under international law, a strait must meet a geographical and a functional requirement to be considered international. In other words, it must be an obvious and useful route for international maritime traffic. Article 37 of UNCLOS states that within such straits, "used for international navigation," all ships and aircraft enjoy the right of transit. As Donat Pharand has written, however, "Before a strait may be considered international, proof must be adduced that it has a history as a useful route for international maritime traffic."[31] With only 185 complete transits through the end of 2012, and most of these traveling via a combination of the southerly routes, it is at least debatable whether or not the "useful" test has been met. This is why the status of the Northwest Passage is unlikely to be resolved in the short term.[32]

At the same time, the actual navigability of the various passages is evolving annually: they are not stable, year-round routes such as one finds, for example, in the Torres Strait between Australia and New Guinea (first mapped in a definitive fashion by James Cook) or the Strait of Malacca, between the Malay Peninsula and Sumatra. But the southern routes are largely ice free for a short time in the late summer and early fall. This has led some commentators to suggest that the Northwest Passage is on its way to becoming internationalized (i.e., it will gradually become an international strait as global warming makes it more viable as a naval and commercial route). If ultimately the international-strait designation were to prevail, Canada might not necessarily lose all rights and powers over the passage, but it would be obliged to respect the navigational rights of other states. Others have raised the possibility that the Northwest Passage could be considered internal waters, subject to a right of passage; the passage would not meet the requirements of an international strait, but neither would it be entirely enclosed within Canada's straight baselines, and foreign ships would therefore enjoy the right of innocent passage.[33]

The United States endows the passage with very high strategic significance. In 1985, the American icebreaker *Polar Sea* sailed through the passage without asking for Canada's permission, an event that caused a furor in Canada in the belief that the United States was making a "statement." In reality the aim was much less aggressive and had more to do with practicality than anything else. The *Polar Sea* was in Thule, Greenland, and needed to get to Seattle. Obviously a Northwest Passage route was the most practical way to go. The Canadian Coast Guard was notified, its representatives were invited to sail on board, and the CCGS vessel *John A. Mac-*

donald accompanied the *Polar Sea* for part of the voyage.[34] In response to opposition to the transit in Canada, however, the United States government was clear about its legal stance: the voyage was "an exercise of navigational rights and freedoms not requiring prior notification." It suggested further that the two countries should "agree to disagree on the legal issues [the status of the passage] and concentrate on practical matters." In the end Canada agreed and granted the permission it was never asked for, stating that Ottawa was "committed to facilitating navigation" through the waterway and was "prepared to work toward this objective."[35]

The *Polar Sea* incident and the straight-baseline claim governing the entire archipelago instituted by Ottawa in 1985 after it took place, however, motivated the United States and Canada to sign an Arctic Co-operation Agreement in 1988, which pledged (without prejudice to either nation's position on the status of the Northwest Passage) "that all navigation by US icebreakers in waters claimed by Canada as internal would be undertaken with the consent of the Canadian government."[36] In a real way, this agreement underlines Canada's position over the last forty years: that it will not withhold consent for any transit as long as the Arctic Waters Pollution Prevention Act (1970) and adequate vessel-construction standards are adhered to. The current tacit agreement by the Arctic players to disagree about status and for Canada to grant de facto permission for all transits, subject to these conditions, seems acceptable moving forward into a future that will inevitably bring further changes and challenges and require further commitment to collaboration by all parties.

In fact, Canada has few resources to prevent a foreign ship from attempting a transit. Since the canceling of the Polar 8 icebreaker project in 1990, also instituted in 1985 in response to the *Polar Sea* transit, Canadian budget concerns have consistently trumped the strategic importance of Canadian Arctic infrastructure. Prime Minister Stephen Harper made Canadian Arctic sovereignty and security one of his core campaign issues during the 2006 federal election.[37] Plans were proposed to construct several Arctic offshore patrol vessels, to establish a military training base in Resolute on Cornwallis Island, at the entrance to the main route of the Northwest Passage, and to build a deep-water harbor and a huge icebreaker. These plans were, at least in part, a response to growing public interest in Arctic issues as a result of reports and media coverage and the publication of a number of new books, such as those cited in this essay.

Until relatively recently, it might have been easy for Canada to secure the region through a limited number of CCGS patrols, because for most of the year the passage routes were not accessible. However, now, because of the retreat of the ice, increased resource development, and changing geopolitical interests, the Arctic is rapidly being opened up to the world. The 2007 plans to build a deep-water port and military training center at Resolute Bay have not moved ahead, calls for a deep-water port at Iqaluit have not been answered, and the intention to build icebreakers and Arctic patrol vessels seems continually to have been downgraded or postponed. A number of commentators fear that Canada is falling behind in the race to meet the practical challenges involved in the new north. If the various routes of the Northwest Passage are ultimately determined to be international waterways, there are questions, legitimately raised by Canada, about who would be responsible, in a practical, on-the-water sense, for security, search and rescue, and cleaning up after polluting incidents such as oil spills. But would Canada be able to finance all these responsibilities if the passages were internal waters? Probably not. A lot of questions remain on the table for discussion. One is the possible implementation of user fees for marine services in such a fragile yet often-hostile environment, an approach used by Russia in the Northern Sea Route. Since Canada will bear almost all the negative environmental impacts of any maritime traffic in the region, it probably should also have a predominant voice in deciding such questions, and user fees might indeed provide the possibility of generating significant revenue and thus the opportunity for more sustainable activity and development in the north.[38]

THE COLLABORATIVE DYNAMIC

Moves by Arctic nations to work together scientifically to meet the challenges posed by continental-shelf delineation are merely examples of a trend that has been growing since the 1970s and most obviously manifests itself today in the work of the Arctic Council, founded in 1996.[39] The issues surrounding resource extraction, primarily exploration and drilling for oil, coincided with an increased awareness among all Arctic governments of the need to protect the fragile Arctic environment as well as the interests of the region's indigenous peoples. Even before the recent dramatic effects of change from global warming were being realized, Native peoples in Alaska and northern Canada had become fearful of the potential dangers to their way of life from resource development and the effects of supertankers and pipelines on the marine environment.[40] The Iñupiat of Alaska were the driving force behind the creation of what became the Inuit Circumpolar Conference (now the Inuit Circumpolar Council or ICC), which had its beginnings in an Arctic Peoples Conference in 1973 in Copenhagen, organized by several organizations based in Greenland and attended by representatives from Finland, Norway, Sweden, and Canada. In 1975, Eben Hopson, a former mayor of Alaska's vast North Slope Borough, was responsible for pushing forward the idea of a pan-Inuit organization. That year he hosted a meeting in Barrow, Alaska, and two years later hosted the actual founding meeting of the ICC, attended by Inuit from Greenland, Canada, and the United States (fig. 18.2). Since that historic gathering, the organization has flourished and grown into a major international nongovernmental organization representing approximately 150,000 Inuit in the United

18.2 Eben Hopson (right) photographed in 1970, was an early champion of environmental protection, Native American land claims, and effective rural governance in Alaska. In 1972, he came to prominence as mayor of the new North Slope Borough on the coasts of the Chukchi and Beaufort Seas, where huge oil deposits had been discovered in 1968. He was then instrumental in raising international awareness of aboriginal issues across the entire Arctic region in the 1970s. In June 1977, he hosted the First Circumpolar Conference in Barrow, Alaska. Alaska State Library Historical Collections: Groups—Native Leaders 4.

States (Alaska), Canada, Greenland, and Russia (Chukotka). The organization holds consultative status II at the United Nations and is a permanent participant in the deliberations of the Arctic Council, along with five other indigenous organizations.[41]

The genesis of the Arctic Council lay in concerns within each of the Arctic states about the opening up of the Arctic environment. Increasingly vocal politicians and government officials realized that individual nations would have limited success in facing numerous challenges, particularly related to economic development and shipping, and that a more coordinated, collaborative approach was needed. Happily this realization coincided with the end of the Cold War, a period of détente that enabled the United States and Russia to work together in an international forum with overarching goals of researching and discussing matters of obvious common interest that did not threaten more parochial national interests.[42]

In 1991, at a conference held in Rovaniemi, Finland, sometimes referred to as the Finnish Initiative, representatives of eight Arctic nations—Denmark, Norway, Canada, Sweden, Finland, Iceland, Russia, and the United States—came together to discuss environmental concerns. The ICC was an active participant.[43] The result of the meeting was an official Arctic Environmental Protection Strategy (AEPS). This was essentially the unofficial founding document of the Arctic Council. The council was created five years later in Ottawa in 1996, with a formal declaration by the original eight states of the Finnish Initiative. They set out three principal commitments: "to the well-being of the inhabitants of the Arctic, including recognition of the special relationship and unique contributions to the Arctic of indigenous people and their communities" (figs. 18.3a and b); "to sustainable development in the Arctic region, including economic and social development, improved health conditions and cultural well-being"; and "to the protection of the Arctic environment, including the health of Arctic ecosystems, maintenance of biodiversity in the Arctic region and conservation and sustainable use of natural resources." In addition, they pledged their desire "to provide for regular intergovernmental consideration of and consultation on Arctic issues."[44]

The Arctic Council, therefore, is a high-level intergovernmental forum designed to provide the means for promoting cooperation, coordination, and interaction among the Arctic states, with the unique involvement of Arctic indigenous communities, on common Arctic issues. It is designed to facilitate consensus leading to final agreement for action. Its work is supervised and directed by the ministers of foreign affairs of the permanent members. With Sweden's having chaired the council from 2011 through 2013, all member states have now been in the chair for a two-year period. The key operations of the council currently take place within six expert working groups: the Arctic Contaminants Action Program, designed to provide information on remedial and preventive actions relating to con-

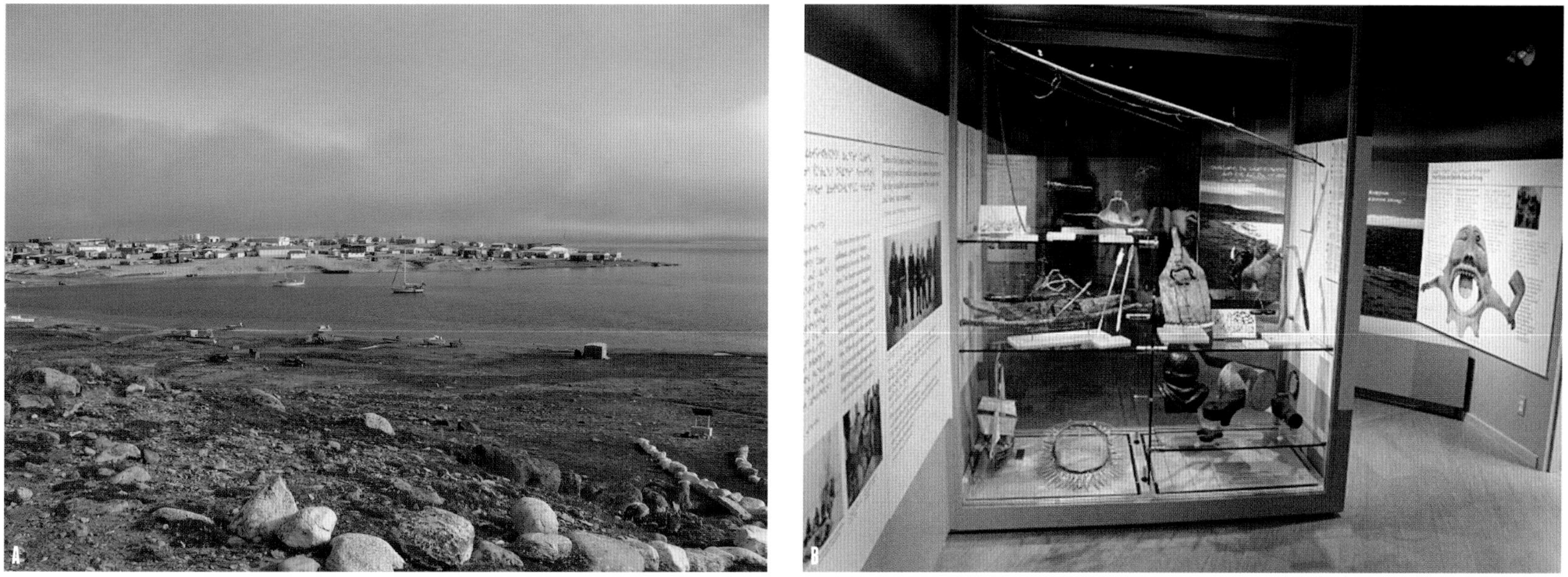

18.3 (a) The Arctic community of Gjoa Haven in Nunavut, Canada was first established as a Hudson's Bay Company post in 1927, and the tiny hamlet reflected the transition of many formerly nomadic aboriginal groups toward a more settled existence. The name derives from the ship in which Roald Amundsen traversed the Northwest Passage between 1903 and 1906. He stayed almost two years in what he called "the finest little harbor in the world." Photo by Gudrun Bucher. (b) The population of Gjoa Haven in 2013 was approximately 1,300 people. The community has responded in its own way to the changes coming to villages across the Arctic by establishing the Nattilik Heritage Centre. It is a place to celebrate and maintain their cultural traditions and to present interpretive exhibitions for the enlightenment of an increasing number of outside visitors. On display are artifacts collected by Roald Amundsen and his companions over one hundred years ago, which have been repatriated from the Museum of Cultural History in Oslo, Norway. Nattilik Cultural Centre: Courtesy of David Jensen, D. Jensen & Associates, Vancouver.

taminants; the Arctic Monitoring and Assessment Program, which focuses on monitoring, assessing, and preventing pollution in the Arctic; Conservation of Arctic Flora and Fauna, dealing with biodiversity conservation and sustainability; Emergency Prevention, Preparedness, and Response, which is assigned the key task of averting and responding to possible environmental emergencies; Protection of the Arctic Marine Environment, which focuses on policy and pollution prevention and control measures related to the protection of the Arctic marine environment; and Sustainable Development, which deals with the living conditions of Arctic residents.

A vitally important pioneering study initiated under the auspices of the council, in cooperation with the International Arctic Science Committee (a nongovernmental organization), was the *Arctic Climate Impact Assessment* (2004), which has led to ongoing high-level research on the effects of global warming on Arctic environments and peoples.[45] This multidisciplinary study, which for the first time codified the results of both natural-science and social-science research and underscored the coming reality of increased marine activity in the Arctic Ocean, led to another groundbreaking study done under the auspices of the council's Protection of the Arctic Marine Environment Working Group: the *Arctic Marine Shipping Assessment 2009 Report*. About two hundred experts, led by contributors from the United States, Canada, and Finland,

18.4 A biannual Arctic Council ministerial meeting was held at Kiruna, Sweden, in May 2013. Here the Russian foreign minister, Sergey Lavrov, addresses the final press conference with the US secretary of state, John Kerry (third from left), and the incoming council chair, Leona Aglukkaq, an Inuk from Nunavut, Canada, looking on. Nunavut was carved out of Canada's Northwest Territories in 1999 to provide for a territorial government that could offer a new level of focused attention on environmental and indigenous issues to a major portion of northern Canada and the Canadian Arctic archipelago. Photograph courtesy of the United States Department of State.

analyzed current shipping activity and made recommendations in three key areas: enhancing marine safety; protecting people and the environment; and building marine infrastructure.

The work of the council is also carried out through task forces, which have included the Task Force on Arctic Marine Oil Pollution Preparedness and Response (2011–13) and the Task Force on Search and Rescue (2009–11). The work of these task forces led directly to the signing of two agreements, subject to ratification by each member nation: the Nuuk (Greenland) Agreement on Cooperation on Aeronautical and Maritime Search and Rescue in the Arctic (May 12, 2011), and the Kiruna (Sweden) Agreement on Arctic Marine Oil Pollution Preparedness and Response (May 15, 2013) (fig. 18.4).

In 2011, and again in 2013, the Arctic Council granted observer status to a number of nations.[46] The prime purposes have been to sensitize a larger group of nations to Arctic issues and, at the working-group level, to tap into their expertise and investment finance. To this end the council produced an *Observer Manual for Subsidiary Bodies.* But the move is controversial. Some members feel that the educational potential and the obligation to uphold the council's core goals of safeguarding the region and its people make the initiative worthwhile; others, sensing pressure from energy-hungry nations far away from the Arctic, which have less interest in its environment and peoples, share the discomfort of the new chair, Leona Aglukkaq of Canada, who in May 2013 expressed concern at the expansion of a tent originally "created by northerners, for northerners, before the Arctic was of interest to the rest of the world." A senior US State Department official has described the Council to date as "a small and friendly forum," musing that "the bigger it gets the dynamic changes."[47]

The new reality is an Arctic that is coming into sharper focus not only for those states with sovereignty rights in the region but also for the wider global community. While there are clear national interests at play and disputes that will not be resolved in the short term, the overwhelming dynamic is for a collaborative approach to the issues under the umbrella of UNCLOS. This approach was underlined in May 2008, when a meeting of the five Arctic Ocean Coastal nations held at Ilulissat in Greenland declared that "the law of the sea provides for important rights and obligations concerning the delineation of the outer limits of the continental shelf, the protection of the marine environment, including ice-covered areas, freedom of navigation, marine scientific research, and other uses of the sea." As a result, they declared: "We remain committed to this legal framework and to the orderly settlement of any possible overlapping claims."[48] In addition, the same collaborative and cooperative dynamic is present in the desire to address the pan-regional challenges ahead—be they safe, secure, and environmentally responsible maritime activity, sustainable economic development, or effectively addressing the interests of the region's indigenous peoples—within the forum of the Arctic Council.

NOTES

1 See *National Strategy for the Arctic Region* (May 2013), which quotes the *National Security Strategy of 2010* as follows: "The United States is an Arctic Nation with broad and fundamental interests in the Arctic Region, where we seek to meet our national security needs, protect the environment, responsibly manage resources, account for indigenous communities, support scientific research, and strengthen international cooperation on a wide range of issues." The document is accessible at www.whitehouse.gov/sites/default/files/docs/nat_arctic_strategy.pdf.

2 See *Canada's Northern Strategy: Our North, Our Heritage, Our Future* (Ottawa: Department of Indian Affairs and Northern Development, 2009), http: //northern stategy.gc.ca/cnc/cns-eng.asp; and *A Northern Vision: A Stronger North and a Better Canada* (Yellowknife: Government of the Northwest Territories, 2007), www.anorthern vision_english.pdf.

3 Michael Byers, *Who Owns the Arctic? Understanding Sovereignty Disputes in the North* (Vancouver: Douglas & McIntyre, 2009), 91.The full text of UNCLOS is accessible at en.wikisource.org/wiki/United_Nations_Convention_on_the_Law_of_the_Sea.

4 Arctic Ocean Conference, *Ilulissat Declaration* (Ilulissat, Greenland, 28 May 2008), available at www.oceanlaw.org/downloads/arctic/Ilulissat_Declaration.pdf, accessed February 14, 2014. See also Rob Huebert, "Canada and the Changing International Arctic: At the Crossroads of Cooperation and Conflict," in *Northern Exposure: Peoples, Powers and Prospects in Canada's North,* ed. Frances Abele et al. (Montreal: Institute for Research on Public Policy 2009), 77–106.

5 Byers, *Who Owns the Arctic?,* 91.

6 "Russia and Norway Reach Accord on Barents Sea," *New York Times,* April 27, 2010, www.nytimes.com/2010/04/28/world/europe/28norway.html.

7 Karl Hinz, "Wem gehört die zentrale Arktis? Geologie, Bathymetrie und das Seerecht," *Logbuch Arktis: Der Raum, die Interessen und das Recht,* ed. Manfred Sapper, Volker Weichsel, and Christoph Humrich (Berlin: Berliner Wissenschafts-Verlag, 2011), 87–92.

8 Uwe Jenisch, "Arktis und Seerecht: Seegrenzen, Festlandsockel, Verkehresrechte," in Saper, Weichsel, and Humrich, *Logbuch Arktis,* 57–76.

9 Yadullah Hussain, "The Great Race North: Reserves Make Arctic New Theatre for Tensions," *National Post* (Toronto), July 27, 2012.

10 See *National Post,* December 9, 2013, www.news.nationalpost.com/2013/12/09 canada-makes-territorial-claim-for-north-pole-despite-not-mapping-area-yet/.

11 Byers, *Who Owns the Arctic?,* 88–98.

12 Ibid., 93.

13 The most comprehensive discussion of this subject can be

found in Shelagh D. Grant, *Polar Imperative: A History of Arctic Sovereignty in North America* (Vancouver: Douglas & McIntyre, 2010), chapters 7 and 8.

14 Ibid., 320; René Dussault and George Erasmus, *The High Arctic Relocation: A Report on the 1953–55 Relocation* (Ottawa: Canadian Government Publishing, 1994). See also Frank James Tester and Peter Kulchyski, *Tammarniit (Mistakes): Inuit Relocation in the Eastern Arctic, 1939–63* (Vancouver: UBC Press, 1994).

15 Gerard Kenney, *Dangerous Passage: Issues in the Arctic* (Toronto: Natural Heritage, 2006), 178.

16 Randy Boswell, "Hans Island Was Ours First, Greenland Says," *Ottawa Citizen,* May 28, 2008.

17 Grant, *Polar Imperative,* 456.

18 Byers, *Who Owns the Arctic?,* 98.

19 *National Security Presidential Directive and Homeland Security Directive on Arctic Region Policy,* NSPD-66, January 9, 2009, clause III.D.2, available at http://www.fas.org/irp/offdocs/nspd/nspd-66.htm.

20 François Côté and Robert Dufresne, *The Arctic: Canada's Legal Claims* (Ottawa: Library of Parliament, Parliamentary Information and Research Service, October 24, 2008), Publication PRB 08–05E, www.parl.gc.ca/content/lop/researchpublications/prb0805-e.htm; Byers, *Who Owns the Arctic?,* 97–99.

21 Randy Boswell, "Work Underway to Resolve Beaufort Sea Boundary Dispute," *Vancouver Sun,* July 26, 2010, also available at http://byers.typepad.com/arctic/2010/07/work-underway-to-resolve-beaufort-sea-boundary-dispute.html, accessed February 14, 2014.

22 R. K. Headland, *Transits of the Northwest Passage to the End of 2012* (Cambridge: Scott Polar Research Institute, University of Cambridge, April, 2013).

23 Parry Channel is a broad seaway running east to west beginning in Lancaster Sound, passing through Barrow Strait into Melville Sound and out into the Beaufort Sea through McClure Strait. It was named after the explorer William Parry, who reached Winter Harbour on Melville Island in 1819–20.

24 Headland, *Transits.*

25 Lawson W. Brigham, "Think Again: The Arctic," *Foreign Policy* 181 (September–October, 2010): 73–74.

26 Headland, *Transits.*

27 See Donat Pharand, *Canada's Arctic Waters in International Law* (Cambridge: Cambridge University Press, 1988). The historic-title argument involves exclusive exercise of state jurisdiction, a long lapse of time, and the acquiescence of foreign states. The fact that the Inuit, now Canadian citizens, have used the waterways of the archipelago since "time immemorial" has been raised as a factor in the dialogue.

28 Byers, *Who Owns the Arctic?,* 52. From 1951 onward, "straight baselines" between outer headlands or fringe islands have been an accepted means for determining a coastal state's internal waters along fragmented coastlines. This was a result of a decision by the International Court of Justice in a dispute between Britain and Norway over fishing rights. The United States, however, immediately rejected Canada's claim, as this would have constituted acceptance of full Canadian control of the Northwest Passage and thus terminated America's navigation rights. The European Union also objected, maintaining that the baselines were too long and diverged too much from the general direction of the mainland coast. Ten other states also protested against the baselines (Byers, *Who Owns the Arctic?,* 53).

29 Côté and Dufresne, *The Arctic,* 3.

30 NSPD-66, clause III.B.5, states unequivocally: "Freedom of the seas is a top national priority. The Northwest Passage is a strait used for international navigation, and the Northern Sea Route includes straits used for international navigation; the regime of transit passage applies to passage through those straits. Preserving the rights and duties relating to navigation and overflight in the Arctic region supports our ability to exercise these rights throughout the world, including through strategic straits."

31 Donat Pharand, "The Arctic Waters and the Northwest Passage: A Final Revisit," *Ocean Development and International Law* 38, nos. 1–2 (2007): 3–69.

32 See Headland, *Transits.*

33 Côté and Dufresne, *The Arctic,* 3–4.

34 Lawson W. Brigham, personal communication, July 10, 2013.

35 Byers, *Who Owns the Arctic?,* 51. In this instance the Canadian government was following the precedent set in

1969 when it gave permission, also not requested, for the US supertanker *Manhattan* to transit the passage and also provided the assistance of the CCGS icebreaker *John A. Macdonald.* The circumstances were somewhat different, however, as Canada at that time was only claiming a three-mile territorial sea, which conveniently left an international navigational corridor through the archipelago (Byers, *Who Owns the Arctic?,* 44–45).

36 Grant, *Polar Imperative,* 378; Byers, *Who Owns the Arctic?,* 56–58.

37 Huebert, "Canada and the Changing International Arctic."

38 Kenney, *Dangerous Passage,* 182–84.

39 See Arctic Council website, www.arctic-council.org.

40 See Grant, *Polar Imperative,* chapter 11, for a detailed discussion of the early history of the connection between oil, native peoples, and the environment in the latter half of the twentieth century.

41 See Inuit Circumpolar Council (Canada) website, www.inuitcircumpolar.com. The five other organizations are the Arctic Athabaskan Council; the Aleut International Association; the Gwich'in Council International; the Russian Arctic Indigenous Peoples of the North; and the Saami Council.

42 Huebert, "Canada and the Changing International Arctic."

43 Grant, *Polar Imperative,* 387.

44 Full texts of the AEPS and the *Declaration on the Establishment of the Arctic Council, Ottawa, 1996,* can be found on the Arctic Council's website at www.arctic-council.org/index.php/en/document-archive/category/4-founding-documents.

45 See Arctic Council and the International Arctic Science Committee, Arctic Climate Impact website, www.acia.uaf.edu.

46 Twelve nations have been granted observer status: in 2011, France, the United Kingdom, the Netherlands, Germany, Poland, and Spain; in 2013, China, India, Japan, Singapore, South Korea, and Italy. The Arctic Council's *Observer Manual for Subsidiary Bodies* is available at www.arctic-council.org/index.php/en/document-archive/category/4-founding-documents.

47 Luiza C. Savage, "Why the World Wants the Arctic," *Maclean's* (Toronto), May 27, 2013.

48 Arctic Ocean Conference, *Ilulissat Declaration.* See www.arcticgovernance.org/the-ilulissat-declaration.4872424.html

Select Bibliography

Amundsen, Roald. *My Life as an Explorer.* New York: Doubleday, Doren, 1928.

Andrewes, William J. H., ed. *The Quest for Longitude: Proceedings of the Longitude Symposium, Harvard University, Cambridge Massachusetts, November 4–6, 1993.* Cambridge, MA: Harvard University, Collection of Historical Scientific Instruments, 1996.

Arctic Council. *Arctic Climate Impact Assessment* (ACIA). 2004. New York: Cambridge University Press, 2005.

———. *Arctic Marine Shipping Assessment (AMSA) 2009 Report.* 2nd printing. Arctic Council, April 2009.

Ballantyne, Tony, ed. *Science, Empire, and the European Exploration of the Pacific.* Aldershot, UK: Ashgate Publishing, 2004.

Barnett, James K. *Captain Cook in Alaska and the North Pacific.* Anchorage, AK: Todd Communications, 2008.

Barr, William. *Arctic Hell-Ship: The Voyage of the HMS* Enterprise, *1850–1855.* Edmonton: University of Alberta Press, 2007.

Beaglehole, J. C. *Cook the Writer.* Sydney: Sydney University Press, 1970.

———. *The Life of Captain James Cook.* Stanford: Stanford University Press, 1974.

Bergreen, Laurence. *Over the Edge of the World: Magellan's Terrifying Circumnavigation of the Globe.* New York: Harper Collins, 2003.

Betts, Jonathan. *Harrison.* Greenwich, UK: National Maritime Museum, 2007.

Black, Lydia T. *Russians in Alaska, 1732–1867.* Fairbanks: University of Alaska Press, 2004.

Bockstoce, John R. *Whales, Ice, and Men.* Seattle: University of Washington Press, 1986.

Byers, Michael. *Who Owns the Arctic? Understanding Sovereignty Disputes in the North.* Vancouver, BC: Douglas & McIntyre, 2009.

Captain Cook Memorial Museum. *Northward Ho! A Voyage towards the North Pole, 1773.* With contributions by Ann Savours, Sophie Forgan, and Glyn Williams. Whitby, UK: Captain Cook Memorial Museum, 2010.

———. *Smoking Coasts and Ice-Bound Seas: Cook's Voyage to the Arctic.* With contributions from Glyn Williams, Geoff Quilley, Sergy Arutiunov, and Sophie Forgan. Whitby, UK: Captain Cook Memorial Museum, 2008.

Cook, James. *The Journals of Captain James Cook on His Voyages of Discovery.* 3 vols. Vol. 1, *The Voyage of the* Endeavour, *1768–1771.* Vol. 2, *The Voyage of the* Resolution *and* Adventure, *1772–1775.* Vol. 3, *The Voyage of the* Resolution *and* Discovery, *1776–1780* (in 2 parts). Edited by J. C Beaglehole. Cambridge: Cambridge University Press for the Hakluyt Society, 1955–67.

Cook, James, and James King. *A Voyage to the Pacific Ocean. undertaken, by the command of His Majesty, for making Discoveries in the Northern Hemisphere, to determine the position and extent of the west side of North America, its distance from Asia, and the practicability of a Northern Passage to Europe.*

Performed under the direction of Captains Cook, Clerke, and Gore, in His Majesty's ships the Resolution *and* Discovery, *in the years 1776, 1777, 1778, 1779, and 1780.* Vols. 1 and 2 written by Captain James Cook, F.R.S. Vol. 3 by Captain James King, L.L.D., F.R.S. London: G. Nicol and T. Cadell, 1784.

Cook, Warren. *Flood Tide of Empire: Spain and the Pacific Northwest, 1543–1819.* New Haven, CT: Yale University Press, 1973.

Coote, Jeremy, ed. *Old Collections, New Knowledge: Cook-Voyage Collections of "Artificial Curiosities" in Britain and Ireland, 1770–2010.* Oxford: Museum Ethnographers Group, 2013.

Crowell, Aron L. "Maritime Cultures of the Gulf of Alaska." *Revista de Arqueologia/Journal of American Archaeology* 17, no. 19 (2000).

Currie, Noel Elizabeth. *Constructing Colonial Discourse: Captain Cook at Nootka Sound.* Montreal: McGill-Queen's University Press, 2005.

David, Andrew, ed. *The Charts and Coastal Views of Captain Cook's Voyages.* Vol. 3, *The Voyage of the* Resolution *and* Discovery, *1776–1780.* London: Hakluyt Society in association with the Australian Academy of the Humanities, 1997.

Day, Alan. *Historical Dictionary of the Discovery and Exploration of the Northwest Passage.* Lanham, MD: Scarecrow, 2006.

Delgado, James P. *Across the Top of the World: The Quest for the Northwest Passage.* Vancouver, BC: Douglas & McIntyre, 1999.

Engstrand, Iris Wilson. *Spanish Scientists in the New World: The Eighteenth-Century Expeditions.* Seattle: University of Washington Press, 1981.

Fisher, D., et al. "Natural Variability of Arctic Sea Ice over the Holocene." *Eos, Transactions* 87, no. 28 (2006).

Fisher, Raymond. *Bering's Voyages: Whither and Why.* Seattle: University of Washington Press, 1977.

Fisher, Robin, and Hugh Johnston, eds. *Captain James Cook and His Times.* Seattle: University of Washington Press; Vancouver, BC: Douglas & McIntyre, 1979.

———. *From Maps to Metaphors: The Pacific World of George Vancouver.* Vancouver: UBC Press, 1993.

Frost, Alan, and Jane Sampson. *Pacific Empires: Essays in Honour of Glyndwr Williams.* Vancouver: UBC Press, 2005.

Gascoigne, John. *Captain Cook, Voyager between Worlds.* London: Hambledon Continuum, 2007.

Gibson, James R. *Otter Skins, Boston Ships, and China Goods: The Maritime Fur Trade of the Northwest Coast, 1785–1841.* Seattle: University of Washington Press,1992.

Gough, Barry M. *Britain, Canada and the North Pacific: Maritime Enterprise and Dominion, 1778–1914.* Aldershot, UK: Ashgate Variorum, 2004.

———. *First Across the Continent: Sir Alexander Mackenzie.* Norman: University of Oklahoma Press, 1977.

———. *Fortune's a River: The Collision of Empires in Northwest America.* Madeira Park, BC: Harbour, 2007.

———. *The Northwest Coast: British Navigation, Trade, and Discoveries to 1812.* Vancouver: UBC Press, 1992.

Grant, Shelagh D. *Polar Imperative: A History of Arctic Sovereignty in North America.* Vancouver, BC: Douglas & McIntyre, 2010.

Haycox, Stephen, James Barnett, and Caedmon Liburd, eds. *Enlightenment and Exploration in the North Pacific, 1741–1805.* Seattle: University of Washington Press for the Cook Inlet Historical Society, 1997.

Hearne, Samuel. *A Journey from Prince of Wales's Fort in Hudson's Bay to the Northern Ocean.* Edited by Richard Glover. Toronto: Macmillan, 1958.

Holmes, Christine, ed. *Captain Cook's Final Voyage: The Journal of Midshipman George Gilbert.* Honolulu: University of Hawaii Press, 1982.

Horwitz, Tony. *Blue Latitudes: Boldly Going Where Captain Cook Has Gone Before.* New York: Henry Holt, 2002.

Hough, Richard. *Captain James Cook: A Biography.* London: Hodder & Stoughton, 1994.

———. *The Last Voyage of Captain James Cook.* New York: William Morrow, 1979.

Howse, Derek. *Greenwich Time and the Longitude.* Oxford: Oxford University Press, 1980.

———. *Nevil Maskelyne, the Seaman's Astronomer.* Cambridge: Cambridge University Press, 1989.

Huxtable, George. "Finding Longitude by Lunar Distance." *Navigation News,* September–October 2007.

Inglis, Robin. *Historical Dictionary of the Discovery and Exploration of the Northwest Coast of America.* Lanham, MD: Scarecrow, 2008.

———, ed. *Spain and the North Pacific Coast: Essays in Recognition of the Bicentennial of the Malaspina Expedition,*

1791–1792. Vancouver, BC: Vancouver Maritime Museum, 1992.

Joppien, Rüdiger, and Bernard Smith. *The Art of Captain Cook's Voyages.* Vol. 3. *The Voyage of the* Resolution *and* Discovery, *1776–1780.* New Haven: Yale University Press, 1988.

Kaeppler, Adrienne L. *Artificial Curiosities: Being an Exposition of Native Manufactures Collected on the Three Pacific Voyages of Captain James Cook, R.N. . . .* Honolulu, HI: Bishop Museum Press, 1978.

———. *Holophusicon: The Leverian Museum; An Eighteenth-Century English Institution of Science, Curiosity and Art.* Altenstadt, Germany: ZKF, 2011.

Kaeppler, Adrienne L., et al. *James Cook and the Exploration of the Pacific.* London: Thames and Hudson, 2009.

Keating, Bern. *The Northwest Passage: From the* Mathew *to the* Manhattan, *1497 to 1969.* New York: Rand McNally, 1970.

Kenney, Gerard. *Dangerous Passage: Issues in the Arctic.* Toronto: Natural Heritage Books, 2006.

King, J. C. H. *First Peoples, First Contacts: Native Peoples of North America.* Cambridge, MA: Harvard University Press, 1999.

Lamb, W. Kaye, ed. *The Journals and Letters of Sir Alexander Mackenzie.* Cambridge: Hakluyt Society, 1970.

Larsen, Henrik A., Frank R. Shea, and Edvard Omholt-Jensen. *The Big Ship.* Toronto: McClelland and Stewart, 1967.

Ledyard, John. *Journal of Captain Cook's Last Voyage.* Edited by J. K. Munford. Corvallis: Oregon State University Press, 1964.

Mackie, Richard Somerset. *Trading beyond the Mountains: The British Fur Trade on the Pacific, 1793–1843.* Vancouver: UBC Press, 1997.

MacLaren, I. S. "In Consideration of the Evolution of Explorers and Travellers into Authors: A Model." *Studies in Travel Writing* 15, no. 3 (September 2011).

Malaspina, Alejandro. *The Malaspina Expedition, 1789–1794: Journal of the Voyage by Alejandro Malaspina.* 3 vols. Edited by Andrew David, Felipe Fernández-Armesto, Carlos Novi, and Glyndwyr Williams. London: Hakluyt Society; Madrid: Museo Naval, 2001–4.

Martínez Shaw, Carlos, ed. *Spanish Pacific: From Magellan to Malaspina.* Madrid: Ministerio de Asuntos Exteriores and Lunweg Editores, 1988.

Maslanik, J. A., et al. "A Younger, Thinner Arctic Ice Cover: Increased Potential for Rapid, Extensive Sea-Ice Loss." *Geophysical Research Letters* 34 (2007).

Miller, Robert J. *Native America, Discovered and Conquered: Thomas Jefferson, Lewis and Clark, and Manifest Destiny.* Westport, CT: Praeger, 2006.

Mirsky, Jeannette. *To the Arctic! The Story of Northern Exploration from Earliest Times to the Present.* New York: Knopf, 1948.

Moziño, José Mariano. *Noticias de Nutka: An Account of Nootka Sound in 1792.* Rev. ed. Edited and translated by Iris Wilson Engstrand. Seattle: University of Washington Press, 1991.

Nicandri, David L. *River of Promise: Lewis and Clark on the Columbia.* Bismarck, ND: Dakota Institute Press, 2010.

Nokes, J. Richard. *Columbia's River: The Voyages of Robert Gray, 1787–1793.* Tacoma: Washington State Historical Society, 1991.

Overland, J. E., and M. Wang. "When Will the Summer Arctic Be Nearly Sea-Ice Free?" *Geophysical Research Letters* 40 (2013).

Pethick, Derek. *First Approaches to the Northwest Coast.* Seattle: University of Washington Press; Vancouver, BC: Douglas & McIntyre, 1979.

———. *The Nootka Connection: Europe and the Northwest Coast, 1790–95.* Vancouver, BC: Douglas & McIntyre, 1980.

Polyak, L., R. B. Abbey, et al. "History of Sea Ice in the Arctic." *Quarternary Science Reviews* 29 (2010).

Quanchi, Max, and John Robson. *Historical Dictionary of the Discovery and Exploration of the Pacific Islands.* Lanham, MD: Scarecrow, 2006.

Quill, Humphrey. *John Harrison: The Man Who Found Longitude.* London: Baker, 1966.

Ragnall, Steve. *Better Conceiv'd than Describ'd: The Life and Times of Captain James King, 1750–84.* Leicester: Troubador, 2013.

Richardson, Brian W. *Longitude and Empire: How Captain Cook's Voyages Changed the World.* Vancouver: UBC Press, 2005.

Robson, John. *Captain Cook's War and Peace: The Royal Navy Years, 1755–1768.* Barnsley, UK: Seaforth, 2009.

Ronda, James P. *Astoria and Empire.* Lincoln: University of Nebraska Press, 1990.

Shalkop, Antoinette, ed. *Explorations in Alaska: Captain Cook Commemorative Lectures.* Anchorage, AK: Cook Inlet Historical Society, 1980.

Skelton, R. A. "Captain James Cook as a Hydrographer." *Mariner's Mirror* 40 (1954).

Sloan, Kim, ed. *Enlightenment: Discovering the World in the Eighteenth Century.* London: British Museum Press, 2003.

Smith, Bernard. *European Vision and the South Pacific.* New Haven, CT: Yale University Press, 1985.

Stephenson, Scott R., Laurence C. Smith, Lawson W. Brigham, and John A. Agnew. "Projected 21st Century Changes to Arctic Marine Access." *Climatic Change* 118, nos. 3–4 (June 2012).

Suthren, Victor. *To Go upon Discovery: James Cook and Canada, 1758–1767.* Toronto: Dundurn, 1999.

Svet, Yakov M., and Svetlana G. Fedorova. "Captain Cook and the Russians." *Pacific Studies* 2, no. 1 (Fall 1978).

Thomas, Nicholas. *Cook: The Extraordinary Voyages of Captain James Cook.* New York: Walker & Company, 2003.

Tovell, Freeman. *At the Far Reaches of Empire: The Life of Juan Francisco de la Bodega y Quadra.* Vancouver: UBC Press, 2008.

Vancouver, George. *A Voyage of Discovery to the North Pacific Ocean and round the World, 1791–95.* 4 vols. Edited by W. Kaye Lamb. Cambridge: Cambridge University Press for the Hakluyt Society, 1984.

Wagner, Henry R. *Cartography of the Northwest Coast to the Year 1800.* Vols. 1 and 2. Berkeley: University of California Press, 1937.

Wheeler, Mary E. "Empires in Conflict and Co-operation: The 'Bostonians' and the Russian-American Company." *Pacific Historical Quarterly* 40 (November 1971).

Williams, Glyndwyr. *Arctic Labyrinth: The Quest for the Northwest Passage.* New York: HarperCollins, 2009.

———, ed. *Captain Cook: Explorations and Reassessments.* Woodbridge, UK: Boydell, 2004.

———. *The Death of Captain Cook: A Hero Made and Unmade.* Cambridge, MA: Harvard University Press, 2008.

———. *The Prize of All the Oceans.* London: HarperCollins, 1999.

———. *Voyages of Delusion: The Northwest Passage in the Age of Reason.* London: HarperCollins, 2002.

Williams, Robert A. *The American Indian in Western Legal Thought: The Discourses of Conquest.* New York: Oxford University Press, 1990.

Contributors

EVGUENIA ANICHTCHENKO is a research fellow at the National Natural History Museum, Smithsonian Institution. Formerly she worked as curator of special exhibits at the Anchorage Museum. She holds two master's degrees: an MA in History from the Central European University, Budapest, and an MA in Maritime Studies and Underwater Archaeology from East Carolina University. She came to Alaska to document the remains of the bark *Kad'yak* while working on her thesis about the fleet of the Russian American Company. Her research interests include the history of Russian America, the maritime history of the Arctic and north Pacific, and the underwater cultural heritage of Alaska and the circumpolar north. She is the author of a number of publications and is currently finishing her doctoral degree at the Center for Underwater Archaeology at the University of Southampton, UK.

JAMES K. BARNETT has been an attorney in private practice in Anchorage since 1974. He is former deputy commissioner of the Alaska Department of Natural Resources and elected member of the Anchorage Municipal Assembly. He is also the longtime president of the Cook Inlet Historical Society. He was coeditor and contributor to the Vancouver symposium volume *Enlightenment and Exploration in the North Pacific, 1741–1805* (1997) and more recently authored *Captain Cook in Alaska and the North Pacific* (2007). He is currently working on the celebration of the centennial of Anchorage's founding and publishing the Burney and Roberts journals from Cook's third voyage.

LAWSON W. BRIGHAM is Distinguished Professor of Geography and Arctic Policy at the University of Alaska Fairbanks. After serving as a career US Coast Guard officer, which included duty as an icebreaker captain on the Great Lakes, in the Arctic, and on Antarctic expeditions, he earned his PhD at the Scott Polar Research Institute at Cambridge University. He was chair of the Arctic Council's

Arctic Marine Shipping Assessment (2005–9) and continues his research on the Russian maritime Arctic, Arctic climatic change, marine transportation, and polar geopolitics.

GUDRUN BUCHER studied cultural anthropology in Frankfurt, Germany, and wrote her PhD dissertation on Vitus Bering's second Kamchatka expedition. Since 1998, she has traveled as a lecturer on expedition cruise ships, tracking the routes of Bering and other explorers in the Arctic and sailing to Antarctica and across the South Pacific. She is conducting research for the University of Göttingen about the institution's Siberian and north Pacific ethnographic collections.

ARON L. CROWELL is an anthropologist who works with indigenous communities of the north in the fields of cultural research, archaeology, oral history, and collaborative heritage. As Alaska director for the Smithsonian Institution's Arctic Studies Center, he has curated or co-led major exhibitions, including *Looking Both Ways: Heritage and Identity of the Alutiiq People; Crossroads of Continents: Cultures of Siberia and Alaska;* and *Gifts of the Ancestors: Ancient Ivories of Bering Strait.* He directs archaeological research around the Gulf of Alaska from the Katmai coast to Glacier Bay and currently leads National Science Foundation–funded research on the human and environmental history of Yakutat Bay. Crowell's doctorate in anthropology is from the University of California, Berkeley, and he is an affiliate faculty member of the University of Alaska.

JAMES P. DELGADO has led or participated in shipwreck expeditions around the world (including the 2010 scientific mapping of the *Titanic* site), as well as surveys of the USS *Arizona* at Pearl Harbor and the polar exploration ship *Maud.* His archaeological work has also included the excavation of ships and collapsed buildings along the now-buried waterfront of gold rush–era San Francisco. Currently director of maritime heritage in the Office of National Marine Sanctuaries for the National Oceanic and Atmospheric Administration, Dr. Delgado oversees heritage programs and active research in US waters, as well as outreach and education on America's underwater and marine heritage. He is a fellow of the Royal Geographical Society and of the Explorers' Club. His thirty-two books and numerous articles include *Across the Top of the World: The Quest for the Northwest Passage.*

RICHARD DUNN is senior curator and head of science and technology at Royal Museums Greenwich. Having worked on the history of navigation since joining the museum in 2004, he has been one of the investigators on a five-year research project on the history of the British Board of Longitude, run in collaboration with the Department of History and Philosophy of Science, Cambridge University, and funded by the Arts and Humanities Research Council.

IRIS ENGSTRAND is professor of history at the University of San Diego. She is the author of *Spanish Scientists in the New World: The Eighteenth-Century Expeditions* (1981) and translator and editor of *Noticias de Nutka: An Account of Nootka Sound in 1792* by José Mariano Moziño (1970). With Donald C. Cutter, she coauthored *Quest for Empire: Spanish Settlement in the Southwest* (1996), and, with Freeman Tovell and Robin Inglis, *Voyage to the Northwest Coast of America, 1792: Juan Francisco de la Bodega y Quadra and the Nootka Sound Controversy* (2012). Dr. Engstrand was recently awarded the prestigious medal of the Order of Isabel la Católica by King Juan Carlos of Spain for her outstanding contributions to the history of Spain in the Americas.

JOHN GASCOIGNE was educated at Sydney, Princeton, and Cambridge universities and since 1980 has taught at the University of New South Wales, where he is now Scientia Professor of History. His publications have focused on the impact of the Scientific Revolution and the Enlightenment, and particularly their impact on exploration. His books include a two-volume study of Sir Joseph Banks and his world and *Captain Cook: Voyager between Worlds* (2007), winner of the Frank Broeze prize of the Australian Association for Maritime History. His most recent publication, from Cambridge University Press, is *Encountering the Pacific in the Age of the Enlightenment* (2014).

BARRY GOUGH is Canada's foremost proponent of maritime history and has written extensively about the seas, great rivers, and lakes of his country. Author of *The Northwest Coast: British Navigation, Trade and Discoveries to 1812* (1992) and the *Historical Dictionary of Canada* (2nd ed., 2011), he has also written in the field of exploration history and has been consulting editor to a number of publishers on the geography and history of exploration. A long-standing member of the Hakluyt Society, for whom, with editor Andrew David, he introduced *William Robert Broughton's Voyage of Discovery to the North Pacific, 1795–1798* (2010), his recent books include *Fortune's a River: The Collision of Empires in Northwest America* (2007) and *Juan de Fuca's Strait: Voyages in the Waterway of Forgotten Dreams* (2013).

RICHARD INGLIS, former head of anthropology at the Royal British Columbia Museum, has worked with the Mowachaht-Muchalaht First Nations on a number of heritage and cultural projects since 1983. He is the coauthor, with James C. Haggerty, of "Cook to Jewitt: Three Decades of Change in Nootka Sound," in *Le castor fait tout: Selected Papers of the Fifth North American Fur Trade Conference, 1985* (1987) and "The Spanish on the Pacific Coast: Reconstructing the Native Perspective" in *Spain and the North Pacific Coast* (1992). His research interests include the historical record relating to the contact and maritime fur-trade period, with a focus on traditional ownership and use of lands and resources.

ROBIN INGLIS is a fellow of the Canadian Museums Association and former director of the Vancouver Maritime Museum and the North Vancouver Museum and Archives. He is author of the *Historical Dictionary of the Discovery and Exploration of the Northwest Coast of America* (2008) and coeditor of *Voyage to the Northwest Coast of America, 1792: Juan Francisco de la Bodega y Quadra and the Nootka Sound Controversy* (2012). He served as regional editor (Northwest Coast) for the Hakluyt Society's edition of *The Malaspina Expedition, 1789–1795*, volume 2 (2003), and curated major bicentennial exhibitions on the voyages of Jean-François de La Pérouse (1986) and Alejandro Malaspina (1991). He has served as research curator for the exhibition *Arctic Ambitions: Captain Cook and the Northwest Passage* for the Anchorage Museum and the Washington State Historical Society.

ADRIENNE L. KAEPPLER is curator of oceanic ethnology at the National Museum of Natural History at the Smithsonian Institution in Washington, DC. In the 1970s she worked as an anthropologist at the Bishop Museum in Honolulu, and in 1978 she curated a bicentennial exhibition featuring the Pacific collections from the voyages of James Cook, publishing *Artificial Curiosities: An Exposition of Native Manufactures Collected on the Three Pacific Voyages of Captain James Cook, RN* (1978). In 2011 she published *Holophusicon: The Leverian Museum; An Eighteenth-Century English Institution of Science, Curiosity, and Art*, the fruit of over forty years of research into the collections of the world's first popular museum of science and the arts, which were dispersed by auction in 1806. In 2009 Dr. Kaeppler curated *James Cook and the Exploration of the Pacific*, an exhibition presented in Bonn, Vienna, and Bern from 2009 through 2011, which brought together over five hundred artifacts and works of art from Cook's voyages.

I. S. MacLAREN has taught at the University of Alberta since 1985 in the departments of history and classics, and English and film studies. His teaching and research pertain to the history of Arctic exploration, the history of national parks systems, the early literature of North America in English, and the genre of travel writing. He collaborated with the editor Stuart Houston to write the commentary for *Arctic Artist: The Journal and Paintings of George Back, Midshipman with Franklin, 1819–1822* (1994) and is currently completing a comprehensive study of the early Canadian painter Paul Kane's mid-nineteenth-century transcontinental travels.

ROBERT J. MILLER is a professor at the Sandra Day O'Connor College of Law at Arizona State University. He has taught and practiced American Indian law since 1993. He has also been a part-time tribal judge for Pacific Northwest tribes since 1995 and is the chief justice of the Court of Appeals for the Grand Ronde Tribe. His first book was *Native America, Discovered and Conquered: Thomas Jefferson, Lewis and Clark, and Manifest Destiny* (2006). His second, *Discovering Indigenous Lands: The Doctrine of Discovery in the English Colonies,* coauthored with indigenous professors from Australia, New Zealand, and Canada, was published in 2010. He is a citizen of the Eastern Shawnee Tribe of Oklahoma.

DAVID L. NICANDRI is the recently retired director of the Washington State Historical Society, where he served as executive editor of the society's critically acclaimed quarterly journal, *Columbia Magazine.* Among other publications, he is the author of *River of Promise: Lewis and Clark on the Columbia* (2010) and is currently working on a stand-alone study of James Cook's voyaging in the high latitudes and the evolution of the cartographic image of the Northwest Passage.

JOHN ROBSON is map librarian at the University of Waikato in Hamilton, New Zealand. He has written and lectured extensively on James Cook and his Pacific voyages and has undertaken pioneering research into the lives and careers of Cook's many traveling companions. He is the author of *Captain Cook's World: Maps of the Life and Voyages of James Cook, RN* (2000); *The Captain Cook Encyclopedia* (2006); and *Captain Cook's War and Peace: The Royal Navy Years, 1755–1768* (2009).

HARRY STERN is a senior mathematician at the Polar Science Center, Applied Physics Laboratory, University of Washington, Seattle, where he studies Arctic sea ice and climate using satellite data. In 2009 he sailed through the eastern half of the Northwest Passage with the Around the Americas expedition. He organizes the annual Polar Science Weekend, a popular outreach event held at Seattle's Pacific Science Center. He has been with the Polar Science Center since 1987.

NICHOLAS THOMAS is professor of anthropology at the University of Cambridge and Director of the Museum of Archaeology and Anthropology. For more than three decades he has worked on many projects exploring cross-cultural histories in the Pacific Ocean. His books include *Entangled Objects: Exchange, Material Culture, and Colonialism in the Pacific* (1991); *Discoveries: The Voyages of Captain Cook* (2003); and *Islanders: The Pacific in the Age of Empire* (2010), which was awarded the Wolfson History Prize, an award given annually in the United Kingdom to encourage excellence in the writing of history for the general public.

GLYN WILLIAMS is professor emeritus of history at Queen Mary University of London. He was general editor of the Hudson's Bay Record Society from 1967 to 1975 and president of the Hakluyt Society from 1978 to 1982. Among his awards and honors are D.Litt. degrees from Memorial University, Newfoundland, and La Trobe University, Melbourne; the Elizabeth Laird Distinguished Lectureship at the University of Winnipeg; and the Caird Medal of the National Maritime Museum, Greenwich. He is the author of a dozen books and more than thirty articles, most of them on the exploration of the Pacific and the Arctic, including *Voyages of Delusion: The Search for the Northwest Passage in the Age of Reason* (2002). His most recent book is *Naturalists at Sea: Scientific Travellers from Dampier to Darwin* from Yale University Press (2013).

Illustrations

Index

Boldface numerals indicate material in this volume by its contributing authors.

B

D

E

H

I

J

K

L

M

S

T

W

Y

Z

IAC· COOK OCEANI INVESTIGATOR ACERRIMVS·
REG · SOC · LOND·
SOCIO SVO·